The Wizard of Oz Catalog

ALSO BY FRASER A. SHERMAN
AND FROM MCFARLAND

*Screen Enemies of the American Way:
Political Paranoia About Nazis, Communists,
Saboteurs, Terrorists and Body Snatching Aliens
in Film and Television* (2011)

*Cyborgs, Santa Claus and Satan: Science Fiction,
Fantasy and Horror Films Made for Television*
(2000; paperback 2009)

The Wizard of Oz Catalog

*L. Frank Baum's Novel, Its Sequels
and Their Adaptations for Stage,
Television, Movies, Radio, Music Videos,
Comic Books, Commercials and More*

FRASER A. SHERMAN

McFarland & Company, Inc., Publishers
Jefferson, North Carolina, and London

The present work is a reprint of the library bound edition of The Wizard of Oz Catalog: L. Frank Baum's Novel, Its Sequels and Their Adaptations for Stage, Television, Movies, Radio, Music Videos, Comic Books, Commercials and More, *first published in 2005 by McFarland.*

LIBRARY OF CONGRESS CATALOGUING-IN-PUBLICATION DATA

Sherman, Fraser A.
The Wizard of Oz catalog : L. Frank Baum's novel, its sequels and their adaptations for stage, television, movies, radio, music videos, comic books, commercials and more / Fraser A. Sherman.
p. cm.
Includes bibliographical references and index.

ISBN 978-0-7864-7517-9
softcover : acid free paper ∞

1. Baum, L. Frank (Lyman Frank), 1856–1919. Wizard of Oz — Bibliography. 2. Baum, L. Frank (Lyman Frank), 1856–1919 — Film and video adaptations. 3. Baum, L. Frank (Lyman Frank), 1856–1919 — Stories, plots, etc. 4. Baum, L. Frank (Lyman Frank), 1856–1919. Wizard of Oz. 5. Baum, L. Frank (Lyman Frank), 1856–1919 — Stage history. 6. Baum, L. Frank (Lyman Frank), 1856–1919 — Bibliography. 7. Baum, L. Frank (Lyman Frank), 1856–1919 — Adaptations. 8. Children's stories, American — Film and video adaptations. 9. Fantasy fiction, American — Film and video adaptations. 10. Children's stories, American — Bibliography. 11. Fantasy fiction, American — Bibliography. 12. Fantasy films — History and criticism. 13. Oz (Imaginary place) — Bibliography. 14. Oz (Imaginary place) I. Title.
Z8080.S54 2013 [PS3503.A923] 016.813'4 — dc22 2005004748

BRITISH LIBRARY CATALOGUING DATA ARE AVAILABLE

© 2005 Fraser A. Sherman. All rights reserved

No part of this book may be reproduced or transmitted in any form or by any means, electronic or mechanical, including photocopying or recording, or by any information storage and retrieval system, without permission in writing from the publisher.

Cover photograph: The Tin Man, Straw Man, Dorothy and the Cowardly Lion on the road to see *"The Wizard of Oz,"* from the Puppetworks production (marionettes by Nicholas Coppola; photograph by L.R. Rush)

Manufactured in the United States of America

*McFarland & Company, Inc., Publishers
Box 611, Jefferson, North Carolina 28640
www.mcfarlandpub.com*

To Cindy Jo, for three decades of friendship;
to Roxanne, for being who she is;
and to Pam, Lisa, Matt, Chris and Phyliss,
for giving me someone to hang out with

Acknowledgments

This book could not possibly have been written without the aid of scores of others: the authors who browsed old theater archives and newspaper articles and published the results, countless Oz fans who contributed to the *Baum Bugle*, public relations people in theaters all over America, and people who just gave generously of their time and knowledge when asked.

To be more specific:

I. The Written Word

Thanks go first to the following authors: Robert Sellers (*The Films of Sean Connery*); Mark Evan Swartz (*Oz Before the Rainbow*); John Fricke (*100 Years of Oz*); Allen Eyles (*The World of Oz*); Michael Patrick Hearn (*The Annotated Wizard of Oz*); Richard Anobile (*The Wiz Scrapbook*); Jonathan Clements and Helen McCarthy (*The Anime Encyclopedia*); Katharine M. Rogers (*L. Frank Baum: Creator of Oz*); John Towsen (*Clowns*); David L. Greene and Dick Martin (*The Oz Scrapbook*); Aljean Harmetz (*The Making of the Wizard of Oz*); Douglas Greene, Peter E. Hanff, Dick Martin, David L. Greene and James E. Haff (*Bibliographia Oziana*); Jeanine Basinger (*The World War II Combat Film*); Tim Hollis (*Dixie Before Disney*); Rick Goldschmidt (*The Amazing World of Rankin-Bass*); and Stephen Nissenbaum (*The Battle for Christmas*).

The Baum Bugle, the International Wizard of Oz Club's magazine, is an invaluable resource. While the full list of contributors this author learned from would run several pages, Daniel Mannix, Michael Patrick Hearn, Tim Hollis and Willard Carroll deserve exceptional thanks.

On-line, thanks go to Mike Voiles (dcindexes.com); Cynthia A. Read (the neitherworld.com); Patrick Lonergan (snlyou.jt.org); Jared Davis (dorothyozma.topcities.com); Carol deGiere (musicalschwartz.com); dunrobin (threestooges.net); the indispensable cartoon buff Ronn Webb (wingnuttoons.com); and the even more indispensible Eric Gjovaag (eskimo.com/~tiktok/) and Scott Hutchins (his Web site is probably gone by now, but without it this book would have far fewer entries).

II. Public Relations Staff, Librarians, Archivists and Other Informative People

Thanks go to Michael D. Brown of the American Heart Association; Dirk Johnson at toyboxxx.com; Ronn Webb at wingnuttoons.com; Dr. Liz Connor of Metro Magazine; Nelson Lafraia of the United Kingdom's Brazilian embassy's video library; Danna Brennan, cultural affairs officer for the U.S. Embassy in Israel;

Linda Habjan, acquisitions editor at Dramatic Publishing; Gary Martin, chair of communications media at Cosumnes River College; Paul McMullen of the Alban Arena; Gary Reed at Caliber Comics; Zane Kesey; Michelle Everhart at the Children's Theatre Company of Milwaukee; Allen Browne at bmg.com; Jerry Viemeister, Charlotte Performing Arts Center managing director; Diane Houk, executive director of the Puppetry Arts Institute; Eric Hart at globo–TV; Anita Frank at Family Communications, Inc.; and Michelle Sweetser and Karen Jania at the Bentley Historical Library at the University of Michigan.

Also Karin Browne at the Shakespeare Centre Library; Alan Shefsky at Northwestern University's Performance Studies Department; Michal Podhradsky at www.animation.cz; Ellen Bailey, Pasadena Playhouse archivist; Julie Habjan Boisselle at the Mt. Holyoke College library; Mark Lutwak, artistic director at the Honolulu Theatre for Youth; Frank Augustyn at Adelphi College; Craig Titley, marketing manager at Watford's Palace Theatre; Jonathan Bowdin at the Bradford Theatres; Bob Griffith and Trudi Olivetti of the Unitarian Church's Chalice Theatre; Patricia J. Albright, archives librarian at Mt. Holyoke College; Christopher Huddert, Applause Unlimited; Vedide Kaymak at Rio Cinema; Reed Sampson at the Society for the Preservation of Barbershop Singing Quartets of America; Faye Barron, University of Utah Department of Theatre; Rachel J. Newman, production manager, Lincoln Theatre; Taryn Essinger, public relations manager, Seattle Children's Theatre; Daniella Topol, New Works program director, National Alliance for Musical Theatre; Allen Schmeltz; Brandon D. Markland at the Bay Agency; and Ashley Maurin, marketing associate, Starlight Theatre.

III. Creators

Thanks to the writers, producers and others who generously took the time to discuss their or their associates' work: Cheryl Ann Silich; Scott Richardson at Richardson Designworks; Jeff Slutsky at Street Fighter Marketing; Jeff Church, producing artistic director at the Coterie; Carmen de Lavallade; Doree Steinman; Matt Kelly; Fred Barton; Douglas Davis; Michael Rotman at Hack Comics; Paul Edwards and David Downs at Northwestern University; Jerry Robbins at Colonial Radio Theatre; Mark Grizzard of Chapter Six; Tom McCabe; Mila Johansen; Alexander O'Brien Feldman at alexthejester.com; Bob D. Mathis-Friedman; Susan Zeder; Mary Carroll-Bower at the Oz Kids Production Company; Louise Reichlin of Louise Reichlin and Company; Barry Kleinbort; Nicolas Coppola of Puppetworks, Inc.; Toby Nichols; and Joe Cascone of the Toronto Civic Light Opera.

IV. And Others

Thanks also go to Fred Patten and Jonathan Clemens for the anime research; Bob Thorne for his knowledge of Supergirl; Ross Bagby for turning up some amazingly esoteric fims; to Lisa Wildman and Sheila Cole-Sherman for loaning their DVD players; to C.J. Holrook and Beverly Suarez-Beard for morale boosting; and to Roxanne Koogler for unfailing support.

Special thanks to Marc Berezin for finding films, going over credits and generally making this book much better than it would have been without him.

And finally, thanks to L. Frank Baum, creator of Oz, without whom this book and many others would not exist. Both fantasy and reality would be poorer without him.

Table of Contents

Acknowledgments — vii
Preface — 1
Introduction — 3

1. The Books of Oz — 7
2. Theatrical and Other Staged Adaptations — 64
3. Oz Comic Books and Comic Strips — 120
4. Audio Adaptations — 127
5. Film and Video: Creative Works — 138
6. Film and Video: Nonfiction and Educational — 182
7. Oz on Television: Series, Episodes, and Specials — 193
8. Oz on Television: Commercials — 236
9. Computer Games and Educational Software — 239
10. Oz Web Sites — 241
11. Oz Allusions and References in Film, Television, and Video — 243
12. Oz Title Allusions — 248

Index — 249

Preface

This book breaks down into several sections:

- Synopses and some basic bibliographical information for the forty Oz books in the original series; a number of related books by the Royal Historians of Oz, and a bibliography of Oz books outside the work of the Royal Historians.
- Synopses and credits for live performances based on the Oz books, and on Baum's non–Oz fantasies.
- Comic-book and comic-strip adaptations of Oz.
- Synopses and credits for radio shows, and for dramatic performances on audiobook or vinyl records.
- Synopses and credits for theatrical films and shorts.
- Documentaries and educational films.
- Synopses and credits for television series and episodes based on Oz, as well as a listing of television commercials inspired by Oz.
- Video and computer games.
- Useful web sites.
- Television, film, and title allusions and references to Oz.

The credits do not identify the novel on which films or series are based if it is obvious from the title of the production. Several Russian or Turkish productions may have somewhat inaccurate synopses owing to the absence of subtitles or dubbing.

Video and DVD cuts and edits for television can lead to a substantial variation in running time, so that information constitutes a best guess. If no cast or backstage credits are listed for a given production, the information was either unavailable or eluded discovery.

This catalog does not contain:

- Film and TV productions with no Oz element except an "It was all a dream and you were there"—theme, or having characters play double roles (e.g., as the Kansas characters in MGM's *The Wizard of Oz* do in Oz), or men who hide behind curtains (e.g., the fake intimidating alien who tries to bluff Captain Kirk in the *Star Trek* episode "The Corbomite Maneuver").
- Audiobooks that are straight readings of the text, rather than dramatic adaptations.
- L. Frank Baum's own non–Oz plays, such as *The Maid of Arran*.
- Newspaper comic strips and cartoons that use a one-shot Oz gag for one episode (listing all of them would probably take a small book in itself).

Introduction

Then there is the other book, the best thing I have written, they tell me, The Wonderful Wizard of Oz.
— Lyman Frank Baum, 1900

Water melts witches. Click your heels together three times. Brains, heart and courage. A good man who's a bad wizard. Winged monkeys. Glinda the good. Follow the yellow brick road.

Even before MGM turned *The Wizard of Oz* into the legendary 1939 film, L. Frank Baum's *The Wonderful Wizard of Oz* had been accepted as a classic of children's literature.

The Wizard of Oz has spawned 39 official sequels, over a hundred unofficial sequels, spin-offs and parodies, well over three dozen films, several TV series, music videos, commercials, computer games, radio shows and more. It's been given an African-American slant and a Russian rewrite, and it has inspired Turkish low-budget fantasy, Japanese anime, American pornography and millions of devoted readers.

Why?

What made the story about a girl from Kansas, three peculiar companions, an evil witch and a humbug wizard a bestseller in its own time, a beloved classic in every generation since, and a success in pretty much every country in the world?

For the start of an answer, let's look at *Wizard*'s creation. By 1900, Lyman Frank Baum had spent his life in assorted careers — salesman, store owner, theatrical manager, playwright, newspaper publisher — without success, the mixed result of bad business sense and pure bad luck. His newspaper folded during a depression and his theater burned down (according to one account taking props, costumes and scripts for Baum's play *The Maid of Arran* with it).

Baum's *Mother Goose in Prose* had done reasonably well with its whimsical stories explaining the strange events in nursery rhymes (inspired by his own children's questions), as did the follow-up, *Father Goose: His Book*. Before *Father Goose* reached the stores, though, Baum — as he described it later — was struck with inspiration for *The Emerald City*, a story that would break fresh ground in the fairy tale genre.

Hundreds of fairy stories, both traditional tales and new literary fictions, had been published over the nineteenth century, and Baum's *Enchanted Island of Yew*, *Queen Zixi of Ix* and *The Sea Fairies*, among others, were solidly in that tradition. Oz, too, was a fairyland (as Baum repeatedly referred to it), but in the introduction to *Wizard* Baum states his intention to break away from convention and create a modern fairy story: no old-fashioned creatures such as genies, dwarfs and fairies; nothing too bloodcurdling or scary; and no moral message. For 1900, that was a groundbreaking agenda.

No moral message? Victorian children's literature was chock-full of moral instruction, and even among adults, light reading was regarded with suspicion (as Patrick Brantlinger describes in *The Reading Lesson*). Even children's stories without an overt moral routinely depicted children as so noble and self-sacrificing they make Sir Galahad look like a reprobate.

Although Baum did include moral themes, both in Oz and his other works, they were rarely as heavy-handed, and his child protagonists, while good and sweet, are almost never saintly. Of the three stated goals for the modern fairy tale, he had the most success with this one.

Nothing scary? Even with some of the more gruesome elements edited out, traditional and literary fairy tales routinely confronted their heroes and heroines with abandonment, murder and cannibalism.

Generations of readers have testified that Baum did in fact curdle their blood: the destruction of the Tin Woodman and Scarecrow by the Winged Monkeys, the Wheelers' attack on Dorothy in *Ozma of Oz*, the shrinking doom that befalls Trot and Cap'n Bill in *The Magic of Oz*.

Nevertheless, Baum did keep his tales much less grim than, well, the Brothers Grimm. The witch who captures Hansel and Gretel almost eats them, but the worst Blinky can do to Dorothy is turn her into a cooking drudge. The Nome King's invasion in *The Emerald City of Oz* is defeated without violence; there's nothing in Oz comparable to the destruction of the Awgwas in Baum's *The Life and Adventures of Santa Claus* (the conquest of Pingaree in *Rinkitink in Oz* is brutal, but *Rinkitink* was originally written as a non–Oz book).

No old-fashioned creatures? Even in the first book, Baum had witches, and later stories would add fairies, dwarves (Nomes), giants and wizards who weren't humbug.

But in Baum, these traditions co-existed with a Kansas farm-girl who enters fairyland in a sensible gingham dress; a Scarecrow who starts in a cornfield and ends up ruler of Oz; and a phony Wizard who's more akin to showman P.T. Barnum than Merlin. In *The Land of Oz* the heroes include a wooden sawhorse and a stick figure; in *Ozma*, we meet a mechanical, wind-up automaton, Tik-Tok (though we're told only in a fairy realm could anyone build such a sophisticated mechanism); and in *The Patchwork Girl of Oz*, Dorothy communicates with Baum by radio ("wireless telegraph") and the city of the Hoppers is decorated with radium.

That two of *Wizard*'s witches were good represents another break with tradition. It's easy to forget today, when TV viewers have grown up with *Bewitched*, *Sabrina the Teenage Witch* or *Charmed*, that "good witch" was once an oxymoron, but in her day, Glinda, the Good Witch of the North, was a radical departure from the child-eating, pointy-hatted stereotype Margaret Hamilton so memorably captured in MGM's *The Wizard of Oz*.

One departure Baum didn't mention in his introduction was his decision not to include romance in Oz. In contrast to countless fairy tales that end with prince and princess tying the knot, Baum firmly believed romance didn't interest children and didn't belong in their stories. There are minor romantic subplots in some books, but the only thing close to a traditional fairy-tale romance is in *The Scarecrow of Oz* (carried over from the film it was based on), and Baum proceeds to parody the heck out of it.

Baum's ground-breaking certainly explains some of his success, but a large part of it is also that *The Wizard of Oz* is simply a very good book. W.W. Denslow's illustrations are delightful, and Baum has the knack every fantasy writer should have: His magic works. Whether writing of living scarecrows, lunchpail trees, Nome armies, plant people or Yookoohoos, Baum's fantasy is always believable (even in his weaker books), and that's trickier than it sounds. Baum's successor on the Oz books, Ruth Plumly Thompson, never did it as well, and her successor, John R. Neill, couldn't do it at all.

The influence of the MGM movie can't be underestimated, either. For millions of people, the Judy Garland film *is* the Oz story. The standard reaction to learning of Baum's sequels is "How can there be sequels? Oz was just a dream!" Shown annually on TV for over 30 years, it's spread Baum's story (or a fairly close copy, at least) throughout American culture. The more familiar it becomes, the easier it is to use the characters as icons, symbols and character types.

In *The World War II Combat Film*, author Jeanine Basinger argues that what distinguishes genre from formula is flexibility: Once the basic images and plots of a genre are in place, they can be parodied, slanted or revised to reflect new issues, new trends, new attitudes and new ideas—and then be revised again when the next new idea comes along.

Oz hardly constitutes a genre, but the MGM movie's images and characters are so firmly in place, we use it and adapt it in much the way Basinger sees genres changing. Give us three characters lacking intelligence, compassion and courage, and we know who they are whether they're visiting Fantasy Island or touring Australia, struggling through high school or trying to make it in sales. The man behind the curtain can be a powerless fraud and trickster, or a manipulator pulling strings from behind the scene.

The Wizard of Oz has been hailed as a feminist journey to empowerment; a quest for spiritual enlightenment; a celebration of America's magical cities or its love for the unexplored frontier; a journey through Freudian therapy; and a world where outcasts and freaks are accepted (one of the reasons given for gay Oz fandom). The creators of several Oz productions mentioned in this book have said they chose Oz as a metaphor precisely because the characters are instantly recognizable, universally familiar.

Small wonder that Oz has been, and continues to be, a popular source for adaptations, whether faithful or off-beat, happy or cynical. And that, of course is the point of this book, a reference guide to Oz in all its many forms: The "Famous Forty" official Oz novels, the numerous unofficial books, the films, stage plays, music videos, commercials and the radio shows. It's only a way station on a very long road. An animated TV movie of *The Patchwork Girl of Oz* and a *Muppet Wizard of Oz* are both supposed to be in production as this book goes to press; by the time of *Wizard*'s bicentennial, there will be many, many more stories of Oz to keep track of.

But here in this book is a snapshot of Oz in all its glory at one moment in time. Now, click your heels together three times...

1

The Books of Oz

The Books of L. Frank Baum, First Royal Historian

The Wonderful Wizard of Oz. Illustrated by W.W. Denslow with 24 color plates. Chicago and New York: Geo. M. Hill, 1900. 261 pages.

The first edition had the text sheets, the 24 color plates and the stamped binding case produced separately. The cover — light green cloth stamped in red and green — shows the Lion on the front, Toto on the spine, and Dorothy, the Scarecrow and the Tin Woodman's faces on the back. The dust jacket has dark green print on pea-green stock.

The Wonderful Wizard of Oz was rechristened *The New Wizard of Oz* for a 1903 reissue to avoid confusion with the 1902 stage play, then became *The Wizard of Oz* after the MGM film came out.

Dorothy (no last name given) lives on a bleak, joyless Kansas farm with her Aunt Em and Uncle Henry, both worn gray and sullen by the harsh prairie life. A cyclone carries the farmhouse off with Dorothy and her dog Toto inside, then eventually drops the house in the beautiful land of the Munchkins, crushing the Wicked Witch of the East.

The Munchkins salute Dorothy as a great sorceress. The friendly Good Witch of the North tells Dorothy that the land of Oz is surrounded by a great desert and only the all-powerful Wizard Oz who rules the Emerald City has the magic to send her home. Replacing her worn shoes with the Wicked Witch's durable silver slippers, Dorothy sets off on a yellow brick road with only Toto and the Good Witch's magic kiss for protection.

Next day, Dorothy helps a talking Scarecrow off his pole. When he confesses how he hates having no brains, Dorothy suggests he come with her and ask the Wizard for some. They meet a rusted Tin Woodman and oil him back to life. The Woodman introduces himself as Nick Chopper and explains how when he fell in love, the Wicked Witch was hired by the girl's guardian to break up the romance. The Witch enchanted Nick's axe to cut him to pieces, which a local tinsmith replaced with metal; when he became all metal, however, he no longer had a heart and couldn't love the girl. In hopes of receiving a heart, he joins the trip to the Wizard.

A lion attacks, but when Dorothy challenges him, he reveals himself as a cringing coward, and agrees to join them to petition Oz for courage. The journey takes them through the wildest parts of Oz, where they face kalidahs (part bear, part lion) and a field of poppies that puts the "meat people" to sleep until the Scarecrow and Tin Woodman work out a plan with some friendly field mice to save their friends.

When they reach the Emerald City, the group has to don green glasses to protect them from its blinding beauty. Inside the city, everything is green, even people and food. Oz meets each of them individually in different shapes (a ball of fire, a monster, a beautiful woman, a disembodied head) and tells each of them that he'll grant their

Dorothy watches as the Winged Monkeys bind the Cowardly Lion. W.W. Denslow, *The Wonderful Wizard of Oz.*

wishes, once they kill the Wicked Witch of the West.

When they enter the land of the Winkies, the one-eyed witch, Blinky, sends armies of wolves, crows, bees and then Winkies against them, but Dorothy's friends triumph each time. The furious witch uses a magic cap to summon the Winged Monkeys, who destroy Tin Woodman and Scarecrow and capture the Lion. They can't harm Dorothy because of the Good Witch's kiss, but bring her safely before Blinky.

Blinky intimidates Dorothy into serving her, then trips her with an invisible rope which dislodges one of the slippers. Angry, Dorothy douses Blinky with a bucket of water, which melts the Witch away. Free, the Winkies repair Scarecrow and Tin Woodman. When Dorothy learns the power of the cap, she summons the Winged Monkeys, who take them to the Emerald City.

Oz refuses to see them until Dorothy threatens to summon the monkeys; when he does see them, he's a disembodied voice reneging on his promises. Toto knocks over a screen, revealing the Great and Powerful Oz as a little old man whose magic is humbug ("A good man — but a bad wizard."). Oz explains he was a circus entertainer hailed as a wizard after his balloon was swept from America to Oz and he descended on the city from the sky. He maintained the illusion with "humbug" (fraud and trickery — the word evolved from criminal slang in the eighteenth century, though the exact origin is unknown) such as the stage magic that created his different shapes and the green glasses that make everything in the city look magically green.

Oz tries to convince Dorothy's friends that they have already proven their intelligence, compassion and courage; when they insist on magic help, however, he provides it (pins and needles to make the Scarecrow's brains sharp, a soft silk heart for Nick Chopper, a courage potion for the Lion), arguing to himself that he can't be blamed for fooling people who insist on him doing the impossible.

Oz and Dorothy then put together a new balloon to return to America, but while Dorothy looks for Toto, the balloon breaks loose and leaves without her. She summons the Winged Monkeys, but they can't cross the desert; a green-whiskered soldier suggests Dorothy seek help from Glinda, the powerful witch of the South.

Dorothy and her friends pass through a forest of fighting trees, a country of living china dolls, a forest ruled by a giant spider — which the Lion slays — and the hill of the Hammerheads, whose elongated necks let them head-butt anyone who comes near. The Winged Monkeys carry everyone over the Hammerhead hill to Glinda.

Glinda agrees to send Dorothy home in return for the golden cap, which she will use to send the others home: The Scarecrow to rule the Emerald City, the Tin Woodman to rule the Winkies, the Lion to rule the forest where he slew the spider (all with their subjects' consent, of course). After she tells Dorothy the magic of the shoes, Dorothy clicks the heels together three times, taking her and Toto home to a delighted Auntie Em (the first sign of affection Em shows).

The first Oz book is very different from the series to follow, and from the MGM version — and not just because Baum's Oz is quite real. This bleak version of Kansas is closer to the frontier in Lillian Gish's *The Wind* (1927) than the happy farm of the Garland film; Baum visited Kansas only once, but he may have based it on his relatives' stories, or on his own life in South Dakota.

Oz is also different from the way later Baum books portrayed it. Instead of one fairyland sharing a continent with many other realms, it's simply an isolated, "uncivilized" land not that far removed from those in the "lost race" novels by H. Rider Haggard, Edgar Rice Burroughs, A. Merritt and other twentieth century writers (Merritt's fantasies certainly included creatures as bizarre as a man of living tin).

There's a long-standing tradition that Baum took the name "Oz" from an O–Z filing cabinet label (or from the "oohs" and "aahs" of his child fans), but his wife Maud said flat out that Baum just made it up. As biographer Katherine Rogers has pointed out, it's not that different from other Baum creations such as Ev, Ix or Yew.

The book draws on Baum's mother-in-law Matilda Gage's vision of witches as wise keepers of ancient knowledge, unfairly persecuted by the medieval church (while some fundamentalist Christians love *The Wizard of Oz*, one group sued to have Baum removed from a school library, objecting that portraying good witches goes against the Bible). Dorothy may have been named after Baum's niece, who died at five months old, or simply because it was a popular name in fiction; Baum himself used Dorothy in *Mother Goose in Prose* and Dot in *Dot and Tot in Merryland* (the Gale surname came from the 1902 stage adaptation).

Certainly a lot of the book's success came from Denslow's charming illustrations, which were worked into the text freely; in some cases, text was printed right over them.

Some fans have argued one change that improved on Baum was MGM cutting the ending trip to Glinda; others have argued it gives Dorothy's friends a chance to prove their brains, heart and courage. The China Country was a foretaste of the whimsical theme kingdoms Baum would use more often in the later books (sometimes simply to fill space).

Baum had no plans for a sequel and instead went on to write *Dot and Tot of Merryland*, *American Fairy Tales*, *The Master Key* and *Life and Adventures of Santa Claus* before the success of the 1902 *Wizard of Oz* musical persuaded him to return to Oz.

The Marvelous Land of Oz. Illustrated by John R. Neill. Chicago: Reilly & Britton, 1904. 287 pages. This book has 16 color plates.

The cover shows the Scarecrow and Tin Woodman on the front and Jack Pumpkinhead on the back, and Jinjur on the spine. The dust jacket was monochrome, with dark green printing on light green stock; the cover casings include light green or red cloth, stamped in navy blue, silver and green; red cloth with identical stamping and the title outlined in silver; the same stamping on rose cloth.

The title changed to *The Land of Oz* in 1906.

Tip, a young boy, lives in the Gilliken quarter of Oz with the old witch Mombi. Returning from a trip, Mombi confronts a pumpkin-headed stick figure Tip built to scare her; to the boy's astonishment, she brings "Jack Pumpkinhead" to life with a powder she obtained from another wizard. Mombi decides to kill Tip and use Jack for her new servant, so Tip steals the powder, animates a wooden sawhorse and rides it with Jack to the Emerald City to seek protection from the Scarecrow.

Unfortunately, their arrival coincides with that of General Jinjur and her all-girl Army of Revolt. Jinjur plans to seize the throne of Oz, distribute the emeralds to her girls, then force the men of Oz to assume housework duties. The army seizes the city, but Tip, Jack and the Scarecrow escape on the Sawhorse to the Tin Woodman.

Returning to reclaim the throne, they meet H.M. Woggle-Bug, T.E., a pompous but well-educated insect who lived in a classroom until a science project magnified him to human size. Their path is blocked by Mombi, who's thrown in with Jinjur and sets an array of illusions in the heroes' path. With the help of the Queen of the Field Mice (from *The Wizard of Oz*) the band escapes the illusions and, once they reach Scarecrow's palace, the sight of the mice sends the Army of Revolt screaming away (women's phobia of mice was a common stereotype of the day). The girls still keep the palace surrounded, but Tip uses the last of the Powder of Life to create a flying steed, the Gump, out of a hunting trophy's head lashed to two couches and palm-leaf wings.

The Gump flies them to Glinda, who tells the Scarecrow he has no more right to the throne than the Wizard or Jinjur: The rightful ruler is Princess Ozma, who vanished as an infant after the Wizard deposed her father, King Pastoria. After Glinda's research

Dorothy picks a meal from a lunch-pail tree. John R. Neill, *Ozma of Oz*.

indicates Mombi knows Ozma's whereabouts, Glinda leads her own female army to the Emerald City and captures Mombi when the witch tries to flee. Mombi confesses that in return for learning some of the Wizard's magic, she agreed to hide Ozma away — transformed into Tip.

After Tip agrees to be transformed back, Glinda captures Jinjur and ends the revolution. Ozma assumes the throne and the Scarecrow happily joins the Tin Woodman in the Winkie country.

After the 1902 *Wizard of Oz* musical became a hit, Baum decided to write a sequel to *Wizard* that could be turned into a second stage show. He hoped it would star Montgomery and Stone, who played the Tin Woodman and Scarecrow in the '02 show; it didn't work out, as detailed in the *Woggle-Bug* entry [under "1905" in Chapter 2]). Hence the working title for this book, *The Scarecrow and the Tin Woodman*; the release of *Denslow's Scarecrow and Tin Woodman* may have helped kill that idea.

Accordingly, the book gave large roles to the Tin Woodman and the Scarecrow and didn't bring back Dorothy (the bland ingenue in the stage *Wizard* was replaced by the feistier Prissie Pringle on stage); it's the only Baum Oz novel with no Americans in the cast. It also had lots of female soldiers suitable for chorus numbers. Jinjur's revolt also parodied the suffragettes (even more so in *The Woggle-Bug*) despite Baum's own support for the movement and his otherwise strong women's characters (when Jinjur shows up in later books, she's still strong-minded and stubborn, instead of being chastened into accepting subservience).

One person who didn't return was Denslow. He and Baum had been somewhat at odds over who should receive the most credit for their joint success, and even more at odds when Denslow demanded an equal share of the royalties from the 1902 musical. Baum also resented that Denslow had co-copyright to *Wizard* and *Father Goose* and so had as much right to the characters as Baum did. When their original publisher folded, Baum and Denslow parted ways and Reilly & Lee hired talented John R. Neill as the new Royal Illustrator. Neill held the post until his death, not to mention writing three Oz books of his own.

The other landmark in *Land* is, of course, the introduction of Ozma, drawn as a blonde here but raven-haired from *Ozma of Oz* on (possibly to contrast her with Dorothy's blonde locks). The boy-to-girl transition (a stage element lifted from British pantomime) seriously unsettled some readers, such as future Royal Historian Jack Snow, who had Tip's indignant spirit return in the short story, "A Murder in Oz."

Not for the last time, Baum ignored his own continuity: Mombi tells Glinda the Wizard taught her real magic as well as stage tricks, and we're told the Wizard overthrew King Pastoria (the name of the monarch in the '02 play) rather than filling an empty throne. Giving an innocent babe to Mombi also hardly qualifies him as "a good man," one reason some adaptations have stressed that the Wizard made Mombi swear to take good care of Ozma.

Ozma of Oz. Illustrated by John R. Neill. Chicago: Reilly & Britton, 1907. 270 pages.

Instead of color plates, there are colored illustrations in the text. The cover is light tan stamped in black, red, blue and yellow, showing Dorothy and Ozma on the front; Ozma's face on the spine; and cowardly Lion, Hungry Tiger and Billina on the back. The full color dust jacket has a different front showing several characters.

On a sea voyage with Uncle Henry, Dorothy is swept overboard in a storm along with Billina, a yellow hen; they wash up in Ev, on the far side of the Deadly Desert from Oz. They discover Tik-Tok, a wind-up mechanical man who protects them from the Wheelers (bullies with wheels for hands and feet) but runs down when Dorothy is captured by Princess Langwidere. The self-centered ruler of Ev wears many different heads and locks Dorothy up until the girl agrees to trade her noggin for one of Langwidere's.

Fortunately, Ozma arrives in Ev with her army (26 officers, one private), Dorothy's three friends and the insatiable Hungry Tiger. Langwidere releases Dorothy, who joins the Ozites on their quest to free the royal family of Ev, sold by the late king to Roquat, the Nome King.

In Roquat's underground kingdom, the jovial monarch reveals he turned the royals into bric-a-brac, and offers to free them if the Ozites can guess which ornaments they are. Anyone who fails to find even one royal, however, will also become an ornament.

Ozma agrees, then discovers how very many ornaments the Nome King has. One by one, she and the others are transformed until Billina eavesdrops on Roquat and learns how to save both Ozites and Evites. Furious, Roquat threatens to kill them all, but the Scarecrow uses Billina's eggs—poison to Nomes—to hold them at bay while Dorothy snatches the Nome King's magic belt, the key to his transformation powers. The battle won, everyone returns to the Emerald City; Dorothy gives Ozma the belt and Ozma sends her home, promising to watch over Dorothy and help if she ever needs it.

Because so many children had written asking for Dorothy to meet Ozma, Baum reintroduced her to Oz. He also introduced his best villain, the Nome King; the "Nome" name reflects Baum's interest in Theosophy, a nineteenth-century mystical movement that believed in the existence of elemental spirits (earth nomes, fire salamanders, etc.). It may also have been inspired by the Nome King in Edith Ogden Harrison's *Prince Silverwings* fairytale collection, which Baum later adapted for the stage (a Nome King also appears in *Life and Adventures of Santa Claus*).

Tik-Tok, the wind-up man, is a textbook example of Baum's modern fairytale concept: Tik-Tok is not magical, but Baum asserts that only in fairyland could so sophisticated a machine be built. While often described as a prototype robot, Tik-Tok probably owes more to sophisticated automatons such as the Turk, a mechanical man that astounded nineteenth century America by beating humans at chess (it was a fake, but that wouldn't be proven for years), or a mechanical man exhibited at fairs and carnivals around the time *Ozma* came out (Ozma's Magic Picture, which shows any person she wishes, may refer to a standard sideshow magic trick).

This was the first book to set Oz on its own continent, rather than being simply isolated by the Deadly Desert — and here the desert is deadly even to touch, not simply dangerous to cross.

Baum subsequently adapted the book into *The Tik-Tok Man of Oz*, a stage play later re-adapted as *Tik-Tok of Oz*.

Dorothy and the Wizard in Oz. Illustrated by John R. Neill. Chicago: Reilly & Britton, 1908. 256 pages.

This has 16 full-color plates. The cover is light blue cloth with a pictorial paper label in colors, and figures and lettering set against a metallic gold background. The dust jacket is full color. The cover shows Dorothy, the Wizard and the piglets he uses in his magic act; the Tin Woodman's face is on the spine.

In California (on the way home from the cruise in *Ozma*), Dorothy, her kitten Eureka, her cousin Zeb and his horse Jim are caught in an earthquake and fall through a crevasse into the realm of the Mangaboo plant people. The Mangaboos want to punish them for the earthquake, but when the Wizard's new balloon descends into the Mangaboo land, he intimidates the plant-folk with his "magic." The humans pluck a new Mangaboo ruler off a bush, but instead of being grateful, she has them sealed inside a cavern to die.

Fortunately, the band finds a passage out of the cavern into the Valley of Voe, with its invisible bears; then the wooden land of the malevolent wooden gargoyles; then a cavern of baby dragons which leads to a dead-end tunnel. Dorothy remembers Ozma's promise to watch over her and signals for help; Ozma teleports everyone to the Emerald City.

Over the next few days, Eureka goes on

trial for supposedly killing one of the Wizard's pet piglets, and Jim foolishly tries racing the tireless Sawhorse. Ozma sees her people are still amazed at the Wizard's humbug and makes him court magician before transporting Dorothy, Jim and Zeb back to California and Uncle Henry.

In answer to requests from his readers, Baum brought the Wizard back to Oz, though he had to fudge a little to do it — Ozma's retelling of Oz history drops the Wizard, turning her over to Mombi. This was the first (but not the last) book to use Ozma as a deus ex machina.

The Road to Oz. Illustrated by John R. Neill. Chicago: Reilly & Britton, 1909. 261 pages.

There are two pages of ads in the back for other Baum books and his pseudonymous Laura Bancroft work. There are no color plates.

The cover has a picture of the yellow brick road with Shaggy Man wearing a donkey head. The spine has Toto; the back shows Ozma and Dorothy. The cover is light green cloth stamped in black, dark green, tan and red; the full-color dust cover shows Dorothy up front with her three friends behind her. (The illustration on page 15 is for a later edition.)

When Dorothy tries to give a friendly tramp called the Shaggy Man directions, she discovers the roads have been magically distorted so now they're both lost. Protected by Shaggy's Love Magnet, which lets him charm anyone who looks at it, Dorothy, Shaggy and Toto pass through assorted odd kingdoms, picking up a sullen lost boy called Button-Bright, and Polychrome, the Rainbow's daughter, along the way. In the course of the trip, Shaggy Man is stuck with a donkey's head and Button Bright with that of a fox.

At the Deadly Desert, Shaggy Man's friend Johnny Dooit builds a magic sled which carries them to the Emerald City. Ozma reveals she's having a birthday party and enchanted the roads to lead Dorothy here (while watching in case Dorothy needed protection). The Oz cast and characters from other Baum books (Santa Claus, Queen Zixi, John Dough and Chick) attend the party; Dorothy heads home afterwards but Shaggy Man stays in Oz, giving Ozma the Love Magnet.

This rather aimless road trip does show the two sides of Baum's modern fairytales with its two new characters: Polychrome is a typical, though charming, fairy in the classic mold, while the Shaggy Man seems to spring from the era's fascination for tramps, often portrayed in popular fiction as free-spirited nonconformists. On the vaudeville stage of that era, tramp comics were as popular as Yiddish and black-face performers.

This book also begins the transition of Oz to a true Utopia. *Land of Oz* established Ozma's reign as a golden age, but here Oz is described as a land where greed, money and overwork are unknown and those who have plenty give freely to those in need (it has been suggested that after his many hard knocks in business, a land free of social Darwinism may have had strong appeal to Baum).

Button Bright here comes off as a dullard who answers "don't know" to everything, but his ornery personality in later books suggests "don't know" is simply a way of brushing people off, not expressing ignorance.

The Emerald City of Oz. Illustrated by John R. Neill. Chicago: Reilly & Britton, 1910. 296 pages.

There are 16 full-color plates. The cover comes in both light blue and dark blue cloth, printed with a pictorial paper label in colors, with metallic green against a silver background. The label shows the Sawhorse pulling Ozma's wagon. The full-color dust jacket reprints a list of Baum books on the back.

Embittered over his defeat in *Ozma of Oz*, Roquat sets his Nomes to digging a tunnel toward the Emerald City while Nome General Guph enlists three monstrous races — the grotesque Whimsies, the inhumanly strong Growleywogs and the sorcerously mighty Phanfasms — to join in the invasion. Everyone except the dimwitted Whimsies intends to double-cross the others once the Emerald City falls.

Back in Kansas, the bank forecloses on the

Jack Pumpkinhead at home: John R. Neill's cover for *The Road to Oz*.

The Growleywogs vow war upon Oz. John R. Neill, *The Emerald City of Oz.*

Dorothy and the ruler of Bunnybury do lunch. John R. Neill, *Emerald City of Oz.*

Gale farm, so Ozma brings Dorothy, Henry and Em to the Emerald City to stay. To celebrate, Dorothy and the Wizard — now a real wizard under Glinda's tutelage — take a tour of Oz, encountering the living desserts of Bunbury (whom Dorothy callously insists she has a right to eat), the rabbits of Bunnybury, the pompous Rigmaroles and the worry-wort Flutterbudgets.

By chance, Ozma checks up on Roquat with her Magic Picture and discovers his plan. She refuses to make war, even in self-defense, so the Scarecrow suggests filling the tunnel with dust, leaving the invaders dry, coughing and thirsty when they emerge ... in front of a glorious fountain, the water of which just happens to erase memories.

With the forces of evil all amnesiac, Ozma

sends them home. To forestall another invasion or airplanes flying into Oz, Glinda renders the realm utterly invisible from beyond its borders. Oz is cut off from us and the series, Baum concludes, is now over.

Baum really did attempt to end the series with this book so he could move on to the Trot and Cap'n Bill books, but though *The Sea Fairies* and *Sky Island* were excellent books, the sales were poor, and Baum returned to Oz with *The Patchwork Girl of Oz*.

The Emerald City of Oz is unusually preachy for an Oz book, with the Rigmaroles, Flutterbudgets and Whimsies all cited as examples of how boys and girls should *not* behave.

The Patchwork Girl of Oz. Illustrated by John R. Neill. Chicago: Reilly & Britton, 1913. 340 pages.

There are five pages of publisher's advertisements at the end of the book, giving synopses of the second through the sixth Oz books. The cover is light green cloth stamped in green, red and yellow, with Scraps on the front and the Woozy on the spine. The dust jacket shows Scraps and Ojo on the front and the Woozy on the back, flashing fire from his eyes to light a candle. There are no color plates, but color is used in many text illustrations.

Munchkins Unc Nunkie and his nephew Ojo visit their nearest neighbor, Dr. Pipt, the creator of the Powder of Life from *The Land of Oz*, and his wife Margolette. When they arrive, Pipt is completing a new batch of powder (despite Ozma's banning magic except for herself, Glinda and the Wizard) to animate "Scraps," a life-sized ragdoll who will become Margolette's servant. When Ojo realizes Pipt plans to create a dull drudge, Ojo sneaks extra brain mixture into the doll's head.

When Scraps comes to life, a startled Margolette spills a petrifying potion on herself and Unc Nunkie. Ojo sets out to find the ingredients for an antidote, accompanied by the magician's selfish glass cat, Bungle, and by Scraps—cynical, flamboyant and fun-loving, and constantly spouting poetry. Along the way they meet the Shaggy Man, the Scarecrow and the Woozy, a cubical creature whose tail hair is needed for the cure.

In the Emerald City, Ojo picks a six-leaf clover for the potion, but gets arrested because the clover is also an ingredient in evil magic. When Ozma learns his motive, she sets him free.

After accumulating all but one ingredient—and stopping a war between the neighboring Hopper and Horner tribes in the process—Ojo asks the Tin Woodman for the last item, the wing of a yellow Winkie butterfly. The Woodman refuses to let any living creature in his lands be harmed, but fortunately Ozma, Glinda and the Wizard have found their own cure. The petrification is reversed, Pipt is stripped of magic and Ojo, Unc Nunkie, Scraps and Bungle the glass cat move to the Emerald City.

After the modest sales on the Trot and Cap'n Bill books, Baum returned to Oz, planning to alternate the two series; sales on *Patchwork Girl* were so much better, however, that Baum was locked into Oz for the rest of his career. Baum explains in the introduction that he re-established contact with Oz through "wireless telegraph" (radio); in another example of Baum's modern fairytale approach, the Horner city is decorated with that most modern of metals, radium.

Scraps is one of Baum's best characters; where Nick Chopper yearned for a heart, the flamboyant rag doll delights in being free from human sentiment (though she does stick her neck out for Ojo) and shows an energy that bounces off the page. The book also shows Baum's lack of continuity: The Dr. Nikidik referred to in *The Land of Oz* has a new name, and seems none the worse for having been reported dead in *The Road to Oz* (leading one fan to suggest he faked death and started a new life so that he could keep working magic).

Baum wrote one chapter, "The Garden of Meats," set in a kingdom where vegetables plant and eat people. When the publisher

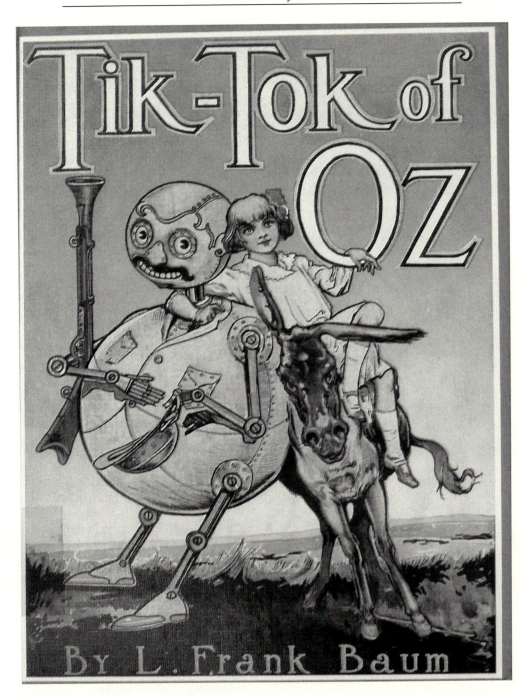

Tik Tok, Betsy Bobbin and Hank the Mule from the cover of *Tik Tok of Oz*.

protested this would be too disturbing for children, Baum suggested an alternative chapter featuring the Marshmallow Twins; instead the chapter was dropped, with only Neill's illustrations remaining (and no hint at all who the Marshmallow Twins would have been).

Tik-Tok of Oz. Illustrated by John R. Neill. Chicago: Reilly & Britton, 1914. 272 pages.

The frontispiece to *Tik Tok of Oz*, by John R. Neill, dedicated to Louis Gottschalk, the composer for the *Tik Tok Man of Oz* stage play.

There are 12 full-color plates. The cover is medium-blue cloth with a pictorial paper label in colors showing Tik-Tok, Hank and Betsy. The full-color dust jacket had an identical illustration.

Betsy Bobbin and her pet mule Hank are washed ashore in Ev (though Hank doesn't talk until they reach Oz). They meet the Shaggy Man, who is out to rescue his brother from the prison caverns of the Nome King, who has resumed his evil ways but not his name (he's now called Ruggedo, and would be for the rest of the series). Along the way they're joined by Princess Ozga, a refugee from a rose kingdom; Queen Ann Soforth of Oogaboo who fantasizes about conquering Oz with her 27-man army; Polychrome; and Tik-Tok, whom they find shattered by the Nome King, to whom Ozma had sent him as an emissary.

Shaggy reassembles Tik-Tok, but Ruggedo sends the entire party into a tunnel that shoots them to the far side of the Earth, much to the anger of that realm's ruler, the all-powerful fairy Tititi-Hoochoo. He sends the group back up the tunnel on dragon-back, bearing a magic locket that enables them to take away Ruggedo's magic. The king flees, leaving his steward, Kaliko, as Nome Ruler; Shaggy finds his brother and frees him from a spell of ugliness; Betsy and Hank settle down in the Emerald City; and Ann gives up her ambitions and returns home with Ozga, who marries one of Ann's soldiers.

This book adapts Baum's stage show, *The Tik-Tok Man of Oz*, which was itself an adaptation of *Ozma of Oz*. Baum's plans to adapt the third Oz book had hit a snag when it turned out all the characters from *The Wizard of Oz* and *The Land of Oz* were contractually tied up with their respective stage shows. His solution was to replace them — Betsy and Hank for Dorothy and Billina, Ann's army for Ozma's, etc.— which explains why Betsy has absolutely no back-story here and why Roquat's name changed (he'd been Ruggedo on stage, so that was apparently good enough).

The Scarecrow of Oz. Illustrated by John R. Neill. Chicago: Reilly & Britton, 1915. 288 pages.

This book has 12 full-color plates. The cover is bright green cloth with a pictorial label in colors that shows the Scarecrow with crows perching all over him; the full-color dust jacket has the identical illustration.

While Trot and Cap'n Bill (from *The Sea Fairies* and *Sky Island*) are boating, a storm traps them in a coastal cave. With the help of the friendly flying Ork, they escape through an underground tunnel, and after a series of adventures, meet their friend Button Bright. The humans and Ork arrive in Jinxland, an isolated Oz kingdom ruled by the usurper, King Krewl.

Krewl wants the rightful ruler, Princess Gloria, to marry the wealthy Googly-Goo, but she loves Pon, a prince forced to labor as an under-gardener. When the three Americans show up, Bill's fearlessness convinces Krewl the sailor must have magic power. The king summons the witch Blinkie to destroy the captain and bring about Gloria's marriage; Blinkie freezes Gloria's heart, killing her love for Pon, and turns Bill into a wooden-legged grasshopper.

When the Scarecrow learns this from Glinda's Book of Records, which records all events in the world, he decides to intervene and thwart Krewl. In Jinxland, he meets the kids and Cap'n Bill, then Krewl, who finds his swordsmen outmatched by the Scarecrow's flexibility and lack of internal organs. Nevertheless, the army overwhelms the straw man, but before he can be burnt to death, a squadron of Orks arrive, scattering Krewl's forces with the wind of their tail propellers.

Blinkie undoes her evil before being stripped of her powers; Pon and Gloria marry and take the throne; and everyone else returns to Oz, where Trot, Cap'n Bill and Button Bright decide to stay.

This book adapted the Oz Film Company's *His Majesty, King Scarecrow*, which is why it is the only Oz book with a major romantic subplot. Baum, who didn't think romance belonged in children's stories, makes it almost a parody, with Trot and Button Bright baffled by Gloria and Pon's high-flown romantic speeches.

With the Trot and Cap'n Bill series kaput, Baum relocated them to Oz for more adventures, but says nothing of what Trot's parents (or Button Bright's) made of this (presumably since they had no reason to move the way Em and Henry did, it was easier just to ignore that detail).

Rinkitink in Oz. Illustrated by John R. Neill. Chicago: Reilly & Britton, 1916. 314 pages.

This book has 12 full-color plates. The cover is very light-blue cloth with a pictorial paper label on the front showing Inga and Rinkitink riding Bilbil. The spine shows Bilbil. The full-color dustjacket has an identical illustration.

The sea raiders of Regos and Coregos descend on the peaceful island of Pingaree and drag the entire population off in chains, save for Prince Inga, visiting King Rinkitink (a jovial glutton avoiding the responsibilities of ruling his own realm) and Rinkitink's dour steed, the goat Bilbil. Inga knows of three

The Scarecrow of Oz and some friends. John R. Neill's cover of *The Scarecrow of Oz.*

magic pearls—granting strength, invulnerability and wisdom—hidden in the palace, and unearths them from the ruins to rescue his people.

With his new powers, Inga captures Regos, but the king retreats with his Pingaree slaves to Coregos. Rinkitink loses Inga's shoes—with the pearls hidden in them—and they wind up on a peasant girl's feet. Queen Coregos captures the now-helpless prince, but

In the aftermath of the invasion of Pingaree, Inga helps Rinkitink out of hiding. John R. Neill. *Rinkitink in Oz.*

Prince Inga to the rescue, powered by the magic pearls of Pingaree. John R. Neill, *Rinkitink in Oz*.

when Inga regains the pearls, he frees himself and his people. The evil monarchs flee to the Nome Caverns, where the current king, Kaliko, promises to keep Inga's parents imprisoned forever.

When Inga and his friends arrive, Kaliko refuses to break his promise, but can't destroy them because of the power of the pearls. Fortunately, Dorothy has been following events in the Book of Records and comes with a basket of eggs to change Kaliko's mind. Pingaree is restored, Coregos and Regos remain free, Rinkitink reluctantly returns to his kingdom and the Wizard discovers Bilbil is a transformed prince himself and restores him to normal.

King Rinkitink was originally an unpublished non–Oz novel written in 1905, transformed into an Oz book by using Dorothy for a deus ex machina (which reduces a great book to a merely good book) and deftly rewriting Roquat's role to fit the less evil Kaliko.

The Lost Princess of Oz. Illustrated by John R. Neill. Chicago: Reilly & Britton, 1917. 312 pages.

This book contains 12 full-color plates. The cover is light-blue cloth with a pictorial paper label in colors showing Dorothy arm-in-arm with the Frogman. The full-color dust jacket has the same illustration.

It's trouble in Oz when Ozma's court discovers that the Magic Picture, the Book of Records, Glinda's and the Wizard's magical equipment and Ozma herself have all vanished overnight. The courtiers split up into search parties to scour the kingdom, with Dorothy bringing along the Nome King's belt, which hasn't been stolen.

Meanwhile, in the pocket Oz kingdom of Yip, the baker Cayke discovers that her gold dishpan — allegedly magical — has vanished too. She sets out to find it along with the Frogman, a conceited, man-sized frog revered by the Yips for his size and (non-existent) wisdom. Unfortunately for the Frogman, he bathes in a Truth Pond which makes him admit his limitations to Cayke and everyone else, giving him a crash course in humility.

Dorothy's searchers (including Button-Bright, the Wizard, Scraps and the Lion) eventually reach the city of the super-strong Herkus. The Herku leader points them toward the wicker castle of Ugu the Shoemaker, who withdrew from the city to follow his ancestors' tradition of sorcery.

It is a good guess that Ugu, having discovered Cayke's dishpan can teleport, stole it and used it to swipe every magic item Ozma and her court could use against him, then kidnapped and transformed Ozma after she caught him at work.

Cayke and the Frogman learn some of this from the clairvoyant Little Pink Bear of Bear Center. The bear king, the Lavender Bear, joins Cayke's quest, bringing the pink visionary along. When they meet Dorothy's group, the Little Pink Bear steers them to Ozma, but all they find is a lost Button Bright.

When they reach the castle, the Wizard neutralizes Ugu's stolen magical defenses, but Ugu still contrives to trap his foes. But his family books taught him about Oz magic, not the Nome King's belt, which Dorothy uses to escape the wizard's snares, then turn him into a dove. Cayke reclaims her pan; the group finds Ozma, transformed into a peach-pit, in Button Bright's pocket; and after she's restored, the now sensible Frogman joins her court. Ugu later tells Dorothy that in his new form, he's finally free of greed and ambition.

Written under the working title *Three Girls in Oz*, this book gave the series its second-best villain in Ugu.

The Tin Woodman of Oz. Illustrated by John R. Neill. Chicago: Reilly & Britton, 1917. 288 pages.

This book includes 12 full-color plates. The cover is red cloth with a pictorial label showing the Tin Woodman and Captain Fyter holding up Woot the Wanderer; the Tin Woodman's on the spine. The full-color dust jacket has the same illustrations. The first edition was the only Reilly & Britton printing before the company changed its name to Reilly & Lee.

When young Woot the Wanderer enters

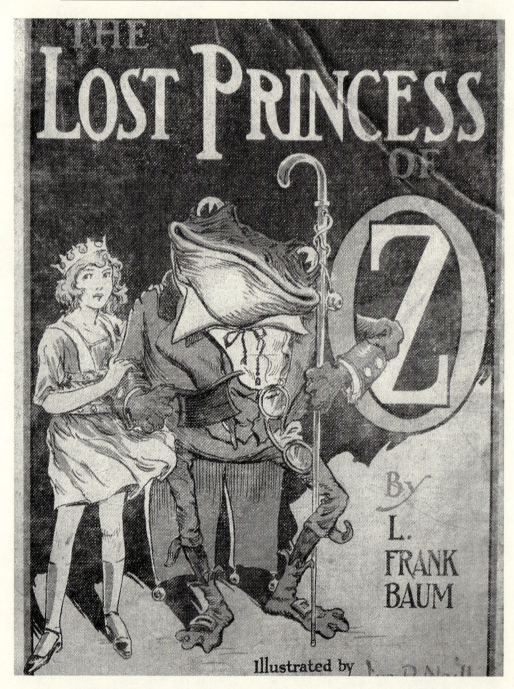

Dorothy and the Frogman, on John R. Neill's cover of *The Lost Princess of Oz*.

Nick Chopper's castle, the Tin Woodman tells the story of how he came to be made of tin (as described in *The Wizard of Oz*) and how, even after receiving a heart, he couldn't love his former sweetheart, Nimmie Amee, because the Wizard gave him a kind heart, not a loving one. Woot replies that it's better to have a kind husband than a loving one, and encourages the Tin Woodman to find his old love and propose.

Nick Chopper, meet Nick Chopper! The Tin Woodman encounters his "meat" head in a scene from *The Tin Woodman of Oz*.

The Woodman and Woot set off with the Scarecrow, but make the mistake of stopping at isolated Yoop Castle. Mrs. Yoop, the wife of a giant who appears briefly in *The Patchwork Girl of Oz*, is both a giant and a Yookoohoo, a mistress of transformations who has already turned Polychrome into a caged canary. Mrs. Yoop now turns Woot into a green monkey, Scarecrow into a straw bear and the Tin Woodman into a tin owl.

Despite the giantess's magic, her victims escape the castle. Glinda and Ozma manage

Nick Chopper, Woot and Captain Fyter on the cover of *The Tin Woodman of Oz*, drawn by John R. Neill.

to restore everyone but Woot; instead, they transform Mrs. Yoop into Woot, then swap her shape with the monkey body, restoring the Wanderer to normal while leaving Yoop in a magicless form.

The Tin Woodman, Scarecrow and Woot resume their mission and run into a rusted tin man not far from where Dorothy once found Nick Chopper. Oiled up, the man identifies himself as Captain Fyter, who loved Nimmie Aimee only to lose all his body parts when the Witch of the East cast a spell on his sword. Fyter and Nick agree Nimmie can choose which of them she wants to marry.

Stopping at Ku-Klip's cottage for directions, the Tin Woodman finds his old head stuck in a cupboard and they argue which of them is the real Nick Chopper. Ku-Klip tells the searchers that he magically recombined their other human parts into a single person, Chopfyt; when they reach Nimmie, they discover she married Chopfyt after the tin men vanished, and is too used to him to change. The search over, Woot resumes wandering, Tin Woodman and Scarecrow return to the Winkie country and Fyter is sent by Ozma to patrol the far north.

Baum said he wrote *The Tin Woodman* to answer the many letters he received asking why Tin Woodman never went back to his sweetheart after getting a heart. The backstory adds the detail absent from *The Wizard of Oz* that Nick Chopper's love was a servant to the Wicked Witch herself.

Transformation was a recurrent threat in Baum's Oz books (Glinda dismisses it in *The Land of Oz* as inherently deceitful), possibly because it allowed him to trap characters in terrible situations without any bloodshed or violence.

In this book Baum asserted that no one ever dies or ages in Oz, with even babies staying infants forever; Ruth Plumly Thompson modified this rather ghastly thought by stating the inhabitants can turn the ageing process on or off at will.

The Magic of Oz. Illustrated by John R. Neill. Chicago: Reilly & Lee, 1919. 266 pages.

This book has 12 color plates. The cover is bound in various shades of green cloth with a pictorial paper label in colors, showing Dorothy and the Wizard with one of the tiny monkeys; a monkey appears on the spine. The full-color dust jacket reproduces the illustrations.

Ozite Kiki Aru of Mt. Munch discovers a secret word that can transform anyone or anything into anyone or anything else. The restless boy morphs into an eagle to cross the Deadly Desert, and meets ex–Nome King Ruggedo. Learning of Kiki's power, Ruggedo suggests using the word to conquer Oz (while trying to learn the word so he can dispose of his new partner) by convincing the Oz animals Ozma will enslave them if they don't attack her first.

Meanwhile, Cap'n Bill, Trot and Bungle head into the Gilliken country to find the perfect gift for Ozma's birthday: a flower that changes blooms constantly from one minute to the next. They discover too late that anyone who steps onto the flower's island becomes rooted to the spot and slowly absorbed into the ground.

Seeking a troupe of monkeys to entertain at the party, Dorothy and the Wizard head into the same forests of Oz where Kiki and Ruggedo have appeared to the beasts as Limon-eags: winged, lion-headed monkeys. They're on the brink of winning over the king, Gugu the Leopard, when the humans arrive with the Cowardly Lion and Hungry Tiger. Kiki panics and turns them, along with Ruggedo and Gugu, into harmless shapes. The Wizard, however, overhears and masters the word, restores everyone to normal, turns Kiki Aru and Ruggedo into nuts and makes peace with the animals.

When the Wizard learns what has happened to Trot and Cap'n Bill, he goes to the island but can't break its spell. Instead he uses the word to turn the humans to bees; they fly away and are turned back to normal, then Bill finds a trick to finally claim the flower. After the big party, the Wizard restores the two villains and tricks them into drinking from the Fountain of Forgetfulness

Kiki Aru and Ruggedo transformed into li-mon-eags, plotting to conquer Oz. John R. Neill, *The Magic of Oz.*

again. This time, Ozma decrees, Ruggedo will be given a home in the Emerald City so they can watch over him and keep him from turning evil.

Baum being seriously ill, this book is heavily padded (the party scene takes up far too much space). The animals' revolt has been interpreted as a parody of the Russian Revolution, though Oz expert Michael Hearn has pointed out the book would have to have been whipped out pretty fast after that event to be published when it was.

The word "pyrzqxgl" has inspired countless Oz fans to try to figure out the pronounciation that will make it work (which actually happens in Zenna Henderon's short story, "The Believing Child").

Glinda of Oz. Illustrated by John R. Neill. Chicago: Reilly & Lee, 1920. 279 pages.

This book has 12 full-color plates. The cover comes in various cloth colors with no priority established; the pictorial paper label on the front cover shows Glinda surrounded

Reality or illusion? Ervic enters the cottage of Red Reera, the Yookoohoo shapeshifter. John R. Neill, *Glinda of Oz.*

by Dorothy, Ozma, the Scarecrow and the Tin Woodman. The full-color dust jacket duplicates the paper label illustration.

When the Book of Records reveals that the Oz races known as the Flatheads (who carry their brains in their pockets) and Skeezers are going to war, Ozma decides it's her duty to make peace. After a long journey north, she and Dorothy confront the Flathead sorcerer-ruler, Su-Dic, who blames the war on the Skeezer queen Coo-ee-oh refusing the Flathead's fishing rights in the lake around the Skeezer island, and turning Su-Dic's wife into a pig.

On the island, however, the girls learn more: Coo-ee-oh trapped her former mentors, the Three Adepts, in the lake as fish, and if they're killed, her power will vanish — hence Su-Dic's passion for fishing. The Flatheads attack the island, which Coo-ee-oh submerges (it's under a protective dome); in a battle with Su-Dic, he transforms the queen into a swan, avenging his wife, but leaving no one who can raise the island back up.

Ozma's court reaches the lakeshore and brainstorms with Glinda, while the Adepts contact the Skeezer Ervic, who's been trapped outside the city. With their guidance Ervic tricks the Yookoohoo shapeshifter Red Reera into restoring them to normal, but even they can't raise the city. Scraps thinks of lowering the lake, then breaking into the city; once inside, the Adepts and Glinda master Coo-ee-oh's secrets and raise the island. Both races are given better rulers and the Flatheads' skulls are restored to normal human shape.

Glinda of Oz was the last Baum book, published after his death.

The Books of Ruth Plumly Thompson, Second Historian of Oz

The Royal Book of Oz. Illustrated by John R. Neill. Chicago: Reilly & Lee, 1921. 303 pages.

This book contains 12 full-color plates. The cover is light-gray cloth with a pictorial label showing Dorothy and the Scarecrow perched on the Cowardly Lion.

When Professor Woggle-Bug writes the genealogy of Ozma and her court, he dismisses the Scarecrow as a nobody with no ancestors. Stung, the straw man returns to the beanpole on which he came to life, seeking proof he's more than he seems. He gets it when the earth caves in, leading to a fall that eventually deposits him far below ground, in the Silver Islands. The Scarecrow learns that the last emperor, Chang Wang Woe, was transformed by magic into a crocus—and the beanpole sprang from the crocus pot, reaching up to Oz and transferring the emperor's soul into the Scarecrow.

As the new emperor, the Scarecrow inspires adoration in his subjects—especially after stopping an invasion—except for his descendants, who realize an ageless Scarecrow can sit on the throne forever. They conspire to restore him to a human body with a local wizard's help, and to marry him off to boot.

Meanwhile, Dorothy and the Cowardly Lion seek their friend so they can brush off the Woggle-Bug's insults. They become trapped in the somnolent realm of the Slow Pokes, but manage to escape along with Sir Hokus, an old knight trapped there by a sorcerer. They meet the Doubtful Dromedary and the Comfortable Camel, then step onto a Wish Way where Dorothy wishes them to Scarecrow's side.

Reunited with his friends, the Scarecrow decides to abdicate, but the islanders refuse to let him go. The wizard tries to turn him into a human being, but a magic parasol Dorothy found enables her to turn the spell back on the Scarecrow's "sons." Scarecrow now insists on abdicating, appointing his whimsical aide Happy Toko as emperor in his place. The Ozites return to the Emerald City where the Woggle-Bug pens the Scarecrow's new history into the Royal Book of Oz.

Reilly & Lee had a stake in keeping the Oz series going despite Baum's death, so they invited Thompson—a rising young fairytale writer in her own right with *The Princess of Cozytown* and *The Perhappsy Chaps* to her credit—and asked her to become the new Royal Historian (Thompson has refuted persistent legends she was chosen because she'd been Baum's secretary, or relative). The publishers attributed her first book to Baum's leftover notes; Thompson didn't receive sole cover credit until DelRey Books' 1985 edition.

Thompson clearly knew her Oz, since she specifically covers why the Book of Records and the Magic Picture can't be used for Ozma to find everyone and save the day. It also shows the plot elements she would use in future books: A magical item, such as the parasol, that conveniently turns up, and theme kingdoms much more hostile than Baum's (keen, like Slow Pokes, on imprisoning anyone who crosses their border).

It's worth noting that Oz is one of the few, if not the only, series where continuations by other authors are actually considered "official" by most fans as much as the original author's work.

Kabumpo in Oz. Illustrated by John R. Neill. Chicago: Reilly & Lee, 1922. 297 pages.

This book has 12 full-color plates. The cover has blue or blue-green cloth with a pictorial paper label in colors showing Pompa, Peg Amy, Wag and Ozma perched on Kabumpo's head and trunk.

On his 18th birthday, Prince Pompadore of Pumperdink (a Gilliken kingdom) learns a prophecy. He must marry a fairy princess or see the kingdom disappear. His family plans for Pompa to marry the aging fairy Faleero, but Kabumpo, the royal elephant, carries Pompa off to the Emerald City to marry Ozma instead.

Meanwhile we learn Ruggedo has regained his memory since *The Magic of Oz* and has decorated a secret lair under the city with stolen furniture and Trot's stolen doll, Peg Amy. When the Nome uncovers a buried box of magic charms, he brings Peg Amy to life, turns his rabbit servant Wag man-size and makes himself so gigantic that Ozma's palace is stuck on his head. Shocked, Ruggedo strides across the desert to Ev and ponders what to do. Peg Amy and Wag follow with the box of magic; they meet Pompa and Kabumpo, who agree to help save Ozma.

On the way to Ev, the group is captured by sentient Runaway Island, which proclaims Peg its princess. When the island catches up with Ruggedo it freezes in shock and its "settlers" disembark. Although Ozma refuses Pompa's proposal, the magic from the box restores Ruggedo and the palace to normal and reveals that Pompa's true bride is the princess of Sun Top Mountain.

Pompa and the others travel to the mountain where they learn Peg Amy is the princess, transformed by the sorcerer Glegg. Glegg appears and reveals he has manipulated everything (including the fake prophecy) to restore the princess to normal. Ozma intervenes at the last minute and Glegg's own magic explodes him. Ozma then sends Runaway Island to the Nonestic Ocean with Ruggedo as its sole inhabitant. Pompa and Peg Amy marry and live happily ever after.

This book showed Thompson's fondness for princes from homey little duchies (villains often live in evil, vaguely Arabian kingdoms such as Mudge in the next book), and her greater use of romantic plots.

The Cowardly Lion of Oz. Illustrated by John R. Neill. Chicago: Reilly & Lee, 1923. 291 pages.

There are 12 full-color plates. The deep emerald-green or drab-green cloth cover has a pictorial paper label in colors showing Bob and Notta on the Lion's back.

In America, circus clown Notta Bit More unwittingly casts an old Oz spell that transports him and orphan Bob to the desert kingdom of Mudge. The brutal ruler Mustafa is obsessed with capturing the Cowardly Lion for his menagerie, but Glinda's magic prevents the Mudgers from leaving their land; Notta and Bob, however are free to leave, so Mustafa sends them forth, showing he can paralyze them magically if they double-cross him.

Meanwhile, the Cowardly Lion becomes convinced the Wizard's old courage potion has worn off, and that only eating a brave man will give him permanent courage. His soft heart undercuts his efforts, but when he meets Notta, the clown's bravery convinces the Lion this is the man to eat. The trio head to the Emerald City, all with hidden agendas.

Before long they wind up in the flying realm of Un, inhabited by people who are Unfriendly and Unreasonable. The trio's Unpleasant schemes cause them to turn into Uns until they repent and become friends. Stealing the Un leader's flying vehicle, they return to Oz, crashing in a stone quarry where they meet Crunch, a stone man who has spent centuries just standing there, but agrees to take the Lion to Mudge while Notta and Bob contact Ozma.

Despite the clown's terrifying the Emerald City residents by disguising himself as a witch, the two Americans convince Ozma they're the good guys. When Glinda discovers the Lion is in danger, Notta uses the spell from the start of the book to teleport everyone to Mudge. They arrive to see Crunch turn Mustafa's menagerie to stone, including the Cowardly Lion, whom he wants for his own pet. Glinda and the Wizard paralyze Crunch, strip away Mustafa's magic and take the Lion back to Ozma's palace where he's depetrified. Notta and Bob, of course, stay in Oz.

Grampa in Oz. Illustrated by John R. Neill. Chicago: Reilly & Lee, 1924. 271 pages.

There are 12 color plates in this book. The cover is light brick-red cloth with a pictorial picture label in color showing Grampa, Bill, Tatters and Pretty Good.

When a storm blows off the head of King Fumbo of Ragbad, it leaves the impoverished Oz province in worse shape than usual. Prince Tatters sets off to find Fumbo's head, accompanied by Grampa, a war veteran, and Bill, an iron weathercock the storm brought from America.

Meanwhile, in Perhaps City, the royal seer Abrog announces that Princess Pretty Good is doomed to marry a monster, and offers to save her by marrying her first. When the king nixes that idea, Abrog and Pretty Good both turn up missing; court poet Percy Vere sets off to find them.

Tatters and his friends are captured by bandits but escape with some of the bandits' magic loot. They enter the underground garden of the wizard Gorba and wake Urtha, a girl of flowers. Meanwhile, Percy Vere meets Dorothy and Toto, only to have a Runaway Road strand all three in the hinterlands of Oz.

Accompanied by Urtha, Tatters and his company undergo repeated trials until they find Fumbo's head in a cloud island (yes, his head is in the clouds!) and persuade it to come home with them. They meet Dorothy and Percy, but get separated from Urtha, who winds up in Perhaps City, where the king recognizes her as the transformed Pretty Good.

Tatters, having fallen in love with Urtha, follows her to the city — and is rushed into a marriage ceremony, King Peer Haps figuring that will stave off the wedding to the monster. As the others arrive, Abrog appears and proclaims Tatters *is* the monster, since he has two heads (having carried Fumbo's with him). Dorothy realizes Abrog is Gorba, spelled backwards, and Abrog admits to hiding Pretty Good in his garden after Peer Haps turned him down. Abrog is magically disposed of, Pretty Good returns to normal and her father gives Tatters a hen that lays gold bricks so Ragbad will be prosperous again.

The Lost King of Oz. Illustrated by John R. Neill. Chicago: Reilly & Lee, 1925. 280 pages.

The book includes are 12 color plates. The cover is medium-blue cloth with a pictorial paper label in color showing Pastoria, Pajuka, Snip and Ozma.

Years after the events of *The Land of Oz*, Mombi, the former witch, has used her cooking and brewing skills to become head cook to King Kinda Jolly in the province of Kimbaloo. She discovers the goose that she plans to cook for dinner is Pajuka, the former adviser to King Pastoria, Ozma's father, Mombi having transformed both men years before.

Pajuka convinces Mombi that if Mombi can remember what she turned Pastoria into, she'll be well-rewarded when he's restored to the throne. They set out to find the king, dragging along Snip, a servant boy who heard her plans. Knowing Snip wants to report all this to Ozma, Mombi plots to dispose of him.

At Ozma's court, a goose-feather quill pen warns Ozma to avert a coming danger by going "to Morrow today." When Scarecrow realizes "to Morrow" is a destination, not a time, the Wizard transports everyone to what Ozma recognizes as her father's old, abandoned castle. Scraps discovers a magic robe that can restore the king to his proper shape, and the group heads back to the city on foot (the Wizard forgot to bring transportation home).

Elsewhere in Oz, Dorothy pockets some magic sand that carries out her idle wish to visit America. Stumbling into a location film shoot (which shows us she left America too soon to know much about movies) she brings a dummy to life (called Humpy for his baggy body) and finds herself growing into her natural age before she manages to wish herself and Humpy back to Oz. Passing through some theme kingdoms, they meet Kabumpo, who agrees to give them a ride to the Emerald City.

Mombi throws Snip down a well, which turns out to lead him to the land of the Invisible Blanks. Here he makes a friend of Tora the Tailor, imprisoned for years but using flying ears to gather news. Snip and Tora escape; in the process, one of Pajuka's feathers caught on Snip's hands flies off to give that message to Ozma's court (we learn later it's a magic pen Pajuka was carrying when transformed). Trying to beat Mombi to Pastoria, Snip and Tora meet Dorothy and her party instead.

When they finally catch up with Mombi, Pajuka pegs Humpy as his old master and Mombi tries to restore him — but lacking the magic robe, she fails. When Ozma and the others catch up with them, they use the robe but Humpy still doesn't transform; Snip realizes it's Tora who is the transformed king. Pastoria, however, decides to remain a tailor, with Humpy and Snip as his assistants; Mombi is doused with water and destroyed forever.

A good attempt at straightening out the inconsistencies in Baum's Oz history.

The Hungry Tiger of Oz. Illustrated by John R. Neill. Chicago: Reilly & Lee, 1926. 261 pages.

There are 12 full-color plates. The cover is dark drab-green cloth with a pictorial paper label in colors showing Betsy and Carter Green reclining on the Hungry Tiger.

Irasha, the usurper tyrant of Rash (which lies just beyond the Deadly Desert) learns his prisons have no room for more inmates, due to Irasha's fondness for jailing anyone who even looks at him funny. The tyrant decides to bring the insatiable Hungry Tiger to Rash to eat the inmates. His vicious aide Ippty crosses the desert by magic and convinces the Tiger that since the prisoners are all condemned to death, his conscience won't be troubled.

In Rash, Irasha traps the Tiger in the prison courtyard and starts throwing in victims. The Tiger realizes the prisoners are pathetic and harmless, and hides them in a cleft in the wall rather than eat them. Back in Oz, Betsy Bobbin meets Carter Green, a grocer who loved vegetables so much his body is now made of them. Carter shows off a ruby he found inside a potato, then a series of magical flukes transports them across the desert to Rash. Irasha throws them to the Tiger along with the rightful ruler of Rash, Prince "Reddy" Evered.

The cleft leads the Ozites and Reddy into the money-making theme kingdom of Downtown, where the Rashian prisoners decide to stay. Reddy discovers Carter's ruby is one of three Rash rubies (scattered by Irasha) that gives the rightful rulers invulnerability in air, water and underground.

Leaving Downtown, the group wind up in the Nome Kingdom. King Kaliko refuses the Nomes' demands that he torture everyone — just for the sake of being mean, but then he learns about the ruby and decides to steal it to match one he already found. Carter swipes that ruby instead and their combined magic enables the group to escape to the surface — where the Hungry Tiger is captured by a girl giant from the city of Big Wigs.

Meanwhile, we learn the reason Ozma hasn't saved everyone is that she has been kidnapped by Atmos Fere, a balloon man who wants a specimen to prove life really exists at the bottom of the air. Ozma contrives to deflate Atmos so he sinks back to Earth, but she repairs him before he deflates to death.

Reddy sneaks into the Big Wig city and discovers its residents are normal people turned gigantic by their wigs. Stealing a wig, he frees the Tiger and rejoins the others, who then meet Ozma and Atmos. Atmos turns out to have the third ruby and willingly flies them over the Deadly Desert. Once in Rash, the power of the rubies and the giant wig make restoring Reddy to the throne easy, after which Atmos carries Irasha and Ippty back to the sky as his specimens.

This is the only story besides *Tik-Tok* to put Betsy center stage.

The Gnome King of Oz. Illustrated by John R. Neill. Chicago: Reilly & Lee, 1927. 282 pages.

There are 12 full-color plates in the book. The cover is bright-emerald green or light-jade green cloth with a pictorial paper label in colors showing Peter and Ruggedo.

When the Queen of Patch — an Oz kingdom devoted to sewing and quilting — falls to pieces from hard work, a magic spool picks Scraps as the new queen. The Patchwork Girl is delighted to rule a patchwork kingdom, until she discovers the Patch queen is literally the servant of her people, and that the malevolent Scissor Bird stands ready to cut her to shreds if she balks.

Over in Philadelphia, baseball-loving Peter is kidnapped by a balloon bird, but wriggles free over the Nonestic Ocean, washing up on Runaway Island, where Ruggedo was imprisoned in *Kabumpo in Oz*. Peter is amazed to learn Oz is real, but not entirely convinced by Ruggedo's story of how cruelly Ozma betrayed and abused him (Peter hasn't read any of Ruggedo's appearances). When an earthquake lifts a sunken galleon from the sea bottom, the duo uses it to escape.

Ruggedo takes a torn magic cloak from the pirate's treasure, planning to use it to reclaim his belt; Peter settles for two magic plant bulbs and a mysterious emerald. They eventually make their way to the Nome Kingdom, where Ruggedo bluffs Kaliko off the throne. He demands Kaliko fix the cloak, but learns it can only be done in Patch. Fortunately, the two bulbs grow plants that take them across the Deadly Desert in safety.

In Oz, Ruggedo and Peter meet Kuma Party, who can disassemble his body parts, then arrive in Rash, where Ruggedo sells Peter as a slave in return for sewing up the cloak. When it's fixed, however, Peter commands it to transport Ruggedo to Zamagoochie (Kuma's birthplace) in hopes of buying time (it works; Kuma's wizard father traps Ruggedo for several hours). Kuma's flying hand shows up and helps Scraps and Peter escape. They meet an oztrich that carries them to the Emerald City, bringing along its egg as a weapon against Ruggedo.

Ruggedo arrives in the Emerald City first, however, and uses the cloak's invisibility power to play pranks on the court until Ozma returns to the city with the belt. When Peter arrives with the egg, the Nome panics until it hatches; then Ozma returns, and Ruggedo snatches away the belt. Visible and triumphant, he prepares to transform his enemies, but Peter beans him with the emerald first — and it turns out its magic is to turn people mute! Peter returns to Philadelphia with two bags of pirate gold; with surprising open-mindedness the newspaper actually prints his story of saving Oz.

This is a rather odd title: In what possible sense is Ruggedo "of" Oz?

The Giant Horse of Oz. Illustrated by John R. Neill. Chicago and New York: Reilly & Lee, 1928. 281 pages.

There are 12 color plates in this book. The cover is brick-red cloth with a pictorial paper label in color, showing a half-dozen characters riding High Boy.

Years ago, when Mombi was Wicked Witch of the North (before the Good Witch defeated her), she kidnapped Queen Orin of the formerly happy Ozure Island and sent the sea dragon Quiberon to torment the islanders, and Orin's husband Cheeriobed. In the present, when the dragon learns of the mortal girls living in the Emerald City, he demands one as a handmaiden. The island seer Akbad uses magic wings to fly to the city, planning to kidnap one of the girls, while Prince Philador has the king of the local seagulls fly him to the Good Witch of the North for help.

Far away in Boston, a tailor finds an old book of spells in a coat he's working on and accidentally animates a local statue which wanders around, stumbling into a pit and crashing through the bottom, falling all the way to Oz. The Scarecrow meets him and names him Benny, since he's the statue of a Public Benefactor.

The Scarecrow and Trot take Benny to the Wizard to make him human, but Akbad snatches up the girl before they get far. Benny grabs the seer's ankle as he takes off and the magic wings carry them all (with Scarecrow hanging on) back to Quiberon's cavern. Trot and her companions escape into the cave tunnels, and Quiberon gets stuck in the passage trying to follow.

Tattypoo, Good Witch of the North, lives in Mombi's old cottage and admits to her pet dragon, Agnes, that she has no memory prior to her first battle with Mombi. When she uses a magic window to probe her past, she and Agnes fall through the window and vanish. Philador arrives to find an empty cottage, then accidentally frees Herby, a medicine man imprisoned in a bottle by Mombi (his torso now holds all his potions, a literal medicine chest).

Heading to the Emerald City for help, they first meet High Boy, a horse with telescopic legs that can ford any obstacle, then meet Trot, Scarecrow and Benny.

Back in the islands, Queen Orin shows up out of the blue, delighting the islanders until Quiberon frees himself and attacks her. Akbad saves her, but Quiberon demolishes the city. Fortunately, Philador and his friends have reached the Emerald City, so the Wizard teleports everyone to the islands and petrifies Quiberon.

Orin explains that Cheeriobod had rejected Mombi's advances years before, so the witch kidnapped Orin as payback and sought to turn her into another evil watch. Orin's good heart turned her into a good witch, Tattypoo, strong enough to defeat Mombi; when she finally learned the truth in the magic window, she reverted to normal and headed home. Everyone celebrates and Benny finally accepts that he is more interesting as a living statue than a real person.

Curiously, one illustration shows Scarecrow and Scraps on High Boy, but Scraps isn't in the story.

Jack Pumpkinhead of Oz. Illustrated by John R. Neill. Chicago and New York: Reilly & Lee, 1929. 252 pages.

The book has 12 full-color plates. The cover is greenish-grey or light-grey cloth with a pictorial paper label in color showing Jack with a sword.

Two years after *The Gnome King of Oz*, Peter finds one coin left in the sacks of pirate gold — a wishing coin that teleports him back to Oz. He lands outside Jack Pumpkinhead's house, so Jack takes him into the city for his "father," Ozma, to send Peter home. The perpetually skitterwitted Jack takes them the wrong direction and they wind up lost and encountering an array of odd kingdoms and creatures. In the course of their travels, they acquire a magic dinner bell created by the Red Jinn, which summons a servant to bring dinner. Peter discovers that the pirate sack, which he brought with him, can swallow up anything, and they also meet an iffin, a griffin that has had the "grrr" scared out of it in the kingdom of Scares.

They next meet Baron Belfaygor, suffering from a super-growing beard as the result of a misfired spell, a beard so long he was too entangled to save his bride, Shirley Sunshine, from being kidnapped by Baron Mogadore. After getting the beard somewhat under control, the band reaches Mogadore's castle in time to see him preparing to ride off with Shirley and his army to conquer Oz.

Peter and his friends try to use the sack on Mogadore, but they get captured and Jack is beheaded. After Mogadore leaves, the others escape and restore Jack's head, which has overheard of a flagon hidden in the castle that will, if spilled, bring doom on both Mogadore and on whoever spills it. Despite Mogadore's safeguards, the group claims the flagon and heads off through more theme kingdoms until it catches up with Mogadore. Peter tries to use the bag but instead it swallows him, Belfaygor and the Iffin.

Jack resorts to summoning the slave of the bell, then hanging onto him when he disappears again. That returns Jack to the palace of Jinnicky, the jovial Red Jinn, who lives inside a red jar. Jinnicky begins planning to save the day when Jack abruptly disappears, much to Jinnicky's indignant dismay.

Back in the Emerald City, Mogadore's surprise attack captures Ozma and her court. Using Ozma's magic belt, Mogadore summons the flagon to him, believing that as king of Oz he's immune to its power (Jack, possessing the flagon, was dragged along). Having been advised by Jinnicky how to duck the curse, Jack shatters the flagon which shrinks Mogadore and his men to brownies, as their ancestors were. The Wizard cures Belfaygor's beard problem and Peter returns home again.

The Yellow Knight of Oz. Illustrated by John R. Neill. Chicago and New York: Reilly & Lee, 1930. 275 pages.

The book has 12 full-color plates. The cover is usually brick-red cloth though rose and mauve cloth have been seen; the pictorial paper label in colors shows Sir Hokus and Speedy at center stage with other characters behind them.

When Sir Hokus announces his intent to set out on a quest and do some knightly deeds, the rest of Ozma's court decides to come, too. Worried that with the Cowardly Lion, the Wizard and the others along, there won't be any risk or challenge, he sets out alone, hiding the Magic Picture so Ozma can't trace him.

Meanwhile, the Sultan of Samandra, who rules not only his own Oz kingdom but neighboring Corabia and Corumbia (whose inhabitants he captured and transformed) discovers that his favorite camel now lives at Ozma's court. He sends his vizier, Tuzzle, to reclaim the Comfortable Camel but doesn't tell anyone his real interest is the treasure in the camel's saddlebags.

In America, young Speedy is about to join his uncle in an experimental space rocket. By accident, Speedy goes off in the rocket alone, and his efforts to land send it burrowing underground. In the kingdom of Subterranea, Speedy discovers a golden statue that comes to life as Princess Marygolden; together they make it back to the rocket and use the ejector seat (or "parashuter") to carry them back to the surface.

Ozma tells Tuzzle that the Camel can return to Samandra if he wishes, but it turns out the Camel has left the stable. Tuzzle heads home while the Wizard works on a magic search-light to find Hokus and Camy.

Camy catches up with Hokus, having decided to serve as the questing knight's steed. A "flying field" carries them to a deserted golden castle surrounded by animate plants. Munching on an old date in the camel's saddlebags, Hokus tosses the pit away; it strikes one bush and turns it into Peter Pun, a jester; unfortunately, the transformation has Peter too dazed to make sense of this. Tuzzle, boating back to Samandra, spots Camy and kidnaps him.

After passing through several theme kingdoms, Speedy and Marygolden enter the enchanted forest. Speedy tosses one of the leftover date pits and turns another plant into Stampedro, proud former steed of Prince Corum the Yellow Knight (the yellow is a fashion statement, not a brand of cowardice). Speedy and Marygolden join Stampedro searching for Corum; when they meet Sir Hokus and share information, it becomes clear that whoever took the Camel knows the secret behind the dates.

To find the answers, they follow Tuzzle to Samandra. Despite the sultan's efforts to hold them, they escape with Camy, more date pits and the sultan's dog, Confido. Marygolden charms the dog into telling how the sultan transformed everyone in Corumbia and Corabia, and that the dates can free them. When they use the magic, it transforms Hokus back into Prince Corum (the Sultan having been the sorcerer who trapped Hokus in Pokes prior to *The Royal Book of Oz*) and frees the rest of the Corumbians as well.

Corum frees the Corabians and wins the hand of the Corabian princess, who turns out to be Marygolden (that this is the princess's real name doesn't apparently tip off anyone). The Wizard's searchlight locates everyone and Ozma strips the Sultan of his magic and confines him to Samandra for 500 years. Corum and Marygolden marry, and Speedy returns home to tell his uncle his amazing stories.

Pirates in Oz. Illustrated by John R. Neill. Chicago: Reilly & Lee, 1931. 280 pages.

There are 12 color plates in the book. There are covers of medium-green, turquoise, off-white and olive-green cloth (priority not established), with a pictorial paper label showing (in color) Peter and Captain Salt in the rigging of the Crescent Moon.

Ruggedo, still mute after *The Gnome King of Oz*, lucks out when he enters Menankypoo, whose inhabitants love having a monarch who can't order them around. The Nome still wants revenge on Oz, and so is delighted to find a wizard's cave where he regains his voice, and allies himself with the Cuckoo Clock Man who "speaks" through notes delivered by the cuckoo. When pirates attack Menankypoo, Ruggedo enlists them to attack Oz instead.

On Octagon Island, the residents have just sailed away out of disgust for lazy King Ato, who lounges languidly while his pet bird, Roger, reads to him. Before long, they're joined by Captain Salt, a pirate abandoned by his crew when he decided to become an honest explorer, and Peter from Philadelphia, lost at sea and stranded on Octagon with a bottle he found. The odd crew sets sail in Salt's *Crescent Moon*, encountering the usual oddities and adding Pigasus, a flying pig, to the crew. Meanwhile, Ruggedo encounters the Octagon Islanders and dragoons them into his army.

Salt sails to Ev so Peter can try to contact Ozma for a way home. In Ev, they discover the boat his crew stole, with the chief mutineers imprisoned while the others follow Ruggedo across the desert by magic. Peter flies Pigasus to the Emerald City but arrives in time to be paralyzed by Ruggedo along with Ozma's court; Ruggedo reclaims his belt and starts transforming people.

Fortunately, Peter's bottle turns the *Crescent Moon* into a flying ship, so Salt, Ato and Roger arrive in time to surprise and defeat Ruggedo. Ozma turns the Nome into a jug for safekeeping, and Peter heads home. Salt becomes Royal Explorer of Oz and Ato and Roger agree to spend half of each year sailing with him.

The Purple Prince of Oz. Illustrated by John R. Neill. Chicago: Reilly & Lee, 1932. 281 pages.

The book has 12 color plates. Covers are light purple or dark-purple cloth, with a pictorial paper label in color (no priority known) showing Randy riding Kabumpo.

In this sequel to *Kabumpo in Oz*, Kabumpo and his new servant Randy are forced on the run when an evil wizard — actually the fairy Faleero, Pompador's one-time fiancée — makes Pompador and his family disappear, puts the king's brother on the throne of Pumperdink, and then marries him.

Magic guides Kabumpo and Randy — actually prince of Regalia, on a quest to prove his worthiness for the throne — to the Red Jinn, who joins them on the return trip to Pumperdink (delighted that unlike *Jack Pumpkinhead in Oz*, he'll get a share of the action). They run into the usual Oz oddities, including the magician Ozwoz who swaps a life-size remote-controlled toy soldier for some of Jinnicky's magic. When they reach Pumperdink, Faleero's magic overwhelms them, but the soldier captures her.

By this time, Ozma has learned about the trouble in Pumperdink, but Jinnicky rushes to disenchant the royal family before the Wizard can show up and do it. Randy's adventures have met the terms of his quest so he returns to Regalia in triumph.

Ojo in Oz. Illustrated by John R. Neill. Chicago: Reilly & Lee, 1933. 304 pages.

There are 12 color plates in the book. The cover is cloth, in several different colors with no set priority; the pictorial paper label in color shows Ojo, Realbad and Snuffers.

When Ojo sneaks away from Unc Nunkie to see the gypsies visiting the Emerald City, the gypsies kidnap the boy, baffling him with hints of a huge reward. Before long, they're captured and robbed themselves by the swashbuckling bandit Realbad, who likes Ojo enough to give him a ring that is a twin to the bandit's own — but nevertheless decides to carry out the gypsies' plan of taking him to Moojer Mountain for a fortune in sapphires. Ojo's only friend in the gypsy camp, the dancing bear Snufferbox, insists on coming along, but can't get the boy free.

When the other bandits try to doublecross Realbad, he, Ojo and Snufferbox escape and begin wandering toward Moojer Mountain, though the bandit and Ojo find themselves bonding with each adventure. Back in the Emerald City, the magic picture locates Ojo but Scraps thoughtlessly magics herself, Dorothy and the Lion over to the gypsy camp rather than to Ojo. After several adventures, they wind up on Moojer Mountain, where the sorcerer Mooj transforms the trio into clocks.

At Snufferbox's insistence, Ojo tries abandoning Realbad; when a giant serpent attacks the boy, his ring brings Realbad to save him (the rings protect the owners from harm, and warn the wearers if the other's in danger). When they enter a unicorn kingdom, however, Snuffers tricks Realbad into removing his ring, ties him up, and carries Ojo off—right up Moojer Mountain. When they reach the top, Mooj snatches Ojo and gives Snuffers the sapphires.

Fortunately, Realbad rides up on the queen unicorn, just as the Wizard and Company, having located Ojo, arrive on the mountaintop. Mooj flees but Ozma turns him into a sparrow.

We then learn that Ojo, Realbad (aka Prince Re Alla Bad) and Unc Nunkie are part of the royal family of Seebania, scattered after Mooj destroyed Realbad's father, the king; after Re Alla Bad's wife gave birth, Unc Nunkie carried the baby (guess who?) away before Mooj could kill him. Realbad assumes the Seebanian throne and Ojo, with Snuffers in tow, reunites with the parents he finally has.

Speedy in Oz. Illustrated by John R. Neill. Chicago: Reilly & Lee, 1934. 298 pages.

There are 12 color plates in the book. The cloth cover has been reported in almost a dozen colors; the pictorial paper label in color shows Speedy, Gureeda and Waddy parachuting through the sky by umbrella.

The Reilly & Lee imprint on the spine is in fancy semi-script, as it would be on all subsequent books until *Merry Go Round in Oz*.

When airborne Umbrella Island crashes into the giant Loxo, Loxo demands King Sizzeroo's son as a slave in return for his injuries. He is unaware that it is the king's boyish daughter, Reeda (nicknamed Gureeda because she loves to "go read a" book). The Umbrellan wizard Waddy persuades the giant to wait three months, hoping to find a solution.

The answer arrives when Speedy from *The Yellow Knight of Oz* is hurled to Umbrella Island by a geyser, along with a dinosaur skeleton that comes to life as Terrybubble. Speedy looks so much like Reeda, Sizzeroo hopes to palm him off on Lozo, so they're quite happy when he agrees to stay, becoming Gureeda's friend and Waddy's apprentice. When the island crashes into the ocean between warring lands of Norroway and Roaraway, Speedy heroically manages to destroy hostile Roaraway's devastating water cannon, buying Waddy enough time to repair the Umbrellan flying system.

When Speedy and Terrybubble learn of Loxo, they parachute into Oz with Gureeda for help, but wind up trapped by the giant. The Umbrellans enlist Ozma's help, but when they confront Lox, Waddy's magic saves the day, shrinking the brute to mortal size. Speedy returns home, but the last paragraph predicts he'll return to the island someday and marry Gureeda.

The Wishing Horse of Oz. Illustrated by John R. Neill. Chicago: Reilly & Lee, 1935. 297 pages.

The book has 12 full-color plates. Various colors of cloth cover have been reported. The pictorial paper plate shows Skamperoo riding Chalk.

When selfish, greedy King Skamperoo of Skampavia discovers the merchant Matiah selling emerald necklaces from Oz, he confiscates them. Matiah gets them back by claiming the necklaces grant wishes but only he can work the magic; to his surprise, the king's wish for a horse (a magnificent white charger called Chalk) comes true.

Matiah decides to stay at court until he figures out the secret, but Chalk figures it out first. Skamperoo uses the magic to imprison Glinda, the Wizard and every monarch in Oz and its provinces, then makes everyone believe that he is the true ruler of everything. Only Dorothy manages to escape the spell;

after she frees Pigasus the flying pig from the magic, they set off to find help. In the Black Forest they confront the witch Glooma, who becomes horrified to realize she's facing Dorothy, the famous witch-slayer. Fortunately, Gloma is actually a good witch, and she sends Dorothy on her way with a magic powder of darkness.

Dorothy and Pigasus then fly to King Kaliko's Nome Caverns, but for once the Nomes win one: Kaliko weasels out of providing more than minimal help and advice. Soon after, however, Dorothy and Pigasus reach the moving castle of the seer, Bitty Bit, who transports them back to the Emerald City. With Gloma's magic dust, they capture Chalk and Skamperoo; the king agrees to give up the necklaces if he's allowed to make five wishes when he returns home (the seer assures Dorothy the wishes are good ones). Dorothy uses the necklaces to undo all Skamperoo's mischief; horse and master return to Scampavia, which Skamperoo transforms by his wishes into a fertile, thriving kingdom just as happy as Oz.

Captain Salt in Oz. Illustrated by John R. Neill. Chicago: Reilly & Lee, 1936. 306 pages.

Starting with this book, there are no color plates. Covers are most commonly found in light blue or medium blue, but also vermilion and green cloth (no set priority). The pictorial paper label shows Salt, Ato and Tandy steering the Crescent Moon.

Three years after *Pirates in Oz*, Captain Salt returns to Octagon Island and invites Ato and Roger to join him in exploring the ocean and winning new countries to Ozma's empire (by consent — no conquest allowed). Along the way, they pick up Nikobo, a talking hippopotamus, and her friend Tandy, a prince of Ozamaland who mysteriously wound up on a desert island with Nikobo. Initially shy and haughty, Tandy soon thaws and learns to love life on Salt's ship as they travel past the usual oddities (a volcanic isle of salamanders, a sea forest).

What Tandy doesn't know is that his council of ministers hired a wizard to remove the prince so the ministers could take over. When the Crescent Moon returns to Ozamaland, Tandy wins the people over; to make matters worse for the traitors, the wizard pays them back for cheating him out of his payment by dropping them into the sea. Rather than return to his dreary monarchical existence, Tandy appoints one of Ozamaland's tribal chieftains as his regent (under Ozma's imperial guidance, of course) and resumes his exciting life aboard the Crescent Moon.

Captain Salt is unique in the series: Despite the title, none of the book takes place in Oz and none of the characters come from there.

Handy Mandy in Oz. Illustrated by John R. Neill. Chicago: Reilly & Lee, 1937. 246 pages.

There have been several cloth covers reported in different colors; the label shows Handy Mandy in head shot with seven hands below her and smaller busts of the other characters to either side.

Mandy, a goatherder and orphan, lives by herself on Mt. Mern, where she and everyone else have seven hands (one iron, one leather, two human, etc.). A geyser hurls her into Kerataria, an Oz kingdom, where arrogant King Kerr condemns her to the dungeons. Nox, the golden-horned royal ox, claims her for his slave instead.

Nox tells Mandy that Keratarian monarchs only live as long as their companion royal ox — and that Nox is actually Boz, companion to the former King Kerry, who vanished mysteriously. When Boz was identified as the new ox for the next king, he decided to play the role until Kerry returns. Mandy discovers Nox's horns are hollow and a message in one directs them to Silver Mountain. They escape Kerateria, picking up a silver hammer en route, and using the magic in the hollow horns to survive various adventures.

Mandy discovers that the hammer summons Himself, an elf, who leads them into Silver Mountain. Here they find the Wizard of Wutz is plotting to steal all Oz magic and rule the realm, and is holding Kerry prisoner so Wutz's agent, Kerr, can rule in his place. Wutz imprisons Mandy and Nox in the depths of his mountain, then has one of his agents bring him Ruggedo (transformed into a jug in *Pirates in Oz*) to exploit his knowledge of Oz magic. Realizing Mandy and Nox have magic of their own, Wutz tries forcing them to restore Ruggedo when his own magic fails to do so, and by a fluke, Mandy succeeds. Ruggedo agrees to help Wutz in return for getting his magic belt back.

After the two villains head off for the belt, Nox's horns guide him and Mandy to Kerry, then Himself carries them to the Emerald City. Himself snatches the belt from the villains, then carries them back to Silver Mountain where he turns them into cacti. The elf reveals he was forced to capture Kerry by a now-dead witch, but enchanted Nox's horns in the hopes that the boy would be saved. Mandy returns to Kerataria with Nox and Kerry and the trio rule happily ever after.

The Silver Princess in Oz. Illustrated by John R. Neill. Chicago: Reilly & Lee, 1938. 255 pages.

The cloth cover is in various colors, with a pictorial paper label showing Randy and Planetty riding Thun. Curiously, the spine shows a head shot of Handy Mandy.

In this sequel to *The Purple Prince of Oz* King Randy of Regalia is bored silly with his court's endless, tedious rituals, so he jumps at a chance to visit Jinnicky with Kabumpo. After the usual misadventures, a gale blows them clear out of Oz and into Ix, where they meet Princess Planetty and her horse Thun, living-metal extraterrestrials stranded on Earth, where the environment will petrify them within a week.

After a cross-country ride in which Planetty and Randy become quite drawn to each other, the group arrives at the Red Jinn's castle, only to discover his treacherous servant Gludwig has thrown Jinnicky into the sea and enslaved the realm.

Gludwig traps the newcomers in the dungeons with Jinnicky's faithful servant Ginger, and the two Anutherians become petrified. Jinnicky, however, manages to escape and defeat Gludwig, then transforms Thun and Planetty to humans—in which form the princess is only too happy to marry Randy.

Ozoplaning with the Wizard of Oz. Illustrated by John R. Neill. Chicago: Reilly & Lee, 1939. 272 pages.

There are over a half-dozen reported colors for the cloth cover. The pictorial label shows the Wizard, Scarecrow and Tin Woodman staring up into the sky.

The Wizard celebrates the anniversary of Dorothy's arrival in Oz by inviting her, the Lion, Tin Woodman, Scarecrow, Jellia Jamb and Wantowin Battles to a private party and revealing his new invention, the ozoplane. When Battles launches himself, Jellia and the Tin Woodman into the stratosphere, the Wizard and the others follow in a second ozoplane.

The first plane eventually lands in the sky kingdom of Stratovania, which the Tin Woodman claims for Oz, much to the displeasure of the monarch, Strut, who decides to annex Oz instead. After he forces the Tin Woodman to fly him to Earth, the second plane arrives and Jellia convinces them that the Cowardly Lion is Strut, transformed by Oz magic. Strut's suspicious queen blows the plane out into space, but the Ozites manage to escape.

After a brief imprisonment by the usurper king of Red Top Mountain, the Ozites race to Glinda's castle, where Ozma is visiting—except neither woman is there, and the Book of Records shows the Stratovanians are attacking the Emerald City. Fortunately, the Wizard manages to summon Ozma's magic belt, then Glinda and Ozma, and Ozma teleports the entire sky army home, forcing Strut to admit he's out of his league. With everyone at peace, the Wizard and the Tin Woodman fly off to find the plane that was blown off Stratovania.

The Later Historians

John R. Neill

The Wonder City of Oz. Illustrated by John R. Neill. Chicago: Reilly & Lee, 1940. 318 pages.

A half-dozen colors have been reported for the cloth cover. The pictorial label shows the living houses of the Emerald City.

When teenaged Jenny Jump catches leprechaun Siko Pompus in her New Jersey kitchen, she wishes not for his pot of gold but to become a fairy herself. Pompus turns half of Jenny into a fairy, then escapes; Jenny's now magical right foot lets her jump miles at a step, which ultimately lands her in Oz, in the middle of Ozma's birthday parade.

After Jenny describes American elections, Ozma decides to hold an ozlection to see if the country wants her for queen; since no one in Oz wants to run against Ozma, Jenny throws her hat in the ring. Jenny and Number Nine (named for being the ninth child in his Munchkin family) discover a magic turnstile that changes the clothing style of whoever walks through it. Jenny uses this to open up an Emerald City boutique and starts canvassing her customers.

While the ozlection campaign proceeds, the Emerald City is attacked by vote-eating Heelers (from ward-heeler, an old term for a political hanger-on) and an army of chocolate soldiers. When it comes time to vote, the Woggle-Bug decides to measure the weight of the opposing voters to pick the winner, and some Ozites must vote for Jenny to prevent a landslide (on the bizarre grounds that a landslide could crush the Emerald City). That leads to a tie until Pompus votes for Ozma, which drives Jenny so mad she knocks herself out, after which the Wizard magically turns her sour personality into a sweet one. Jenny settles down in her boutique and Nine gets to work both as her assistant and the Wizard's.

John R. Neill clearly set out to put his own stamp on the series as Royal Historian, with new concepts (teleporting with an Ambassadoor) and characters that recur in his next two novels. Unfortunately, his writing isn't up to his superb artwork: Neill throws in random events and magical weirdness with no regard for plot or plausibility (his magic never feels as real as Baum's), though other elements of *Wonder City*, such as the ozlection and the Wizard's magic brain-surgery on Jenny, were written in by the publisher.

Neill also had an odd taste in names, here christening an Irish leprechaun after "psycho-pomp," a Greek spirit.

The Scalawagons of Oz. Illustrated by John R. Neill. Chicago: Reilly & Lee, 1941. 309 pages.

There are a half-dozen color cloth covers reported. The pictorial paper shows Dorothy and Ozma riding in a Scalawagon.

The Wizard invents Scalawagons—living flying cars—planning to present the first model to Ozma at her next party. When he puts Tik-Tok in charge of the factory, the mechanical man soon runs down and the bad-tempered Bell-Snickle (a living tire with bells on, more or less) enters and sends the Scalawagons flying over the Deadly Desert before their fuel turns him into a balloon.

Jenny Jump leads some of the other Ozites in recapturing the Scalawagons and steering them back to the Emerald City where everyone gushes over the cars for several chapters. The Bell-Snickle comes back to Earth, steals a Scalawagon and then sends a living forest against the Emerald City (the Tin Woodman meets them at the city gates and starts chopping). Defeated, the Bell-Snickle agrees to work for Jenny as a rubber stamp and everyone has a party.

The Bell-Snickle name comes from a Santa Claus-figure in Pennsylvania folklore.

Lucky Bucky in Oz. Illustrated by John R. Neill. Chicago: Reilly & Lee, 1942. 289 pages.

The cloth cover comes in several colors of unknown priority. The pictorial paper label shows Lucky Bucky sitting on the front rail of Davy Jones, the wooden whale.

An explosion on his family's barge hurls "Lucky" Bucky Jones all the way to Ev, where he lands inside a volcano occupied by a tribe of cooks. When rat pirates attack in Davy Jones, a living wooden whale, the bakers capture the rats and Bucky boards the whale. They sail toward the Emerald City but wind up getting washed into the Nome caverns and imprisoned.

Number Nine, who's been watching Bucky clairvoyantly, teleports through the Ambassa-door and frees them. Meanwhile, Ozma's court decorates the city with magic paint that brings an image of Mombi to life; when Davy Jones emerges from underground, the witch hides inside.

Davy Jones reaches the Winkie Land with Polychrome's help, but discovers Scarecrow and Tin Woodman have locked away the Winkie rivers because they hate water. They release one river so Davy can reach the city. When Davy floods on the journey, Mombi flies out, but Ozma recaptures and repaints her (adding a smile to neuter her). The baker's volcano gets transferred to Lake Quad and Davy Jones and Bucky are assigned to convey the baked goods to the Emerald City.

JACK SNOW

The Magical Mimics of Oz. Illustrated by Frank Kramer. Chicago: Reilly & Lee, 1946. 242 pages.

The cover is light-gray cloth with a pictorial label showing the Scarecrow in Pineville.

The back flap of the dust jacket, which would normally show a list of Oz books, has a long statement about Jack Snow, Kramer and Baum's literary importance.

When the fairy queen Lurline summons Ozma to a Grand Council (leading Ozma to remember how Lurline transformed Oz from a mundane realm to a full fairyland years before), Ozma appoints Dorothy as regent.

This draws the attention of the evil, shapeshifting Mimics of Mt. Illuso, who are prevented by Lurline's magic from attacking Ozites as they would otherwise do from sheer malice. Mimic King Umb and Queen Ra realize Lurline's power doesn't protect Americans living in Oz, so they replace Dorothy and the Wizard, imprisoning them inside Mt. Illuso, in order to find the secret that will free the Mimics from Lurline's restraints. Toto, however, soon realizes his mistress is an imposter.

Inside Illuso, the paralysis spell on Dorothy and the Wizard fades away and a magic elevator takes them to Pineville, a land of wooden figures atop Illuso. Pineville is the creation of Ozma's cousin Ozana, assigned by Lurline to watch over the Mimics. Unable to penetrate Ra's cloaking spells, Ozana sets off for Oz with the two Americans.

Meanwhile, however, the Mimics secure the counterspell and escape back to the mountain. Ra unleashes a giant spider whose web binds Lurline's magic, freeing the Mimics to attack Oz. They duplicate and paralyze all the humans in the Emerald City, then capture the nonhumans, but Ozma and Glinda return and intervene before the Mimics can burn the Scarecrow to ash. Ozana restores the binding spell on the shapeshifters, then banishes them back to Illuso. Ozma points out that the Book of Records will let Ozana monitor any further evil deeds, so Ozana moves to Oz along with her friends in Pineville.

After Neill's death, Reilly and Lee waited three years before trying a new Oz book. Snow includes several continuity touches, and Ozma's exposition at the beginning explains why Oz in *The Wizard of Oz* is so much darker than the later stories.

The Shaggy Man of Oz. Illustrated by Frank Kramer. Chicago: Reilly & Lee, 1949. 254 pages.

The cover is gray cloth with a green cast. The pictorial paper label shows Shaggy meeting the King of the Beavers.

American twins Twink and Tom are persuaded by Twiffle, a toy clown, to visit Conjo Island and its master, the wizard Conjo, by passing through their TV set. Meanwhile, in Oz, the Love Magnet breaks in an accident and Ozma tells the Shaggy Man that only Conjo, who created it, can fix it — and he might refuse out of sheer selfishness. When Shaggy learns American kids are on Conjo

Island too, he decides to ask Conjo for a repair job as an excuse to keep an eye on the twins.

As fans of the Oz books, the twins are thrilled when Shaggy shows up on the island, but Conjo isn't. However, he agrees to repair the magnet and fly Shaggy home in an airmobile in return for a magic compass Ozma loaned the old tramp. Shaggy refuses, but Conjo repairs the magnet and secretly swaps it for the compass anyway.

Twiffle tells Shaggy that Conjo plans to keep the children on the island as an audience for his magical marvels, so Shaggy takes the twins and the clown with him in the airmobile. After numerous adventures, they arrive in a beaver kingdom on the far side of the Deadly Desert from Oz. The King Beaver reveals that his subjects have dug into the Nome invasion tunnel from *The Emerald City of Oz*, which gives Shaggy a way to cross the desert with the others in safety. When they reach Glinda's invisible barrier, everyone turns invisible and collides with each other, but the king's magic gets them through it.

When they reach the Emerald City, they discover Conjo has taken over the Wizard's workshop as the self-proclaimed new Wizard of Oz. The King Beaver magically jets water from the Fountain of Oblivion into Conjo's mouth, erasing his memory; Twiffle volunteers to take him back to the island and teach him right from wrong, and the twins attend a royal Oz banquet before going home.

The original manuscript included chapters showing Dorothy on an adventure with Baum's Father Goose character, and Ozma and her court tracking the Gilliken River to its source, but they were dropped to concentrate on the main storyline.

RACHEL COSGROVE

The Hidden Valley of Oz. Illustrated by Dirk (Dirk Gringhuis). Chicago: Reilly & Lee, 1951. 313 pages.

The cover is medium-blue cloth. The label shows Jam riding what looks like a tiger (but is probably a minor character, the Leopard That Changes His Spots) with Percy, Scarecrow and Tin Woodman walking with them.

A windstorm catches Jonathan Andrew "Jam" Manley's kite and carries it and Jam away to Hidden Valley in the Gilliken land. The lab rat Jam brought with him starts talking and christens itself "Percy the Personality Kid." Jam discovers the giant Terp the Terrible has enslaved the valley dwellers to make jam for the muffins Terp plucks from a muffin tree, which is guarded by a two-headed monster. Terp captures Jam and decides to see how he tastes on muffins.

Percy frees his pal and they set off for the Tin Woodman, whom the Gillikens believe can cut down the muffin tree, ending Terp's need for jam. On the trip, Percy eats a stolen muffin and turns man-sized; Jam realizes the muffins are the key to Terp's giant size.

The duo reach the Tin Woodman and lead him, Dorothy and Scarecrow back to Hidden Valley. Percy discovers the muffin's effects are temporary, but hopes Ozma can make him permanently large. After assorted adventures, they reach Hidden Valley where the Gillikens trap Terp in the jam factory long enough for the Tin Woodman to overcome the monster guardian and chop the tree down. When they return to the Emerald City, the Wizard grows Percy to the size the rat wishes and Ozma gives Jam a magic kite that can carry him back and forth between America and Oz.

Longtime Oz fan Cosgrove satisfied a childhood fantasy by writing *Rocket Trip to Oz* and selling it to Reilly and Lee. The publisher, however, said it had just rejected a book with a rocket-ride to Oz and asked Cosgrove to make it a flying saucer (presumably to avoid plagiarism charges), but decided that was still too close. Cosgrove went on to write over 40 more children's novels.

Many fans have objected to Percy's use of contemporary slang, such as calling everyone "kid," but his dialog looks as fanciful now as the muffin tree ("Personality Kid" seems to have been a showbiz term — an overbearing actress describes herself as "the personality kid" in the Buster Keaton film *Speaking Easily*).

The original story of how Percy and Jam got to Oz, *Rocket Trip to Oz*, was reprinted in the anthology *Oz-Story #6*.

Eloise Jarvis McGraw and
Lauren McGraw

Merry Go Round in Oz. Illustrated by Dick Martin. Chicago: Reilly & Lee, 1963. 303 pages.

The cover is white cloth, printed in full color on the back, front and side with a wrap-around drawing showing a merry-go-round with Robin riding Merry, Fess riding the Unicorn, Dorothy riding the Lion and Gules riding Fred.

The last of the official Oz books has not one but three sets of travelers: American orphan Robin Brown, who snags the brass ring on a carousel and is magically catapulted to Oz with the horse he's riding (which comes to life under the name Merry Go Round); Dorothy and the Cowardly Lion, visiting the Easter Bunny to order eggs for Ozma's Easter party; and Squire Fess and Prince Gules of the knightly Oz kingdom of Halidom, leading a quest for three lost magic talismans Halidom desperately needs to recover.

After surviving the boisterous fox-hunters of View Halloo, Robin and Merry arrive in the glass-domed city of Roundabout, where the seer Roundelay proclaims Robin is the king mentioned in his new prophecy, destined to finally bring the city prosperity. Unable to cross the whirling road around the city, Robin and Merry are stuck there.

Following a cryptic prophecy, Gules and Fess encounter Dorothy and the Lion bearing a handcrafted egg for Ozma. While escaping the nightmarish Good Children Land (where armies of Nannies threaten to make them eat spinach and take lots of baths), the group discovers that the gold band around Ozma's egg is one of the Halidom talismans, a discovery that fits the prophecy perfectly.

When they arrive in Roundabout, the prophecy makes them initially suspect Robin has a talisman, then Gules recognizes Roundelay from Halidom. The seer admits he stole the talisman but insists Roundabout needs it more than Halidom. The group successfully reclaims the talisman from its mechanical guardian (it fits the prophecy, but is not the talisman they expect) and Merry shows the other steeds how to cross a rotating road in safety.

Back in Halidom, Dorothy realizes the rest of the prophecy still points to Robin, and it turns out the brass ring he grabbed from the roundabout is the third talisman (Eloise McGraw said later they either dropped the explanation as too complicated or simply forgot about it). The talismans restore Halidom's prosperity, Ozma arranges the same for Roundabout and Robin and Merry settle in the Emerald City.

McGraw said in an interview that the genesis of the story came from using the roundabout as a new way to reach Oz, then tying the circlets of Halidom in with Robin's brass ring. Another influence was Lynn McGraw's fondness for English material such as fox hunting.

The charming end result is this author's personal favorite of the post–Baum books. Eloise McGraw went on to a highly successful career as a children's author; her 1964 short story, "The Magic Land," fictionalizes how Baum wrote *The Wizard of Oz*.

Apocrypha by the Royal Historians and Others

In addition to the "famous forty" in the official Oz series, the Royal Historians of Oz wrote a number of other Oz books published outside the canon. This section also includes several Baum non–Oz fantasies that were adapted for the screen.

Baum, Frank J. **The Laughing Dragon of Oz.** Illustrated by Milt Youngren. Racine, WI: Whitman, 1934.

The story of Rosine, an American girl, her monkey, Jim, and the lighthouse keeper Cap'n Bob; together they seek to rescue

Princess Cozytoes with the help of the Laughing Dragon.

The Royal History that wasn't: Frank Baum had hoped to follow his father as Royal Historian, but L. Frank Baum died while his son was stationed in France, and Reilly & Lee gave the post to Ruth Plumly Thompson. After Reilly & Lee turned down Baum's *Rosine in Oz*, Baum turned to publisher David Graham Fischer, but the announced *Rosine and the Laughing Dragon* never appeared, and no record of it remains but the cover design. *The Laughing Dragon* eventually came out as one of Whitman's Big Little Books; anticipating a legal fight with Reilly & Lee, Baum trademarked the word "Oz" and published a short story, "Jimmy Bulber in Oz" (Bulber being a light bulb-headed man created by a witch) to prove he was actively using the trademark.

When Reilly & Lee, having learned about *The Laughing Dragon*, sued, however, Whitman settled out of court, agreeing not to reprint *The Laughing Dragon* or to publish the planned sequel, *The Enchanted Princess of Oz*. Reilly & Lee won a court decision that Oz was their common-law trademark. The question of whether Baum's son had a right to continue the series was never resolved in court since Whitman settled and agreed not to publish any more copies of *The Laughing Dragon*.

Baum, L. Frank. **The Enchanted Island of Yew.** Illustrated by Fanny Y. Cory. Indianapolis: Bobbs-Merrill, 1903.

A fairy bored with immortality turns herself into a mortal prince for a year in order to find excitement and adventure. Roaming over the magical island of Yew she battles evil kings, strange civilizations and roguish bandits before the year is up.

____. **John Dough and the Cherub.** Illustrated by John R. Neill. Chicago: Reilly & Britton, 1906.

By coincidence, a magic elixir winds up in an American bakery where it brings a life-sized gingerbread man, John Dough, to life. Fleeing the elixir's owner, John arrives on the Isle of Phreex where he meets androgynous child Chick the Cherub, the world's first incubator baby. The gutsy kid leads John on a series of adventures across the sea before arriving in a kingdom divided into Hiland (ruled by ectomorphs) and Loland (a kingdom of dwarves). John's arrival fulfills an ancient prophecy of a promised king, with Chick serving as his trusted right hand.

Oz expert Martin Gardner suggests this may have been written, like *The Land of Oz*, with a stage show in mind (but if that was the case, a 1906 *Gingerbread Man* musical probably precluded another gingerbread man hitting the boards). A big publicity contest offered a prize for whoever gave the best answer as to whether Chick was a boy or a girl (Baum never said); according to Baum's son Frank, the $100 first prize was divided between a child who picked "boy" and one who argued for "girl."

____. **The Last Egyptian: A Romance of the Nile.** Illustrated by Francis P. Wightman. Philadelphia: Edward Stern, 1908.

An Egyptian seeks revenge on the English nobleman who seduced and ruined his grandmother by ruining the Englishman's granddaughter in turn. Baum published this drama anonymously.

____. **The Life and Adventures of Santa Claus.** Illustrated by Mary Cowles Clark. Indianapolis: Bowen-Merrill, 1902.

When the immortal woodsman Ak finds an abandoned child in the forest, the baby is raised by the combined efforts of the forest animals and the forest spirits. As Claus grows to manhood, the harsh lives of other children in the human world touches his heart and he begins creating the first toys for them to play with. This brings on the wrath of the monstrous Awgwas, monsters who promote misbehavior. They interfere with his work to the point Ak has to lead the immortals in battle and destroy the Awgwas utterly.

Continuing his work, Claus adopts most of the customs we associate with Christmas for one reason or another, such as coming down chimneys, using reindeer and flying one night of the year. At the end of the book, Ak prevails on the immortals to grant Claus immortality, that he might continue helping children everywhere.

_____. **The Little Wizard Series.** Illustrated by John R. Neill. Chicago: Reilly & Britton, 1913.

This was a series of six original 29-page books written by Baum and illustrated by Neill, similar to the Little Golden Books. In 1914, these stories were released in one volume as *The Little Wizard Stories of Oz*. Later printings included give-aways tied into the Jell-O-sponsored *The Wizard of Oz* radio show, and a re-release in 1939 when the MGM film came out.

> **The Cowardly Lion and the Hungry Tiger.** The two beasts go searching for a baby the Tiger can eat and an adult the Lion can attack, but instead they wind up returning a lost child to his mother.
>
> **Jack Pumpkinhead and the Sawhorse.** Jack and his steed go into the forest to rescue two children who have been captured by squirrels.
>
> **Little Dorothy and Toto.** The giant Crinklink kidnaps Dorothy and Toto, but it turns out to be the Wizard in disguise, showing them the danger of wandering alone in a fairy country.
>
> **Ozma and the Little Wizard.** The Wizard and Ozma try to vanquish three imps who remain mischievous in every form, until they're transformed into buttons.
>
> **The Scarecrow and the Tin Woodman.** The two friends run into various troubles while trying to take a peaceful boat ride.
>
> **Tiktok and the Nome King.** Tik-Tok delivers a message to Ruggedo from Ozma; the angry king tears the robot to pieces, but Kaliko reassembles him and the Nome King becomes convinced he's faced with a robot ghost.

_____. **Queen Zixi of Ix.** Illustrated by Frederick Richardson. New York: Century, 1905.

A band of fairies bestows a magic wishing cloak upon a miserable orphan, Fluff, shortly before a fluke of fate makes her brother, Bud, the new king of Noland. As Bud learns to balance his mischievous nature with a just treatment of his subjects, the cloak winds up passing from hand to hand, with whimsical effects for those who wish upon it.

This draws the attention of Queen Zixi, a 600-year-old witch who realizes the cloak can make her truly beautiful, instead of having to hide her age with illusion. After several attempts, she obtains the cloak, but finds its power won't work for a thief; casting it aside, she comes to peace with her appearance. When the monstrously rotund Roly-Rogues invade Noland, Bud and Fluff recover the cloak, but find it too damaged to work. Zixi's magic defeats the Rogues, then fairies reclaim the cloak, after allowing Bud one last wish; to become the best monarch of Noland ever.

Baum's most old-fashioned fantasy, very much in the Victorian fairy-tale tradition.

_____. **The Sea Fairies.** Illustrated by John R Neill. Chicago: Reilly & Britton, 1911.

Mermaids overhear peg-legged Cap'n Bill tell his young friend Trot how devilishly dangerous mermaids are, so to prove him wrong, they bring Bill and Trot into the undersea kingdom. Protected by magic, the humans explore the sea's wonders, but the monstrous sorcerer Zog the Terrible traps them in his sub-sea lair. The mermaids match Zog's magic with their own and finally escape. When Zog pursues them, Anko the Sea Serpent, monarch of all sea creatures, destroys the monster and Trot and Cap'n Bill return home safely.

After Baum wrapped up the Oz series (he thought) in *The Emerald City of Oz*, he kicked off this delightful new series. Sales were disappointing.

_____. **Sky Island.** Illustrated by John R. Neill. Chicago: Reilly & Britton, 1912.

In the follow-up to *The Sea Fairies*, Trot

and Cap'n Bill meet Button-Bright from *The Road to Oz* after he flies to California on a magic umbrella found in his family's attic. When they give the umbrella the wrong instructions it carries them to Sky Island, an aerial fairyland divided between the Blues—cruelly oppressed by the arrogant Booleroo—and the Pinkies, who keep their queen in abject poverty so that she won't imagine herself better than they are. The Booleroo steals the umbrella, forcing the earthlings to set things right on the island before they can return home.

Considered by many to be Baum's best story, but sales of these two books were so much less than *The Patchwork Girl of Oz* that Baum gave up the series and moved Trot and Cap'n Bill to Oz.

____. **The Woggle-Bug Book.** Illustrated by Ike Morgan. Chicago: Reilly & Britton, 1905.

The Woggle-Bug wanders through America (and sometimes other countries) pursuing a plaid dress whose bright colors fascinate him.

This picture book was written to promote the 1905 play, *The Woggle-Bug,* in which the Wogglebug is similarly fixated on a plaid dress. The storyline also tied in with Baum's *Queer Visitors from the Land of Oz* strip, stating at the start that it takes place while the Woggle-Bug is separated from the other visitors and ending with his return to their hotel room.

Denslow, W.W. **Denslow's Scarecrow and the Tin-Man.** New York: G.W. Dillingham Co., 1904.

This book describes the humorous exploits of two actors playing Scarecrow and Tin Woodman after they run away from *The Wizard of Oz* stage play. It has no relation to Denslow's *Scarecrow and Tin Woodman* cartoon strip. It was also issued in 1904 in a bound volume with several other Denslow picture books as *Denslow's Scarecrow and the Tin-Man and Other Stories.*

Kellogg, Jean. **The Visitors from Oz.** Illustrated by Dick Martin. Chicago: Reilly & Lee, 1960.

A novel based on Baum's *Queer Visitor* strips.

McGraw, Eloise Jarvis. **The Rundelstone of Oz.** Illustrated by Eric Shanower. San Diego: Hungry Tiger Press, 2001.

When the Troopadoor mannikins arrive in a small Gilliken village, everyone's delighted. But when the entire troupe disappears, Pocotristi the puppet must save them, despite the schemes of an evil wizard Slyddwynn and the vanishing of the magic Rundelstone.

____, and Lauren Lynn McGraw. **The Forbidden Fountain of Oz.** Illustrated by Dick Martin. Kinderhook, IL: International Wizard of Oz Club, 1980.

A young girl opens up a limeade stand in the Emerald City, unaware she's made her juice with water from the Fountain of Oblivion. And then Ozma buys a glass.

Neill, John R. **The Runaway in Oz.** Illustrated by Eric Shanower. New York: Books of Wander, 1995.

When the Patchwork Girl decides to run away, she triggers all kinds of unexpected chaos.

Payes, Rachel Cosgrove. **The Wicked Witch of Oz.** Illustrated by Eric Shanower. Kinderhook, IL: International Wizard of Oz Club, 1993.

Singra, the Wicked Witch of the South, returns seeking revenge on Glinda for defeating her—and God help those who get in her way. Dorothy, Percy the Personality Kid and Leon the Neon (a man formed of animated neon tubing) set out to stop Singra.

Russell, Thomas. **Pictures from the Wonderful Wizard of Oz.** Illustrated by W.W. Denslow. Chicago: George W. Ogilvie & Co., 1903.

After Baum and Denslow parted company and *The Wizard of Oz* publisher Geo. M. Hill went bankrupt, another publisher acquired uncut sheets of Denslow's color plates and issued them with a completely unrelated, non–Oz story on the back.

Snow, Jack. **Who's Who in Oz.** Illustrated by John R. Neill. Chicago: Reilly & Lee, 1954.

This reference guide gives brief descriptions of the roughly 600 characters in the Oz series to date.

Thompson, Ruth Plumly. **The Cheerful Citizens of Oz.** Illustrated by Rob Roy MacVeigh. Kinderhook, IL: International Wizard of Oz Club, 1992.

A collection of poems about the Oz characters.

____. **The Enchanted Island of Oz.** Illustrated by Dick Martin. Kinderhook, IL: International Wizard of Oz Club, 1976.

A young boy meets a talking camel at the circus. They journey to Oz but get carried off on the flying island of Kapurta.

The Enchanted Island was an unpublished manuscript from the late 1940s that Thompson rewrote into an Oz book shortly before her death.

____. **Yankee in Oz.** Illustrated by Dick Martin. Kinderhook, IL: International Wizard of Oz Club, 1972.

Tommy, a drummer boy, and Yankee, an Air Force dog, join forces with Jinnicky against a wicked giant threatening both America and Oz. This book was written in the 1960s, and published 33 years after Thompson's previous Oz book saw print.

The Further Books of Oz

Abbott, Donald. **The Amber Flute of Oz.** New York: Emerald City Press, 1998.

In the time between *Wizard* and *Land of Oz*, the Scarecrow, Tin Woodman and Cowardly Lion must help Glinda find the amber flute to save Oz from Blinkie, the Wicked Witch of the South.

____. **Father Goose in Oz.** New York: Emerald City Press, 1994.

Baum's character Father Goose is brought to Oz by his magic pen, and unintentionally restores the Wicked Witch of the West to life.

____. **How the Wizard Came to Oz.** New York: Emerald City Press, 1991.

The story of how balloonist and showman Oscar Diggs was blown to Oz at a time when the Wicked Witches still ruled — and how Diggs wound up as the mysterious Wizard of Oz.

____. **How the Wizard Saved Oz.** New York: Emerald City Press, 1996.

In the time before *The Wizard of Oz*, the Wizard and the Queen of the Field Mice join forces against Mombi.

____. **The Magic Chest of Oz.** New York: Emerald City Press, 1993.

When an evil spirit escapes the chest that serves as her prison, it's up to the Scarecrow, the Tin Woodman and the Cowardly Lion to seal her back inside again.

____. **The Speckled Rose of Oz.** New York: Emerald City Press, 1995.

Glinda must prevent a sorcerer from destroying all the flowers of Oz.

Anfuso, Dennis. **The Winged Monkeys of Oz.** Wilton, NH: Interset Press, 1996.

A girl in Tacoma befriends a Winged Monkey stranded by a storm, which leads her on a series of adventures in the islands of the Nonestic Oceans.

Barlow, Nate. **Veggy Man of Oz.** Albuquerque, NM: Buckethead Enterprises of Oz, 1988.

The sinister Mirror Men have conquered Oz, and the Veggy Man and his animated vegetable friends have the job of liberating the kingdom.

Barstock, Jeff. **Song of Oz.** Albuquerque, NM: Buckethead Enterprises of Oz, 1989.

On a mission to save Aunt Em, Dorothy and Toto enter a distorted Oz where Glinda has become an evil witch. With a living porcelain angel, Dorothy sets out to put things right.

____. **Starglory of Oz.** N.p.: Tails of the Cowardly Lion and Friends, 2002.

A girl of living starlight is stranded in the underground realms and will die unless she returns home soon.

Baum, Kenneth Gage. **Dinamonster of Oz.** Albuquerque, NM: Buckethead Enterprises of Oz, 1991.

Ruggedo's giant unstoppable Dinamonster appears to be the weapon that will finally conquer Oz.

Baum, Roger S. **Dorothy of Oz.** New York: Books of Wonder, 1989.

A mad jester uses the Wicked Witch of the West's magic wands to turn Ozians into china figures. Dorothy returns to Oz and joins her friends to try to save the day.

____. **The Green Star of Oz.** Johnson City, TN: Overmountain Press, 2000.

L. Frank Baum and the children of his neighborhood are transported to Oz, where Dorothy is slowly disappearing from existence.

____. **The Lion of Oz and the Badge of Courage.** Palm Desert, CA: Yellow Brick Road, 1995.

In this version of O.Z. Diggs's arrival in Oz, his balloon lands carrying a lion from the same circus. When a witch kidnaps Diggs, the Lion is forced to find a magic talisman that will help the Wizard conquer all Oz.

____. **The Rewolf of Oz.** New York: Simon & Schuster, 1991.

The Rewolf tries to destroy the Ozian countryside — but why?

____. **The Silly OZbul of Oz and the Magic Merry-Go-Round.** Westlake Village, CA: Yellow Brick Road, 1992.

Two children are magically transported back in the time to arrival of the Wizard in Oz.

____. **Silly OZbul of Oz and Toto.** Westlake Village, CA: Yellow Brick Road, 1992.

Toto and a SillyOZbul set off to see Glinda.

____. **Silly OZbuls of Oz.** Westlake Village, CA: Yellow Brick Road, 1991.

The Silly OZbuls want to give love to the people of Oz — but a sorcerer has a plan to exploit them.

____. **The Wizard of Oz and the Magic Merry-Go-Round.** Johnson City, TN: Overmountain Press, 2003.

Two children discover an old merry-go-round in a junkyard, and find themselves riding it alongside their own parents, when they were children. The reason lies in Oz. This is a picture-book version of *The Silly OZbul and the Magic Merry-Go-Round* with the plot rewritten to drop the OZbul.

Baxley, Ron, Jr. **The Talking City of Oz.** N.p.: Vanitas Press, 1999.

Dorothy comes to the rescue when Oz disappears into a hole in the ground, courtesy of Nome King Kaliko.

Begley, Vincent. **Dorothy: This Side of the Rainbow.** United States: Xlibris Corp., 2002.

A book directed to an adult audience, telling the story of Dorothy and her experiences as an orphan.

Berends, Polly. **Ozma and the Wayward Wand.** New York: Random House, 1985.

While Ozma and her court go to greet a visiting Dorothy, a young boy steals Ozma's magic wand.

Berg, Margaret. **Ozallooning in Oz.** Belen, NM: Tails of the Cowardly Lion and Friends, 2003.

The Wizard's special new hot-air balloons bring adventure to everyone, including a Native American boy and a Norwegian-American girl.

Blaine, Richard, and March Laumer. **The Cloud King of Oz.** N.p.: Vanitas Press, 1997.

The Emerald City gets stolen just before Ozma's birthday, and she must journey to the Cloud King's realm to get it back.

Blossom, Henry S. **The Blue Emperor of Oz.** N.p.: Blossom, 1966.

Jam (from *The Hidden Valley of Oz*) finds the Gump's head on sale in Cleveland and agrees to return him to Munchkinland. The first Oz book published outside the "famous forty."

Briggs, Liatunah Johanna. **Ozma Gets Really Pissed Off and Cusses and Totally Offends (Almost) Everyone in Oz.** Tucson, NM: Palo Verde Emeralds, 1990.

A humorous book; one reviewer says that "nothing actually happens apart from the scene implied by the title."

Brzozowski, Annie. **The Joust in Oz.** Belen, NM: Buckethead Enterprises of Oz, 1997.

In the sequel to *Pegasus in Oz*, Sir Plus and Sir Hokus decide to settle an old argument with a duel.

____. **Pegasus in Oz.** Belen, NM: Buckethead Enterprises of Oz, 1996.

Donald, a young boy, encounters Pegasus, the inhabitants of Oz and a very hungry cyclops in this story.

Buck, Amanda Marie. **The Cloud King of Oz.** Belen, NM: Tails of the Cowardly Lion and Friends, 2002.

When four of Dorothy's friends go missing, she organizes a search party. A friendly rabbit helps them out.

Buckley, Christopher Wayne. **Beach Blanket Babyloz.** Belen, NM: Tails of the Cowardly Lion and Friends, 2000.

Ozma, Dorothy and the other Ozians are stranded on a California beach.

Campbell, Bill, and Irwin Terry. **The Lavender Bear of Oz.** New York: Emerald City Press, 1998.

When the living Teddy Bears of Bear Center disappear, the Lavender Bear (from *The Lost Princess of Oz*) sets out to find them with the help of the Tin Woodman and the Scarecrow.

____. **Masquerade in Oz.** New York: Emerald City Press, 1994.

At a costume party, the Oz characters all dress up as each other—then a magic spell convinces them that they're really the people they're dressed as.

Carlson, Karyl, and Eric Gjovaag. **Queen Ann in Oz.** New York: Emerald City Press, 1993.

Queen Ann of Oogaboo sets out to find her long-lost parents.

Carroll, Willard. **I, Toto.** New York: Stewart, Tabori & Chang, 2001.

An "autobiography" of Terry, the dog cast in the MGM film, written by a longtime Oz fan, writer and film-maker (*The Oz Kids*).

Carter, Lin. **The Tired Tailor of Oz.** Belen, NM: Tails of the Cowardly Lion and Friends, 2001.

Pastoria, Jinnicky and Pigasus join forces against an evil sorcerer who traps the heroes of Oz inside a giant metal ball.

D'Amato, Barbara, and Brian D'Amato. **Hard Road.** New York: Scribner, 2001.

In this mystery novel, reporter Cat Marsala investigates a murder at an Oz festival.

deCamp, L. Sprague. **Sir Harold and the Gnome King.** Newark, NJ: Wildside Press, 1991.

Harold Shea, who knows the secret for traveling between parallel earths (as described in a series of stories written by deCamp and Fletcher Pratt) visits Oz, where he finds Ozma has married Evardo of Ev and Kaliko has kidnapped their son.

Dulabone, Chris. **The Bunny King of Oz.** N.p.: Xlibris, 2001.

Extraterrestrials kidnap the rabbit ruler of Bunnybury.

____. **The Colorful Kitten of Oz.** Albuquerque, NM: Buckethead Enterprises of Oz, 1990.

The secret history of Eureka, the pink kitten, which actually starts 1,000 years ago in Pingaree.

____. **Dagmar in Oz.** Albuquerque, NM: Buckethead Enterprises of Oz, 1991.

The Queen of the Scoodlers returns from *The Road to Oz*, seeking revenge.

____. **The Deadly Desert Around Oz.** Albuquerque, NM: Buckethead Enterprises of Oz, 1989.

Dorothy gets kidnapped by a Dust Devil while Ruggedo escapes—but still in the form of a cactus from *Handy Mandy in Oz*.

____. **Do It for Oz.** Belen, NM: Tails of the Cowardly Lion and Friends, 2003.

Johnny Dooit's helpful exploits include visits to the Sea Fairies, Merryland and the Enchanted Island of Yew.

____. **Egor's Funhouse Goes to Oz.** Belen, NM: Buckethead Enterprises of Oz, 1994.

Egor, a friendly monster, runs a funhouse for children—which gets carried to Oz, and the adventures begin…

____. **Fairy Circle in Oz.** Belen, NM: Buckethead Enterprises of Oz, 1996.

Wooglet must restore the powers of the Love Fairy to save love in Oz and everywhere else.

____. **The Fantastic Funhouse of Oz.** Belen, NM: Buckethead Enterprises of Oz, 1996.

Furious at being made into part of a carnival funhouse, the Wicked Witch of the West replaces her animatronic counterpart and prepares to avenge herself upon the children.

____. **Hurray for Oz.** Belen, NM: Tails of the Cowardly Lion and Friends, 1998.

A young girl steps in for the Tooth Fairy when the fairy is injured during her rounds.

____. **Lunarr and Maureen in Oz.** Albuquerque, NM: Buckethead Enterprises of Oz, 1992.

Toto and Lunarr (from *Toto in Oz*) become involved in a professor's scheme to track down a favorite student and plagiarize his research.

____. **The Lunechien Forest of Oz.** Belen, NM: Buckethead Enterprises of Oz, 1993.

A sequel to Baum's *Animal Fairy Tales*, set in Oz.

____. **The Marvelous Monkeys in Oz.** Belen, NM: Buckethead Enterprises of Oz, 1994.

The first book in a trilogy about the winged monkeys.

____. **A Queer Quest for Oz.** Belen, NM: Buckethead Enterprises of Oz, 1996.

A sequel to *Captain Salt in Oz* involving an evil necromancer and a game of Snakes and Ladders.

____. **The Three Imps of Oz.** Belen, NM: Tails of the Cowardly Lion and Friends, 1998.

Three mischievous imps from the *Little Wizard* stories return with their powers back.

____. **Toto in Oz.** Albuquerque, NM: Buckethead Enterprises of Oz, 1986.

Feeling second-rate among the animals of Oz, Toto runs away and winds up in the canine realm of Africa, where he becomes the new magistrate.

____. **A Viking in Oz.** Albuquerque, NM: Buckethead Enterprises of Oz, 1988.

Victor the Viking is lost at sea and enters the amazing world of Baum's *The Sea Fairies*. As Victor makes his way around the Nonestic Ocean, Button Bright gets lost and has an adventure of his own.

Eager, Edward. **Seven Day Magic.** New York: Harcourt, Brace & World, 1962.

In this fantasy, a group of siblings discovers a library book with magic powers. In one of several adventures, they arrive at what might be Oz in the years before *The Wizard of Oz*.

Einhorn, Edward. **Paradox in Oz.** San Diego: Hungry Tiger Press, 1999.

When the enchantment that makes Ozians ageless is disrupted, Ozma must travel back in time to restore it, but without interfering with recorded Oz history.

Evans, Bob, and Chris Dulabone. **Abducted to Oz.** Belen, NM: Tails of the Cowardly Lion and Friends, 2000.

A wicked witch kidnaps an American boy and takes him to Oz, where they wander through Thoughtformland, Americanindianland and other enlightening realms.

_____. **The Forest Monster of Oz.** Belen, NM: Buckethead Enterprises of Oz, 1997.

The giant spider the Cowardly Lion killed in *Wizard of Oz* returns for revenge.

Evans, Robert J. **Dorothy's Mystical Adventures in Oz.** N.p.: Xlibris, 2000.

Dorothy and her friends have new adventures and discuss certain cosmic issues.

Farmer, Philip Jose. **A Barnstormer in Oz, or, A Rationalization and Extrapolation of the Split-Level Continuum.** New York: Berkley Books, 1982.

In the 1920s, Dorothy's son, a pilot, finds himself swept into Oz (in this version Dorothy never returned after *Wizard* so Baum made up the other books) and works with Glinda to protect Oz from an evil witch and an American government plan to loot Oz of its gems.

Freedman, Jeff. **The Magic Dishpan of Oz.** New York: Emerald City Press, 1994.

Two Oregon girls are transported by Cayke's dishpan (from *The Lost Princess of Oz*) to Oz, where they must prevent a band of magicians from destroying Oz with discord and hate.

Gannaway, Atticus. **The Silver Sorceress of Oz.** New York: Emerald City Press, 2002.

When Sonora, the Silver Sorceress, discovers that her precious Silver Hammer has fallen into the hands of Ozma, she sets off to the Emerald City to recover it.

Gannaway, Ryan. **As the Clock Strikes Oz.** N.p.: Ozian Seahorse Press, 1993.

A powerful villain creates a timepiece that can change the course of Oz history.

_____. **The Magic Bowls of Oz.** N.p.: Ozian Seahorse Press, 1997.

The Wizard's new spell transfers Ozma and Button-Bright into each other's bodies.

_____. **Sinister Gasses in Oz.** N.p.: Ozian Seahorse Press, 1995.

The Nome King has developed a gas that can make him master of Oz.

_____. **Time Traveling in Oz.** N.p.: Ozian Seahorse Press, 1992.

Dorothy and the Wizard must stop a plot against Oz that has already happened.

_____. **A Wonderful Journey in Oz.** Albuquerque, NM: Buckethead Enterprises of Oz, 1990.

Button Bright, Trot and Cap'n Bill take another ride on the magic umbrella from *Sky Island*.

Gardner, Martin. **Visitors from Oz: The Wild Adventures of Dorothy, the Scarecrow, and the Tin Woodman.** New York: St. Martin's, 1998.

As part of the celebration of the *Wizard of Oz* centennial, a slick publicist persuades Dorothy and her friends to come to America to promote a new Oz movie.

Gardner, Richard A. **Dorothy and the Lizard of Oz.** Cresskill, NJ: Creative Therapeutics, 1980.

In this sequel to the MGM film, Dorothy realizes that her return home hasn't solved all her problems — and her Oz friends haven't resolved theirs, either.

Gick, Greg. **Bungle and the Magic Lantern of Oz.** Albuquerque, NM: Buckethead Enterprises of Oz, 1992.

The glass cat is caught up in a wizard's scheme to release an evil genie from its lamp.

Grandy, Melody. **The Seven Blue Mountains of Oz: Book I, the Disenchanted Princess of Oz.** Belen, NM: Buckethead Enterprises, 1995.

The first of a trilogy, exploring what happened to Tip when Ozma was restored to herself.

____. **The Seven Blue Mountains of Oz II: Tippetarius of Oz.** Belen, NM: Tails of the Cowardly Lion and Friends, 2000.

In the second installment in the Blue Mountain trilogy, a sorcerer arrives at the Emerald City just as the inhabitants are all shrinking.

____, and Chris Dulabone. **Thorns and Private Files in Oz.** Belen, NM: Tails of the Cowardly Lion and Friends, 1998.

A follow-up to *Tik-Tok of Oz* in which Ozga, Files and Hank the Mule have a new adventure.

Haas, Dorothy. **Dorothy and Old King Crow.** New York: Random House, 1986.

Old King Crow traps the Scarecrow and challenges Dorothy to a spelling contest to free him.

____. **Dorothy and the Seven-Leaf Clover.** New York: Random House, 1985.

To free Toto from a leftover spell cast by the Witch of the West, Dorothy and her friends must find a rare seven-leaf clover.

Haas, Mark. **Leprechauns in Oz.** Atlanta: Protea, 2000.

A teenage boy accompanies a leprechaun on a quest to seek Ozma's help against a banshee terrifying a leprechaun village.

____. **The Medicine Man of Oz.** Atlanta: Protea, 2001.

Herby, the medicine man from *The Giant Horse of Oz*, goes up against the Nome King's latest plan.

Hardenbrook, Dave. **The Unknown Witches of Oz: Locasta and the Three Adepts.** Lakeville, MN: Galde Press, 2001.

An average American guy helps a stranded witch return to Oz and has a romance with Ozma.

Heinlein, Robert. **The Number of the Beast.** New York: Fawcett Columbine, 1980.

In this science fiction novel, a quartet of heroes fleeing a mysterious enemy bounce between parallel worlds, including a visit to Oz.

Hess, Robin. **Christmas in Oz.** New York: Emerald City Press, 1995.

When Santa sets up a new workshop in Oz, the Wicked Blue Witch sets out to drive him off.

Howe, James. **Mister Tinker in Oz.** New York: Random House, 1985.

Believing the guarantee on Tik-Tok is about to run out, his creator enlists Dorothy to help reach the mechanical man in time. Illustrations by David Rose.

Hulan, David. **The Glass Cat of Oz.** New York: Emerald City Press, 1995.

The Bad Lads overrun Oogaboo, leaving it to the Glass Cat and two California children to save the day.

Hunter, Greg. **The Enchanted Gnome of Oz.** Albuquerque, NM: Buckethead Enterprises of Oz, 1988.

The Goblin King sends Ruggedo, the former Nome King, to find a magic lamp, and Ruggedo threatens to ruin Ozma's Christmas with magic blue snow.

____. **Two Terrific Tales of Oz.** Albuquerque, NM: Buckethead Enterprises of Oz, 1987.

In *Betsy Bobbin of Oz*, Betsy finds her parents with the help of a living doll. In *Unc Nunkie and the White King of Oz*, Nunkie and Ojo visit the King of the White Mountains.

Inglis, Julia. **The Magic Ruby of Oz.** Belen, NM: Buckethead Enterprises of Oz, 1997.

Dorothy, Betsy Bobbin and the Sawhorse go up against a pair of sorcerers with a particularly nasty plan to destroy Oz.

Joel, Gil S. **The Case of the Framed Fairy of Oz.** Belen, NM: Buckethead Enterprises of Oz, 1993.

When Ozma is put on trial for practicing witchcraft, she hires Perry Mason as her defense attorney.

____. **The Healing Power of Oz.** Belen, NM: Buckethead Enterprises of Oz, 1995.

Four troubled individuals from our world become the only barrier to the Nome King's latest plan for conquest.

____. **Roots of Wonder in Oz.** Belen, NM: Tails of the Cowardly Lion and Friends, 1998.

A story about the Fairy Queen who founded Oz and about the creation of the Emerald City.

Kaminsky, Stuart. **Murder on the Yellow Brick Road.** New York: St. Martin's, 1977.

In the second of the Toby Peters murder mysteries, gumshoe Peters investigates when one of the MGM Munchkins turns up dead.

Karr, Phyliss Ann. **The Gardener's Boy of Oz.** Albuquerque, NM: Buckethead Enterprises of Oz, 1988.

Pon, the Gardener's Boy from *The Scarecrow in Oz*, rescues his father Phearse and Queen Gloria's father Kynd from the pond where they've both been sunk.

____. **Maybe the Miffin.** Tucson: Palo Verde Emeralds, 1994.

The Iffin from *Jack Pumpkinhead in Oz* goes looking for a mate.

Kline, K. **Kaliko in Oz.** Belen, NM: Buckethead Enterprises of Oz, 1994.

Kaliko must cope with his Nomes' enthusiasm for war, a giant egg creature attached to the Nome King and a sorceress demanding the return of the magic belt.

Laumer, Keith. **The Other Side of Time.** New York: Berkley, 1965.

Not an Oz book, but this science fiction story is noteworthy for a scene in which a traveler trapped in a parallel world discovers that in that timeline, Baum's one and only Oz novel was *The Sorceress of Oz*.

____, and March Laumer. **Beenie in Oz.** N.p.: Vanitas Press, 1997.

Beenie (based on the author's sister) dons a Scarecrow costume that carries the Scarecrow's personality, meets a boy from Oz (Australia) and tells the "generic story of Oz" in which Ozma saves the day at the last minute.

Laumer, March. **Aunt Em and Uncle Henry in Oz.** N.p.: Vanitas Press, 1983.

When Henry reminds Aunt Em that a thimble she lost years ago may still be somewhere in the old farmhouse that crashed in the Munchkin country, they set off to find the house and the thimble.

____. **The Careless Kangaroo of Oz.** N.p.: Vanitas Press, 1988.

Along with the eccentric kangaroo from *The Emerald City of Oz*, this story includes the Shaggy Man falling for Dorothy, Polychrome falling for the Shaggy Man, Eureka trying to return to Oz and Almira Gulch from the MGM film studying witchcraft.

____. **Charmed Gardens of Oz.** N.p.: Vanitas Press, 1988.

A recreation of the "Garden of Meats" chapter dropped from *The Patchwork Girl of Oz*, based on the Neill illustrations.

____. **Dragons in Oz.** N.p.: Vanitas Press, 1999.

After vanishing in *Woozy of Oz*, Ozma returns five years later.

____. **A Fairy Queen in Oz.** N.p.: Vanitas Press, 1989.

Written to resolve several inconsistencies, this story includes a visit by Queen Lurline to a town in Sweden and Ozma discovering something about how people travel to Oz.

____. **A Farewell to Oz.** N.p.: Vanitas Press, 1993.

For the hundredth anniversary of Dorothy's arrival in Oz, Baum, John R. Neill, Ruth Plumly Thompson and other contributors to the Oz legend are brought to Oz for a party.

____. **The Frogman of Oz.** Lund, Sweden: Vanitas Press, 1986.

The Frogman from *Lost Princess*, a Navy frogman from the United States and the prince Quelala—transformed into a frog for much of the book—are the heroes of this story.

____. **The Good Witch of Oz.** N.p.: Vanitas Press, 1984.

A Big Wig giantess seeks the Scarecrow while Dorothy visits the Good Witch of the North.

____. **The Green Dolphin of Oz.** N.p.: Vanitas Press, 1978.

Most of this book focuses on the adventures of a band of time and space travelers, but the latter part of the story blends their adventures with an unpublished manuscript of Baum's, *An Oz Book*.

____. **The Magic Mirror of Oz.** N.p.: Vanitas Press, 1985.

This story involving the Adepts of Magic explains why some of Baum's later books locate Munchkinland in the east of Oz.

____. **The Ten Woodmen of Oz.** N.p.: Vanitas Press, 1987.

Dorothy is sent to warn our world that pollution is threatening disastrous consequences to Oz.

____. **The Umbrellas of Oz.** Chicago and Lund, Sweden: Vanitas Press, 1991.

Assorted umbrellas from the Oz books figure into a story that also includes Speedy attending a reunion with other Oz visitors and Button Bright meeting Omby Amby in Missouri.

____. **The Vegetable Man of Oz.** N.p.: Vanitas Press, 1990.

Dorothy, Betsy and Trot visit California in 1942 with Carter Green, who becomes a mere vegetable; a Japanese tengu also appears in California. The book includes summaries of unwritten chapters.

____. **The Woozy of Oz.** N.p.: Vanitas Press, 1999.

Trouble strikes after Ozma lifts her ban on magic.

____, and M. Michanczyk. **The Crown of Oz.** N.p.: Vanitas Press, 1991.

Economic, personal and geographic problems hammer Oz, but who's behind them?

____, and Ruth Tuttle. **The China Dog of Oz.** N.p.: Vanitas Press, 1990.

A revisionist look at *The Patchwork Girl of Oz* showing Ozma as a dupe and Dorothy as a rather annoying meddler.

Lionel, Rufus K. **The Braided Man of Oz.** Albuquerque, NM: Buckethead Enterprises of Oz, 1987.

The Braided Man from *The Road to Oz* goes in search of his prototype flutters and confronts a killer robot that, being lifeless, can survive in the Deadly Desert.

Madden, Onyx. **Mysterious Chronicles of Oz.** Santa Monica, CA: Dennis-Landman, 1985.

Shortly after her coronation, Ozma dresses up as Tip and rides out on the Sawhorse for adventures, including her first meeting with the Cowardly Lion and the Hungry Tiger.

Maguire, Gregory. **Wicked: The Life and Times of the Wicked Witch of the West.** New York: ReganBooks, 1995.

This pretentious, talky (but commercially successful) revisionist novel depicts a girl rejected for her green skin who grows up into a good witch. When she pits herself against that repressive, conniving dictator, the Wizard of Oz, the Wizard's propaganda machine brands her as Oz's greatest villain, the Wicked Witch of the West.

The most successful "unofficial" Oz book, *Wicked* was a best-seller, inspired a Broadway musical, and now has a film adaptation in the works.

Martin, Dick. **The Ozmapolitan of Oz.** Kinderhook, IL: International Wizard of Oz Club, 1985.

Dorothy suspects a hidden agenda when Oz's only newspaper sets out to increase circulation.

McBain, Allison. **Cory in Oz.** Belen, NM: Buckethead Enterprises of Oz, 1993.

A new Nome King casts his spell on the good witches of Oz, just as young Cory discovers a secret that makes her different from everyone else.

Mebes, Marcus. **Brewster Bunny and the Case of the Outrageous Enchantments in Oz.** Belen, NM: Buckethead Enterprises of Oz, 1994.

A solve-it-yourself mystery containing all the clues readers should need to help Oz detective Brewster Bunny restore many enchanted people and objects to normal.

_____. **The Haunted Castle of Oz.** Belen, NM: Buckethead Enterprises of Oz, 1995.

A ghost haunts Ozma's castle.

_____. **Lurline and the White Ravens of Oz.** Tucson, NM: Palo Verde Emeralds, 1995.

The story of how Lurline came to enchant Oz, and the price she paid.

_____. **The Mysterious Caverns of Oz.** Albuquerque, NM: Buckethead Enterprises of Oz, 1990.

Bud of Noland and Zixi of Ix are visiting Oz when a mysterious sinkhole swallows a house, and Bud and Polychrome join the investigation.

_____. **Sail Away to Oz.** Tucson, NM: Palo Verde Emeralds, 1993.

A dream-poem with an appearance by King Rinkitink.

_____, and Chris Dulabone. **The Magic Tapestry of Oz.** Albuquerque, NM: Buckethead Enterprises of Oz, 1992.

A magic time machine carries some of the Oz characters back to the birth of the land of Oz.

Mongold, Harry E. **Button-Bright of Oz.** Privately printed, 1979.

In order to obtain a powerful magic mirror, villainous Trickolas Om contrives to send Button-Bright to secure it for him.

_____. **The Sawhorse of Oz.** Privately printed, 1981.

The Tin Woodman investigates a silver chest that appears before him, while the evil Krook is sent on a quest by a spray can that answers any question asked of it.

Morris, Ruth. **Dr. Angelina Bean in Oz.** Belen, NM: Tails of the Cowardly Lion and Friends, 2003.

Psychiatrist Angelina Bean sets off for Oz in the belief that Ruggedo has been cruelly mistreated for years, and that she alone can redeem him.

_____. **The Flying Bus in Oz:** or, **Joy Marie and the Noyzy Boys.** Belen, NM: Buckethead Enterprises of Oz, 1993.

A Canadian schoolbus flies to Oz, giving the passengers the adventure of a lifetime.

Muller, Romeo. **Dorothy and the Green Gobbler of Oz.** New York: Scholastic Book Services, 1982.

An adaptation of *Thanksgiving in the Land of Oz.*

Otto, Frederick E. **The Lost Emeralds of Oz.** Belen, NM: Buckethead Enterprises of Oz, 1995.

In the early days of her reign, Ozma comes up against a cabal of sorcerers too powerful for her to defeat.

Pendexter, Hugh, III. **The Crocheted Cat in Oz.** Albuquerque, NM: Buckethead Enterprises of Oz, 1991.

A new Oz visitor, the Crocheted Cat, leads a band to recover one of Ozma's stolen birthday gifts.

____. **Oz and the Three Witches.** Savannah, GA: Pen Press, 1977.

Set after the Wizard returns to Oz, this book retells the story of his early days in Oz and explains some of the questions about Ozma's childhood.

____. **Wooglet in Oz.** Belen, NM: Buckethead Enterprises of Oz, 1993.

Wooglet and her uncle end up in Oz, and must find a way home.

Phipps, Charles. **The Wooing of Ozma.** Bloomington, IN: 1st Books Library, 2003.

Ozma falls in love with Milo, a young man who must then rescue her from the dungeon of her evil cousin Zoam. First in a trilogy.

Piro, Rita E. **The Summer of Oz.** New York: TB Books, 2002.

A young adult novel in which a young movie fan must choose between meeting Judy Garland at MGM or seeing her brother off as he joins the military.

Powell, Ray. **Mister Flint in Oz.** Albuquerque, NM: Buckethead Enterprises of Oz, 1987.

Hardas Flint, a man of living quartz, sets out to find his father with the help of the Scarecrow and the Tin Woodman.

____. **Raggedys in Oz.** Tucson, NM: Palo Verde Emeralds, 1968.

An evil mage teams up with the Nome King in a story whose cast includes Raggedy Ann, Raggedy Andy and Percy the Personality Kid from *The Hidden Valley of Oz.*

Quinn, Richard G. **Red Reera, the Yookoohoo and the Enchanted Easter Eggs of Oz.** Belen, NM: Buckethead Enterprises of Oz, 1994.

A story featuring Reera from *Glinda of Oz* and the Easter Bunny from *Merry Go Round.*

Richardson, Nikki Ray. **Vampires and Oz.** N.p.: Xlibris, 2000.

A good vampire flees to Oz, pursued by evil vampire killers.

Romer, Ken. **Dorothy and the Wooden Soldiers.** N.p.: Star Rover Press, 1987.

This story combines elements of both Oz and Alexander Volkov's Russian version, the Magic Land.

Ross, Dev. **The Birthday Ban in Munchkin Land.** N.p.: Treasure Bay, 1999.

A beginning reader book in which twins decide to thwart the Wicked Witch of the East's ban on birthdays.

Ryman, Geoff. **Was.** New York: Knopf, 1992.

A dark story about Dorothy Gael, an abused orphan living a harsh life with her relatives Henry and Emma Gulch—a life that inspires L. Frank Baum to spin a fantasy giving her a happy ending. This mixes in with a dying AIDS victim in the present trying to locate the real Dorothy.

Saunders, Susan. **Dorothy and the Magic Belt.** New York: Random House, 1985.

Dr. Nikidik's son turns the members of the Emerald City court into babies so that he can steal Ozma's magic belt and free his father to resume practicing sorcery.

Schulenberg, Peter. **The Corn Mansion of Oz.** Belen, NM: Buckethead Enterprises of Oz, 1998.

The origin of Scarecrow's corn-shaped mansion and Jack Pumpkinhead's pumpkin-house.

____. **The Tin Castle of Oz.** Belen, NM: Buckethead Enterprises of Oz, 1998.

The Tin Woodman tells the story behind his tin castle.

____. **The Unwinged Monkey of Oz.** N.p.: Patchwork Press, 2001.

The adventures of a winged monkey that was born "unwinged."

Seltzer, Richard. **The Lizard of Oz.** West Roxbury, MA: B & R Samizdat Express, 1974.

It's up to the Lizard of Oz to save some children from the schemes of the Humbug.

Shanower, Eric. **The Giant Garden of Oz.** New York: Emerald City Press, 1993.

A story in which Dorothy becomes a giant. Shanower's previous graphic novels are listed in the comic-book chapter.

____. **The Salt Sorcerer of Oz and Other Stories.** San Diego, CA: Hungry Tiger Press, 2003.

A collection of short stories from writer/artist Shanower.

Silva, Carol P., and Marin Elizabeth Xiques. **The Magic Topaz of Oz.** Belen, NM: Tails of the Cowardly Lion and Friends, 2003.

Tweaty, the canary from *The Forest Monster of Oz*, acquires a magic topaz that can not only break him free of an enchantment but also help the Cowardly Lion.

Skipp, John, and Marc Levinthal. **The Emerald Burrito of Oz.** Northridge, CA: Babbage Press, 2000.

In the near future, travel between Oz and Earth is common, but one vacationer gets caught up fighting the latest menace to threaten Oz. A revisionist, adult version of the Oz legends.

Sprague, Gilbert M. **The Nome King's Shadow in Oz.** New York: Emerald City Press, 1992.

When Billina frightens the Nome King's shadow away from the king, the shadow decides to strike at Oz on its own.

____. **The Patchwork Bride of Oz.** New York: Emerald City Press, 1993.

The Scarecrow and Scraps decide to tie the knot!

Steadman, Jeremy. **The Emerald Ring of Oz.** Belen, NM: Buckethead Enterprises of Oz, 1993.

A lost boy becomes involved with pirates, magic treasures—and Oz.

Tedrow, Thomas L. **Dorothy: Return to Oz.** New York: Family Vision Press, 1992.

A young girl becomes increasingly worried by her grandmother Dorothy's delusions about some strange magic land called Oz. But during a cyclone, the young girl finds her grandmother's ruby slippers and tries them on…

Vinge, Joan D. **Return to Oz.** New York: Del Rey, 1985.

A novelization of the movie.

Volkov, Alexander. **Fiery God of the Marrans.** Moscow: Soviet Russia Publishers, 1968.

The fourth Volkov novel, in which Urfin Jus launches a new scheme to take over the Magic Land.

____. **The Seven Underground Kings.** Moscow: Soviet Russia Publishers, 1964.

The realm underneath the Magic Country is ruled by seven monarchs, six of whom sleep at a time—but when they all awake at once, a crisis strikes. The third Volkov novel.

____. **Taina Zabroshennovo Zamka aka The Secret of the Deserted Castle.** Moscow: Soviet Russia Publishers, 1982.

A posthumous book by Volkov in which aliens planning to conquer Earth make the mistake of landing in the Magic Land. There would be many subsequent Magic Land books by other authors, but they're slightly outside the sphere of this bibliography.

____. **Urfin Jus and His Wooden Soldiers.** Moscow: Soviet Russia Publishers, 1963.

Evil Urfin Jus uses the powder of life to create a wooden army and sets out to conquer the Magic Land in the second Volkov novel. Can Elli stop him?

____. **The Wizard of the Emerald City.** Moscow and Leningrad: Ts. K.V.L.S.M. Publishing House of Children's Literature, 1939.

This was a Russian "translation" of *Wizard* that comes closer to a reworking: Elli and her dog Totoshka travel to the Magic Land where they meet a Scarecrow, a Cowardly Lion and an Iron Woodchopper. Volkov wrote several sequels moving even further from Oz and many other authors would follow with stories of the Magic Land.

____. **Zholtiy Tuman aka The Yellow Fog.** Moscow: Soviet Russia Publishers, 1970.

Reawakening from centuries of sleep, the sorceress Archna creates a deadly yellow fog with which to conquer the magic land in the fifth Volkov book.

Wauchpe, Virginia, and Robert Wauchope. **Invisible Inzi of Oz.** Albuquerque, NM: Buckethead Enterprises of Oz, 1992.

When Glinda's magical texts disappear, the Wizard, Dorothy, Scarecrow and Scraps set out to stop the wizard responsible, and receive help from Invisible Inzi. Written by two children, this 1920s story is the first known Oz book written by someone other than the Royal Historians.

White, Ted. **The Oz Encounter: A Doc Phoenix Novel.** Weird Heroes, vol. 5. New York: Pyramid, 1977.

Doc Phoenix, a psychologist who projects himself into people's minds to cure their delusions, discovers his new patient's mindscape is a twisted version of Oz where the Shaggy Man has used the Love Magnet to enslave everyone.

Wickwar, Gina. **The Hidden Prince of Oz.** Kalamazoo, MI: International Wizard of Oz Club, 2000.

In a glass valley, the Glass Cat and an American orphan join forces to learn the secret of a vanished prince.

The Wiz Kids. **Valuable Gift from Oz.** Albuquerque, NM: Wiz Kids of Oz, 1995.

In the last Wiz Kid book, the Kids receive a magic microscope from Oz.

____. **The Enchanted Emeralds of Oz.** Albuquerque, NM: Wiz Kids of Oz, 1990.

Another Oz fantasy by the Wiz Kids.

____. **John R. Neill Visits Oz.** Albuquerque, NM: Wiz Kids of Oz, 1994.

Royal Illustrator and Historian Neill joins the kids on a visit to Ozmico.

____. **The Liberty Bell in Oz.** Albuquerque, NM: Wiz Kids of Oz, 1992.

A story about Ruth Plumly Thompson's adventures in Oz.

____. **Many Lands in Oz.** Albuquerque, NM: Wiz Kids of Oz, 1991.

Elementary school students travel through time and learn about mathematics and L. Frank Baum.

____. **Our Trip to Oz.** Albuquerque, NM: Wiz Kids of Oz, 1989.

A book about Oz written and illustrated by fourth and fifth graders who were introduced by their teacher to the wonderful world of the Oz books.

____. **W.W. Denslow in Oz.** Albuquerque, NM: Wiz Kids of Oz, 1993.

The Wiz Kids travel with Oz illustrator W.W. Denslow to Ozmico, a region of Oz created by Ozma especially for them.

Xiques, Marin Elizabeth. **The Silver Shoes of Oz.** Albuquerque, NM: Buckethead Enterprises of Oz, 1990.

Ozma discovers the lost silver shoes in the deadly desert, and Betsy Bobbin accidentally uses them to wish away every magic-worker in Oz.

____, and Chris Dulabone. **Brewster Bunny and the Purloined Pachyderms of Oz.** Belen, NM: Tails of the Cowardly Lion and Friends, 1999.

Detective Brewster Bunny goes looking when one of Kabumpo's friends disappears.

____. **A Foolish Fable from Oz.** Belen, NM: Tails of the Cowardly Lion and Friends, 1999.

This story of the Wicked Witches in pre–*Wizard* Oz tells the origin of the silver slippers.

____. **The Green Goblins of Oz.** N.p.: Ozian Seahorse Press, 1997.

The adventures of two goblins trying to reach the Emerald City.

____. **I Want to Grow Up in Oz.** Belen, NM: Tails of the Cowardly Lion and Friends, 1999.

An evil panther contrives to thwart a spell Ozma used to keep the cruel cat small and harmless.

____. **The Land Before Oz.** Belen, NM: Tails of the Cowardly Lion and Friends, 1999.

The Scarecrow and his friends go back in time to help some orphaned dinosaurs find a new home.

____. **A Mystical Magical Super Adventure in Oz.** Belen, NM: Tails of the Cowardly Lion and Friends, 1999.

A field trip to the forests of Oz leads to danger.

____. **Ridiculous Rivals in Oz.** Belen, NM: Tails of the Cowardly Lion and Friends, 1998.

The Cowardly Lion, Scarecrow and Tin Woodman try to drive a three-eyed sorceress out of the forest she rules.

____. **A Silver Elf in Oz.** Belen, NM: Buckethead Enterprises of Oz, 1994.

Two children set off to find Father Christmas.

Anthologies

Acinad Goes to the Emerald City. Albuquerque, NM: Buckethead Enterprises of Oz, 1988.

A book by Oz author Chris Dalabone's grade school students in which Acinad, rightful ruler of the Nomes, races a witch to find a magic diamond.

Dorothy Returns to Oz. Albuquerque, NM: Buckethead Enterprises of Oz, 1990.

Another collection of stories by gradeschoolers, each story springing off from asking what would have happened had Dorothy not returned to Oz until she was an adult.

Fwiirp in Oz. Belen, NM: Buckethead Enterprises of Oz, 1996.

When Miss Cuttenclip's magic paper blows to America, a would-be Oz Historian finds it — and whatever she writes upon it happens to come true. A group of characters try to use a Skeezik tree to make sense of all this.

In Other Lands Than Oz. N.p.: Vanitas, 1984.

A collection of several stories, most of them, despite the title, based on Oz.

The Magic Diamond of Oz. Albuquerque, NM: Buckethead Enterprises of Oz, 1989.

An Oz fantasy written by fourth and fifth grade children, students of Oz author Chris Dulabone.

The Odd Tale of Osoenft in Oz. Belen, NM: Buckethead Enterprises of Oz, 1994.

Polychrome, Kaliko and Scraps are among those visiting Osoenft's Skeezik tree.

The Shifting Sands of Oz. Belen, NM: Buckethead Enterprises of Oz, 1995.

Another Skeezik anthology involving stories told while crossing the deadly desert.

Skeezik and the Mys-Tree of Oz. Albuquerque, NM: Buckethead Enterprises of Oz, 1992.

The first of several anthologies centered around the Skeezik trees, which enable anyone who visits them to relive the existence of any object they find in the tree (allowing for several non–Oz stories within the Oz framework). In this book, two royal children seek help from the tree with a mystery of their own.

2

Theatrical and Other Staged Adaptations

Plays are far more ephemeral than movies or television, and so is information about them. For that reason, many of these entries lack the in-depth information found in other sections of this book. In some cases, finding the first performance of any given version has proven elusive; such plays are listed by publication date.

1902

The Wizard of Oz. 6/6/02. Grand Opera House, Chicago.
Cast: Dorothy Gale (Anna Laughlin), Scarecrow (Fred Stone), Tin Woodman (Dave Montgomery), Cowardly Lion (Arthur Hill), Tryxie Tryfle (Mabel Barrison), Pastoria (Neil McNeil), Sir Wylie Gyle (Stephen Maley), The Wizard (John Slavin), Cynthia Cynch (Helen Byron), Sir Dashemoff (Bessie Wynn), Locasta, the Good Witch of the North (Aileen May), Glinda (Doris Mitchell), Imogene the Cow (Edwin J. Stone).
Credits: Director: Julian Mitchell; *Producer:* Fred Hamlin; *Writers:* L. Frank Baum, Paul Tietjens, Glen MacDonough, Robert B. Smith, A. Baldwin Sloane, Edgar Smith, Nathaniel D. Mann; *Costume design:* W.W. Denslow, Will R. Barnes; *Scenic designer:* Walter Burridge.
Songs: Niccolo's Piccolo; In Michigan; The Man Who Stays in Town; To the Princess Within; Carrie Barry; Alas for the Man Without Brains; The Road through the Forest; Love Is Love; When You Love, Love, Love; The Poppy Chorus; The Guardian of the Gate; Hayfoot Strawfoot; When We Get What's a'Comin' to Us; Courtyard of the Wizard's Palace; Phantom Patrol; Mr. Dooley; The Witch Behind the Moon; The Different Ways of Making Love; Sammy; Connemara Christening; Spanish Bolero; Wee Highland Mon; Rosalie; The Lobster; The Wizard Is No Longer King; I'll Be Your Honey in the Springtime; She Didn't Seem to Mind; The Traveller and the Pie; Finale.

A cyclone carries Kansan Dorothy Gale (a young adult) to Oz, along with her cow, Imogene; Pastoria II, the rightful king of Oz (after the Wizard landed in Oz, he conned Pastoria into riding the balloon back to Kansas and exile); and Tryxie Tryfle, a Kansas waitress engaged to Pastoria. Pastoria plans to regain his throne from the usurping Wizard with the help of one-man army General Riskitt.

In Oz, they meet Cynthia Cynch, deranged since her piccolo-playing lover, Niccolo Chopper, disappeared; Oz poet laureate Dashemoff Daily, who falls for Dorothy; and Locasta, the Good Witch of the North, who gives Dorothy a wishing ring. Unfortunately, Dorothy wastes the ring's two charges, first by wishing to learn one of Dashemoff's songs, then by bringing a Scarecrow to life.

Dorothy and the Scarecrow head off to the Emerald City, picking up the Tin Woodman on the way. Pastoria heads in the same direction accompanied by Imogene, Tryxie and the Cowardly Lion, posing as a circus to hide from the Wizard's police. A field of deadly poppies paralyzes everyone, but the magic ring alerts Locasta, who kills the poppies with snow. The different groups go on to the Emerald City.

In the city, inventor Sir Wiley Gyle tells the audience he plans to overthrow the Wizard despite the latter's fake magic. When the Wizard starts performing tricks for his court, however, Gyle can't convince anyone he's a phony. Dorothy's party arrives, so the Wizard whips up some brains and a heart for the Scarecrow and Tin Woodman, proclaims a royal ball to celebrate the achievement and invites Pastoria's circus to perform.

In between the ball's musical numbers, Gyle shows some of the Ozians how the Wizard's tricks work and they agree to overthrow him. Unfortunately for Gyle, just as the Wizard is unmasked as a humbug, Pastoria reveals himself and reclaims the throne. The Wizard escapes in his balloon. Dorothy and her friends journey to Glinda's realm of Dreamland to ask for help; Cynthia discovers the Tin Woodman is really Niccolo, Glinda promises Dorothy a return home, the Wizard shows up to ask for help for himself and everyone breaks into song for the big finale.

Baum and composer Paul Tietjens were already working on a musical (*The Octopus*, never produced — though "Love is Love" and "The Traveler and the Pie" from that show made it into *The Wizard of Oz*) when they hit on the idea for working on a stage version of *The Wizard of Oz* instead. The inspiration has been credited to Baum, Tietjens or artist W.W. Denslow, and Baum himself gave three different stories of its genesis.

After some non–Oz projects failed to go anywhere, Baum set to work on an Oz comic opera (in the style of Gilbert and Sullivan or Victor Herbert) with Tietjens and Denslow, who contributed some design and costume suggestions. Some of this early version may be preserved in a wall-paper designed by Denslow that includes a Wicked Witch, the Motor Man, Queen Golinda and Gabriel the Poet Boy, none of whom made it to the stage.

Baum and Denslow, however, had been at odds for some time: Baum resented how much credit Denslow received for the success of their collaborations, and his ownership of the illustrations for the books. Although Denslow's contributions were minor, he received a third of the royalties and pushed Baum to make it two-fifths for each of them, one-fifth for Tietjens (who only went along with the one-third division for fear a fight would stop the whole show cold). This contributed to the decision to bring in John R. Neill as illustrator on *The Marvelous Land of Oz*.

The finished result was a fairly faithful adaptation, but without Toto or the Wicked Witch of the West (Dorothy outs the Wizard the first time they meet), more romance (the Tin Woodman keeps offering his heart to everyone) and lots of Tin Woodman/Scarecrow banter.

Fred Hamlin, a producer and manager at Chicago's Grand Opera House, expressed an interest in the show, though he didn't like the script, and asked director Julian Mitchell for a second opinion. Mitchell decided *The Wizard of Oz* would work better as a musical extravaganza, a popular genre in which a minimal plot served as a framework for dance numbers, songs, comedy routines and visual spectacle. Mitchell began shaping the show in that direction, despite occasional protests from Baum and Tietjens.

Mitchell knew his stuff: the end result wasn't high art, but the mix of colorful effects, flocks of chorus girls and romantic subplots made for a major hit. Mitchell added many popular elements, such as mistaken-identity shticks, self-descriptive names such as Dashemoff and Riskitt and a parody of Chicago's then-notorious ticket-scalping scandal (Pastoria plans to finance the revolution by scalping coronation tickets).

The show included spectaculars such as the dance of the poppies (chorus girls), spectacular visuals and a first-rate PR campaign by the theatre's business manager, Townsend Walsh. The greatest asset, though, was comedy team Fred Stone and David Montgomery as the Scarecrow and Tin Woodman. Both were talented, experienced vaudeville performers, who incorporated several of their old routines into the show (other scenes were written especially for them). Stone's boneless dancing was widely praised. *The Land of Oz*, which Baum hoped to adapt into a second show with Montgomery and Stone, was dedicated to the two actors.

The show opened in Chicago, June 16, 1902. It ran for 14 weeks, then toured the Midwest before moving to New York in 1903 for 293 performances on Broadway, then toured the country. Baum admitted later that the show's success convinced him that Mitchell had been right in his revisions.

When the show went to New York, several changes were made to the third act: after Pastoria becomes king, the Scarecrow and Tin Man are locked away in the dungeons, while the Wizard and Gyle are reduced to street sweepers. The Tin Man cuts the Scarecrow to pieces and passes him to Dorothy, then escapes himself when the sentry goes looking for the Scarecrow.

The Tin Woodman and Dorothy reassemble the Scarecrow (this special effects scene was considered a high-point, and duplicated by Baum in *The Tik-Tok Man of Oz*); Cynthia hears the Tin Woodman play the piccolo and they realize they're old sweethearts. Pastoria then enters and sentences everyone to be beheaded. At the last minute, Dorothy calls on Locasta, who asks Glinda to hide the prisoners in darkness, then carry Dorothy home in a cyclone; terrified of facing another tornado, Pastoria relents and frees everyone.

The show's success encouraged a flood of similar fantasy extravaganzas, starting with Hamlin and Mitchell's *Babes in Toyland* (generally considered a superior work because of the Victor Herbert score) and later *The Pearl and the Pumpkin* and *Wonderland*; Baum himself contributed two more Oz shows, *The Woggle-bug* and *Tik-Tok Man of Oz* in the same vein (Baum biographer Katherine M. Rogers suggests it would have been better if Baum had followed his own instincts rather than trying to imitate Mitchell). Although that made *The Wizard of Oz* look more and more routine as the years passed, it kept touring through 1909, then in 1911 was released for stock and amateur productions around the country.

The show would also influence the subsequent Oz series. It was the hope of a second stage hit that convinced Baum to write *The Marvelous Land of Oz*; and it was *The Wizard of Oz* script that named Dorothy as Dorothy Gale ("That must be why you're so breezy."), Tin Woodman as Nick Chopper and Ozma's father as Pastoria (later referred to in *The Marvelous Land of Oz*). It introduced the snow-on-the-poppies used in the MGM film and was the first of several adaptations to show Dorothy's home as a happy, lively place rather than Baum's bleak version.

1905

The Woggle-Bug. 6/18/05. Garrick Theatre, Chicago.

Cast: Woggle-Bug (Fred Mace), Tip (Blanche Deyo), Mombi (Phoebe Coyne), Jack Pumpkinhead (Hal Godfrey), Prissy Pring (Mabel Hite), General Jinjur (Beatrice McKenzie), Sawhorse (Ed Cunningham), Dinah (Walter Smith), Maetta (Helen Llyn), Regent Sir Richard Spud (Sidney Deane), Lord Stunt (W.H. Thompson), Professor Knowitt (Sidney Bracey).

Credits: Director: Frank Smithson; *Producer:* Henry Raeder; *Book:* L. Frank Baum; *Score:* Frederic Chapin; *Costumes:* Archie Gunn; *Set design:* Walter Burridge.

Songs: Opening Pantomime (The Creation of Jack Pumkinhead); Opening Chorus; Mr. H.M. Woggle-Bug; T.E.; Sweet Matilda; Ting-a-Ling-a-Ling; My Little Maid of Oz; The Hobgoblins; Soldiers; Act I Finale; To the Victors Belong the Spoils; The Household Brigade; Patty Cake Patty Cake Baker's Man; I'll Get Another Place; Jack O'Lantern; There's a Lady-Bug a Waitin' for Me; The Doll and the Jumping Jack; The Things We Learned at School; Transformation; The Equine Paradox; The Sandman Is Near; Finale.

Tip, a young boy, sets up a man-sized stick figure, topped with a carved pumpkin head, to startle his guardian, Mombi. When Mombi shows up, it works, but then the witch animates the figure with a magic Powder of Life.

A teacher projects the magnified image of

a woggle-bug on a screen for his students to study; when the Woggle-Bug steps off the screen, still magnified, everyone panics and runs. After some witty banter between teacher and bug, General Jinjur — who plans to conquer Oz with her all-girl army — enters the schoolhouse with her tough-talking soldier, Prissy Pringle. Prissy's plaid skirt enraptures the Woggle-Bug, who's ready to marry her for that reason and spends the rest of the show falling for anyone wearing the skirt. Jinjur and the teacher reveal they were once sweethearts.

Tip and Jack fall asleep outside the City of Jewels, then Jack's alarm clock goes off and he shouts, "Six o' clock!" a catchphrase he uses throughout the show. Tip tells Jack he dreamed of being Princess Ozma, rightful ruler of the city. Trying to enter the city, Tip uses the powder to bring a sawhorse to life. The Regent appears, delighted to learn Tip will assume the burdens of rulership once he becomes Ozma. Tip and the Regent enter the city, while Jack waits outside, where he meets the Woggle-Bug.

Mombi appears in Prissy's skirt and the Woggle-Bug falls in love with her; they flirt, and Woggle-Bug blows kisses to Mombi as they both go off-stage. Jack meets Prissy and falls in love with her. The Regent demands Mombi restore Tip to his true self, but Mombi threatens to unleash the Army of Revolt, which enters carrying banners proclaiming "Give us victory or give us fudge." Tip and his friends retreat inside the city and the curtain falls; when it rises again, the city is in flames, the Regent in chains and Jinjur in power.

The second act opens with Jinjur on the throne, eating fudge but frustrated by her idle life and by men demanding equal rights. Jinjur offers to keep the Regent in luxury if he'll succumb to her desires, but the Regent nobly refuses, though admitting he might fancy her if she were still a humble milkmaid. Jinjur orders the guards to ply the Regent with food and drink until he's ready to sacrifice his virtue.

The Woggle-Bug enters, now chasing after Dinah, a black cook wearing the dress. Tip and Jack catch up with him and together plan to escape by flying machine to the palace of Maetta, the Good Sorceress. The escape succeeds, but Mombi's coven crashes the flying machine, so when we see Tip and his friends next, they're traveling by rabbit-drawn chariot. The rabbits overturn the chariot and run off, then girls dressed as chrysanthemums surround Tip, Jack and the Woggle-Bug. The bug drives them off with a spell that brings down a drenching rain.

Tip and his friends reach Maetta, as does the Regent; Maetta's forces then bring in Jinjur, Prissy (in the plaid) and the Woggle-Bug who creates five more sawhorses for the song, "The Equine Paradox." Maetta condemns Prissy to become a housemaid; strips Mombi of her power; turns Tip back into Ozma; and demotes Jinjur back to a milkmaid, at which point the Regent pops the question. Prissy takes off her skirt and the delighted Woggle-Bug dons it as a vest.

Following the success of the 1902 *The Wizard of Oz* musical, Baum wrote several unproduced plays such as *The King of Gee-Whiz* before deciding to write a second Oz novel that could be made into another stage hit. Since Dorothy hadn't contributed much to the stage show, Baum didn't use her in either the new book or the new play, but the Tin Woodman and Scarecrow had large roles suitable for the Montgomery/Stone comic team who had played the parts in *The Wizard of Oz*. Montgomery and Stone were already chafing to leave their *Wizard* roles, however, so Jack and the Woggle-Bug became the comic team.

Following in the spirit of *The Wizard of Oz*, Baum threw in female armies suitable for chorus numbers, tough-talking Prissy (a clone of Tryxie Trifle), plenty of puns and jokes and a "rain of cats and dogs" which was dropped from the show because of poor critical response. It also sent up the suffragette movement, despite Baum's strong support for women's right to vote (he doubtless knew mocking the women's movement would be a bigger laugh-getter than supporting it, as would be true for much of the century).

After three out-of-town performances in Milwaukee, the show opened in Chicago to universally bad reviews: critics dismissed it as a flat copy of *The Wizard of Oz* (and better imitations, such as *Babes in Toyland*, had already made the whimsy of the first Baum show overly familiar), but lacking any of the first show's strength. In particular, it lacked Montgomery and Stone; Mace and Godfrey as the Woggle-Bug and Jack weren't at the same level, and weren't a pre-existing comic team with established rhythms and routines to fall back on.

Another difference was that this was very much Baum's work, without the extensive rewrites and changes *The Wizard of Oz* underwent—and although he tried faithfully to follow the formula, he didn't have the touch for extravaganza that Mitchell and Hamlin did. In the end, the show "failed to woggle" as one critic put it, and closed July 12, after less than a month; even before that, some of the stage lights had been repossessed, forcing the producers to cut out a couple of scenes. Baum had better luck in 1913 with *The Tik-Tok Man of Oz*.

1908

Fairylogue and Radio Plays. 9/24/08. Grand Rapids, Michigan (try-out); 1/10/08. Orchestra Hall, Chicago.

Cast: Narrator (L. Frank Baum), Dorothy (Romola Remus), Scarecrow (Frank Burns), Tin Woodman (George E. Wilson), Cowardly Lion (Joseph Schrode), Ozma (Delilah Leitzell), Tip (Will Morrison), John Dough (Joseph Schrode), Chick the Cherub (Grace Elder), Para Bruin (Frank Burns).

Credits: Directors: Otis Turner (John Dough), Francis Boggs (Land of Oz); *Producer:* L. Frank Baum; *Writers:* L. Frank Baum, Otis Turner (based on *Wizard of Oz*, *Land of Oz*, *John Dough and the Cherub*, *Ozma of Oz*); *Set design:* E. Pollack; *Music:* Nathaniel D. Mann, performed by Theodore Thomas Orchestra; *Cinematography:* Selig Polyscope Company, film hand-colored by Duval Freres; *Slides painted:* E. Pollock; *From:* Radio Play Company of America.

This one-of-a-kind stage show opened with Baum, in person, telling the audience how a fairy visited him and told him the story of Oz. Then a film begins, with a pageboy opening a book to show Dorothy in black-and-white; the image of Baum, onscreen, beckons Dorothy out of the book, at which point she turns to color. The same happens with Tin Woodman, Cowardly Lion, Glinda and other characters, who then bow to the audience.

Baum then narrates *The Wizard of Oz*, starting with a slide show: Dorothy lands in Oz, though not on the Witch (no witches appeared in the show), receives the silver slippers and sets off on the yellow brick road. The story switches to film: Dorothy panics when she sees the Scarecrow move, but he persuades her to help him off his pole. Despite his stumbling walk, they set off for the Emerald City with Dorothy helping him. A slide shows them having lunch, then the film shows them finding and oiling up the Tin Woodman, then meeting the Cowardly Lion.

When the foursome (and Toto) reach the Emerald City, the Wizard is exposed as a humbug, but nevertheless manages to fulfil the wishes of the Lion, Tin Woodman and Scarecrow. The Wizard plans to take Dorothy home, but an accident sends him ballooning alone, so Dorothy seeks out Glinda, who tells her how the silver slippers can take her home.

A shortened slide/film version of *The Land of Oz* followed. Scenes included Tip turning into Ozma and the Gump Flying; Mombi was captured by the Winged Monkeys, rather than by Glinda on the Sawhorse. Then came a more detailed adaptation of *Ozma of Oz*, fairly faithful to the book (two deletions were the giant with the hammer and Dorothy's begging the Nomes to let them into the caverns).

Then came the intermission, illustrated by slides of the newest book, *Dorothy and the Wizard in Oz*, in which the Wizard performs some magic tricks before melting back into the book cover with Dorothy. Intermission also gave the audience a chance to buy the new book in the lobby.

After intermission, Baum narrated *John Dough and the Cherub*, the story of a gingerbread man brought to life by a magic elixir, hitching a ride on a Fourth of July skyrocket from America to the Island of Phreex (this special-effects scene was a high point) and wandering through a series of oddball adventures with a feisty child, Chick the Cherub, and the rubber bear Para Bruin.

The *John Dough* storyline followed the book but dropped an encounter with pirates and a scene where an imprisoned girl regains her strength by eating part of Dough's body. At the end of the show, Dough and Chick arrive in Hi-Lo land right after the old king dies, and Chick persuades the people to accept John as the new monarch (a much simplified version of the ending events in the book).

This production adapted the Oz books into "fairy tale" films heavy on fantasies and special effects; since it also fit the format of a lecture tour or travelogue, it became a "fairylogue." Baum claimed he took "radio play" from Michel Radio, who hand-tinted the filmstrips, but he may have been joking. Film projectors being rather shaky in those days, the 113 slides gave the audience a break: some were painted to match the Neill and Denslow illustrations, some showed the film actors in costume.

Some of the costumes, several sight gags and the Scarecrow's rubber-limbed walk were borrowed from *The Wizard of Oz* musical, which was still running.

The show was a hit, particularly with children, and the opening sequence was considered at the cutting edge of special effects. It didn't bring in enough to keep the show going, however, and the cost of the hand-colored filmstrips was so high that Baum closed the *Fairylogue* in debt (business sense had never been his strongpoint). To settle his debts with Selig Polyscope, which had provided the film, Baum gave it the right to adapt *The Wizard of Oz*, *John Dough and the Cherub* and *The Land of Oz* for new films (contrary to some reports, Selig Polyscope didn't simply re-release the *Fairylogue* film strips).

The scripts and slides from the *Fairylogue* survive, but the Baum family disposed of the films in the late 1960s.

1913

The Tik-Tok Man of Oz. 3/31/13. Majestic Theatre, Los Angeles.
Cast: Hank the Mule (Fred Woodward), Tik-Tok (James C. Morton), Shaggy Man (Frank Y. Moore), Private Files (Charlie Ruggles), Betsy Bobbin (Lenora Novasio), Queen Ann Soforth (Josie Intropedi), Ozma (Vera Doria), Polychrome (Dolly Castles), Princess Ozma (Beatriz Michelena), the Metal Monarch (John Dunsmure).
Credits: Director/Producer: Oliver Morosco; *Writer:* L. Frank Baum, added lyrics by Oliver Morosco; *Composer:* Louis F. Gottschalk, added music by Victor Schertzinger.
Songs: The Magnet of Love; When in Trouble, Come to Papa; The Waltz Scream; Dear Old Hank; So Do I; The Clockwork Man; Oh My Bow; Ask the Flowers to Tell You; Rainbow Bride; Just for Fun; Army of Oogaboo; An Apple's the Cause of It All; Work, Lads, Work; My Wonderful Dream Girl.

Having been lost at sea in a storm, Betsy Bobbin and her beloved mule Hank open the show by drifting to land in a chicken coop. They meet the Shaggy Man, who's off to rescue his brother Wiggy from Ruggedo, the Nome King. They enter the Rose Kingdom, where a gardener tells them the ruler has condemned them to death — though technically the realm is kingless, since none of the monarchs on the royal rose bush are ripe for picking.

Shaggy uses the Love Magnet to charm the gardener, who leads them to the bush, with a chorus of female roses in tow. Shaggy and Betsy find one ripe princess, Ozma, and plucks her, but the roses refuse to be ruled by a girl and drive Ozma out with Shaggy and Betsy. Traveling onward, the group meets Tik-Tok, sent to assist Shaggy; Polychrome, the Rainbow Fairy, who was stranded when the rainbow disappeared; and Ann of Oogaboo, whose 17-man army (16 of them officers) she hopes will conquer the world. The Love Magnet passes from hand to hand, giving whoever carries it unwanted attention; Tik-Tok runs down a lot.

When the cast reaches the Nome King's vast caverns, they find them full of glittering jewels, with a chorus of girl Nomes beating out gold and silver on the anvils. Shaggy and Tik-Tok get into a fight with each other that ends with the automaton flying to pieces. Betsy and Ruggedo reassemble him in the dark, so that Shaggy, when he sees Tik-Tok again, assumes it's a ghost.

Polychrome charms Ruggedo, who spells out the advantages of being an old man's mistress in "When in Trouble, Come to Papa." The greedy Nome is also impressed Polychrome's touch turns common rocks to gold, but finds the gold reverts to rocks when he grabs it. After more comic adventures and songs, Shaggy's brother is rescued and the group escapes over a rainbow sent by Polychrome's father.

Baum started adapting *Ozma of Oz* into *The Rainbow's Daughter* (in which Shaggy is out to rescue his wife and 10 children) in 1908, then renamed the show simply *Ozma of Oz*. Then he realized the characters from his first two Oz books were contractually tied up with *The Wizard of Oz* and *The Woggle-Bug* and couldn't be used on stage in a new show. But he was already using Shaggy Man and Polychrome from *The Road to Oz*, so he simply created substitutes to fill the other roles—Betsy for Dorothy, Ozma the Rose Princess for Ozma of Oz (the Rose Kingdom itself was based on the Mangaboo realm from *Dorothy and the Wizard in Oz*), Ann's army for Ozma's, etc.

The show also borrowed extensively from *The Wizard of Oz* stage musical: numerous chorus girls, a character disassembled and rebuilt, Shaggy and Tik-Tok as a comic team and an ingénue accompanied by a pantomime animal. The Love Magnet plotline also resembles the plaid dress that passes from person to person in *The Woggle-Bug*. Oz expert Daniel Mannix has suggested the underground scenes were also strongly influenced by the Metropolitan Opera's production of *Ring of the Nibelungs*, and that the dragon in the novel *Tik-Tok of Oz* was a Wagnerian element Baum didn't have the budget to use on-stage.

The play didn't find a producer until 1912, when Oliver Morosco took it on, opening the show at his Majestic Theatre in Los Angeles the following year. Between Morosco's staging and Gottschalk's score, it was an immense hit, and *The Wizard of Oz* hadn't played so much on the coast that the similarities bothered people.

After the show toured, however, Morosco, who was already producing the smash hit *Peg O' My Heart,* closed it rather than take it to Broadway. The high production costs may have been a factor, and audiences further east probably found it too similar to *The Wizard of Oz* (Chicago critic Amy Leslie sniffed that if she still had her old *Wizard* review, she could just reprint it for *Tik-Tok*).

Fred Woodward (Hank) would go on to play animal roles in several Oz film Company productions.

1920s

Schooldays in the Land of Oz.
Credits: Writer: Eleanor T. MacMillan.

A short skit designed to promote the Oz books.

1925

An Adventure in the Land of Oz. 2/7/25. Forum Theatre, Los Angeles.

Cast: Dorothy (Andree Bayley), Tin Man (Roy Sager), Scarecrow Man (Harry L. Wagner), Wizard of Oz (Josef Johnson), Prince Kynd (Jean Winslow), Queen of Song and Flowers (Ethel Jenks), Tulip (Irene Alexander), Rose (Beth Williams), Daisy (Eleanor Phillips), Violet (Doris Cleveland), Marigold (Inez Creber), Orchid

(Margaret Mason), Daffodil (Lucille Hodgeman), Penny (Mary Watson), Iris (Marjorie Davis), Buttercup (Mildred Davis), Spanish lover (Carl Yanow), Oz inhabitants (Lloyd McKinnion, Margaret McCubbin).

Credits: Director, producer, writer: Norman K. Whistler.

A "spectacular musical fantasy" with an Oz theme that played at the Forum Theatre in Los Angeles to accompany the 1925 Larry Semon *Wizard of Oz* film. Action begins in Kansas, then moves to Oz for the remaining 11 of 12 scenes, mixing the book's characters with Prince Kynd from the film, the Queen of Song and several ethnic numbers. The program also featured newsreels and a short film travelog.

Incorporating movies into a variety show format such as this was common at the time.

1928

The Magical Land of Oz. Jean Gros French Marionettes.

Credits: Writer: Ruth Plumly Thompson (based on *Ozma of Oz* by L. Frank Baum); *Song lyrics:* Norman Sherrerd, Ruth Plumly Thompson; *Music:* Irene Griffin Gros.

This loose adaptation included puppets of Scarecrow, Tin Woodman, Scraps, Jack Pumpkinhead, Tik-Tok and the Sawhorse and a 14-piece puppet orchestra.

The Jean Gros company described itself at the time as the world's largest traveling marionette company, with 150 puppets in full-stage presentations.

The Wizard of Oz.

Credits: Writer: Elizabeth Chapman.

This adaptation of Baum is one of a number of adaptations from the Samuel French theatrical publishers—most of them no longer in print—described as "Junior League" plays because they were popular productions with local Junior Leagues (some of them were also adapted for radio).

The Land of Oz.

Credits: Writer: Elizabeth Fuller Goodspeed (who also wrote *The Wizard of Oz* above); from Samuel French.

A Junior League play based on Baum's second Oz book.

Late 1920s

The Wizard of Oz.

Credits: Director: Ellen Van Volkenburg.

A marionette production described by one critic as the first faithful adaptation of *The Wizard of Oz*.

1929

A Day in Oz [Also known as **Scraps in Oz**].

Credits: Writer: Ruth Plumly Thompson; *Music:* Norman Sherrerd.

The Scarecrow comes on stage looking for Scraps, who bursts out of a ragbag for some bantering and puns. Dorothy and the Tin Woodman join them, then Ozma appears with some souvenirs and a new Oz book. Scarecrow sings, then the Tin Woodman; Ozma's father Pastoria rushes onstage to announce that Jack Pumpkinhead's head is gone—and so is his entire body! Just as the Cowardly Lion joins the worried group, Jack shows up and tells them about his amazing recent adventures—enough to fill a book! The retelling done, he and the others head off to a party.

Starting in the early 1920s, Ruth Plumly Thompson wrote a series of *Day in Oz* skits to be staged in department stores as promotions for the year's new Oz book (the version above was used for *Jack Pumpkinhead of Oz*). The title refers to "scraps" as in bits and pieces, not the Patchwork Girl herself.

Puppeteer Bill Eubanks later performed one of the *A Day in Oz* scripts as a puppet show.

1935

Ozma of Oz.

Credits: Writer: March Buchanan.

Another Junior League adaptation (reportedly, the series also adapted *The Patchwork Girl of Oz*).

1937

The Enchanted Island of Yew.
Credits: Writer: Mary Buchanon.

The adventures of a fairy who transforms into the heroic Prince Marvel for a year of mortal adventures battling dragons, evil kings and bandits on the island of Yew.

1942

The Wizard of Oz. 1942. St. Louis Municipal Opera.
Cast: Dorothy (Evelyn Wycoff), Mayor of Munchkins (Al Downing).
Credits: Book: Frank Gabrielson; *Score:* Harold Arlen, E.Y. Harburg.

This play was the first (but not the last) stage play to fit the Harburg/Arlen score from the MGM film *The Wizard of Oz* into a new script, though this one was heavily derivative of the movie.

This adaptation would be used many times by various theaters over the years. Margaret Hamilton played the Wicked Witch of the West in one production (riding a vacuum cleaner rather than a broom) as did Roseanne Barr more recently.

1950

The Wizard of Oz. Suzari Marionettes, New York City Center Theater.
Credits: Director: Dorothy Zaconick.

This marionette version used a score based on American folk tunes. The Suzari Marionettes continued performing the show until 1962, when the company disbanded and became the Nicolo Marionettes.

1951

The Wizard of Oz. Reed Marionettes.
Credits: Puppeteers, writers: Robin and Edith Reed.

A puppet production described as faithful to the spirit of the Baum book, even when it departed from the letter. The Wizard appears to Dorothy and her friends individually, as in the movie, but in different shapes (as a fireball to the Scarecrow, a dragon to the Lion and a waterfall to the Tin Woodman).

After a year of writing, researching animal movements and building marionettes, Robin and Edith Reed staged this as their first puppet show, including two stages, 15 scene changes and over 30 characters. They would continue performing it for many years.

1959

The Wizard of Oz. Brooklyn College Women's Synchronized Swimming Group.

In this version, Dorothy is sent back to Kansas by swim fins and snorkel.

There are at least two other underwater versions, one by the Swarthmore Swim Club and one by the Weeki Wachee mermaids.

1960

The Wizard of Oz. Ice Capades, New York.
Cast: Dorothy (Lynne "Patsy" Finnegan).
Credits: Producer: John H. Harris.

In this 13-minute production, Dorothy arrives in Oz with a poodle under her arm, meets her three friends and ice-dances "If I Only Had a Brain/Heart/The Nerve" with each of them (backed by a chorus line). When they confront the Wizard's giant head, Dorothy immediately dismisses it as "humbug." The Wizard then skates out from behind the curtain and grants their wishes.

The Wizard of Oz on Ice. United Kingdom.
Credits: Director, producer: Gerald Palmer; *Choreography:* Ross Taylor.

This ice-skating adaptation used the score of the MGM film.

The Wizard of Oz. Ringling Brothers and Barnum & Bailey Circus.

Dorothy and Toto emerge from their farmhouse and the cyclone (a man on stilts waving cloths) carries it off (it's actually moved by horses). Walking around the circus tent on a yellow carpet, Dorothy meets the Good Witch; her three friends; the poppies (girls garlanded with flowers) and the field mice (midgets) who save her from eternal sleep; and finally she and her friends meet Oz within the first ring.

Setting off to find the Witch of the West, the group meets talking trees, girls costumed as crows and Winged Monkeys riding elephants. The Witch captures them, but Dorothy throws a bucket of paper strips over her. The group returns to the Emerald City where the Wizard departs by balloon and Glinda appears on an elephant and shows Dorothy how to use the silver slippers (Dorothy is then lifted away by a rope).

1962

Ozma of Oz. 10/20/62. Nine O'Clock Players, Los Angeles.

An adaptation of the book.

1963

The Wizard of Oz. Nicolo Marionettes.
Credits: Writer: Nicolas Coppola; *Music:* Bruce Haack.

A tornado carries Dorothy and Toto to Oz, but Toto disappears; Dorothy sets off to

Dorothy and her friends are off to see the Wizard, in Puppetsworks' adaptation of *The Wizard of Oz*. (Photograph credit: Guido.)

The Wizard thanks Dorothy for destroying the Witch of the West in Puppetworks' *The Wizard of Oz.* **(Photograph credit: Guido.)**

the Emerald City to ask the Wizard to help find him. On the way she picks up a silly Scarecrow, a grouchy Tin Woodman, and a Cowardly Lion, but the Wizard tells them he'll only grant their wishes if they kill the Wicked Witch of the West. After they defeat her — with the Cowardly Lion throwing the water — Dorothy goes back to Kansas and her friends all receive their wishes.

Nicolas Coppola began as a puppeteer with the Suzari Marionettes in 1954, and this version used the same folk themes as the Suzari production, but with a more country-western sound. Space restrictions limited the show to one Munchkin and one Winged Monkey, but it did have an on-stage tornado and a melting witch.

The company toured with the show through

Dorothy and her friends on the yellow brick road, from Puppetworks' *The Wizard of Oz*. (Photograph credit: L.R. Rush.)

1978. In 1980, after the company became Puppetworks, Inc., it revived the show; although it no longer tours, Puppetworks still presents *The Wizard of Oz* at its Brooklyn theater and at the Children's Aid Society in Manhattan.

The Wizard of Oz.
Credits: Writer: Anne Coulter Martens.

Dorothy crashes down on the Wicked Witch of the East (offstage), then meets Melinda, Good Witch of the North, who gives her the witch's silver shoes. Dorothy meets the Scarecrow, Tin Man and Cowardly Lion, and when Belinda, the Wicked Witch of the West, sends a field of poppies to put them to sleep, the Lion scatters them with a roar.

At the Emerald City, the Great and Powerful Oz takes a different form to greet each of them, and tells them he'll grant their wishes if they steal the source of Belinda's powers, her magic cap.

In the Winkie lands, Belinda poses as a sweet old woman to lure the group into her castle and capture them. When Belinda tricks Dorothy out of one of the slippers, Dorothy douses her with water, melting the Witch. When they return to the city with the cap, Oz is exposed as a fraud, able to grant Dorothy's friends' wishes but utterly unable to help the girl. Fortunately, Glinda, the rightful owner of the magic cap, tells Dorothy how to use the slippers and gives her a ring that will return her to Oz when she wishes.

The Yellow Knight of Oz. 1/26/63. Eaglet Civic Theater, Sacramento, CA.
Credits: Director, writer: Richard Fullmer.

The play opens with two children, Speedy and Betty, arguing over whether the rocket Speedy's uncle has built should go first to Mars or to Oz, which is Betty's pick. Speedy tells her that's stupid, so Betty leaves in a huff. Needless to say, when Speedy enters the rocket and accidentally blasts off, it isn't to Mars.

After landing in Oz, Speedy is initially amazed that Oz is real. In the isolated province of Samandra, Speedy frees Marygolden, an enchanted princess who had been turned into a statue. They join Sir Hokus, an Oz knight accompanied by the Comfortable Camel and seeking a maiden to save, a monarch to serve and a monster to slay.

In the ruined realm of Corumbia, a pit from one of the dates in the camel's saddlebag restores the transformed Corumbian jester, Peter Pun. The Sultan of Samandra, it turns out, has enchanted the entire kingdom, but Speedy and his friends lift the enchantment. They discover Sir Hokus is actually Prince Corum of Corumbia, and disenchant him and Marygolden, his true love.

After adapting *The Wizard of Oz* for the Eaglet Theater in Sacramento, theater manager Richard Fullmer found himself dissatisfied with the other children's scripts available so he sought permission from Thompson and Reilly & Lee to adapt *The Yellow Knight of Oz*, a book he greatly admired and believed would work well on stage.

After extensive negotiation, Fullmer secured the rights, then trimmed down the book by eliminating most of the theme kingdoms (Subterranea, Quick City and Marshland). The production used puppets for some of the characters, such as the Comfortable Camel.

This is the only Thompson book adapted to date. *Merry Go Round in Oz* has been adapted as a school play, and Neill's *Wonder City of Oz* became an unproduced TV script.

The Wizard of Oz. 8/2/63. Starlight Theater, Kansas City, MO.

Cast: Dorothy (Connie Stevens), Scarecrow (Will B. Able), Tin Woodman (Jim Powers), Cowardly Lion (Dean Dittman), Wicked Witch of the West (Lois Daniel), Uncle Henry (Joseph Macaulay), Aunt Em (Lois Daniel), Sorceress of the North (Nancy Myers), Wizard of Oz (Joseph Macaulay), Joe (George Wasko), Farmer (Murray E. Simon), Munchkin Mayor (William Morris), Munchkin (Justin Morley, Jr.), Banana Man (A. Robins), Queen of the Butterflies (Ista), Private (Steve Rydell), Old Lady (Joycelyn Merge), Lord Growlie (George Wasko), Gloria (Maybelle Franz), Witches (Judy Granite, Jackie Alloway), Tibia (Ronald Highley), Little Witch (Mary Jeanne Williams), Chorus (Sherron Baslee, Suanna Flake, Maybelle Franz, Sylvia Hutchinson, Katherine Kiblinger, Nancy Myers, Howard Hensel, Walter Hook, James A. Linduska, Tom McGill, William Morris, Howard Nevison, Peter C. Orte, Stan Orton, Jack Packer, Steve Rydell, Delton D. Shilling, Murray E. Simon, Vester Swingle, Ronnie Young), Dancers (Theresa Vreeland, Jann La Prade, Dorothy Allen, Skiles Ricketts, Jeanne Ocasek, Mitzi Fein, Sherry Fine, Melissa Stoneburn, Judy Cole, Harriet All, Paula Perrine, Mimi Camston, Ted Kivitt, Paul Krumm, Tom Rehill, Orrin Kayan).

Credits: Director: Glenn Jordan; Music director: Roland Fiore; Producer: Richard H. Berger; Adapted by Frank Gabrielson from the stage version by L. Frank Baum and Paul Tietjens; Music: Harold Arlen, E.Y. Harburg; Choreography: Harding Dorn; Set design: G. Philippe De Rosier; Costume design: Audre; Lightning design: Marc Cohen.

Songs: Over the Rainbow; Munchkinland; If I Only Had a Brain; If I Only Had a Heart; We're Off to See the Wizard; If I Only Had the Nerve; Jitterbug; Specialty; Changing of the Guard; Song Macabre; Ghost Dance; Ding, Dong the Witch Is Dead; Specialty; Emerald City Ballet; Finale.

A cyclone sweeps Dorothy to Kansas where she crashes down on the head of the Wicked Witch of the East, killing her, which earns Dorothy the gratitude of the Munchkins and the hostility of the Witch of the West. Setting out to seek the Wizard of Oz, Dorothy picks up the Scarecrow, Tin Man and Cowardly Lion and together they reach the Emerald City despite the obstacles in their way, only to have themselves almost danced to death when they enter the city's "Jitterburg."

The Wizard agrees to grant their wishes once they kill the Wicked Witch of the West. Learning of their approach, the Witch tries to trap them all in a deadly cauldron, but winds up meeting that fate herself. When they return to the Emerald City, Dorothy unmasks the Wizard as a fake, but he manages to grant her friends' wishes anyway, and promises to take Dorothy home to Kansas in his balloon.

Kansas City's Starlight Theatre performed this version as part of its annual Salute to Children. Although the program credits the original 1902 show, the storyline and songs seem solidly based on the MGM film, plus specialty acts (Banana Man and the dancing Human Butterfly) and a couple of extra songs by Stevens ("I'm Shootin' High" and "Don't Take Your Love from Me," according to the *Baum Bugle*).

Snow White Meets the Wizard of Oz. 8/21/63. Galley Productions, Willow Grove Park Playhouse, NJ.

A production mingling characters from both stories. The seven dwarfs also appear in the Turkish Oz film, *Aysecick and the Wizard of Dreamland*.

The Wizard of Oz. 10/18/63. New Masque Players at St. Thomas the Apostle Church, Chicago.

This adaptation had an original musical score, including a Flying Monkeys Chorus and a Witches' Ballet, but it did include "Over the Rainbow" from the MGM film.

Adventures in Oz. 11/17/63. Montgomery County Ballet, Maryland.

A dance adaptation performed at a Washington, D.C., book fair.

1964

Ozma, Ruller of Oz. 4/11/64. Moppet Players, Minneapolis, MN.
Credits: Writer: James Crabb (based on L. Frank Baum's *Ozma of Oz*).

Dorothy is shipwrecked in the Land of Ev, where she falls into the clutches of Princess Langwidere, who wears heads as others wear hats. Langwidere wants Dorothy's head for her collection, but the Kansas girl refuses. Fortunately, Ozma and her court arrive, free Dorothy and take her with them to liberate the royal family of Ev from the evil Nome King.

Langwidere's switching heads was faked by trading wigs styled in a bubble hair-do, with a high collar to make the illusion more effective.

Patchwork Girl of Oz. 6/4/64. El Camino College, Torrance, California.

The Wizard of Oz: Fashion and Fantasy. 8/3/64. May-D & F department store, Denver, CO.

This musical, which included plugs for back-to-school clothes, was presented in two matinees, then aired on KOA-TV on August 6. It followed the plot of the Baum book but used dialog from MGM's musical and added two new songs, "In Oz, in Oz," and "Here We Go" (the latter substituted for "We're Off to See the Wizard.")

Several similar "fashion and fantasy" shows toured the country in August, with some differences (a performance in New Orleans was intended to raise money for a special-ed school, for instance). In each case, a pre-taped film was made for TV.

The Wizard of Oz. 8/14/64. Northern Illinois University Stadium, Dekalb, IL.

This adaptation involved a cast of 1,700 performing at a Tupperware convention with an Emerald City stretching the length of a football field and gifts awarded to salespeople as the story progressed.

Merry Go Round in Oz. 11/13/64. Kent School third grade, Denver.

This must have been an unusual adaptation, since it didn't include Merry Go Round, the title character.

1965

Land of the Wizard Witch. Hazelle Little Play Theatre, Kansas City, KS.

A tornado carries young Dotty away to the Land of the Wizard Witch. Dotty asks the

Wizard Witch for a spell to take her home, but the witch tells Dotty to prove herself first by making new friends. As proof of her power, the Wizard Witch brings a nearby scarecrow to life as "Mr. Strawman."

Once the Wizard Witch strengthens Strawman's legs, he and Dotty dance, accidentally waking a nearby Lion. The Lion agrees to be their friend. He confesses he's really a boy named Mike, transformed by the Wizard Witch for throwing rocks at her, and stuck as a lion until someone kisses him. Dotty does so, and the lion becomes Mike. Since they have no other friends, Dotty suggests they all go home to Kansas together, and they head off to find the Witch.

The late Hazelle Hedges Rollins began manufacturing marionettes in the 1930s, eventually turning her business into Hazelle Incorporated, which for many years was the largest puppet-maker in the world. Rollins created over 300 original puppet-character designs and three U.S. patents (marionette mouth mechanism, airplane control and ankle/shoe movement); *Land of the Wizard Witch* used puppets of her own design.

The Wizard of Oklahoma. 2/25/65. University of Oklahoma.

Dorothy and her three companions encountered Infirmaryland and Parking Meter land while seeking the Wizard of the Student Senate.

That Wonderful Wizard of Ourz. 3/12/65. Denver Pick and Hammer Club, Denver, CO.

A geologist seeking a high administrative position makes the trip to the Emerald City down the Purple Prose Road in this parody, which includes parodies of several MGM songs.

The Marvelous Land of Oz. 3/19/65. Concordia Players Children's Theatre.

The Land of Oz. 5/8/65. Pasadena Festival of Arts Youth Theatre Workshop, Workshop Repertory Company, at Huntington School Auditorium, San Marino, CA.

Credits: Book, score: Dulcie Odriozola, Robert F. Denniston.
Songs: Oh What a Witch; I Don't Know What I Know; Militant Dilletante.

This musical was based on the book, and included the Cowardly Lion as a character.

Dorothy in the Mysterious Land of Oz. 5/27/65. Toby Nicholson School of Dance and Musical Theatre, Winnetka, KS

Cast: Dorothy (Robin Stewart), Jeb (Gary Alesi), Eureka (Dotti Sue More), Mangaboo Queen/Cowardly Lion/Chief Steward (Alice Untermyer), Sorcerer (Jane Dickson), Mangaboos (Janet Katzenberg, Susan Bernard), Wizard of Oz (Greg More), Mangaboo Princess (Gretchen Beris), Mangaboo Children (Melanie Byrne, Elizabeth Richman, Jenny Campbell, Susan Maggiore), Ev Guards (Leslie Cunninghan, Susan Bernard, Amy Untermyer), Little Guard (Frank Untermyer), Nanda (Elizabeth Richman), Princess Langwidere (Connie Byrne, Barbara Halperin), Ozma (Cathy Masamitsu), Scarecrow (Alison Ickes), Tin Woodman (Wendy Byrne), Nome King (Craig Axelrod), Little Princess of Ev (Lisa Byrne), Queen of Ev (Daryl Gorden), Ev Children (Julie Mitchell, Debbie Gorden, Jenny Campbell, Pam Groen, Colleen Brophy, Sarah Marshall, Melanie Byrne), Mangaboos and Nomes (Alison Ickes, Wendy Byrne, Leslie McBride, Leslie Cunninghan, Jane Dickson, Susan Bernard, Gretchen Berris, Susan Maggiore, Janet Katzenberg, Jennifer McNerney, Amy Untermyer, Melanie Byrne, Elizabeth Richman).

Credits: Director, writer, costume design, set design, choreography: Toby Nicholson; based on *Dorothy and the Wizard in Oz* and *Ozma of Oz* by L. Frank Baum; *Lyrics:* Hal Robinson.

When the ground cracks (offstage) during an earthquake, Dorothy, her cousin Jeb and Dorothy's cat, Eureka, fall into the underground realm of the Mangaboos. The Mangaboos blame the children for the "rain of stones" that damaged the city. As the Mangaboo sorcerer interrogates them, the former Wizard of Oz's balloon drifts down through the crevice with the Wizard aboard.

The Wizard coolly asserts his superiority over Mangaboo magic ("I'm delighted to find humbug inside the earth, just the same as on top of it.") and uses his stage magic to impress the Mangaboo queen. The sorcerer tries slaying the Wizard with magic, so the Wizard stabs the sorcerer to death, discovering thereby that the Mangaboos are actually plant people.

After the Mangaboos plant the sorcerer to grow replacements, the Queen decides to kill the surface-dwellers, so Dorothy plucks a princess from a bush. The princess takes the Mangaboo throne, but still plans to kill the humans, so the Wizard leads the children and Eureka through a cave to safety, emerging in the Land of Ev.

Ozma (Cathy Matsamitsu) knows one jewel will free the Nome King's captives — but which? From *Dorothy in the Mysterious Land of Oz.* (Photograph credit: Toby Nicholson.)

The Wizard tells the children the royal family of Ev has been imprisoned by the Nome King, leaving only lazy Princess Langwidere as the effective ruler. When they visit Langwidere, she demands Dorothy's head for her collection (she changes them like clothes). Dorothy refuses to trade, but the princess offers to let her go if she can outdance Langwidere; after they dance, Langwidere decrees Dorothy didn't dance well enough.

Ozma and her court arrive from Oz and demand Dorothy's freedom. When Langwidere realizes Ozma seeks to free the royal family, the princess releases Dorothy willingly; once the family is back in charge, Langwidere can admire herself all day without taking time to run the kingdom. Langwidere tells Ozma the royals have been turned into ornaments in the Nome King's palace.

Along the path to the underground, Eureka catches a mouse, which the Scarecrow agrees to keep in his pocket. Dashing past the Iron Giant, Ozma's forces confront the Nome King as he finishes a musical number with his Nomes. The king invites everyone to dinner; his steward grumbles that the Ozites should be transformed immediately, but the king replies he'll do it after they try and fail to find and restore the royal family.

Dorothy successfully touches one of the princes and restores him, but everyone else fails and becomes an ornament in turn. Eureka overhears the king mention one ornament that will undo all the transformations, touches it and frees everyone, but the king announces they will never leave alive. His magic belt paralyzes everyone but the Scarecrow and Tin Woodman, then the mouse leaps out of Scarecrow's pocket. The Nomes freeze in fear of the mouse, giving Scarecrow a chance to seize the belt; with everyone free, they return to Oz, with Dorothy heading home to Kansas afterwards.

As a dancer in the Sybil Shearer Company, Nicholson ran the company's dance and theater school, and adapted children's stories for performance. He picked *Ozma of Oz* because Kathy Masamitsu looked so much like the Neill illustration of Ozma. He used the entire student body for the show, with several different actresses playing Langwidere with different heads.

The Wizard of Oz. 6/65. Fifth Annual Oz Club Convention, Bass Lake, IN.

Dorothy, Eureka and Scarecrow (Robin Stewart, Dottie Sue More, Alison Ickes), surrounded by Nomes in *Dorothy in the Mysterious Land of Oz*. (Photograph credit: Toby Nicholson.)

Credits: Puppeteer: Bill Eubanks.

Puppeteer Eubanks introduces the rod-puppet show himself as "Mr. Tell-a-Tale," dressed in a costume similar to Uncle Henry's in *The Emerald City of Oz*. The story that follows is a faithful adaptation (with a tape-recorded script), but with Dorothy brunette rather than blonde: Eubanks realized even his daughters thought Dorothy should look like Judy Garland.

The Wizard of Oz. 7/65. Chicago.

At a Kappa Delta Sorority Convention, members performed a skit based on the MGM film in which the KD Wizardess rewards them with sorority honors after they reach the Emerald City.

The Wizard of Oz. 7/1/65. Los Angeles County Fairground, Crippled Children's Society of Los Angeles County.

In this short play, the Tin Woodman had a cast, Dorothy had high heels and the Lion wore braces.

Follow the Yellow Brick Road. 7/25/65. Parent-Child Workshop, Des Moines Art Center, Des Moines, OH.

This workshop included opportunities to meet the Oz characters and a puppet show during which the Wicked Witch throws a pie in the Wizard's face.

Adventures in the Land of Oz. 8/7/65. Marin Junior Theatre, Ross, CA.

Uncle Henry and Aunt Em tour Oz, meeting many of the characters including Scarecrow, Tin Woodman, Tik-Tok, Jack Pump-

Eureka, the Wizard of Oz, Scarecrow and Dorothy (Dottie Sue More, Greg More, Alison Ickes, Robin Stewart), together again in *Dorothy in the Mysterious Land of Oz*. (Photograph credit: Toby Nicholson.)

kinhead, the Woggle-Bug, Scraps, Polychrome and more, as well as Nomes, the Cuttenclip paper dolls, Utensians and Bunnybury bunnies.

The Wizard of Oz. 8/19/65. Swarthmore Swim Club, Swarthmore, PA.

In this underwater adaptation (which included scenery, costumes and music), the Wicked Witch goes up in a puff of carbon dioxide. This was the second swimming rendition of the story.

The Wizard of Oz. 12/9/65. El Paso High School, El Paso, IL.
Cast: Dorothy (Barbara Bollheier).

An Oriental-styled version, including tech crews dressed in black for concealment.

1966

The Wizard of Oz. Royal European Marionette Theatre.

This production included 55 marionettes

and a $35,000 set that took two years to build.

The Wizard of Oz. Page One Bookshop, FL.

This was one of several puppet shows bookshop owner Shirley Adama put on in her store.

The Wizard of Oz. 3/20/66. Mahwah Ballet School, Mahwah, NJ.

This was a two-act dance adaptation.

The Wizard of Oz. 5/66. Sayre Elementary School.

This version was written by Janice Thorn, the Sayre drama teacher.

Much to Do About Oz. 7/30/66. Youth Theatre Workshop, Alhambra, CA.
Credits: Director, writer: Dulce Odriozola; based on *Ozma of Oz.*

This show included most of the characters from *Ozma of Oz.* Songs included "My Elaborate Laboratory" and "The Magical Land of Oz."

In addition to this show and 1965's *Land of Oz,* Odriozola also adapted a musical version of *Dorothy and the Wizard of Oz* in 1966.

The Wizard of Oz. 10/1/66–9/30/67. Weeki Wachee Springs, FL.

This adaptation, in which Dorothy is swept to Oz by a whirlpool, was performed underwater by the Weeki Wachee Mermaids (swimmers in mermaid tails). Weeki Wachee's marketing tie-ins included dolls of Dorothy and her friends in swim fins.

Though it has fallen on hard times, Weeki Wachee Springs was one of the most famous of the attractions that Florida offered travelers in the days before Disneyworld (other attractions included Petticoat Junction, Cypress Gardens and the Sunken Gardens). This production was fairly typical of the Mermaids' repertoire; they have also performed *Alice in Wonderland,* and more recently *The Little Mermaid.*

The Wizard of Oz. 10/22/66. Stockholm Marionette Theatre, San Francisco.

This puppet adaptation of the book combined marionettes, giant figures and live actors.

The Wonderful Land of Oz. 11/19/66. Beverly Unitarian Church, Chicago.
Credits: Puppeteer: Bill Eubanks.

A second puppet show by Eubanks, adapting the second Baum book.

The Great Wizard. 12/8/66. St. Nicholas County Primary School, Oxford.

Described as a fairly faithful adaptation. Nonmusical.

1967

The Wizard of Oz in Hippieland. St. Scholastica High School, Chicago.

Christmas in Ozland. Eugene Field School, Glendale, CA.

A fourth-grade production.

1968

The Wizard of Oz. 11/27/68–3/2/69. Bil and Cora Baird Marionettes, Bil Baird Theatre, New York.

Dorothy (a blonde) is carried to Oz along with her goat Tanglefoot, where she meets her three friends and escapes a monstrous kalidah. Upon reaching the Emerald City, the group petitions the Wizard (who appears before them individually, as in the Baum book, though not using exactly the same disguises) to grant their requests. After they defeat the Wicked Witch of the West, the Wizard is exposed as a humbug, but persuades Dorothy's friends to believe in themselves, then Glinda shows Dorothy how to get home.

This off–Broadway show used the MGM film score, but paired it with a new script more faithful to the Baum book. The Baird Marionettes were a highly successful company in the 1940s and 1950s; Bil Baird is probably best known for the "lonely goatherd" puppet show in *The Sound of Music*.

1969

The Wizard of Oz. 2/8/69. New Shakespeare Company, Hamilton Playground, CA.

This production used dialog straight from the book (though as in the MGM movie, there was only one good witch) and threw in some Shakespearian elements, such as a witch's chant from *Macbeth*.

The Patchwork Girl of Oz. 3/1/69. Museum of the City of New York.
Credits: Puppeteers: Eleanor Boylan, Jeanette Nizel.

This was a marionette adaptation of the Baum book.

The Emerald City of Oz. Pioneer Memorial Theatre, Salt Lake City, UT.
Credits: Writer: Gayle Cotterell Nemelka.

1970

The Land of Oz. 6/15/70 (opening), Banner Elk, NC.

Visitors to this North Carolina theme park were taken to the "Gale farm," then rushed into the cellar to avoid an onrushing storm (rear projection created the illusion of farm animals blowing past the windows). Visitors emerged from the cellar to find the house tilted 15 degrees; Dorothy then led them to visit Scarecrow, Tinman and the Cowardly Lion; to the Wicked Witch's castle; then to the Emerald City where Munchkin girls (with antennae) would hand out "greenie glasses" to make sure everything looks emerald. Dorothy and her friends then performed the Magic Moment show in which the Wizard grants everyone's wishes and sends Dorothy home by balloon.

The Land of Oz is typical of the quirky theme parks (Ghost Town in the Sky, Santa's Workshop, Petticoat Junction) populating the South before such parks as Disneyworld and Universal became the big destinations. The recession of the 1970s and high gas prices killed attendance, then fire and recurrent vandalism finished it off. The Land of Oz closed its doors in 1980, though developers have preserved some of what survived, as has the Appalachian Cultural Museum.

Oz theme parks and amusement park rides have a long history: In 1905, outsize figures from *The Wizard of Oz* and *The Land of Oz* decorated the Water Chutes amusement park as a promotion for the stage show *The Woggle Bug*. There was a rumor — probably a hoax — the same year that Baum was going to build a theme park off the California coast; Cincinnati's Coney Island amusement park included a land of Oz section starting in 1934; and Disney designed but never put in place a Land of Oz exhibit in Disneyland. More recently, plans for a Kansas Wonderful Wizard of Oz theme park collapsed in a financial muddle in 2003.

The Wizard of Oz.
Credits: Writer: Dorothy E. Skinkle.

A musical, fairly close to the book.

1973

Trolmanden Fra Oz. Det Lille Theater, Copenhagen, Denmark.

This Danish production was adapted from the Classics Illustrated Jr. comic-book version.

The Wizard of Oz. Second Story Players of Union College, Schenectady, NY.

The masks designed for the characters by Bill Brenders are said to have given this show a unique look.

The Wizard of Oz in the Wild West.
Credits: Writer: Willard Simms.

Moments after the end of MGM's *The Wizard of Oz* film, Dorothy, Scarecrow, Tin

Man and Cowardly Lion materialize together in Kansas—but 100 years before Dorothy's time, in a small town dominated by wealthy Miss Grimshaw, who takes an intense interest in the ruby slippers.

Dorothy's refusal to bow down to Grimshaw inspires some of the townfolk to defy the woman. Dorothy tries to use the slippers to leave, but only bounces herself and her friends around the Wild West, meeting Wild Bill Hickock, Billy the Kid and Annie Oakley.

When Dorothy and her friends confront Grimshaw, the sinister spinster reveals that she used magic to defeat her rivals and become wealthy. When she turns her talismans on Dorothy, the power of the slippers, backed by Dorothy's friends' love, destroys Grimshaw's magic. Images of the Wizard had the Good Witch Clarise appear and explain that Grimshaw's magic was originally stolen from Oz, so they engineered Dorothy's trip to bring about its destruction.

1974

A possible sequel to *The Wizard of Oz*.

Julian Oldfield reportedly directed and wrote a sequel to *The Wizard of Oz* in 1973, but nothing about it, even the title, seems to be known.

The Marvelous Land of Oz. Smithsonian Puppet Theatre.
Credits: Writer: Martin Williams.

This was a faithful adaptation using three-foot tall marionettes, and primarily performed on college campuses.

The Wiz. 10/21/74. Morris A. Mechanic Theatre, Baltimore, 1/5/75; Majestic Theatre, New York City.
Cast (Baltimore): Scarecrow (Charles Valentino), Lion (Ken Prymus), Dorothy (Renee Harris), Tin Man (Ben Harney), Queen of the Field Mice (Butterfly McQueen).
Broadway: Scarecrow (Hinton Battle), Tinman (Tiger Haynes), Lion (Ted Ross), The Wiz (Andre de Shields), Addaperle (Clarice Taylor), Aunt Em (Tasha Thomas), Dorothy (Stephanie Mills), Evillene (Mabel King), Glinda (Dee Dee Bridgewater).
Credits: Directors: Gilbert Moses III, Geoffrey Holder; *Producer:* Ken Harper; *Book:* William F. Brown; *Score:* Charlie Smalls; *Choreography:* George Faison.
Songs: Prologue; The Feeling We Once Had; Tornado; He's the Wizard; Soon As I Get Home; I Was Born on the Day Before Yesterday; Ease On Down the Road; Slide Some Oil to Me; I'm a Mean Ole Lion; Be a Lion; So You Wanted to See the Wizard; What Would I Do If I Could Feel; Don't Nobody Bring Me No Bad News; Everybody Rejoice; Y'All Got It!; If You Believe; Home.

The play opens on a ramshackle Kansas farm as Aunt Em chides 13-year-old Dorothy for playing with Toto instead of doing her chores. When a cyclone hits, Em and Uncle Henry shelter in the cellar, but Dorothy is caught in the farmhouse as it is swept away to Oz, crashing down on Evvamene, the Wicked Witch of the East. The Munchkins are so happy, they promise to wear white to Evvamene's funeral.

Evvamene's death brings out flamboyant Addaperle, stage magician and Good Witch of the North. Her ineffective magic can't send Dorothy home ("That'd be transporting a minor across state lines!"), but she tells the girl the all-powerful Wiz in the Emerald City can do the job. Addaperle gives Dorothy Evvamene's silver slippers and sends her down the yellow brick road.

Dorothy meets a Scarecrow who dreams of buying brains so he can amount to something, and suggests he ask the Wiz for help. They find a rusty Tinman who, once oiled back to life, tells Dorothy how a witch cursed his axe to chop away body parts every time he used it—and although replacing them with tin kept him alive, his tin chest lacks a heart. After he joins the journey, a lion attacks the trio, but when Dorothy slaps him he collapses into a coward and blames all his problems on an unhappy homelife. Dorothy suggests a visit to the Wiz would work where the Lion's three years of therapy have failed miserably.

The monstrous kalidahs attack, but are

driven off by Scarecrow and Tinman (the Lion claims he was sidelined by a hairball). When they enter a poppy field, the Lion hallucinates sensuous dancing flower children, which distracts him until he passes out, only to be dragged to safety and chided for his immoral behavior by Emerald City's "Mice Squad" (a pun on vice squad). At the entrance of the city, the gatekeeper allows them in, once they don green sunglasses. The stylish Emerald City residents (also in green shades) sneer at the idea that four hicks will get to meet the Wiz, but change their tune when they see Evvamene's slippers on Dorothy's feet.

When the quartet enters the Wiz's throne room, the Wiz threatens them and mocks Dorothy's wish to go home ("Home is faded memories and broken furniture.") but agrees that if they kill Evillene, Wicked Witch of the West, they'll all get their wishes.

In Act Two, one of the Winkies tells Evillene that her armies have failed to stop Dorothy or get the slippers; the witch has him hanged. Evillene sends the Winged Monkeys to capture her enemies, which they do, then reduces the Lion and Dorothy to slaves. Her bullying the lion outrages Dorothy, however, so she hurls a bucket of water on the witch, destroying her.

When they return to the city, the Gatekeeper has been told to keep them out, but he hides rather than stand up to a powerful witch-killer. The group re-enters the throne room where the Lion finds the Wiz in hiding, forcing the man to confess he's nothing but a small-time Omaha hustler; when all his schemes failed, he tried religion, and was blown to Oz while preaching from a hot-air balloon.

The Wiz reveals that after the city embraced him as a flying wizard, it was easy to con them them into wearing green glasses and thinking that he'd created an Emerald City: It's what people believe, not what they see, that really matters. He tries to persuade Dorothy's friends to believe in themselves, but when that fails, he uses potions and powders from his bag to convince them that they've been magically transformed.

Dorothy convinces the Wiz that if he can rule Oz, he can succeed back in America, and without hiding away, lonely, inside an empty throne room. The Wiz holds a revival meeting before he and Dorothy fly the balloon home; of course, she misses the launch. Addaperle summons Glinda, the Witch of the South, who tells Dorothy the slippers can take her home if she believes in herself. Dorothy realizes she could have gone home already if she'd known, but tells her friends that helping them made everything they went through worthwhile. They tell her to use the slippers to return some day, and Dorothy clicks her heels together three times...

The Wiz was born in 1972, when black DJ Ken Harper saw his girlfriend in an abridged version of *Cabaret* that kept only enough story and dialogue to frame the songs. Harper decided to pitch the TV networks on doing other abridged musicals in a series of specials, including one all-black show (since an all-black revival of *Hello, Dolly!* had done well recently). He picked *The Wizard of Oz* as the first special and decided that making it the African-American show would lower resistance to a "remake" of the MGM film.

Because federal rules had shifted a half-hour of prime time from network control to local stations, the networks now had less programming time and a backlog of specials. Harper set his sights on Broadway instead and enlisted composer Charlie Smalls to write some songs. 20th Century–Fox agreed to put up $650,000 in returns for the rights to make a movie out of the show if it was a success.

By the time the show opened in Baltimore, costumer Geoffrey Holder (an accomplished choreographer and dancer best known today as Baron Samedi in the James Bond film *Live and Let Die*) had taken over as director, adding the "tornado ballet" in which Dorothy gets whirled away to Oz and cutting Butterfly McQueen, cast as Queen of the Field Mice. According to Harper, technical rehearsal was so bad that they considered postponing the opening, but the first night went wonderfully, with a standing ovation generating four curtain calls.

The show opened on Broadway the next year to mixed reviews. Although the lack of big names probably hurt with regular theater patrons, it had strong support from the African-American press, which generated heavy word of mouth, and Fox put enough money into the show to guarantee a five-week run. Audiences grew, and the show won seven Tonys, including 1975 Best Musical.

The show deserved its success. With song styles including gospel, rock and blues, snappy dialogue and sharp humor, it is appealing in its own right, but also surprisingly faithful to Baum, both in plot and in details (the rescue by the field mice, silver slippers instead of ruby, distinguishing Glinda from the Witch of the North).

Despite the show's success, 20th Century–Fox decided not to exercise its movie options: the executives who financed *The Wiz* had left the company, several other filmed musicals (*Star!* and Fox's own *Hello, Dolly!*) had flopped recently and Fox may have figured a big-budget African-American film would probably lose money, given the usual grosses for black movies. More surprisingly, Fox didn't even exercise its options to release an album of the show (Atlantic Records did, and won a Grammy).

Motown's Rob Cohen, however, believed *The Wiz* was the only way to pull off a new *Wizard of Oz* film, so he worked out a deal for Universal to acquire the rights (the disastrous results are covered in the entry on *The Wiz* film).

1975

The Road to Oz. A production at the University of Utah.

1976

The Wizard of Oz. Nicolo Marionettes, Macy's Herald Square, NY.

The Nicolo Marionette Company performed a 20-minute version of its long-running *The Wizard of Oz* show 10 times daily for a week as part of a Macy's promotion. The marionettes were redesigned to match the film, with Dorothy in Judy's gingham dress and the Cowardly Lion walking on two legs instead of four.

Wizard of the Emerald City. Malaya Bronaya Theater, Moscow.

This was a stage version of Alexander Volkov's Russian adaptation of L. Frank Baum, in which Elli and her dog Totoshka are swept away by a cyclone to the Magic Land ruled by the wizard Goodwin. This production was later performed in England as *The Scarecrow, the Lion, the Tinman and Me*.

1977

Christmas in the Land of Oz.
Credits: Writer: Ruth F. Perry.

It's Christmas, a year after the events of *The Wizard of Oz*, and Uncle Henry's farm has almost been wiped out by drought. Dorothy finds the silver slippers and returns to the Emerald City for help. Unfortunately, things aren't much better there: Scarecrow, having no heart, can't get into the Christmas spirit; the Tin Woodman loves Christmas so much he's holding it every week, and can't think why his subjects object; and someone's stealing Christmas ornaments and food.

Dorothy solves her friends' problems by sewing a brain into Tin Woodman's head and a heart into Scarecrow's chest. The Cowardly Lion reveals that the Winged Monkeys are responsible for the thefts, but the Tin Woodman's Winkie archers send the monkeys running. Glinda tells Dorothy where Uncle Henry needs to graze his cattle, and the Scarecrow gives Dorothy a bag of emeralds to take home. When she returns to Kansas, the emeralds will more than cover the price of the new farmland Glinda has recommended.

The Wizard of Oz. 8/2–14/77. Melody Top Theater, Milwaukee.

Cast: Dorothy Gale (Marsha Kramer), Zeke/Cowardly Lion (Stubby Kaye), Hickory/Tin Woodman (Cris Groenendaal), Huck/Scarecrow (Clyde Laurents), Professor Marvel/Wizard/etc. (Jerry Tullos), Miss Gulch/Wicked Witch of the West (Nancy Kulp), Glinda (Kathy Taylor).

Credits: Director/set design: Stuart Bishop; Costumes: Ann Bruskiewitz, Jan Valentine.

Songs: Somewhere Over the Rainbow; Ding Dong the Witch Is Dead; If I Only Had a Brain; If I Only Had a Heart; If I Only Had the Nerve; We're Off to See the Wizard; The Merry Old Land of Oz; If I Were King of the Forest; While You Are Young; Jitterbug; Optimistic Voices.

This adaptation used the entire MGM script, book and lyrics (though with a couple of added songs, including the dropped "Jitterbug" number), as well as many of the costumes. The special effects duplicated much of the film's look, including the change from black-and-white to color: in Kansas the set is covered by a brown drop cloth and Dorothy wears brown and white gingham, changing into blue and white when she emerges from the farmhouse into Oz.

1978

Dorothy and the Wizard of Oz.
Credits: Writers: Steve Hotchner and Kathy Hotchner (based on *The Wizard of Oz*).

This was an audience-participation version in which children in the audience were constantly asked to assist, pose as trees, answer questions from the cast — and at the climax, to make rain noises and gestures for when rain comes down to melt the Wicked Witch. At the end, instead of the Wizard going home to Omaha, Glinda gives him a "wizard hat" that gives him the same self-confidence that his humbug tricks have given the Tin Man, Scarecrow and Cowardly Lion.

1979

Ozma of Oz. 10/5/79. Poncho Theatre, Seattle.

Cast: Dorothy (Pamela Bridgham), Uncle Henry (Edward Sampson), Bill (Linda Hartzell), Tic Toc (Paul Fleming), Princess Langwidere (Linda Hartzell), Ozma (Gretchen Orsland), General (Ramone Marue), Army (Randy Hoffmeyer), Roquat of the Rock (Ramone Marue), Feldspar (Pamela Pulver), Nanda (Diane Petrie), Guard (Pamela Pulver), Rock People (Diane Petrie, Randy Hoffmeyer), Sam (Randy Hoffmeyer), Steve (Ramone Marue), Wheelers (Randy Hoffmeyer, Pamela Pulver).

Credits: Director: Jenifer McLauchlan; *Writer:* Suzan Zeder; *Costume design:* Susan Nininger; *Set design:* Mark Sullivan; *Music/sound:* John Engerman.

The play opens in the present day with Dorothy and Uncle Henry, in a wheelchair, sailing to Australia on a cargo freighter. Henry is thrilled to be traveling overseas at last, but Dorothy wants to go home instead of babysitting a foolish old dreamer. A storm washes them overboard to the shores of Oz, along with Bill, a chicken; although the storm hit at noon, they arrive in Oz at dawn.

Dorothy uses a key she found to wind up Tic Toc, a robot time machine who reveals that before he was created, Oz existed in perpetual daylight and endless youth. When he was activated, so was time; when the first night fell, the Nomes emerged from underground to conquer Oz, but Ozma held them back until dawn came, then threw the key into the sea, freezing time at dawn. Now, time has returned, and Roquat taunts Dorothy from below that come nightfall he'll reconquer Oz.

When Roquat's Wheelers (who wear roller-skates on hands and feet) try to capture the group, Dorothy tries to protect her helpless uncle, but instead the Wheelers assume that his wheelchair makes Henry the Big Wheel who will liberate them from Roquat. The group sets out to contact Ozma, but gets captured by the soldiers of Princess Langwidere. The vain princess realizes the return of time means she'll soon become as old as Uncle Henry, and locks them all away until Dorothy gives her the key to turn Tic Toc off (it can't be taken by force).

Ozma arrives, accompanied by her general

and her one-man army, intending to thwart Roquat; Ozma frees Dorothy by bending the bars of her cell with her bare hands, then uses her powers to make Langwidere confess to selling Tic Toc, Bill and Henry to Roquat.

Overcoming all obstacles, Dorothy and Ozma reach Roquat's caverns, where the king challenges Dorothy to guess which of four ornaments is a transformed Uncle Henry (he turns Bill back to normal to prove he's not bluffing)—or give him the key if she fails. Dorothy realizes the object that captures Henry's essence is a quartz crystal, because of its inner light and beauty, and sure enough, her uncle returns to normal. Roquat seals the caverns to starve Dorothy into submission, but after Uncle Henry finds Tic Toc, Dorothy tricks Roquat into opening the doors, then races the Nomes to the surface. They emerge into night, but Dorothy speeds Tic Toc up so that it becomes day, destroying Roquat.

Ozma deactivates Tic Toc, making oz timeless again, and offers Dorothy and Henry a chance to stay. Dorothy wants to grow up and Henry has too much living to do, so they say no; now that Dorothy respects her uncle's strength, she has Ozma return them to the ship instead of Kansas, so that she can accompany Henry on further adventures.

Zeder says that she wrote this play to focus on the relationship between age and youth, while using the Baum characters she loved. She rewrote the play as a 1999 musical, *Time Again in Oz.*

Ozma of Oz was later performed in one of Mt. Holyoke College's annual Oz festivals.

1980

We're Off to See ... the Most Happy Fellows. The Most Happy Fellows

Cast: (in 1999 video) Dorothy (Larry Hassler, lead), Lion (Tom Wilkie, bass), Tin Man (Bob Hodge, tenor), Scarecrow (Jack Lyon, baritone).

In this barbershop quartet adaptation, the Most Happy Fellows dress up as Dorothy, the Lion, Tinman and Scarecrow from the MGM movie and sing some of the high points (Merry Old Land of Oz, Follow the Yellow Brick Road, etc.), narrating to bridge the gaps and adding a few extra barbershop numbers as well. The four members sometimes play different musical parts; the ones given here are from a 1999 video recorded at the Washington Center for Performing Arts, Olympia, Washington.

Ken Hawkinson was the original Cowardly Lion when the Most Happy Fellows began what is now their signature performance. Arranger Steinkamp has credited the idea to their coach, who had been "waiting on a quartet he felt was appropriate to do the job."

1981

L. Frank Baum's The Marvelous Land of Oz. Children's Theatre Company, Minneapolis, MN. 104 mins. (on video), color.

Cast: Mombi (Wendy Lehr), Tip/Ozma (Christopher Passi), Jack Pumpkinhead (Carl Beck), Scarecrow (Gary Briggle), Tin Woodsman (Stephen Boe), Jellia Jamb (Rana Haugen), General Jinjur (Julee Cruise), Guardian of the Gates (Steve Huke), Glinda (Kathleen Wegner), H.M. Wogglebug, T.E. (Tom Dunn), Dr. Nikidik (Garth Schumacher), Colonel Cardamon (Suzanne Petri), Soldier (Oliver Osterberg), Sawhorse/Mouse Queen (James McNee, voice only), Women's Army/Citizens of Oz (Lynn Anderson, Andrea Bebel, Gary Costello, Libby Croteau, Lisa Dante, Michael deLeon, Sally Dworsky, Melissa Finnson, David A. Gray, Tracy Harrison, Amy Harsha, Keith Herron, Catie Hinchey, Stacey Howat, Sonya Kostich, Kate McKillip, James McNee, Sean McNellis, Sarah Napier, Kris Neville, Peter Passi, Elizabeth Piper, Devi Piper, Lilly Iran Vakili, Mary Walker, Julie Warde, Jon Westgaard, Elizabeth White, Lori Williams, Chris Ryan, John Cunningham, Kristen B. Froebel, Andrea Franchett, Heather Gorecki, Michael Monroney, Angela B. Prokop, Truda Stockenstrom, Gabrielle Zuckerman)

Credits: Director, producer: John Clark Donahue; *Director for TV:* John Driver; *Writer:*

Thomas W. Olson; *Music:* Richard A. Dworsky; *Lyrics:* Gary Briggle; *Producers:* Richard A. Carey, Jonathan Stathakis; *Executive producers:* Douglas Draper, Ronald Tanet, Francis M. McGovern; *Assistant director:* Len Dell'Amico; *Associate producers:* Charles Hairston, J.F. Limata; *Choreography:* Myron Johnson; *Costume designer:* Barry Robison; *Musical director:* Thomas F. Florey; *Editor:* Veronica Loza; from the Children's Theatre Company and School of Minneapolis, Television Theatre Company.

Songs: All Alone; A Family; Stand Aside; Good Morning; Woggle-Bug; Not Since the Good Old Days; Look to Your Own Heart.

Tip, a lonely young orphan, lives alone with the old witch Mombi ("Witchcraft is illegal — I'm just an old woman who makes her own remedies.") but doesn't know why, or why she won't let him leave. Mombi tells Tip to bake a pumpkin while she's visiting a neighboring wizard, Dr. Nikidik; instead Tip decides to play a practical joke on her, creating a pumpkin-head stick figure to startle the witch. Meanwhile, Mombi persuades Nikidik to give her a free sample of his Powder of Life. When she meets the pumpkinhead on the way home, she uses the figure to test the powder — and it works.

To Tip's dismay, Mombi decides to turn the boy into a marble statue and use the pumpkinhead as her new servant. Unenthused by the thought of life as a lawn ornament, Tip runs away, taking "Jack Pumpkinhead"— whom he realizes is effectively his son — and the remnants of the powder sample. He uses it to bring a wooden Sawhorse to life, but it runs off with Jack, leaving Tip behind. He meets General Jinjur, who informs Tip her army is about to overthrow King Scarecrow and the rule of men over women. She assures Tip there will be no violence, since no man will want to fight an army of pretty girls.

In the Emerald City, Jack meets the Scarecrow but assumes they don't speak the same language since they come from different parts of Oz. Palace maid Jellia Jamb amuses herself by "translating" everything Jack says into an insult until the two men catch on. Realizing they're both artificial men, they agree to be friends.

Tip rushes in to warn the Scarecrow the women of Oz are revolting, but the Scarecrow assures him "In a few years I'm sure you'll find them more attractive." (Baum used the same joke in *Woggle-Bug*). Sure enough, the Army of Revolt takes out the city's ineffective guardians, then Mombi shows up, determined to recapture Tip. The boy flees on the Sawhorse with Jack, Jellia and the Scarecrow. Mombi reminds Jinjur that Scarecrow and Tin Woodman have defeated mightier foes than the army, and offers to help in return for Jinjur delivering Tip.

The Scarecrow leads his friends to the Tin Woodman, now ruler of the Winkies, and the Tin Woodman heads back with them to reclaim the throne. Along the way they meet a man-sized, well-dressed insect, H.M. Woggle-Bug, T.E., who joins them but drives them mad with constant puns. They meet the Scarecrow's old friend, the Queen of the Field Mice (a puppet), who agrees to let Scarecrow carry some of her subjects to the city inside his straw.

Mombi obstructs the group with illusions of fire, drenching rain to rust the Woodman, and other tricks, but her magic doesn't stop them. When they reach the Emerald City, Mombi tells Jinjur to hold them within the city for one night, then victory will be assured.

When the group enters Jinjur's throne room, her army overwhelms them until the Scarecrow unleashes the mice, which send the girls screaming away (an old stereotype that all women are muscophobic). They lock the doors behind them, however, leaving everyone trapped, except Jellia, who has slipped out with the army. The Scarecrow devises a way to escape, using the Powder of Life to create a flying vehicle out of a Gumphead hunting trophy, palm-frond wings and a body made from two couches.

Meanwhile, Mombi kills Nikidik and steals the potions for her master spell, unaware that by then Tip and the others are already flying to Glinda, Good Witch of the South. When they land, Glinda shows she already knows everything about the revolution and their troubles—and tells the Scarecrow that the only one with a true right to the throne is Ozma, long-lost heir to Pastoria, the king from whom the Wizard took the throne.

Nevertheless, Glinda agrees to overthrow Jinjur to put a stop to Mombi. Tip tells Glinda privately that he's afraid after the battle ends, his friends will go and Jack will spoil, leaving him alone again. Glinda tells him to find courage inside himself. Back in the Emerald City, where the men are exhausted from doing "women's work," Jinjur receives an offer of amnesty if the army turns over Mombi; instead Mombi persuades Jinjur to trick Glinda in order to stay in power. Jellia sends the Sawhorse off to Glinda, but gets captured herself.

No sooner does the Sawhorse come with the message, than Jellia shows up, free, and tells Tip the only way to save his friends from destruction is to surrender. When he realizes that she's controlled by Mombi, Jellia tries to kill him, but Glinda blasts them and traps Mombi's spirit, freeing Jellia.

Glinda gives Mombi two choices: execution, or going free stripped of magic, if she confesses why the Wizard of Oz visited her secretly so many times. When Glinda proves capable of spotting any lies, Mombi confesses that the Wizard brought her the infant Ozma, whom she concealed by turning him into a boy—Tip! Tip is horrified at the idea of changing sex, even to his "true self," but draws comfort from the fact that he now knows his family and where he belongs. Before Mombi's power expires, she uses her magic to transform Tip back into Ozma.

Glinda's forces ambush Jinjur in the palace and drag her before Ozma. Jinjur defends herself ("A life of scrubbing floors is a dismal future for anyone—and a government by me is no worse than a government by men!") and Ozma decrees an amnesty once the army disbands and returns the emeralds looted from the city. Jinjur dourly turns over the crown, then Ozma proclaims that all men, women, races, pumpkinheads and giant insects are welcome in the Emerald City. Jack assures her she's the same as she always was "only different" and everyone celebrates the dawn of Ozma's glorious reign.

A delightful production, very faithful to Baum up until the end (shapeshifting and a griffin-Sawhorse race would probably have taxed a stage production) and to Neill's illustrations—Wogglebug looks closer to the book than seems possible.

The 40-year-old Children's Theatre Company performed the Royal Shakespeare Company's version of *The Wizard of Oz* in 2000. Both productions are available on video.

The Wizard of Oz.

Credits: Puppeteers: Jon Ludwig, Peter Hart, Jane Catherine Shaw, Bobby Box, Mary Harrison; *Designer:* Stephanie Kaskel.

This puppet adaptation used rod puppets, and patterned their design after the W.W. Denslow illustrations in the original Baum novel.

1982

The Wonderful Wizard of Oz. 11/16/82.
Cincinnati Playhouse in the Park.

Cast: Dorothy (Diane Della Plazza), L. Frank Baum/Wizard (Tom Flagg), W.W. West (William Alan Coats), Scarecrow (Jack Hoffman), Tinman (Peter Moran), Cowardly Lion (Tony Hoty), Elementals (Scott Bartlett, Michael Kelly Boone, Sarah Combs, Jan Horvath, Sally Knight, Harrison Lee, Ellen Marguiles, William Schaeffer, Sarah Simon, Sally Sockwell, Gregg Ward, Deborah Watassek, Tim Zay).

Credits: Director/producer/conductor: Worth Gardner; Book: Frank Gabrielson; *Score:* Harold Arlen and E.Y. Harburg, additional music and lyrics by Worth Gardner; *Lighting design:* William Mintzer; *Set/costume design:* Paul R. Shortt.

Songs: Over the Rainbow; Ding Dong, the Witch Is Dead; Yellow Brick Road, We're Off to See the Wizard, If I Only Had a Brain/A Heart/The Nerve; Optimistic Voices; Merry Old Land of Oz; If I Were King of the Forest; I Want Those Ruby Shoes; Ding Dong the Witch Is Dead; The Role and the Self.

Musicians: Conductor/Keyboard: Worth Gardner; *Keyboard:* Rick Snyder; *Reeds:* Michael Andres, Steven Hoskins, Eugene Marquis; *Percussion:* Ken Bovinger; *Bass:* Michael Sharfe; *Harp:* Kate Conway; *Trumpets:* Frank Brown, Charles Johnson; *Trombone:* Ken Kappel; *French Horn:* A.C. Myers.

As the play opens, Baum's publisher, W.W. West, informs L. Frank Baum that Baum's manuscript is overdue and that Baum has run out of credit. Baum begins desperately improvising his new story, *The Wizard of Oz*, despite West's sneers about the certainty of rejection and the probability of bankruptcy.

Fighting against his doubts, Baum tells the story of Dorothy Gale of Kansas, swept by cyclone to Oz, meeting her three friends and going through the story of the MGM musical. Baum himself provides the voices for some of the characters, from Auntie Em to the Wizard himself, constantly putting ideas forth on ways to keep the story going, save his creations from the Witch (played by the same actor as Mr. West) and to bring Dorothy back from Oz. In weaving the story, Baum taps into his own strength, heart and courage, and comes to realize that if the most his writing ever does is amuse some children, he has triumphed.

This, the first of several plays to use Baum as a character, filled in his dialogue with quotes from his other writings and made his struggle to create, rather than the adventures of Dorothy and her friends, the real heart of the story.

This is said to be a striking visual version, with an immense spiral serving as both the yellow brick road and the cyclone, a six-armed, Oriental idol as one of the forms of the Wizard and some impressive costuming. In the Playhouse's 1990 revival, an added touch was that the stage magician playing Scarecrow figured out how to have the witch throw real fireballs.

1983

The Wizard of Oz. Mt. Holyoke College Summer Theatre, South Hadley, MA.
Credits: Writer: Tom McCabe.

This adaptation by McCabe, a children's theater veteran, broke all box office records at the theater (4,000 children attended). That prompted Mt. Holyoke to stage Oz plays regularly for over a decade; this, in turn, became the nucleus of a South Hadley Oz Festival.

Scraps. Annenberg Center, University of Pennsylvania.
Credits: Writer: Jane Martin.

This was an original monolog.

Oddyssey in Oz. Quirk Theatre, Ypsilanti, MI.
Credits: Writer: Virginia Koste.

This wasn't a direct adaptation but a play-within-a play inspired by Baum's work, later revised into *On the Road to Oz*.

The Wonderful Wizard of Oz. Eastern Michigan University Theatre, Ypsilanti, MI.
Cast: L. Frank Baum (Bobb James), Dorothy (Hollee Frick), Toto (Tod Barker), The Scarecrow (Tim Monision), The Tin Woodman (Phil Walker), The Cowardly Lion (Dale Foren), Good Witch of the North (Paula Kline), Wicked Witch of the West (Theresa McElwee), Glinda the Good (Sandara Herron), Aunt Em (Sally McNamara), Uncle Henry (Marvin Miller), Guardian of the Gates (Dominic Depofe), Stagehand (Paul Brohan), Winkies (Rick Zemke, Heidi Cowing, Gerri Gushman, Mark Loeb, Kate McElya, Jaime Weiser, Kathi Aron), Munchkins (Tara Egnor, Jeramy Evans, John Holkeboer, Kristen Joseph, Scott McCloud, Larissa Sims, Hannah Yager).
Credits: Director, writer: Virginia Glasgow Koste; *Scenery, lighting, technical direction:* P. George Bird; *Costume design:* Katherine Holkeboer.

Coming on stage in 1900, just before the show starts, stage manager L. Frank Baum picks up a copy of the script and begins to narrate as Dorothy gets carried to the Munchkin lands, receives the silver slippers and heads off down the yellow brick road to the Wizard. Frank continues to provide narration as Dorothy meets Scarecrow, Tin Woodman and the Cowardly Lion and bridges occasional gaps in the script ("We're

Almira Gulch lives! Fred Barton in costume for his one man show, *Miss Gulch Returns*.

not showing the kalidahs ... it's not just to get out of making more costumes!").

After Oz (appearing to each character in an individual shape, as in the original novel) sends them to kill the Wicked Witch of the West, the group successfully defeats the witch's army of wolves (offstage) and enters her castle. The Witch captures them but when she threatens Scarecrow with fire, Dorothy picks up a bucket of water. Back in the Emerald City (after more bridging narration) the group exposes the Wizard, but Dorothy's friends still insist on their rewards. Amused that they still think he can do it, the Wizard whips up his placebos, then breaks character and presents himself to the audience as L. Frank Baum in disguise. Baum skips the next few chapters until the characters stand before Glinda; as the Good Witch shows Dorothy how to return home, Baum realizes he loves the characters too much to let the story end. He tells the audience to tell the story to their children, so that Oz will live on, forever.

Koste said that in adapting the book rather than the MGM film, she chose to do a deliberately "theatrical" production (so the Wizard's outfits are obviously stagey, for instance), and brought in Baum to reflect on the extent to which authors become their creations

The Wizard of Oz. 7/24/83-9/11/83. Tokyo, Japan.
Cast: Dorothy (Chika Takami).

A new stage production produced by Seiyu, a theatrical subsidiary of the Seiby department store chain of Japan.

Miss Gulch Lives! 11/83. Palsson's Supper Club, New York, NY.
Cast: Miss Gulch (Fred Barton).
Credits: Writer, director, producer: Fred Barton.
Songs: You're the Woman I'd Wanna Be; Take Me Please; I'm a Bitch; Born on a Bike; Pour Me a Man; Everyone Worth Taking; It's Not My Idea of a Gig; Don't Touch Me; I'm Your Bitch; Pour Me a Man, Part 2; Give My Best to the Blonde; Finale (Everyone Worth Taking, Part II).

This delightful show opens when pianist

Fred Barton, star of *Miss Gulch Returns*, out of cosutme.

Fred Barton spots Almira Gulch from MGM's *The Wizard of Oz* across a bar-room and admits that "you're the woman I'd like to be" before donning a Gulch costume himself to tell her story: How she was born on a bicycle, perpetually disappointed in love and at having her big solo, "I'm a Bitch," cut from the MGM film and finding the only acting roles she can get are with a Judy Garland-adoring gay cabaret.

To Almira's astonishment, she does find a man, but soon loses him again: "I knew before I met him, he was one of those men who thought monogamy was a game put out by Parker Brothers." Despite the blow, Almira refuses to give up, hoping that someday, somehow, love will find her again and stay.

Barton, an immense fan of Margaret Hamilton, wrote "I'm a Bitch" while in college, then started playing it at after show parties when he worked on a regional production of *The Wizard of Oz* (as music director, then stepping into the Gulch role after the original actor was fired). Barton later combined "I'm a Bitch" with a series of songs he called "a theatrical metaphor for being single with an inferiority complex" to create *Miss Gulch Lives!* After two performances Barton learned of Hamilton's death, and when he next performed the show in 1985, it became *Miss Gulch Returns!*

1984

A Recall to Oz.
Credits: Writer: Michelle Wan Loon.

Dorothy returns to Oz as an old woman.

Journey Back to Oz. Mt. Holyoke College Summer Theatre, South Hadley, MA.

Another Mt. Holyoke production, based on *The Land of Oz* and *The Road to Oz*.

1985

The Patchwork Girl of Oz. Mt. Holyoke College Summer Theatre, South Hadley, MA.

A third Mt. Holyoke production, adapting the Baum novel but adding a Scarecrow/Scraps romance that would culminate in a wedding in *Royal Wedding of Oz*.

El Mago de Oz Cuento de Frank Baum [also known as El Mago De Oz]. Mexico, 70 mins., color.

Cast: Dorotea (Angelica Vale), Espantapajaros/Panta (David Rodrigo), Bruja/Dona Brujilda (Ana Gloria Blanch), Hombre de Hojalata (Lucio Boliver), Professor Maravilla/Mago de Oz (Manuel D'Flon), Leon/Leoncio (Carlos Espindola), Guardia/Jorobado (Jorge Rosette), Ema/Hada Glinda (Pilar Boliver).

Credits: Director, writer, lyrics: Ange'lica Ortiz; *Producer, TV director:* Ramon Tellez; *Musical director:* Mario Tovar; *Assistant director:* Leopoldo Falcon; *Choreography:* David Rodrigo, Lucio Boliver, Jorge Rosette; *Music:* Harold Arlen; *Editor:* Andres Menendez. From: Amarillo Rojo Cafe, Estudio 5 y 3.

This bad filmed stage play followed the MGM template (with Dorothy's mother Ema doubling as Glinda) but included a hunch- backed servant for the witch and a song from Disney's *Cowardly Lion of Oz* record.

1986

Scraps! The Ragtime Girl of Oz. 5/15/86. Theatre of the Young, Eastern Michigan University, Ypsilanti, MI.

Cast: Scraps (Lisabeth Rohlck), The Author (Jeanne M. Jenne), Ojo (Fred Bock), Unc Nunkie (Tom Krawford), Dr. Pipt (Neil Carpentier-Alting), The Woozy (Kathy A. Klein), Plant Monsters (Kathy Fouche Kerr, Kathleen J. Rowe, Todd A. Nielsen), Scarecrow (Mitchel Roberts McElya, Jr.), Hip Hopper (Kathleen J. Rowe), Jak Horner (Jim Angell), The Puppet (Todd A. Nielsen), Princess Ozma (Peggy L. Kasenow).

Credits: Director: Patricia Moore Zimmer; *Writer:* V. Glasgow Koste, based on *The Patchwork Girl of Oz*; *Assistant director/stage manager:* Lynne A. Pace; *Costume design:* Katherine Strand Holkeboer; *Scenery/lighting design:* John P. Charles.

Scraps, the Patchwork Girl, enthusiastically launches into her story as the play begins, only to have Baum insist on starting earlier, before her first appearance. So we begin in the home of young Ojo the Unlucky and his uncle Unc Nunkie, who go to visit Unc's magician friend, Dr. Pipt. Pipt tells Ojo the Powder of Life he's brewing will animate a cloth doll made out of a patchwork quilt, with just enough brains to be a docile drudge. When Pipt isn't looking, an indignant Ojo rifles the mage's powders and adds considerably more brains.

With ragtime on his record player, Pipt brings Scraps to bouncing exuberant life, but she accidentally spills a petrification potion on Unc Nunkie while bouncing around. Ojo sets out to find the ingredients for the antidote; Scraps follows, despite Pipt's protests. As Scraps glories in her new life, they meet the bizarrely cubic Woozy, man-eating plants and the Scarecrow who falls into what Koste calls a "passionate platonic relationship" with Scraps. The questers visit the land of the ultra-serious Hoppers and their annoying, punning neighbors, the Horners, to obtain one ingredient, and Scraps persuades the two races to understand each other better.

All Ojo needs now is a six-leafed clover, so despite the laws against plucking one, he does so, only to be dragged before Ozma, who explains that picking the plant is outlawed because of its use in numerous evil spells. Even without the clover, Ozma is able to restore Unc Nunkie, and Scraps is free of Dr. Pipt, as free as ragtime itself.

A fairly faithful adaptation and very much a love poem to the Patchwork Girl (as Koste notes in her afterword to the script, Scraps is innately theatrical).

The Royal Wedding of Oz. 8/19/86. Mt Holyoke College Summer Theatre, South Hadley, MA.

Credits: Director, writer: Tom McCabe.

It's time for Scarecrow and Scraps to tie the knot, but an insanely jealous Mombi sets out to spoil the happy day, stealing a wedding dress, switching places with Scraps, and later kidnapping and hiding the Patchwork Girl. Despite her efforts, however, the wedding takes place, with the Cowardly Lion and Tin Woodman as the best men.

1987

The Flight of the Gump. Sylmar Chamber Ensemble, Minneapolis, MN.

Cast: The Scarecrow (Flautist), Tin Woodman (Oboist), Woggle-Bug (bassoonist), Gump (pianist).

Scarecrow, Tin Woodman and Woggle-Bug create the Gump in a scene from *The Land of Oz* in order to escape the besieged castle of the Scarecrow.

Narration and acting passed from one performer to the other as the rest of the ensemble provided musical continuity. The show culminates in a boogie-woogie version of "Over the Rainbow."

Lessons of Oz.

Credits: Writer: Christina Hamlett.

After her return from Oz, Dorothy writes a successful book, *Kansas Never Looked So Good*, about her trip. She becomes frustrated and tired at an autograph session in the local library, but fortunately Scarecrow, Tin Woodman, Cowardly Lion and the Wizard show up and spirit her away.

The Enchanted Island of Yew. 7/12/87. White Barn Theatre, Westport, CT.

Credits: Written and performed by Carmen de Lavallade.

Frustrated with immortal life, a bored fairy enlists the help of a young girl to turn herself into a mortal for one year. As the noble knight Prince Marvel, the fairy crisscrosses the Island of Yew, battling bandits; facing the monstrous King Terribus, whom she transforms into a handsome, compassionate man; journeying to Twi, where all living creatures have an exact physical double; and defeating the gigantic Red Rogue. When the year ends, Prince Marvel has had enough adventures to face immortality with new enthusiasm.

De Lavallade read the narration and took all the characters' parts in this one-woman show. She said she followed the 1903 Baum novel "practically word for word" subject to some cutting to fit a one-hour slot.

The Wizard of Oz. 12/17/87–2/27/88, Royal Shakespeare Company, Barbican Theater.

Cast: Dorothy (Imelda Staunton), Zeke/Cowardly Lion (Jim Carter), Hunk/Scarecrow (Paul Greenwood), Hickory/Tinman (John Bowe), Glinda/Aunt Em (Dilys Laye), Wicked Witch/Miss Gulch (Billie Brown), Professor Marvel/Wizard of Oz (Tony Church), Toto, Uncle Henry/Guard (David Glover), Apple Trees (Julia Lintoff, Nadine Shenton, Julia Lewis), Barrister (Nicholas Panayiotou), City Fathers (Justin Degen, Ross Sando), Coroner (Justin Hillier), Crows (Philip Tsaras, Christopher Tudor, Peter St. James), Farmhands/Poppies (Julia Lewis, Julia Lintoff, Jo-Anne Sale, Nadine Shenton, John Cumberlidge, Philip Tsaras, Mark Haddigan, Christoper Tudor, Andrew Thomas James, Peter St. James, Terry Cavanagh, Mary Ann Kraus, Karen Halliday), Flying Monkeys (Nicholas Panayiotou, Nicole Chasan, Sophie Dunn, Justin Hillier, Debbie Chasan, Keith Banks), Lollipop

Guild (Christian Jaquest, Matthew Brice, Keith Banks), Lullaby League (Sara Alexander, Tara Gaffney, Claudia Hill, Jodie Clark), Mayor (Richard Stoughton), Munchkins (Debbie Chasan, Nicole Chasan, Sophie Dunn, Elizabeth Ebbs, Simon Gaffney, Ewan Maclean, Sarah Rodgers, Victoria Avery, Kezi Salih, Remy Beard, Jay Westbrook, Kelly Bright, Kathryn Charlton), Nikko (Richard Stoughton), Winkie General (Mark Haddigan).

Credits: Director: Ian Judge; *Writer:* John Kane, based on MGM script; *Music:* Harold Arlen, E.Y. Harburg; *Artistic director:* Terry Hands; *Designer:* Mark Thompson; *Lighting designer:* Nick Chelton.

Dorothy is a young Kansas girl, restless on the small Gale farm. After local spinster Miss Gulch threatens to have Dorothy's dog destroyed, Dorothy runs away and gets caught in a tornado (the entire stage revolves, showing fishing boats and a rocking chair caught in the storm; Almira Gulch bicycles around, then emerges as the Witch on a broomstick). She lands in Oz, on top of the Witch of the East, and sets out for the Wizard with Toto, picking up her three friends along the way (the Tin Woodman tells her how he lost his limbs to an enchanted axe) and escaping the snares of the Witch of the West (who travels, like Glinda, in a bubble—a black bubble)

When they arrive at the Emerald City the Witch bombards the city with "Surrender Dorothy" leaflets, and the Wizard tells the quartet they can have their wishes if they destroy the Witch. The Witch captures them when they reach her castle, but when she tries to burn the Scarecrow, Dorothy douses him with water and melts the witch.

When the band returns to the Wizard, they discover he's nothing but a fraud. The Wizard cons Dorothy's friends into thinking he's magically enhanced their brains, heart and courage, then offers to take her home in his balloon; when he accidentally leaves without her, Dorothy learns from Glinda that her ruby slippers can take her home.

The Royal Shakespeare Company wasn't the first to adapt MGM's script for the stage, but their version has become a perennial, performed many times since by many groups, including a Gay Men's Chorus version in 2002 in Washington, D.C., and a British version using a video projection of Patrick Stewart (star of the television series *Star Trek: The Next Generation*) as the Great and Powerful Oz.

1988

On the Road to Oz.
Writer: V. Glasgow Koste.

Elliott "Yotty" Marlowe sits down to write an adaptation of *The Wizard of Oz*—which results not only in Dorothy materializing and asking for attention, but "actors"—his mental images of the people who'll be playing the roles—shifting in and out of different characters as the story rolls from *Wizard* to *The Road to Oz*. In the course of it, Yotty realizes the message of his play is about wandering and seeking, rather than finding.

Koste describes this rather plotless play as a metaphor for the playwright's art and the human voyage of discovery.

Holiday in Oz. Balcony Theatre, Pasadena Playhouse, Pasadena, CA.
Cast: B.J. Turner, Steve Cassling.
Credits: Director, writer: B.J. Turner.

This two-man adaptation of *The Wizard of Oz* included Mr. and Mrs. Claus and some of the characters from the Robin Hood legend.

This pantomime ran in a small theatre at Christmas for two years to sold-out houses, so it moved to the larger Mainstage Theatre for the third year, 1990.

Dorothy Meets Alice or, The Wizard of Wonderland. Glassboro Summer Children's Theatre, Glassboro, NJ.
Cast: Dorothy (Lea Antolini), Alice (Laura Diamond), Judson (James Bohanek), Mad Hatter (A. Wade Hancock), Scarecrow (Patric Pinto), White Rabbit (Donielle LaVancher), Tin Man (Mark Jacobs), Dormouse (Jose Rosario), Cowardly Lion (Bill Winegardner), Wicked Witch (Gwen Hasheian), Red Queen (Kirstin Lynch).
Credits: Musical direction: Rosalind Metcalf;

Writer: Joseph Robinette; *Co-producer:* William C. Morris; Music: Karl Jurman; *Set, lighting design:* Bart Healy; Costumes: Joan Sommers.

Songs: Opening; Stay with Me; Jabberwocky; We Could Have Been Like Them; Perfect Together; Curtain Call.

Judson, a New Jersey boy, finds himself in the Tulgey Wood on the border between Wonderland and Oz. He realizes that this is the result of having a book report due tomorrow in school, and being unable to decide which book to work on.

When Dorothy and Alice show up seeking Toto and the White Rabbit respectively, Judson persuades them not to leave the wood, for fear he'll wake up with his book report undone (he also has to come to school as a character from the book and has no idea who he will be). This disgruntles Dorothy's and Alice's supporting casts, who are anxious for their adventures to get going. It also annoys the Red Queen (whom the play's author has confused with the Queen of Hearts) and the Wicked Witch of the West, who don't have the power to attack Alice or Dorothy in the wood.

As the characters try to make sense of their increasingly mangled plot, the Red Queen and the Witch try to terrify everyone by posing as the monstrous Jabberwock, but get exposed; while they argue about who's to blame, the characters escape back into their respective stories, but not before dressing up Judson in elements from both books so he can go to school as the Wizard of Wonderland (of course, he still hasn't read the books).

A fairly silly children's show, one of several Oz adaptations to combine Lewis Carroll and L. Frank Baum.

The Patchwork Girl. 12/16/88–1/14/89, Palace Theatre, Watford, UK.

Cast: Ojo the Unlucky (Clare Grogan), Scraps (Carla Mendonca), Scarecrow (Simon Butteris), Bo-Hoko/Dodo (John Conroy), Woozy/Canary (Ben Thomas), Tollydiggle/Gardener (Lesley Nicol), Tin Woodman/Soldier/ MMM/Prime Minister (Paul Keown), Princess Ozma/Nightingale (Margaret Houston), Unc Nunkee/Mangaboo Prince (David Shaw-Parker), Dr. Pipt/Shaggy Man/Yoop (Richard Syms).

Credits: Director: Lou Stein; *Book/lyrics:* Adrian Mitchell; *Music:* Andy Roberts; *Musical director:* Stewart Mackintosh; *Choreographer:* Pat Garrett; *Lightning designer:* Davy Cunningham; *Stage manager:* Jonathan Stott.

Songs: Long Away and Far Ago; Very First Journey; Mixing Mixtures; Miss What's Your Name; Spell Recipe; Patchwork Moonlight; The One and Only Woozy; Off to the Emerald City; Everybody Greets You in the Garden; John Sebastian Box' Rap; The Famous Shaggymobile Song; Straw; Great to be Small; The Robber's Ballad; Ozma of Oz; Go Happy; Hoppers Are the Best; Yoop-te-Hoop, I Am the Yoop; Cloudsurfing.

When food runs out in their isolated forest home, young Ojo and his Unc Nunkie set out to visit Nunkie's friend Dr. Pipt. Pipt feeds them, then announces he's about to animate a patchwork doll as his new servant with the use of his Powder of Life. Disapproving of Pipt's intent to keep his servant a stupid drudge, Ojo secretly adds a lot more intelligence powder than Pipt had intended to give his creation.

When Scraps come to life, she knocks a bottle of petrifying fluid onto Unc Nunkie and turns him to stone. She and Ojo set off for the ingredients for an antidote, with Scraps constantly filled with delight at her strange new world. Their quest is joined by the bizarre Woozy and the Scarecrow, threatened by the Mangaboos—plants who grow humans for food—and constantly bedeviled by Bo-Hoko, a joker who turns up in different disguises to befuddle the questers.

Ojo completes the quest except for the wing of a yellow butterfly, but the tender-hearted Tin Woodman refuses to let him hurt such a beautiful living creature. Ozma realizes the butterfly's wing was added to the list as one of Bo-Hoko's jokes; Dr. Pipt restores Unc Nunkie without using the wing, Bo-Hoko is magicked so that practical jokes will set his pants on fire, and Nunkie, Ojo and Scraps return to Ojo's home together.

An adaptation very much in the British pantomime tradition (such as having Ojo played by a girl). The scene with the Mangaboos is from a dropped chapter, "The Garden of Meats," deleted from *The Patchwork Girl* (though the Mangaboos take their name from *Dorothy and the Wizard in Oz*).

1989

The Wizard of Oz Live! 3/22/89. Radio City Music Hall, New York.
Credits: Director, producer: Michel M. Grilikhes.

This was another stage version of the MGM film, released to commemorate its 50th anniversary and using prerecorded dialog and musical numbers. Highly publicized (including a proclamation of Wizard of Oz Day in New York), it disappointed audiences and most of the planned 70-city tour was cancelled. One critic wrote that the show "has no brains, no heart and a hell of a nerve."

On the Road to Wizdom … Against All Oz. 5/12 & 13, 1989. 120 mins. University of Virginia School of Medicine Class of 1989/Charlottesville Performing Arts Center.
Cast: Dorothy (Gail Gresens), Tinman (Vic Bernet), Lion (Mike Menz), Scarecrow (Becky Schroeder), Commencement Speaker/Barely Hidden (Andy Cutler), Dean Pullen (Randy Cook), Mike Iwanik (Al Baker), Cadavers (Kyusang Lee, Martha Fernandez, Darby Sider, Tom Garigan), Fresh Stiffs (August Sanusi, Jane Tuller, Tom Franck, Jill Anderson), Toto (Andy Lee), Jacob Creutzfeld (Bill McClelland), Frank AIDS (Joe Fiorazo), Dr. Brain (Read McGehee), Hung Lee (Kyusang Lee), Resident (John Greenfield), Anesthesia Resident (Justin Osborn), Puppy Pat (Helen Kaulbach), Dr. Wright (Randy Cook), Totette (Andy Lee), Malcolm Inger/Nurse (Bill Plonk), Scarecrow (Becky Schroeder), Psychiatry Resident (Karen Dembeck), Pediatrics Narrator (John Evett), Obstetrician (John Torres), Mother (Darby Sider), Father (Tom Garigan), Resident (Vic Bernett), Med Students (Andy Cutler, Joe Gunn), Nurse (Benn Burns), Dr. Wilson/Dr. Loud (Don Dingus), Rod Serling (Shawn Gersman), Dr. Testa (Shaival Kapadia), Dr. Craig (Ed Dodson), The Great Craig (Dr. Craig), Ann Thomas (Jane Tuller).
Credits: Director: Mike Mallare; *Producer:* Debbie Marzulli; *Video:* Aspen Photography; *Produced, directed, videotaped Pediatrics segment:* John Torres; *Writers (Pediatrics segment):* Martha Fernandez, Jill Anderson.
Songs: I'm Sliding Down the Bellcurve; I Don't Need No Doctor; He's Lost That Loving Thing; Working at the VA Blues; Don't Hurry … Be Happy; The Times of Our Lives.

Graduating medical student Dorothy nods off during a boring commencement address. A whirlwind descends (shown on video) and we're swept away (along with Dorothy, Toto, Scarecrow, Cowardly Lion and Tin Man) to medical school, for a humorous medical rotation through neurosurgery, pediatrics, obstetrics, etc., before everyone graduates and celebrates with some serious partying.

A graduation performance by med school students, with proceeds going to the Ronald McDonald House. Several of the songs were parodies ("Workin' at the VA Blues" for Jim Croce's "Workin' at the Carwash Blues").

The Wizard of Oz. Eric Smith Puppet Theater.

This puppet company started performing *The Wizard of Oz* in the 1980s, including two productions in Israel.

1990

The Wizard of Oz: Dorothy's Adventure.
A Japanese puppet show that was released on video the following year.

Wizard of Oz. 8/90. Koma Theatre, Tokyo.
A large-scale musical adaptation that proved wildly popular.

1992

Over the Rainbow. Departmento de Cine of the Universidad de los Andes.
Dancers: Julie Barnsley, Leyson Ponce.
Credits: Director: Haydee Pino.

A 12-minute performance, caught on video.

The Ozard of Wiz. 5/1–23/92. Nevada County Performing Arts Guild, Miners Foundry Stage, Nevada City, CA.

Cast: Dorothy (Mila Johansen), Cowardly Lion (Darryl Stines), Tinman (Collin Dusenbury).

Credits: Director, writer: Mila Johansen.

Despite an approaching tornado and a line full of clothes to be picked up, Dorothy can't tear herself away from a book by Einstein discussing the possibility that other, unseen worlds exist all around us. Uncle Henry joshes her out of her studies by teaching her how to say spoonerisms, but then the storm hits.

Dorothy wakes up among the Munchkins, all of whom speak in spoonerisms (so the dead witch, Zelda, is the Icked Itch of the Wheest) and tell her she can only go home with the help of the Ozard of Wiz. Glinda and her sister, Penny Pearl—good witch of the South and shopaholic—show up, so that when the Witch of the West, Zorna, appears, they distract her long enough to slip the ruby shoes on Dorothy (though Pearl is quite dismayed when she realizes she gave away powerful magic).

Setting off to the "Ozard," Dorothy meets her three friends, bypasses the Poppy Cats vocal group that tries to keep her from the city, and finally meets the Wizard. He, of course, sends her to destroy Zorna, after which he gives Dorothy's friends their hearts' desires despite being exposed as a humbug, all before Dorothy learns the silver slippers are her way to get home.

Johansen, a writer who credits Baum for sparking her imagination, subsequently adapted *The Land of Oz* into *The Lost Princess of Oz* and followed that with *Ozma of Oz* (but dates aren't available).

Oz. 10/27–11/8/92. Paul Taylor Dance Company, New York City Center.

Cast: Dorothy (Caryn Hellman), Zeb (Tom Patrick), Patchwork Girl (Rachel Berman Benz), Crooked Magician (Elie Chaib), Giant Porcupine (David Grenke), Jellia Jamb (Karla Wolfangle), Tik-Tok (Andrew Asnes), Daughter of the Rainbow (Constance Dinapoli).

Credits: Choreographer: Paul Taylor; *Music:* Wayne Horvitz; *Costumes:* Santo Loquasto.

Dorothy arrives at the train station, is met by her cousin Zeb, and both sleep. The world around them changes, and they find themselves in Oz, watching a series of freewheeling dances—Tik-Tok short and choppy, Jellia fast and nervous, Dr. Pipt giving life and taking it, Scraps whirling and spinning, Polychrome ethereal.

Originally commissioned by Mikhail Baryshnikov, this jazz/rock ballet piece was plotless but used a variety of Baum characters, from the Patchwork Girl to the Blue and Pink Pearls of *Rinkitink in Oz*. Taylor told interviewer Barbara Arnstein he avoided characters used in the MGM film so as not to compete, and chose some characters to match his dancers—Tik-Tok was picked to match a stout dancer, for instance.

Der Zauberer Von Oss.

This German production paired an original script with the MGM score.

Dorothy and Alice. Glassboro, New Jersey, Center for the Arts.

1993

Pay No Attention to That Man Behind the Curtain.

Credits: Writers: Paulette Aniskoff, Rebecca Davis.

A high-school play in which the MGM scenes were mimed.

1994

Was. 5/12/94. Northwestern University.

Cast: Jonathan (Jeremy Johnson), Aunt Em (Rachel Moore), Uncle Henry (Michael Ness), Dorothy Gael/Judy Garland (Sophia Skiles), Tom and others (Greg Berlanti), Bill and others (Scott Duff), Wilbur and others (Aaron Morgan), Ira and others (Anthony Prud'homme), Jonathan's mother and others (Jean Villepique), Millie/others (Sarah Weaver), Etta/others (Amanda Weier), Jonathan's father/others (Dan Weiss).

Credits: Director: David Downs; *Writer:* Paul Edwards, based on Geoff Ryman's novel; *Set design:* Karen Cox; *Costume design:* Jodi Kar Jala; *Lighting design:* Gregg R. Essex.

Jonathan, an actor dying of AIDS, arrives in Manhattan, KS, seeking, he says, to find "history." That history begins in 1875 when orphan Dorothy Gael arrives in Manhattan with her feisty dog Toto to stay with her Aunt Emma Gulch and her husband Henry.

Dorothy soon discovers that though Em sees life in Kansas as a glorious frontier with a proud heritage of strength, it's actually harsh and lonely. Life grows worse after her friend Will kills himself, and after Em shoots the irascible, disobedient Toto. The more Dorothy fights the constricting rules around her, the harsher her life becomes.

When Uncle Henry starts raping her, her anger erupts, not at the Gulches but at the weaker children at school. She becomes the school bully and even mocks the teachers, who paddle her, but realize when that doesn't work that there's nothing they can do to control her. One teacher quits in despair, so next morning the children meet their substitute, "Frank," a showboating, smart-mouthed actor stuck in Kansas after a tour of *The Maid of Arran* (one of Baum's own plays) ran out of money.

Frank is immensely entertaining, discussing such off-topic matters as the Turkish language, which includes words such as "Ev" and "Uz," and his own acting experiences. Intrigued by Dorothy, Frank tells her to write a story; when she writes about Toto, he's touched, which triggers a burst of outrage, not only about Toto's fate but what Henry does to her every day. The school refuses to believe her, and fires Frank. He leaves, wishing there were some way he could help Dorothy, or to rewrite history to give her the happy life she should have had.

Dorothy finally runs away, longing to return to her mother and Toto in the past, "the land of Was." Instead she's caught up in a tornado, watched by tiny hallucinatory figures; when the cyclone ends, her mind is clear and her confidence restored.

Years later, Bill, a new intern at a psychiatric ward, befriends Dorothy, now a crotchety old patient and former troublemaker. When they watch *The Wizard of Oz* on TV, she becomes distraught, claming the movie has stolen her life. Although she and Bill grow closer, she eventually snaps, sneaks out into the snow and kills herself.

All this is interspersed with the story of Jonathan: Lover of Oz, colorblind, actor, star of a *Nightmare on Elm Street*–style horror series — and dying of AIDS. He confesses to his counselor — Bill again — that he's spent his entire life accompanied by hallucinatory versions of the Lion, Tin Woodman and Scarecrow, at which point Bill tells him about Dorothy. Jonathan grows obsessed with finding the real Dorothy; when he realizes his slow wasting away is destroying his love, Ira, Jonathan walks out and goes to Kansas to find Dorothy's home. Bill joins him combing through old records. When Jonathan finally locates the Gulch home, he starts seeing in color, and a cyclone lifts him away, but as far as Bill can tell, Jonathan simply vanished.

This was an extremely faithful adaptation of Geoff Ryman's novel, subsequently directed by scriptwriter Edwards (with some revisions) in Chicago, where it won a Chicago Equity Award. Ryman, however, actually found it too faithful (he dismissed it as squeezing 400 pages into two hours of performance) and refused to grant rights for more productions (a new version of *Was* was staged in New York a few years later).

Although well done, the show does suffer the same weaknesses as the novel, such as the implausibly happy ending for Jonathan and Dorothy's strange burst of sanity in her tornado, neither of which really makes much sense.

Twister! A Musical Catastrophe for the Millennium's End [also known as TWISTER! A Ritual Reality in Four Quarters]. Summer. Eugene, OR.
Cast: Oz/Voice of Bones (Ken Kesey), Frankenstein/Thor (Ken Babbs), Tin Man (George Walker), Glenda the Good Witch (Carol Provance),

Scarecrow (Phil Deitz), Liasonette (Stephane Kesey), Mountain Girl (Carolyn Garcia), Legba/Crow (Arzinia Richardson), Ring Girl (Candace Lambrecht), Technoidician (Zane Kesey), w/ Sunshine Schuster, Angelina (Emily Messmer), Don Pardo (Obie Babbs), cyber (Todd Kushnir), Fed-Ex delivery boy (Lewis Messmer), Tubing kid (Lennon Messmer), Izzy the Religious Nut (himself), Elvis (Simon Babs), with Obie Babs, John Swan, Zane Kesey.

Credits: Director, writer: Ken Kesey.

Songs: Call the Wind Starvation; If I Only Had a Cure; Every Mornin' finds Me Moanin'; Earth Dance; G-L-O-R-I-A.

Bones, a skeleton, tells the story of religious fanatic King Otto the Bloody and his fanatical purges of heretics and sinners at the end of the first millennium. Bones says this will give perspective on the upcoming end of the second millennium.

"Glenda" and the Great and Powerful Oz are seen studying Dorothy, debating whether it's kinder to wake her or let her "dream her way into oblivion like everyone else." Oz announces he doesn't care about being kind and tries to wake her, but nothing works until Oz badgers Thor, now working as a TV weatherman, into waking the girl with a thunderbolt. The Gale house whirls around in a cyclone (with Miss Gulch and other Oz images playing against a psychedelic background) and Dorothy tells Toto it's finally time for the sequel!

When they land in Oz, however, Toto disappears; when he finally returns, Dorothy discovers a storm-blown violin has castrated him (it's a stuffed dog, stuck to a fiddle). Glenda insists she and Oz will prevent anything that bad from happening to Dorothy, who replies that if that were true, she wouldn't have crashed her car when she was driving to Mexico for her fourth abortion (Dorothy's character in *Twister* seems fused with Judy Garland, an aging show-biz figure with a tragic personal life). Oz replies that during the Cold War, fantasy figures were too busy churning out government propaganda to play guardian angel.

Regardless, Dorothy tells them she's through with show business and that if Oz wants another witch killed, he can do it himself. Oz says he wants her to warn the real world that the end is coming, and to teach people how to survive it, which doesn't impress Dorothy either, but Oz promises to send her some assistance.

Scarecrow — now a member of Emerald City College — enters with a litany of woe: His old nemeses, the crows, have stripped his fields bare of corn; famine is so bad he has to stuff himself with Styrofoam popcorn; and Oz windstorms are growing increasingly destructive. All he can contribute to Dorothy's quest is the insight that we can save the world by spinning like dervishes "We've got to give it a chance!"

Dorothy's second helper, Thor, shows up with his weather map and confirms that America is being hit with record floods and tornadoes, prompting Scarecrow to break into "Call the Wind Starvation" (a parody of "Call the Wind Mariah" from *Paint Your Wagon*).

In the second act, Glenda warns Dorothy another menace is viruses, because of their ability to constantly adapt "like the Borg!" Tinman enters, patched, rusty and hooked up to a plasma bottle; he explains that his new heart "loves not wisely but too much and too many," saddling him with something combining a sexually transmitted disease with a computer virus. He and Glenda rattle off the biological threat to humanity in "If I Only Had a Cure."

Tinman tells Dorothy human suffering is breaking his heart, but she finds his "bleeding heart liberal drivel" as dumb as Scarecrow's spinning. Tinman tries to lead the audience in a sing-along, but the voodoo spirit Legba comes in and informs him he has a "tin ear." He keeps making fun of the Tinman despite the latter's offer to give him sensitivity training; when Tinman tries to get physical, Legba ducks every attack despite being lame. He tells the Tinman that since they both have physical pain, they can sing a blues duet. While they do so, Bones tells how Otto's life went into a downward spiral as death and disease plagued his family.

As the third act opens, Dorothy is outraged that after showing her her friends suffering, Oz is now off getting stoned. Then the third helper arrives — not the Lion (Glenda reveals that his courage has made him leader of an American militia group) but Frankenstein's monster. Dorothy calms the hostile giant by suggesting they dance; he teaches her the "Earth Dance" and warns her that earthquake damage is increasing across the world.

Elvis Presley appears to tell the monster the song needs more "rock" and less Earth. The monster replies that Elvis is an enemy of family values so not worth listening to. As they argue, Dorothy becomes fed up and demands the cast assemble on stage, then demands Oz cough up the answers about their mission. Oz comes on stage and asserts things that have changed since the start of the show, but the others reply the only change is that things have gotten worse. Oz tells Dorothy that to survive the hard times ahead, people will have to be on their feet and alive, not passive couch potatoes.

The group's argument devolves into spontaneous musical numbers, all clashing and cacophonous; it drives Dorothy up the wall but Oz insists that making noise is what counts, not whether it has meaning. As Dorothy reaches her breaking point, a young angel appears with the ruby slippers. The angel reveals her that name is Angelina Ramirez, and that she was killed before her sixth birthday in an earthquake. Touched, Dorothy returns the shoes (which she's been pining for throughout the show) and vows to stick with her friends no matter what.

Dorothy and her equally moved friends now start singing in harmony and explain the incomprehensible moral message (the only point that makes sense is Dorothy's statement that those who can't find the rainbow are the ones who've let themselves grow too old). A Fed-Ex courier gives Dorothy a fully healed Toto, and Oz encourages the audience to join in singing. Bones wraps it up by telling how Otto, driven insane by hardship, returned to his castle to find the clergy in control and as fanatical as he ever was. When he cries out "What about the baby?" the peasants rise up with him and drive the priests off, proving (Bones says) that "glory rises anew."

Kesey (best known as the author of *One Flew Over the Cuckoo's Nest*) has said this play sprang from his perception that disaster survivors came out stronger and saner than ordinary people and that disastrous natural events were increasing in the pre-millennium decade, with the touching story of Angelina tying everything together. At least, that's his theory: In practice the play wanders erratically before coming to a pointless end. It is, however, the single weirdest production noted in this book and that's saying something.

Oz. 6/14–7/10/94. Coterie Theatre, Kansas City, MO.

Cast: Dot (Amani Starnes), L. Frank Baum (William Harper), Bridgey (Brenda Mason).

Credits: Director: Jeff Church; *Writer:* Patrick Shanahan (based on *The Wizard of Oz*); *Set designer, technical director:* Brad Shaw; *Costume designer:* Gayla Voss; *Resident lighting designer:* Art Kent; *Resident composer:* Greg Mackender.

It's 1899 and author L. Frank Baum is hard at work on his new fantasy, *The Emerald City*—or will it be *From Kansas to Fairyland*? When Dot, a motherless girl living with her father (after a stay in Kansas with her dour Aunt Em), sneaks into his study, Baum spins out the story to entertain the cynical girl (plucking the name of his fantasy land from an O–Z filing cabinet), acting it out with every thing around them turned into costumes, props or even Toto (a footstool). His enthusiasm sweeps Dorothy up and she steps into the Dorothy Gale role, and even his housekeeper joins in as the Wicked Witch, despite her initial reluctance: "I am employed in this household to be a maid, not to release hounds from hell!".

Dorothy becomes outraged, however, when Baum ends the story with Oz unmasked and none of the characters getting their wishes: "I'm a good man, Dorothy, I'm

A real-life Dorothy (Amani Starnes) pops in on L. Frank Baum (William Harper) in Patrick Shanahan's *Oz*. (Photograph credit: World Premiere by the Coterie Theatre, Kansas City, MO.)

just not a very good author." She persuades Baum to keep the story going, and he improvises the ending we all know. When the fictional Dorothy goes home, however, the real Dorothy says she doesn't want to because her father is working long hours and she's all alone. Baum and Bridgey convince Dorothy that her father truly loves her, and promise that she can return to them to play, any time life gets too rough.

The story-within-the-story follows Baum rather than MGM, except for using the film's ruby slippers (the author wrote that they're too good an icon to pass up). The play's interesting approach allows the entire story to be performed on a simple set with only three actors.

Hakosem! 11/29/94. Cinerama Auditorium, Tel-Aviv, Israel.

Cast: Dorothy (Michal Yannai), Sam the Wizard (Arik Lavi), Pachi/Pach-Pach the Tin Man (Adam), Arik/Aryeh the Cowardly Lion (Tzahi Noy), Kashi/Kash-Kash the Scarecrow (Saar Ben-Yossef), Uncle Henry/Smee/Dr. Samuel/Guardian of the Gates/Admiral Smoo (Shmuel Eiser), Machshemashot Sisters/Witches (Sharon Elimelech, Sharon Malki, Vicky Bahir, Limor Elroi), Farmers/Green People/Scarecrows/Fieldmice/Palace Attendants/Fighting Monkeys/Angels (Nir Sha'ibi, Ilan Mamman, Gal Atari, Yigal Marley, Lior Tzioni, Vladimir Margolin, Noam Inbar).

Credits: Director, writer: Uri Paster (based on L. Frank Baum's *The Wizard of Oz*); *Lyrics/music:* Yaron Kafkafi (with "Over the Rainbow" by Harburg and Arlen); *Costumes:* Yuval Caspin; *Choreographer:* Sigi Nissan; *Set design:* Erez Yaniv; *Lighting:* Eya Tavori; Produced by Talit Productions.

Songs: A Country Celebration; Little Witch; On the Way to the Wizard; I'm Free; Wild Rhythm; The King Is Us; War Is War; Sam the Wizard; The Magic of Magic; How Good It Is to Love; Give Us a Chance; Somewhere Over the Rainbow; How Good It Is at Home.

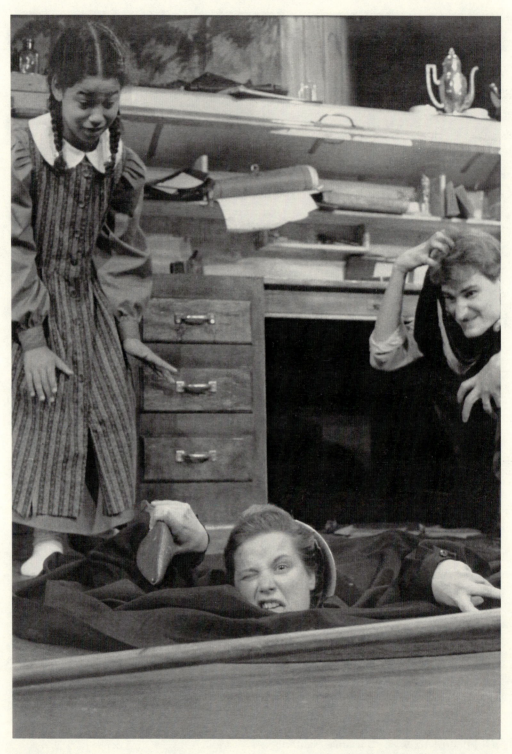

She's meeelting: Bridgey (Brenda Mason) gets into character as Dot (Amani Starnes) watches in Patrick Shanahan's *Oz*. (Photograph credit: World Premiere by the Coterie Theatre, Kansas City, MO.)

During the harvest celebration, Dorothy goes looking for her dog Toto, who she believes can talk, but neither forgetful Kashi nor timid Arik can help. The Machshemoshot Sisters tease Dorothy about young Pachi giving her a pocket-knife, but Dorothy insists Pachi is not in love with her. Dorothy finds Toto in the barn and they fall asleep in a pile of hay, which a cyclone carries away.

Three witches (the Machshemashots) see the haystack coming, and worry the Wizard has summoned a good witch to destroy them. They steer the hay into the realm of their little sister; when Dorothy lands on the fourth sister, crushing her, the other witches swear revenge. Dorothy awakens in the land of the Green People where Smee (Uncle Henry) directs her to Great Wizard Sam in the City of Fire, the only man who can send her home.

Dorothy frees a group of scarecrows from their poles. Although most of them head off to Scarecrowland, one (Kashi) stays behind, ashamed of his own stupidity. Dorothy invites him along to ask Sam for brains. Next they detach the metal man Pach-Pach (Pachi) from a wrecked car and the heartless metal man joins them to get a heart. They catch a lion act in the circus and agree to help one timid lion come along to ask Sam for courage.

The witches send mice to attack the group, but Dorothy persuades them to go ask Sam for free cheese instead. The witches set the poppies in Dorothy's path, but Pach-Pach plugs up the blossoms with some of his metal parts and his friends awake.

When they reach the Emerald City, Sam tells them the only magic he believes in is inner magic: They must bring him the three witches, thereby proving the qualities they want, they already have. Sure enough, in the course of tracking the witches, Dorothy's friends show their brains, hearts and courage, and trap the witches in butterfly nets while they're stealing strawberry tarts. When they bring the witches to Sam he gives the Lion a crown, the Scarecrow a diploma, a cassette of love songs to the Tin Man, a bone to Toto — and tells Dorothy all she has to do to go home is wake up.

Dorothy wakes and reunites with her friends, telling them the lesson learned is that "Life is a dream and dreams are life and whoever can't make life into a dream and dreams into life knows nothing about either life or dreams."

A phenomenally successful show in Israel during its one year run. Paster did an updated revival in 2000.

1995

The Wizard of Oz on Ice. 9/95. Florida opening, followed by U.S. tour.

Cast: Dorothy (Laurnea Wilkerson, voice; Jeri Campbell, skater), All other voices (Bobby McFarin).

Credits: Producer: Kenneth Feld, owners of Ringling Bros. and Barnum and Bailey Circus; *Choreographer:* Robin Cousins; *Costume designer:* Frank Krenz; *Lighting designer:* LeRoy Bennett.

This $9 million ice-skating adaptation was based on the MGM film version. Choreographer Cousins was an Olympic gold medalist. It played on TV in 1996, and was the subject of a documentary, *Creating the Wizard of Oz on Ice.*

The Wizard of Oz in Concert. 11/5/95. Broadcast 11/22 on TNT; 96 mins.

Cast: Dorothy (Jewel), Scarecrow (Jackson Browne), Glinda (Natalie Cole), Tin Man (Roger Daltrey), Professor Marvel/Wizard of Oz (Joel Grey), Cowardly Lion (Nathan Lane), Wicked Witch of the West (Debra Winger), Toto (James Waller), Munchkins (Boys' Choir of Harlem), Auntie Em (Lucie Arnaz), Crows/Winkies (Ry Cooder, Images), Guard Captain (Ronnie Spector), Mayor (Daniel Lane), Coroner (Kevin Miller), Host (Alfre Woodard), Singers (Larry J. Alexander, John Anthony, Christy Baron, Jay Kiman, Neal Mayer, Julia K. Murney, Jennifer L. Neuland, Catherine Ruivivar, Stephanie Seeley, Robin Skye, Tom Treadwell), Announcer (Dick Tufeld), Jitterbug Dancers (Jamilah Clay, Tamika Jones, Mecca Leach, Dwayne Perkins, Trevel Price, Kenyatta Prince, Lawrence Riddles, Dana

Rogers, Asia Thomas, Charles Thomas with Dr. John, David Sanborn, Phoebe Snow.

Credits: Director, writer, producer: Darrell Larson (based on MGM film); *Director (TV):* Louis J. Horvitz; *Lyrics:* EY Harburg; *Music:* Harold Arlen, Herbert Stothart, George Bassman, George Stoll, Bob Stringer, Keith Levenson; *Executive producer:* Johnathan Brauer; *From:* Turner Pictures Worldwide, TNT.

This charity fund-raiser was performed live and filmed for TV. It followed the MGM script and songs. Despite the fine cast (and the presence of a pre-stardom Jewel as Dorothy), the results were largely undistinguished.

1996

The Wizard of the Emerald City. State Academic Children's Musical Theatre.

Cast: Olga Tolkonnikova, Mikhail Chesnokov, Yevgeny Ushkov, Anton Chabanenko, Vladimir Betev, Gennady Piskunov, Galina Sverbilova.

Credits: Director: Victor Riabov; *Writers:* Roxana Satz, Victor Riabov; *Art director:* Vladimir Arefiev; *Composer:* Igor Yaroshenko; *Conductor:* Andrei Yakovlev; *Ballet director:* Boris Liapaev; Produced by GTRK, Petersburg, Channel Five.

This appears to be a musical/ballet adaptation of the Alexander Volkov novel. It has been recorded on tape.

The Wizard of Oz on Ice. 5/5/96. Color, one hour, CBS.

Cast: Dorothy (Oksana Baiul), Dorothy's voice (Shanice), Scarecrow (Victor Petrenko), Tin Woodman (Brent Frank), Cowardly Lion (Mark Richard Farrington), Jitterbugs (Paul Martini, Barbara Underhill), Wizard of Oz/Host (Bobby McFerrin).

Credits: Director: Paul Miller; *Writer:* Jerry Bilik (based on the MGM film); *Producers:* Kimber Rickabaugh, Paul Miller; *Executive producers:* Kenneth Feld, Jerry Bilik; *Choreographer:* Robin Cousins, with added choreography by Sarah Kawahara and Cindy Stuart; *Lighting designer:* Allen Branton; *Production design:* Mark Fisher; *Costume design:* Frank Krenz; From Rick Mill Productions, Irvin Feld & Kenneth Feld Productions, CBS-TV.

This was a TV version of the *Wizard of Oz on Ice* ice-skating show.

1997

Return to the Land of Oz. 7/30/97. Mt. Holyoke College Summer Theatre, South Hadley, MA.

Credits: Writer: Noah Smith.

Dorothy and Glinda introduce children to Oz in the 10th Mt. Holyoke Oz festival.

Hakosem Me'Eretz Utz [also known as The Wizard of Oz: The Musical]. Israel; 58 mins on video.

Cast: Itzik Aloni, Azriel Ashrov, Gili Blaushstein, Yaacov Cohen, Haldas Kalderon, Milli Parnes, Reuven Partok.

Credits: Director: Ariel Ashrov; *Writer:* Ariel Ashrov (based on *The Wizard of Oz* by L. Frank Baum); Music: Harold Arlen, Misha Balchrovich; Lyricist, musical adaptor, Misha Balchorvitch; Choreographer: Avi Lapidot; From IAC Film.

Another Israeli stage adaptation of the MGM film, released on video.

The Wizard of Clods.

Credits: Writer: R. Eugene Jackson.

In this oddball parody, students at Emerald City High enduring the apathetic teaching of Mrs. East get a jolt when a cyclone drops a girl on top of the teacher (though the accident doesn't kill her). The girl, Dorothy, insists Toto, a spunky student, is really Dorothy's dog, and leads Toto, dimwit Gaga, hard-hearted female grease monkey Equilla and shy Brunson on a quest for the Wizard (Mr. Willard, the principal). The principal tells the students he'll grant their wishes once they kill Mrs. West, who's ruining the school's academic record by holding out against grade inflation.

When Dorothy and her crew bring West back to Willard, they discover his secretary, Ms. Sentinel, has been faking his existence because after he quit, the school board never replaced him. The students realize what they need to succeed is more dedicated teachers like West; Gaga, Equilla and Brunson overcome their weaknesses; and the student body buys Dorothy a bus ticket back to Kansas. In the conclusion, Sentinel, Dorothy and

Willard congratulate themselves on tricking the students into demanding tough teachers, while the students congratulate themselves on tricking the school into giving them a good education!

1999

Christmas in the Land of Oz — That Was. Training Wheels Amateur Community Theatre Group, Heyfield, Australia.

Cast: Dorothy (Christine Thexton), Cowardly Lion (Jesse Bryer), Tinman (Justin Azlin), Scarecrow (Lisa Snow), Wicked Witch of the Northwest (Judith Smyk), Glenda the Good Witch (Erin Warren), Auntie Em (Claire Van Baalen), Mayor/Lady Lion (Sharlene Clayton), Uncle Henry (Drewe Hetherton) Wanda June (Debbie Chambers), Captain Simeon (Tim Oliver), Billy Joe/Munchkin (Aaron Whelan), Clem (Joe Stoddart), Moonbeam (Kimberly Whelan), Police Munchkin/Sergeant Ape (Yvonne Dennett), Fisher Munchkin/Jim Bob (William Smyk), Toymaker (Mathew Dennett), Gardener Munchkin/Flying Monkey (Tammie Dennett).

A Christmas production for children by an Australian group.

Time Again in Oz. 12/3/99. Seattle Children's Theatre, Seattle.

Cast: Dorothy (Beth DeVries), Uncle Henry (Allen Galli), Tic Toc/Man (Mark Anders), Captain/General/Wheeler (Jason Collins), Sailor/Feldspar/Wheeler (Lisa Estridge-Gray), Sailor/Major/Wheeler (Bobbi Kotula), Bill/Nanda (Leslie Law), Grand Dame/Langwidere (Anna Lauris), Tycoon/Roquat/Army (Robert Shampain), Ozma (Maya Sugarman).

Credits: Director: Linda Hartzell; *Musical director:* Jeff Caldwell; *Book:* Suzan Zeder (based on *Ozma of Oz*); *Score:* Richard Gray, with additional lyrics by Suzan L. Zeder; *Choreography:* Marianne Roberts; *Set design:* Carey Wong; *Lighting design:* Amarante Lucero; *Costume design:* Susan Tsu.

In the early 1900s teenager Dorothy Gale is fed up with traveling alongside wheelchair-bound Uncle Henry on a cruise to Australia with a boatful of tycoons, grand dames and other annoyances. Henry, on the other hand, is eager for adventure and travel. Shortly after a mysterious stranger gives Dorothy a key, she, Uncle Henry and his prize chicken Bill are washed overboard in a storm and land on the shores of Oz.

The Wheelers, who have wheels instead of hands and feet, hail Henry in his wheelchair as "the Big Wheeler," but Dorothy knows that in Oz danger can lurk amidst beauty. When she finds Tic Toc, the mechanical man, and winds him up with the key, time comes to Oz, which was previously timeless and immortal.

Princess Langwidere, who owns and changes multiple heads, is horrified and angry to find all her heads are aging; determined to stop time, she captures Dorothy and the others to force Dorothy to give up the key. Meanwhile Roquat, the Nome King, emerges from the underworld to force Oz back through history to the Stone Age.

To help Henry, Dorothy uses the key to rewind time until Henry is young and healthy; he leaves his wheelchair but as time rewinds, Roquat kidnaps Uncle Henry and Tic Toc. Ozma arrives and joins forces with Dorothy to battle, and ultimately defeat Roquat. The battle over, Dorothy and Henry have the option to stay in Oz and remain young and healthy forever — but instead choose to return to our world, where they face aging and death but also growth, change and life.

Zeder says that when asked to turn her *Ozma of Oz* into a musical, she decided on a major overhaul rather than just adding songs to the script, so she focused even more on the original play's themes of growth and time.

2000

The Wonderful Wizard of Oz. 12/00. Civic Light Opera Company, Toronto.

Cast: Dorothy (Kelly Sanders), L. Frank Baum/Wizard of Oz (Joe Cascone), Scarecrow (Cameron McKinnon), Tin Woodman (Bryan Chamberlain), Cowardly Lion (David Haines), Aunt Em (Carol Kugler), Uncle Henry (Lloyd Dean), Toto (Jesse), Farmers (Gary Prudence, Stephen Monk),

Wizard of Oz (Lloyd Dean, Gary Prudence, voices only), Wicked Witch of the West (Julie Lennick), Monkey King (Christopher McKinnon), Hungry Tiger (Gary Prudence), Glinda, Good Witch of the South (Joanne Kennedy), Cyclone (Susan Sanders), Boq (Christopher McKinnon), Locasta the Good Witch of the North (Sandi Horwitz), Mrs. Stork (Susan Sanders), Mouse Queen (Carol Kugler), Royal Army of Oz (Stephen Monk).

Credits: Director, book: Joe Cascone; *Score:* James P. Doyle; *Choral director:* Liane Fainsinger; *Choreography:* Leslie Fordon; *Lighting:* Mark Tingle; *Scenery:* Blain Berdan.

Songs: Just a Touch of Humbug; Gray; Round and Around; Free; Wizard Who Lives in Oz; Rags and Hay; Love Doesn't Count; 'Fraid Not; Dream for Me; Further Along the Way; Pull Together; Act One Finale; Emerald City; Come Along with Me; The Golden Cap; Nothing Special; Wicked Is What I Do; Dream for Me (reprise); This Land of Oz.

L. Frank Baum appears on stage and sings to the audience of his lifelong love of theater, where a "touch of humbug" can create magic out of illusion, if the audience is willing to believe.

Dorothy broods on life on the prairie and worries it will turn her as bleak and gray as the world around her. The cyclone strikes, carrying Dorothy (but not Toto) to Oz in the farmhouse, landing on and crushing the Wicked Witch of the East. Boq, a Munchkin elder, thanks Dorothy, as does Locasta, the Good Witch of the North. They give Dorothy the witch's silver shoes and send her down the yellow brick road to seek help from the Great and Powerful Oz.

Along the way, Dorothy meets the Scarecrow, Tin Woodman and Cowardly Lion, inviting them along to ask Oz for brains, a heart and courage respectively. After battling rivers, the monstrous kalidahs and deadly poppies (from which the Queen of the Field Mice has her subjects pull the lion) they reach the Emerald City, which is so magnificent the gatekeeper insists they wear glasses to shield themselves from its brilliance.

The quartet confronts the Wizard one at a time, and he agrees to grant their wishes—once they destroy the Wicked Witch of the West. Dorothy and her friends set out to do so, but the Witch sends her servants, the Winged Monkeys, to capture Dorothy and the Lion and destroy Scarecrow and Tin Woodman.

Captured by the Witch, Dorothy realizes that no matter how gray Kansas is, it's her home, and the home of the people she loves most. The Witch bullies Dorothy incessantly, then tricks her out of one of the slippers, at which point the angry child douses the Witch with a bucket of water, melting her.

Once the Scarecrow and Tin Woodman are restored, the quartet returns to the Emerald City. Even after they discover that the Oz is a humbug, Dorothy's friends let him convince them that he can magically give them the qualities they long for. Oz also tries taking Dorothy home in his balloon, but by accident, he flies off without her. The foursome then journeys to Glinda, the Good Witch of the South, despite more perils in the path (a giant spider, fighting trees and the wonder of a kingdom of China figures). When Dorothy learns the powers of the silver shoes, she willingly uses them to take herself home.

Creators James Doyle and Joe Cascone conceived this project as a faithful adaptation of *The Wizard of Oz*, with a few cosmetic changes (the Wicked Witches are sisters, as in the MGM film; the Good Witch of the North has the name Locasta, as in the 1902 stage musical; and the Tin Woodman gives the expanded backstory from *The Tin Woodman of Oz*), and one larger one, leaving Toto in Kansas (to give Dorothy more incentive to go home, and to minimize the problems of using a dog on stage).

Doyle based the score on what would have been contemporary music for Baum — waltzes, marches, Tin Pan Alley and ragtime — as well as the work of Paul Tietjens and Louis F. Gottschalk (composers for the '02 Wizard stage play and for *Tik-Tok Man of Oz* respectively), whose work Doyle also presented on the *Before the Rainbow* CD at the same time.

The show originally had Dorothy and her friends meet the Wizard individually, but the number, "Oz, the Great and Terrible," never worked on stage, so they met him in a group, as in the MGM film. They also cut back the Witch of the West to the second act of the show, following Baum's book, moving "Wicked Is What I Do" from her first act appearance to the second (replacing "Wicked Waltz of the West").

We're Off to Save the Wizard.
Credits: Writer: Craig Sodaro.

In this adaptation of *Tik-Tok of Oz*, Ruggedo taunts Ozma with the news that he's captured the Wizard and his assistant, the Shaggy Man's brother. Shaggy, Dorothy and Tik-Tok go off to rescue them, meeting the Rose Kingdom folk, Anne of Oogaboo and her army and Polychrome before the Nome King tries to dispose of them by plunging them through the Earth into the land of the Great Jinn. The Jinn then sends them back with the power to neutralize Ruggedo's magic; they successfully defeat him and save the Wizard and Shaggy's brother Hank.

2001

Kaspar in the Wonderful World of Oz.
Savoar, Sweden.
Cast: Dorothy (Trulsa Rabe), Wizard of Oz (Anders Rabe).

In this Scandinavian puppet show, Kaspar (equivalent to Punch in the traditional Punch and Judy show) is blown to Oz by a strong wind and lands on the Woggle-Bug. Over the course of the show, Toto steals the Nome King's magic belt and gives it to Ozma, who returns the king to the underground.

This show mixed human actors with puppets of Toto, Kaspar, Woggle-Bug, Nome King and Ozma.

The Patchwork Girl of Oz. 3/24/01 (Part 1). Louise Reichlin & Dancers, Colburn School of Performing Arts, Los Angeles, CA; 30 mins.
4/7/02 (Part 2). University of Southern California's Alfred Newman Recital Hall, University Park; 30 mins.
11/02 (Part 3). Miles Memorial Playhouse, Santa Monica; 10 minutes.

Cast: (Tape production of all three): Scraps, the Patchwork Girl: (Tara Page, Janell Burgess, Mandy Langen); Dorothy Gale (Natalie Pausch, Ellen Rosa, Carlene Lai); Scarecrow (Sarah Jenkins, Shelby Williams); Ojo (Tina Tsunoda, Adrienne Fisher, Yuki Tomino); Unc Nunkie (Wilson Williams); Dame Margolotte (Shannon Schwait, Shelby Williams, Karen Acosto); The Crooked Magician (Steven Nielsen, Brian Pelletier, Carlene Lai, Shaun Curtin); The Glass Cat (Natalie Pausch, Jennifer Flanagan, Ellen Rosa); The Woozy (Shannon Schwait, Shelby Williams); Glinda, Sorceress of the South (Elizabeth Brookman, Katina Childs, Karen Acosta, Sioux Wing); Glinda's Assistant (Sarah Jenkins, Carlene Lai, Shaun Curtin); The Shaggy Man (Wilson Williams); The Soldier (Wilson Williams); The Wizard (Steven Nielsen, Brian Pelletier); Princess Ozma (Shannon Schwait); The Hungry Tiger (Elizabeth Brookman); The Champion Hopper (Wilson Williams); The Horners (Brian Pelletier, Shannon Schwait, Elizabeth Brookman and children from Vermont Avenue Elementary School, the Idaho Falls School of Ballet, Franklin and John Muir Elementary Schools in Santa Monica); Narrator (Louise Reichlin).

Credits: Director, writer, choreographer: Louise Reichlin; Multimedia collaboration, including multimedia design and authoring, modeling and animation, video editing and compositing: Richard Wainess; Costumes: Linda Borough; Opening video, Part 2: Michael Masucci; Tin Woodman video: Shinji Murakoshi; Multimedia operators: Bertran Harden, Andrea Avila: Music: Varttina, Alfred Desio, Hedningarna, Benoit Jutras, Djura Abouda, Afro Celt Sound System, Barachois, Kodo.

Two Munchkins — a boy named Ojo the Unlucky and his uncle, Unc Nunkie — visit Nunkie's friend the Crooked Magician, who works in his lab to combine computer technology and magic. His latest project is using the computer to design the perfect servant for his wife, Margolette, then bringing her to life. Distressed that the magician plans to create a docile drudge, Ojo tries to expand her intellect by adding extra chips and floppies to the Crooked Magician's system.

We're off to save Unc Nunkie! The Glass Cat (Ellen Rosa), Patchwork Girl (Janell Burgess) and Ojo (Adrienne Fisher) from the Louise Reichlin & Dancers production of *The Patchwork Girl of Oz*. (Photograph credit: Sallie DeEtte Mackie.)

When the Patchwork Girl comes to life, the added bytes make her the smartest person in the world. Unfortunately, her creation unleashes a computer virus that infects and petrifies Unc Nunkie and Margolette.

The Patchwork Girl uses the Crooked Magician's computer to find an antidote formula on the Web, then sets out with Ojo and the magician's Glass Cat to find the ingredients: A six-leafed clover, the wing of a yellow butterfly, bottles of computer chips, three hairs from the tail of a blue Woozy and a magical notebook computer.

The trio soon meets the Woozy, who agrees to join the quest, which also brings them into contact with Dorothy, Ozma, the Wizard of Oz and the Shaggy Man. They journey to the lands of the warring Hoppers and Horners for one of the ingredients, then visit the Tin Woodman only to discover he won't allow them to harm any of the Winkie land's yellow butterflies. Scraps and her friends find an alternative solution and restore Nunkie and Margolette to life.

While visiting collector Willard Carroll's Oz exhibition at the Los Angeles Public Library, Reichlin remembered her own fondness for the Oz books and was struck by the "dance nature" of Neill's flowing illustrations. That led to her creating this production for her company (which performs family-oriented dance numbers), combining the dancers on stage with the dancers' enhanced video images on a 70-inch on-stage screen

Dancing through her life: Scraps, the Patchwork Girl (Mandy Langen) from Louise Reichlin & Dancers, *The Patchwork Girl of Oz*. (Photograph credit: Sallie DeEtte Mackie.)

(so a dancer could appear on the screen as Neill's Woozy or the Glass Cat), or other images such as clocks going backwards to indicate a flashback. Dorothy's appearance also used video footage of her initial visit to Oz by cyclone.

Oz: A Twisted Musical. 4/01. Hudson County Schools of Technology Jay Todd Theatre, North Bergen, NJ; 7/16/03–8/9/03. Producer's Club II Theatre, New York.

Cast: Dorothy (Kyla Garcia), Toto (Matt Kelly), Scarecrow (Frank Criscione), Tinman (Jeffrey Vicente), Lion (Gio Perez), Glinda (Desiree Santiago), Wicked Witch (Marissa Gonzalez), Oz (Ashley Vitha/Lazaro Marquez), Aunt Em (Chelsea Richardson), Wicked Witch of the East (Katie Hurley), with Miriam V. Cortez, Tyler Flagg, Veronika DeLeon, Jean-Marie Stodolski.

The Woozy (Shannon Schwait) and Ojo the Unlucky (Adrienne Fisher), from the Louise Reichlin & Dancers production of *The Patchwork Girl of Oz*. (Photograph credit: Sallie DeEtte Mackie.)

Credits: Director/choreographer/producer: Alex Perez; *Musical director:* Rod Shepard; *Production manager:* Matt Kelly; *Book:* Tim Kelly; *Score:* Bill Francoeur, with additional songs by Christina Ruiz and Rod Shepard; *Lighting design:* Matt Kelly; *Costumes:* Barri Yanowitz; *Set design:* Peter King.

Songs: The Cyclone; Sing, Sing Everybody; Follow the Road; I Ain't Got a Brain; That's Wonderful; A Little Bit O'Courage; Lullaby; China Princess; Modeling Music; I Got the Power; There's a Light in the Distance; The Castle of No Return; The Ol' Soft Paw; The New Soft Paw; I'm Going Home.

In this musical, Dorothy is a streetwise Kansas teenager with a bare navel and fishnet stockings, swept by a tornado to Oz where she crashes atop the Wicked Witch of the East. The grateful Munchkins (who eat at Dunkin' Donuts) and Glinda give Dorothy the witch's silver platform shoes and turn Toto into a bouncy human companion.

Seeking help from the Wizard of Oz, Dorothy and Toto set out along the yellow brick road, picking up the Scarecrow, Tin Woodman and Lion (who do *not* get along with each other, or her), and being pursued by the Wicked Witch of the West, whose lair is an S&M dungeon. Along the way to the Emerald City they encounter a Chinese princess and a Tina Turner wannabe who thinks she should be ruler of Oz.

Oz sends Dorothy off to kill the Witch of the West, who captures her enemies and reduces them to slaves. When she tricks Dorothy out of one of the silver shoes, Dorothy douses her with the usual bucket of water. They return to the Wizard, who contrives to grant Dorothy's friends wishes even after he's outed as a humbug. By now, Dorothy realizes she truly misses her home and family, and is delighted when Glinda tells her that the silver shoes can send her home.

Perez, the musical theater director at North Bergen, New Jersey's High Tech High School, choreographed this show in 1995 at an off-off Broadway workshop, then staged the show for school in 2001, adding the numerous modern quirks (the original Kelly script plays the show straight). A 2002 pro-

Dorothy (Ellen Rosa) from the Louise Reichlin & Dancers production of *The Patchwork Girl of Oz*. (Photograph credit: Sallie DeEtte Mackie.)

duction won three Rising Star Awards from the State Theatre for Best Overall Musical Production, Best Director and Best Costume Design; Perez then raised the money to perform off–Broadway and reunited his cast and crew.

Was. 12/01. Lincoln Center Theater, New York. *Cast:* Jonathan (Malcolm Gets), Young Dorothy (Andrea Bowen), Emma Gulch (Barbara Walsh), Henry Gulch (Matthew Bennett), Wilbur Jewell (Kirk McDonald), Angel (Marcy Harriell), Ira Bernstein (David Pittu), Dorothy Gael at 13 (Brooke Sunny Moriber), L. Frank Baum (Henry Stram), Dotty (Phyliss Somerville), with Ryan Perry, Andrea Burns, Rachel Ulanet, John Jellison, James Moye.

Credits: Director: Tina Landau; *Musical director:* David Loud; *Book:* Barry Kleinbort; *Score:* Joseph Thalken.

Songs: There's a Star; Far Away from Here; Pioneer Beauty; Ain't No Time for Tears; Snow Scene; Father on High; Lucky Day; Tickle Song; School Anthem; Dorothy; Far Away from Here (reprise); Frank's Turkish Song; On to the Next One; Dorothy's Essay; Dorothy's Breakdown; I Got It; Magic (Finale, Act One); A Silver Strand; Chasing a Dream; On Saturday Night; In Black and White; Was; The Story of D. Gael; Time; Finale.

Was follows two interwoven stories: Dorothy Gael, an orphan living in despair with her aunt and uncle in Kansas, slipping into rage and then insanity after her uncle rapes her. A chance meeting with L. Frank Baum during his acting days (when a touring company folds, he turns to substitute teaching to make ends meet) gives her a brief moment of joy, but horrifies Baum when he realizes the brutality of Dorothy's life — and inspires him to write a book telling of the happy life Dorothy should have had.

The second story involves Jonathan, a moderately successful actor and a lover of Oz, dying of AIDS and slipping slowly into delirium. When he learns from his therapist that Dorothy had a real prototype (who died, years ago, in an asylum), he sets out to Kansas on an obsessive quest to find her home.

This play was performed in a theater workshop attended only by producers and theater professionals, with no sets, costumes or stage lighting. It won a Gilman and Gonzalez-Falla Commendation Award and went on to a full stage performance in 2003 at the National Alliance for Musical Theatre.

Writer Kleinbort describes this production as faithful to the spirit (which he describes as "We all need fantasy to get us through reality") but not quite the letter of Geoff Ryman's dark novel. For example, the play eliminates the Judy Garland scenes in Ryman's book, which don't tie into the Jonathan and Dorothy storylines that come together at the end of the show.

Kleinbort and Thalken decided that a musical would be the ideal vehicle to tackle the multiple layers of Ryman's novel, because the music would allow the same sort of layering (as when music and lyrics ironically convey different moods), would help buffer the shock of some of the story's many brutal events, and could link Jonathan and Dorothy together (by singing a duet on stage even though they're decades apart).

2002

The Wizard of Oz. Oz Kids Production Company, MO.

Credits: Writer: Mary Carroll-Bower.

This was an adaptation of the MGM film, but Carroll-Bower also borrowed from several juvenile stage plays to make it simpler and shorter. The name of the production company refers not only to Baum, but to the group's location within the Ozarks.

The Wizard of Oz. 2/02. Chapter Six, Millikin University, Decatur, IL.

Cast: Narrator (Aaron Stonecipher), Dorothy (Luke Menard), Tin Woodman (Jarrett Johnson), Scarecrow (Nathan Pufall), Cowardly Lion (Chuck Bosworth), Wicked Witch of the West (John Music).

Credits: Arranger: Mark Grizzard.

Grizzard, the arranger for the a cappella group Chapter Six, describes this as a condensed six-minute version of the MGM film ("We get the plot across and have some fun with it") in which the narrator describes the plot and Chapter Six sings the big numbers, including "Somewhere Over the Rainbow" and "If I Were King of the Forest."

Grizzard said the group originally wanted to do a "jazzy arrangement of 'Somewhere

A costume crew readies Dorothy (Kyla Garcia) to go on in *Oz*. (Photograph credit: Laura Kim.)

Tin Man (Jeff Vicente), Dorothy (Kyla Garcia), Toto (Matt Kelly), Lion (Gio Perez) and Scarecrow (Frank Ciscione) in a group shot from *Oz*. (Photograph credit: Laura Kim.)

Over the Rainbow,'" then decided it wanted to sing more of the score. Since Chapter Six plays to audiences of all ages, there were obvious advantages to performing a show that all age groups would enjoy.

Sing-a-Long Wizard of Oz. 12/12/02. Ford Center for the Performing Arts, Chicago.

An "interactive" version of the MGM film in which the audience is encouraged to come in costume, sing along, hiss the witch, cheer when appropriate, etc. The MC provides bubble-blowers, kazoos and wands for the audience.

This is the third recent Sing-a-long production (after *Sing-a-Long Grease* and *Sing-a-Long Sound of Music*), though the tradition dates back at least to the cult classic *Rocky Horror Picture Show*.

2003

Wicked. 5/27/03. San Francisco; 10/30/03. New York City.

Cast: Glinda (Kristin Chenoweth), Elphaba (Idina Menzel), Wizard (Joel Grey), Madame Morrible (Carole Shelley), Doctor Dillamand (William Youmans), Fiyero (Norbert Leo Butz), Nessarose (Michelle Federer), Boq (Christopher Fitzgerald), with Ioana Alfonso, Stephanie J. Block, Ben Cameron, Cristy Candler, Mellissa Bell Chait, Marcus Choi, Kristoffer Cusick, Kathy Deitch, Melissa Fahn, Rhett George, Kristen Lee Gorski, Kisha Howard, Manuel Herrera, L.J. Jellison, Sean McCourt, Corrine McFadden, Mark Myars, Jan Neuberger, Walter Winston O'Neil, Andrew Palermo, Peter Samuel, Michael Seelbach.

Credits: Director: Joe Mantello; *Musical director:* Stephen Oremus; *Book:* Winnie Holzman (based on Gregory Maguire's *Wicked*); *Producers:* Marc Platt, Universal Pictures, David Stone; *Choreography:* Wayne Cilento; *Scenic design:* Eugene Lee; *Costume design:* Susan Hilfert.

Songs: No One Mourns the Wicked; Dear Old Shiz; The Wizard and I; What Is This Feeling; Which Way Is the Party; We Deserve Each Other; Popular; I'm Not That Girl; One Short Day; A Sentimental Man; The Chance to Fly; Defying Gravity; Thank Goodness; I Couldn't Be Happier; Wonderful; As Long as You're Mine; No Good Deed; March of the Witch Hunters; For Good; Finale.

This Broadway play opens with the Winkies celebrating the death of Elphaba, the Wicked Witch of the West, as Glinda descends to join them. The Good Witch reluctantly admits she was once Elphaba's friend, and blames Elphaba's wicked life on the fact that she was born with green skin after her adulterous mother shared her lover's green cordial while pregnant.

That only whets the crowd's curiosity, so Glinda continues the story from the moment Elphaba and her paraplegic sister, Nessarose (crippled by the remedy Mom took to prevent another green child), enroll at Shiv College in the Emerald City. Nessa gets jeweled slippers from their father for attending, but Elphaba only gets mockery from the other students for her skin, but she vows some day Oz will celebrate her (the audience knows it's her death they're going to celebrate).

Not everyone's against Elphaba: headmistress Madame Morrible enrolls her in sorcery classes and perky, popular Galinda eventually becomes her friend, even though both girls are in love with swaggering Prince Fiyero. Fiyero loves Elphaba back, but she refuses to believe he could care for a green freak. Boq, another student, falls for Galinda while Nessa falls for Boq.

When anti–animal rights bigots target Professor Dillamond, a talking goat, Elphaba vows to defend him. Seeing that this impresses Fiyero, Galinda "honors" Dillamond by changing her name to match the way he mispronounces it. "Glinda" and Elphaba win an audience with the Wizard, who tricks Elphaba into using the great Oz spellbook to painfully mutate ordinary monkeys into winged spies. Realizing the Wizard is behind

The Wicked Witch (Marissa Gonzalez) readies for an entrance in *Oz*. (Photograph credit: Laura Kim.)

Elphaba (Ida Menzel) and Glinda (Kristin Chenoweth) square off in a scene from Stephen Schwartz's *Wicked*. (Photograph credit: Joan Marcus.)

the anti–animal movement, Elphaba flees with the spellbook. Morrible immediately demonizes her in the media as the Wicked Witch of the West.

Years later, Elphaba remains an outcast, Nessarose is Munchkin governor (with Boq forced to serve as her caregiver) and Glinda is a prominent government figure, advancing her career by helping smear Elphaba, who is so evil, pure water would melt her! Although Fiyero resents Glinda's refusal to support Elphaba, he reluctantly agrees to marry her.

Elphaba asks Nessa to help fight the Wizard, but Nessa not only refuses, she uses guilt to persuade Elphaba to enchant the jeweled shoes (turning them red) to let her walk. Boq decides since Nessa no longer needs him, he's free to woo Glinda one final time. Furious, Nessa uses Elphaba's spellbook to shrink Boq's heart; Elphaba tries to protect him and the clashing magics turn the Munchkin into a heartless Tin Man. Nessa blames her sister, but also berates herself for becoming a second "wicked witch."

The Wizard meets with Elphaba again, and almost convinces her to join him (in return for freeing the winged monkeys) until she discovers he's keeping the now-mute Dillamond caged. Fiyero finally leaves Glinda for Elphaba, so the bitter Good Witch tells the Wizard he can control Elphaba by threatening Nessa. Morrible doesn't believe threats are enough, and begins working a weather spell.

Just as Fiyero and Elphaba reunite, Elphaba spots the tornado carrying a house across the sky and senses Nessa in danger. She arrives to find Nessa dead and Dorothy (never seen on stage) off to the Emerald City in Nessa's ruby shoes. The Wizard's soldiers capture the Witch, but Fiyero saves her. In punishment, the soldiers stake him out in a cornfield under the blazing sun to make him talk; Elphaba saves him from death by turning him into a scarecrow (though we don't learn that until later).

Chapter Six performs its six-minute Cliff Notes version of MGM's *Wizard of Oz*: Aaron Stonecipher, John Musick, Chuck Bosworth, Nathan Pufall, Luke Menard, Jarret Johnson. (Photograph credit: Chapter Six.)

Elphaba captures Dorothy, but Boq raises a mob to storm her castle. Glinda, repentant, arrives at the castle and promises to clear Elphaba's name if she'll only flee. Elphaba refuses: Only Glinda has the power and the will to reform Oz, and she'll lose that power if she's linked with the Wicked Witch.

After seeing her friend destroyed by that fateful bucket of water, Glinda discovers proof the Wizard was Elphaba's mother's lover, and the Wicked Witch's father. When she confronts the Wizard with the truth, he collapses in grief, enabling Glinda to exile him, imprison Morrible and take over the government, vowing to rule, at last, as a genuinely good witch. She doesn't know that Fiyero and Elphaba used a trapdoor to fake the melting, and, rather than reveal that the Wicked Witch still lives, they flee Oz together, happy in each other's arms.

Gregory Maguire told the *New York Times* he wrote the novel *Wicked* because of his revulsion at seeing the MGM film in the 1970s and seeing a clear parallel between the Wizard and Glinda lying to Dorothy (Glinda's lie being not telling her at once that the slippers can take her home) and the lies of the Nixon regime (the novel is even more pretentious and heavy-handed than that makes it sound). Schwartz, whose credits include *Godspell* and *Pippin*, said the book attracted him because it shows how appearances deceive and "life is always more nuanced and complex than we like to think it is."

Reviews when the $14 million show opened in San Francisco were mixed but generally favorable; the biggest complaints concerned the loss of the source novel's alleged philosophical depth, heavy-handed references to current politics (such as Dorothy inflicting a "regime change" on the Munchkins), and that Fiyero wasn't strong enough to hold up the romantic triangle (which plays a much bigger role than in the book). Chenoweth won solid enthusiasm for her turn as the shallow Glinda, with her song "Popular" considered one of the show's best.

For Broadway, the producers made cast changes (replacing Robert Morse as the Wizard, Kirk McDonald as Boq and John Horton as Dillamond), added some on-stage flying (there was none in San Francisco) and tried for a better balance between Elphaba's straight-woman role and Chenowith's scene-stealing Glinda.

The changes seem to have helped, since the show snagged 10 Tony nominations in 2004: Best Musical, Best Book, Best Original Score, Best Leading Actress in a Musical (both Chenowith and Menzel), Best Scenic Design, Best Costume Design, Best Lighting Design, Best Choreography and Best Orchestrations. Menzel, scenic designer Lee and costumer Hilfert all won an award.

The 2004 Tony Awards show included Chenoweth as Galinda introducing one presenter, and a performance of "Defying Gravity."

Another role-reversal Oz story, *Pamela West* (the Witch is good, Dorothy's a bitch, Toto's a pit bull) was supposedly on Hollywood's drawing boards at the turn of the century, but as often happens, it seems to have vanished into limbo.

3

Oz Comic Books and Comic Strips

1904

Queer Visitors from the Marvelous Land of Oz. 9/4/04–2/26/05. 26 Sunday episodes.

Credits: *Writer*: L. Frank Baum; *Artist*: Walt McDougall.

In the opening episode of this weekly comic strip, the Gump from *The Land of Oz* flies the Tin Woodman, Scarecrow, Saw-Horse, Woggle-Bug and Jack Pumpkinhead to the United States where they land in a large arena, alarming a guard and a buffoonish black worker. At the end of the installment the Woggle-Bug announces that he's figured where they've landed, but readers of the 1904 episodes were left until the next week to learn "What did the Woggle-Bug Say?" (In this case, that it was Stadium Athletic Field). Readers were invited to write in their guesses in a contest held by many newspapers.

In subsequent adventures, the Oz characters wandered America undergoing entertaining (or so Baum hoped) adventures: The Scarecrow replaces his stuffing with dollar bills, which get pulled out by visitors to a church fair; the group visits Kansas and saves Dorothy from a bull; the Tin Woodman saves a poodle from fire with his tin body; the visitors see Santa and provide him with Oz dolls for Christmas (though no tie-in dolls were actually made).

This series was part of Reilly & Britton's extensive promotional campaign for *The Marvelous Land of Oz*, the first book the new publisher would release. The campaign included heavy build-up for the "What Did the woggle-bug Say?" contest (including a song by Paul Tietjens, who'd collaborated with Baum on the '02 *Wizard* stage show), and seemingly serious newspaper articles, starting in August, reporting a flying object approaching the United States (it turns out to be the Gump, flying in from Oz).

The stories, however, were rather rambling and the art simplistic and slapstick, which may have suited Baum fine (he frequently complained that the illustrations in the Oz books should be more humorous). The strips were later collected in *The Third Book of Oz* in 1986.

Denslow's Scarecrow and the Tin-Man. 12/10/04–2/18/05. 14 Sunday episodes.

Credits: *Writer, artist*: W.W. Denslow.

The Scarecrow, Tin-Man and the Cowardly Lion wandered through North and South America in this comic strip. In various installments, Aztec villagers try to keep the Lion fed for fear he'll eat them; Bermuda customs officials suspect Scarecrow and Tin-Man of hiding contraband in their bodies; and a blacksmith adapts Nick Chopper's feet for skating.

Denslow and Baum shared the copyright on *The Wizard of Oz*, so after Baum released his *Queer Visitors* strip, Denslow came up with a similar one of his own (quite unrelated to the book, *Denslow's Scarecrow and the Tin-Man*). This was a better looking cartoon than *Queer Visitors* and ran slightly longer, but it appeared in far fewer papers.

1932

The Wonderland of Oz. 5/31–10/33. Monday–Saturday comic strip.

Credits: Artist: Walt Spouse.

This strip faithfully adapted *The Land of Oz*, *Ozma of Oz*, *The Emerald City of Oz*, *The Patchwork Girl of Oz* and *Tik-Tok of Oz*. Unfortunately, the very faithfulness made the installments look rather static (it took seven strips for Dorothy to walk to Bunbury), which may have been why the series only ran 16 months.

Dell Comics reprinted the strips from 1938 to 1940 in *The Funnies*, frequently relettering the strips so that the dialog, which had all been in captions, would be in letter balloons. More recently, Hungry Tiger Press's *Oz-Story* has reprinted them, too.

1938

The Funnies. 1938–40. Dell Comics.

This book, which reprinted runs of newspaper strips such as *Tailspin Tommy*, *Alley Oop* and *Mutt and Jeff* also featured Walt Spouse's *The Wonderland of Oz* for a while.

1940

Hi Spot Comics. 11/40, #2. Hawley Publications.

Another reprint of several episodes of *The Wonderland of Oz*.

1946

Wow Comics: The New Wizard of Oz. 10/46, #48. Fawcett Comics.

Mary Marvel, the World's Mightiest Girl (and sister to the better known Captain Marvel) in an Oz pastiche.

1956

Dell Junior Treasury Comics: The Wizard of Oz. 7/56, #5. Dell Publishing.

Credits: Writer: Gaylor Dubois. Based on the book.

A straight adaptation of the Baum book.

1957

Classics Illustrated, Jr.: The Wizard of Oz. #535. Gilberton Co.

This was another adaptation of the original novel. *Classics Illustrated, Jr.* was a spin-off of the legendary *Classics Illustrated* series (said to have been the source of countless book reports in the days before Cliff Notes) adapting children's books, myths and fairy stories.

1962

The Wizard of Oz. March/May, #1308, Dell Publishing

This one-shot book told stories based on the Rankin-Bass *Tales of the Wizard of Oz* TV cartoon (comics adapting sitcoms, Westerns and other TV series were quite common at one time).

1965

The Adventures of Jerry Lewis: The Wizard of Ooze. July/August1965, #89. DC Comics.

Credits: Artist: Bob Oksner.

Jerry Lewis (yes *the* Jerry Lewis — though presented in this series not as an actor, but as the schmuck he played on-screen) and his sorcerous housekeeper Witch Kraft visit the Land of Ooze, where the Wizard — a giant head resembling *Mad*'s Alfred E. Neumann — sends them on a quest (which requires Jerry to dress up as Dorothy at one point) for a variety of odd items such as the "blue cheese of happiness." When Jerry finally unmasks the Wizard, it turns out to be Bob Hope.

DC's *Jerry Lewis* (originally *Martin and Lewis*) and *Bob Hope* comics were the last of the movie-star comic books that sprung up in the 1950s, showcasing the actors in adventures suited to their on-screen personas (Lewis as a goofball, Hope as a fast-talking womanizer, Alan Ladd as a tough adventurer, etc.).

Walt Disney Comics and Stories: The Wizard of Bahs. 4/66, #307. Gold Key.
Credits: Plot/story: Vic Lockman; *Art:* Tony Strobl; *Ink:* Mike Royer.

In this parody of Baum, Daisy Duck plays Dorothy with Pluto as her Toto, the Seven Dwarfs become the Munchkins and inventor Gyro Gearloose turns out to be the Wizard.

1967

Harvey Hits. Harvey Publications.

This magazine ran a Baum parody in one of its *GI Joe, Jr.* stories.

1969

Mad Magazine: The Guru of Ours. 7/69, #128. E.C. Comics.

Dorothy (Liza Minnelli) lives with Aunt Em (pop singer Tiny Tim) until she and the farmhouse are swept away to Oz by a cyclone. She sets off to seek the Guru of Ours (Ed Sullivan), and when he turns out to be a fake, she and her friends join him anyway in his Underground City palace.

A parody that took pot-shots at a lot of familiar 1960s' celebrities along with *The Wizard of Oz* itself.

1970

Adventure Comics: The Mysterious Motr of Doov. 6/70, #394. DC Comics.
Credits: Writer: Cary Bates; *Artist:* Win Mortimer.

Supergirl and Streaky (an Earth cat endowed with super-powers) fight a tornado only to have it pull them into another dimension where their normal powers vanish, replaced by other abilities. Accompanied by a stranded Earth man and several unique creatures (including a neon-lit man and an intelligent animal) they battle a monster and get hurled through a fountain, at which point they return to Earth. Supergirl later realizes that the man she met was L. Frank Baum, and that their adventure, with a few changes, was the basis for Baum's *The Wizard of Oz*.

Supergirl, Superman's cousin from Krypton, was a popular DC character for many years (she was eventually killed, though a different superhuman assumed the Supergirl name).

Cycle Toons: Hogg in Oz
Credits: Writer, Artist: Bill Stout.

A 10-page parody in which a biker visits Oz.

1975

MGM's Marvelous Wizard of Oz. Marvel Comics/DC Comics.
Credits: Writer/editor: Roy Thomas; *Artist:* John Buscema; *Inker:* Tony deZuniga.

This tabloid-sized comic (a format often used for various special editions during the 1970s) retold the story of the MGM film. Special features included stills from the film and profiles of L. Frank Baum and the MGM cast.

Oz enthusiast and Marvel Comics writer Thomas had been pushing to do an Oz book for several years before publisher Stan Lee gave the go-ahead for a faithful adaptation of *The Wizard of Oz* (Thomas describes Buscema's original art as a mix of Denslow and Neill). DC announced it was also planning an Oz book (though Thomas suspected they were bluffing), and the two companies decided to collaborate rather than compete (a first — this book came out several months ahead of the better-known *Superman vs. Spiderman*).

At some point (Thomas, detailing this a decade later, didn't recollect how), MGM became involved and the companies agreed to adapt the movie rather than the book. Buscema then redrew the story as a faithful rendition of the film, despite not having seen it in years.

Marvel Treasury of Oz Featuring the Marvelous Land of Oz. 11/75. Marvel Comics.

Credits: Writer: Roy Thomas; *Artist:* Alfredo Alcala.

Marvel's second tabloid-sized Oz adaptation (without DC, this time) retold the story of Tip's adventures and his transformation into Ozma quite faithfully, though with a lot of added dialog; the biggest change is that in telling about the transformation, Mombi tells Glinda that when the Wizard brought Ozma to Mombi's cottage, he made Mombi swear not to hurt her (and this makes no reference to his teaching her magic).

Artist Alcala does a superb job following Neill's illustrations, except for matching Scarecrow and Tin Woodman to the MGM movie (part of the contractual arrangements from Marvel's *The Wizard of Oz* adaptation).

Following the *Wizard of Oz* tabloid, Marvel decided to launch a series of Oz adaptations, and the last page of *The Land of Oz* announces *Ozma of Oz* for early 1976. Although *Ozma* was drawn and lettered, and Thomas had a synopsis drawn up for *Dorothy and the Wizard in Oz*, various complications, possibly including that nothing past *The Land of Oz* was out of copyright, stopped the series in its tracks.

Special features include a reprint of a Neill illustration, another MGM still and a text page by Roy Thomas explaining the differences between Baum's Oz and the MGM version.

1983

Muppet Magazine: The Wizard of Fox. Telepictures Publication.

Miss Piggy of the Muppets searches for the Wizard in this parody.

1986

The Oz-Wonderland War. Jan–March, 1986, #1–3. DC Comics.

Credits: Story: E. Nelson Bridwell; *Script:* Joey Cavalieri; *Art, additional dialog:* Carol Lay.

The Zoo Crew, super-heroes from a "funny animal" world (i.e., anthropomorphic animals like Porky Pig or Huckleberry Hound) are contacted by the Cheshire Cat, who tells them Roquat the Nome King has conquered Oz and may soon move against Wonderland. With the help of the Wonderland characters, the Zoo Crew sets out to rescue Ozma and her court, who've been transformed into ornaments and hidden all over Oz.

This mini-series, actually six issues in three double-size books, was originally going to be part of the recently cancelled *Captain Carrot and his Amazing Zoo Crew* (the penultimate issue of that book revealed the super-villain Gorilla Grodd had restored Roquat's memory after *The Emerald City of Oz*), but after the cancellation, it received its own brief run. Arrow Comics' *Wonderland* (and several stage plays) would also mingle Wonderland and Oz characters.

Lay's art was certainly distinctive, drawing the Zoo Crew as themselves, the Oz characters in the Neill style and the Wonderland characters along the lines of Lewis Carroll's original *Alice in Wonderland* illustrator, John Tenniel.

1986

First Comics Graphic Novels: The Enchanted Apples of Oz. #5. First Comics.

Credits: Writer, illustrator: Eric Shanower.

Dorothy and her friends are caught in a duel between Valynn, guardian of the title magic apples, and Bortag, a sorcerer (riding a flying swordfish) who wishes to wake the lost Wicked Witch of the South with the apples, even though eating even one will turn Oz into a mundane, non-magical realm.

First Comics Graphic Novels: The Secret Island of Oz. #7. First Comics.
Credits: Writer, artist: Eric Shanower.

Dorothy and her friends are seeking a rare fish for Ozma's pond, but when their quest leads them inside a mountain they're caught by a whirlpool and encounter adventures, a spoiled princess and a living boy toy.

1987

First Comics Graphic Novels: The Ice King of Oz. #13. First Comics.
Credits: Writer, artist: Eric Shanower.

When the malevolent Ice King develops a brand of magic neither Glinda nor the Wizard can stop—and kidnaps Ozma—Dorothy, the Scarecrow, Tin Woodman and Flicker (one of Shanower's own creations) must try to rescue their princess without the help of magic.

1988

First Comics Graphic Novels: The Forgotten Forest of Oz. #16. First Comics.
Credits: Writer, artist: Eric Shanower.

A wood nymph steals the amnesia generating waters of the forbidden fountain. How are Burzee and the troll king involved?

1991

Taboo: Lost Girls. Spiderbaby Graphics.
Credits: Writer: Alan Moore; *Artist:* Melinda Gebbie.

In 1913, Alice Liddell (of *Alice in Wonderland*), Wendy Darling (from *Peter Pan*) and Dorothy Gale meet as adults for a serious of erotic explorations one reviewer describes as "an attempt to reinvent pornography as something exquisite, thoughtful and human." Their experiences conjure up an erotic dream world of childhood fantasy, juxtaposed against the coming war.

Six chapters of the 240-page, 30-chapter story were published by Spiderbaby (in the magazine *Taboo*). The series then moved to Kitchen Sink Press, which reprinted the first six chapters, but couldn't afford to publish the remainder. Moore and Gebbie then finished the series and proposed publishing it as a single graphic novel, which Top Shelf Productions has on its coming projects list.

Moore has said that combining the three fictional girls in this story was one of the inspirations for *The League of Extraordinary Gentlemen*, in which several 19th-century characters become an adventuring team (the basis for the film of that name).

1992

The Blue Witch of Oz. Dark Horse Comics.
Credits: Writer, artist: Eric Shanower.

Dorothy and Scarecrow set off on a quest to find the Good Witch of the East, and help her find her lost son.

The Life and Adventures of Santa Claus. Tundra Publishing.
Credits: Writer, artist: Michael Ploog (based on the Baum book).

This graphic novel adapted Baum's fantasy, keeping to the main plot, but adjusting the order of events (introducing several characters early, for instance). The book also has references to the Emerald City and the Scarecrow.

Oz Squad. #1–3, Brave New Worlds; #4, Second series #1–10, Patchwork Press, 1992–1996.
Credits: Steven Ahlquist, Terry Loh.

Years after Dorothy's recorded adventures, Oz, which exists in a parallel dimension, opens diplomatic relations with Earth. Realizing the potential danger from using Oz magic in our world, the U.S. government recruits Dorothy (still a young adult, despite having lived in Oz for a century) to lead a team of Oz characters on troubleshooting missions. In our world, the Lion and Hungry Tiger can morph into humans but the Scarecrow becomes depressed and Tik-Tok goes haywire.

A wildly unpopular book with Oz fans. Patchwork Press also published the one-shot *Little Oz Squad* showing the characters as children.

1994

Legion of Super-Heroes Annual. #5. DC Comics.

This was an "Elseworlds" story (putting DC characters in different times, settings or alternate histories) in which Light Lass, a member of the 30th-century Legion of Super-Heroes, takes a trip to Oz in the Dorothy role.

Oz. #0–22, 1994–97. Caliber Press.
Credits: Writers: Ralph Griffith, Stuart Kerr; *Art:* Bill Bryan (1–5).

A trio of friends from Earth — Mary, Peter and Kevin — land in Oz to discover the yellow brick road in ruins, Scarecrow, Tin Man and the Lion gone and the Nome King in power: The lands of Oz are desolate and barren, monsters roam freely, Mombi has Dorothy in her power and Ozma is imprisoned.

Mary falls in with Pumpkinhead, who introduces her to the Freedom Fighters, including Woggle-Bug, Tik-Tok and Hungry Tiger. Kevin and Peter join Scarecrow and rescue Tin Man. Eventually the heroes defeat Mombi's spells, but the battle with the Nome King lies ahead.

Along with the main *Oz* series, Caliber also published several one-shots tied into the series: *Freedom Fighters, Lion, Scarecrow, Tin Man* and *Daemonstorm*, and two three-issue miniseries (*Romance in Rags* and *Straw and Sorcery*). The series was later collected into *Gathering of Heroes* and *Mayhem in Munchkinland.*

Arrow Comics continued the story in five issues of *Dark Oz* (written by Ralph Griffith and drawn by Bill Bryan), then in nine issues of *Land of Oz* (a story in *Arrow Anthology* #4 linked the two series) drawn by Bryan and written by Gary Bishop. In *Land of Oz*, Ozma falls into a coma while the new threat of the sorcerers Donlar and Singra threatens Oz.

The distributor cancelled the series with #12 due to low sales, but the creators decided stopping at #9 made better dramatic sense.

Spinoffs at Arrow included the one-shot *Wogglebug* and three issues of *Wonderland* in which Dorothy and other Oz characters show up in a similarly dark and sinister Wonderland.

1997

Mad Magazine: The Buzzard of Oz. #300. E.C. Comics.

Another parody from the "usual gang of idiots."

What If…? #100. Marvel Comics.

This series presented stories of the Marvel Comics super-heroes as if their lives had gone differently at crucial points. In one of the two stories in the centennial issue, the Fantastic Four visit Oz, with Sue Storm as Dorothy.

1998

Pinky and the Brain: The Terrific Takeover of Oz. #23. DC Comics.

Brain, a super-genius labmouse, works with his addlepated sidekick Pinky to take over Oz. The series was based on the TV cartoon.

2002

Fables. #1, 7/02–, (on-going). DC Comics (Vertigo Imprint).
Credits: Writer: Bill Willingham; *Penciler:* Lan Medina; *Inkers:* Steve Leialoha, Craig Hamilton.

This fantasy series is set in Fabletown, a section of New York where for centuries fairy-tale characters such as Snow White, Old King Cole and Prince Charming have lived secretly ever since a monstrous adversary drove them out of their world. Oz and Lilliput were among the literary fairy-tales overrun by the Adversary, and the Winged Monkeys are regularly seen doing go-fer work for the Fabletown sheriff (Tin Woodman and Jack Pumpkinhead have been glimpsed in other scenes).

2004

The Lizard of Oz. Fantagraphics Press.
Credits: Writer, Artist: Mark Bode.

A graphic novel using characters created by Bode's father, Vaughn Bode, in a parody of Baum.

Dates Uncertain

Peter Pan and the Warlords of Oz. #1. Hand of Doom Publications.
Credits: Writer: Don Christensen; *Artist:* Al Hubbard.

Peter Pan and the Warlords of Oz: Dead Head Water. #1, Hand of Doom Publications.
Credits: Writer, artist: Robert Hand.

Alice and the inhabitants of Wonderland use a dimensional gateway to enter Oz, seeking an evil grimoire that could be used to destroy all life. Thinking they're under attack, the Oz inhabitants fight back; when they learn what Alice is looking for, they try to reach the grimoire first. As if this wasn't bad enough, Peter, the Lost Boys and the ticking crocodile enter from Neverland.

This is a fairly obscure indie comic (neither comic-book guide this author consulted listed publication dates), and one of several to combine Lewis Carroll with Baum.

4
Audio Adaptations

1926

Topsy Turvy Time. WMAQ, 1926–27.

This daily children's show included excerpts read from the Oz books as a regular feature. In addition, Thompson wrote *The Enchanted Tree of Oz* (based on an unpublished non–Oz novel of hers) for the show as part of a contest: The Scarecrow and Dorothy disappear into the magical Tree of Whutter Wee, at which point the story stops and children were invited to submit endings.

1927

The Wizard of Oz. WTAM, 15 mins., thrice weekly for 13 weeks.

WTAM originally planned to adapt the "Junior League" plays from Samuel French, but instead negotiated with Maud Gage Baum for the right to perform an original adaptation. After 12 weeks, the sponsor dropped it.

1929

Children's Hour. 10/29. NBC.

This show regularly featured readings from the Oz books (*Grampa of Oz* was running in the given time period). Another NBC show, *Jolly Bill and Jane*, featured an Oz Day every Wednesday.

1933

Wizard of Oz. 9/25/33–3/23/34. NBC.

Cast: Dorothy/Jinjur (Nancy Kelly), Scarecrow (Bill Adams), Cowardly Lion (Jack Smart), Uncle Henry/Jack Pumpkinhead (Jack Smart), Tin Woodman/Sawhorse/Tik-Tok (Parker Fennelly), Toto/Woggle-Bug (Junius Matthews), Announcer (Ben Graver), Tip (Walter Tetty), Mombi/Langwidere (Agnes Moorehead), Billina (Junius Matthews), Wizard (Ian Wolfe), Nome King (Bradley Barker), Ozma (Irma Uran), Soldier (Edwin Witney), Jim, the cabhorse (Bradley Barker), Mangaboo leader (Junius Matthews), Gwig (Junius Matthews), Wizard of Oz (Ian Wolfe), King of the Winds (Junius Matthews), piglet (Junius Mathews), Braided Man (Ian Wolfe), Shaggy Man (Jack Smart), Fox (Edwin Whitney), King Dox (Bradley Barker), Music Man (Ian Wolfe), Scoodler (Bradley Barker), Queen Scoodler (Agnes Moorehead), Camel (Ian Wolfe), Fish/Johnny Dooit (Bradley Barker), Whimsie Leader (Ian Wolfe), Button Bright (Jack Smart), Soup Ladle (Bradley Barker), Growleywog leader (Edwin Witney), King Bristle (Bradley Barker), Rabbit Warbler (Ian Wolfe), Johnny Cake (Bradley Barker), Flutterbudget (Ian Wolfe), Scarlet Crocodile (Bradley Barker), Ork (Bradley Barker), Firefly leader (Bradley Barker), Ozma (Betty Wragge), Growleywog (Ian Wolfe), Princess Potato (Marian Hopkinson).

Credits: Director: Donald Stauffer; *Music/conductor:* Frank Novak.

A cyclone sweeps Dorothy and Toto to Oz in the farmhouse, with Toto acquiring speech almost immediately. Landing in Oz atop the Wicked Witch, Dorothy meets the Good Witch of the North and the Munchkins, receives the silver shoes and heads off to meet the mysterious, powerful Wizard of Oz, acquiring Scarecrow, Tin Woodman and Cowardly Lion as companions along the way. Dorothy keeps trying to use the magic of the shoes, but with minimal success: Her attempt to go home only raises another cyclone, and when she summons more stuffing for the Scarecrow, the group is almost buried in straw.

Along the way to the Emerald City, they face the field of poppies; an army of animals who require the Lion to kill a giant spider before the travelers can pass; the Hammerheads; balloon people; and flying umbrellamen. In the city, the Wizard meets them and sends them off to kill the witch. The group successfully defeats her armies of crows, bees and wolves, but the Winged Monkeys tear apart Scarecrow and Tin Woodman and bring the others to the witch. Fortunately, once Dorothy melts her with water, the slippers summon her friends and the Winkies repair them.

The Winkies give Dorothy the golden cap that commands the Winged Monkeys, who carry Dorothy and her friends back to the Emerald City. Although they discover Oz is a fake, he contrives to grant Dorothy's friends' wishes, then take her home in his balloon—but of course, he winds up leaving alone. Dorothy's friends take her to Glinda (encountering a guardian tree, the China Country and the River of Rubber Ducks before reaching the sorceress). Glinda tells Dorothy how to use the slippers, but Dorothy has lost one so the magic won't work.

Searching for the missing slipper, the travelers meet Tip, a young boy fleeing the witch Mombi with the Powder of Life he stole from her. Tip uses the powder to bring Jack Pumpkinhead to life and also finds the missing shoe; Dorothy gives Tip and Jack directions to the Emerald City, then uses the shoes to go home. Tip brings a sawhorse to life as a steed, but Mombi ambushes them with woodpeckers.

Escaping the witch, Tip and his two companions meet General Jinjur and her child army. The Sawhorse carries its riders to the Emerald City (picking up the Woggle-Bug along the way), but even after they warn the Scarecrow, Jinjur's army conquers the city. Mombi forms an alliance with Jinjur.

Tip and his companions cobble together furniture and a hunting trophy to create the Gump, a flying creature Tip brings to life with the powder. Despite Mombi's interference and some bad luck, they reach Glinda, who tells them the history of King Pastoria and his lost daughter Ozma. They return to the Emerald City where Jinjur unmasks the shapechanged Mombi; the witch turns into a griffin, but can't outrace the Sawhorse. Mombi reveals Tip's true nature and reluctantly transforms him into Ozma. The princess returns to the Emerald City; Scarecrow gives up his crown and rides off on the Sawhorse to see the Tin Woodman.

When Scarecrow falls into a river, Dorothy paddles up on a raft to rescue him. She tells the Scarecrow she and her companion, Billina the chicken, were washed overboard at sea. Together, the threesome escape the malevolent Wheelers and discover Tik-Tok, a wind-up automaton, hidden in a cave. Despite winding down at key moments, Tik-Tok defeats the Wheelers. The travelers visit Princess Langwidere, who demands to swap one of her many heads with Dorothy's. When the girl refuses, Langwidere locks her guests away.

Dorothy has the field mice send word to Ozma, who arrives with the Cowardly Lion in time to save the day. Together, they all head for the Nome kingdom to free the rulers of Ev from the Nome King. After passing a hammer-wielding giant, the group enters the Nome King's domain. He tells them that if they can guess which figures in his collection are the Ev royals, everyone goes free; fail, and the Ozites become statuettes, too.

Dorothy and her friends try but fail to peg the right statues, but Billina overhears the Nome King explain how to find them, and does so, freeing her friends as well. The Scarecrow having collected Billina's eggs—poison to Nomes—the Nomes let the outsiders escape with the king's magic belt.

4. Audio Adaptations

Dorothy decides to visit the Tin Woodman with Scarecrow and the Lion, and sends everyone else back to Oz with a cyclone—which also brings Dorothy's old horse Jim from Kansas. Riding Jim, they head for the Tin Woodman's castle, but find him rusted by the roadside on his way to help with the Nomes.

Jim tries to use magic to take them the rest of the way, but they land in the realm of the Mangaboo vegetable people instead. The Mangaboo sorcerer Gwig orders them thrown into a garden of twisting vines, but the magic belt brings the Wizard of Oz to Dorothy by balloon to help. The Wizard defeats Gwig and the group plucks a replacement for the Mangaboo ruler, but she proves just as unfriendly.

The travelers make a narrow escape which leads them through the cave of the Wind King; the Valley of Voe where everyone is invisible; the country of the wooden Gargoyles; a cave of infant dragons; the country of the Furious Frogs; and a land where wishes come true. The Wizard and Jim wish themselves to the Emerald City, the Lion goes home to his forest and Dorothy wishes for excitement. Another whirlwind carries her, Scarecrow and Tin Woodman away to meet the wandering Shaggy Man.

Traveling with Shaggy they use his magic Love Magnet to charm such menaces as a giant turkey and an army of foxes, but Shaggy still winds up getting a donkey head stuck on his shoulders before the magic belt takes everyone to safety. They escape the man-eating Scoodlers and reach the Deadly Desert, where wonder-builder Johnny Dooit constructs a sandboat for them to cross the desert. They crash on the far side, where Shaggy Man falls into the Truth Pond and returns to normal, but drops the Love Magnet.

The Whimsies, brutes whose pinheads are covered by pasteboard fakes, capture everyone while Shaggy dives for the magnet. The others learn that the Whimsies are part of the Nome King's invasion of Oz. Dorothy ruins the Whimsies' fake heads with a storm summoned by the belt, then teleports her friends away (Shaggy's still in the pond). Racing to Ozma, the group meets Button Bright, a lost boy, but gets captured by an army from the Kingdom of Pot and Pan, also allied with the Nomes.

The group escapes the army, gets caught by the inhumanly strong Growleywogs, escapes again and hides in the Rabbit Kingdom. After wandering through the realms of Bunbury and the Flutterbudgets, they're confronted by the leader of the evil shapeshifting Phanfasms who gives them all the heads of mice. Dorothy uses the magic belt to return to the Truth Pond to restore their heads; Shaggy reveals he was with Dorothy the whole time, transformed into Button Bright. Dooit returns and sends everyone back to the Emerald City in giant soap bubbles, but a popcorn blizzard brings the bubbles down in the Land of Mo. Dorothy cons a flock of Orks into carrying them back to Oz, where the group re-enters the land of wishes and wishes themselves to the Emerald City.

After much discussion with Ozma, the Scarecrow hits on using the Fountain of Oblivion as a trap for the invaders, filling the tunnel they're digging with so much dust their first thought will be to drink. The Nomes and Phanfasms forget their evil ways, and return peaceably to their homes.

This show ran 5:45–6 P.M., Monday, Wednesday and Friday, adapting the stories in serial fashion, running from *Wizard* through *Emerald City*, though not always in a faithful form. There were many repetitive running gags and teasing and banter between the leads, not to mention constant references to Jell-O, which was sponsoring the show: When the Nome King turns the cast into figurines, the narrator points out that the real tragedy is that the characters can no longer eat Jell-O!

Audiences and NBC executives liked the show, but after a year, Jell-O decided to sponsor Jack Benny's radio show instead (a good call; it would prove a classic of radio comedy) and no other sponsor emerged. *Oz* was replaced by *Frank Merriwell*, a series devoted to the eponymous clean-cut collegiate hero.

The Wizard of Oz. Date unknown. CBS.
Credits: Writer, director: John Elkhorn; *Music:* Charles Paul and his Munchkin Music Men.

Two 15-minute episodes of a CBS adaptation are known to exist as recordings, the first running from Dorothy's life in Kansas through celebrating the death of the Wicked Witch of the East, the second, broadcast some three weeks later, in which Dorothy and her friends enter the poppy field and meet the Queen of the Field Mice. The series probably ran five episodes a week.

1939

Maxwell House Good News. 6/39. CBS.
Cast: Judy Garland, Frank Morgan, Ray Bolger, Bert Lahr, Fred Stone.

This was a Maxwell House-sponsored series that did promotional and spotlight episodes focusing on MGM films. This episode previewed the upcoming *The Wizard of Oz* film; it included interviews with cast members and Fred Stone (the Scarecrow in the 1902 stage play), the first public performance of some of the Arlen/Harburg songs; and Fanny Brice playing her popular radio character, Baby Snooks, in a routine in which Daddy reads Snooks *The Wizard of Oz*. The show also threw in several made-up vignettes about backstage life on the film.

Ripley's Believe It or Not. 9/22/39. CBS.

Robert Ripley's *Believe it or Not*, which presented allegedly amazing but true stories to the audience (in newspaper cartoons, books, radio and later a TV series) presented a dramatization in which Baum's widow Maud Baum (playing herself) persuades her husband to go for his dreams and risk everything on publishing a new children's book. Months later, with Christmas approaching, a penniless Baum goes to ask the publisher for an advance on royalties, hoping it will be enough to buy the kids some presents—and comes home with a $13,000 royalty check for *The Wonderful Wizard of Oz*!

Then Mrs. Baum talks to Ripley about her husband, including dismissing the suggestion he based any of his characters on real life, rather than imagination.

This was a spin-off of MGM's PR blitz for *Wizard of Oz*.

1949

Dorothy and the Wizard in Oz. Three 12" 78 rpm records. Capitol.
Cast: Rosemary Rice, Billy Lynn, Patricia Jenkins, LeRoi Operti.
Credits: Adaptation: Ralph Rose; *Producer:* Walter Rivers; *Musical background:* Nathaniel Shilkret and his Concert Orchestra.

A condensed but faithful adaptation with an original song thrown in.

Long before audiobooks on cassette or CD, vinyl records offered the same sort of entertainment (both straight readings and dramatizations), of which this and the other albums in this chapter are typical examples.

1950

Lux Radio Theater: The Wizard of Oz. 12/25/50.
Cast: Host (William Keighley), Dorothy (Judy Garland), Tin Woodman (Herb Vigran), Scarecrow (Hans Conried), Liza Minnelli (herself).
Credits: Music: Rudy Schrager.

This series started in the 1930s (hosted by Cecil B. DeMille) adapting Broadway shows for radio, then moved to the West Coast to adapt movies instead. This adaptation of MGM's *The Wizard of Oz* condensed the film to fit a 60-minute slot, throwing in some added "Look! The Witch!" dialog to compensate for the lack of visuals (according to the *Baum Bugle* it still worked in more of the film's dialog than the official soundtrack album). In an interview at the end of the hour, Garland tells Keighley that the Scarecrow has been teaching Garland's daughter, Liza (who has a cameo), to dance, making the Cowardly Lion quite jealous.

1964

Wizard of Oz. 33⅓ rpm, 6¾". General Electric Show 'n Tell Picturesound.

This recording was made for a special combination record player/slide viewer that advanced 15 frames of pictures as the record told the story.

The Wizard of Oz in Story and Song. 33⅓ rpm, 12". Cricket Records.

Cast: Hanky Pank Players, Cricketone Chorus and Orchestra.

A dramatization including three of the MGM film songs and four original ones.

1964–65

The Wizard of Oz/Babes in Toyland. 33⅓ rpm, 12". MGM Children's Series.

Cast: Gwen Davis, Jack Grimes, Danny Davis.

A dramatization of the book, with four songs from the MGM film.

1965

Walt Disney Presents the Scarecrow of Oz. 33⅓ rpm, 12". Disneyland Records.

Cast: Narrator (Ray Bolger), Scarecrow (Ray Bolger), Glinda/Princess Gloria/Button Bright (Robie Lester), Blinkie (Martha Wentworth), Cap'n Bill/Ork (Dal McKennon).

Credits: Writer: Jimmy Johnson; *Music:* Tutti Camarata.

Songs: Happy Glow; Over the Rainbow.

Trot, Cap'n Bill and the flying Ork travel through an underground river to Oz, where they become embroiled in a battle for the throne of the Jinxland kingdom and for the heart of Princess Gloria. Fortunately, the Scarecrow learns what's happening and saves the day, despite the evil schemes of Blinky the Witch.

Although Disney had obtained rights to all the Baum Oz books after *The Land of Oz*, by the late 1950s the only attempt to adapt them had been the abortive *Rainbow Road to Oz*. Johnson, the head of Disneyland Records, believed Oz was a natural fit with Disney, and decided to adapt some of the books for long-playing records, of which this was the first.

1969

The Wizard of Oz. 33⅓ rpm, 12". Disneyland Records.

Voices: Dorothy (Robie Lester), Scarecrow/Wizard of Oz/Guardian of the Gate (Dal McKennon,), Scarecrow (Mike Sammes, singing voice) Good Witch of the North/Glinda/Wicked Witch of the West (Ginny Tyler), Tin Woodman/Cowardly Lion (Sam Edwards).

Credits: Writer: Jimmy Johnson; *Music:* Tutti Camarata.

A second book-on-record adaptation from Disney. Although the studio had never secured rights to the Baum book, it was now in public domain.

The Cowardly Lion of Oz. 33⅓ rpm. Disneyland Records.

Voices: Cowardly Lion (Sam Edwards, Mike Sammes singing)), Forget-Me-Not/Princess Flora (Robie Lester), Glarm/Prince Paul (Dal McKennon), Glinda/Smarmy (Ginny Tyler, Carol Lombard singing), Cowardly Lion (Mike Sammes, singing voice).

Credits: Writer: Jimmy Johnson; *Music:* Tutti Camarata.

Glinda enlists the Lion's help to head off a war between Oz and the neighboring Prattling Country. With the help of the absent-minded Forget-Me-Not, the Lion successfully defeats the wicked witch Smarmy, thereby staving off the war.

Unlike Disney's other recorded Oz books, this has no relation with the Ruth Plumly Thompson novel. It included several songs written for the never-made *Rainbow Road to Oz* film.

Late 1960s

The Wizard of Oz Returns. 33⅓ rpm. Golden Records.

Voices: Laine Roberts, Connie Zimmet, James Dukas, Tom Cippola, Jerry Roberts.

Credits: Writer: Sid Frank; *Songs:* Ralph Stein; *Music:* Golden Orchestra and chorus.

The Wizard and Dorothy return to Oz, but with both wicked witches dead, the Ozites no longer see the need for a wizard. Dorothy and the Wizard visit the Good Witch of the North along with the Lion (now chief of the Oz Army), Scarecrow (president of Oz University) and Tin Woodman (who writes an advice column). The Good Witch agrees to pose as a Wicked Witch to scare Oz into wanting the Wizard back, but she takes so many Mean Pills she actually turns evil. When she attacks the Emerald City, Dorothy and the Wizard hit her with water, washing the evil out of her.

This album's double-jacket opened into a game board with a spinner and a card with instructions and cut-out playing pieces. The record was rereleased in 1972 as *Further Adventures of the Wizard of Oz*.

Early 1970s

The Tin Woodman of Oz. 33⅓ rpm, 12". Disneyland Records.

Cast: Woot (Ron Howard, Bill Lee singing), Tin Woodman/Cowardly Lion/Hip-po-gy-raf (Sam Edwards), Scarecrow/Tin Soldier (Dal McKennon), Polychrome/Nimmie Amee (Robie Lester, Sally Stevens singing), Ozma/Mrs. Yoop/Jinjur/Lioness/Scarecrowess (Ginny Tyler).

Credits: Writer: Jimmy Johnson; *Music:* Tutti Camarata.

Songs: I Found My True Love; I'm Mrs. Yoop the Yookoohoo;

Woot, a young boy, persuades the Tin Woodman to find and marry Nimmie Amee, the Munchkin girl he loved when he was human. They set off with the Scarecrow, but are trapped with Polychrome by Mrs. Yoop, a giantess and master of shapeshifting. They escape with Ozma's help and track Nimmie Amee, now married to the murderous Captain Fyter, the Tin Soldier (a cold-blooded killer in this version). In the end, not only does Tin Woodman get married, but so do Woot, Polychrome, the Scarecrow and the Cowardly Lion.

The last of Disney's Oz records, with (obviously) a radically different ending from the book. And yes, that is the famous Ron Howard, performing between *The Andy Griffith Show* and *Happy Days*.

1972–73

The Wizard of Oz. 33⅓ rpm. United Artists Records.

The Famous Theatre Company, backed by the Hollywood Studio Orchestra, performs a dramatization of the book, in which Dorothy lands in Oz (met by the Good Witch of the South) and acquires her friends on the way to the Emerald City, where the Wizard appears as a phantom voice and sends them to destroy the Wicked Witch of the West. The witch enslaves Dorothy and her friends with the golden cap (no Winged Monkeys), but when she decides to burn the Scarecrow, Dorothy douses him and melts the witch.

The Scarecrow gives Dorothy the cap which takes them back to the Emerald City but doesn't have the power to take her home. After the Wizard is exposed as a humbug, he has Dorothy use the cap to visit the Good Witch of the North, who tells her the power of the silver shoes to take her home.

This recording was released as part of UA's Tale-Spinners for Children line.

The Wonderful Wizard of Oz. Jabberwocky.

Voices: Cowardly Lion (Terry McGovern), Narrator (Fay DeWitt).

Credits: Writer: Patty Mortensen; *Producer:* Bob Lewis.

This adaptation (reissued in the early 1990s), is long enough to include many episodes early books-on-tape omit (the China Country, the Hammerheads, etc.).

One reviewer found the voices and the production good, despite several dated one-liners referring to then-contemporary commercials (such as Alka-Seltzer's "I can't believe I ate the whole thing!" catchphrase).

1985

Walt Disney Pictures Return to Oz. 33⅓ rpm record, or cassette tape.
  Cast: Narrator: William Woodson. With Dana Howarton, Pat Lentz, Linda Gary, Corey Burton, Tony Pope, Bob Telson, Arthur Burghardt.
  Credits: Produced by Ted Kryczko.

A recreation of the Disney *Return to Oz* film on LP and cassette.

1995

The Wizard of Oz. Piglet Press.

This small press released an audiobook dramatization of the book, followed later by a dramatization of *The Emerald City of Oz*.

1996

The Wizard of Oz. BBC Radio 4.
  Cast: Wicked Witch of the West (Maureen Lipman). With Philip Franks, Kerry Shale.

Another radio adaptation of the Baum book, later released on audiobook.

2000

Adventures in Odyssey: The Great Wishy Woz. 10/28, 11/4/00. Kids Radio.
  Voices: Dotty (Mandy Straussberg), Manny Kin (Tom Riley), Metal Guy (Bernard Walton), Mystical Mountain Lion (Jack Allen), Great Wishy Woz, Aunt Bea, Fairy Oddmother, Nono, Wicked and Mean and Generally Not Very Nice Woman, Leopold, Melvin Nerfwiddle, Murray, Mr. Iam.
  Credits: Director/writer: Mandy Straussberg; Music: John Campbell; Songs composed by John Beebee, arranged by John Campbell.

Songs: Somewhere; Follow the Big Fat Road; If I Only Had Some Smarts; We're Off; Always.

Young Dotty is horrified to realize that she and her dog Nono are staying with Aunt Bee because her parents are getting divorced. She's still in shock when a tornado strikes the farm, knocking her out. She wakes up in Littleland, where people believe in doing and thinking as little as possible. Kindly Fairy Oddmother gives Dotty some ruby tennis shoes and advises her to follow the Big Fat Road to the Great Wishy Woz; at all costs she should avoid the Little Narrow Gate used only by narrow-minded people, and the Fisherman who lurks on the Big Fat Road.

On the road, Dotty does meet the seemingly pleasant Fisherman, who gives her a whistle for emergencies. She also meets shop-window dummy Manny Kin, Metal Guy — magnetized to a lamp-post by the Wicked, Mean and Generally Not Very Nice Woman — and Mystic Mountain Lion who babbles pop mysticism with Yoda-style grammar. Seeking brains, love and mystic power, they join Dorothy to petition the Wizard.

In the Green and Environmentally Correct City, the quartet meet the gigantic Woz, who agrees to grant their wishes once they realize they can only find brains, heart and enlightenment through personal effort. To prove this, they have until sunset to bring back a book of Philosophy, a Valentine's Day card, a candle from the Temple of Eternal Truth and a compass (symbolic of Dorothy's need to find home).

They obtain the book (and many more) from the library, a card from the Mall of Pleasure ("Love is loving yourself enough to do what feels good"), a flame-thrower from the Temple, which can't spare the candles (believing true illumination comes from within, they forgot to pay the light bill) and a compass that points in all directions "so you're free to go anywhere you want." When the group returns to the Woz, he tries brushing them off, and they expose him as a fake.

When they head back down the Big Fat Road, the Not Very Nice Woman appears and claims them as slaves—as is everyone in the realm, from the Littles to the Woz. Dotty calls on the Fairy Oddmother, but the Woman reveals she played that role to deceive them; as the Woman summons her army of flying pigs, Dotty thinks of the Fisherman's whistle, blows it, and the Woman shrinks to nothingness.

Dotty realizes the Wee Skinny Road must be the real way home, but Scarecrow can't get his books through the gate, Metal Guy's huge Valentine card won't fit either, and the Lion believes he has all he needs. Passing with Nono onto the Wee Skinny Road, she meets the Fisherman—Mr. I Am—who makes it clear he's the only one who can take her home. Dotty follows I Am into the teeth of a terrible storm—and wakes in Aunt Be's house, happy now that she knows she'll never be alone again. For those who don't get the message, the host spells out that no matter what alternatives people think there are, Jesus is the only way to reach Heaven.

The conservative Focus on the Family organization produced this Christian twist on Oz (Baum, no admirer of organized Christianity, would probably not have been amused) as two *Adventures in Odyssey* episodes; the writer said she'd always wanted to stage a musical, but realized a radio musical would be more cost-effective. The "narrow road" is an old metaphor for the difficulty of reaching heaven, and the show takes numerous potshots at secular and non–Christian alternatives. The Woz's statement about attaining brain, heart and courage through personal growth may be a shot at Baum himself—some fundamentalists have attacked *Wizard of Oz* precisely for suggesting people can grow and develop without divine help.

2000

The Wonderful Wizard of Oz. National Public Radio.

Cast: Wizard (Harry Anderson), Dorothy (Michelle Trachtenberg), Scarecrow (Rene Auberjonois), Tin Woodman (Nestor Serrano), Cowardly Lion (Robert Guillame), Glinda the Good (Annette Bening), Wicked Witch (Phyliss Diller), Queen of the Field Mice (Joanna Gleason), Guardian of the Gates (John Goodman), Munch the Munchkin (Mark Hamill), Soldier With Green Whiskers (Maurice La Marche), Aunt Em (Michael Learned), King of the Winged Monkeys (Mako), Toto (Phil Proctor), Creatures of Oz (Dee Bradley Baker), Mrs. Quadling (Candace Barrett), Uncle Henry (Raye Birk), Old Crow (Norman Corwin), Hammerheads (Firesign Theatre), China Milkmaid (Jennifer Hale), Good Witch of the North (Alison Larkin), Mrs. Stork (Edie McClurg), Glinda's girl (Lara Jill Miller), Mrs. Farmer (Melinda Peterson), Mr. Joker (Rob Paulsen).

Credits: Directors, producers: David Ossman, Judith Walcutt; *Adapted:* David Ossman.

NPR staged this unabridged adaptation to celebrate the 100th anniversary of the book; proceeds went to benefit the Los Angeles Children's Museum. The audiotape/CD version includes an interview with Oz admirer Ray Bradbury.

The Wonderful World of Oz. 9/10/00, 10/8/00, 10/29/00, 11/6/00, 11/20/00. Colonial Radio Theatre.

Voice Cast: (in order of production) *Dorothy and the Wizard in Oz*: L. Frank Baum/Prince/Gump (Jerry Robbins), Announcer/Jim (George Fennell), Dorothy (Amy Strack), Zeb (Chris Bradley), Eureka (Diane Capen), Gwig (Armand Fillian), Messenger (David Driscoll), Wizard (Robert Mackie), Princess (Cynthia Pape), Piglet (Leigh Ann Price), Advisor/Father/Hungry Tiger (David Driscoll), Child (Courtney Cameron), Mother (Michelle Mulvaney), Soft voice/Servant (Deborah Roy), Piglets (David Driscoll, Judson Pierce, Leigh Ann Price), Little Dragon (Jordan Russell), Jellia Jamb (Ashley Ayers), Ozma (Leigh Ann Price), Scarecrow (Tom Berry), Tin Woodman (Frederick Rice), Billina (Diane Lind), Woggle-Bug (Lincoln Clark), Servant (Deborah Roy), Sawhorse (Judson Pierce), Cowardly Lion (David Krinitt).

Wizard of Oz: Dorothy (Amy Strack), Scarecrow (Tom Berry), Cowardly Lion (David Krinitt), Tin Woodman (Frederick Rice), Toto (Diane Capen), Narrator (Cynthia Pape), Aunt Em (Marcia Friedman), Uncle Henry (Jerry Robbins), Witch of the North (Diane Capen), Munchkins (Chris Bradley, Marcia Friedman, Joseph Zamparelli, Jr.), Boq (Bill Hammond), Farmers (Nick Aalerud, Eddie Bennett, Joseph Zamparelli, Jr.), Stork (Diane Capen), Queen of the Field Mice (Deborah Roy), Mice (Nick Aalerud, Eddie Bennett), Woman (Marcia Friedman), Husband (Joseph Zamparelli, Jr.), Guardian (Armand Fillian), Soldier (Joseph Zamparelli, Jr.), Oz as giant head (Robert Mackie), Oz as lady (Teresa Goding), Wicked Witch of the West (Diane Lind), Lord Growler (Joseph Zamparelli, Jr.), Captain Croaker (Peter Mancini), Winkies (Bill Hammond, Chris Bradley), General Clutcher (Joseph Zamparelli, Jr.), Monkey (Chris Bradley), Oz (Robert Mackie), Milkmaid (Marcia Friedman), China Princess (Deborah Roy), Mr. Joker (Peter Mancini), Tiger (Bill Hammond), Girl (Diane Capen), Glinda (Deborah Roy)

Road to Oz: Dorothy (Amy Strack), Shaggy Man (Joseph Zamparelli, Jr.), Button Bright (Evan Cole), Polychrome (Shonna McEachern), Captain (Barbara Dempsey), King Dox (Doug Rainy), Counselor (George Fennell), Donkeys (Tom Berry, Armand Fillian), Kik-a-Bray (Robert Mackie), Allegro da Capo (Jeffery Gage), Scoodlers (Bill Hammond, Doug Rainy, George Fennell, Barbara Dempsey, Tom Berry), Queen

An illustration by W.W. Denslow decorates the cover of Colonial Radio's *Wonderful World of Oz* audiobook set. (Photograph credit: Colonial Radio.)

Scoodler (Barbara Dempsey), Johnny Dooit (Bill Hammond), Tik-Tok (Bill Hammond), Billina (Diane Lind), Ozma (Leigh Ann Price), Jack Pumpkinhead (Jerry Robbins), Hungry Tiger (Joseph Zamparelli, Jr.), Guardian of the Gates (Armand Fillian), Jellia Jamb (Ashley Ayers), Servant (Tom Berry), Tin Woodman (Frederick Rice), Cowardly Lion (David Krinnit), Scarecrow (Tom Berry), Woggle-Bug (Lincoln Clark), Wizard (Robert Mackie), High Chamberlain (George Fennell), King Dough (Robert Mackie), Santa Claus (Joseph Zamparelli, Jr.), Candy Man (Tom Berry).

Ozma of Oz: Announcer (George Fennell), Dorothy (Amy Strack), Tik-Tok/Helmsman (Bill Hammond), Billina (Diane Lind), Princess Langwidere (Shana Dirik), Ozma (Leigh Ann Price), Tin Woodman (Frederick Rice), Scarecrow (Tom Berry), Cowardly Lion/Sailor (David Krinnit), Hungry Tiger/Wheeler/General (Joseph Zamparelli, Jr.), Roquat (Doug Rainey), Girls (Kristen Cameron, Courtney Cameron, Jordan Russell), Captain Hill (Tom Berry), Maid (Diane Capen), Colonel/Private (Jerry Robbins), Stewards (Jerry Robbins, David Krinnit), Evring (Evan Cole), Queen of Ev (Lis Adams), Jinjur (Kate Mahoney), Glinda (Deborah Roy).

Land of Oz: L. Frank Baum/Soldier/Jack Pumpkinhead/Guard/Gump (Jerry Robbins), Announcer (George Fennell), Tip (Jonathan Randell Silver), Mombi (Shana Dirik), Sawhorse (Judson Pierce), Scarecrow (Tom Berry), Jellia Jamb (Ashley Ayers), General Jinjur (Kate Mahoney), Tin Woodman (Frederick Rice), H.M. Woggle-Bug, T.E. (Lincoln Clark), Professor/Sad Man (Bill Hammond), Captains (Diane Capen, Marjorie Fairfax), Guardian of the Gate (Armand Fillian), Queen of the Field Mice/Glinda (Deborah Roy), Girls (Leigh Ann Price, Diane Capen).

Credits: Director, writer, producer: Jerry Robbins; *Music composed by:* Jeffrey Gage; *Executive producer:* Mark Vander Berg.

This was an 11½ hour, 10-cassette adaptation of the first five Oz books, with *Emerald City of Oz* recorded later, but at press time, unreleased. Robbins said the inspiration was his cousin Samantha's demand for Oz-related items after seeing the MGM movie, which eventually sent him back to the original Baum books. Robbins then decided to adapt them for Colonial Radio Theatre, which had previously focused on dramas

Colonial Radio's Jerry Robbins in performance for the *Wonderful World of Oz.* (Photograph credit: Colonial Radio.)

taken from American historical topics (e.g., the Alamo, Gettysburg).

This was first recorded in March of 2000, then rerecorded with different voice casting. The shows were recorded in single sessions, as if performed live (although the cast did stop for retakes). Recording took three to four hours; editing took up to two weeks per book.

The shows were released as audiobooks in February of 2001, but with running times of over two hours, haven't been broadcast on radio, except for a *Radio Works* condensed version mentioned below.

Robbins said he hopes to release the entire Oz series by Baum eventually.

2001

Radio Works. 9/10/01.

A 30-minute version of Colonial's *Dorothy and the Wizard in Oz* aired on this show repeatedly starting on this date.

2002

The Emerald City of Oz. 7/8/02. Colonial Radio Theatre.

Voice Cast: Announcer/Tik-Tok (Bill Hammond), L. Frank Baum/Jack Pumpkinhead (Jerry Robbins), Nome King/Flatiron/Pop Over (J.T. Turner), Guard/Rye Loafer (Jim Murphy), Kaliko/Banker/Cowardly Lion/Owl Man (David Krinitt), Blug/C. Bunn (Susan Sanders), Dorothy (Amy Strack), Uncle Henry (Rik Pierce), Aunt Em (Cynthia Pape), Ozma/Captain/Graham Gem/Jellia Jamb (Leigh Berry), Crinkle (Lis Adams), Guph/ Corkscrew/Can Opener/B. Pudding (Shana Dirik), Hungry Tiger/Shaggy Man/Masher (Joseph Zamparelli, Jr.), Billina (Diane Lind), Counselor/Whimsy Chief/Sawhorse/ Judge Sifter/Roll (Judson Pierce), Gallipoot (Sam Donato), Counselors (David Krinitt, Tom Berry, Jim Murphy), Wizard of Oz (Robert Mackie), Omby Amby (Tom Berry), H. M. Woggle-Bug, T.E. (Lincoln Clark), Soldiers (Susan Sanders, Lis Adams), Miss Cuttenclip/Rolling Pin/Boston Bun (Jennifer Powers), Foremost (Jim Murphy), Cook/Capt. Dipp (Lis Adams), Chigglewitz/Kettle/Muffin (Sam Donato), Spoons (Leigh Berry, Jennifer Powers), Toto (Diane Capen), Kleaver (Jim Murphy), Paprica (Frederick Rice), Karver (Susan Sanders), Chop Knife (Tim Berry), Saucepan (Robert Mackie), Kitchen Fork (Lis Adams), Rigmaroles (Shana Dirik, Sam Donato), Flutterbudgets (Lis Adams, Jim Murphy, Susan Sanders, Joseph Zamparelli, Jr., Jennifer Powers), Tin Woodman (Frederick Rice), Scarecrow (Tom Berry), Glinda (Lis Adams).

Credits: Director, writer, producer: Jerry Robbins; *Music composed by:* Jeffrey Gage; *Executive producer:* Mark Vander Berg; *Foley crew:* Diane Capen, David Driscoll; *Distributor:* Penton Overseas, Carlsbad, CA.

Colonial Radio's Jeffrey Gage in performance for the *Wonderful World of Oz*. (Photograph credit: Colonial Radio.)

Colonial's unreleased follow-up to *The World of Oz*, adapting the sixth Oz book.

2003

The Wizard of Oz. Monterey SoundWorks.

Another full-cast audio adaptation of the book.

5

Film and Video: Creative Works

1910

The Wonderful Wizard of Oz. 3/24/10. One reel, 1,000 feet, b&w.

Cast: Dorothy (Bebe Daniels), Scarecrow (Hobart Bosworth, probably), Tin Woodman (Robert Leonard, probably), with Eugenie Besserer, Winifred Greenwood, Lillian Leighton, Olive Cox.

Credits: Director: Otis Turner (poss.); *Writers:* L. Frank Baum, Otis Turner; *Producer:* William Nicholas Selig; *From:* Selig Polyscope Company.

The film opens with Dorothy and some farm-folk chasing after a mule, only to have it turn and chase them. Dorothy breaks away to play ball with Toto, then a Scarecrow talks to her. Initially shocked, she helps him down from his pole; he tries to walk, but his clumsy efforts scare off the nearby farm animals.

A cyclone drives Dorothy, the Scarecrow, Toto and some of the animals to hide in a haystack, but the whirlwind sweeps them all up and drops them into Oz. Cut to the Wizard of Oz in his palace, yearning to return to Omaha. He proclaims that whoever frees him from the power of Momba the witch can rule Oz in his place, but Momba flies in on her broomstick and forces him back on the throne.

The Cowardly Lion attacks Dorothy; Glinda turns Toto into a bulldog and the Lion collapses in fear, then agrees to join Dorothy. They find the rusted Tin Woodman, who sets everyone dancing with a piccolo tune as soon as he's oiled up.

Momba and her monsters capture the travelers. The witch tries enslaving Dorothy, but the girl tosses a bucket of water over Momba with the usual consequences. The Tin Woodman breaks free of Momba's prison and drives off the witch's soldiers. The Scarecrow realizes that Dorothy can claim the throne of Oz, but when they reach the Emerald City, Dorothy takes the crown from the Wizard and passes it to the Scarecrow. The city seamstresses stitch together a balloon, but the Wizard leaves without Dorothy. The film ends with a big production number and Dorothy still stranded in Oz.

After Baum's *Fairylogue and Radio Plays* tour left him $3,000 in debt to Selig Polyscope Co., he gave the company the rights to adapt the books in *Fairylogue* for the big screen (contrary to some reports, Selig did not simply rerelease the *Fairylogue* films). This slapstick version shows the 1902 musical was still influential: the Tin Woodman plays a piccolo, Scarecrow and Tin Woodman clown together a lot and some of the costumes and scenery also show the musical's influence.

Dorothy and the Scarecrow in Oz. 4/14/10. One reel, 1000 feet, b&w.

Cast: Dorothy (Bebe Daniels, probably).

Credits: (alleged) *Director:* Otis Turner; *Writer:* L. Frank Baum (based on *Wizard of Oz* and *Land of Oz*); *Producer:* William Nicholas Selig; *From:* Selig Polyscope Company.

As the film opens, Dorothy and her friends are still living in the Emerald City (with the Wizard, despite leaving in the first film). Together they journey through Oz, still hoping to get their wishes granted. An earthquake hurls them into the underground Glass City of the Mangaboos, where Dorothy picks the plant-people a new princess. She and her companions are driven into a black pit, but escape and meet Jim the cab-horse. (Annotation based on reviews in *Motion Picture World*, culled by Dick Martin.)

Other sources say this included the field of poppies, a battle with a giant spider and Glinda sending Dorothy home. No trace of this film or the next two survives today.

The Land of Oz. 5/19/10. One reel, 1000 feet, b&w.

Cast: Dorothy (Bebe Daniels, probably).

Credits: Writer: L. Frank Baum; *Producer:* William Nicolas Selig; *From:* Selig Polyscope Company.

Dorothy and her friends, along with the Wizard, return from the Mangaboo realm to the Emerald City. They encounter General Jinjur's all-girl revolutionary army, and the army's maneuvers generate a "spectacle worthy of the best artists of picturedom." (Annotation based on reviews in Motion Picture World, culled by Dick Martin.)

Another lost production from Selig.

John Dough and the Cherub. 12/19/10. One reel, 1000 feet, b&w.

Credits: Writer: L. Frank Baum (based on the book); *Producer:* William Nicolas Selig. *From:* Selig Polyscope Company.

A baker unwittingly mixes a magic elixir into his life-size gingerbread man, bringing "John Dough" to life. After Dough is accidentally carried off on a Fourth of July rocket, he meets the feisty kid Chick the Cherub. Their adventures culminate in Dough becoming a king, fulfilling a prophecy Ozma made to Chick.

Another lost film from Selig. The combined profits from the four one-reelers didn't wipe out Baum's debt to the company, so he still owed them $1,000 when he declared bankruptcy the following year.

1914

The Patchwork Girl of Oz. 8/6/14 (premiere, Los Angeles Athletic Club), 9/28/14 (general release). Five reels, b&w, 59 mins.

Cast: Scraps, the Patchwork Girl (Pierre Couderc), Ojo (Violet McMillan), Unc Nunkie (Frank Moore), Cowardly Lion/Tottenhot (Hal Roach), Dr. Pipt (Raymond Russell), Margolotte (Leontine Dranet), Jesseva (Bobbie Gould), Danx (Dick Rosson), Mewel/Woozy/The Zoop (Fred Woodward), Jinjur (Marie Wayne), Soldier with the Green Whiskers (Frank Bristol), Ozma (Jessie May Walsh), Wizard of Oz (Todd Wright), Scarecrow (Herbert Glennon), Tin Woodman (Lon Musgrave), Bell Ringer (Juanita Jansen), Rozyn the Fiddler (Ben Deeley), Tottenhot (Harold Lloyd), Hungry Tiger (Andy Anderson), Royal Chamberlain (William Cook)

Credits: Director: J. Farrell MacDonald; *Writer:* L. Frank Baum (based on the book); *Assistant director:* Harold Ostrom; *Producers:* L. Frank Baum, Louis F. Gottschalk; *Executive producers:* Clarence Rundel, Harry F. Haldeman; *Cinematography:* James A. Crosby; *Music:* Louis F. Gottschalk; *From:* Oz Film Company, Paramount Pictures.

Faced with starvation, young Ojo convinces his Unc Nunkie that they should leave their forest home for the Emerald City where food is plentiful. Elsewhere in Munchkinland, the sorcerer Dr. Pipt is hard at work finishing up a batch of his wondrous Powder of Life, while his wife magically sews together a life-size patchwork doll to become her servant once the powder animates her. Jesseva Pipt, meanwhile, receives a marriage proposal from young Danx.

Ojo and Nunkie arrive at the Pipts', trailed by the aggressive donkey Mewel. Jesseva's friends chase off the donkey while Ojo and Nunkie are invited to watch "Scraps" come to life. Ojo secretly stuffs magic powders of intelligence into Scraps's head, so that she'll be more than the stupid drone Margolotte plans to create.

When Scraps comes to life, she accidentally spills a petrification potion over Danx, Nunkie and Margolotte. Pipt sends Ojo, Jesseva and Danx in search of the ingredients for a cure, shrinking Danx so Jesseva can carry him in a basket.

Scraps befriends the bizarrely cubic Woozy, whose tail-hairs are one of the ingredients; since they're too strong to yank out, the Woozy joins the journey. After passing through an illusory wall around the Emerald City they meet Jinjur, a girl who falls in love with Danx's figurine. When Ojo illegally plucks a six-leaf clover for the cure, Jinjur has them arrested and snatches Danx away. Scraps reclaims Danx, but Ozma's all-girl army captures the others and marches them into Ozma's throne room.

Dr. Pipt's quest for some of the ingredients leads him into the House of Magic with its animated furniture. After a brief look at the Lonesome Zoop (a scaly humanoid that runs around scaring people for no reason), we see Pipt enter Hoppertown, whose one-legged inhabitants decide to amputate his "extra" leg. Fortunately Scraps comes running from Jinjur and persuades the Hoppers to take her leg off instead.

Outside Hoppertown, Pipt sews Scraps's leg back on; they meet the Tottenhot tribesmen, then Jinjur recaptures Danx. Pipt and Scraps press on and find the next ingredient, water from a Dark Well, in the land of the Horners. The duo head back to the Emerald City.

Ojo and the others are brought before a royal jury, including Scarecrow and Tin Woodman. When the Scarecrow steps outside to think, he meets Scraps, and the two stuffed figures hit it off at once, even trading a kiss. When Pipt arrives, Ozma gives him permission to brew the antidote. The Wizard transports Margolette and Nunkie to the throne room and when Jinjur enters, Pipt reclaims Danx as well. Scraps and the Scarecrow enter, cuddling, Pipt restores everyone to normal and happily-ever-after is on the way.

Baum and some of his friends founded Oz Film Manufacturing in 1914, hoping to adapt his Oz books and plays for the screen. This adaptation adds romance, irrelevant special effects and the equally irrelevant Zoop to the original storyline; Baum may have been trying once again to duplicate the whimsy of the 1902 *Wizard of Oz* musical, but this kind of fairy-tale fluff was out of fashion by 1914.

Like many independent production companies, then and now, Oz Film also had a hard time finding a distributor; Paramount eventually agreed to handle the film, but it was perceived strictly as children's film (not the last time this would bedevil an Oz film), and box office was poor. Because of that, Oz Film was unable to find a distributor for *His Majesty, the Scarecrow of Oz* or *The Magic Cloak of Oz* (Box Office Attraction Co. may have briefly distributed the former film, but if so, withdrew it promptly).

The company switched gears, turning to adult fare starting with *The Last Egyptian*, while working on a series of fantasy one-reelers as well.

The copyright on *Patchwork Girl* was later renewed under the title *The Ragged Girl of Oz* but it wasn't released under that title.

The Last Egyptian. 12/7/14. Five reels, b&w.

Cast: Kara (J. Farrell MacDonald), Winston Bey (Howard Davies), Viscount Consinor (Jefferson Osborne), Lord Roane (Frank Moore), Tadros (J. Charles Hayden), Sebbet (Fred Woodward), Sheik Antur (Pierre Couderc), Aneth Consinor (Vivian Reed), Nepthys (Jane Urban), Princess Hatacha (Mai Wells), Mrs. Everingham (Ora Buckley), Tilga (Mrs. Emmons).

Credits: Director: J. Farrell MacDonald; *Writer:* L. Frank Baum (based on his book); *Producers:* L. Frank Baum, Louis F. Gottschalk; *Assistant director:* Harold Ostrom; *Executive producers:* Clarence Rundel, Harry F. Haldeman; *Cinematography:* James A. Crosby; *From:* Oz Film Manufacturing Company.

Kara, last descendant of the Egyptian pharaohs, lives in poverty with his grandmother Hatatcha. Dying, Hatatcha extracts a vow of revenge from her grandson on Lord Roane, the Englishman who seduced and abandoned her years before. Hatatcha also tells Kara of a lost tomb; after her death, Kara takes enough wealth from the tomb to buy a slave, Nepthys, from the trader Tadros, and to travel to Cairo and set himself up as a prince.

Kara meets Roane, his son Consinor and his granddaughter Aneth in Cairo. After Kara wins two thousand pounds gambling with Consinor — money Consinor can't repay — Kara demands Aneth's hand in payment, planning to ruin her with a fake marriage as Roane ruined Hatatcha. Aneth agrees but her sweetheart, Winston, learns Kara's scheme from Tadros and persuades Aneth to fly with him.

Kara sends a band of Arabs to capture them, but the Arabs demand payment before turning over the girl. Kara returns to the tomb for money, but Consinor follows him, attacks him in the tomb and leaves the injured Egyptian to die. When Consinor reemerges, however, Nepthys mistakes him for Kara and kills him. Tadros arranges the lovers' freedom, and they leave free of the menace of the last Egyptian.

After the failure of *Patchwork Girl*, the Oz Film Manufacturing Company shifted to contemporary melodrama, adapting *The Last Egyptian* from Baum's 1908 anonymous novel and planning to follow it up with *Daughters of Destiny* and *The Fate of a Crown*, written by Baum under his Schuyler Staunton pseudonym. Distributors didn't bite, believing audiences would assume any Oz Film product was another fairy-tale fantasy.

Late in 1914, Alliance finally struck an agreement to release *The Last Egyptian* and to assign Oz Film's future productions (suffice to say, more Oz adaptations were not on the agenda). Production at Oz Film stopped for several months, while management changed hands (P. Sumner Brown replaced Baum as president, and Baum's son Frank became general manager), and the studio rented out its facilities to other companies. In March, 1915, the company, now known as Dramatic Films, began work on another drama, *The Gray Nun of Belgium*.

His Majesty, The Scarecrow of Oz [Also known as The New Wizard of Oz]. 10/5/14 (preview); 3/15 general release. Five reels, b&w, 59–82 mins.

Cast: Dorothy (Violet McMillan), Scarecrow (Frank Moore), Tin Woodman (Pierre Couderc), Cowardly Lion/Animals/Lonesome Zoop (Fred Woodward), King Krewl (Raymond Russell), Googly-Goo (Arthur Smollet), Wizard of Oz (J. Charles Hayden), Pon (Todd Wright), Princess Gloria (Vivian Reed), Mombi (Mai Wells), Button-Bright (Mildred Harris).

Credits: Director: J. Farrell MacDonald; *Writer:* L. Frank Baum (based on *Wizard of Oz*); *Producers:* Louis F. Gottschalk, L. Frank Baum; *Executive producers:* Clarence Rundel, Harry F. Haldeman; *Assistant director:* Harold Ostrom; *Cinematography, optical effects:* James A. Crosby; *Music:* Louis F. Gottschalk; *From:* Oz Film Manufacturing Company.

King Krewl of Oz demands his daughter, Gloria, wed the foppish courtier, Googly-Goo, who has bribed Krewl generously for Gloria's hand. Gloria, however, loves only Pon, the gardener's boy. Krewl discovers this and forbids their love; Pon flees, but Gloria vows to stay true.

Cut to a new Scarecrow, coming to life in the cornfield, then to Dorothy — present in Oz without explanation — sobbing her heart out. Mombi (who looks like Denslow's Blinky in *Wizard of Oz*) captures Dorothy for her scullery maid. When Krewl asks the witch to destroy Gloria's love for Pon, Mombi throws Dorothy out of the house in order to work.

Dorothy and Pon watch as Gloria defies her father again. Mombi and her coven force Gloria to drink a potion that freezes her heart, then the coven drives Dorothy and Pon away. Unfortunately they also pick on a wandering donkey, which retaliates by driving Mombi out of her house. Gloria wanders off listlessly and spurns Pon when he finds her.

Dorothy drags Pon away, with Gloria following. Dorothy takes the Scarecrow off his pole, whereupon he tries and fails to melt Gloria's heart. Mombi catches up with them and rips out the Scarecrow's stuffing, but Dorothy and Pon repair him after she leaves.

Accompanied by a lost boy named Button Bright, the group arrives at the Tin Woodman's castle and finds the owner rusted outside. Dorothy oils him up, and when Mombi reappears, he chops off her head. Mombi soon restores herself, however, and angrily turns Pon into a kangaroo. After a brief clip of the Cowardly Lion fighting the Lonesome Zoop (from the *Patchwork Girl* film), we cut back to the Tin Woodman, who vows to overthrow Krewl and set Gloria on the throne. The group sets off on a raft, but the pole snags and hooks Scarecrow off the raft in midstream. After a waterlogged encounter with a mermaid, Scarecrow hitches a ride with a crow that takes him to the others on land.

The group encounters a hostile cow, then the upward flowing Wall of Water, then the Wizard, whose wagon is drawn by a wooden horse. When Mombi appears, the Wizard magically traps her in a can of preserved sandwiches, rewriting the label to read "preserved witch." Dorothy and her friends travel on, meet the Cowardly Lion and befriend him, but Krewl's guards capture Gloria and take her back to the king.

When the good guys reach the castle, the Scarecrow, unaffected by arrows, storms the castle, buying the others time to come over the wall. Krewl yields his crown to the straw man. The Wizard arrives and Mombi agrees to restore Gloria's heart in return for freedom. Googly-Goo is imprisoned, the Wizard restores Pon to normal, Pon and Gloria marry and bow with the others to His Majesty, King Scarecrow.

This film amounts to Baum's own adaptation of *Wizard of Oz*, though it uses Mombi instead of the Witch of the West. Although tighter-written than most of Oz Films' output, it still shows the weakness for throwaway bits (the Zoop, the mermaid, etc.) that bedeviled the other adaptations. Baum later novelized the story as *The Scarecrow of Oz*.

Unlike *Patchwork Girl of Oz*, this film received enthusiastic reviews at its 1914 preview, but even publicizing it as an adaptation of the hit 1902 musical (which it wasn't) didn't attract a distributor. As part of its agreement with Oz Film, Alliance released the film at last in 1915 as *The New Wizard of Oz*, a name that lasted through 1920. Sales were still poor, which probably led the company to dissociate itself further from Oz by changing its name to Dramatic Features Company.

1915

The Country Circus. 9/10/15. One reel, b & w.

Cast: Claribel (Violet McMillan), Circus animals (Fred Woodward).

Credits: Writer: L. Frank Baum; *From:* Oz Film Company, released by Universal Film Manufacturing Co.

Young Violet, who's been forbidden to visit the circus, dreams of sneaking into the big top disguised as a boy. Here she befriends the animals only to be confronted by a trainer who makes her admit to being a girl. Instead of sending her home, though, the circus folk give her a grand tour; then she wakes up.

While working on *The Last Egyptian*, Oz Film also produced *Violet's Dreams*, a series of shorts about a young girl's dream adventures (though Violet was the actress's name, not the character's). Baum had used a similar concept in several stories published under his Laura Bancroft pseudonym. *Magic Bon Bons*, based on one of Baum's *American Fairy Tales*, was made first, but released later.

Like most of the studio's output, this film failed to find a distributor; Oz Film sold the shorts outright to Victor (which at one point planned to label the series *The Dream Girl*); Victor released them through Universal.

The Magic Bon Bons. 10/22/15.

Cast: Claribel (Violet McMillan).

Claribel learns Dr. Daws has magic bon bons, each of which will turn the user into a gifted singer, dancer, actor, pianist, etc. She buys a box of the wonder candies, then loses it. It winds up at a friend's house where her family samples the box and starts compulsively performing. When Claribel visits her friend, she sends the family to Dr. Daws for an antidote, takes the remaining chocolates to make herself multi-talented — and wakes.

Based on a story in *American Fairy Tales*, this was the first filmed in the series.

The Gray Nun of Belgium. 4/26/15 (announced release date); five reels, b & w.

Cast: The Gray Nun (Cathrine Countiss), Mother Superior (Betty Pierce). With: David Proctor.

Credits: Director: Francis Powers; *Writer:* L. Frank Baum (possibly); *Producer:* Frank J. Baum; *Assistant director:* Nat G. Deverich; *From:* Dramatic Feature Films.

A nun helps Allied soldiers escape from behind German lines during the Great War.

Shot in two weeks, this was the first production from Oz Film in its new identity as Dramatic Feature Films. Unfortunately, Alliance Films, though it had supported the project, decided not to distribute it, possibly because the quick shoot resulted in a poor product or exhibitors still didn't want to touch an Oz Film, even after the renaming.

Whatever the reason, the company had now failed to sell films to either adults or children. It gave up its charter in the summer of 1915, though its unreleased fantasies would eventually make it to the screen. It is generally believed *The Gray Nun* no longer exists, but there are unconfirmed reports that it turned up on video in the early 1980s.

Pies and Poetry.

Cast: Betty Pierce.

Credits: From: Dramatic Feature Films.

This one-reeler is another lost and never-released film, probably a slapstick comedy.

1917

Like Babes in the Woods. 8/6/17. Two reels, b&w.

Cast: Claribel (Violet McMillan), Billie (Gordon Griffin), Hank the Mule (Fred Woodward), Fortune Teller (Jack Nelson).

Credits: Directors: Chester M. Franklin, Sidney Franklin. *Writer:* Karl R. Coolidge; *Producer:* George Cochrane.

A fortune-teller gives Violet and her friend Billie what she claims is a wishing ring. When Violet wishes a bearskin rug to life, the bear chases them into the woods. They wish to become the "Babes in the Woods," from the fairytale and find themselves barefoot and in rags. A tiger approaches, but just as in the tale, the forest birds hide them in leaves and then distract the tiger. Hank brays, and wakes them from their dream.

Victor edited together its last two Claribel shorts (identified by Oz film expert Scott Hutchins as *Box of Bandits* and *In Dreamy Jungletown*) making a two-reeler. It's sometimes mistakenly identified as one of the shorts cut from *The Magic Cloak of Oz*.

The Magic Cloak of Oz [Also known as The Magic Cloak; The Witch Queen]. 1917. Five reels, b & w.

Cast: Fluff (Mildred Harris) Bud (Violet McMillan), Nickodemus (Fred Woodward), Queen Zixi (Juanita Hansen), Quavo the Minstrel (Vivian Reed); Speculative cast: Woozy/Zoop (Fred Woodward), Jikki (Raymond Russell), Mary's Father (Dick Rosson), Mary's Mother (Leontine Dranet), Lulea (Jessie May Walsh), Aunt Rivette, (Mai Wells), Cowardly Lion (Hal Roach), Hungry Tiger (Andy Anderson).

Credits: Director: J. Farrell MacDonald; *Writer:* L. Frank Baum (based on *Queen Zixi of Ix*); *Producers:* L. Frank Baum, Louis F. Gottschalk; *Executive producers:* Clarence Rundel, Harry F. Haldeman; *Assistant director:* Harold Ostrom; *Cinematography, optical effects:* James A. Crosby; *Music:* Louis F. Gottschalk; *From:* Oz Film Manufacturing Company.

The fairies of the forest of Burzee weave a magic cloak that grants each wearer one wish, and decide to give it to the most unhappy person they can find.

Young Fluff and Bud live nearby with their ferryman father and their donkey, Nickodemus. After their father dies, Aunt Rivette takes the kids to Noland, where the king has just died without an heir. Discovering the grieving Fluff considers herself the saddest girl in the world, the fairies give her the cloak. Fluff wishes to be happy again. To her astonishment, when they enter the East Gate of Noland next morning, the royal council proclaims that as 47th person to enter, Bud is now the new king.

The children love their new life, and empty the treasury buying toys, but Nickodemus decides to go home. Bandits capture the donkey, but another prisoner, Mary, frees him. Nickodemus gathers an army of forest animals to defeat the robbers and rescue Mary, then returns to his owners.

Cut to 600-year-old Queen Zixi of Ix, magically young and beautiful to others, but cursed to see her true age in every mirror. Zixi realizes the cloak could wish her curse away and contrives to steal it, then discovers its power won't work for thieves. Meanwhile, the fat, malevolent, soup-loving Rolly Rogues descend from the mountains above Noland to conquer the city and take its soup. Bud and Fluff discover the cloak, which could save Noland, is missing, and set out to track it down. Zixi tells them she threw it away when its magic failed; by the time they find it, Dame Dingle has cut it into scraps.

Zixi's magic reassembles the cloak and Fluff uses another wish to summon Nickodemus and his animal army. The animals drive the Rogues out; the fairies, realizing mortals aren't responsible enough for the wishing magic, take the cloak back; but before giving it up, Bud makes a final wish, to be the best king Noland ever had.

Much of what made *Zixi of Ix* good (such as Bud's royal council's unwittingly making foolish wishes on the cloak) was cut from this film, which did, however, find space for more dated scenes of pantomime animals romping.

Because of the failure of *Patchwork Girl of Oz*, Oz Film couldn't find a distributor for *Magic Cloak*, and instead cut it into two two-reelers, *The Magic Cloak* and *The Witch Queen*, and marketed them as fillers. After Oz Film folded, National Film Co. bought *The Magic Cloak of Oz* and finally released it in its original form.

The Wizard of Oz. 2/7/25. Seven reels, 70–93 mins. b&w. Forum Theatre, Los Angeles.

Cast: Old Man/farmhand/Scarecrow (Larry Semon), Prince Kynd (Bryant Washburn), Dorothy (Dorothy Dwan), Lady Vishuss (Virginia Pearson), Wizard (Charles Murray), Farmhand/Tin Woodman (Oliver Hardy), Prime Minister Kruel (Josef Swickard), Ambassador Wikked (Otto Lederer), Aunt Em (Mary Carr), Uncle Henry (Frank "Fatty" Alexander), Snowball (G. Howe Black), Phantom of the Basket (Frederick Ko Vert), with William Hauber, William Dinus, Wanda Hawley, Chester Conklin.

Credits: Director, producer: Larry Semon; *Writers:* Frank Joslyn Baum, Leon Lee, Larry Semon; *Executive producer:* I.E. Chadwick; *Cinematography:* H.F. Koenenkamp, Frank Good, Leonard Smith; *Assistant directors:* William King, Robert Stevens; *Art director:* Robert Stevens; *Editor:* Sam Zimbalist; *From:* Chadwick Pictures Corporation.

An elderly toy-maker places dolls of a Scarecrow, Dorothy and the Tin Woodman on a table, then opens a copy of *The Wizard of Oz* (revealing the film's credits) to read to his little niece. The film cuts back to this scene whenever the setting switches between Kansas and Oz, rationalized by the girl's requests of the storyteller.

Cut to Oz, years after the disappearance of the infant heir to the throne. Prince Kynd and the "townsfolk of Oz" confront the usurper Prime Minister Kruel and his aides, Lady Vishuss and Ambassador Wikked, to demand the return of the rightful queen. Kruel summons the all-powerful Wizard of Oz to find the girl, but the fake Wizard instead distracts the crowd with stage tricks, such as summoning a dancer out of an empty basket.

In Kansas, Dorothy, almost 18, lives on a farm with sweet Uncle Em, brutal Uncle Henry, cowardly black farmhand Snowball and two unnamed hands (since they're played by Hardy and Semon, this synopsis will use their names for convenience). Both the workers love Dorothy, but Semon is too tongue-tied to approach her, and even farm animals pick on him.

Dorothy complains to Em about Henry's cruelty; Em replies that Dorothy isn't blood kin, but was given to them by a stranger as a baby, with an envelope to be opened on her 18th birthday. Dorothy promises Semon she'll tell him the contents before anyone else.

Back in Oz, Kynd demands Kruel produce the queen by the new moon; Kruel tells Vishuss to "get the papers or destroy the girl," so Wikked hops a plane to Kansas. He arrives on Dorothy's birthday and tries unsuccessfully to bribe Henry into giving him the envelope. Hardy, jealous that Dorothy's going to let Semon in on the contents, offers to steal it; Wikked tells Hardy that if he fails, the envelope will keep Dorothy from him forever. Henry unearths the letter, but has to hide it again from Wikked's thugs. Wikked threatens Dorothy with death, but Semon saves her, and saves the letter when Hardy finds it.

Wikked corners Dorothy, Henry and the farmhands in a shed, then a cyclone carries them and Snowball off to Oz, crashing down outside the Emerald City. Semon gives Dorothy the letter which reveals — surprise!— that she's the rightful ruler of Oz. Kruel demands the Wizard turn the Americans into animals, but the "hokum hustler" assures Semon that's not possible. Kynd escorts Dorothy into the city, but Kruel insists he still rules Oz.

Fleeing Kruel guards, Semon disguises himself as a scarecrow while Hardy hides in a junkpile. Kruel scoffs when the Wizard claims to have turned the men invisible, so the Wizard "magically" conjures a living Scarecrow (Semon) and a Tin Woodman (Hardy, covered in junk). This display of magic sends Kruel running, but only as far as the nearest cannon, which he uses to blast the men into surrendering. Kruel condemns Snowball and the Wizard to the dungeons, then gives up the throne to Dorothy and knights Hardy and Henry — all the while scheming to regain his power.

In the dungeon, the Wizard disguises Snowball in a lion skin, after which the "Cowardly Lion" scares off the guards. Hardy chases Semon into the dungeons, where after many comic bits (such as Semon swatting a lion he assumes is Snowball), Semon, the Wizard and Snowball escape. Up above, Kynd and Kruel fight a duel over Dorothy; a guard attacks Kynd from behind, but Semon drops heavy vases on him and Kruel. The prime minister confesses to hiding Dorothy in Kansas and gets dragged away by the guards; Dorothy gives Semon a kiss, then leaves embracing Kynd.

Wikked and Hardy chase Semon up what looks like a medieval oil derrick, then blast it with a cannon. As Semon escapes to a second tower, Snowball sends a plane with a rope ladder flying overhead; Semon catches the ladder but as he flies off, the rope snaps. Back in the toy store, the Scarecrow doll hits the floor, waking the sleeping girl. She goes to bed; then her uncle reopens the last page of the book, revealing that Dorothy and Kynd lived happily ever after (Semon presumably wound up as a bloodspot on the Emerald City cobblestones).

Frank Joslyn Baum had hoped to take over the Oz series after his father's death, but publisher Reilly and Lee hired children's author Ruth Plumly Thompson instead. As a consolation prize, Frank's mother, Maud Gage Baum, gave Frank permission to sell the film rights to the Oz books, and Chadwick Pictures Corp. snapped up *The Wizard of Oz*. Chadwick turned the project over to one of its contract players, slapstick comic Semon, who'd scored a modest success writing, directing and starring in Chadwick's *The Girl in the Limousine*. Also in the cast was the same Oliver Hardy who would later find success as one half of Laurel and Hardy.

The film went into production in 1924, with Chadwick planning a Christmas release, but despite abundant publicity (*Variety* proclaimed it "The greatest sensation among screen classics since *The Birth of a Nation*") Semon worked slowly and *Wizard* opened the following February. A week before the opening, William LaPlante of the National Film Corp. claimed his company had film rights to the Baum book (apparently tied to National's distributing *The Magic Cloak of*

Oz) and threatened to sue; Chadwick threatened a counter-suit and its film opened as scheduled at Los Angeles's Forum Theater.

The film enjoyed enough moderate success to move to New York, but it ran into the same problem as *Patchwork Girl* and MGM's *The Wizard of Oz*: good audiences, but they were children playing half-price. Chadwick couldn't find a national distributor and farmed the film out to state distributors instead, with reasonable success and generally favorable reviews.

Unsurprisingly, the film plays to Semon's strengths—broad physical comedy and madcap chases—and appears to draw at least somewhat on the 1902 musical *Wizard*, in which intrigues around the throne of Oz propelled the plot. Possibly the failure of *The Patchwork Girl of Oz* made this look a safer bet than a fantasy, but this film dates just as badly as Oz Film's product: the racist portrayal of Snowball is particularly grating, and unlike Baum's Dorothy, Dorothy here just stands passively while the men decide her fate.

The picture did air on one of the early TV broadcasts in 1931, and it may have influenced MGM's more successful version: Semon's production is the first to set much of the story in Kansas and to give the farmhands a role in the story, and the ending scene at least implies the whole story was the little girl's dream.

1932

The Land of Oz [Also known as The Scarecrow of Oz]. 2/25/33. Two reels, b&w.

Cast: Scarecrow (Donald Henderson), Tin Woodman (Fred Osbourn), Dorothy (Maryeruth Boone), General Jingur (Louise Ringland), Sorceress (Sissie Flynn), Tip (Matt Flynn), Jellia Jamb (Glenna Vaughn), Soldier with the Green Whiskers (Caryl Roberts).

Credits: Director, producer: Ethel Meglin; *Art direction:* Danny Hall; *Set design:* Ernest Smythe.

"Princess Dorothy" returns to the Emerald City to find the Scarecrow under siege from General Jingur [sic] and her all-girl army. Jingur captures Dorothy and turns her over to a sorceress who imprisons Dorothy alongside Tip in a lair just across from the Scarecrow's throne room. Dorothy escapes by tightrope to the throne room, but the sorceress cuts the rope in mid-crossing; fortunately, the Scarecrow rides the (flying!) Tin Man and rescues her.

Dancer Ethel Meglin ran a successful Los Angeles children's dance studio (which would later become a franchise of over 130 schools) from which came the Meglin Kiddies, a troupe that performed in stage productions and variety acts, as well as short films. This adaptation of Baum — originally announced as *The Scarecrow of Oz*—was Meglin's one and only attempt to produce and direct the kids in a film herself (the results, according to one Oz fan who saw it, were imaginative art direction and mediocre performances). The abrupt ending may mean that like Selig's series of one-reelers, this was planned as one in a series of shorts.

The film received a limited, largely non-theatrical release, mostly in Beverly Hills and Pasadena, then disappeared (there are unconfirmed reports it was rereleased in 1934 as *The Scarecrow of Oz* and some reference books still list it under that title). It was believed to be a lost film until a print turned up in 1998.

1933

The Wizard of Oz. 8.5 mins., animated, Technicolor.

Credits: Director: Ted Eshbaugh; *Story:* Col. Frank J. Baum; *Producer:* J.R. Booth; *Executive producers:* Ted Eshbaugh, J.R. Booth, Carl W. Stalling; *Drawing:* Frank Tipper, Bill Mason, Cal Dalton, Vet Anderson, "Hutch"; *Music:* Carl Stalling; *From:* Film Laboratories of Canada.

In this dialog-free cartoon, Dorothy (looking very much like Denslow's plump version) is carried from blue-tinted Kansas to Technicolor Oz by the cyclone, knocking the Scarecrow from his pole as she falls from the air. Setting off with Toto, they find the vine-covered Tin Woodman and oil him up. After watching bees, swans and bluebirds pair-bond, the group enters the Emerald City in a parade surrounded by cheering crowds.

The bearded, Merlinesque Wizard conjures up chairs for them, then conjures tiny dolls who dance as a chorus line, a chicken who lays magic eggs and other wonders. The Wizard enchants one undersized egg to grow, but when Toto runs off with his wand and the eggs keeps expanding. After Tin Woodman and Scarecrow try in vain to crack the shell, Toto taps it with the wand and it shatters, revealing a tiny chick inside.

Although this good-looking cartoon has the cast we know, the story has little relation to anything Baum wrote, despite his son Frank's contribution. Because Disney had exclusive rights to make Technicolor cartoons at the time, this one wasn't released until the 1980s.

1936

Oz University. 6/2/36. 9.5 mins., two-strip Technicolor.
Cast: Cast: Members of University of Michigan Women's Athletic Association.
Credits: Director: Sarah Pierce; *Writers:* Betty Jane Mansfield, Marcia Connell, Barbara Paterson, Elizabeth Rorke, Carolyn Ross, Margaret Bryant.

Sitting on the throne of Oz, the Wizard, with Dorothy and the Woggle-Bug beside him, commands the Magic Picture to show him the University of Michigan. The Wizard watches jocks, debs and scholars grumble about college life and decides to transport them to Oz University to study under the Woggle-Bug: "They'll change their characters you will see, and their true selves they all will be."

The Wizard's magic transforms the students into Tin Woodman, Jack Pumpkinhead, Shaggy Man and others (in what look like homemade costumes). The new students endure the tedium of registering for classes, interrupted by dances, Betsy Bobbin and Shaggy tumbling, and other stunts; then the Woggle-Bug begins to lecture, putting many of them to sleep. Then comes a test, which turns into another dance routine, at which point the students decide there's no place like their alma mater. They beg the Wizard to send them back to Michigan, which he does, and the show ends.

This freshman pageant was produced by the University's Women's Athletic Association, in conjunction with their annual Lantern Night.

1938

Land of Oz: A Ken McClellan Cartoon. Never released.
Producer: Kenneth McLellan; *Executive producer:* Maud Gage Baum.

Dorothy and Toto are caught in a blinding windstorm that takes them to Oz. Anthropomorphic flowers swirl to *Dance of the Hours*; a Lion chases Dorothy, but turns out to be friendly; the Scarecrow gets torn apart during the chase; the Tin Woodman rides up on the Sawhorse and sorts everything out.

During the 1930s, Ruth Plumly Thompson tried to interest Hollywood in turning the Oz books into an animated series, but Baum's widow, Maud Gage Baum, shot down several proposals Thompson liked (including one from Walt Disney) before striking a deal with independent filmmaker Kenneth J. McLellan to adapt all Baum's books following *Wizard of Oz*. According to McLellan, the shorts would be made using 12-inch character figures and a specialized form of stop-motion animation; another description of his plans for *Land of Oz* refers to using ink and paint on the animation cells.

McLellan's planned series never materialized, possibly because he couldn't find a backer. Reportedly, however, some footage was completed; whether or not it was from *Land of Oz*, McLellan's synopsis for that initial short gives some idea of where he was heading.

1939

The Wizard of Oz. 8/12/39 (Oconomowoc, Wisconsin premier); 8/15/39 (Los Angeles premiere). 101 mins., b&w/color.

Cast: Dorothy Gale (Judy Garland), Scarecrow/Hunk Andrews (Ray Bolger), Tin Man/Hickory Twicker (Jack Haley), Cowardly Lion/Zeke (Bert Lahr), Wicked Witch of the West/Almira Gulch (Margaret Hamilton), Professor Marvel/The Great and Powerful Oz/Cabbie/Guard/Doorman/ Soldier (Frank Morgan), Glinda the Good (Billie Burke), Uncle Henry (Charley Grapewin), Auntie Em (Clara Blandick), Nikko (Pat Walshe), Mayor (Charley Becker), City Fathers (Matthew Raia, Billy Curtis), Barrister ("Little Billy" Rhodes), Heralds (Karl Kosiczky, Carl M. Erickson, Clarence C. Howerton), Army Captain (Victor Wetter), Commander Navy (Johnny Winters), Sergeant-at-Arms (Prince Denis), Soldiers ("Idaho Lewis" Croft, Willi Koestner, Nicholas Page, Garland Slatten, Parnell Elmer St. Aubin, August Clarence Swenson, Gus Wayne, Murray Wood), Coroner (Meinhardt Raabe), Coach Driver (George Ministeri), Back Seat Driver (William H. O'Docharty), Fiddlers (Friedrich Ritter, Mickey Carroll), Bearded Man (Tommy Cottonaro), Munchkin Maid (Fern Formica), Townsmen (Joseph J. Koziel, Frank Cucksey, Lajos "Leo" Matina), Lollipop Guild (Jerry Maren, Harry Doll, Jakob Gerlich), Lullaby League ("Little Olga" C. Nardone), Nita Krebs, Yvonne Moray), Munchkins (Walter Miller, Hazel I. Derthick, Margaret Williams, Matthe Matina, Bele Matina, Charles E. Kelley, Jessie E. Kelley, Dolly Kramer, Tiny Doll, Daisy Doll, Gracie Doll, Alta M. Stevens, Emil Kranzler, "Little Jeane" LaBarbera, Betty Tanner, Joseph Herbst, Ruth E. Smith, James R. Hulse, Ethel W. Denis, Marie Denis Maroldo, John Ballas, Franz Balluck, John T. Bambury, Henry Boers, Theodore Boers, Eddie Buresh, Colonel Casper, Eugene S. David, Jr.; Eulie H. David, Major Doyle, William A. Giblin, Jack Glicken, Jakob Hofbauer, Robert Kanter, Frank Kikel, Bernhard Klima, Adam Edwin Kozicki, Johnny Leal, Charley Ludwig, Dominick Magro, Carlos Manzo, Howard Marco, Nels P. Nelson, Franklin H. O'Baugh, Frank Packard, Johnny Pizo, "Prince Leon" Polinsky, Sandor Roka, Jimmie Rosen, Charles F. Royale, Albert Ruddinger, Charles Silvern, Elmer Spangler, Carl Stephan, George Suchsie, Arnold Vierling, Harvey B. Williams, Gladys W. Allison, Freda Besky, Josefine Balluck, Christie Buresh, Lida Buresh, Nona Cooper, Elizabeth Coulter, Addie E. Frank, Thaisa L. Gardner, Carolyn E. Granger, Helen M. Hoy, Marguerite A. Hoy, Emma Koestner, Mitzi Koestner, Hilda Lange, Ann Rice Leslie, Margaret C.H. Nickloy, Hildred C. Olson, Leona M. Parks, Lillian Porter, Margie Raia, Gertrude H. Rice, Hazel Rice, Helen J. Royale, Stella A. Royale, Elsie R. Shultz, Ruth E. Smith, Charlotte V. Sullivan, Grace G. Williams, Gladys V. Wolff, Betty Ann Cain, Joan Kenmore, Shirley Ann Kennedy, Pricilla Montgomery, Valerie Shepard, Viola White), Cat Owner (Lois January), Ozites (Lorraine Bridges, Tyler Brook, Ralph Sudam, Bobby Watson, Oliver Smith, Charles Irwin, Elvida Rizzo, Dona Massin), Winged Monkeys (Harry Monty, Sid Dawson, George Noisom, Buster Brody, Lee Murray, Walter Miller), Winkie Captain (Mitchell Lewis).

Credits: Directors: Victor Fleming, Richard Thorpe, King Vidor; *Writers:* Noel Langley, Florence Ryerson, Edgar Allan Woolf, Irving Brecher, William H. Cannon, Herbert Fields, Arthur Freed, E.Y. Harburg, Samuel Hoffenstein, John Lee Mahin, Herman J. Mankiewicz, Jack Mintz, Ogden Nash, Sid Silvers; *Producer:* Mervyn LeRoy; *Associate producer:* Arthur Freed; *Cinematography:* Harold Rosson; *Art direction:* Cedric Gibbons; *Costumes:* Adrian; *Music & lyrics:* Harold Arlen, E. Y. Harburg, George Bassman, George E. Stoll, Herbert Stothart, Robert W. Stringer; *Editing:* Blanche Sewell. *From:* MGM, Loew's Inc.

Songs: Somewhere Over the Rainbow; Ding Dong the Witch is Dead; If I Only Had a Brain; If I Only Had a Heart; If I Only Had the Nerve; We're Off to See the Wizard; The Merry Old Land of Oz; If I Were King of the Forest.

(The author realizes how unlikely it is that anyone in the Western world doesn't know the plot of this film, but just in case...)

Dorothy Gale would sooner live anywhere than her Uncle Henry's dreary Kansas farm, despite the loving attention of her Uncle, her Auntie Em, their good-natured farmhands and Dorothy's dog, Toto. After bitchy spinster Almira Gulch threatens to have Toto killed for supposedly attacking her, Dorothy runs away with the dog. They soon meet sideshow mentalist Professor Marvel, a shrewd fraud who convinces Dorothy that Aunt Em has literally fallen sick with worry over her leaving.

Dorothy rushes home just as a tornado hits, gets caught in the farmhouse and knocked cold as the twister yanks the house up by its roots. When she wakes and walks out of the house (at which point the film switches from black and white to Technicolor) she finds herself in Oz. The Munchkins thank Dorothy for crushing the Wicked Witch of the East with her house, but the witch's sister, the Wicked Witch of the West, appears and vows revenge. She grows even madder when Glinda the Good Witch transfers the dead witch's magic ruby slippers onto Dorothy's feet.

Glinda tells Dorothy only the Great and Powerful Oz has the power to send her home. Traveling down the yellow brick road to the Emerald City, Dorothy acquires three friends, all lookalikes for the farmhands back in Kansas: A Scarecrow seeking a brain, a Tin Man who wants a heart and a tough-talking but Cowardly Lion yearning for courage. They go with Dorothy to petition the Wizard for help, and aid her as they encounter hostile trees, the Wicked Witch and a field of sleep-inducing poppies.

The Emerald City turns out to be a happy, light-hearted town, but Oz — a giant, glowering, bodiless head — is not. Oz mocks the foursome for their wishes, but tells them they'll get what they want — once the Wicked Witch of the West is dead.

When the foursome enter the witch's eerie realm, her flying monkey servants tear the Tin Man and Scarecrow apart, beat up the Lion and carry Dorothy to their mistress. The witch begins plotting how to destroy Dorothy without damaging the magic of the shoes. Fortunately, Dorothy's friends recover and sneak into the castle to save her; when the witch catches them, she sets the Scarecrow on fire, prompting Dorothy to douse her friend with a pail of water. When the water washes over the witch, she melts away.

When the conquerors return to the Emerald City, Oz tries to welch, but Toto discovers the real Wizard (a double for Marvel) hiding behind a curtain, manipulating the fake head. Oz tells Dorothy he's a stage magician from Omaha whose balloon drifted into Oz years ago, convincing the inhabitants that he must be a wizard. He tries to persuade Dorothy's friends to give up their wishes, but when they insist, he presents them with a college diploma, a heart-shaped testimonial watch and a medal for valor, convincing them that they should believe in themselves.

Oz offers to fly Dorothy and Toto home in his balloon, but Dorothy, distracted by Toto, misses the launch. Glinda appears and reveals that the ruby slippers can take Dorothy back to Kansas, now that she realizes "there's no place like home" and no point looking anywhere else for happiness. Dorothy taps her heels together three times, and wakes up at the farm. She assures her worried friends and family she's fine, and tells them she had a strange dream "and you were there, and you, and you...."

MGM's predecessor, Metro-Goldwyn, first tried for film rights to *The Wizard of Oz* in 1924, but lost out to Chadwick Films. In 1933, when the company was Metro-Goldwyn-Mayer, it tried cutting a deal to make an animated Oz series, but Baum's widow sold the animation rights to Ken McLellan instead (MGM considered another bid in 1937, but decided cartoons based on the *Captain and the Kids* comic strip would have wider appeal).

The following year, producer Samuel Goldwyn (who'd left Goldwyn Pictures before it became Metro-Goldwyn) bought film rights to *Wizard* with plans to cast Eddie Cantor as the Scarecrow, W.C. Fields as the Wizard and Helen Hayes or Mary Pickford as Dorothy. Cantor's declining popularity put that plan on the shelf, but after the success of Disney's *Snow White*, Goldwyn found himself fielding offers for Oz from other studios, including MGM, suddenly interested in children's fantasies. The studio not only bought the rights to the book but to all existing dramatic adaptations, meaning they could borrow elements of the 1902 stage show or any of the films. The price: $75,000.

Top screenwriter Herman Mankiewicz tackled the first draft, which established Kansas as black-and-white but (according to *The Making of the Wizard of Oz*) gave Dorothy a perkiness reminiscent of Harold Gray's comic-strip character, Little Orphan Annie, which may have been a ploy by Mankiewicz to get out of the project.

British playwright Noel Langley (who also wrote the children's fantasy *The Land of Green Ginger*) took over from Mankiewicz. Langley's treatment established Oz as a dream, with two farmhands becoming Tin Woodman and Scarecrow in Oz (despite the resemblance to the Semon film, Langley credited the idea to Mary Pickford's *Poor Little Rich Girl*). The Cowardly Lion, who's actually the Oz hero Florizel under a transformation spell, had no Kansas counterpart; in some versions, he kills the Wicked Witch.

Langley's initial drafts had Auntie Em wanting Toto destroyed, but his subsequent revisions introduced Almira Gulch; Bulbo, the Witch of the West's son (in various drafts either Uncle Henry's counterpart or Miss Gulch's son); Lizzie, a waitress reminiscent of the stage musical's Tryxie Trifle; made the wicked witch a running threat (in Baum, she's only in a couple of scenes); gave Glinda the magic bubble in which she flies, patterned after the silent fantasy *Queen of the Sea*; and had the Wizard exposed as a fraud early on, then joining the fight against the witch.

In one draft, Dorothy and her friends sneak into the Wicked Witch's castle in circus disguise, as in the 1902 *Wizard*; according to *Oz Before the Rainbow*, some drafts also had the Scarecrow and Tin Woodman as ordinary humans in costumes, like the Semon film.

Among subsequent writers on the project, Edgar Allan Woolf and Florence Ryerson came up with Professor Marvel, had the Wizard appear in multiple roles; stressed Dorothy's desperation to return home; and had the witch focus on claiming the ruby slippers, where Langley had her sending an army to conquer the Emerald City. Songwriter Yip Harburg contributed the medal/diploma/testimonial scene, tailoring to W.C. Fields's sarcastic delivery when he was in the running for the Wizard's role.

Casting could, in fact, have turned out quite differently. About the only role everyone agreed on from the start was comedienne Billy Burke as Glinda. Several MGM executives, for instance, are said to have wanted Shirley Temple for Dorothy (though there's nothing on paper to confirm that), but 20th Century–Fox head Darryl Zanuck rejected loaning her out (he later cast her in *The Blue Bird*, a children's fantasy widely seen at the time as "Temple's Oz").

Buddy Ebsen and Ray Bolger were initially cast as Scarecrow and Tin Man respectively, but Bolger was a great admirer of Fred Stone, the Scarecrow in the 1902 musical, and fought to follow in his idol's footsteps. Eventually MGM had the men switch parts; then, after Ebsen turned out to be allergic to the Tin Man makeup, Jack Haley replaced him. Both W.C. Fields and Ed Wynn were offered the Wizard's role, but both turned it down; Morgan, on the other hand, begged for the part and won over the reluctant studio.

As for the Wicked Witch, Mervyn LeRoy wanted glamorous screen villainess Gale Sondergaard to play the witch as a sexy fallen woman. According to Sondergaard, LeRoy's coworkers eventually convinced him that the witch should be an ugly hag, and she and he agreed that wasn't the role for her.

The film also went through its share of directors: Richard Thorpe was fired after 12 days (Mervyn LeRoy later said Thorpe didn't have a feel for children's fantasy); George Cukor did three or four days of test shooting, during which he ditched Garland's blond wig; and then LeRoy and Louis B. Mayer persuaded Victor Fleming (*Red Dust*, *Test Pilot*, *Captains Courageous*) to take over. Later in the production, however, Fleming traded jobs with King Vidor, who wanted to leave David O. Selznick Productions' *Gone with the Wind*.

Through the shooting, other changes took place. The "Jitter Bug" dance number (no relation to the jitterbug dance craze, but a reference to a creepy-crawly giving people the jitters) was cut to trim running time but it's on some DVD and VHS editions, and Harold Arlen's home movies of the number appeared on 10/2/83 in *Ripley's Believe it Or Not*. "Over the Rainbow" was cut too ("Why is she singing in a barnyard?") but Freed pushed it back in.

The film opened with a bang, breaking the house record for opening day at New York's Loew's Capitol Theater (probably helped by Garland and Mickey Rooney, her co-star in several other films, making a personal appearance) and grossing $93,000 the first week. Thousands of children turned out for the show, but as with earlier Oz films, a packed house paying kids' prices proved a mixed blessing.

Indeed, by the time *Wizard of Oz*'s theatrical run ended, it qualified, at best, as a modest success. Although the film had grossed $3 million, the net loss after advertising and distribution came out to $1 million. Now, after multiple TV showings, it ranks second as a money-maker only to *Gone with the Wind* among 1939 releases.

Although the film scored some good reviews, most major critics gutted it for recycling old vaudeville routines (in the jokes and dances among Dorothy's friends) and ranked it far below the level of *Snow White*. Critics also found the message that we shouldn't look for happiness "beyond our own back yard" unbearably saccharine. When Frank Morgan died in 1949, his obituary didn't even list *Wizard* among his major credits.

Nevertheless, *Wizard of Oz* received six Oscar nominations including best picture, color cinematography, interior decoration, best song ("Over the Rainbow"), best original score, and best special effects. The film won Oscars for best score (though the award went to Herbert Stothart, who composed the bridging and background music, rather than to songwriters E.Y. Harburg and Harold Arlen) and best song, but *The Rains Came* took the special-effects Oscar and the others went to *Gone with the Wind*. Judy Garland did receive a special Oscar for her work as a juvenile.

MGM reissued the film in 1949 — after which *Wizard* finally showed a profit — then again in 1955. Nevertheless, when CBS decided to air a major movie as an annual TV event (a novel idea in the 1950s, when Hollywood still looked on TV as an adversary), they had no interest in *The Wizard of Oz* until MGM turned down the network's first choice, *Gone with the Wind*. At that point, CBS executive Robert Weintman turned to *Wizard* because the fantasy setting wouldn't date it.

CBS agreed to run *Wizard* twice at $225,000 a showing, with an option for seven more showings at $150,000 each, though the network didn't expect it would be worth running more than three or four times.

The Wizard of Oz debuted on CBS on Nov. 3, 1956, with Bert Lahr and Judy Garland's daughter Liza Minnelli serving as hosts (Justin Schiller, a teenage Oz collector who would later found the International Wizard of Oz Club, joined them on stage). The tradition of on-air hosts continued through 1967.

The debut airing did well, but contrary to expectations, future showings did better. In 1975, *Wizard* was the 11th-highest rated film ever shown on TV — and also the 12th, 14th and 16th highest (multiple airings, multiple slots).

In 1967, CBS refused to up the payments to renew its contract, so NBC purchased the rights through 1976, after which CBS then bought the film back. Since CBS's rights lapsed again in 1998, *Wizard* has appeared on TNT, Turner Classic Films and the WB Television Network, all branches of the Time-Warner conglomerate which controls most of MGM's film library. The WB's 2002 airing flashed back to CBS's use of on-air hosts, with stars of various WB shows bracketing the commercial breaks with reminiscences of watching the film in childhood.

Today, the movie *is* Oz, eclipsing the books to the point that many people don't realize Baum's Oz isn't a dream; many movies, TV shows, comic books and stage plays supposedly adapting Baum actually use the movie as their source, rather than the novel.

In 1975, a toy manufacturer found dolls based on the film had an 80 percent recognition factor, and the dialog—"Lions and tigers and bears, oh my!" "Follow the Yellow Brick Road!" "Click your heels together three times"—is as universally familiar as the images. A 2000 *USA Today* poll ranked "There's no place like home" as one of filmdom's all-time top 10 catchphrases.

Much of the credit goes to the annual TV showings; Margaret Hamilton has said the real buzz didn't start until after the third or fourth time the film aired. For some families it became a tradition (something much easier to establish back in the days of only three networks), and the annual viewings guaranteed a new generation of fans every few years. *The Making of the Wizard of Oz* points out that the critics who reviewed it in 1939 were adults; more favorable reviews in later years came from critics who'd grown up with the film.

Even so, there is more to the movie's success than just familiarity. No other movie ever earned multiple slots in the list of the 25 highest-rated films. And although Christmas movies air every year, even *It's a Wonderful Life* isn't as quotable, or as well entrenched in contemporary culture.

In 1989, *Wizard of Oz* was one of the first 25 movies designated as a National Treasure by the National Film Registry and Library of Congress.

1962

Number 13 [Also known as The Tin Woodman's Dream, Fragments of a Faith Forgotten, Magic Mushroom People of Oz]. Color.

Credits: Director, writer, production designer: Harry Smith, from *The Wizard of Oz*; *Producer:* Lionel Ziprin; *Executive producers:* Elizabeth Taylor, Arthur Young; *Costumes:* Stuart Reed; *Animation:* Harry Smith, Joanne Ziprin; *Music:* Charles Gounod, from *Faust*; *From:* Film Makers Cooperative Production.

As described by Philip Smith (*After Harry Smith*), watching the fragments of this film involves visiting Oz "in the form of a Tibetan mandala," passing into a series of green glass domes in which Oz characters (animated in the style of Denslow's drawings) are mixed with cut-outs from the Hieronymous Bosch painting *Garden of Earthly Delights* or, in another dome, designs based on biologist Ernest Haeckel's studies of symmetric, microscopic lifeforms. Kaleidoscopic camera effects further reduce the film to a series of wild images and colors.

This was eccentric auteur Harry Smith's 13th film project (sometimes referred to as *Oz*), of which only fragments survive, the backer, Arthur Young, having dropped the project before completion (Smith stated that he spent Young's last payment for finishing the film on taking a vacation instead). The four fragments:

#13: a five minute sequence, *The Approach to Emerald City*, using ballet music from Gounod's *Faust*. 15 minutes of non-color-corrected rushes are known to survive from several hours.

#16: *The Tin Woodman's Dream*, from about 1967, is 14.5 minutes, and includes *Approach to Emerald City* plus kaleidoscopic footage.

#19: includes several excerpts from #13.

#20: *Fragments of a Faith Forgotten* from 1981, combines both 19 and 16 for a 27 minute short film.

1965

The Wizard of Mars [Also known as Horrors of the Red Planet; Alien Massacre]. 88 mins., color.

Cast: Steve (Roger Gentry), Doc (Vic McGee), Charlie (Jerry Rannow), Dorothy (Eve Bernhardt), Wizard (John Carradine).

Credits: Director, writer, producer: David L. Hewitt; *Story:* David L. Hewitt, Armando Busick (based on Baum's *The Wizard of Oz*); *Executive producer:* David L. Hewitt, Joe Karston; *Assistant director:* Ernie Reed; *Cinematography:* Austin McKinney; *Music:* Frank A. Coe; *Editor:* Tom Graeff; *From:* Karston-Hewitt Organization/ American General Pictures/Republic Pictures.

In 1975, Mars Probe 1 crashes on Mars, leaving the crew—Steve, Charlie, Doc and Dorothy—struggling to survive. After passing through a series of caverns, they reach an abandoned probe and convert its liquid oxygen fuel into an air supply. When a storm uncovers a worn road of yellow brick, the crew follows it to a ruined alien city. In the city center, they find aliens housed in crystal containers, and are telepathically steered to the center of the complex.

Here, a disembodied head (veteran horror star John Carradine) materializes and tells the astronauts that the Martians used their limitless scientific brilliance to freeze time around themselves, giving them infinite time to ponder the universe. Now they're bored, frustrated and unable to escape unless someone with a physical body adjusts the time controller. Once the astronauts do that, the city collapses; the humans run out — and suddenly, they're back in the spaceship heading for a landing. And although only a few minutes have passed, they're grizzled and filthy — as if they'd spent days in the wilderness (gasp!).

No synopsis can convey how deadly dull this film is (long, long stretches of wandering and struggling-to-survive across Mars).

1966

Fantasia III. Spain, 82 mins., color.

Cast: Dianik Zvrakowska, José Palacio, Juan Diego, Tomás Blanco, Luis Prendes.

Credits: Director, writer: Eloy German de la Inglesia; *Writer:* Fernando Martin Iniesta; *Art director:* Eduardo Torre de la Fuente; *Cinematography:* Santiago Crespo; *Music:* Fernando Garcia Morcillo; *Editor:* Franciso Jaumandreu; *From:* Pan Latina.

This Spanish anthology film adapts Hans Christian Andersen's *The Little Mermaid* and *Three Hairs of the Devil*, but between them is a segment based on *The Wizard of Oz* (contrary to some reports, it isn't the third in a series of separate films).

This film appears to be unavailable on video, even in Spain, but one on-line review describes it as having bad cinematography, awful costumes, bad scenery, horrible scripts and bad enough that the memory of it "causes nightmares."

1969

The Wonderful Land of Oz. 11/1/69. 72 mins., color.

Cast: Tip (Channy Mahon), Jack Pumpkinhead (George Wadsworth), Mombi (Zisca), Tin Woodman (Al Joseph), Scarecrow (Mike Thomas), Woggle-Bug (Gil Fields), General Jinjur (Caroline Berner), Glinda (Hilary Lee Gaess), Ozma (Joy Web).

Credits: Director, writer, producer, cinematography: Barry Mahon; *Script:* Clelle Mahon; *Set designer:* Ray Menard; *Music:* George Linsenmann; *Lyrics:* Ralph Falco; *Editor:* Steven R. Cuiffo; *From:* Cinetron.

Songs: The Land of Oz; The Powder of Life; A Real, Real Boy; Try To Touch a Star; On the Great Takeover Day; I've Watched Over You.

Under the watchful eyes of a purple cow, young Tip carves a jack o'lantern and puts it atop an elegantly dressed stick-figure, a practical joke on his stepmother, the witch Mombi. When the witch confronts "Jack Pumpkinhead," it shocks her cold, then she uses a magic powder to bring Jack to life. She tells Jack that although Tip built him, he owes his life to her magic; she tells Tip that although she's honor-bound to watch over him, that will be much easier once she turns him into a lawn statue.

Tip sensibly decides to run away first, bringing Jack and taking Mombi's powder with him. They head for the Emerald City to seek King Scarecrow's protection, but while Tip sleeps, Jack (who doesn't need sleep) keeps walking. Tip wakes up alone, then meets Jinjur, general of an all-girl army out to overthrow the Scarecrow; unlike the motive in Baum's book, it's not for women's rights, but so she and her girls won't ever have to listen to their parents. Jinjur drags Tip along to be her servant.

Jack reaches the Scarecrow's throne room, where the Scarecrow's maid, Jellia, interprets for them — i.e., making up insulting remarks — before telling them they both speak the same tongue. Jinjur inspires her army with visions of never babysitting or doing chores again; when the army reaches the city, the Guardian of the Gates can't bear to fight girls, so they shove him aside and invade.

Tip races ahead to warn the Scarecrow the palace is surrounded. The Scarecrow takes off his crown, admitting he's always found it heavy, and they flee to the Tin Woodman's castle. Along the way, Tip persuades the Scarecrow to fight the revolution with the Woodman's help, and they meet H.M. Woggle-Bug T.E., an insect whose experiences in an Oz schoolroom made him not only educated but highly magnified as well. Tip also adopts a mouse as his pet, carrying it in his pocket.

By the time they reach the city, Jinjur has found ruling less enjoyable than expected: none of her girls can cook, and none of them, including her, has any idea how to run a kingdom. Nevertheless, she tells the Scarecrow she has as much right to the throne as he does, and condemns them all to the dungeons. Tip saves them by letting his mouse run free, driving the girls off (conforming to the old stereotype of all women as mouse-phobic).

The army surrounds the palace, but Tip and his friends use the Powder of Life to turn a couple of sofas, some palm-frond wings and a hunting trophy's head into a flying Gump that carries them to Glinda, whom we've seen in glimpses watching them throughout the film.

Scarecrow asks Glinda about his right to the throne; Glinda tells him the rightful ruler is Ozma, heir to Pastoria, whom the Wizard deposed. Ozma has been missing since the Wizard took her, as a baby, to Mombi.

Glinda teleports everyone to Mombi and forces her to confess that in return for the Wizard teaching her magic (all of which turned out to be fake), Mombi promised to hide Ozma away, and always watch over her — which she did by turning him into Tip. Tip is horrified at the thought of becoming a girl, but Glinda promises the transformation will put part of his male spirit into every boy in Oz: "You'll have hundreds of adventures, everywhere!"

Back in the palace, Jinjur is wilting under her responsibilities, but when Ozma appears on the throne, the general still objects until Glinda and the others appear. The army of revolt slinks home, and Ozma begins studying under the Woggle-Bug while Jack and the Scarecrow leave to proclaim her reign to the kingdom.

In 1961, Florida businessman K. Gordon Murray persuaded movie theaters across America to start offering a "kiddie matinee" on weekend afternoons, providing them with low-budget fantasy films imported from Mexico to fill the slot. This was so successful (at one point NBC considered giving Murray a TV showcase like *Wonderful World of Disney*) that several imitators sprang up. Barry Mahon, otherwise known for sexploitative fare such as *Good Times With a Bad Girl*, churned out a number of low-budget American fantasies in the years before Hollywood persuaded the theaters to go back to showing the regular evening features at matinees.

This particular Mahon production is surprisingly faithful to the book, and most of the changes probably relate to what couldn't be accomplished on a shoestring budget, such as a Sawhorse, a griffin and talking field mice. That only proves that fidelity isn't a guarantee of quality: The uniformly wooden acting and the cheap appearance make this resemble a very bad school play (much worse than any school play this author has ever worked on).

The musical score is sometimes confused with a record released by the Land of Oz theme park.

1971

Aysecik Ve Sihirli Cuceler Ruyular Ulkesinde [Also known as Aysecik and the Bewitched Dwarfs in Dreamland; The Turkish Wizard of Oz]. Turkey, 100 mins., color.

Cast: Aysecik (Zeynep Değirmencioğlu), Iron Man (Süleyman Turan), Lion Man (Ali Sen), Scarecrow (Metin Serezli), Oz (Cemal Konca), Magician (Suna Selen), Angel (Mine Sun), Dolls (Sitki Sezgin, Ilhan Hemseri), Dwarves (Tayar Yildiz, Hari Turyut, Memet Aik, Salih Carpar, Ali Abbas Bayer, Harlun Atalay), with Seyhan Gümüs, Ferdi Celep, Murvet Issever, Kucuk Cudidiler, Semra Karseler, Seda Kardesler.

Credits: Director: Tunc Basaran; *Music director:* Yilzabram Gurses; *Writer:* Hamdi Degirmencioglu (based on *The Wizard of Oz* by L. Frank Baum); *Producer:* Ozdemir Birsef; *Cinematography:* Mustafa Yilmaz, Rafet Siriner; *Lighting director:* Mazhar Eroz; *Choreography:* Semra Maytalmah; *Music:* Torgut Oren; *From:* Hisar Film.

[Watched in the original Turkish]

Aysecik (a brunette teen with Judy Garland-style pigtails) lives on her uncle's farm with her beloved dog Banju. The live-action film switches to animation long enough for a tornado to carry the farm-house, with Ay-

Time for a curtain call: Aysecik (Zeynep Degirmencioglu), her friends and the Seven Dwarves take a bow. From *Aysecik and the Bewitched Dwarfs in Dreamland*. (Photograph credit: Riocinema.)

Aysecik (Zeynep Degirmencioglu), Lion Man (Ali Sen), Scarecrow (Metin Serezli) and Iron Man (Suleyman Turan) drift on the water in *Aysecick and the Bewitched Dwarfs in Dreamland*. (Photograph credit: Riocinema.)

secik and her dog inside, to the dreamland of Ulkesinde, where they land on top of the Wicked Witch. This delights the Good Witch of the North and her friends, the Seven Dwarfs, who wear toy-soldier outfits (the scene where they meet Aysecik is missing from most videos available in America).

After Glinda and the dwarves vanish, Aysecik takes the witch's silver slippers (real ballet slippers) and sets out on a clay path to find the mighty Wizard of Dreamland. She frees Scarecrow from his pole in a field of grass; they find and oil up the rusted Tin Man; when a Lion attacks Toto, Aysecik slaps the big cat, who turns into a coward. All three join Aysecik's journey, and when a tree grabs her, the Tin Woodman forces it to let her go.

When the travelers come to a high wall, the Tin Woodman makes a ladder to climb over it. Inside it, a miniature land of dolls comes to life for a while when the clock strikes; whatever they say to Aysecik provokes the Tin Woodman to cry until he rusts. Next the group tries rafting across a river, but get stranded in midstream until the dwarves show up, magically take them to land and conjure up dinner. After Aysecik and her friends move on, the dwarves disappear.

The travelers reach the Emerald City, which looks like a big toy fort (inside, it resembles an ancient stone city). In the Wizard's throne room, they face a skull on a table with a fire burning in the fireplace in front of it. A voice (from the skull?) tells them to kill the Wicked Witch of the West, much to their dismay.

When the witch (whose face appears to be covered with fake putty warts) spots them in her crystal ball, she sends something (never

Aysecik (Zeynep Degirmencioglu) leads her friends in search of the Wizard of Dreamland. (Photograph credit: Riocinema.)

shown on-screen, unless that's another missing segment) to attack them, but Scarecrow has the others hide under his straw, then repair him afterwards. Watching this by telescope, the Witch sends soldiers to destroy the Scarecrow and Tin Woodman, and capture the others. They can't harm Aysecik because Glinda kissed her forehead, but they do bring her back to the witch.

Aysecik refuses to give up the slippers, but the witch eventually trips her with a hidden wire, knocking one of the shoes loose. The witch snatches it up, then a voice (the Wizard's?) tells Aysecik to throw water at her; the witch doubles over in pain and the camera cuts away; when it pans back, the witch has melted. The grateful soldiers restore Aysecik's friends, who dance with the dwarves.

When the group returns to the Wizard, he refuses to grant their wishes until Banju finds the real Wizard and forces him out of his hidden room. The Wizard gives Aysecik's friends what appears to be an inspiring speech about brains, heart and courage, which apparently cures their problems. He offers Aysecik a balloon ride home, but as usual, she misses it while collecting Banju.

The dwarves send Aysecik and the others back to the doll country, where she and the dwarves take turns dancing with the china dolls. Further down the road, cliff-dwelling cavemen attack Aysecik and her friends but the dwarves drive them off. Everyone meets Glinda at the edge of the lake and Aysecik learns the power of the slippers. She returns home to embrace her aunt and uncle with the dwarves watching from a distance, crying a little at having to say goodbye.

Degirmencioglu's Aysecik films were a popular children's series in Turkey, inspiring many imitations. The dwarves first appeared in the previous Aysecik film, an adaptation of *Snow White*, and proved so popular they returned in this film.

The finished product confirms Turkish cinema's reputation for low-budget, rather eccentric adaptations of American characters (this author has been told that their version of Superman is even wilder).

1972

Journey Back to Oz [Also known as Return to Oz]. 1972 (UK), 1974 (USA); 88 mins., color.

Voices: Dorothy Gale (Liza Minnelli), Aunt Em (Margaret Hamilton), Scarecrow (Mickey Rooney) Mombi (Ethel Merman), Cowardly Lion (Milton Berle) Tin Man (Danny Thomas), Glinda (Risë Stevens), Uncle Henry (Paul Ford), Signpost (Jack E. Leonard), Pumpkinhead (Paul Lynde), Woodenhead (Herschel Bernardi), Crow (Mel Blanc), Omby Amby (Dallas McKennon), Amos (Larry Storch).
Credits: Director: Hal Sutherland; *Writers:* Fred Ladd, Norm Prescott (based on *The Land of Oz*, with additional dialogue by Bernard Evslin; *Score:* Sammy Cahn, James Van Heusen, arranged and conducted by Walter Scharf; *Producers:* Norman Prescott, Lou Scheimer; *Art director:* John Christenson; *Supervising animator:* Amby Paliwoda; *Layout:* Alberto De Metto, Don Bluth, C.L. Hartman, Kay Wright, Herb Hazelton, Dale Baer; *Animators:* Bob Bransford, Bob Carlson, Jim Davis, Otto Feuer, Ed Friedman, Fred Grabe, Laverne Harding, Lou Kachivas, Les Kaluza, Anatole Kirsanoff, George Kreisl, Paul Krukowski, Bill Nunes, Jack Ozark, Manny Perez, Virgil Raddatz, Bill Reed, Virgil Ross, George Rowley, Ed Solomon, Ralph Somerville, Reuben Timmins, Lou Zukor.
From: Filmation Associates/Warner Brothers.

When another cyclone approaches Uncle Henry's farm, Dorothy ignores it, building a tin-can man beside the farm's scarecrow and remembering Oz. When the twister hits, the wind cracks the pasture gate against Dorothy's head, knocking her cold and sweeping her, Toto, the Scarecrow and the tin figure away. When Dorothy wakes, she realizes she's not in Kansas any more.

Dorothy finds the yellow brick road but when she reaches an intersection, the talking sign post decides it would be boring to point her in one direction and gives her three paths to the Emerald City. Ignoring the post, Dorothy stumbles down a hill and discovers Pumpkinhead, hiding in terror from Mombi, "the very wickedest witch in Oz." He tells Dorothy that Mombi made him through magic to serve as her assistant, but the loathsome nature of her deeds convinced him that he should run away. Dorothy suggests that if they go together to King Scarecrow, Pumpkinhead will be safe.

Unfortunately, when Toto chases Mombi's cat into the witch's cottage, it leads to Mombi (looking a lot like MGM's Wicked Witch) confronting Dorothy and realizing this is the girl who destroyed her cousins (the Witches of West and East). Mombi traps Dorothy in a magic chair and shows her a bubbling cauldron brewing an army of green elephants with which to demolish the Emerald City and overthrow the Scarecrow. Mombi decides to add Toto to the brew, but she and her pet crow have to find more firewood first to keep the cauldron boiling. Once they go, Pumpkinhead sneaks inside and frees Dorothy.

On the way to the Emerald City, Dorothy, Toto and Pumpkinhead find what looks like a merry-go-round horse stuck in the ground by its pole. After they free him, Woodenhead tells them that being a carousel horse was his latest unsuccessful career, culminating in flying off the carousel and getting stuck pole-first in the ground. He agrees to carry them to the Emerald City in return for Dorothy asking Scarecrow to give him a job.

Scarecrow is delighted to see Dorothy, though he tells her running Oz is so tiresome, he's beginning to regret having the brains for it. Mombi's elephants begin demolishing the city; the good guys ride off on Woodenhead, but an elephant plucks Scarecrow and Toto off the horse. Dorothy reluctantly keeps going, conceding she can't help if she's captured, too.

She and Pumpkinhead flee to Tinland, where the Tin Woodman dwells in a realm of robots and metal sculptures. Although eager to help, he tells Dorothy he's no match for Mombi's elephants. Dorothy is surprised his heart doesn't inspire him to try anyway, but the Tin Woodman replies that at times like this, his heart is a painful burden. He sends Dorothy to the Lion, but the thought of fighting the magic elephants drains away the beast's courage; like the others, he tells Dorothy the Wizard's gift has been more a burden than a blessing.

Glinda appears to Dorothy, but says even her magic has limits; the secret to Dorothy's triumph, she says, is to realize that believing in herself is "the greatest magic of all." Glinda does give Dorothy a silver box, not to be opened until she reaches the Emerald City.

Mombi sends animated magical trees to surround Dorothy and her friends, but when Glinda sends a golden hatchet into the forest, the trees fight over the gold, using the axe to hack themselves apart (which turns them into masses of happy flowers). Dorothy and her friends ride on to the Emerald City, where the elephants surround them. Dorothy opens the box and a mouse army pops out, sending the elephants fleeing in panic (an old wives' tale has it that elephants are terrified of mice).

Mombi, gloating over the tortures she'll inflict on Scarecrow and Toto, suddenly realizes her army has fled, but vows to destroy her captives, nonetheless. When a mouse enters the room, it startles Mombi into splashing both her pet crow and pet cat with shrinking potion, reducing them until the mouse can beat them up. Mombi turns herself into a rose bush with poison thorns to hide from the mice, but part of the elephant herd stampedes that way, and crushes Mombi, thorns and all, beneath their feet. The witch withers, the elephants vanish and the damage from their rampage is undone. Pumpkinhead reverts to a lifeless stick figure, but Dorothy's love for her friend brings him back to life.

Back on the throne, Scarecrow makes Woodenhead the royal steed and Pumpkinhead the minister of agriculture. Glinda summons a cyclone to carry Dorothy and Toto back to Kansas and the girl awakes lying by the gate with Toto, the cyclone having passed. Happy to be home, she runs to rejoin her family.

Producer Norm Prescott began work on *Return to the Land of Oz* in 1962, but ran out of money after finishing only 11 minutes. It took another decade to complete the film, and it did little business either side of the Atlantic.

The animation isn't bad, and the movie uses actors for vocal talent long before that became a standard practice. The plum casting, of course, is Judy Garland's daughter, Liza Minnelli, as Dorothy (sounding uncannily like her mother) and giving Margaret Hamilton a cameo as Aunt Em. The story, however, is a mess, from replacing Jinjur's army with Mombi's ludicrous elephants to Dorothy's friends all regretting the Wizard's gifts (this might have worked if the movie resolved it, but there's no payoff).

This is the first *The Land of Oz* adaptation with Dorothy written into the story, and the only adaptation that makes no use of either Tip or Ozma.

When ABC TV broadcast this on December 5, 1976, it included a live-action framing sequence with Bill Cosby playing the Wizard with some "Munchkin" kids (later both *Alftales* and *All That!* did Oz parodies with Cosby as the Wizard).

1973

Zardoz. 1973 (UK); 1974 (USA); 108 mins., color.

Cast: Zed (Sean Connery), Consuella (Charlotte Rampling), May (Sara Kestelman), Friend (John Alderton), Avalow (Sally Anne Newton), Arthur Frayn (Niall Buggy), George Saden (Bosco Hogan), Apathetic (Jessica Swift), Star (Bairbre Dowling), Old Scientist (Christopher Casson), Death (Reginald Jarman).

Credits: Director, writer, producer: John Boorman; *Assistant directors:* Simon Relph, Redmon Morris; *Associate producer:* Charles Orme; *Production design:* Anthony Pratt; *Art Director:* Martin Atkinson; *Cinematography:* Geoffrey Unsworth; *Costumes:* Christel Kruse Boorman;

Design and story associate: Bill Stair; *Music:* David Munrow; *Editor:* John Merritt. *From:* 20th Century–Fox.

300-year-old Arthur Frayn introduces the film, describing himself as tired of life — and the manipulator responsible for the events we're about to see. Those events begin in the barren wastelands of A.D. 2293, as Zardoz, a gigantic, flying stone head, gives the barbaric Exterminators "the gift of the gun" to make genocidal war on the other "Brutals."

One Exterminator, Zed, hides inside the idol-head before it flies off; finding Frayn inside too, Zed guns him down. Zardoz carries Zed through a force-field, the Vortex, to land in a pastoral community of Eternals, immortals wielding advanced technology but choosing to perform cooking and other chores by hand. Two Eternals, the lovers May and Consuella, capture Zed.

Consuella wants the savage executed, but May favors studying Zed to learn how effectively Frayn controls the Brutals. The violent memories her probe dredges up show the Brutals aren't the peaceful drones Frayn has claimed; the memories also fascinate the listless Eternals, who vote to keep Zed alive.

Zed learns that although the Tabernacle supercomputer keeps the Eternals from aging or death — it resurrects Frayn — not all of them are happy about it. The Renegades who've challenged the system have been aged to their dotage but still can't die; the Apathetics are catatonic from boredom; and even sane Eternals have lost the urge to procreate. Consuella tries studying Zed's sex drive, but discovers, to her outrage, that she arouses him a lot more.

Zed tells May he wants to destroy the Tabernacle; she offers to take him to it in return for letting her probe him further. In his mind, May sees a masked figure teaching Zed to read, which makes Zed realize there's more to life than mindless slaughter. Then Zed was given *The Wizard of Oz* to read, and realized Zard-Oz was just another humbug. Determined to look behind the curtain, he stowed away on Zardoz to discover the truth.

May, in turn, tells Zed how the elite who survived the world's collapse inside the Vortex had to repress any concern for the rest of humanity, which turned them into the cold creatures they've become. Consuella finds May and Zed together and, furious, rouses the Eternals to kill him, but the Renegades help Zed escape. Rejoining May, Zed impregnates her in return for a telepathic download of her vast education.

Frayn then appears and gives Zed a crystal; he reveals that he both created Zardoz and showed Zed the truth about him, in order to use the Exterminator to shatter the stifling Eternal society. When Consuella attacks Zed, she and he realize they're now perfectly matched: Zed's education makes him Consuella's intellectual equal just as anger has made her capable of Brutal savagery. They fall in love.

Zed realizes the crystal is the Tabernacle, but the computer traps his mind inside the crystal. Zed finds the flaw in the crystal and frees himself, destroying the Tabernacle. May, Consuella and Zed escape as the Exterminators ride through the failing Vortex to give the Eternals the death they long for. In the epilog, Zed and Consuella raise a child, age and die: the cycle of nature is restored.

John Boorman, who scored a Best Picture nomination with the 1972 hit thriller *Deliverance*, said he wrote *Zardoz* after wondering how California's communes might evolve if the rest of civilization fell away. Boorman planned to cast *Deliverance*'s Burt Reynolds as Zed, but submitted the script to Connery after Reynolds was sidelined by illness.

Connery loved the film so much that like Boorman, he passed on his usual salary (though some sources say he received a small one) in favor of a percentage of the profits. Warner Brothers and Columbia had rejected the film because Boorman insisted on full creative control, but Connery's financial concessions meant Boorman could forgo studio financing and make the film for only $1.1 million. Connery claimed the budget was so tight, some extras had painted legs instead of boots.

Rampling and Connery were both nominated for *London Evening News* awards as best actor and actress, and received good reviews, but despite the film's fine visuals (particularly remarkable for a low-budget, pre-computer-effects production), the rather aimless story, confusing narrative and "gloriously pretentious" style (in the words of author Robert Sellers) left the audience and the critics cold. Test audiences were so cold, Boorman added the prologue with Frayn, but it didn't help.

The film grossed only $1.5 million in the U.S. One film historian suggested *Zardoz*'s problem was timing, coming too late for 1960s psychedelics but too early for the *Star Wars*-fueled SF film boom.

1975

The Wonderful Wizard of Oz [Also known as The Wizard of Oz]. 15 mins., color.

Credits: Writers: Katherine Jose, Irene Lewis. *From:* Teaching Resources Films.

Six segments of film (*The Cyclone, Dorothy's New Friends, Along the Yellow Brick Road, They Meet the Wizard, Three Wishes Granted, Dorothy and Toto Come Home*) that showed scenes from *The Wizard of Oz* to accompany narration on records or cassettes (a fairly common educational tool at the time).

1976

Oz [Also known as 20th Century Oz]. 9/29/76 (Australia); 1977 (USA). 103 mins. (85 mins. USA, 90 mins. director's cut), color.

Cast: Dorothy (Joy Dunstan), The Wizard/Wally/salesclerk/ conductor/doorman/party guest (Graham Matters), Blondie/bass player (Bruce Spence), Killer/guitarist (Gary Waddell), Greaseball/drummer (Michael Carman), Glynn the Good Fairy (Robin Ramsay), Jane (Paula Maxwell), Truckie/bouncer (Ned Kelly), Waitress (Lorraine West), Receptionist (Beris Underhill), Gays (Russell Thomson, Gino Lattori), Promoter (Jim Slade), Manager (Roland Bonnet), Boys at dance (Martin Allen, Alan Pentland, Neil McColl) Trucker's mates (Stephen Millichamp, James Williamson, Phil Motherwell).

Credits: Director, writer: Chris Lofven (based on *The Wizard of Oz*); *Songs:* Ross Wilson, Wayne Burt, Gary Young, Baden Hutchins; *Producers:* Chris Lofven, Lyne Helms; *Associate producer:* Jane Scott; *Cinematography:* Dan Burstall; *Production design, art director:* Robby Perkins; *Music:* Ross Wilson; *Editor:* Les Luxford. *From:* Count Features, Inc., Australian Film Commission and BEF Film Distributors/Inter Planetary Pictures, Inc./Davis Equities Corporation Investment Partnerships/O&O Associates, Ltd.

Dorothy, a small-town Australian teen, is ready to cut loose for somewhere exciting, but the aunt and uncle she lives with don't see it that way. Heading home from a dance, Dorothy hitches a ride with the band, but the van crashes, knocking her out.

Dorothy wakes to find the band gone and the streets deserted. She enters the Good Fairy clothing store where the effeminate Glynn tells her the van hit and killed the town bully, and everyone assumes Dorothy was the driver. Glynn gives Dorothy a pair of red-sequined platform shoes as her reward. A hulking trucker enters and tells Dorothy the bully was his brother, and she's going to pay for his death, but Glynn promises the shoes will protect her.

Then Dorothy spots a photo of the Wizard, a rock icon ("The most sensational thing ever to hit Oz!") on the shop wall. Glynn tells her tonight's farewell performance in a nearby city will be Dorothy's last chance ever to see the Wizard in concert. He tells her to "follow the highway" and hitch rides whenever she can.

Dorothy hitches a ride with Blondie, a spaced-out surfer. When they stop for lunch, the trucker shows up and manhandles Dorothy, but she escapes. When Blondie stops for gas, Greaseball, a surly mechanic, sets his sights on Dorothy, and Killer, a tough biker, pushes the girl around but breaks into tears when she slaps him. Blondie's car malfunctions, so when the trucker turns up, Dorothy goes with Greaseball, then with Killer on his bike after Greaseball's car dies, too. While they get stoned on the beach,

Blondie and Greaseball catch up, but so does Glynn, who reminds Dorothy time is running out and gives her a ride in his Mustang. The other guys follow.

Dorothy reaches the city, and when she can't buy tickets for the concert, talks her way past the arena doorman, soon followed by her friends. The Wizard's spectacular performance blows Dorothy away, so she sets out to locate his hotel room and meet him in person. Thugs ambush her friends and drag her to the trucker, who drives her to his house to rape her. Dorothy's friends break in, which distracts the trucker long enough for her to plant one of her platform shoes in his groin.

The foursome tracks the Wizard to his hotel, where Killer bluffs his way past the desk clerk. They crash the Wizard's party, and Dorothy finds the man himself behind the curtain — his shower curtain. Dorothy joins him in the shower, but finds him much less impressive; he dismisses his on-stage persona as a showbiz illusion. Glynn, the Wizard's agent, storms in and demands the Wizard get out and mingle with the press. The Wizard does so, leaving Dorothy standing there, miserable and alone.

Dorothy's friends enter and try to comfort her; dressing, she beats the heels of her shoes together angrily, muttering "fame and fortune fuck you up ... fame and fortune fuck you up..." and waking by the van, watched by the musicians (who were all there in the dream, though she doesn't give the "you and you and you" speech). She dazedly repeats her thought about fame and fortune, to which one of the band promptly responds, "Bullshit!"

This Australian story took Dorothy out of Oz (though of course, "Oz" is also slang for Australia itself) and into the modern world, which, along with the rock score, profanity and sex, went over like a lead balloon with critics and viewers. It was released in America as *20th Century Oz* with music remixed into four-track stereo, and 12 minutes trimmed by the director.

1978

The Wiz. 10/24/78. 133 mins., color.

Cast: Dorothy (Diana Ross), Scarecrow (Michael Jackson), Tin Man (Nipsey Russell), Cowardly Lion (Ted Ross), Evillene (Mabel King), Aunt Em (Theresa Merritt), Miss One (Thelma Carpenter), Glinda the Good (Lena Horne), The Wiz (Richard Pryor), Uncle Henry (Stanley Greene), Peddler (Clyde J. Barrett), Crows (Derrick Bell, Roderick-Spencer Sibert, Kashka Banjoko, Ronald "Smokey" Stevens), Gold Footmen (Tony Brealond, Joe Lynn), Green Footmen (Clinton Jackson, Charles Rodriguez), Head Winkie (Carlton Johnson), Munchkins (Ted Williams, Mabel Robinson, Damon Pearce, Donna Patrice Ingram), Cheetah (Harry Madsen), Rolls Royce Lady (Glory Van Scott), Green Lady (Vicki Baltimore), Partygoers (Carlos Cleveland, Marianna Aalda, Aaron Boddie, Gay Faulkner, Ted Butler, T.B. Skinner, Jamie Perry, Daphne McWilliams, Douglas Berring, James Shaw, Johnny Brown, Gyle Waddy, Dorothy Fox, Frances Salisbury, Beatrice Dunmore, Traci Core, Donald King, Claude Brooks, Billie Allen, Willie Carpenter, Denise Dejon, Kevin Stockton, Alvin Alexis).

Credits: Director: Sidney Lumet; *Book:* Joel Schumacher (based on *The Wiz*, book by William F. Brown, score by Charlie Smalls); *Score:* Charlie Smalls, additional songs by Quincy Jones, Nick Ashford, Valerie Simpson; *Producer:* Rob Cohen; *Executive producer:* Ken Harper; *Production design, costumes:* Tony Walton; *Art director:* Philip Rosenberg; *Choreography:* Louis Johnson; *Special effects:* Albert Whitlock; *Music arrangements:* Quincy Jones; *Editor:* Dede Allen. *From:* Universal, Motown.

Songs: The Feeling That We Have; Can I Go On?; He's the Wizard; Soon as I Get Home; You Can't Win; Ease on Down the Road; What Would I Do If I Could Feel; Slide Some Oil to Me; I'm a Mean Ole' Lion; Poppy Girls; Be a Lion; End of the Yellow Brick Road; So You Wanted to See the Wizard; Is This What Feeling Gets?; Don't Nobody Bring Me No Bad News; Brand New Day; Believe in Yourself; Home.

At 24, black Harlem schoolteacher Dorothy Gale is so terrified of life that she still lives with her aunt and has never gone south of 125th street. When her dog, Toto, runs into a snowstorm, Dorothy follows;

they're both caught in a tornado and swept to an Oz that looks like a wild dream version of New York itself. Coming down, they strike the top of a neon sign which crashes fatally on the Wicked Witch of the East, freeing the Munchkins the witch had turned into graffiti art.

Miss One, Good Witch of the North and head of the Munchkins' numbers racket, tells Dorothy only the all-powerful Wiz can send her home. None of the cabs on the yellow brick road will stop for her, so Dorothy puts on the Wicked Witch's silver slippers and starts walking. She rescues a Scarecrow who's been convinced of his own stupidity by bullying Jim Crows; frees the Tin Man — a hard-hearted carny hustler — from under a massive female statue ("I have an irresistible attraction to the wrong women," says the Tin Man) and discovers a frightened lion hiding inside one of the stone lions fronting the New York Public Library. All three join Dorothy to ask for help from the Wiz.

After escaping a menacing subway station, the Lion, Dorothy and Toto are drugged by the Poppies (nightclub dancers) but revived by Tin Man's tears. They enter the ultra-hip Emerald City, whose residents race to keep up with the Wiz's fashion dictates: "Green is dead! My color is red!" The Wiz — a giant steel head dwelling in an immense skyscraper — agrees to grant their wishes once they kill Evillene, the Wicked Witch of the West.

When they enter Evillene's realm, however, the witch's winged-monkey bike gang drags them all to the witch's sweatshop. The witch tortures Dorothy's friends to make her give up the slippers, but at Scarecrow's suggestion, Dorothy triggers the fire alarm, setting off the sprinklers and melting Evillene away. They return to the Wiz's chamber, but discover he's nothing but a phoney, a failed American politician blown to Oz during a campaign balloon ride.

Dorothy then convinces her friends that they don't need magic because they've had brains, heart and courage all along. Glinda the Good Witch appears and tells Dorothy the same is true of her: She'll be able to return home once she accepts that she's strong enough to make a home anywhere. Realizing the sniveling Wiz proves no one can find one's self by living a lie, Dorothy clicks her heels together, ready to return home and face the world.

When Motown and Universal first struck a deal to bring Broadway's *The Wiz* to the big screen (for details, see the entry for *The Wiz* in Chapter 2), they envisioned a $6 million musical with a screenplay — written by Motown's Rob Cohen and prospective director John Badham — that stayed close to the stage version. There would also be a national talent search for a girl to play Dorothy.

That plan went out the window when Motown singing star Diana Ross, who'd already starred in *Lady Sings the Blues* and *Mahogany*, said she wanted to play Dorothy. The advantages of having a major star in the lead persuaded Cohen to drop the talent search (making *The Wiz* one of many productions that announced a search for a talented unknown but wound up casting a very known), but at the cost of losing Badham: Unlike Garland, Ross would have to play Dorothy as an adult, and Badham foresaw that wouldn't work.

Cohen then invited Sidney Lumet (*Dog Day Afternoon*, *Serpico*) to direct, on the grounds that Lumet's *Network* showed a flair for fantasy (certainly his resume is no more at odds with the material than Victor Fleming's was for MGM's *Wizard*). Lumet decided no one could relate to Kansas farms any more (he also stated, inaccurately, that there hadn't been black farmers in Kansas in the 1930s), so he set the whole film in New York City. Screenwriter Joel Schumacher then rewrote the script, claiming the play wouldn't work on the big screen and that he wanted a film close to Baum's book (of course the Broadway show was quite faithful to Baum, certainly more so than the film turned out to be).

The $24 million film (1978's most expensive feature next to *Superman*) included extensive on-location shooting, a color-wash process to blend the yellow brick road into the New York streets, and 1,200 costumes designed by Bill Blass, Halston and other top designers for the Emerald City's dancers (400 dancers constantly changing costumes to stay in fashion).

The end results, alas, are a textbook example of how not to do it: The film went far over-budget and many of the visuals looked clunkingly charmless. Pryor, whose comic flair could certainly have pulled off a modern "humbug," is wasted as a sniveling weakling, neither a good wizard nor a good man. And Ross's turn as Dorothy is fatally bad — her efforts to act terrified of life come off frantic and unconvincing. Reviews were tremendously unfavorable.

Another all-black *Wizard of Oz* was announced in the late 1990s, to star rappers Snoop Doggy Dog and Queen Latifah; a revised version of the project was announced as a 2002 Fox TV movie, *The O.Z.*, but it has yet to materialize.

1981

The Wizard of Malta. 20 mins.
Cast: Narrator (Diane Keaton).
Credits: Director, writer, producer: Douglas Davis.

This experimental split-screen film consisted of three screens showing parodies of *The Wizard of Oz* (MGM version), *The Maltese Falcon* and *Napoleon* by Abel Ganz, all running simultaneously. Davis says he created the film as a tribute to Abel Ganz, whose silent classic *Napoleon* used the same triple-screen format, but didn't show the film much precisely because coordinating the timing on all segments was so difficult.

"It was shown at the Ronald Feldman Gallery for one month," Davis said. "How in the hell they managed to get the timing right each day ... it was not easy."

Under the Rainbow. 7/31/81. 98 mins., color.
Cast: Bruce Thorpe (Chevy Chase), Annie Clark (Carrie Fisher), Duchess (Eve Arden), Duke (Joseph Maher), Otto Kringling (Billy Barty), Nakamuri (Mako), Rollo Sweet (Cork Hubbert), Tiny (Pat McCormick), Henry Hudson (Adam Arkin), Assassin (Robert Donner), Lester Hudson (Richard Stahl), Otis (Freeman King), Homer Hingle (Peter Isacksen), Louie (Jack Kruschen), Akido (Bennett Ohta), Wedgie (Gary Friedkin), Fitzgerald (Michael Lee Gogin), Lana (Pam Vance), Telephone Operator (Louisa Moritz), Inspector Collins (Anthony Gordon), Steward (John Pyle), Mail Clerk (Bill Lytle), Hitler (Ted Lehmann), Rosie (Patty Maloney), Iris (Zelda Rubinstein), Ventriloquist (Bobby Porter), Hilda's Ride (Charlie Messenger), Lefty (Robert Murvin), Dispatcher (David Haney), Man at Radio (Gordon Zimmerman), Whittler (Jom Boeke), Truck Driver (Tony Ballen), Waitress (Geraldine Papel), Cleaning Woman (Ruth Brown), Studio Guard (Pat Hern), Director (Peter W. Wooley), Actor (Gary Wayne), Actress (Suzanne Leonard), Servant (Deloris Crenshaw), Cigarette Girl (Twink Caplan), Bartender (John F. Goff), Prostitute (Beth Nufer), Flying Morleys (Denise Cheshire, Victor Hunsberger, Jr.), Pops (Leonard Barr).

Credits: Director: Steve Rash; *Writers:* Pat McCormick, Harry Hurwitz, Martin Smith, Pat Bradley, Fred Bauer; *Story:* Fred Bauer, Pat Bradley; *Producer:* Fred Bauer; *Executive producer:* Edward H. Cohen; *Production design:* Peter Wooley; *Cinematography:* Frank Stanley; *Costumes:* Mike Butler; *Music:* Joe Renzetti; *Editor:* David Blewitt. *From:* Innovisions/USA, Orion Pictures Company, Warner Brothers.

In a 1938 Midwestern charity mission, Rollo, a midget hoping to be cast in the MGM *Wizard*, falls off the roof repairing a radio aerial. Cut to Adolf Hitler assigning midget spy Kringling to deliver American defense secrets to Japanese agent Nakamuri in Los Angeles (Nakamuri will know Kringling by his height). Cut again to Secret Service agent Thorpe, newly assigned to bodyguard a pair of exiled European aristocrats obsessed with the ridiculous idea that there's an assassin hunting them. They're right, but Thorpe accidentally thwarts the killer without realizing he's there.

Meanwhile, MGM underling Annie Clark learns her next assignment is as a minder for the hundred-plus midgets cast as Munchkins in *Wizard of Oz*. Annie's assistant, Homer, books hotel reservations, but assistant manager Henry doesn't get the word. Annie meets the midgets—and Thorpe—at the train station; Rollo shows up, hunted by cops for hopping a freight, but the Munchkins hide him and invite him to join the cast.

Annie, Thorpe and their respective charges all show up at the hotel, which Henry has renamed Hotel Rainbow. Unfortunately, a Japanese tour group lead by Akido has already booked it solid. Nakamuri arrives and doesn't know which midget to contact; the equally confused Kringling turns the plans over to Akido, just before the assassin kills Akido by mistake. Over the course of the evening, Annie and Thorpe strike sparks and the midgets party like teens on a Ft. Lauderdale spring break. Kringling and Nakamuri connect, and deduce (wrongly) that Annie has the plans; the midgets spot the spies, but assume they're out to sabotage the movie.

The spies capture Rollo, Annie and the Duke, saving him from the assassin in the process, and demand Thorpe deliver the map. Thorpe tells them its hidden in the Duke's dog's collar—the same dog the spies just threw out into the street. While Kringling chases the dog, the assassin tries again, and he and Nakamuri wind up killing each other. The Munchkins now know Kringling's real agenda, so the good midgets chase the Nazi midget onto and through the MGM backlot, disrupting an Esther Williams musical, a Western and *Gone With the Wind* before Rollo hits the Emerald City set, knocking himself out.

Rollo wakes in the mission and realizes it was all a dream and you were there, and you, and you (since his was the only face seen in the opening, this comes as a surprise, albeit a lame one). Then the radio announces FDR's New Deal, which means everyone will have jobs soon! Better yet, the Munchkin bus shows up to collect Rollo (his letter of acceptance got lost in the mail); as it drives off, we discover the building is ... the Rainbow Mission, Kansas.

The antics of the 124 midgets cast as Munchkins in MGM's *Wizard* are Hollywood legend (or fiction; *The Making of the Wizard of Oz* suggests that most of their sex-capades were a myth). This unfunny comedy takes their antics, adds the Oz dream motif and throws comic scenes at the screen in the hope some of them stick (few do).

1982

Ozu No Mahotsukai [Also known as The Wizard of Oz]. 5/82. 60 mins. (78 in USA), animated, color.

Voice Cast: (American): Dorothy (Aileen Quinn), The Wizard (Lorne Greene), Tin Man (John Stocker), Scarecrow (Billy Van), Cowardly Lion (Thick Wilson), Wicked Witch/Good Witch of the North (Elizabeth Hanna), Glinda (Wendy Thatcher).

Credits: Director: Fumihiko Takayama (John Danylkiw, USA); *Writer:* Akira Miyazaki; *Lyrics:* Sammy Cahn, Allen Byrns; *Producer:* John Danylkiw; *Executive producers:* Yoshimitsu Banno, Katsum Ueno, Alan L. Gleitsman (USA); *Key animator:* Koji Kobayashi; *Music:* Jx Hisaishi, Yuichiro Oda; *Editor:* Johann Lowenberg; *From:* Toho, Alan Enterprises, Paramount.

Songs: A Wizard of a Day; I Dream of Home; It's Strictly Up to You.

While Dorothy's loving aunt and uncle are in town, a twister strikes the farm, knocking Dorothy out as she tries to reach the storm cellar. The farmhouse goes up, up, up, then down, down, down onto the Wicked Witch of the East in Munchkinland. As Dorothy emerges, the Good Witch of the North hands the incredulous girl the Wicked Witch's magic ruby shoes. Dorothy asks to go home, but the Good Witch has no idea how to send her across the Deadly Desert; instead, she recommends visiting the Emerald City to consult the great Wizard of Oz. To protect her, the witch places a magic kiss on Dorothy's forehead, and reminds her any difficulty can be overcome "with wisdom, love and courage."

Dorothy soon meets the Scarecrow, who has wanted brains ever since a wise old crow told him they were the only thing worth having. Next morning, they find and oil the rusted Tin Woodman, who believes that with no heart, he never has and never can love; though both Dorothy and the Scarecrow question this, the Woodman decides to go with them to Oz to get a heart. In a forest, a lion attacks them, but backs off when Dorothy slaps him; a coward at heart, he decides to ask the Wizard for courage.

Despite assorted problems—a chasm in the roadway, the Tin Woodman crying himself rusted when he steps on a bug, the monstrous kalidahs—they reach the city, where the Wizard agrees to see them, but only one at a time. A giant bodiless head astounds Dorothy by knowing where Kansas is, but demands she kill the Wicked Witch of the West before sending her home. The other three are given the same demand, but from different shapes: A beautiful angel for the Scarecrow, a monstrous beast facing the Tin Woodman, a ball of fire for the Lion.

Entering the Winkie lands, they face a pack of magical wolves, a murder of crows that merge into one gigantic bird, and then the winged monkeys. Although they can't hurt Dorothy because of the Good Witch's kiss, she lets them take her to the castle along with her friends. She and Toto help the others escape, then the one-eyed witch binds everyone with magic. Protected by that kiss, Dorothy escapes and topples a vat of water in the pursuing witch's path, which destroys her. Dorothy and her friends return to the Wizard, surrounded by admiring, cheering crowds.

The Wizard tells them to come back another day, but Toto trips a button that reveals the real "Oz," a stage magician from Omaha, brought to Oz by balloon. He convinces Dorothy's friends that they don't need magic: The Lion lacks confidence, not courage, the Scarecrow is learning from experience and the Tin Woodman's compassion is more important than a physical heart.

The Wizard prepares to take Dorothy home in his old balloon, but winds up leaving alone while Dorothy chases Toto. Glinda then appears and tells Dorothy that the power of the slippers is enough to take her home; she returns to Kansas to tell Henry and Em about her amazing adventure somewhere over the rainbow.

This is overall a faithful adaptation of the original novel, with Glinda and the Witch of the North straight out of Denslow's illustrations. It's one of several adaptations (e.g., *The Wiz*) in which Glinda appears to Dorothy, cutting out the journey to her castle, but it doesn't really work here: Dorothy knows from the start there's no place like home, so why didn't Glinda appear to her sooner to tell her about the shoes?

This version, which wasn't shown in Japan until 1986, is sometimes confused with the 1984 anime TV series, which had the same writer.

1984

Os Trapalhões E O Magico De Oroz [Also known as The Tramps and the Wizard of Oroz; The Bunglers and the Wizard of Oroz; The Nutcases and the Wizard of Oroz]. 93 mins., Brazil.

Cast: Didi Mocó (Renato Aragão), Espantalho/Scarecrow (Zacarias), Homem de Lata/Man of Can (Mussum), Delegado Leão/Sheriff Lion (Dedé Santana), Sóro (Arnaud Rodrigeus), Tatu (José Dumont), Maria (Bia Seidl), Aninha (Xuxa Meneghel), Carcaras the Vulture (Tony Tornado), Magico de Oroz (Dary Reis). With: Maurício do Valle, Jofre Soares, Wilson Viana, Roberto Guilherme, Dino Santana, Fernando José, with Déa Peçanha, Sônia Aires, Carmem Palhares, Olívia Pineschi, Péricles Flaviano, Zanatha, Sérgio Luis Pereira, Ricardo Cabral, Alison Vingador, Roberto Lee, Ubirajara Gama, Roberto Bigode, Roberto Piau, Mano Melo.

Credits: Directors: Dedé Santana, Vitor Lustosa; *Writers:* Vitor Lustosa, Gilvan Pereira, Renato Aragão, Dede Santana, Gracindo Jr.; *Executive producer:* Paulo Aragão; *Cinematographer:* Antônio Gonçalves; *Music:* Arnaud Rodrigues; *Incidental music:* Caxa Aragao; *Art director:* Renato Aragão; *From:* Renato Aragão Produções/Demuza.

A drought has left northeast Brazil in such a pitiable state that vagrants Didi, Soro and

Tatu have to catch vultures for food. The desperate trio head off to Oroz, hitching their small hut to their horse, Salvation. They are astounded when a Scarecrow hanging in a field of withered corn talks to them, but when vultures swoop down to torment the brainless "Clowbrush" (clown face, hair like a brush), the Trapalhões kill the birds. They take Clowbrush along with them so that in Oroz, he can find a doctor who will give him some brains.

Soon after, the group enters an abandoned house and finds Vat, a metal man immobilized because his oil drum torso has leaked and dried him out. The Trapalhões plug it with straw from Clowbrush, refill it with rum (Vat's "blood") and invite him along to ask the doctor for a heart.

Oroz, however, has problems of its own: Wealthy landowner Ferreira controls all the water and sells it at exorbitant rates, and his cowardly stooge, Sheriff Leão, ruthlessly punishes water thieves. Ferreira tells the town's sexy schoolteacher, Aninha, that he'll provide free water to all her students if she'll marry him, but she insists that she loves Lion despite his cowardice.

When the Trapalhoes arrive, they rip off the local bakery, then hide out in Aninha's school. Their defiance terrifies the sheriff, but the citizens force him to confront the thieves. To impress Aninha, Leão challenges Didi to single combat, resulting in a slapstick brawl that ends when Didi stops to genuflect to a priest, giving Leão a chance to deck him. Everyone goes to court, where the judge orders Didi, Clowbrush and Vat to help Leao find water, while Soro and Tatu stay as hostages.

After trying and failing to rob Ferreira's wells, the group goes into the desert, where a hermit directs them to the underground lair of the Wizard of Oroz. When they enter, the Wizard (dressed like a sideshow conjurer) appears before them, hears their requests, then responds incomprehensibly ("Having a heart in your chest doesn't mean the plenitude of creation!"). When Didi asks him to bring rain, the Wizard's magic mirror shows a metal monster that legend says will spout water at the "time of the elections." The seekers leave the cave, still clueless.

Ferreira and his men attack, but the Wizard gives Didi a magic bone that enables him to triumph. Didi then uses the bone to fly them all to Rio de Janeiro, where they spot the metal monster, a downtown water pump. After riding bicycles all over town and causing increasing quantities of chaos, they steal one of the pumps and return to Oroz.

Of course, the pump can't do much when detached from a water supply, so the furious townsfolk tie up Didi and his friends in the town square. As they lament their state, Didi convinces his friends that they have brains, heart and courage after all — and if they have faith, too, they can accomplish anything, even willing it to rain. The prisoners concentrate until a cloudburst descends, leading to a celebration in which even Ferreira joins in until he's pelted with mud.

This is one of a series of slapstick films made by the clowning Trapalhões (variously translated as tramps, nutcases or bunglers) in their native Brazil. Director Aragão said this parody was intended to dramatize contemporary drought conditions too terrible to approach realistically (which certainly wasn't a problem with this film).

And yes, the actress Xuxa is the popular children's TV host whose series briefly ran in the United States.

1985

Return to Oz. 6/21/85. 110 mins., color.

Cast: Dorothy Gale (Fairuza Balk), Dr. Worley/Nome King (Nicol Williamson), Nurse Wilson/Princess Mombi (Jean Marsh), Aunt Em (Piper Laurie), Uncle Henry (Matt Clark), Tik-Tok (Michael Sundin and Tim Rose; Sean Barrett, voice), Billina (Mak Wilson; Denise Bryer, voice), Jack Pumpkinhead (Brian Henson, Stewart Larange; Brian Henson, voice), Gump (Stewart Larange; Lyle Conway, voice), Scarecrow (Justin Case), Cowardly Lion (John Alexander), Tin Man (Deep Roy), Ozma (Emma Ridley),

Mombi's other heads (Sophie Ward, Fiona Victory), Head Wheeler (Pons Mar), Wheelers (John Alexander, Rachel Ashton, Robbie Barnett, Ailsa Berk, Peter Elliot, Roger Ennals, Michele Hine, Mark Hopkins, Colin Skeaping, Ken Stevens, Philip Tan, Robert Thirtle), Policeman (Bruce Boa), Supporting puppeteers (Susan Dacre, Geoff Felix, David Greenaway, Swee Lim), Polychrome (Cherie Hawkins).

Credits: Director: Walter Murch; *Writers:* Walter Murch, Gill Dennis (based on *Ozma of Oz* and *The Land of Oz*); *Producer:* Paul Maslansky; *Executive producer:* Gary Kurtz; *Claymation:* Will Vinton Productions; *Cinematography:* David Watkin; *Production design:* Norman Reynolds; *Music:* David Shire; *Editor:* Leslie Hodgson; *From:* Walt Disney.

Six months after Dorothy returned from Oz to Kansas, Dorothy's constant talk of tin men and talking scarecrows has Aunt Em convinced that the girl has gone mad. Dorothy insists a key that she found is a message from Oz; Em responds by taking her to town for electroshock. Once the doctor hears Dorothy's deranged tale of a woodman whose entire body was chopped up and replaced with tin, he agrees with Em.

A young girl materializes to comfort Dorothy; after a thunderstorm shuts down the power, the girl returns to help Dorothy escape. Dorothy stumbles into a river and floats out to sea on a crate, accompanied by a chicken. When Dorothy wakes, the chicken, Billina, can talk, which tells Dorothy they've washed up in Oz. They land on a stone outcropping which they use to cross the Deadly Desert, unaware the stones are watching them.

Dorothy finds her old farmhouse where it fell in the Munchkin land, but the yellow brick road beyond it is shattered and overgrown. At the end of the road, the Emerald City is a ruin and Tin Man, Cowardly Lion and her other friends are turned to stone. The grotesque Wheelers, who have wheels instead of hands and feet, chase Dorothy and Billina through the city, warning them the Nome King won't tolerate chickens in Oz.

Dorothy's key opens a hidden chamber where she finds and winds up Tik-Tok, a mechanical man who drives off the Wheelers. The Wheeler leader reveals that the Nome King conquered Oz, and only his servant, Princess Mombi, can tell Dorothy what happened to King Scarecrow.

Mombi—a princess who switches heads to match her moods—tells Dorothy the Scarecrow is imprisoned in the Nome King's mountain fortress. The princess locks Dorothy and Billina up in the attic, intending to take Dorothy's head once it ages a little; Tik-Tok tries to help, but runs down. In the attic, Dorothy finds Jack Pumpkinhead, a pumpkin-headed stick figure. Jack explains that his "mother" created him to surprise Mombi, who then animated Jack as a test of her magic Powder of Life. Mombi then disposed of Jack's mother, locked Jack up—and forgot about him.

Dorothy escapes the attic and rewinds Tik-Tok. He and Jack cobble together a flying creature from sofas, brooms and a stuffed deer head, and Dorothy steals Mombi's powder to animate it. They escape the attic, heading for the Nome mountain. Furious, Mombi confronts Dorothy's girl friend in a mirror and tells "Ozma" that not even Dorothy can save her.

The Nome King, an elemental spirit of stone, drops Dorothy through a chasm into his throne room. He justifies attacking Oz to reclaim the emeralds "stolen" from the Earth, briefly reunites Dorothy with the Scarecrow, then turns the straw man into one of the countless ornaments in his caverns. He gives Dorothy and her friends (except Billina, nesting unseen in Jack's head), three chances each to find Scarecrow or become bric-a-brac themselves.

While Dorothy's friends play the game and fail, the king reveals that he found Dorothy's ruby slippers when they fell off on the flight back to Kansas; they gave him the power to conquer Oz. He offers to use them to send Dorothy home, but she insists on taking her turn at the game. Mombi arrives, and the Nome King informs her that once Dorothy loses, Ozma will be forgotten and the king will become fully human (a statement that's never explained).

Dorothy wins the game when she deduces that the king has turned her friends into green trinkets for the Emerald City. Furious at losing, the king becomes a stone giant and snatches up Jack; this dislodges Billina's new egg (poison to Nomes) onto the king, turning him and his army to dust. Dorothy reclaims the slippers, takes everyone back to the Emerald City, with Mombi in chains, and restores the petrified populace.

The slippers then show her Ozma — Jack's mother — inside a mirror and Dorothy helps her into reality. Glinda reveals Ozma, the rightful ruler, was turned over to Mombi by the Wizard when he took the throne; Mombi then turned her into a mirror image at the Nome King's behest. Dorothy gives Ozma the ruby slippers, and Ozma promises to watch over Dorothy in Kansas and bring her to Oz any time she asks. Ozma sends Dorothy home —

— and Dorothy wakes on the side of the river. Henry and Em find her, overjoyed that she survived the clinic burning down. When they return home, Dorothy sees Ozma in the mirror, but lets her aunt believe she's over all that silly Oz fantasy.

Director/co-writer Walter Murch said he decided to combine elements of *The Land of Oz* and *Ozma of Oz* to give Dorothy an active hand in Ozma's ascension. Putting Dorothy into *Land* is a fairly common change, actually; Murch has suggested that Baum might have done it himself if he had known at the time that she would return in the third book. Murch also decided against a musical or writing the film as a direct sequel to MGM's *The Wizard of Oz*, but he did try to keep the two films compatible, with ruby slippers (which required an agreement with MGM, since they introduced them) and a brunette Dorothy.

The film's set designs were based on buildings at the 1893 Chicago World's Fair, and the Oz characters were designed like the Neill drawings, except for the Nomes: Spectacular claymation made them into living earth elementals who impressed even critics who hated the film.

And there were plenty of those, ranging from critics who knew nothing of Baum and judged the film purely as a sequel to MGM's 1939 movie (Chicago critics Gene Siskel and Roger Ebert wondered why anyone would make an Oz film that wasn't a musical) to Oz fans who found that the dark tone (Dorothy faced with electroshock?) failed to capture the spirit of the book. Others quite enjoyed the film's effort to look beyond MGM's version.

The box office was dismal, but some industry watchers blame that less on the film than timing: *Return to Oz* came out immediately after a management change at Disney, so the new team had no stake in its success. Writer Harlan Ellison suggested that the new team wanted it to fail, so their first projects would look better by comparison.

The ending celebration scenes include a number of familiar faces such as Scraps, the Frog-Man, Rinkitink and Polychrome. For the Japanese release, the song "Keep on Dreamin'" was added over the ending credits.

1986

My Favorite Fairy Tales, Volume 4: The Wizard of Oz. Eight mins., animated, color.

Voices: Alice Smith, Kris Noel Pearson, Benjamin Walker, Kimberly Crystal, Xavier Garcia, Wayne Kerr.

Credits: Director: Robert Barron; *Writer:* Winston Richard; *Producer:* Haim Saban; *Executive producer:* Shuki Levy; *Music:* Haim Saban, Shuki Levy; *From:* Saban Productions.

A cyclone strikes Kansas, ruining Dorothy Gale's plans to spend the day with Toto; when she hides in the farmhouse, it carries her off, without Toto, and drops the house in Oz on the Wicked Witch of the East. Dorothy receives the witch's ruby shoes and goes to the Wizard of Oz for help getting home. Along the way she picks up the Scarecrow, Tin Woodman and Cowardly Lion who agree to join her and seek the Wizard's help finding brains, heart and courage respectively.

When they reach the Emerald City, a shadow-figure on a throne agrees to grant their wishes, once they destroy the Witch of the West. The quartet passes through a magic gate in the castle and enters the witch's realm. The witch blasts them with fireballs; Scarecrow deduces that the best weapon against a fire-witch is water, and after several failures, Dorothy successfully douses the witch and destroys her.

The foursome returns to the throne room where the Wizard reveals he's an ordinary man using trick lighting to create the shadow-image. He tells Dorothy's friends that having proved their brains, heart and courage fighting the witch, they no longer need his help. The Wizard then summons Glinda, who shows Dorothy how to use the slippers to return home to Toto.

A badly animated, very condensed version, culled from an anime to which Saban had bought the rights.

1987

Hello Kitty's Furry Tale Theater: The Wizard of Paws. 12 mins., animated, color.

Voices: Hello Kitty (Tara Charendoff), Tuxedo Sam (Sean Roberge), Chip (Noam Zylberman), My Melody (Mairon Bennett), Grandpa Kitty (Carl Banas), Grandma Kitty/Mama Kitty (Elizabeth Hanna), Papa Kitty (Len Carlson), Catnip (Cree Summer Francks), Grinder (Greg Morton), Fangora (Denise Pidgeon).

Credits: Director, producer: Michael Maliani; *Writer:* Phil Harnage; *Executive producer:* Andy Heyward; *Art directors:* Istvan Fellner, Pascall Morelli; *Animation supervisor:* Norman Drew; *Music:* Haim Saban, Shuki Levy. *From:* Sanrio Productions/DiC Enterprises/MGM/UA Television.

Oh-so-cute, anthropomorphic Hello Kitty and her friends (penguin Tuxedo Sam, Chip the cat, hulking bulldog Grinder and others) stage adaptations of various fairy tales in the Furry Tale Theatre (though once the play starts, it looks "real," not stage-bound). In *The Wizard of Paws*, Kitty plays Hello Dorothy, who lives on a farm in Catfish with her grandparents until the cyclone carries her and the farmhouse away.

The twister drops the house on the Wicked Witchie of the West in the Land of Paws, much to the joy of the Tin Penguin, the Scarecrow (Chip) and the Cowardly Rabbit. After the Good Witch of the North gives Dorothy Witchie's ruby collar, Witchie (Kitty's rival Catnip) reconstitutes herself and flies off, vowing revenge.

Dorothy and her friends visit the Wizard of Paws in Anchovy City, where the emerald towers are all fish-shaped. The Wizard agrees to grant their wishes once they bring him Witchie's brooms; the quartet heads off, but the Winged Monkeys capture Dorothy and throw the others into a swamp. They escape the swamp and sneak into the castle to remove Dorothy; Witchie blasts them with a spell, but it rebounds off the mirror behind them and turns her into a toad.

Back in Anchovy City, the Wizard gives Scarecrow a straight-A report card; gives the Rabbit mirrored sunglasses so no one can see how scared he is; gives Tin Penguin a Valentine card proclaiming "You must have a heart if someone loves you." He offers to fly Dorothy home on the witch's broom, but it rockets off with him before she can board. The Good Witch tells Dorothy how to use the ruby collar to go home, and Dorothy wakes up in her bed. The cast comes out to take their bows, and the actor playing the Wizard crashes through the set on the broom.

Hello Kitty has been promoting Sanrio products for 15 years, making her one of the most successful characters in anime.

Dorothy Meets Ozma of Oz. 8/11/87. 28 mins., animated, color.

Voices: Narrator (Michael Gross), Dorothy (Janice Kawaye), Scarecrow (Matt Stone); with Sandra J. Butcher, Nancy Chance, Jay David, Fredie Smootie, Debbie Lytton.

Credits: Directors: Pierre DeCelles, Georges

Grammat, Chiou Wen Shian, Myrna Bushman, Lisa Wilson, Bill Knoll, Joe Cisi; *Writers:* Jim Carlson, Terrence McDonnell (based on *Ozma of Oz*); *Producers:* Diana Dru Botsford, Thomas A. Bliss; *Executive producers:* Donald Kushner, Peter Locke; *Artistic director:* Philip J. Felix; *Music:* Al Kasha, Joel Hirchhorn, Michael Lloyd; *Production manager:* Nelson Shin; *From:* Atlantic-Kushner-Locke, Inc., Lorimar Telepictures, A-KOM Productions, Ltd., Prairie Rose Productions, Inc.

This was a 30-minute adaptation of *Ozma of Oz*, initially offered as a premium for Ban deodorant.

1988

The Wizard of Oz. 59 mins., animated, color.

Credits: Writer: Corrine J. Naden (based on *The Wizard of Oz*); Illustrations by Bill Morrison.

This set of four filmstrips, running slightly under an hour, told the story of the first Baum book. *Off to See the Wizard*, *Dorothy and the Wicked Witch*, *Dorothy and the Wizard*, and *Over the Rainbow* are the strip titles.

Video Anime E-Bon. Japanese, 12 mins., animated, color.

Credits: Director: Noriaki Kairo; *Writers:* Noriaki Kairo, Shin Yukuba; *Animator:* Shunji Saita; *Music:* Masahito Maekawa; *From:* Mushi Productions.

This video series covered over 50 different classics, including *Three Musketeers*, *Jack and the Beanstalk*, *Little Women* and a 12-minute version of *Wizard of Oz*.

1989

The Wonderful Wizard of Oz.

Walker Co. made an obscure animated adaptation.

1990

Wild at Heart. 5/90. 125 mins., color.

Cast: Sailor Ripley (Nicolas Cage), Lula Fortune (Laura Dern), Bobby Peru (Willem Dafoe), Marcello Santos (J.E. Freeman), "Jingle" Dell (Crispin Glover), Marietta Fortune (Diane Ladd), Glinda (Sheryl Lee), Reggie (Calvin Lockhart), Perdita (Isabella Rossellini), Johnny Farragut (Harry Dean Stanton), Juana (Grace Zabriskie), Mr. Reindeer (W. Morgan Sheppard), Girl in Accident (Sherilyn Fenn), Dropshadow (David Patrick Kelly), George Kovich (Freddie Jones), Sparky (John Lurie), Spool (Jack Nance), Buddy (Pruitt Taylor Vince), Bob Ray Lemon (Gregg Dandridge), Pace (Glen Walker Harris, Jr.), Madam (Frances Bay), Janitor (Blair Bruce Bever), Aunt Rootie (Sally Boyle), Hotel Manager (Peter Bromilow), Reindeer Dancer (Lisa Ann Cabasa), Old Bum (Frank A. Caruso), Timmy Thompson (Frank Collison), Rex (Eddy Dixon), Punk (Brent Fraser), Man at Shell Station (Cage S. Johnson), Valet (Valli Leigh, Mia M. Ruiz), Wheelchair Man (Nick Love), Cowboy (Daniel Quinn), Singer (Koko Taylor), Irma (Charlie Spradling), Desk Clerk (Ed Wright), Billy Swan (himself), Singer's Manager (Darrel Zwerling).

Credits: Director, writer: David Lynch (based on Barry Gifford's novel *Wild at Heart: The of Sailor and Lulu*); *Producers:* Monty Montgomery, Steve Golin, Sigurjon Sighvatsson; *Executive producer:* Michael Kuhn; *Production design:* Patricia Norris; *Cinematography:* Frederick Elmes; *Costume designer:* Amy Stofsky; *Music:* Angelo Badalamenti; *Editor:* Duwayne Dunham; *From:* Polygram/Propaganda Films, Samuel Goldwyn Co.

Small-time hood "Sailor" Ripley loves Lula, the daughter of wealthy, white-trash widow Marietta Fortune. Marietta loathes Sailor and believes he witnessed her murder Lula's father. As the film opens, Marietta sends a thug to kill Sailor; he beats the man to death, for which he gets two years in jail.

On a crystal ball (as in several later scenes) we see Lula defy her mother and meet Sailor when he leaves prison. Breaking his parole, they leave for California. Lula fantasizes their journey parallels Dorothy's trip to the Wizard, and imagines Marietta pursuing them on a broomstick. Marietta has, in fact, taken out a contract on Sailor; after repeated attempts on his life and increasing violence, Lula worries that they've "broken down on the yellow brick road." After a sleazy motel clerk rapes Lula, she sobbingly clicks the heels of her red shoes together (to no effect).

Bobby, one of Marietta's goons, befriends Sailor and learns Lula is pregnant. He persuades Sailor to join him in a bank robbery to support his new family, planning to kill Sailor during the heist. A cop guns down Bobby instead; Sailor lands a five-year prison term and Lula goes back to her mother. She and her son meet Sailor when he leaves prison, but he believes he's no good for Lula and sends her away. After Sailor provokes and loses a brawl with a local gang, Glinda appears and tells him if he's truly "wild at heart," he'll fight for his dream. Sailor catches up with Lula and wins her back—and we see a photograph of Marietta melting away.

This repellent film showcases Lynch's flair for graphic violence and bizarre imagery, neither of which were in the source novel. The contrast between the Oz elements and Sailor and Lulus' grimy reality doesn't work very well, nor does the film's insistence that their love is so pure it can redeem them from all the ugliness (Gifford's novel wasn't so optimistic: He had Sailor and Lulu break up for good).

The Dreamer of Oz. 12/10/90. Two hours, b&w/color, NBC.

Cast: Lyman Frank Baum (John Ritter), Maud Baum (Annette O'Toole), Matilda Joslyn Gage (Rue McClanahan), Dorothy (Courtney Barilla), Badham/Cowardly Lion (Charles Haid), W.W. Denslow (David Schramm), Ned Brown/Farmer (Ed Gale), Mr. Munchkin (Jerry Maren), Reporter (John Cameron Mithcell), Marreit Baum (Nancy Lenehen), Dorothy Leslie Gage/Dorothy Gale (Courtner Barilla), Helen (Nancy Morgan), Charlie (Pat Skipper), Frank, Jr. at three (Joshua Boyd), Frank, Jr. at 5 to 9 (Tim Eyster), Salesman (Roger Steffans), Sullivan (Frank Hamilton), Publisher (Steven Gilborn), Mrs. Munchkin (Elizabeth Barrington), Photographer (Terry Willis), Actress (Laura Owens), Stage Manager (Richard Marion), Carpenter (Rod Gist), Publisher (Bill DeLand), Scarecrow (David Ellzey), Ton Man (Derek Loughram), Announcer (Dale Tarter), Teenage Frank Jr. (Christopher Pettiet), Robert Baum (Ryan Todd), Girl (Alexis Kirchner), Harry Baum (Jason Ritter).

Credits: Director: Jack Bender; *Writer:* Richard Mattheson; *Story:* David Kirschner, Richard Matheson; *Producer:* Ervin Zavada; *Co-producers:* Laura Moskowitz, David Brooks; *Executive producers:* David Kirchner, Robert M. Myman; *Cinematography:* Thomas Burstyn; *Artistic designer:* David Negron; *Set design:* Bill McAllister; *Production design:* James Julsey; *Music:* Lee Holdridge; *Editor:* Jerrold L. Ludwig; *From:* Bedrock Productions, Adam Productions, Spelling entertainment, NBC.

The film opens in black-and-white as a reporter interviews Maud Gage Baum at the premiere of the MGM *Wizard of Oz*. Maud (slipping into color) tells how she married L. Frank Baum over her mother's objections; how they moved from Syracuse to Aberdeen, South Dakota, where Baum ran a newspaper; how he almost had to fight a duel over one article, until his opponent, Badham, ran away and how he moved to Chicago working in various jobs after the paper failed.

Along the way, Baum turns the elements of his life into stories to amuse children (Badham becomes the model for the Cowardly Lion, for instance), and retells many of them to his dying, six-year-old niece, Dorothy. After her death, he gambles everything he has on turning the stories into a book with a heroine based on Dorothy. Once it's published, success arrives and the rest is history.

For the most part, this Christopher Award-winning film is fairly faithful to Baum's life, the big changes being the portrayal of Maud's mother as something of a harridan (she and Baum were actually quite close) and presenting his niece, who died in infancy, as a young girl. It also avoids anything that would tell audiences that MGM's film wasn't a faithful adaptation of Baum.

The Dreamer of Oz also follows most of the clichés of Hollywood "biopics": Years of struggle and heartbreak (though of course, Baum did have a lot of those), exhortations to follow your dream, and showing that all of Baum's ideas somehow came from real life. Given that screenwriter Richard Mattheson was one of the 20th century's best fantasy writers, with numerous TV and film credits, it's surprisingly unimaginative.

Nevertheless, the affectionate portrayal of Baum won a strong following among Oz fans, which makes it all the more surprising that this film has never been released on video in America.

1991

Wizard of Oz. 4/10/91. 30 mins., animated, color.

Credits: Director, producer: Jim Simon; *Writer:* Roger Scott Olsen; *Executive producers:* Diane Eskenazi, Ron Layton; *Animation:* Dai Won Animation Co.; *From:* American Film Corporation.

A tornado hits a Kansas farmhouse and carries it away, with Dorothy Gale inside. It lands in Oz on the Wicked Witch of the East, which wins Dorothy the gratitude of the Munchkins and the Good Witch of the North, who gives Dorothy the East Witch's silver shoes and a protective kiss.

Setting off to find the Wizard of Oz, Dorothy and Toto join a befuddled Scarecrow; the Tin Woodman, cursed by the Wicked Witch into a metal body without a heart; and the Cowardly Lion. All agree to ask the Wizard for help. Their journey is threatened by the monstrous part-bear, part-tiger kalidahs, but the travelers escape across a chasm on a tree the Woodman fells, then the Tin Woodman hews it through while the kalidahs are midway across.

In the Emerald City, they confront the Wizard as a blazing ball of energy who demands that they destroy the Wicked Witch of the West before he grants their wishes. When Dorothy and her friends enter her realm, they defeat her Winkie servants but are captured by the Winged Monkeys, who destroy the Tin Woodman and Scarecrow, truss up the Lion and drag Dorothy before the witch. When Dorothy refuses to give up the slippers, the Witch attacks Toto, which prompts Dorothy to pick up that fatal bucket of water.

With the witch dead, the Winkies willingly restore her friends and give Dorothy the cap that controls the Winged Monkeys. Back in the Emerald City, the Wizard refuses to keep his word; when Dorothy tells him he's no wizard at all, he confesses to being a fake. He tells Dorothy that with both witches dead, he's no longer afraid to leave the city and return to America, taking her with him.

First, however, he gives the Scarecrow glasses to make him look intelligent, gives the Tin Woodman a small stuffed heart and crowns the Lion king of the beasts. Dorothy misses the balloon ride, but as the Wizard flies off, he tells her to seek help from Glinda. The monkeys carry her to Glinda, who tells Dorothy the secret of the slippers, and she returns home.

This forgettable 30-minute version ran as a special on Nickelodeon. Although Dorothy is visually and vocally modeled on Judy Garland, the plot hews closer to Baum than MGM.

The Wizard of Oz. 10/12/91. 24 mins., animated, color.

Voices: Narrator (Norma MacMillan), Dorothy (Christine Lippa), Toto/Wolf (Lee Tockar), Uncle/Munchkins (Scott McNeil), Aunt Em (Cathy Weseluck), Glenda (Kate Robbins), Scarecrow (Ian James Corlett), Tin Man (Britain Durham), Lion (Mike Donavan), Oz/Guard (Doug Parker), West Witch (Barbara Whiting).

Credits: Voice director: Doug Parker; *Additional direction:* Richard Newman, Alvin Sanders, Mike Donovan; *Writer:* Barbara A. Oliver; *Producer:* Eric S. Rollman; *Supervising producer:* Winston Richard; *Executive producer:* Jerald E. Bergh; *Story editor:* Tony Oliver; *From:* Fuji Eight Company Ltd., Fuji Project, Fuso Publishing, Inc., Pony Canyon, Inc. Studio Junio, Saban Productions.

An addlepated narrator tells how Dorothy scoffed at an oncoming tornado to the point that Uncle Henry and Aunt Em slammed the storm-cellar door on her, leaving her stuck in the house with Toto as the cyclone carries it away. When they land in Oz on the Witch of the East, Glenda, the Witch of the North, tells the "tourist" about Oz, gives Dorothy the silver slippers and sends her off to the Wizard: "And so Dorothy lived happily ever after — no, I'm on the wrong page."

Needless to say, Dorothy runs into the Scarecrow, who wants "to understand the simple things in life like TV game shows" the Schwarzenegger-accented Tin Woodman ("Without a heart, how can I understand trashy novels?") and the insecure Cowardly Lion. In the Emerald City the Wizard (as a ball of fire) tells them they must prove themselves worthy of his help, either by singing and chewing gum simultaneously or by killing the Wicked Witch of the West.

When they approach the witch's castle, she sends a Winged Monkey to kidnap Dorothy. The Tin Man vows to save her: "I shall be the Tinmanator." The witch sends a wolf-pack after them. The Lion finds the courage to kill them, then the Scarecrow thinks of a way into the castle. The witch traps them, but when she avoids stepping in a puddle, they realize her weakness and destroy her.

When they return to the throne room, Toto finds the real Wizard hiding behind his throne. The Wizard (in an Elmer Fudd voice) insists he's not a fake, to which Dorothy replies "If you're a real wizard, I'm Judy Garland!" The Wizard points out her friends have already proven they have the qualities they seek, then offers to take Dorothy home by balloon. She misses the ride of course, but a plaque tells her how to use the shoes and she heads home. The narrator informs us the moral is "use a travel agent on long trips!"

This weirdly drawn cartoon (the Tin Man looks like a bad version of Tik-Tok) is very much a parody (and a pretty funny one) in dialog, at least in the American version.

1992

Liquid Dreams. 90 mins., color.
Cast: Eve Black (Candice Daly), Cab Driver (John Doe), Scavenger (Mark Manos), Tina (herself), Cecil (Tracey Walter), Frank Rodino (Richard Steinmetz), Escorts (Zane W. Levitt, Bob Kay, B.J. Davis, Jerry Spicer, Don Stark), Juno (Juan Fernandez), Coffee shop girl (Denise Truscello), Waitress (Rowena Guinness), Coffee shop manager (Rohanne Descy), Paula (Frankie Thorn), Maurice (James Oseland), Violet (Marilyn Tokuda), Angel (Paul Bartel), Taxi dancer (Annaluna Karkar, Lisa Melville), The Major (Barry Dennen), Felix (Mink Stole), Yelling Man (Ted Fox), Neurovid reactors (Gina Marie De Vita, Robin Bazy, Diane Firestone, Lisa Stagno, William Black, Merrie Lawson), Scarecrow (Harvey Leder), Crows (Vernon Gallegos, Aejandro Velasquez).

Credits: Director: Mark Manos; *Writers:* Zack Davis, Mark Manos; *Producers:* Zane W. Levitt, Diane Firestone; *Executive producers:* Ted Fox, Cassian Elwes; *Production designer:* Pam Moffat; *Costumes:* Merrie Lawson; *Choreographer:* Alexandre Magno; *Music:* Ed Tomney; *Editor:* Karen Joseph. *From:* Zeta Entertainment, LTD.

Eve, a Kansas woman trying to put a history of drinking and drugs behind her, arrives in the big city to stay with her sister, Tina — whom Eve finds dead. Hardboiled cop Rodino dismisses the death as an overdose; refusing to believe it, Eve hunts for clues in the city's sexual underbelly, working as a taxi-dancer under the name Dorothy (and wearing red stilettos). Her bosses soon move her up to stripping and erotic videos, using drugs and subliminal messages to put her in the mood. In one video she plays a farm girl in a gingham dress and red shoes, seduced by a scarecrow.

More mysterious deaths pile up, but Rodino, who's trying desperately to turn a blind eye to everything, can't persuade Eve to back off. Eve learns that a crime boss, "the Major," drained Tina's endorphins as a source for the super-narcotic he sells, killing her in the process. The Major has the same fate in mind for Eve, but she manipulates him and his inner circle into killing each other off, leaving only Rodino alive.

Having avenged her sister, Eve flags down the taxi she arrived in. The driver tells her he had a curious dream in which she helped people, himself included, find the way home; Eve replies that going home sounds like a very good idea.

This erotic thriller pretty much inverts *Wizard of Oz* by plunging "Dorothy" into a fantasy so horrible, Kansas looks like paradise. There may be other Oz quasi-themes (the first men Eve meets after her sister's death are a rather nutty scientist, seemingly heartless Rodino and a tough-talking bully), but they don't make it worth watching.

Oz. Two 35-minute episodes, color (released on video).
Voices: Muto (Yasunori Matsumoto), Felicia (Yuko Minguchi), 1019 (Toshiko Fujita), Leon (Yuji Mitsuya), Neito (Kxuchi Yamadera), 1024 (Keiko Toda), 1021 (Mari Yokobi), Lt. Commander Misuto (Asami Mudono), 1024 (Megumi Hayashibara), 1026 (Yubi Hita), Keku (Shiki Kutsu), Surxn (Kyosei Shinkyxsei), Mercenaries (Aruno Tahara, Giosu Kawashi, Matsuhiko Kawtsu, Kiku Yoshimizu), Captain (Daiju Nakamura), Rupert (Osama Saka), Dr. Dantrey (Tamio Aki), 1030 (Yubi Hita); with Megumi Hayashibara, Asami Mudono.
Credits: Director: Katsuhisa Yamada; *Writer:* Asami Watanabe (based on manga by Natsumi Itsuki in *Comic Lala*); *Design:* Toyomi Sugiyama; *Animators:* Toyomi Sugiyama; *Music:* Yoichiro Yoshikawa; *Editor:* Toyabi Sugiyama; *From:* Madhouse Studios.

A nuclear war kills 60 percent of humanity and splits the USA into six warring states. By 2021, the one hope amidst the hunger and devastation is the legendary city of Oz, where famine and war are unknown. Scientist Felicia, mercenary Muto and Droid 1019 set out to find Oz—and discover a city ruled by a madman with enough firepower to plunge the world even deeper into chaos.

This anime video was based on a 1988 manga (Japanese comic strip), which may explain the format (releasing just a couple of anime episodes is a common way to encourage viewers to go to the source material). The manga probably owes less to Baum than to Madhouse Studio's *Wind of Amnesia*, in which the protagonists also make a road trip across a ravaged USA (in that case, because of a wind that steals human memories) to find a sanctuary that turns out to be a hellhole.

1994

Voshebnik Izumrudnogo Goroda [Also known as The Wizard of Emerald City].
63 mins., color, Russian.
Cast: Elli (Katya Mikhailovskaya), Strasheela (Vyacheslav Nevinne), Zhyelyezne Drovosyek, the Iron Woodman (Yevgyeni Gyerasimov), Cowardly Lion (Vyacheslav Nevinne), Goodwin (Viktor Pavlov), Ogre (Valyerii Nosik), Bastinda/Gingyema (Natalya Varlye), Mother/Stella (Olga Kabo), Worra (Syergyeii Varchak), Cyclone (Vladimir Antonik), Guard (Boris Shchyerbakov), Totoshka (Armen Dzhigarhanyan, voice only).
Credits: Director: Pavel Arsenov; *Writer:* Vadim Korostelyev (based on a novel by Alexander Volkov); *Producer:* Alexander Malugin; *Assistant directors:* Nikolai Yemelyanov, Viktor Safronov, Vladimir Ptitsen; *Cinematography:* Urii Posnikov; *Music:* Yevgyenii Krelatov; *Editing:* Valentina Stepanova, Andrei Ivanov; *From:* Committee of Russian Federation of Cinematography, Experimental Performers Association, Ladya, Imeni, Gorky Films Studios.

[Seen in the original Russian]
Young Elli lives happily with her mother and her dog Totoshka until the evil witch Gingemma in the Magic Land sends a cyclone to bring Elli to her. The wind-spirit reports to Gingemma's sister, Bastinda, that Elli's farmhouse fell on Gingemma and killed her (we don't see this). Bastinda sends an ogre after Elli.

Elli emerges from the house and finds silver slippers on the porch; at Totoshka's suggestion, she puts them on. She leaves the house, meets Strasheela the Scarecrow and helps him down from a pole in a field of sunflowers. The Cowardly Lion joins them and they set out to ask the mighty wizard Goodwin in the City of Emeralds for help. They find a rusted Iron Woodman in the forest and oil him back to life, after which he decides to join the visit to Goodwin. The ogre kidnaps Dorothy but her friends drive him off.

Bastinda next sends a platoon of sword-wielding tiger-men after the travelers, but Elli and her friends escape them across a ravine on a chopped-down tree; the Iron Woodman then destroys the bridge as the monsters are crossing. The Winged Monkeys attack, destroying Strasheela and the Woodman and dragging the others to Bastinda's castle. The witch uses an invisible rope to trip Elli and dislodge one of the magic slippers. The angry girl throws a bowl of water at Bastinda, which not only melts the witch, but also turns the monkeys human again. The ex-monkeys lead Elli, Totoshka and the Lion to safety before the castle collapses.

The group then arrives at the City of Emeralds and meets Goodwin—a giant, rubbery head—in his throne room. They discover he's an ordinary man manipulating the head from inside it. Goodwin provides the Lion with a courage potion, sticks pins in Strasheela's brain (for sharpness) and gives the Woodman a cloth heart—but when he reaches Elli, he only looks at her sadly. Fortunately, the Good Witch Stella appears and tells her to click her heels together, at which point Elli opens her eyes on her mother's porch, where she's apparently been dreaming the whole story.

Alexander Volkov wrote *The Wizard of the Emerald City* in 1939, a nominal translation of Baum that rewrote the book quite a bit and renamed the characters (later Magic Land stories go even further afield — Strasheela remains king of the Emerald City and Ozma never appears).

The Magic Book of Oz. Color.
Cast: Dorothy (Kristine Hogan), Trot (Chandi J. Patel), Betsy Bobbin (Caroline Younts).
Credits: Director, writer, producer: Bruce Carroll.

A short video made for the Oz Club featuring Baum's favorite mortal girls, but including several other characters.

1996

Which Way to Oz. Color.
Cast: Psycho Girl (Kimberly Kates); with Kelly Nelson.
Credits: Director: James Hickox; *Writer, producer:* Justin Carroll.

This short film made by Justin Carroll is extremely obscure, to the point this author has been unable to determine if there's any real Oz connection.

1999

The Oz Witch Project. Nine mins., color.
Cast: Dorothy Gale (Meredith Salenger), Cowardly Lion (Curtis Eames), Scarecrow (Ron Repple, Jr.), Tin Man (Guy Stevenson).
Credits: Director, writer: Michael Rotman, M.J. Butler; *Story:* Michael Rotman; *Producers:* David M. Barsky, Michael Rotman; *Cinematography:* Michael Barsky; *Editor:* Earie. *From:* Monkeys in Silk.

The opening text informs us that in 1994, Dorothy Gale and her friends entered the forest near the Emerald City to investigate the legend of the Wicked Witch of the West for a documentary to be called *The Oz Witch Project*. A year later, this footage was found.

We see Dorothy and her three friends (MGM versions) driving off into the woods with a camera, the Lion sweating bullets at the thought of witch-hunting. Before long, they're hopelessly lost, and finding clumps of Munchkin lollipops stuck in the ground.

That night, there's a disturbance outside the tent and a distorted version of the Wicked Witch's theme in the MGM film is heard. Next morning, weird stick figures are hanging in the trees, the map is gone (Scarecrow lost it) and everything goes black—because Dorothy has the lens on the camera. Dorothy insists they just have to find the yellow brick road and Scarecrow tells her in a line from the MGM film, "Some say it's this way—some say that way—many people go both ways."

The final fate of the Tin Man: A scene from Michael Rotman's *Oz Witch Project*. (Photograph credit: Michael Rotman, Monkeys in Silk Productions at www.hackcomic.com.)

That night something attacks the tent while more distorted music plays, and next morning Tin Man and the Lion have vanished. Dorothy finds a bundle of sticks near the camp, and inside them is Tin Man's crushed heart; Dorothy tries to calm herself by singing "Over the Rainbow," but Scarecrow angrily cuts her off. Dorothy stares into the camera, apologizing to Tin Man's mother, Lion's mother, to Auntie Em and to Toto.

The next night, Dorothy and Scarecrow are searching an old house for the Lion, when everything falls silent. The camera shows Scarecrow, unmoving on a pole, with "Surrender Dorothy" scrawled in blood on the wall; the camera pans down to Dorothy lying on the floor. The ruby slippers click once, twice ... and Dorothy stops moving.

1999's *The Blair Witch Project* was a low-budget horror film made by Florida State University film students; it went on to become a box-office hit thanks to a successful Internet ad campaign and its low-key, nothing-seen-on-screen horror atmospherics. After seeing the film, Rotman thought of parodying it as *The Witchy Poo Project* (named for Martha Raye's villain in the 1970s Saturday morning series *HR Pufn'stuff*), but decided that would be too obscure for many people, so he went with an Oz parody instead.

The film sends up several specific scenes in *The Blair Witch Project* as well as MGM; Salenger does a dead-on knockoff of Garland's chirpy tones as Dorothy.

The same concept occurred to *Mad Magazine*, which did a cartoon comparing the two films, and to the creators of the on-line film *The Wicked Witch Project*.

The Wicked Witch Project. 11/17/99. wickedwitchproject.com.

Cast: Dorothy (Casey Porn), Scarecrow (Brian Ludviksen), Tin Woodman (Kevin Darbro), Cowardly Lion (Michael G. Smith).

Credits: Director, editor: Joe Barlow; *Writers:* Joe Barlow, Casey Porn, Brian Ludviksen, Kevin Dabro, Michael G. Smith, Stef Maus, Matt Routh, Lindsay Duggan; *Producers:* Joe Barlow, Kevin Darbro; *Costumes:* Stef Maus, Matt Routh, Lindsay Duggan; *Make-up:* Lindsay Duggan.

This parody of *Blair Witch Project* and MGM's *The Wizard of Oz* has a documentary crew (Dorothy and her friends) investigating the legendary horrors of the Wicked Witch of the East and her crimes among the Munchkins.

Dorothy (Meredith Salenger) sets off to film *The Oz Witch Project.* Big mistake! (Photograph credit: Michael Rotman, Monkeys in Silk Productions at www.hackcomic.com.)

2000

The Lion of Oz and the Badge of Courage [Also known as Lion of Oz]. 8/20/00. 75 mins., animated, color.

Voice Cast: Cowardly Lion (Jason Priestley), Wimsik (Jane Horrocks), Oscar Diggs (Dom DeLuise), Caroline (Kathy Griffin), Silly Ozbul (Bobcat Goldthwaite), Wicked Witch of the East (Lynn Redgrave), Narrator (Henry Beckman), Oak Tree (Gerard Plunkett), Sunbeam (Mik Perlus), Moonbeam (Eleanor Noble), Starburst (Elizabeth Robertson), Gloom (Scott McNeil), Captain Fitzgerald (Tim Curry), Tog (Peter Ketamis), Pin Cushion (Don Brown), Seamstress (Maxine Miller).

Credits: Director: Tim Deacon; *Writers:* Elana Lesser, Cliff Ruby (based on the book by Roger S. Baum); *Score:* Jennifer Wilson; *Producer:* Michel Lemire; *Executive producers:* Jacques Pettigrew, Michel Lemire, Loris Kramer; *Cinematographer:* Heidi Blonkvist; *Editor:* Claudette Duff. *From:* Sony Wonder, CineGroupe.

Songs: The Courage to Be Friends; My Wicked, Wicked Ways; Believe; Something About You.

Oscar Diggs, the balloonist at a small Nebraska circus, is the only one who knows the ferocious circus lion is actually quite timid. The Lion considers Diggs his only friend, so he's overjoyed when Diggs not only takes him for a balloon ride, but also awards him a "badge of courage" for taking the flight. A storm sweeps the balloon away to Oz, where the Lion falls out while the wind carries Diggs onward.

No sooner does the Lion discover he can talk than the Wicked Witch of the East appears with the news she has Diggs imprisoned; to free him, the Lion must find the lost Flower of Oz for her. After she leaves, the tree explains that the Flower is the essence of the good in the land, and if the witch obtains it, she and her spirit ally Gloom will complete their conquest of Oz.

After the Lion rescues a fairy from Gloom, the fairy tells him only a truly brave heart can find the Flower, which vanished in an ice storm. The Lion promises to use the Flower against the witch, so the fairies direct him to Wimsik, the young gardener at Castle Grey. The Lion, accompanied by Silly Ozbul, an addlepated stuffed bear, arrives at the castle; Wimsik decides to join the quest in hopes of recovering her forgotten past. Her doll Caroline and toy soldier Captain Fitzgerald come too—but then the witch appears and destroys Fitzgerald (actually teleporting him to her dungeon). She tells the Lion that each day she waits for the Flower, another friend dies.

Ozbul almost dies without the witch's help, when the search takes him across an illusory bridge. In the gorge below, the seek-

Clicking her heels together didn't help: Dorothy (Meredith Salenger) lies dead at the end of *The Oz Witch Project*. (Photograph credit: Michael Rotman, Monkeys in Silk Productions at www.hackcomic.com.)

ers meet the toy-sized Mini-Munchkins, who built a real bridge for travelers to reach the Flower, but the witch destroyed it and shrank them too small to build another. When Wimsik learns that the Mini's wish to rebuild creates the illusion, she convinces them that they can wish a real bridge into existence. They do (regaining normal size) and the Lion's group crosses the bridge. Outraged, the witch blasts Caroline into the river; the Lion almost drowns saving her, but Wimsik's touch restores his strength.

Meanwhile, Fitzgerald discovers Diggs isn't really in the witch's dungeon, and sets out to get word to the Lion.

The next menace in the group's path is the Seamstress, who turns Ozbul and Caroline into patches in her magic quilt until Wimsik reawakens the good in the sorceress buried by the Wicked Witch's corrupting magic. Wimsik scoffs when the Lion suggests she's showing some sort of special power, but when they reach the Flower's frozen garden, Wimsik thaws it into spring. When they discover the Flower's throne is empty, the Lion realizes it's Wimsik who's the Flower of Oz.

The Wicked Witch and Gloom appear, and the witch threatens to destroy Diggs if the Lion protects Wimsik. Fitzgerald has stowed away in the witch's magic chest, however, and he tells the Lion the truth. The Lion and the others run interference until Wimsik reaches the throne (getting a gown, tiara and glowing aura when she does). The witch snatches away the Lion's badge of courage in revenge, vowing he'll be a sniveling coward forever. She and Gloom attack Wimsik, but find themselves powerless against the Flower of Oz; Gloom disintegrates at the touch of her aura, so the witch flees, vowing she will yet conquer Oz.

The Lion scoffs when Wimsik tells her he still has his courage. He leaves to find Diggs, and spends long months wandering without success—then one day, he sees a girl, a dog, a scarecrow and a tin man walking down a road of yellow brick…

Stories about Oz before *The Wizard of Oz* are a thriving sub-genre in Oz fiction, but this is the only one so far to make it to the screen. It's not very good, but Horrocks does have a fabulous singing voice.

Silly Ozbul appears in several Oz books by Roger Baum (great-grandson of L. Frank).

The Life and Adventures of Santa Claus. 76 mins., animated, color.

Voices: Santa (Robby Benson), Necile (Dixie Carter), Ak (Hal Holbrook), Wisk (Carlos Alazaraqui), Old Santa Claus (Jim Cummings), Martha (Mary Kay Bergman), Gardenia (Melissa Disney), Wagif (Jess Harnell), Peter (Nick Jamison), Mogorb (Maurice Lamarche), Ethan (Brianne Siddall), Shlegra (Cynthia Songe), Natalie (Kath Soucie); Voice direction: Susan Blue; Lyrics: Harriett Schock; Art direction: Andre Clavel; Animator: Anna Saunders; Production manager: Sylvie Boyer.

Credits: Director, producer: Glen Hill; *Writer:* Hank Saroyan; *Executive producer:* Mike Young; *Music:* Misha Segal; *Editor:* Richard Finn. *From:* Universal.

Ak, the lord of all forests, tells the story of a time when humans shared the world with elves, nymphs, fairies and other spirits. In that long-gone past, Ak tells the fairy folk of how harsh and brutal human lives are, so harsh that one of them abandoned an infant in the Forest of Burzee that very morning. Ak tells the fairies he gave the babe to the lioness Shlegra, and that the beasts of the wood have been charged to protect the boy.

The nymph Necile wants to care for the child, and although it bends the laws of Burzee, Ak consents. The shapeshifter Whisk arrives in Burzee fleeing the troll-like Awgwas; when he sees the baby, he takes a fancy to it and decides to stay in Burzee. When he asks the boy's name, the nymphs name it "Nacile's little one," or "Nicholas Claus."

As Nick grows, he realizes how different he is from the fairy-folk, but Necile tells him this might be a blessing: The fairies cannot intervene in the human world, but he can. Ak shows him that the children of the world lead harsh, cruel lives, made worse by the Awgwas, who like to play pranks, then frame the children. Nick decides to help the children of the world, and moves with Whisk to the Valley of HoHoHo. He befriends the local children, and gives one of them a wooden carving of Nick's pet cat—the first toy ever. Nick decides making toys to give children happiness will be his life's work, a goal that infuriates the Awgwas.

Enraged by the children's happiness, the Awgwas banish Nick to the far jungle with sorcery, but Ak's decree of protection persuades the jungle spirits to send Nick home unharmed. He resumes work on the toys, recruiting his immortal friends for help as the orders become more than he can handle. The forest spirits also agree to let him use reindeer to pull a sleigh when the volume grows beyond what Nick can carry on foot. When he enters one locked house by the chimney to drop off the toys, the happy children's parents proclaim him to be Saint Nicholas—or "Santa" Claus. The forest spirits are less happy when he brings the reindeer back late, and his right to use them is revoked.

When Nick resumes delivery on foot, the Awgwas steal the toys, then attack them, too. Ak agrees to let Nick use the reindeer again, providing he makes only one trip a year, on Christmas Eve. Nick agrees, but realizes that the due to the thefts, he doesn't have enough stock to meet the children's wishes.

Ak and Necile decide it's time to put an end to the Awgwas, and call the immortals of Burzee to war. Despite the Awgwas powerful giant and dragon allies, the fairy-folk destroy them, but decide not to tell soft-hearted Nick about it. Necile brings back the toys and Nick learns the reindeer can fly fast enough to make all the deliveries in time and return by morning.

Over the coming years, Nick introduces more Christmas traditions: Providing Christmas trees with candles to families without lamps; dropping little presents into stockings hanging up to dry, etc. As Nick's age catches up with him, Ak convinces the Council of Immortals that Nick's work creating a better world must not be allowed to die: They must award him the Mantle of Immortality that will let him live forever. As the Angel of Death approaches Nick's bedside, Ak appears and gives Nick the mantle. Nick wakes the next morning in great shape, and the closing scenes show that even today, centuries later, he remains devoted to caring for children.

This cartoon version was much less faithful to Baum's novel than the Rankin-Bass TV version, not to mention duller and visually uninspired (the lumpy rock-people Awgwas here are much less interesting than the Rankin-Bass freaks).

6

Film and Video: Nonfiction and Educational

1970

Favorite Children's Books: The Wizard of Oz. 49 frames, Coronet Instructional Films.

A short educational filmstrip.

1974

It's a Heart. 5/74. Six mins., animated.
Voices: Tin Woodman (Ron Marshall).
Credits: Writers: Robert Waldman, Joel Herron, Irwin Lewis; *Art direction, animation:* Myron Waldman; *Music, lyrics:* Joel Herron; *Camera:* Seymour Mandel, *Editor:* Dick Cohen; *Backgrounds:* Myron Waldman, R. Socolov; *Animation coordinator:* Susan Blaney; *Producer:* Joel Herron; *Executive producer:* Irwin Lewis; *Photographed at:* Hal Seeger Studios; *From:* Joleron Production Company.

The Tin Woodman shows the Scarecrow and Cowardly Lion the telescope, microscope and fluoroscope in his workshop, then uses the fluoroscope to study his heart. All three agree it's the most important part of the body, and the Tin Woodman describes how the circulatory system keeps us strong. He tells the watching children to take care of their hearts, then heads off to spread the heart-healthy gospel to others.

One of a series of health-education shorts from the American Heart Association

The Heart That Changed Color. 5/74. Six mins., animated, color.

Cast: Tin Woodman (Ron Marshall), Scarecrow (Earl Hammond), Queen Nicotina (Helene Miles).
Credits: Writers: Robert Waldman, Joel Herron, Irwin Lewis; *Art direction, animation:* Myron Waldman; *Music, lyrics:* Joel Herron; *Camera (Seymour Mandel), Editor:* Dick Cohen; *Backgrounds:* Myron Waldman, R. Socolov; *Animation coordinator:* Susan Blaney; *Producer:* Joel Herron; *Executive producer:* Irwin Lewis; *Photographed at:* Hal Seeger studios; *From:* Joleron Production Company.

The Tin Woodman and Scarecrow tell some forest animals how they once visited the Land of Nicotine, crossing a bridge of cigarettes to reach the murky City of Smog. A cigar captain and cigarette soldiers lead them before Queen Nicotina (a lookalike for the queen from Disney's *Snow White*, except her crown is a big cigarette). Everyone but the two Ozites lights up (turning Nicotina green) and Tin Woodman realizes that the second-hand smoke is speeding up his heartbeat. Glinda sends a rain that clears away the smog and quenches the cigarettes, freeing Nicotina of her addiction. But the Ozites remind us that in the real world there's no Glinda to save us — so don't start smoking!

The most interesting of AHA's several educational cartoons.

The Adventures of a Man in Search of a Heart. 12/74. Six mins., animated, color.
Voices: Tin Woodman (Ron Marshall).
Credits: Directors, writers: Joel Herron, Robert

Waldman; *Producer:* Joel Herron; *Executive producer:* Irwin Lewis; *Animator:* Myron Waldman; *Animation coordinator:* Susan Blaney; *Backgrounds:* R. Owen, Myron Waldman; *Photography:* Seymour Mandel; *Editor:* Dick Cohen; *Music, lyrics:* Joel Herron; *Art director:* Myron Waldman; *From:* Joleron Production Company.

The Tin Woodman visits three skilled metalworkers to ask for a heart, but none of them can help him. When he broods in the forest, animals surround him and quiz him on whether he'd care for his heart if he had it: "Would you exercise, exercise, each and every day?" Answers the Woodman, "If the doctor said it was good for my heart, you betcha, every day!" Satisfied, the animals send him to the Wizard. The Woodman tells how the events of *Wizard of Oz* led to his getting a heart, then reminds viewers to exercise, eat healthy food and never smoke.

The third of the Heart Association's Joleron productions; two more followed in 1975 (this author remembers a revised version of this third cartoon from the 1980s, using stop-motion animals and a live actor for the Tin Woodman, but AHA couldn't find any record of it).

1975

Tin Woodman. 1975. 20 seconds and 10 seconds, animated, color.

Two spots similar in style to the above American Heart Association shorts, with the Tin Woodman encouraging kids to care for their heart.

1987

The Real, the True, the Gen-u-ine Wizard of Oz: L. Frank Baum. 17 mins., color.
Cast: Scarecrow (Bill Eubank).
Credits: Director: Margaret Albrecht; *Writer:* Eleanor Kulleseid. *From:* Random House School Division.

Another educational short for schools.

1989

Trouble in Oz. 35 mins.
Credits: From Center for Drug Free Living, Inc., Orlando, FL.

Evil Morticia, a drug dealer in Big City, claims she'll even "go over the rainbow" to sell drugs. Magically she and her associates are transported to Oz, where Dorothy and her friends lead the Munchkins to fight against drug abuse.

Toto's Rescue. 43 mins., color.
Cast: Dorothy (Pamela Peters), Wicked Witch (LaVona Kessel), Good Witch (Sandee Moore), Scarecrow (Tim Strauch), Lion (John Draper), Tin Man (A.J. Smart), Hansel (Richard Lanza), Gretel (Meredith Miller), R.R. Hood (Ruth Blodgett), Grandmother (Janet Burau), Snow White (Melani Huetter), Rapunzel (Regina Wooten), Jack (Doug McGee), Jill (Amy Lyberger), Farmer (John Weisker), Wife (Carol Belveal), Child (Andromeda Rogers), Nurse (Donna Schubring), Boy Blue (Patrick Johnson), Cinderella (Sally McIsaac), Prince (Bill Silva), Pinocchio (Russ Novak), Toto (Toby Tiger Tail).
Credits: Directors: John Weisker, L.Q. "Missy" Cruz, John Jimenez, Jeff Weigt; *Writer:* Doree Steinmann; *Producer:* Pam Baker; *Executive producer:* Doree Steinmann; *Costume, Set Design:* Pam Baker, Doug McGee; *Music:* John Draper, Mark Hatchfield; Produced at Cosumnes River Colletge, Sacramento, CA by Advanced TV Production students; *From:* Steinmann Productions.
Songs: Witch Is Gone; Living in the Woods; Here Is Where I Want to Be; Beautiful; Always Tell the Truth; Right in Front of Her Nose.

A new Wicked Witch appears in Kansas and kidnaps Toto. A Good Witch demands Dorothy be given a chance to save him, so the Wicked Witch agrees to set the dog free if Dorothy can identify 10 storybook characters without help from anyone over 12.

In Storybook Land, Dorothy reunites with the Scarecrow, Tin Man and the Cowardly Lion, who are too old to help, so she asks the children in the audience to help her make guesses. The quartet sets out, meets different characters such as Rapunzel and Jack and Jill, and Dorothy, with help from the audience, identifies nine stories. The Wicked Witch gloats that she's one short, but then Dorothy realizes *The Wizard of Oz* is the 10th tale. The witch reluctantly returns Toto and Dorothy thanks the audience for its help.

Steinman (a "Storybook Lady" on both a New York radio station and a California TV station) made this educational, interactive video with her students at Cosumnes River College; it combined a crash course in children's stories with basic counting as the children add up Dorothy's wins. The video won first place in the 1991 Broadcast Education Association's scriptwriting contest. Steinman directed another, similar video, *Toby's Rescue from the Planet*, in 1993.

1990

The Hollywood Road to Oz.
Cast: Host (Charlton Heston).

Another documentary about Oz films.

The Wonderful Wizard of Oz: 50 Years of Magic. 2/20/90. Color.
Credits: Director, producer: Jack Haley, Jr.; *Writers:* Jack Haley, Jr., Ralph Ross (from *Making of the Wizard of Oz* by Aljean Harmetz, and *The Official 50th Anniversary Pictorial History of the Wizard of Oz* by John Fricke, Jay Scarfone, and William Stillman); *Associate producer:* John Fricke; *Executive producer:* David Niven, Jr.; *Editor:* David E. Blewitt; *From:* Jack Haley, Jr. Productions, Turner Entertainment, CBS, Warner Home Video.

A salute to the MGM film and its popularity over the years.

1992

L. Frank Baum: The Royal Historian of Oz.

A documentary on Baum produced by Angelica Shirley Carpenter and based on her book, which Carpenter co-wrote with Jean Shirley.

1993

We're Off to See the Munchkins. 77 mins., color.
Cast: Narrator, John Fricke; with Lewis Croft, Jerry Marren, Nels Nelson, Margaret Pellegrini, Meinhardt Raabe, Clarence Swensen, Karl Slover and Betty Tanner.
Credits: Directors: John J. Anderson, John Fricke; *Writer:* John Fricke; *Producer:* John J. Anderson; *Executive producers:* John J. Anderson, Kimberly C. Anderson; *Editor:* Paul Combel; *Music:* Herbert Stothart, Harold Arlen; *Lyrics:* E.Y. Harburg.

This documentary on the Munchkins' experiences in making MGM's *Wizard* includes actors' recollections, film clips, vintage photos and festival and background footage.

Workteams and the Wizard of Oz. 18 mins., color.
Cast: Dr. Ken Blanchard.
Credits: Director, writer: Steven Katten; *From:* The Hathaway Group, CRM Films L.P.

This management training video used clips from MGM's *The Wizard of Oz* to show examples of different personality types and how to work with them.

1994

I Married a Munchkin. 27, 34 or 47 mins. for different cuts, color and b&w.
Credits: Director: Tom Palazzolo; *Producers:* Susan Biszewski-Eber and J. Eber; *Music:* Mike Colligan.

A documentary about Mary Ellen St. Alban, who runs the Midget Club of Chicago and married one of the actors who played a Munchkin in the MGM film.

Hakosem Mae'achorei Hakosem! [Also known as The Magic Behind the Wizard!]

A documentary on the making of *Hakosem!*, the Israeli stage version of MGM's *Wizard of Oz*.

Education Reform in Kentucky: A

Teacher's Search of the Wizard of Oz. 14 mins., color.
Cast: Linda Eden.
From: The Partnership for Kentucky School Reform.

A documentary on educational reform.

1995

Creating the Wizard of Oz on Ice.

A film about the making of *The Wizard of Oz on Ice*. It features Bobby McFerrin, who provided the voices for the ice-skating adaptation.

1996

The Making of the Oz Kids.
Cast: Narrator: Benjamin Salisbury.
Credits: Director: Todd Hare; *Writer, producer:* Kacy Andrews; *From:* Hyperion Pictures, Sunset Post, Warner Brothers, Straightline.

This documentary, which appears as an extra on the Oz Kids videos *Who Stole Santa?* and *Christmas in Oz*, chronicles how Hyperion decided to create a new Oz series using the children of Baum's characters and storylines from Baum's books, both Oz and non–Oz. The documentary also showcases the Oz collection of Hyperion founder Willard Carroll, which was also featured in *100 Years of Oz*.

Beyond Phonics: The Wonderful Wizard of Oz. One min., color.
Credits: From Quality Time Education, Inc.

The Wizard of Oz is used in one segment of a learn-to-read video.

The Gifts Are Divine, the Plan Is Awesome. 2/96. 21 mins., color.
Cast: National Ministries Associate (Judy Atwell), Scarecrow (Jamie Eller), Tin Man (Janice Sidebottom), Cowardly Lion (Bill Watson), Dorothy (Lee Robison).
Credits: Director, writer: Judy Atwell; *From:* The Presbyterian Church, USA.

In this workshop, four professional storytellers play Dorothy and her three friends, and express the gifts—heart, courage, etc.—that God has given them. Judy Atwell, an associate in the church's vocation unit, came up with the idea because the characters would be instantly recognizable to everyone.

A video of the workshop generated a number of orders from Christian educators, but the church says it is no longer available.

1997

Oz: The American Fairlyand. 6/7/97. 113 mins., b&w/color.
Cast: Narrator (Lee Lively).
Credits: Directors, producers: Gayle O'Neal, Leonard A. Swann, Jr.; *Writer:* Janet Anderson; *Editors:* Tom Tucker, Duncan Brown, Craig King; *From:* Sirocco Productions.

An award-winning documentary discussing Oz as an American fairy-tale that celebrates the virtues of hard work, honesty and loyalty. It won an award in the History/Biography category in the 19th international Telly competitions.

Charles Santore Illustrates the Wizard of Oz. 6/7/97. 27 mins., color.
Credits: Director, producer: Gayle O'Neal, Leonard A. Swann, Jr.; *Editors:* Duncan Brown, Tom Tucker; *From:* Sirocco Productions.

A spin-off of *Oz: The American Fairyland*, focusing on Santore—an illustrator who was one of the interviewees in that film—and his work on one edition of *The Wizard of Oz*.

1999

Fairuza Returns to Oz. 8/10/99. Color, Anchor Bay Entertainment.
Cast: Fairuza Balk.
Credits: Director, producer: Marc Cerulli; *Cinematography:* Mark Milkin; *Executive producer:* Jay Douglas; *Editor:* Bill McCullough; *From:* Anchor Bay Entertainment.

Fairuza Balk hosts a talking-heads discussion of Oz and particularly *Return to Oz*. This was released as an extra on some *Return to Oz* tapes.

2000

Le Corsaire, Le Magician, Le Voleur Et Les Enfants [Also known as The Priate, the Wizard, the Thief and the Children]
Credits: Director: Julie Gavras; *From:* KG Productions, Rhone-Alpes Cinema.

Children are shown *The Crimson Pirate*, *The Wizard of Oz* and *The Bicycle Thief* and comment on the films.

The Wizard of the Web. 7/00. OCLC President's Luncheon, Chicago.
Credits: Director: Mary Ann Henry; *Writer:* George Promenschenkel; *Executive producer:* Nita Dean; *Creative consultant:* Phil Schieber; *Produced by:* Henry Ryan Films at Lyon Video, Inc.

Three patrons at a Kansas public library ask librarian Dorothy for help wading through the flood of information available on the Web: One feels stupid because he doesn't know which sites are accurate, an aluminum siding salesman, or "tin man," has lost heart faced with information overload, and the excess data has also intimidated a man in a Lions cap.

Dorothy tells them she wishes she could help them reach the right home page, then the quartet suddenly finds themselves in a wild storm that lands them on a giant keyboard against a vast, printed-circuit backdrop. Dorothy has Judy Garland's pigtails and costume and the men have elements of the MGM characters' costumes. Dorothy assures them that the Wizard of the Web will be able to help.

The Wizard materializes on a computer screen and flaunts his expertise in every known subject, but is less than enthused about answering specific requests (particularly the salesman's interest in Romantic literature). Dorothy tells the Wizard that her friends need to find specific information, so he suggested the Wicked Search Engine of the Web. Dorothy replies that most search engines "melt away" into uselessness when tried. The Wizard continues boasting until he's unmasked as a computer operator hiding behind a curtain, at which point Dorothy denounces him as a bully: "You're so big you make it impossible for anyone to use you!"

The Good Witch appears and assures the Wizard he can be truly great and powerful; she then tells Dorothy that by libraries working together (for instance with the Online Computer Library Center), they can master the Web. Dorothy realizes there's no place like a home page, clicks her slippers together ... and wakes to tell her patrons that you were there, and you, and you, and she can make the Web work for all of them. Linking arms, they dance down a yellow brick road along the library floor.

A video promoting the advantages of using OCLC to tame the web.

The Wizard of Sales. 8/6/00. NSA Foundation Event.
Cast: Scarecrow, Hunk (Don Daniels), Tin Man, Hickory, Munchkin (Matthew Ellison), Dorothy (Amy Beth Goldberger), Glenna, the Good Meeting Planner (Cindy Kubica), Lion Zeke, Munchkin (Steve Rizzo), Almira Gulch/Wicked Meeting Planner (Susan Rudick), Wizard/Professor Marvel/Gatekeeper/Munchkin (David Titus).
Credits: Director: Michael Leeds; *Musical director, pianist:* Phil Reno; *Writer, producer:* Jeff Slutsky; *Set design:* William Barclay; *Lighting design:* Tim Hunter; *Costume design:* Alvin Colt; *From:* Street Fighter Marketing.
Songs: Somewhere Over My Sales Goals; It's Out, It's Out; Ding Dong, the Pitch Is Dead; Go Make More Calls on the Road; If I Only Had More Leads; With Objections to the Sale; If I Only Made More Calls; Objections, Rejections and Nos; In Your New Prospect's Eyes; If I Were Boss of the Region.

Street Fighter Marketing adjusts this production to suit different audiences, so exact features and plot details may vary with different productions.

Dorothy (Amy Beth Goldberger) meets Glenna the Good Meeting Planner (Cindy Kubica) at troubled Munchkin Corp (Munchkins David Titus, Matthew Ellison, Steve Rizzo) in *The Wizard of Sales*. (Photograph credit: Street Fighter Marketing.)

All grown-up, Dorothy Gale is now a sales rep in a blue gingham business suit with a virtual Toto on her PDA. She's depressed that she can't close sales; sales manager Mr. Marvel is too busy to help; and then Almira Gulch steals the big Flying Monkey Aerospace account. Overstressed, Dorothy blacks out from a panic attack.

She awakens in a strange new territory and discovers the office furniture that landed with her has crushed the Wicked Sales Manager of the East. Glinda, the Good Sales Manager, and the oppressed Munchkin Corp. executives are overjoyed, but the Wicked Sales Manager of the West shows up, threatens Dorothy, and tries to reclaim her sister's ruby sales manual. The program materializes inside Dorothy's wicker briefcase, but the manager vows to regain it by prioritizing. Glinda tells Dorothy to seek guidance on making her sales quota from the Wizard of Sales in Ephemeral City (adding that Dorothy can boost her quota herself by making more calls on the road).

Along the way, Dorothy meets a Scarecrow (stuffed with shredded documents and memos) who can't find good leads, a Tin Man (in a double-breasted metal suit) who froze when his prospect raised objections, and a Lion who talks tough until Dorothy makes him confess he's too cowardly to make sales calls. Despite obstacles—the Wicked Sales Manager derails them with coffee breaks, and the Wizard's gatekeeper doesn't want to schedule a meeting—they reach the Wizard of Sales.

The Wizard's image agrees to help them if they secure a booking contract from the Wicked Meeting Planner. When they reach her, she agrees to trade a contract for the ruby manual, then tries to burn the contract she just signed. Dorothy tries quenching the fire with Binaca, dousing the planner too—and her outfit is dry-clean only (this is at

Can Dorothy (Amy Beth Goldberger) use the ruby sales manual to help Scarecrow (Don Daniels) and Tin Man (Matthew Ellison), or will they have to seek *The Wizard of Sales*? (Photograph credit: Street Fighter Marketing.)

least the third production to use some variation of that joke)! The planner melts away and the quartet returns to Ephemeral City where the Wizard shows how they've already had all the qualities they need inside themselves.

Slutsky developed this show as a humorous way to remind sales professionals of the key techniques. The exact script and the characters' sales problems are adapted to fit each audience, just as the Wizard is an electronic image of the company's CEO.

We All Dream of Oz. 11/19/00. 8 mins., TNT.
Cast: Narrator (Sally Kellerman).

Actors including Anne Archer, Linda Fiorentino, Susan Sarandon and Gwyneth Paltrow describe their feelings about the MGM *Wizard*. This short film also shows out-takes, studio stills, deleted scenes and shots of early theatrical scenes.

2001

Adventures in Oz with Cheryl. 37 mins. (part one), 41 mins. (part two), 46 mins. (part three), color.

Cast: Dorothy/Storyteller (Cheryl Ann Silich; Rae Dawn Wedwe, singing voice), Boz (Mark Bosler), Munchkids (Bria Uzzell, Ryan Waldoch), Faithless Hound (Tasha), Lizard of Oz (Brian Kelly, voice), Archie (Victor Varnado, voice), Lefty (Joe Wilson, Jr., voice), Key to Fitness (Momar Jirafee, voice); Singing Munchkid (Kit May), Scarecrow (Joey Babay), Tin Kid (Victor Varnado), Lion (Joe Wilson, Jr.), Gate Keeper (Ian Larson), Wizard (Scott Allard), Ice Witch (Taylor Corwin).

Credits: Director: Eric Goldstein; *Writers:* Eric Goldstein, Tory Sheehan, Wayne Thompson, Stanley Goldstein (based on a concept by Cheryl Ann Silich); *Costumes:* Deborah Fiscus; *Choreographers:* Alyce Finwall, Susie Coury, Kathy L. Silich; *Music:* Dick Jones, Jim May; *From:* Oz-Some Exercise Productions.

Dorothy in the world of *The Wizard of Sales*. (Photograph credit: Street Fighter Marketing.)

Part One: *Munchkidland*; Part Two: *Yellow Brick Road*; Part Three: *Emerald City*.

A cyclone uproots a Kansas farmhouse with exercise instructor Dorothy inside it. While it flies through the air, Dorothy passes the time with a workout and encourages the audience to join her (audience-participation workouts occur regularly throughout this health-instructional video). When the house crashes down in Oz, it dislodges a fez-wearing lizard and an old key from a nearby tree.

The key informs Dorothy it's the Key to Fitness and encourages her to clean up her house. The Lizard introduces itself as the Lizard of Oz (a running gag is that his accent makes it sound like Wizard of Oz), a nutritionist and former head librarian at the University of Oz. He tells Dorothy how the Ice Witch deluged Oz with lazy rain, after which no one had the drive to visit the library; left alone, he read so many books he now knows something about almost everything.

The Lizard and Dorothy enter the lovely but nutritionally empty Junk Food Forest, where Munchkids (Munchkins transformed by the lazy rain) sit around watching TV and pigging out. The Key reminds Dorothy too much sugar is bad for you (its homilies are another running element); she tries and fails to shake the Munchkids up with an exercise class. The Lizard tells Dorothy the Ice Witch cast the spell after some tragedy prevented her playing outside, so she decided no one else would go outdoors either.

Dorothy finds the Witch's talking silver sneakers, Archie and Leftie, but can't touch them through the Witch's magic shielding. She persuades Munchkid Mayor Boz to start an exercise program, and decides it's her duty to bring fitness back to all of Oz. The re-energized mayor gives Dorothy the sneakers and sends her and the Lizard down the yellow brick road to seek help from Oz.

In Part Two, Dorothy finds a Scarecrow mocked by crows for his stale jokes. He tells her he can't learn new jokes—or anything—because he's illiterate, so Dorothy suggests that he join her in seeking the Wizard's help. They next meet a muscular but rusted Tin Kid, who tells them the one muscle he's failed to develop is his heart. A Lion attacks but panics in fear at the sight of the Lizard; unable even to speak in front of groups, he agrees to ask the Wizard for some confidence.

In Part Three, the group reaches the Emerald City, whose closed gates sit behind steps resembling a giant keyboard. The guard tells the group it must enter in harmony; the group realizes this means moving up and down the steps until the notes it plays blend together.

The Great and Powerful Oz, alas, is a fat giant head that refuses to stop watching TV to help them. The guard tells Dorothy that the Ice Witch was once a Nice Witch until the Munchkins teased her for stumbling while skipping outside. The furious witch blasted them with the lazy rain and forced the Emerald City folk indoors with a freezing storm that iced over the city gardens, freezing herself into the Ice Witch in the process.

Dorothy and her friends find the frozen

Dorothy back in the real world in *The Wizard of Sales*. (Photograph credit: Street Fighter Marketing.)

sorceress and discover Scarecrow's jokes, even his worst ones, thaw the witch by making her laugh. When she finally thaws out, she angrily demands Dorothy give back the sneakers—or else! Dorothy reminds the Ice Witch that her last tantrum hurt her as much as her targets; then the Scarecrow cracks more jokes, thawing the witch's heart completely. Dorothy teaches the restored Nice Witch how to skip down the garden path, and they return to the Wizard's chamber, where the Lizard releases the air from the balloon-like head, restoring Oz to normal, too.

For their rewards, the Wizard gives Scarecrow some learn-to-read tapes, Tin Kid gets a heart, the Lion gets a crown and the Lizard gets a set of English-as-a-second-language tapes. Dorothy gives the Nice Witch her sneakers and is then transformed into Ozma, Princess of Fitness! A storyteller (Silich, whose narration opens and closes each episode) tells us Ozma became a famous fitness guru, the Lion a celebrated speaker, Tin Kid a champion bodybuilder (and mayor of Emerald City) and the Scarecrow a student of the Lizard, who became dean of the university. Health was restored—and that's

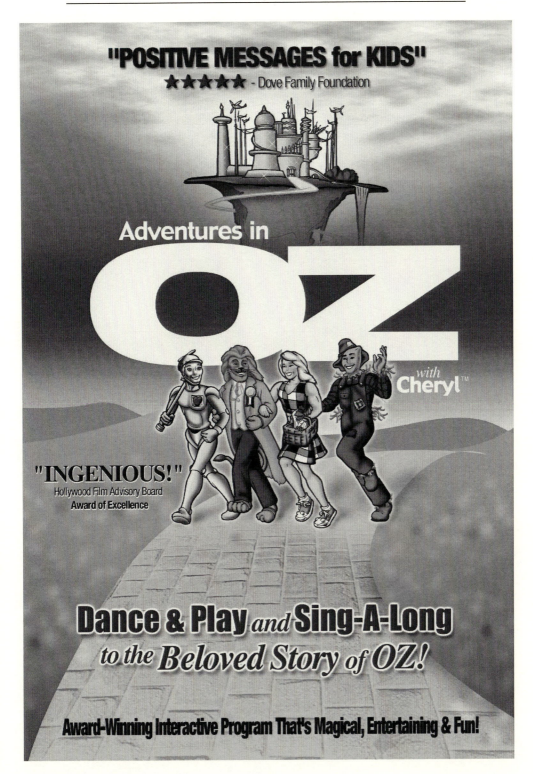

A promotional poster for Cheryl Anne Silich's exercise/health video series for children, *Adventures in Oz with Cheryl.*

just one of the wonderful places kids can visit by reading, Silich adds.

Silich, a real-world fitness instructor and an Oz enthusiast and collector, found a way to combine both her passions in this three-part video series.

7

Oz on Television: Series, Episodes, and Specials

1950

Kukla, Fran and Ollie. 5/22/50. 30 mins., b&w, NBC.

Cast: Narrator: Fran Allison.

Credits: Puppeteer: Burr Tilstrom; *Director:* Lewis Gomavitz; *Producers:* Beulah Zackery, George Latsham.

Fran Allison narrates the story from *The Land of Oz* of how Tip and Mombi created Jack Pumpkinhead (Scarecrow and Tin Woodman make cameos in the opening and closing credits). The skit was performed by marionettes.

Kukla, Fran and Ollie was a beloved puppet show in which Allison engaged in unscripted, live conversation and games with balding puppet Kukla, affable, educated dragon Ollie (both hand puppets rather than marionettes) and other characters, eventually known as the Kuklapolitans. The show adapted many other stories over the years, including *The Mikado* and *The Arabian Nights*. One Tilstrom fan who saw the Oz skit found it surprisingly disappointing, however.

1957

Disneyland Fourth Anniversary Show. 9/11/57. One hour, color, ABC.

Cast: Walt Disney (himself), Narrator (Sterling Holloway), Scraps (Doreen Tracy), Scarecrow (Bobby Burgess), Dorothy (Darlene Gillespie), Ozma (Annette Funicello), Polychrome (Karen Pendleton), Button-Bright (Carl "Cubby" O'Brien), Zeb Hugson (Cubby O'Brien), Cowardly Lion (Jimmie Dodd), with Bobby Van, Doodles Weaver, Gloria Wood.

Credits: Directors: Sidney Miller, Hamilton S. Luske; *Writer:* Albert Duffy; *Producer:* Bill Walsh; *Cinematographer:* Ray Fernstrom; *Music, lyrics:* Tom Adair, Buddy Baker, Sid Miller; *Editor:* Al Teeter; *From:* Walt Disney Productions.

As part of this TV special (which is actually a third anniversary episode), the young Mouseketeers from *The Mickey Mouse Club* TV show turn up on one of the Disney studio sound stages and present Walt Disney himself with a book called *The Rainbow Road To Oz*. The kids suggest that since Disney owns the copyright to Baum's stories, he should make an Oz movie starring the Mouseketeers.

To sell the idea, they perform the musical number "Patches" (sung by Bobby Van, Doodles Weaver and Gloria Wood) in which the Scarecrow meets the Patchwork Girl on the yellow brick road and picks patches of cloth from a tree to mend her dress. Then the kids perform a scene in which the Cowardly Lion has become King of Oz but an enchantment has made him cruel and conceited. Dorothy, Ozma and their friends try to break the spell by leading the lion in the "Oz-Kan Hop," a dance that's "part Kansas, part Oz!"

Disney agrees to make the movie, and the Mouseketeers tell him that now he can have his cake. They then perform a big production number, "The Rainbow Road to Oz," singing and dancing around a huge birthday cake.

Disney had been interested in adapting Oz ever since the 1930s (Baum's widow chose to go with another animator, but that project never got off the ground). In the 1950s, Disney thought of adapting the books as two-part specials for his *Disneyland* anthology show; in 1954, he purchased the rights to all the Baum books except the first two (which weren't available) and *Dorothy and the Wizard in Oz*, which had been purchased by the Lippert Company. In 1956, Disney bought the rights from Lippert for almost as much as the other 11 books combined, eliminating the risk of a rival production coming out.

Dorothy Cooper wrote a script outline for *Dorothy Returns to Oz*, then a finished script, *The Rainbow Road to Oz*, largely based on Baum's *Patchwork Girl*. Disney thought it would be too expensive for TV, and decided to make a big-screen musical instead, and to use the *Disneyland* special as a promotional stunt (something Disney did many times).

Not long afterwards, the studio dropped the project. Possible reasons included the budget, the script, fear the Mouseketeers couldn't carry a theatrical release (especially with ratings for *Mickey Mouse Club* declining) or a fear that the new film wouldn't be able to compete with MGM's *Wizard of Oz*, which had just started playing on TV.

In 1969, Disney released *The Story and Songs From the Cowardly Lion of Oz*, a book-and-record set that was supposedly based on the Thompson novel of that name, but actually had an original script and used two of the songs planned for *The Rainbow Road to Oz*, "The Ozphabet" and "The Pup-Pup-Puppet Polka."

De Crawley films of Canada also proposed a film of this title in the 1930s, but that project never materialized, either.

1960

The Shirley Temple Show: The Land of Oz. 9/18/60. One hour, color, NBC.

Cast: Tip/Ozma (Shirley Temple) Mombi (Agnes Moorehead), Scarecrow (Ben Blue), Tin Woodman (Gil Lamb), Jack Pumpkinhead (Sterling Holloway), Lord General Nikidik (Jonathan Winters), Graves the Butler (Arthur Treacher), Jellia Jamb (Mari Lynn), Glinda (Frances Bergen), Colonel (Charles Boaz), Lightning Bug Repairman (Norman Leavitt), Royal Army (William Keene), Court Doctor (Lou Merrill), Sawhorse/Book (Mel Blanc, voice only), Gump (Maurice Dallimore, voice only).

Credits: Director: William Corrigan; *Writer:* Frank Gabrielson; *Producer:* William Asher: *Executive producer:* William H. Brown, Jr.; *Art director:* E. Jay Krause; *Costumes:* Bob Carlton; *Lighting:* John Casagrande; *Musical director:* Vic Shoen; *From:* NBC Productions.

Gilliken ruler General Nikidik, who's so evil that feeling good depresses him, strikes a bargain with Mombi to overthrow Princess Ozma and turn the princess into a statue. Mombi magically summons Ozma to her cottage but decides she'd be more useful transformed into a boy, Tip; his past forgotten, Tip becomes Mombi's servant.

Nikidik demands that Mombi make Tip a statue. Tip startles Mombi with a pumpkin-headed stick figure when she comes home, then Mombi surprises him by animating it with the Powder of Life. She threatens Jack Pumpkinhead with being made into a pie unless he helps her brew the petrifying potion. That night, however, Tip and Jack run away, taking the Powder of Life, and decide to seek protection from Princess Ozma.

Tip turns a sawhorse into a living steed with the powder, but falls off as it speeds away. Jack arrives at the Emerald City and learns the Scarecrow has become king; royal maid Jellia Jam amuses herself "translating" for Jack and Scarecrow (who speak the same tongue), then Tip arrives and warns of the invasion. Scarecrow sends a message to the Tin Woodman, but when the Woodman arrives, Mombi's image appears and tells them she made Nikidik's army invisible: the palace is already surrounded.

Tip and his friends combine some couches, palm fronds and a mounted trophy head and bring them to life as the flying Gump. They fly off, but Mombi's magic almost crashes them into a volcano before Glinda saves them. Mombi assures Nikidik Glinda's army—a boy with toy sol-diers—won't stop them, but when Glinda reaches the city, the toys became life-size warriors.

Mombi confesses to everything and offers to turn Tip back (though he'd sooner be a statue than a girl), but instead transports him to the throne room, where she and Nikidik plan to shrink the boy into nothingness. As Tip dwindles away, Glinda appears, casting a spell that destroys Mombi's powers, then turns Tip back to Ozma. Ozma regains her throne and Nikidik, to his horror, is forced to do a good deed a day and be known as Nikidik the Good ever after.

Shirley Temple is believed to have been MGM's first choice for Dorothy in *The Wizard of Oz* (though there's nothing in the studio records to confirm that), and her unsuccessful 1940 fantasy, *The Blue Bird*, is widely seen as "Shirley Temple's Oz," a way to duplicate the success of MGM's film. A fan of Oz herself, Temple once said she never wanted to play Dorothy at the time, she wanted to *visit* Dorothy (whom she assumed was a real person).

After Temple's ABC anthology series, *Shirley Temple's Storybook* became a hit (it became *The Shirley Temple Show* when it moved to NBC), and Ruth Plumly Thompson asked if Temple would be interested in adapting some of Thompson's Oz stories. Temple opted for the public-domain *Land of Oz* instead. The end results are generally considered fairly good, though the boy-to-girl switch distressed some reviewers.

1961

Tales of the Wizard of Oz. Syndicated, 1961. 130 five-minute episodes.

Voices: Dorothy (Susan Conway), Glinda (Pegi Loder), Wicked Witch/Rusty the Tinman (Larry Mann), Socrates the Strawman (Alfie Scopp), Wizard/Dandy Lion (Carl Banas), Munchkins (Susan Morse).

Credits: Producers: Arthur Rankin, Jr., Jules Bass, Larry Roemer, Anthony Peters, Bernard Cowan; *Animation:* Crawley Films, Canada; *From:* Rankin/Bass.

Episodes in Chronological Sequence: The Wizard of Oz, The Witch Switch, The Wizard's Wand, Magic Hat, The Balloon Buzz, Machine Gun Morris, Movie Maid, Shadow Shakes, The Big Cake Bake, Desmond's Dilemma, Misfire Miss, Gung-Ho Gang, Heart-Burn, Stuffed, Fountain of Youth, Munchkinville, Topsy-Turvy Town, The Rubber Man, The Happy Forest, Dandy's Dilemma, The Search, To Bee or Not to Bee, The Bag of Wind, The Music Men, Have Your Pie and Eat it Too, Sound of Munchkins, The Count, Storm in a Tea Cup, Places Please, The Green Golfer, The Flying Carpet, The Monkey Convention, Love Sick, It's a Dog's Life, The Fallen Star, Don't Pick the Daisies, The Munchkin Robin Hood, The Cool Witch, The Wizard's Tail Fins, The Witch's Boy Friend, Brain Child, Salad Happy, Two Heads Are Better than One, The Clock Watchers, The Chariot Race, Double Trouble, The U.N., Going to Pieces, Mail-Order Lovers, The School Marm, An Optical Delusion, Watch the Bouncing Bull, All in a Lather, The Brick Stealer, The Green Thumb, Leap Frog, The Big Shot, On the Wing, To Stretch a Point, The Flipped Lid, Down in the Mouth, The Gusher, Ozzie the Ostrich, The Family Tree, Boomer Rang, The Great Laruso, The Pudgy Lion, Beauty and the Beach, The Hillies and Billies, The Cultured Lion, Chowy Mein, The Super Duper Market, The Jail Breakers, The Reunion, Episodes 75–110 titles unkown, The Green Tomato, The Poet, Episodes 113–4 titles unknown, The Yellow Canary, The Mail Man, Episodes 117–121 Titles Unknown, A Wiff of Courage, Episodes 123–6 titles unknown, Bake Your Cake and Eat it Too, The Pony Express, The Last Straw, The Brain.

"They're three sad souls/Oh me oh my/No brains, no heart/He's much too shy...." In this series, heartless, irascible Rusty, slow-witted Socrates ("I want the Wizard to give me — what was it again?") and utterly timid Dandy were promised the usual cures by the Wizard — who could work real magic and stage trickery, but was a little inept at both — but somehow he never got around to providing them, any more than he was able to send tough, not-so-helpless Dorothy back to Kansas.

While waiting around for the Wizard, Dorothy and her friends had to cope with the Wicked Witch's schemes (stealing the ruby seeds needed to make Rusty's new heart, killing the Wizard with a poison cake, snagging a date with the handsomest man in Oz). In other episodes, characters were drafted; competed in a TV quiz show; visited a coffee house filled with cool "Munchniks"; Dandy turned to self-help books to gain confidence; and a Chicago gangster visited the Emerald City.

This was the second TV series from Rankin-Bass, a company founded by former ABC art director Arthur Rankin, Jr. and adcompany messenger Jules Bass and better known for stop-motion animation specials such as *Santa Claus Is Coming to Town*. Like the first series, *The New Adventures of Pinocchio*, *Tales*' 130 five-minute episodes fit a common children's-show format of the time: A local host and a crowd of kids sitting around talking, pushing the sponsors' products and watching cartoons along with the viewers at home.

The show's art had nothing to do with Oz illustrators Neill or Denslow, but reflected the minimalist designs of the popular UPA cartoons of the 1950s and 1960s. It looks rather crude today, which along with the now-dated topical references may explain why it remains an obscurity (it's also just plain nuts, though that's not necessarily a bad thing, of course). The series has been aired more frequently in Canada, because some top Canadian animation talent worked on it (which led to Canadian voice actors being used in several later Rankin-Bass shows).

A 1964 TV special, *Return to Oz*, reused the characters with elements of MGM's *Wizard* thrown in. Other Baum-related material from the studio includes *The Life and Adventures of Santa Claus* and *That Girl in Wonderland*.

Tales was the only Oz cartoon series until the 1990s, but not for lack of trying: MGM proposed a series in 1961 with Judy Garland providing Dorothy's voice; Hanna-Barbera announced plans for a series both in the 1960s and then in the 1980s (by the latter date, they'd gone to the effort of securing animated rights to all the Baum books, but it still didn't come off); Depatie-Freeling also proposed a series at one point.

1963

Discovery. 3/29/63.

This episode of the informational series guest-starred Margaret Hamilton in Wicked Witch costume for a discussion of L. Frank Baum's role in literature. The "discovery" of the title was that Baum wrote many books besides *Wizard*.

1964

Return to Oz. 2/9/64. One hour, animated, NBC.

Voices: Dorothy (Susan Conway), Glinda/Wicked Witch (Pegi Loder), Socrates the Strawman (Alfie Scopp), Rusty the Tinman (Larry Mann), Wizard/Dandy Lion (Carl Banas), Munchkins (Susan Morse).

Credits: Directors: F.R. Crawley, Thomas Glynn, Larry Roemer; *Writer:* Romeo Muller; *Score:* Gene Farrell, Edward Thomas, James Polacks, George Wilkins; *Producers:* Arthur Rankin, Jr., Jules Bass; *Animation:* Barrie Nelson, Rod Willis, William Mason, Blake James, Don Stearn, Vic Atkinson, Milton Stein, George Ruble; *Camera:* Ron Hames, Gary Morgan, Bill Clark; *From:* Rankin/Bass.

Songs: I Wanna Go Back; Moonbeam; We're Munchkins Naturally; You Can't Buy a Brain; Wickedest Wicked Old Witch; I'm Heartless, Through and Through; Dan, Dan Dandy Lion.

In this sequel to *Tales of the Wizard of Oz*,

Dorothy's finally back in Kansas but receives a letter from Socrates asking her to return to Oz. Another twister hits the Gale farm and takes Dorothy and Toto to Munchkinville.

Glinda tells Dorothy that the winter winds have restored the Wicked Witch of the West. Using power borrowed from another evil witch, the Witch of the West burned Socrates's diploma, melted Rusty's heart-shaped watch and turned Dandy's medal to a dandelion, leaving them stupid, heartless and cowardly once more. The letter Dorothy received was a trick to lure her back so the witch can use her remaining power to steal the magic slippers.

Dorothy and Glinda reunite her helpless friends. Glinda tells them it's the Wicked Witch who is heartless, brainless and cowardly because she's been corrupted by evil. They set off for more help from the Wizard, so the witch attacks (riding a malfunctioning flying umbrella), blasting Dorothy with a lightning bolt, which Rusty heroically intercepts. The witch then enters the Emerald City and captures the Wizard, then has his big giant head direct Dorothy and the others into a trap.

When the trap — a flying crocodile flock — closes, Socrates hides his friends under his straw, then sends the crocs down a false trail. The witch then uses the wizard to lure the group into her castle, where she captures the slippers. Dandy heroically tries to reclaim them, despite the Wizard's warnings that the first person to touch them will turn to stone — and sure enough, the witch seizes them and gets petrified.

The Wizard promises to grant everyone's wishes, but at the awards ceremony uses a phonograph record of his voice to hide the fact that he's sneaking away. Glinda reappears and shows Dorothy's friends that they've proved they still have brains, heart and courage; then another twister sends Dorothy home.

This was the first Rankin/Bass TV special (and also the first collaboration by the song-writing team of Maury Laws and Jules Bass), done, like *Tales*, in the style of UPA's animation, except with a more realistic Dorothy.

The plotline, though, is more a sequel to the MGM *The Wizard of Oz* than *Tales*.

ABC's 1990 *Wizard of Oz* cartoon also used the idea of the Witch of the West stealing the Wizard's talismans.

The Judy Garland Show. 3/1/64. One hour, CBS.
Cast: Judy Garland, Jane Powell, Ray Bolger.
Credits: Director: Dean Whitmore; *Producers:* Gary Smith, George Schlatter; *Executive producer:* Norman Jewison; *Music:* Mel Torme, Harold Arlen; *Lyrics:* E. Y. Harburg; *Musical director:* Mort Lindsey; *Costumes:* Ray Agahayan.

In the "Tea for Two" segment of this variety show, Garland and Bolger share memories of shooting MGM's *The Wizard of Oz* and sing a couple of songs from the film. Along with fellow guest Jane Powell, they do a dance based on the "Jitterbug" number cut from the film.

The Wizard of Oz. 4/1/64. WICB-TV.
Credits: Director, producer: Sharon Staz; Based on Jean Kellog's abridgement of *The Wizard of Oz*.

In this local TV production, freshman and sophomore drama majors gave dramatic readings from the book while children from the Ithaca, NY, area acted, sang and danced.

1967

Off to See the Wizard. 9/2/67–9/20/68. One hour, color, animated (intro and ending), ABC.
Voices: Dorothy (June Foray), Scarecrow (Daws Butler), Don Messick.
Credits: Producer: Abe Levitow; *Executive producer:* Chuck Jones; *From:* MGM.

To the tune of "Over the Rainbow," Dorothy and Toto slide down a rainbow into Oz at the opening of each episode, reuniting with their friends (to the tune of "Off to See the Wizard") and race down the yellow brick road to the Emerald City. Entering the Wizard's private theatre, they engage in a few minutes of banter with him (highlighting the Wizard's bumbling efforts at magic) before settling down to watch a film. After a brief appearance during a commercial break, the

Oz characters return at the end, with the Wizard presenting a trailer for next week's film and the characters sliding down a banister as the show closes.

MGM conceived this series as a way to showcase the studio's family films like *Wonderful World of Disney*; the films, often cut into two episodes to fit the time slot, included *Flipper*, *Clarence the Cross-Eyed Lion* and a few films shot for the TV series, such as *Untamed World*. Given that MGM's *Wizard of Oz* was still riding high on television, the Oz framing sequence, created by animation legend Chuck Jones, seemed a great way to bring in audiences. Whether because of stiff competition or a poor film selection, however, the show died after a year.

Tie-in merchandise — figurines, Halloween costumes, paint-by-number kits — went on selling into the 1970s, divorced from the series and marketed as straight *Wizard of Oz* items.

The Gene London Show. 11/23/67. WCAU-TV.

Cast: Gene (Gene London).

Gene, who runs Mr. Dibley's General Store, buys Dibley's daughter Debbie a $20 bracelet on credit, then can't pay it off. When creditors come calling, Gene's job is in jeopardy, and so is Debbie's dog, Toto, when an elderly woman kidnaps it for digging holes in her lawn. A twister hits, knocking Debbie cold; she awakens to find herself living out MGM's *The Wizard of Oz* (with some variations — Dorothy marries the Scarecrow) before she comes to and finds herself safe in Gene's arms.

Gene London's children's show (also called *The Wonderful World of Gene London* and *Cartoon Corners* — this episode may have appeared under one of those titles) ran from 1959 to 1977 on WCAU in Philadelphia, with stories of Gene's working in the Dibley store (for 8½ cents a week!) mixed with a sprinkling of cartoons and films, particularly those from Disney.

1970

Death Valley Days: The Wizard of Aberdeen. 1/12/70. 30 mins., syndicated.

Cast: Host (Dale Robertson), L.Frank Baum (Conlan Carter), Maud Gage Baum (Beverly McKinsey), with Jennifer Edward, Robert Sorrells, Bill Zuckert.

Credits: Director, writer: Stephen Lord; *Writer:* Vernon H. Jones.

This anthology episode focuses on Baum's time as editor at *Aberdeen Saturday Pioneer*, a difficult job because even though the town loved the paper, readers preferred to share copies rather than buy their own. Baum's greatest happiness comes from telling stories to children, drawing inspiration for his tales from a scarecrow in a field, or making up a Cowardly Lion to comfort a timid boy. When the paper incurs the wrath of Ruggedo, an Aberdeen businessman, Ruggedo challenges Baum to a duel, but in the end, both men settle their differences and discharge their pistols into the air.

Near the end of the show, Baum comforts a sick girl named Glinda with a wonderful story about Dorothy, a girl carried by a twister to a magical land named Oz (Baum plucks the name off an O–Z filing cabinet). The show closes with a tin funnel (like the Tin Woodman's hat) hanging on a fence next to the Scarecrow.

Death Valley Days began on radio in 1930, and continued telling stories of the Old West (mostly related to Death Valley, and all supposedly based on some scrap of truth) until the mid-1970s on television. Dale Robertson was one of several hosts over the years.

The story that Baum plucked the name of Oz from a file cabinet far predates this one, though Baum's wife asserted he simply made it up (in a 1939 interview she also dismisses stories that Baum based his characters on real people). Baum biographer Katharine Rogers has pointed out Oz isn't that different from Baum's other nation-names, such as Ix, Mo, Ev and Yew.

1971

The Jackson Five: The Wizard of Soul.
11/20/71. 30 mins., color, animated, ABC.

Voices: The Jackson Five (Tito Jackson, Jackie Jackson, Michael Jackson, Marlon Jackson, Jermaine Jackson) as themselves, with Paul Frees, Edmund Silvers, Joe Cooper, Donald Fullilove, Mike Martinez, Craig Grandy.

Credits: Directors: Joy Batchelor, John Halas; *Writers:* Romeo Muller, William J. Keenan, Hal Hackady, Lou Silverstone, Susan Milburn; *Animation director:* Robert Balser; *Producers:* Jules Bass, Arthur Rankin, Jr.; *From:* Rankin-Bass, Motown, Halas and Batchelor Cartoon Films.

Shortly before the Jackson Five play a big Las Vegas singing gig, a tornado picks up Michael Jackson and his pet snake Rosey and deposits them in the desert. A nearby oasis leads into the Land of Soul, where Munchkins surround them until the Tin Man drives them off. The Tin Man tells Michael he used to play guitar, but the music-hating Wicked Witch of the East cursed him so he can't play a note.

Tin Man, Michael and Rosie go to find the Wizard of Soul, the one man who can help them, and on the way pick up Straw Man (a singer) and Lion (a bass player), whom the witch has also cursed. When they reach the Wizard, he lifts the spell but tells Michael only the witch can send him home. The witch's winged mice kidnap the boy and bring him to the witch's glass castle; she tells Michael she hates music, particularly rock, because the vibrations damage her castle.

This makes it a really bad idea for the witch to teleport the other characters to join Michael in the dungeon: He leads them in the Jackson's "Oh, How Happy You Have Made Me" and the castle shatters. Michael wakes up in the desert as his brothers arrive, brushing aside his story as a mirage ... much to the annoyance of the Witch as she flies overhead.

Before Michael Jackson went solo, the Jacksons came to Saturday morning in this Rankin-Bass series. Each episode featured Michael in a weird adventure with his brothers turning up as other characters, only for him to wake and realize it was all a dream ... or was it? Which is probably why the "It was all a dream ..." line doesn't show up as one might expect.

1974

Volshebnik Izumrudnogo Goroda [Also known as The Wizard of the City of Emeralds]. 10 episodes, Ekran TV, USSR.

Voices: Elli (Klara Rumyanova), Strasheela (Roman Tkachuk), Iron Woodman (Garry Bardin), Villina (Emilya Milton), Goodwin (Zinovi Gerdt), Wolf (Vladimir Vysotsky), with A. Vlasova, A. Konchakova, Vera Vasilyeva, Roman Fillippov, Rina Zelenya, Zinajda Naryshkina, G. Vlasova, Vladimir Ferapontov, Rogvold Sukhoverko, Zinovi Gerdt, V. Bardin, Vladimir Filimonov, Venyamin Smekhov, Spartak Mishulin, Vladimir Vyosotzky, Igor Yasulovich, Vladimir Gorelov, Valeri Zolotukhin, Andrei Kanevskii, O. Gramova, Olga Aroseva, N. Udakov, I. Narishkina, V. Nosachev, Anatoli Barantsev, Sergei Tzeits, A. Elinosoi, Yuri Savelyev, Mariya Vinogradova, Valentin Nikulin, Viktor Sergachyov.

Credits: Directors: V. Popov, L. Smironov; *Writer:* Aleksandr Kimma (based on Alexander Volkov's *The Wizard of the City of Emeralds*, *Urfin Jus and His Wooden Soldiers* and *The Seven Underground Kings*); *Producers:* K. Malyantovich, L. Aristov, U. Kalisher, U. Trofimov, A. Bogolobov, U. Kleputzkii, K. Sulakauri; *Assistant directors:* G. Beda, V. Nazaryk, B. Moiseyev, U. Trofimov, G. Smolyanov, V. Levinskaya, Y. Bogolobova; *Cinematographers:* I. Golomb, I. Nikolayev, E. Turevich, Ilya Minkovotzkii, L. Kolvinovskii, G. Kasradze, Y. Turvevich, K. Turevich; *Lighting:* I. Tokmakovai, L. Derbeneva, A. Sanina, I. Shaferan; *Music:* Igor Yefremov, L. Bukanov, I. Kosmachev, A. Bukanov; *Editors:* S. Simukhinoai, M. Trusovoi, G. Drobininoi, N. Butakovoi.

[Viewed in the Russian language version.]

ELLI IN MAGIC LAND

Little Elli lives happily with her mother and dog Totoshka on a small farm, until the day the malevolent witch Gingemma sends a cyclone to Elli's farm to bring her to Gingemma in the Magic Land. Fortunately, the

Muncher dwarves tell Good Witch Villina, whose magic blasts Gingemma before Dorothy lands, leaving only the witch's silver shoes behind.

Villina and the Munchers greet Elli, and Totoshka, who discovers he can talk, fetches Elli the witch's slippers. A magical yellow brick road unfurls in front of Elli as Villina directs her to the City of Emeralds, where the great wizard Goodwin may be able to help her.

Elli and Totoshka befriend Strasheela, a plump, legless Scarecrow, rework his bottom to add stubby legs and teach him to walk. He joins them seeking brains from Goodwin. When they oil up a rusted Iron Woodman, Zhyelyeenee Drovosyek, he joins them too. An ogre kidnaps Elli for his dinner, but her friends rescue the girl from the ogre's fortress and Drovosyek traps the ogre under his own portcullis.

THE YELLOW BRICK ROAD

The travellers cross a river on a raft the Woodman has made, but the pole wedges in the river bottom, yanking Strasheela away as the others drift to land. A Lion greets them, confessing to being not only harmless but cowardly; as a proof of his good intentions, he brings Strasheela back to land.

Farther on, the pollen from a poppy field puts Elli, the Lion and Totoshka to sleep, forcing Drovosyek to build a wagon to wheel the Lion out. Riding the wagon, they encounter a rabbit fleeing a saber-toothed tiger; the Lion holds off the tiger long enough for the others to cage it. Strasheela compliments the Lion's heroism, but he brushes it off.

THE EMERALD CITY

The travelers reach the City of Emeralds, which looks like a big green circus tent (much of the city is designed on a circus/sideshow motif) but the guards don't let them in. The city residents have been irrigating the desert, but as Elli and her friends wait to enter, flying monkeys (no wings) throw sand on the new greenery, turning it barren. The Iron Woodman has the idea of using the irrigation hose to blast the monkeys, who then flee, at which point the flowers start growing again.

Goodwin then invites his guests into the big top, changing shapes (giant clown, beautiful woman, monster, fireball) as they speak, with the real Goodwin in clown makeup watching from behind the scenes. Goodwin offers to grant their wishes if they destroy Bastinda, the Wicked Witch of the West; Elli's friends persuade her to try.

KINGDOM OF BASTINDA

A wolf-man guards the gateway into Bastinda's realm, but the gate is set on a dotted line with no wall around it; nearby, Winker slaves break rocks. The guard rushes off to report Elli's approach, leaving Drovosyek free to break the gate padlock, letting his friends inside. When Bastinda hears the wolf's report, she almost skewers him with his umbrella; he heads back and forces Elli and the others back out of the gate at gunpoint. Strasheela then suggests walking around the gate instead, and they reach Bastinda's fortress without trouble.

Bastinda's flying monkeys smash the Iron Woodman, dismember Strasheela and drag Totoshka and the Lion into the fortress. The Winkers take Elli into hiding, and rebuild Strasheela and Drovosyek. The guard finds them and apparently tricks them into visiting the castle with a bucket of water, thereby steering Elli into an invisible rope-trap. Instead, Bastinda gets caught on the rope, falls into the bucket and dissolves. Elli uses the witch's golden cap to summon the flying monkeys to take them back to Goodwin.

DISCLOSURE OF THE GREAT AND TERRIBLE

The monkeys drop everyone off in the city, forcing Goodwin (moustachioed and in a top hat) to rush to set up his illusions, but Totoshka finds him before the wizard is prepared. Goodwin shares his history (more or less identical with the Wizard of Oz's), then provides Elli's friends with the necessary talismans to bolster their confidence. He offers Elli a balloon ride home, but his excited guards let go the basket early, before Elli is inside. The flying monkeys tell her they can't fly out of the Magic Land, but the Good Witch Stella tells Elli how to use the shoes. After giving the golden cap to the monkey king, Elli uses the shoes to send herself and Totoshka home.

The Secret of Gingemma the Witch

The sixth episode opens with Elli and Totoshka playing outside the farmhouse on a mock ship built by their friend, weathered sailor Charlie Black. Then a raven delivers a message showing Strasheela and Drovosyek behind bars.

We flash back to see woodcarver Urfin Jus discovering a powder of life in Gingemma's lair that, sprinkled on an old bear rug, animates it as a living bear, Totopun. Urfin promptly carves a platoon of life-sized wooden soldiers, and brings them to life. Riding Totopun, Urfin Jus leads his army against the City of Emeralds, but the Scarecrow swats them off the walls when they try to scale them, then lights his own straw and throws it to scare off the wooden warriors.

Unfortunately, Gingemma's pet owl is working with Urfin Jus: It drugs the night watchman's tea, allowing the army to conquer the city and capture Strasheela. The owl alerts the Iron Woodman to his friend's peril, leading him into a trap; after he's thrown in to prison however, a bird enters the cell window and agrees to take a message to Elli.

The Ship of the Old Sailor

Charlie puts wheels on his ship and sails it across the steppe with Elli, Totoshka and the bird aboard. Back in the Magic Land, the wooden soldiers continue to destroy children's playthings and other symbols of joy throughout the city, then capture the Courageous Lion (as he's now known) in his forest. As Black's ship approaches the city, it crashes on a magnetic outcrop that also pins Elli and the others to it. Elli's bird friend contacts the Good Witch Stella, who gives him a basket of magic that turns the rock to a strawberry bush, freeing everyone. Elli and her friends sneak through an underground passage into the dungeon, rescue them and return to Charlie's ship.

Soldiers to Gardeners

While Urfin Jus has the Munchers level trees to provide more soldiers, Totoshka sneaks back into the city and brings Drovosyek's axe to the woodman. Charlie wheels his ship in front of the City of Emeralds, and there's a pitched cannon battle between the ship and Urfin Jus's army; the good guys lose and the ship is wrecked. The wooden soldiers enter the forest to find the escaped crew, but they're tricked and trapped; then the Iron Woodman recarves their faces into happy grins. Now the soldiers only want to dance and garden.

Elli and her friends lead an army of children armed with sticks to storm the palace. Urfin Jus flees, but Totoshka sniffs out the secret passage Urfin Jus and Totopun have taken. A desperate Urfin Jus abandons the bear, which reverts back to a rug. The City of Emeralds returns to its happy ways and Elli, Charlie and Totoshka head home in the rebuilt boat.

The Mysterious Cave

Urfin Jus knocks himself out running from an underground monster. The scene cuts to Elli and Totoshka gathering fruit. Elli's cousin Fred invites them for a boat ride, but when the river flows underground, Fred's yell causes a cave-in that closes off their way out. Totoshka talks, a sign they've entered the Magic Land.

In between encountering the strange underground creatures, they meet an old man who takes them to a large chamber with a rotating hourglass and seven curtained alcoves, the home of the Seven Underground Kings. The kings govern in rotation, six sleeping while one rules; as Elli watches, one king drinks from a magic well and falls asleep, then a new king is installed. The spring makes the kings amnesiac, so they must have their roles explained to them.

Sneaking around, Urfin Jus accidentally shatters the cistern beneath the well, causing the water to drain away. He climbs out through the well, and gets captured by the king's servants, but tries to sway the still-confused monarch to his side.

ELLI MEETS THE FRIENDS

More of the kings wake up, and with no water to put them back to sleep, they quarrel over who should lead, and listen to Urfin Jus's venomous whispers. While Elli and Fred try to reason with the monarchs, Elli also sends Totoshka for help. As Urfin Jus persuades the kings to seize Elli and Fred, the Courageous Lion appears and sends them fleeing with a roar. Iron Woodman and Strasheela join him.

The Iron Woodman drills a new well and all the kings drink, as does Urfin Jus when he realizes he's lost again. At Strasheela's suggestion, the kings are stripped of their regalia and given workmen's tools (tape measure, sheers, fishing net, etc.); when they wake, they're told they live in a republic as plain working men. Urfin Jus wakes up utterly bewildered, then Elli, Fred and Totoshka find themselves back on the surface of the magic land.

Alexander Volkov wrote *The Wizard of the Emerald City* in 1939, a "translation" that was actually a rather free adaptation of *Wizard of Oz* (some of the elements, such as Gingemma being responsible for the cyclone, were introduced in Volkov's later revision of the book). Volkov went on to write five more stories that branched further away from Baum; there's no Ozma, for instance, so Strasheela remains king of Oz.

This stop-motion TV series adapted not only the first book but the next two, *Urfin Jus and his Wooden Soldiers* and *The Seven Underground Kings*.

1974

The ABC Saturday Superstar Movie: That Girl in Wonderland. 1/13/74. One hour, animated, ABC.

Voices: Ann Marie (Marlo Thomas); with Patricia Bright, Dick Hehmeyer, Rhoda Mann, Ted Schwartz.

Credits: Directors, producers: Arthur Rankin, Jr., Jules Bass; *Writer:* Stu Hample; *Associate producer:* Basil Cox; *Music:* Maury Laws; *Lyrics:* Jules Bass; *From:* Rankin-Bass.

In this episode of the Saturday morning anthology cartoon, Ann Marie (Thomas's character in her popular sitcom, *That Girl*) is working as a children's book editor, rather than as the actress she was in prime time, and imagines herself the heroine of various classic fairytales—*The Wizard of Oz, Snow White, Sleeping Beauty, Cinderella* and *Goldilocks and the Three Bears*.

In the 1970s, characters from prime-time routinely turned up in Saturday morning cartoons; *The Brady Bunch, My Favorite Martian, I Dream of Jeannie* and *The Partridge Family* are just some of the live-action shows that became cartoon series. This single episode was, however, Ann Marie's only foray into toon-hood.

1977

The Brady Bunch Hour. 1/23/77. One hour, ABC.

Cast: Mike Brady (Robert Reed), Carol Brady (Florence Henderson), Alice Nelson (Ann B. Davis), Greg Brady (Barry Williams), Peter Brady (Chris Knight), Bobby Brady (Michael Lookinland), Marcia Brady (Maureen McCormack), Jan Brady (Geri Reischl), Cindy Brady (Susan Olsen), Mr. Merrill (Rip Taylor), Krofftette Dancers and Water Follies (Robin Blythe, Susan Buckner, Christine Gow, Linda Hoxit, Dee Kay, Lynn Latham, Charkie Phillips, Judy Susman).

Credits: Director: Jack Regas; *Writers:* Ronny Graham, Bruce Vilanch, Steve Bluestein, Mike Kagan, Carl Kleinschmitt; *Producer:* Lee Miller; *Executive producers:* Sid and Marty Krofft; *Associate producer:* Tom Swale; *Art director:* Rene Lagler; *Choreographer:* Joe Cassini; *Costume Design:* Pete Menefee; *Special musical material:* George Wyle; *Music arrangements:* Sid Feller, Van Alexander; *From:* Paramount, Sid & Marty Krofft.

In the opening episode of this series, the Brady family (of *The Brady Bunch*) are packing to move to Hollywood where they'll star in their own variety show. Alice, the housekeeper, finds Marcia playing with her old Oz dolls and tells her there's only room to pack one. Marcia insists on taking the whole set, and tells the Toto doll that Alice is "acting witchy."

Marcia fantasizes herself as Dorothy, working with Scarecrow (Greg Brady), Tin Man (Peter) and Cowardly Lion (Jan) at the Emerald City Carwash, where they sing the theme song from the recent hit film *Carwash*. When the Wicked Witch (Alice) throws up, a bucket of water destroys her. The fantasy lifts Marcia's mood and she goes to help pack.

This bad variety show reunited the cast of *The Brady Bunch* (except Eve Plumb, the original Jan) for what *TV Guide* later listed as one of the 50 worst shows ever (though it didn't stop the Bradys from later turning up in two reunion films, two more sitcoms and two big-screen parodies).

The Donny and Marie Show. 9/30/77. One hour, ABC.

Cast: Donny Osmond, Marie Osmond, Jim Connell, Hank Garcia, Lucille Ball, Paul Williams, Paul Lynde.

Credits: Producers: Sid and Marty Kroft; *Executive producer:* Raymond Katz.

A tribute to the MGM film on an episode of this wholesome variety show.

Nationwide: The Wizard of Oz. 12/25/77. BBC.

Cast: Cyril Smith, Tom Jackson, Denis Healey.

This Christmas production showcased political and union leaders in an Oz parody with lots of puns: for instance, when Dorothy pushes a door, Healey, the Chancellor of the Exchequer, tells her "You'll never budget." In the course of the story, the Wicked Witch reforms instead of being melted, Dorothy stays in Oz, and Healey's Wizard encourages viewers to give to the IMF, the International Magician's Fund: "The money will magically disappear!"

1978

Yogi's Space Race: Race Through Oz. 10/28/78. 30 mins., color, animated, NBC.

Voices: Yogi Bear/Huckleberry Hound (Daws Butler), Scarebear (Joe Besser), Quack Up (Mel Blanc), Captain Snerdly (John Stephenson), Jabberjaw/Buford/Nugget Nose/Captain Good/Phantom Phink (Frank Welker), Goofer (Roger Pelz), Sludge (Frank Welker), Rita/Cindy Mae (Pat Paris), Woody (Dave Landsburg).

Credits: Directors: Ray Patterson, Carl Urbano; *Story editors:* Andy Heyward, Ray Parker, Jim Ryan; *Story:* Herb Armstrong, George Atkins, Haskell Baakin, Jack Bonestell, Doug Booth, Chuck Couch, Mark Fink, Gary Greenfield, George Greer, Andy Heyward, Len Janson, Mark Jones, Glenn Leopold, Ray Parker, Sam Roeca, Jim Ryan, Susan Stewart; *Producer:* Art Scott; *Executive Producers:* William Hanna, Joseph Barbera; *Animation supervisors:* Bill Keil, Jay Saabay, Mark Glamack; *From:* Hanna Barbera Productions.

A space cyclone sweeps the cast (who compete each week in a race through outer space) over a galactic rainbow to Planet Oz. The race runs across the yellow brick spaceway to the Emerald City with a computer-selected dream date as the winner's prize; the route is dangerous, but anyone who quits will have to face the Wicked Witch of the Spaceways.

When heroic racer Captain Good falls behind the others, he reverts to his secret identity as treacherous Phantom Fink. The Witch agrees to derail the competition if the Fink brings her another racer's ruby-framed glasses (but when the Fink delivers, the Witch simply disappears from the plot). The Fink resorts to various tricks to slow down his rivals, such as conning them into a fight with a brutal space wrestler, but his rule-breaking gets him disqualified. Undeterred, he reverts to Captain Good and wins the race, only to discover his date is the witch!

Starting with *Yogi's Ark Lark* in the early 1970s, Hanna-Barbera has produced several shows teaming up characters from its vast cartoon library. This was one of the weaker ones.

Hanna and Barbera told the *Los Angeles Times* in the 1960s that they planned to create an Oz series in which a live Dorothy interacted with a cartoon Oz, but it never materialized, nor did later plans for an animated Oz in the 1980s.

The World's Greatest Superfriends: The Planet of Oz. 11/11/78. 23 mins., animated, ABC.

Voices: Wonder Woman (Shannon Farnon), Superman (Danny Dark), Aquaman (Bill Callaway), Batman (Olan Soule), Robin (Casey Kasem), Mr. Mxylpk/Zan/Gleek (Michael Bell), Narrator (Bill Woodson), Jayna (Liberty Wiliams).

Credits: Directors: Ray Patterson, Carl Urbano, Oscar Dufau, George Gordon; *Story direction:* Rick Hoberg, Will Meugnio, Don Sheppard, Emilie Kong, Larry Latham; *Story:* Jeffrey Scott; *Producer:* Don Jurwich; *Executive producers:* William Hanna, Joseph Barbera. *Animation supervisors:* Bill Keil, Jay Saabay, Bob Goe; *From:* Hanna-Barbera Productions.

The malevolent fifth-dimensional imp Mxylplk sends an unstoppable cyclone to carry the Hall of Justice — headquarters of the Super-Friends team — to the Planet of Oz with Wonder Woman, Aquaman and Superman trapped inside. The imp tells them the only escape is to travel the yellow brick road to the Wizard.

A giant plant attacks, and the Super-Friends discover most of their powers don't work on Oz. They flee into a gingerbread house where a witch turns them into Tin Woodman (Superman), Scarecrow (Aquaman) and Cowardly Lion (Wonder Woman), and Mxylplk warns them not to leave the road again.

The trio resumes its journey, then a flock of crows deposits Aquaman in a river, leaving him waterlogged until he commands a jellyfish to coat him with waterproof ooze — to Mxylplk's secret delight. The imp is just as pleased when Wonder Woman saves herself from a herd of boars by channeling lightning through her golden lasso.

A rainstorm rusts Superman and turns the yellow bricks to green kryptonite. Superman almost tricks a gloating Mxylplk into saying his name backwards (which banishes him to his home dimension and negates all his magic), then transmutes his tin body to lead to protect himself from the kryptonite.

When the heroes finally reach the Wizard, he turns into Mxylplk, restores them to normal and combines the jellied straw, transmuted lead and electrified lasso into a potion that will let him stay forever in our dimension. To prove it, he says his name backwards—and discovers Superman turned the lead back into tin, so the potion was worthless. Mxylplk returns to his own world, and the heroes and the Hall of Justice rematerialize on Earth.

This was a rather off-beat riff in this long-running super-hero cartoon (loosely based on the *Justice League of America* comic-book). Mxylplk was a simplified-spelling version of Superman's comic-book foe Mxyzptlk.

1979

The Making of the Wizard of Oz.

A TV documentary about the MGM movie, based on the book of the same title by Aljean Harmetz. Harmetz, Ray Bolger, Jack Haley and Margaret Hamilton appeared on camera.

1980

Thanksgiving in the Land of Oz [Also known as Dorothy in the Land of Oz; Christmas in Oz]. 11/25/80. 30 mins., color, animated, CBS.

Voices: Dorothy (Mischa Bond), Jack Pumpkinhead/Tyrone the Terrible Tinkerer (Bob Ridgely), Wizard/U.N.Krust (Sid Caesar), Tik-Tok/Ozma (Joan Gerber) Hungry Tiger (Frank Nelson), Aunt Em (Lurene Tuttle), Uncle Henry (Charles Woolf), with Maitzi Morgan, Julie Cohen.

Credits: Directors: Fred Wolf, Charles Swenson; *Animation director:* Takashi Abe; *Writer:* Romeo Muller; *Lyrics:* Romeo Muller; *Producers:* Romeo Muller, Fred Wolf, Charles Swenson; *Executive producer:* Robert L. Rosen; *Animation producer:* Tomo Fukumoto; *Animation:* Toshio Mori, Tatsuji Kino; *Cinematography:* Masatoshi Fukui; *Production manager:* Kosei Otanu; *Music:* Steven Lawrence, David Campbell; *Editor:* Chikako Matsubura; *From:* Toei Doga Animation, Murakami-Wolf-Swenson, Muller-Rosen Productions; *Cinematography:* Masatoshi Fukui.

Dorothy and Aunt Em prepare for their last Thanksgiving dinner: The bank is foreclosing on Uncle Henry so Dorothy is moving in with her cousins and Henry and Em are going to the old folk's home. When someone swipes a pie cooling on the windowsill, Dorothy chases him and confronts the Wizard, broke and hungry because he can't interest anyone in using his new, garishly green turkey-shaped balloon.

An accident sends the balloon skyward with Dorothy, Toto and the pie onboard until it touches down in Oz. Jack Pumpkinhead (with a Southern accent) tells Dorothy that Tyrone the Terrible Toy-Tinker now rules the Winkies even more ruthlessly than the Witch of the West. Jack tells Dorothy her giant bird scared Tyrone off before he could capture Jack, who holds the last supply of the magic Powder of Life Tyrone wants to use to animate a toy-soldier army.

When Dorothy tells Jack the balloon isn't a real bird, Tyrone, hiding nearby, seizes the Powder of Life and turns the balloon into the Green Gobbler of Oz. It flies him off to his mountain lair where the toy soldiers await. Jack leads Dorothy up a secret passage into the mountain, guarded by a tiger; Dorothy considers bribing the cat with the pie, but the powder brought the pie to life too, and it refuses. When they confront the Hungry Tiger, the cat admits he can't bring himself to eat people—but the pie suggests that eating someone as evil as Tyrone shouldn't pose a problem.

Wandering through the maze of tunnels, they discover Tik-Tok, a mechanical man who leads them to Tyrone's volcanic lair. The Gobbler carries Dorothy to the toymaker, but instead of cowering, Dorothy gives him a good talking-to on changing his evil ways. Tyrone slowly warms to the idea of using his skills to become a Santa-esque Christmas gift-giver, but then the Tiger arrives, charges him, and Tyrone spills the powder into the volcano, bringing it back to life.

The Gobbler carries everyone safely to Ozma in the Emerald City; Ozma suggests that instead of Dorothy going home, she bring Henry, Em and the farm to Oz (the Wizard winds up tagging along). Once the oldsters grasp that Oz isn't just a dream, they invite Ozma's court over for Thanksgiving dinner. Dorothy concludes that "home is where the heart is—and we're home at last!"

This Thanksgiving special has aired under several titles less attached to any particular holiday. It's an oddball but appealing mix of elements from *The Land of Oz* and *Ozma of Oz* (Tyrone is a dead ringer for Neill's Nome King), though Tyrone's toy army also resembles one villain's scheme in one of the Russian Magic Land books that spun off from Oz.

1981

Richie Rich/Scooby-Doo Hour: Scooby's Trip to Ahz. 1/17/81. Seven mins., color, animated, ABC.

Voices: Scooby Doo (Don Messick), Shaggy (Casey Kasem), Scrappy Doo (Lennie Weintrib).

Credits: Directors: Ray Patterson, Carl Urbano, Oscar Dufau, George Gordon; *Story:* Tom Swale, Doug Booth, Diane Duane, Mark Evanier, Willie Gilbert, Glenn Leopold, Duane Poole, David Villaire; *Producer:* Don Jurwich; *Executive producers:* Joseph Barbera, William Hanna; *Animation supervision:* Bill Keil, Jay Sarbry, Bob Goe. *From:* Hanna Barbera.

While preparing to watch a TV broadcast of MGM's *The Wizard of Oz*, cowardly great dane Scooby Doo falls and hits his head. A cyclone then carries Scooby, his feisty nephew Scrappy Doo and their human friend Shaggy over the rainbow to a yellow brick road. Shaggy is now a Scarecrow, Scooby a lion and Scrappy has become a Tin Dog.

A Yellow Brick Toad offers to lead them to the Wizard, until he hears the Wicked Witch of the North coming, and runs off. The witch zaps Scooby & Co. into a magic sleep while they're standing in a poppy field, and her winged monkey drags them to her castle. When they revive, Scooby and Shaggy try to escape, dragging Scrappy with them (he wants to fight); the witch catches up with them, but there's a bucket of water handy and Scrappy's seen the MGM film...

As the witch melts, the Wizard shows up and offers them a balloon ride. The balloon isn't built to support four people, though, and Scooby falls through the overtaxed basket. He wakes up outside the van, with the movie about to start — but if it was all a dream, why does he still have a lion's tail?

Scooby Doo debuted on Saturday mornings in 1969's *Scooby Doo Where are You?* wherein he and his human friends investigated supernatural mysteries that always turned out to be hoaxes. The series ran for years in various permutations (and after a few years' absence, returned to Saturday mornings in 2002), including adding the widely despised Scrappy Doo. This season, Scooby's adventures were part of an hour show, combined with cartoons about megawealthy Richie Rich.

1983

Fame: Not in Kansas Anymore. 2/24/83. One hour, NBC.

Cast: Lydia Grant/Glinda (Debbie Allen), Coco Hernandez (Erica Gimpel), Danny Amatullo/Cowardly Lion (Carlo Imperato), Bruno Martelli/Tin Woodman (Lee Curreri), Julie (Lori Singer), Doris Schwartz (Valerie Landisburg), Leroy Johnson/Scarecrow (Gene Anthony Ray), Mr. Shorofsky/The Wizard (Albert Hague), Elizabeth Sherwood/Wicked Witch (Carol Mayo Jenkins), Julie Miller/Winkie Slave (Lori Singer), David Reardon/Guardian of the Gate (Morgan Stevens); Guest cast: Elizabeth Daily (Darlene Smolensky).

Credits: Director: Robert Scheerer; *Writers:* William Binn, Paul Rubell; *Story:* William Bin (based on MGM's *The Wizard of Oz*; *Songs:* Lee Curreri (based on the MGM film); *Choreography:* Debbie Allen.

Fame chronicled the struggles of students and teachers at the New York School for the Performing Arts; in this episode, smart-mouthed but goodhearted student Doris is shell-shocked when English teacher Sherwood informs her that she'll have to drop out of the current school production because of her low grades in English.

Still arguing the case, Doris falls off the stage, hits her head and finds herself wandering through a largely empty school ruled by a tyrannical witch (Sherwood), seeking help from the Wizard (affable teacher Shorofsky), and accompanied by the Scarecrow (class clown Danny), Tin Man (pianist Bruno) and Cowardly Lion (tough guy Leroy). In the course of their adventures, Doris realizes she was wrong and Miss Sherwood was right; she comes to in the auditorium and realizes it was a dream but you were there, and you, and you ...

This episode had some amusing touches such as cello student Julie playing air cello as the witch's slave, and the witch holding up her smoking as proof that she's evil!

Ripley's Believe It or Not. 10/2/83. NBC.

One episode of this show — focusing on the weird, the implausible and the unusual — devoted a segment to some of composer Harold Arlen's home movies from MGM's *Wizard of Oz*, including the deleted "Jitterbug."

1984

Oz No Maho Tsukai [Also known as The Wizard of Oz]. 52 half-hour episodes. Animated, NHK/TV Tokyo, Japan.

Voice Cast: (Cinar English-language version): Dorothy (Morgan Hallet), Tinman (George Morris), Lion (Neil Shee), Scarecrow (Richard Dumont), Narrator (Margot Kidder), Jinjur (Susan Glover), General Guph (Dean Hagopian), Tik-Tok (A.J. Henderson), Kaliko (Walter Massey).

With: Steven Bednarski, Harvey Berger, Maria Birguer, Mark Denis, Kathleen Fee, Carol Ann Francis, Gayle Garfinkle, Susan Glover, Arthur Grosser, Dean Hagopian, A.J. Henderson, Adrian

Knight, Terrence Labrosse, Linda Lonn, Liz Macrae, Brownen Mantel, Walter Massey, Gordon Masten, Steve Michaels, Carla Napier, Linda O'Dwyer, Barbara Pogemiller, Rob Roy, Michael Rudder, Howard Ryshpan, Vlasta Vrana, Tim Webber, Jane Woods.

Voice Cast: (Japanese) Dorothy (Sumi Shimamoto), Kakashi (Tadashi Yasuhara), Woodman (Takumi Kamiyama), Lion (Ichiro Nagai).

Credits (Japanese version): Directors: Masaru Tenkauchi, Masaharu Endo, Hiromitsu Morita; *Writers:* Akira Miyazaki, Takafumi Nagamine, Hiroshi Saito; *Design:* Shuichi Seki; *Animators:* Shinya Takahashi, Minoru Kobata, Akio Sakai, Joji Yanase, Toshio Kaneko; *Music:* K.S. Yoshimura; *From:* Itoman, Panmedia, TV Tokyo.

Credits: (Cinar version): Director: Tim Reid; *Animation director:* Gerald Potterton; *Writers:* Don Ariolli, Tim Reid; *Producer:* Ronald A. Weinberg; *Exeutive producer:* Micheline Charest, Ronald A. Weinberg; *Associate producer:* Elizabeth Klinck; *Animation supervisor:* Christine Laroque; *Storyboards:* Elaine Gasco; *Music:* Hagood Hardy, Richard Homme, Brian Leonard, Ray Parker, Robert Piltch, Tom Szczesniak; *Music composition:* Hagood Hardy, Tom Szczesniak, Ray Parker; *From:* Cinar Productions, RCA-Columbia Pictures, Lightyear Entertainment, HBO Nagai.

Episodes: Dorothy Meets the Munchkins; Dorothy Finds a Friend; Adventures Along the Yellow Brick Road; Saved by the Mouse Queen; The Emerald City at Last; The Wicked Witch of the West; Dorothy's Magic Powers; Freedom from the Witch; Mombi, Tip and the Golden Cap; Back to Emerald City; The Wizard's Disappointing Secret; The Wizard Tries to Help; Journey to the South; Glinda, the Good Witch; Home Sweet Home Again; Dorothy Meets the Wizard Again; Back to Oz; General Jinjur Attacks; Escape from the Emerald City; Tinman to the Rescue; Mombi's Terrible Magic; Trapped in the Palace; The Magical Escape; Glinda Agrees to Help; The Emerald City Captured; Mombi's Attempt to Trick Glinda; Ozma, Princess of Oz; Tik-Tok, the Mechanical Man; The Kidnapped Prince; The Deadly Desert; The Talking Hen; Monsters of Stone; The Underground Country of the Nomes; The Deadly Guessing Game; Dorothy Outsmarts the King; The Secret Fear of the Nomes; The Nome King Sets a Trap; Saved by the Sun; The Nome King Plans Revenge; Princess Ozma's Secret; Miss Cuttenclip and Mr. Fiddle; The Growleywog Joins the Nomes; The Water of Oblivion; Nomes on the March; A Winky Helps His King; The Crowning of Ozma; The Nomes Attack; Dorothy and Her Friends Defend the Palace; A Very Happy Ending.

While Dorothy's aunt and uncle are off in town, a tornado carries off the farmhouse with Dorothy and Toto inside. The cyclone releases the farmhouse in Oz atop the Wicked Witch of the East, to the undisguised delight of her Munchkin subjects and the Good Witch of the North. The Good Witch gives Dorothy the wicked one's shoes (which turn to silver) and a protective kiss, then sends her off to seek help from the Great and Powerful Wizard of Oz.

Resting in a cornfield, Dorothy befriends the Scarecrow, who's so ineffective crows use him as a perch. He agrees to join her journey to seek some brains. Next they meet a rusted Tinman, oil him up and hear how after he fell in love, the Witch of the East, who despised love, turned him to heartless tin from spite. No sooner does he agree to join Dorothy than a lion attacks Toto, only to cringe away when Dorothy slaps him. The Cowardly Lion then signs on for the trip.

Journeying down the road, they must confront the tiger/bear kalidahs; save the Scarecrow when he's stranded in the middle of a river; and the Tinman has to carry his flesh-and-blood friends out of a field of poppies that plunges them into sleep. When they reach the Emerald City (looking rather bleached white), the Guardian of the Gate insists that the Tinman and Scarecrow must be sorcerers and refuses to let them in. Dorothy talks the man around, but the Wizard only allows them in one at a time (as in the novel—although he appears in the same shape each time, as a giant head). As usual, the price of his help is the death of the Witch of the West.

When the witch spots Dorothy and her friends coming, she summons the Winged Monkeys to destroy them. The monkeys demolish the Scarecrow and Tinman, and drag the others to the Wicked Witch; although the witch can't harm Dorothy because of the

Good Witch's kiss, the witch intimidates the girl into working as a servant (mostly having her remove all sources of water from the castle). The witch tries and fails to steal the shoes, so she turns the caged Lion to stone and traps Toto in a ring of fire. The panicked dog runs through the fire to his drinking bowl, splashing the witch, and thereby destroying her.

Back in the city, the Wizard refuses to grant any wishes despite being presented with the witch's broom and the cap commanding the monkeys. When Toto finds the real man hiding in an alcove, he admits to being a mere humbug from Omaha, but nevertheless commits to deliver on his promises.

The Wizard fills the Scarecrow's head with a mix of sawdust and needles, puts a soft velvet heart inside the Tinman and provides Lion with a placebo potion of courage. The Scarecrow hits upon repairing the Wizard's balloon to take Dorothy home, but of course the Wizard winds up flying off alone. The Winged Monkeys fly Dorothy & Co. to Glinda in the South of Oz; Glinda tells how the shoes can take Dorothy home, and offers to use the cap to send her friends to their new realms (Scarecrow ruling the Emerald City, Tinman the Winkies and the Lion the Forest of Oz). Dorothy says goodbye and goes home with Toto.

Uncle Henry and Aunt Em are overjoyed by Dorothy's return until Dorothy starts telling crazy stories about a land where she's friends with a talking Scarecrow. One of the silver shoes fell off in flight; when Em finds it, Dorothy decides to return to Oz and bring back proof. She tries to test the shoes, but they carry her at once to Oz, without Toto, and fall off before she lands. Em and Henry find the shoes, and realize not only is Oz real, their niece has no way home.

Dorothy has no idea where in Oz she is, but a young boy, Tip, instantly recognizes her from a poster proclaiming her great deeds. Tip tells her he's an apprentice to another witch, Mombi, who believes Dorothy must be a powerful sorceress to have destroyed the witches of East and West. Since Mombi's out meeting other mages, Tip prepares a surprise for her, a pumpkin-headed stick figure he places in the path.

The strange figure startles Mombi until she figures it out, and decides to use it as a test of the Powder of Life she traded for. To the astonishment of Dorothy and Tip, "Jack Pumpkinhead" comes to life; Mombi is almost as stunned to meet the mighty Dorothy. They all return to Mombi's cottage (with Jack annoying Tip by calling him "Dada") where Mombi tries bartering for some of Dorothy's magic.

Eventually Mombi decides the Powder of Life gives her enough power to dispense with Dorothy and Tip. As she concocts a petrification potion, the children run off with the powder, Jack trailing behind. When they find a wooden sawhorse, they bring it to life with the powder, but it runs away with Jack, leaving Tip and Dorothy far behind. Worse still, they encounter General Jinjur, who's preparing to seize the Emerald City with her all-girl army.

When Jack reaches the city, the word of Dorothy's return wins him an audience with King Scarecrow. Scarecrow confesses himself bored to tears ruling a kingdom where everything runs smoothly; as if on cue, Jinjur storms the city gates and proclaims herself queen (but instead of a suffragette agenda, she announces that Oz is too happy, so smiling and laughing are forbidden). Dorothy and Tip reach the palace to alert the Scarecrow; when he and Jack ride the Sawhorse to the Tinman for help, Dorothy and Tip get left behind, but sneak out of the city and catch up with their friends.

Mombi arrives in the Emerald City chasing the children; she's too late to catch them, but in time to sell her services to Jinjur. When the Tinman joins his friends heading back to the city, Mombi traps them in an illusion of sentient flowers until Jinjur sneezes and scatters the spell ingredients. The Scarecrow realizes that the Queen of the Field Mice lives nearby, and asks one of her subjects to travel with him as a secret weapon.

When they reach the throne room, Jinjur

summons her army to imprison them, but when the girls see the mouse, they run in panic. Jinjur surrounds the palace, however, and calls on the citizens to back her up in recapturing it. Inside, the good guys create a flying vehicle out of furniture and the head of a hunting trophy, all sprinkled with the Powder of Life.

They fly to Glinda, who tells them she's willing to overthrow Jinjur, but not to restore Scarecrow to the throne: Her sorcery has revealed that the rightful heir, Ozma, is alive, though hidden by Mombi to keep her from threatening the Wizard's reign (though a later recap of Ozma's backstory softens this: The Wizard believed Mombi's magic would protect Ozma from the East and West Witches better than his stage tricks could).

Dorothy & Co. return to the palace, with Glinda watching over them. Jinjur tells them Mombi has transformed herself with sorcery and agrees to surrender, along with the witch, if Dorothy and her friends can find her. Otherwise, Jinjur remains in power. The good guys spot Mombi hiding as a corsage on Jinjur's dress, but instead of surrendering, Mombi turns into a dragon. Glinda shields her friends from Mombi's attack, then captures the dragon as soon as it becomes exhausted. Mombi is forced to confess that after the Wizard turned Ozma over, Mombi used magic to turn him into a boy.

Tip objects that he was the only boy at the cottage ... and when the truth sinks in, he reluctantly agrees to become the rightful ruler Oz needs. Once the transformation is done, Glinda sends Dorothy home and transports the Scarecrow and Tinman to the Tinman's Winkie palace.

Some time later, Dorothy is magically transported from her Kansas bed by a strange ticking sound, and wakes surrounded by Wheelers (hairy dwarves on unicycles). They accuse her of being a witch working with a metal man (she admits to the last part, of course), and try to run over her. Dorothy reaches a rocky slope they cannot ride on, and follows the ticking to an inert Tik-Tok, the metal man they spoke of.

When Dorothy winds Tik-Tok up, the nervous, jittery automaton reveals that the ticking is his in-built safety mechanisms, which brought her from Kansas to save him. He tells Dorothy he needs a Wheeler's hat for his mistress Princess Lulu, a compulsive collector. When the Wheelers approach, Dorothy uses their fear of her to negotiate a truce: She and Tik-Tok go free and Lulu will forget about their hats.

When she and Tik-Tok reach Lulu's castle, Tik-Tok warns Dorothy that Lulu's personality changes to fit whatever hat she wears. Lulu is less than thrilled to learn that Tik-Tok failed and suggests taking Dorothy's hair as a consolation prize; when Dorothy refuses, Lulu cries, then consigns her and Tik-Tok to the dungeon (despite Tik-Tok's description, Lulu's mood is mercurial even without changing hats).

A mouse recognizes Dorothy from the Queen of the Field Mice's description, and goes to Oz to ask the Cowardly Lion to help. Ozma, Jack, Tinman and Scarecrow arrive at Lulu's castle, and Lulu asks them to rescue her brother, the Prince of Ev, from the Nome King. As Ozma tells Lulu she can't leave Oz for that long, the Lion shows up; Tinman realizes that if Dorothy and the Lion join them, they have a team capable of beating the Nome King, even without Ozma. Lulu happily releases Dorothy and Tik-Tok, while Ozma and Jack go home.

Near the entrance to Noland, Dorothy and her friends meet Billina, a hen exiled from the Nome realm after the king discovered that eggs are toxic to Nomes. Clearly smitten with Tik-Tok, she gives the bemused robot an egg as a gift.

The jovially malevolent monarch refuses to let the Prince of Ev go free, but offers to let his guests guess which of his many ornaments is the transformed prince; find the prince and he goes free, fail and be transformed themselves. Tik-Tok tries first and becomes transformed.

The Lion tries tracking the prince by scent, despite the efforts of Kaliko, the king's advisor, to distract him; as a last-ditch measure,

Kaliko touches the Lion's tail to an ornament, transforming him.

Tinman then tells Kaliko his knowledge of the human heart will find the prince: He's going to push Kaliko toward different ornaments, and see if the Nome is afraid of being transformed. The Nome runs, and in following him, Tinman touches an ornament. Scarecrow deduces the prince is a small tiger figurine, but as he reaches to touch it, Kaliko drops a hanging ornament on his head.

Dorothy starts playing, and gives the Nomes a tongue-lashing when they start mocking her. Ashamed, they redeem themselves by convincing the King that the Scarecrow is guiding her to the prince, even in his transformed shape; the Nome King and Kaliko race to hide the figurine, which leads Dorothy to it. The prince helps Dorothy free her friends, but the Nome army surrounds them. The king demands the two metal men to study in his workshop; to save the others, Tik-Tok and Tinman surrender, but when the king opens Tik-Tok's head, he flees in terror from Billina's egg.

Despite the Nomes' pursuit, Dorothy's group reaches the surface, at which point sunlight holds the Nomes back. The Nomes trigger a sinkhole that almost sucks everyone back down, but the heroes escape with Billina and return to Oz. The Nome King, however, tells Kaliko he will have his revenge.

Back in the Emerald City, Dorothy finds Ozma very immature and tries training her into a proper queen. They discover an underground chamber recounting the history of Ozma and her father, which inspires her to accept the responsibility that comes with her royal blood. The chamber also activates Ozma's gift for magic; in the courtyard, she and Dorothy build a giant origami bird, which Ozma makes fly.

Meanwhile, the Nome King summons Mr. Guff, an "invasion specialist" who suggests they invade Oz by tunnel to avoid the sunlight. Guff provides a massive slug-like creature to eat a tunnel through the rock; he also suggests that to prevent Dorothy exploiting the Nome weakness for eggs, they send the monstrous Growleywog to eat every egg in the city before the attack. Growleywog (a hulking man-frog, more or less) agrees to Guff's proposal, which includes disposing of the Nomes after the conquest and dividing the city's emeralds two ways.

Ozma prepares for her coronation, which requires finding the lost Fountain of Oblivion with her magic: Its amnesia-inducing water is part of the ceremony (the only time it doesn't wipe memories). Meanwhile, Growleywog emerges into the Winkie lands and begins eating everything in sight, from buildings to flowers (curiously, no mention of eggs). Against the warnings of his subjects, the Tinman confronts the monster, which almost devours him, but doesn't like his taste. Tinman almost crushes the monster's throat in his metal grip, but after they stumble into the water, he rusts to helplessness. Dorothy, having been contacted by the Winkies, flies up on the paper bird, and Tinman uses his last free movement to keep her from being caught.

The Nomes discover a subterranean iron wall around the Emerald City, impervious to their drills or the worm's maw. Guff offers to scout out the city while they wait for the Growleywog, but his real goal is to pocket some emeralds for himself. He finds an ewer of water from the fountain and drinks, which erases his memory.

Dorothy brings a tinsmith to oil her rusted friend. They find Growleywog using Tinman as a pillow and oil him up without waking the monster; when they leave on the bird, the Growleywog does wake, but they manage to escape. Back in the palace, Dorothy finds Guff amiably sitting in the throne room, harmless but unable to explain himself.

When the coronation begins, the Nome King, watching by periscope, assumes the big crowds are Ozma's army and tells Kaliko there's no time to waste. Guff's slug digs a tunnel to just outside the city, which accidentally catches the Growleywog and drags him underground. The king and the monster strike a deal, and that night, they swarm into the Emerald City.

The city soon falls, but Dorothy and Scarecrow remain free, gathering eggs, which leaves the Nomes too terrified to fight them. When the duo are cornered in a castle chamber, the king leads a charge up the stairs, only to recoin from a fake wooden egg Scarecrow rolls down the stairs. The Growleywog, which has been off emerald-hunting, shows up and eats the fake egg, then devours all Dorothy's real eggs, too. Dorothy and Scarecrow try to find more, but when they try using the paper bird, the Growleywog catches and eats it, leaving them to fall. Dorothy hears Glinda promise safety and finds herself in one piece at the city gates.

When the Growleywog attacks Dorothy, Guff regains his memory and steers the monster to an underground chamber of emeralds instead, unaware that Ozma has sent the Nome King in the same direction. The Growleywog and Nomes battle at the entrance, and when they stumble inside, fall into the pool that feeds the Fountain of Oblivion, leaving them amnesiac and harmless. Glinda explains that their memories will return, but their evil has been washed away; Dorothy returns home, secure in the knowledge Ozma will bring her back any time she asks.

This series—based on Baum's first three books and *Emerald City of Oz*—has a curious history: It's apparently co-produced by Japan and an American company, but the credits, even to the copyrights, are different (anime expert Jonathan Clemens has suggested one of the partners, or both, didn't want to admit they were using foreign talent). It was first broadcast in the West in 1984, then shown in Japan on NHK television in 1986. Dropped by NHK, it was later screened on TV Tokyo, with the last two episodes run as one hour-long special.

Cinar later released it on Canadian TV in 1987, after which it showed up on HBO and was then broken down to four videotapes (one for each book). The series doesn't adapt well to video, however: What would have been weekly reminders about the Witch of the West's dislike of water, for instance, become very repetitive in a 90-minute video.

Jumping from *Ozma* to the Nome King's revenge in *Emerald City* makes a certain sense, and the *Wizard* adaptation is fairly faithful, though the changes it does make are odd; for example, why have Dorothy and her friends make four visits if the Wizard uses the giant head every time? The series grows increasingly off-Baum as it progresses, though, and not for the better: The Growleywog in the *Ozma* episodes is a poor substitute for the Growleywogs and other monsters the Roquat rallied to his cause in the book.

The animation is execrable throughout.

Fantasy Island: Games People Play.
1/14/84. One hour, color, ABC.
Cast: Regular: Mr. Roarke (Ricardo Montalban), Lawrence (Christopher Hewett); *Guests:* Nora Leonard (Lynda Day George), Barbara Jessup (Jennilee Harrison), Sandy Hoffman (Belinda Tolbert), Mr. Wagner (Dick York).
Credits: Directors: Don Weis, Cliff Bole; *Writers:* Stephanie Garman, Hollace White.

Friends Nora, Barbara and Sara arrive at the fabulous Fantasy Island resort, ostensibly for a toy-industry trade show, but secretly hoping the resort owner, Mr. Roarke, can grant their fantasies: Barbara wants to prove she's more than a dumb blonde, Sara wants the courage to confront her boss, Mr. Wagner, and widowed Nora wants to know her heart didn't die with her husband (Roarke points out the Oz analogy to his butler, Lawrence).

With Roarke's encouragement, Barbara tries impressing men with her brains, Sara confronts Wagner and Nora begins a new love affair. Unfortunately, men still do not take Barbara seriously, Sara gets fired and Nora learns her lover seduced her to steal a new toy design. Barbara, however, comes up with a plan to recover the design, Wagner rehires Sara and Nora realizes she does have a heart "because it's breaking."

Aaron Spelling revived the anthology show format in the 1980s with *Love Boat* and *Fantasy Island*, which mixed guest-stars and a regular cast for two or three stories each episode. Lawrence was the largely forgotten replacement for Roarke's better-known sidekick, Tattoo (Herve Villechaize's salary demands having gotten him kicked off the show).

The Guiding Light. 5/84. One hour, color, CBS.

Cast: Nola Reardon/Dorothy/Wizard of Oz (Lisa Brown), Quinton Chamberlain/Scarecrow (Michael Tylo), Tony Reardon/Tin Man (Greg Beecroft), Henry/Chamberlain/Cowardly Lion (William Roerick), Glinda/Bea Reardon (Lee Lawson).

In a dream sequence, soap character Nola Reardon dreams of herself as Dorothy, journeying to the Wizard (who turns out to look just like her) with the usual companions (played by other cast members), to ask for the right name for her newborn baby.

1985

The Whimsical World of Oz. One hour, color and b&w, PBS.

Cast: Narrator (Mason Adams).
Credits: From: Production Associates, Ltd.

This PBS documentary, timed to tie-in with *Return to Oz*, showed clips from that film, *The Wiz*, the Aussie *Oz*, *Journey Back to Oz* and the never-completed *Rainbow Road to Oz*, among others. It also interviewed authors, Oz Club members, actors from various productions (including Romola [Remus] Dunlap from the *Fairylogue and Radio Plays*) and Baum family members.

Muppet Babies: By the Book. 11/30/85. 30 mins., animated, color, CBS.

Voices: Animal/Bunsen/Skeeter (Howie Mandel), Beaker/Kermit (Frank Welker), Fozzie/Scooter (Gerg Berg), Gonzo/Robin (Russi Taylor), Nanny (Barbara Billingsley), Piggy (Laurie O'Brien), Rowlf (Katie Leigh).

In this series about the nursery days of Jim Henson's Muppets, the babies are passing a rainy day reading and fantasizing themselves as characters in the stories. When they turn to *The Wizard of Oz*, Baby Piggy imagines Pigorothy and her dog Ralph-Ralph being carried to Oz by the usual cyclone. The Silly Sorcerer of the South (Scooter) sends them to meet the Wizard; on the way, Pigorothy is joined by Scarecrow (Kermit), the Cowardly Comic (Fozzie Bear) and Gonzo the Tin Weirdo, seeking a job, courage and a new nose respectively.

In the Emerald City the group discovers the Wizard is really Muppet scientist Bunsen Honeydew. Aided by his assistant Beaker, Honeydew invents a New-Job-Courage-New-Nose-Going-Home Machine, Pigorothy and Ralph-Ralph are sent home, and we move on to the next book.

The opening titles for this popular Saturday morning cartoon include a shot of the Muppets dancing down the yellow brick road, but not in the roles they had here.

The Muppets' Wizard of Oz is scheduled to air on ABC May 20, 2005, with Ashanti Douglas as Dorothy, Jeffrey Tambor as the Wizard and Miss Piggy as all four witches.

The Life and Adventures of Santa Claus. 12/17/85. One hour, color, stop-motion animation, CBS.

Voices: Santa Claus (Earl Hammond), Young Claus (J.D. Roth), Great Ak (Alfred Drake), Necile (Lesley Miller), Tingler (Robert McFadden), King Awgwa (Earle Hyman), Wind Demon Commander (Larry Kenney), Queen Zurline/Wife (Lynne Lipton), Peter Nook/Awgwas/Gnome King/Husband (Peter Newman), Weekum (Joe Grasso), Children (Amy Anzelowitz, Josh Blake, Ari Gold, Jamie Lisa Murphy), Chorus (Al Dana, Margaret Dorn, Arlene Martell, Marty Nelson, David Ragaini, Robert Ragaini, Annette Sanders).

Credits: Directors, producers: Arthur Rankin, Jr., Jules Bass; *Writer, lyrics:* Julian P. Gardner (from the Baum book); *Music:* Bernard Hoffer; *Supervising producer:* Lee Dancher; *From:* Rankin-Bass Productions, Lorimar-Telepictures, CBS.

On Christmas Eve in the Forest of Burzee, Ak the Woodsman tells the Council of Immortals that the aging Santa Claus will make his last sleigh ride that night, unless they use the Mantle of Immortality to save him from death. To justify this unprecedented requested, Ak tells the Council Santa's story.

Said story begins 60 years before, when Ak found an abandoned human child and gave it to the lioness Shlegra to raise. The elf Nacile is fascinated by the child, whom she names Claus, "Little One," and she and the other forest spirits help Shlegra raise him. As Claus grows, Ak shows him the cruelty and coldness that fill the human world and the lives of human children. Horrified, Claus vows to change things.

Claus leaves Burzee for the Valley of Ho-HaHo, moving in with Shlegra, the elf Tingler and Blinky the cat. When an orphan befriends Blinky, Claus gives the boy a wooden cat to play with — the first toy: "Yes, I like the sound of that word," says Claus. Other children ask for toys, and Claus happily complies.

The spreading happiness enrages the monstrous Awgwas, who drive children to misbehave. The Awgwas steal toys invisibly whenever Claus tries to deliver them, despite Ak's orders to cease; finally Ak leads the immortals into battle and destroys the Awgwas utterly.

Claus then finds his stock of undelivered toys is too heavy to carry, so Peter Nook, lord of beasts, provides reindeer to tow the toys in a sleigh. Claus still arrives in town after dark, with doors locked, and has to deliver the toys down chimneys. Next morning, parents tell their children that clearly a saint like Claus needs no doors, from which the children rename him Santa Claus. Peter agrees to let Claus use the reindeer every Christmas Eve, and Claus's friends find the stolen toys to provide stock for this year's ride.

The Council agrees to bestow the mantle on Claus, and Nacile wraps it around him as he slips into his last sleep, assuring him he will live forever as the patron saint of children. Strength restored, Santa assures Ak he will do his best to prove worthy of the gift, "for in all the world, there is nothing so beautiful as a happy child."

Most of our Christmas traditions (Santa, buying presents, Christmas stockings) were created out of whole cloth in the 19th century (as Stephen Nissenbaum describes in *The Battle for Christmas*); *The Life and Adventures of Santa Claus* was the first attempt to create a fiction to make sense of them (a genre that would later include Seabury Quinn's short story "Roads," and Rankin-Bass's *Santa Claus is Coming To Town*).

This Rankin-Bass adaptation stays close to the book, giving it a darker feel than the cheery stop-motion specials they were known for (starting with *Rudolph the Red-Nosed Reindeer*). As the last of their specials, it was a good note to go out on.

The same book has also been adapted for *Young Santa Claus*, the 2002 *Life and Adventures of Santa Claus* and *Oz Kids: Who Stole Santa?*

1986

What's Happenin' Now: The Improbable Dream. 30 mins., color, syndicated.

Cast: Roger "Raj" Thomas (Ernest Thomas), Freddie "Rerun" Stubbs (Fred Berry), Shirley Wilson (Shirley Hemphill), Dwayne Clemens (Haywood Nelson), Nadine Thomas (Anne-Marie Johnson), Carolyn (Reina King), *Guest cast*: Paramedic (Harold Surratt), Munchkins (Lou Carry, Kevin Thompson, Buddy Douglas).

Credits: Director: Gary Shimokawa; *Writers:* David Silverman, Stephen Sustarsic.

Several years after ABC cancelled its African-American teen comedy series, *What's Happenin'* (loosely based on the movie *Cooley High*), the syndicated series *What's Happenin' Now* revisited the characters as 20-somethings. In this episode, all of them have problems: Dwayne can't get a date, used-car salesman Rerun can't get get a sale, Raj has writer's block and Carolyn's foster mother, Nadine, won't let her keep "Jojo," a homeless puppy because their yard is unfenced. After Carolyn tries and fails to find Jojo a new owner at Rob's Diner, the local hangout, she gets knocked unconscious in the back room, looking for dog food, and wakes to discover she and Jojo aren't in the diner any more.

Looking for the Wizard, Carolyn meets a

Good Witch working her way through college; a Wicked Witch who wants to confiscate Jojo; and a dateless Tin Man, a Lion who can't sell his car and a Scarecrow with writer's block (all counterparts of the regular characters, of course). The Wizard appears to them as a scary, fire-breathing giant face, but Jojo unmasks the real Wizard (Shirley, the diner waitress). The Wizard helps out Carolyn's friends, but the Wicked Witch appears and snatches Jojo away. Carolyn wakes to find a paramedic watching over her; to her delight, he tells her Jojo would be the perfect gift for his little girl.

Misfits of Science: Against All Oz.
2/7/86. One hour, color, NBC.

Cast: Billy Hayes (Dean Paul Martin), Elmo "El" Lincoln (Keven Peter Hall), Johnny "B-Man" Bukowski (Mark Thomas Miller), Gloria Dinallo (Courtney Cox), Stetmeyer (Max Wright), Miss Nance (Diane Civita).

Credits: Director: Michael Switzer; *Writer:* Morrie Ruvinsky.

Billy Hayes, the leader of the super-powered Misfits of Science team (living lightning bolt Johnny, telekinetic Gloria, size-shrinking Elmo), undergoes a sleep-deprivation experiment for his employer, Humanidyne, which leaves him lapsing in and out of dreams. In his dreams, the Misfits don't exist: Billy is a low-level lab flunky; klutzy Elmo is a former star athlete and Billy's boss; sweet Gloria is a bullying security guard; cool rocker Johnny is a geek; administrator Stetmeyer is a janitor. None of them listen when Billy insists he remembers them all differently.

When the super-weapon Humanidyne's building threatens to destroy the lab, dream-Billy remembers his real-world leadership skills and organizes the others to deactivate the device. When they fail, Billy snaps to wakefulness, and tells the others you were there, and you, and you...

This episode was a "clip show" using numerous flashbacks to previous episodes, justified by having dream-Billy tell the others these strange memories he has in which they're all different.

1987

The Wizard of Oz. Fuji TV, Japan.

Comedian Alexander O'Brien Feldman says he appeared in this TV production along with other variety performers carrying out their various tricks and specialties on the yellow brick road (which leads him to think it wasn't particularly faithful to the Baum book).

1988

Jim Henson Presents Mother Goose Stories. 30-minute episodes, color, Muppets.

Voices: Prince (Scott McAfee), Stella (Anndi McAfee); with John Christian Graas, Jodie Sweetin, Ilan Ostrove, Laura Goodwin, James Conway, Katy Broughton Smith, Nicholle Tom, Ethan Glazer, Michelle Wesson, Naomi Kerbel, Simon Bright, James Goodwin; Mother Goose (Angie Passmore), Goslings (Mike Quinby, Mak Wilson, Karen Prell).

Puppeteers: Credits: Directors: Brian Henson, Michael J. Kerrigan; *Writer:* David Angus (based on *Mother Goose in Prose by Baum*); *Producer:* Roberta Kurtz; *Executive producers:* Paul Stewart Lang, Peter Coogan; *Cinematography:* Peter Ward; *Puppets:* Jim Henson's Creature Shop; *Set design:* Dennis King, Gordon Toms, Malcolm Stone; *Costumes:* Jaqueline Mills; *Puppeteers:* Mak Wilson, Karen Prell, Mike Qinby, Angie Passmore; *Music:* Linda Danly, Mimi Danly. *From:* Jim Henson Productions, TSW Ltd.

Episodes: Humpty Dumpty; Pussy Cat, Pussy Cat/Little Bo Peep/Willie Winkle; Pat-A-Cake/The Giant/It's Raining, It's Pouring; Queen Of Hearts/Ride A Cock Horse To Banbury Cross/Hickety Pickety; Tommy Tittlemouse/Mother Hubbard/The Prince And The Beggars; A Song Of Sixpence/Jack & Jill/Twinkle, Twinkle, Little Star; Mary, Mary/Mary's Little Lamb/Man In The Moon; Margery Daw/Hector Protector/Baa Baa Blacksheep; Dicky Birds/Rub A Dub Dub/Humpty Dumpty; Hickory Dickory Dock/Duke Of York/Hey, Diddle Diddle; Old King Cole/Eenie Meenie/Little Nut Tree; Little Girl With A Curl/Crooked Man/Tommy Tucker; Eensy Weensy Spider/Little Jack Horner/Little Boy Blue; Little Miss Muffet/Jack Be Nimble/Peter, Peter Pumpkin Eater.

In each episode, Mother Goose tells her chicks the whimsical "true" stories behind the different nursery rhymes. Based on the tales in Baum's *Mother Goose* (plus some original ones). The series first aired in England, then on Disney Channel.

China Beach: Somewhere Over the Radio. 5/11/88. One hour, color, ABC.

Cast: Colleen McMurphy (Dana Delany), Lila (Concetta Tomei), Cherry (Nan Woods), KC (Marg Helgenberger), Laurette (Chloe Webb), Boomie (Brian Wimmer); Guest cast: Deejay (David Marciano), Banks (Kenny Ransom), Kim (Marion Kodama Yue), Lieutenant (Scott Brittingham), Pilot (David Reynolds, Chuck Tambarro), Serviceman (J. Tommy Morgan), Clerk (David Alan Novak), Operator (Terrance Vorwald).

Credits: Director: Rod Holcomb; *Writer:* Ann Donahue; *Producer:* John Lugar; *Co-producer:* Geno Escarrega; *Supervising producer:* Rod Holcomb; *Executive producer:* John Sacret Young; *Cinematography:* John J. Connor; *Production design:* James William Newport; *Music:* Paul Chihara. *From:* Sacret, Inc.

In this episode of the Vietnam War series (set at the eponymous medical/R&R facility), Laurette, a USO singer, can't imagine what life on the front lines was like for her boyfriend Boomer. When she learns head nurse Lila is heading up-country to visit her old friend, Captain Osborne, Laurette seizes the chance to join her and see "the real Vietnam." When their helicopter crashes, the women are stranded in the jungle along with Red Cross volunteer Cherry.

Trying for home, the women find Osborne's platoon instead. The hardboiled crew prove an unnerving lot, and Osborne's fast-talking right hand, Deejay, tells Lila that he's the only one allowed to actually talk face-to-face with Osborne.

Laurette, however, sneaks in to meet the captain, but discovers Osborne ("Ozborne?") is just an animal skull wearing a captain's hat; when Deejay insists Osborne's somewhere else, Laurette replies "Pay no attention to the man behind the curtain, right?" Deejay admits Osborne is dead, but rather than give in to despair or put up with a green officer, the men choose to accept the illusion he creates that Osborne is still in command.

Back at China Beach, Cherry's friend KC uses her black-market connections to pull strings and arrange a rescue mission. The women return home safely, though Laurette realizes she still doesn't understand war.

"Osborne" also turns up as a pun in *The New Adventures of Beans Baxter*.

Marvelous Misadventures of Ed Grimley: Blowin' in the Wind. 11/12/88. NBC.

Voices: Ed Grimley/Additional voices (Martin Short), Count Floyd (Joe Flaherty), Mrs. Freebus (Andrea Martin), Wendell Gustav (Danny Cooksey), Miss Malone (Catherine O'Hara), Sheldon (Frank Welker), Mr. Freebus/Roger Gustav/Additional voices (Jonathan Winters).

Credits: Executive producers: Joseph Hanna, William Barbera; *From:* Hanna-Barbera Studios.

A tornado carries nerdy Ed Grimley to a small Kansas farm, whose owners, Henry and Em, are not only struggling to keep bitchy Almira Gulch from foreclosing on their mortgage, but worrying about their niece Dorothy, who's been babbling deliriously about yellow brick roads and wizards since she was injured during the tornado.

When Grimley finds a Broadway director driving through town, he persuades the man to put on a show in Henry's barn, paying enough rent to cover the mortgage. Not only is the show a success, the director and Almira fall in love, and she celebrates by tearing up the mortgage. Dorothy wakes up and tells everyone she had this curious dream "and you were there, and you, and you—but I never saw you before!" she tells Grimley.

This one-season Saturday morning cartoon took Short's *Saturday Night Live* nerd off for his own adventures (mostly in New York City rather than Kansas). This not only parodies MGM's *The Wizard of Oz*, but sends up the Judy Garland/Mickey Rooney "Let's put on a show! We can use the barn!" musicals of the 1930s.

1989

Who Shrunk Saturday Morning? 9/8/89. 30 mins., color, part-animated, NBC.

Cast: Zack (Mark-Paul Gosselaar), Screech (Dustin Diamond), Slater (Mario Lopez), Lisa (Lark Voorhees), Kelly (Tiffani Amber-Thiessen), Master Programmer (Sherman Helmsley), Truant Officer (Marsha Wakefield), plus voices and characters from Several Saturday morning shows.

High-school geek Screech traps himself and his friends inside a TV, with no idea how to get out and little time before they have to be in school. The alien ALF recommends they follow the yellow circuit path to the Master Programmer to send them home. After encountering several characters from that season's Saturday-morning shows, the kids reach the programmer; he agrees to send them home if they'll fill his one remaining slot by starring in the new show *Saved by the Bell*. They agree, and arrive in school just in time to escape truancy.

The networks ran these Saturday-morning promotional shows for many years before Saturday cartoons became a less profitable part of their business. The clips include one from the *Alftales* Oz episode described below.

Paradise: A Gathering of Guns/Home Again. 9/10/ & 9/16/89. One two-hour, one one-hour episode, color, CBS.

Cast: Ethan Cord (Lee Horsley), Claire Carroll (Jenny Beck), Joseph Carroll (Matthew Nemark), Ben Carroll (Brian Lando), George Carroll (Michael Patrick Carter), John Taylor (Dehl Berti), Amelia Lawson (Sigrid Thornton), Scotty McBride (Mack Dryden), Tiny (John Bloom), Depty Charlie (James Crittenden), Mr. Lee (Benjamin Lum), Wade Stratton (Randy Crowder), Carl (Will Hunt) Guest Cast: Wyatt Earp (Hugh O'Brien), Frank (Mark Herrier), Bat Masterson (Gene Barry), Pierce Lawson (Charles Frank), Pat Garrett (John Schneider), Sheriff Cochran (Charles Napier), Skragg (Jack Elam), Gray Feather (Rawley Valverde), Sam Clanton (Robert Fuller), Tom Clanton (Jon Maynard Pennell), Josie Earp (Summer Thomas), Drummer (Richard Lineback). With: Ray Walston.

In this series, gunslinger Ethan Cord set his violent past aside when he became guardian to his late sister's children in the town of Paradise. In the second-season opener, that past intrudes on the present, as Ethan is arrested and thrown into a notorious hell-hole prison (he learns later it's because the warden wants to find a lost Civil War gold shipment that Ethan, as a boy, helped hide).

Ethan's love interest, local banker Amelia, asks her estranged gambler husband, Pierce, for help; Pierce calls in some markers to recruit Wyatt Earp, Bat Masterson and Pat Garrett to rescue Ethan. A Wild West show owner (Ray Walston) offers assistance, hoping to benefit from the publicity, and Frank, a reporter, tags along in hopes of a big scoop.

The gunmen successfully rescue Ethan and another captive using the Wild West show's balloon, then locate the gold and have a showdown with the bad guys at the hidden treasure. The battle won, Earp accepts Ethan's offer to stay in Paradise, and Frank decides to follow them — a wise move, since his articles have drawn Tom and Sam Clanton to town, seeking to avenge their family's deaths at the OK Corral shootout. Frank pushes Earp and the Clantons into a big gunfight despite Ethan telling Wyatt that if the Clantons really wanted revenge, they'd have found him years ago.

Claire, the oldest of Ethan's children, berates Frank for exploiting the old gunmen. Frank replies that his newspaper won't stay afloat without big stories to boost circulation. The reporter whiles his time away watching Ethan's boys prop up a decrepit Scarecrow, and young George building a tin man from a hardware store display. As the gunfight is about to begin, Claire shames the men into calling a truce (Earp and the Clantons exchange obviously insincere promises to have a final showdown some other time).

Frank tells Claire that even though his paper went belly-up, she has inspired him to write a story, a tale of "courage, heart and wisdom." Claire tells him not to use her name, so he walks off, thinking, and settles on ... Dorothy. The show ends with clips of the balloon ride, the scarecrow, the tin man, Claire, and the cover of *The Wizard of Oz*.

Westerns, once a staple of prime-time TV, continued to pop up during the 1980s and 1990s with modest success. This two-part episode brought back several stars of earlier Western shows (Barry, O'Brien) and refers to Baum only as "Frank" throughout the show.

Alftales: The Wizard of Oz. 9/23/89. 30 mins., color, animated, NBC.

Voices: Gordon Shumway (Paul Fusco), Bob/Larson Petty (Thick Wilson), Augie/Rhonda (Paulina Gillis), Flo (Peggy Mahon), Sloop (Dan Hennessey), Skip (Rob Cowan), Stella (Ellen-Ray Hennessey).

Credits: Director, producer: David Feiss; *Writers:* Brad Kesden, Skip Shepherd (from a story by Steve Roberts); *Animation director:* Masakazu Higuchi; *Supervising producers:* Andy Heyward, Haim Saban; *Art director:* Mike Longden; *Music:* Shuki Levy, Haim Saban; *From:* DIC Animation City, Inc., Saban Productions, Alien Productions and NBC.

Gordon, an ET from Melmack stranded on Earth (where he's known as ALF, for Alien Life Form), is caught inside a farmhouse when a cyclone takes him to Oz, dropping the house on the Wicked Witch of the East. Wearing her magic ruby hightop sneakers, Gordon flees from the Wicked Witch of the West with the help of the short hippie Munchies, who send him along the yellow brick road to Cubic Zirconium City.

After picking up the requisite trio ("We're Tin, Straw and Fur, the new folk-rock sensation!") Gordon reaches the Wizard, who turns out to be an off-stage Bill Cosby. The Wizard sends the four after the witch, who forces them to meet her in a basketball game. In the course of the game, Gordon melts her down with a bucket of Gatorade so the Wizard not only sends him home, but also promises to make him a sitcom star as well.

Obnoxious, sarcastic Alf became a TV star in 1986 in NBC's *Alf*, which ran until 1990. This Saturday morning spinoff ignored the prime-time show in favor of episodes showing Gordon on Melmack and parodies such as this one. This mix of Oz with 1960s satire wasn't one of the better episodes.

Maxie's World: Surfside Over the Rainbow. 10/28/89. 30 mins., color, animated, syndicated.

Voice Cast: Maxie (Loretta Jafelice), Rob (Simon Reynolds), Carly (Tara Charendoff), Ashley (Susan Roman), Ferdie (Yannick Bisson), Mushroom (Geoff Kahnert), Jeri (Nadin Rabinovitch), Mr. Garcia (John Stocker).

Credits: Music: Haim Saban, Shuki Levy; *From:* DIC Enterprises.

Maxie, alpha girl at Surfside High School and star of a SURF-TV news show, finds a stray puppy as she leaves work and puts "Tutu" safely inside the station. When she finds a message from SURF owner Mr. Garcia about the dog, Maxie worries that Tutu has made a mess and heads back to the station — only to have a cyclone carry off the building with her and Tutu inside. It lands on a green beach, from which Maxie deduces "We're not in Surfside any more."

Midget Surfkins tell Maxie SURF just crushed the Wicked Witch of the Northeast, and give Maxie the witch's sapphire sneakers. The windsurfing Wicked Witch of the Southwest (Maxie's egocentric friend Angie) demands the sneakers — or else! — but Carlina the Good Witch (Maxie's bosom buddy Carlie) bicycles up and sends the Wicked Witch running. The Surfkins tell Maxie to follow the yellow brick bike path to the Wizard of Surfside TV.

Before long, Maxie meets up with dimwit Lifeguard (her boyfriend Rob), heartless Beach Bully (her friend Ferdy), and the Cowardly Shark (hulking Mushroom) who join her quest for the Wizard. The witch's sandcrabs capture Maxie; the witch takes Tutu and condemns Maxie to an unfinished basement ("No carpeting, no television, no furniture — and no phone!") until she gives up the dog.

Realizing they have brains, heart and courage enough to save Maxie, the guys rescue her from the dungeon only to be caught by the witch. When she threatens Lifeguard with a bucket of water (for no discernable reason), Maxie snatches Tutu away from her, spilling the bucket on the Wicked Witch and shrinking her brand new outfit.

The witch flees upstairs to change, then Carlina appears and tells Maxie to do aerobics in the magic sneakers to get home. Maxie wakes up in her own bed, goes down to the station and discovers Garcia wants to talk about Tutu because he plans to adopt the pup, and to have Maxie do a news special on abandoned animals. The delighted girl proclaims Garcia the real Wizard of Surfside TV!

After three seasons of the toy-line based *Jem!* cartoon (about an heiress with a secret identity as a glamorous rock star), Hasbro decided to switch to a more Barbie-esque line and came up with this insufferably cute, cotton-candy series. *Surside Over the Rainbow* is in the *What a Girl, What a World!* videotape collection.

1990

The Wizard of Oz. 9/8/90-8/31/91. 13 episodes, color, animated, ABC.
Voices: Dorothy (Liz Georges), Scarecrow (David Lodge), Tin Man (Hal Rayle), Cowardly Lion (Charlie Adler), Wizard (Alan Oppenheimer), Toto (Frank Welker), Wicked Witch of the West (Tress MacNeille), Glinda the Good Witch (B.J. Ward), Truckle (Pat Fraley).
Credits: Producer: Andy Heyward; *Music:* Tom Worrall; *Supervising producer:* Michael Maliani; *Music:* Tom Worrall; *Editors:* Gregory K. Bowron, Richard Bruce Elliot, Allan Gelbart; *From:* DIC Enterprises and Turner Entertainment.

In the opening credits to this animated series, Dorothy finds the ruby slippers outside her front door in Kansas, clicks the heels together, and materializes in Munchkin land with Toto. She learns the winged monkeys resurrected the Wicked Witch of the West, who stole the watch, diploma and medal the Wizard gave Dorothy's friends, leaving them convinced that they no longer have their brains, heart and courage. The witch has also forced the Wizard on the run, staying one jump ahead of her in his balloon.

Dorothy and her friends set off to find the Wizard, knowing he can inspire Oz to rise up against the Witch, while also ducking the Witch's schemes to steal the ruby slippers (usually carried out by Truckle, the dimwitted head of the Winged Monkeys). Fortunately, the power of the ruby slippers could always teleport them out of danger or provide some other magic trick when needed.

This Saturday-morning cartoon owes everything to the MGM film — the looks of the characters, the vocal characterizations, the stories— and has absolutely none of the film's talent, charm or style. Up against the popular *Muppet Babies*, it died deservedly after a season. The episode list:

RESCUE OF THE EMERALD CITY
(TWO PARTS)
Writers: Cliff Ruby, Elana Lesser.

Dorothy returns to Oz to find everything in chaos, with the witch's magic wind keeping the Wizard in the far corners of Oz, her three friends convinced they've lost their brains, heart and courage, and the folk of the Emerald City turned into statues. The witch takes Toto hostage and demands that Dorothy bring the slippers to the Emerald City.

On the way to the Emerald City, Truckle captures the Lion; the witch offers him his medal back if he'll help her get the slippers. His friends reach the city, however, and Scarecrow wrecks the plumbing, flooding the palace and forcing the witch to flee. Dorothy uses the slippers to depetrify the citizens, and Glinda creates an Emerald Star that shines as long as the Wizard is safe.

FEARLESS
Writer: Doug Molitor.

CRYSTAL CLEAR
Writers: Pat Allee, Ben Hurst.

WE'RE NOT IN KANSAS ANYMORE
Writers: Lisa Maliani, Michael Maroney.

The Wicked Witch tricks Dorothy into returning to Kansas to care for poor, sick Auntie Em; Dorothy doesn't realize Kansas is a fake, the witch is Em and Truckle is Uncle Henry. Feeling safe, Dorothy takes off the slippers, which materialize on the Lion's feet; realizing she's in danger, the Lion teleports himself, Tin Man and Scarecrow to her side.

The witch forces the Lion to give up the shoes, but by luck, they wind up on Truckle's feet, and he reduces the witch to his servant. Dorothy and her friends, however, manage to trick the monkey out of the shoes and escape before the witch can take them.

The Lion That Squeaked
Writer: Bob Carrau.

With the help of the Wicked Witch, practical joker Laughing Hyena steals the Lion's roar, which enables him to intimidate the forest animals into proclaiming him king. Hyena captures Dorothy for the witch, but Scarecrow and Tin Man trick the witch into donning fake ruby slippers full of itching powder, which she blames on Hyena. With the witch and Hyena busy, Dorothy is rescued and the Lion recovers his roar.

Dream a Little Dream
Writer: Michael Murer.

A Star Is Gone
Writer: Michael O'Mahoney.

To Dorothy's dismay, the Wizard's Emerald Star disappears; it turns out the Wicked Witch tried kidnapping a red color spirit to drain the magic from the ruby slippers, but caught a green one instead, erasing green from Oz. Dorothy and her friends sneak into the witch's castle, but find the witch has caught the red spirit and the shoes lose power. The red luminary breaks free just long enough for Dorothy to use the shoes to teleport the spirits, herself and her friends to safety.

Time Town
Writer: Rick Merwin.

The Wicked Witch begins erasing the history of Oz, destroying the Emerald City, turning the Wizard into a simple farmer and Glinda into an old woman. Dorothy, her friends and the Wizard travel through Time Town to the witch's new lair, despite Truckle's opposition; on Pendulum Mountain, Dorothy distracts the witch long enough for the farmer Wizard to douse the magic fire fueling the spell, restoring Oz history to normal.

The Marvelous Milkmaid of Mechanica
Writer: Jules Dennis; *Story:* Karen Willson, Chris Weber.

When Dorothy and her friends visit the realm of Mechanica, the Tin Man falls for a robot milkmaid.

Upside Down Town
Writer: Gordon Bressack.

Dorothy and her friends pursue the Wizard to Upside Downtown, where everyone speaks backwards, uses shoes as head wear and dogs have licenses for people. When they find the Wizard trapped by giant crows, Scarecrow enlists some flying scarecrows (who steal corn instead of guarding it) to fight the crows off. The Wicked Witch realizes the ruby slippers don't work normally in Upside Down Town, but when she attacks, Dorothy figures at the last minute how to work the slippers' magic again, and returns everyone to Oz.

The Day the Music Died
Writer: Laurie Sutton.

The Winged Monkeys attack Musicland, stealing the baton of the ruling Maestro, without which the Musickers cannot play a note. The Wicked Witch shows up in disguise with a new baton, but says it can only be used by whoever can fit into her slippers. When Dorothy tries them on, the witch snatches the ruby slippers. Knowing the Witch hates music, Dorothy calls on the Musickers to play, play, play; the Wicked Witch drops the slippers in pain and the Musickers realize the music is in them, not in the baton.

HOT AIR

The Wizard takes part in a balloon race, unaware he's flying into the Witch's trap.

The Wonderful Wizard of Oz: The Making of a Movie Classic

Cast: Narrator: Angela Lansbury.

An informative documentary on the making of the film, aired after the MGM movie's broadcast in 1990 and 1996 (which was the 40th anniversary of the MGM film's first TV broadcast). Angela Lansbury narrated the story of the making of the film, with clips of the "Jitterbug" number.

1991

Beetlejuice: The Wizard of Ooze.

11/19/91. Fox-TV.

Voices: Beetlejuice (Stephen Ouimette), Lydia Deetz (Alyson Court), Charles Deetz (Roger Dunn), Ginger/Delia Deetz (Elizabeth Hanna), Claire Brewster (Tara Strong), with Len Carlson, Paulina Gillis, Keith Knight, Ron Rubin, Joseph Sherman.

Credits: Directors: Alan Bunce, John Halfpenny, Rick Marshall, John van Bruggen; *Writers:* Alan Bunce, J.D. Smith; *Assistant directors:* Gerry Fournier, Steve Whitehouse, Jamie Whitney; *Producers:* Michael Hirsh, Patrick Loubert, Clive A. Smith; *Executive producers:* Tim Burton, David Geffen; *Editors:* Tedd Anasti, Patsy Cameron, Dan DiStefano, Michael Edens, J.D. Smith; *From:* Warner Brothers, Nelvana Productions, Geffen Film Company, Tim Burton, Inc.; *Theme:* Danny Elfman.

Beetlejuice, an irreverent, troublemaking ghost from the "Neitherworld" finds his human best friend, Lydia, has fallen asleep reading Baum. He enters her dreams—dull ones about school—and jazzes them up by having a cyclone hurl the school into the Neitherworld, crushing the Wicked Witch (Neitherworld's mayor) to the joy of the Munchkins in the Land of Public Domain (presumably a joke on their out-of-copyright status). Giving Lydia the mayor's possibly magical shoes, the Munchkins send her down the Gray Asphalt Road to the Wizard of Ooze.

Lydia is joined by regular cast members in the forms of a dog (Ginger, a tap-dancing spider), Bone Woodsman (skeletal Jacques LaLean), Cowardly Lion (the Monster Across the Street) and Scarecrow (Beetlejuice himself, but too brainless to remember he's a ghost). The Wicked Witch of the West (Clare, the nasty girl at Lydia's school) vows to destroy them, using the adorable Boola Bears (who turn into hideous monsters), the dimwitted Oogly Ogre Brothers and the Big Stripey Thing, all of which lose out to the travelers' odd mix of talents.

The witch attacks in person on her flying vacuum cleaner, but Lydia throws a bucket of water at her. Clare's makeup washes off, exposing a zit, and she flees in shame. Lydia and her friends reach the Wizard's palace, where the Wizard of Ooze (Barry Me Not) agrees to grant their wishes if they destroy the Mayor ... okay, done, how about the Wicked Witch of ... okay, how about the Boola Bears.... When he realizes they've passed all the tests, he throws them out.

Lydia realizes her friends have already proved they have brains, heart and courage; the Good Witches (who appeared briefly, earlier) tell her all she has to do to go home is click her heels and say "Ripple dissolve to scene 328!" Lydia wakes up, but everything still seems like a dream—because the whole story has been a dream of Beetlejuice's.

Beetlejuice and Lydia first appeared in Tim Burton's 1988 film *Beetlejuice*, then spun off into this animated series for several seasons. Another episode, *Prairie Strife*, has Beetlejuice inheriting a farm from his Aunt Em.

1992

Space Oz No Boken [Also known as Galaxy Adventures of Space Oz]. 26 25-minute episodes. Color, animated, TV Tokyo.

Voice: Dorothy (Mariko Kouda), Aunt Emira (Ai Sato).

Credits: Directors: Soji Yoshikawa, Yoshiaki

Okumura, Katsumata Kanezawa, Shinichi Suzuki; *Writers:* Soji Yoshikawa, Yasuko Hoshikawa, Seiji Matsuoka, Hirokazu Mizude (based on *The Wizard of Oz*); *Design:* Yoshiaki Okumura; *Animators:* Ichiro Fukube, Osamu Kamijo, Seiji Kikuchi; *Music:* Ryuichi Katsumasa; *From:* E&G, Enoki, TV Tokyo.

Eight-year-old, blonde Dorothy Gale and her genetically enhanced dog Talk-Talk live on the planet New Kansas, until swept off by a storm that carries them into the distant galaxy of Oz. Dorothy joins forces with Dr. Oz, boy companion Mosey, android Chopper, the cowardly, macho-posturing Lion-man, and Plantman. Together they defeat the witch Gloomhilda and her henchmen, Bungle, Skum and Sludge, and obtain the three magic crystals of Wisdom, Love and Courage. With the witch defeated, Dorothy uses the Rainbow Crystal to return home.

1993

The Triplets. 22 mins., color, animated.
Credits: Directors: Robert Balsar, Baltasar Roca; *From:* Cromosoma/Televisio de Catlunya.

In each episode, the Bored Witch plays tricks on three little sisters (Anna, Teresa and Helena), sending them into a fairytale, a classic fictional story or back in time to meet famous people. *The Wizard of Oz* was one of the stories covered.

This was a phenomenally successful series popular around the world

Across Indiana — Round Barns in a Square. Color, WFYI-TV, Indianapolis.
Cast: Michael Atwood.
Credits: Director, producer: Dave Stoelk.

This local TV documentary included a feature on the annual Chesterson Oz festival.

Arena: In Search of Oz. One hour, color, BBC.

This biography on L. Frank Baum includes vintage photographs from the years he grew up in South Dakota, comments from admirers including Ray Bradbury, Salman Rushdie and Gore Vidal and clips from MGM's *The Wizard of Oz* and some of Oz film Company's productions. It aired in America on the A&E channel in 1994.

Saturday Night Live. 11/12/94. 90 mins., color, NBC.
Cast: Dorothy (Janeane Garafolo), Glinda (Sarah Jessica Parker), Lollipop Kids (Tim Meadows, Chris Farley, Mike Meyers), with David Spade, Helen Cleghorne.

After Dorothy's farmhouse lands on the Wicked Witch of the East, the Munchkins (cast members on their knees) snub her on the grounds that she liberated them by accident, not intention, so they don't owe her even a thank-you.

1994 is not considered one of the long-running sketch-comedy show's better years; this skit was edited out of the episode for syndicated and cable reruns.

Townsend Television. 11/14/93. One hour, color, Fox-TV.
Cast: Wizard (Sherman Hemsley), Robert Townsend (himself), Good Witch (Marla Henderson), Guard (Jimmy Walker), with Roxanne Beckford, Barry Diamond, Biz Markie, Paula Jai Parker, John Witherspoon

A tornado carries comedian Robert Townsend out of his studio to Oz, where he meets a Scarecrow with a brain but no job, a Tin Woman seeking a good man and a Lion seeking a weapon; "It's a jungle out there," he says. Oz sends the quartet off to battle the Wicked Witch; they defeat her, of course, and bring back her magic dust-buster to the Wizard. They are then provided with a way home, a job, self-esteem (for Tin Woman) and a self-defense course (for the lion).

Not very funny.

1995

Roundhouse: Running Away. 30 mins., Nickelodeon.
Cast: Anydad (John Crane), Anymom (Shawn Daywalt), Son (Ivan Dudynsky), Daughter (Amy

Ehrlich), with Jennifer Cihi, Mark David, Micki Duran, Alfred Carr, Jr., Seymour Willis Green, Shawn Munoz, Natalie Nucci, Julene Renee, David Sidoni.

Credits: Directors: Bruce Gowers, Linda Mendoza, Rita Sheffield; *Writers:* Becky Hartman, Sheila R. Lawrence, Ray Lee Buddy Sheffield, Heather Sheffield.

In one episode of this hip-hop sketch comedy series, which focused on the lives of the Anypeople family, the daughter rebels against the family rules, runs away and enters the Land of Show Biz where she meets characters including Tin Can Man and the Wicked Witch of the West Coast.

Where on Earth Is Carmen Sandiego?: The Remnants. 9/23/95. 30 mins., animated, color, Fox-TV.

Cast: Carmen Sandiego (Rita Moreno), Zack (Scott Menville), Ivy (Jennifer Hale), Chief (Rodger Bumpass).

Credits: From DIC Entertainment.

Brilliant master-thief Carmen Sandiego kicks off her latest crime spree by stealing the ruby slippers used in MGM's *Wizard of Oz*, then a Monet painting of a poppy field, then (after her henchmen skywrite "No Place Like Home" over Mt. Rushmore), the original Teddy Bear inspired by Teddy Roosevelt (stolen from Roosevelt's own home).

Carmen's chief adversaries, teen detectives Zack and Ivy of the Acme Detective Agency, deduce that the theme of Carmen's crimes is indeed "no place like home," and track her to the only home she ever knew, an orphanage due for demolition. They find Carmen there, reading her favorite book from childhood (*The Wizard of Oz*, of course); the detectives reclaim her stolen goods, but Carmen escapes and her helicopter fleet carries the orphanage away.

Carmen Sandiego began as an educational computer game that spun off a PBS game show and this Saturday morning cartoon (its roots were shown in having Carmen challenge "the player" at home and by dropping numerous educational factoids about whatever Carmen was stealing).

1996

All That: The Wizard of Cos. 30 mins., color, Nickelodeon.

Cast: Amanda Bynes, Lori Beth Denberg, Leon Frierson, Katrina Johnson, Kel Mitchell, Alisa Reyes, Josh Server, Kenan Thompson, Kevin Kopelow, Malcolm-Jamal Warner.

Credits: Director: Brian Robbins; *Producer:* Nick Donatelli; *Executive producers:* Brian Robbins, Michael Tollin; *Cinematography:* Barbara Drago, Dave Kinney, Paul Klekolta, Ken Kraus, Mike Lacey, Mike Murray; *Production design:* David Ellis; *Art directors:* Babo Brown, Rusty de Young; *Music:* Richard Tuttobene; *Editor:* Andrew Hirsch.

A sketch on this comedy series has Dorothy, accompanied by a toad-man and a man made of pasta, meet the Wizard of Cos (a parody of Bill Cosby).

The Oz Kids. 28 23-minute episodes, Japan, color, animated, TBS Television.

Cast: Andrea (Shay Astar), Bela (Shayna Fox), Neddie (Eric Lloyd), Jack Pumpkinhead (Aaron Michael Metchik), Dot (Julianne Michelle), Boris (Bradley Pierce), Tin Boy (Benjamin Salisbury), Scarecrow, Jr. (Jonathan Taylor Thomas), Frank, Jr. (Alex Zuckerman), Rick (Lawrence Tierney), Zeb (Ross Mapletoft), Scarecrow (Andy Milder), Dorothy (Erica Schikel), Tin Man (Steve Stoliar), Nome King (Marc Allen Lewis), Prince Otto (Chauncey Leopardi).

Credits: Directors: Bert Ring, Phoydon Shishido, David Teague; *Writer:* Willard Carroll; *Producer:* John Bush; *Executive producers:* Willard Carroll, Thomas Wilhite; *Art direction:* Lucy Tanashian-Gentry; *Film editor:* Charlie King; *Music:* Michael Muhlpriedel; *From:* Hyperion Entertainment.

Oz, the next generation: This series told the exploits of the children of the original Oz characters: Dorothy's offspring Neddy and Dot; the Lion's cubs, bold Bela and shy Boris (who also shows Hungry Tiger's appetite); the Scarecrow's know-it-all son; The Wizard's computer-savvy son, Frank; Tin Boy and Pumpkinhead, Jr.; Glinda's daughter Andrea, obnoxiously fond of using her magic for mischief; and the Nome Prince Otto, torn between tormenting his father's enemies and becoming friends with them.

Creator and Oz-enthusiast Willard Carroll has described this series as a way to dramatize Baum without being compared to or constrained by the MGM *Wizard of Oz*. It may also owe something to the wave of next-generation cartoons in the 1980s and early 1990s (*Flintstone Kids, Muppet Babies, A Pup Named Scooby Doo*). The storylines included original plots and some based on Baum's non-Oz books, such as *The Sea Fairies* and *The Life and Adventures of Santa Claus*.

The series aired first in Japan, with a well-known vocal cast including popular anime actor Noriko Hidaka (one of the stars of the hit *Gunbusters*), Akiko Yajima, Misa Watanabe, Ayumi Yoshida and Mika Kanai. It wasn't picked up by American TV, but did show up on a series of videos (each holding one story arc). Following is a guide to the videos (a Japanese episode breakdown wasn't available):

Toto Lost in New York

Guest Cast: Mother/Wife (Lori Alan), Munchkins (Gabrielle Boni, Jarrett Lennon), The Ork (Peter MacNicol), Daughter (Ashley Malinger), Guards (Ross Mapletoft), Barnabas/Snicklefritz/Vendor (Andy Milder), Angie (Remy Ryan), Mother Crab (Erica Schikel), Husband/Pilot (Steve Stoliar), Dungy (Michael Cade), Billy (John Link Graney), Crusty (Gavin Harrison), Freddie (Jonathan Charles Kaplan).

The Wizard's son Frank equips his father's old balloon with a computerized guidance system that can steer it anywhere on Earth. When the kids shut Andrea out of their plans, she magically uses the computer to fly the balloon away, unaware Toto (son of Dorothy's pet) is playing inside. When the kids discover him missing, Andrea agrees to help if they'll give her a place in future balloon rides. Frank summons the balloon back, but Toto hopped out when it reached New York, so the kids pile into the balloon to go recover him.

After crashing in Central Park, they wander around, trying to make sense of modern America without drawing attention. Aging vagrant Rick befriends Toto, but two bullying kids swipe the dog to sell. Toto escapes, so the kids, Rick and the bullies all chase him through New York, culminating with Andrea rescuing him from the Statue of Liberty (the sight of actual magic stuns the bullies so much they reform).

After repairing the crash-damage to Frank's computer (a difficult job, since they have no idea what money is or how to buy replacement chips), the kids head home, with Rick (having been horrified at the idea that someone could be homeless and no one helps). A collision with an Ork crashes them in the Deadly Desert where sand crabs pull the kids underground and try to eat them; they escape, and the Ork's flock carries the balloon to the Emerald City.

The Nome Prince and the Magic Belt

Guest Cast: Hammerheads (Marc Allen Lewis, Steve Stoliar).

While Rick explores Oz, the kids are stuck indoors during a torrential rain. Boris suggests taking the Nome King's belt from its sealed container and using it to stop the rain; the kids object, but Boris's fumbling opens the chamber anyway. Meanwhile, Nome Prince Otto, finding his dad too busy to play while plotting a new attack on Oz, decides to launch his own attack and uses the Nome tunnel from *Emerald City* to sneak into Ozma's palace—where he sees an opportunity and swipes the belt.

When the stones of the tunnel warn the kids against following Otto, Dot cons the location of a second tunnel out of Dorothy. The tunnel is next to the Hammerhead hill, but the kids manage to distract the 'heads long enough to enter. Dot lags behind, which proves fortunate: When she catches up with Otto, he has turned everyone else into ornaments, and now suggests that Dot play the guessing game from *Ozma of Oz*. To Otto's displeasure, she deduces the identity of each of her transformed friends.

The kids and Otto grapple over the belt, and Otto's unthinking wish to be bigger and stronger turns him into a giant. The kids flee back to the surface but Otto follows, convinced that he's big enough to conquer all Oz. When Otto catches up (after both sides have braved assorted Oz perils), Dot points out that even if he conquers Oz, a 60-foot-tall Nome will never be able to play with anyone, or make it back underground to his father. Faced with eternal loneliness, Otto breaks down in tears; the kids let him use the belt to restore himself, and everyone returns home. The belt is restored and the parents are oblivious to the day's events.

It is no surprise that Ruggedo, Baum's best villain, had his own son in this series, though it is surprising that he's an affectionate, if sometimes preoccupied, father. The kalidahs who appear here are the nastiest looking of several animated versions.

Virtual Oz

Guest Cast: Tommy Kwikstep (Andy Milder), Otto (Chauncey Leopardi), Scraps (Lori Alan).

As the kids are playing with Betty, the Patchwork Girl's baby, they receive a floppy disc from Otto. When Frank inserts it in his computer, they discover it's an enchanted computer game that sucks the kids into a virtual reality. To Otto's horror, however, Betty gets drawn in too, which is more players than the game's programmed for — and if the protocols are violated, the game could become deadly.

As Otto works to fix the software, the kids travel across a game board involving famous Earth landmarks and puzzle-solving. Otto contacts the kids, but when he follows Frank's instructions, it only transforms the game board into a model of Emerald City. The virtual reality world begins collapsing, so Frank tells Otto to go home for a backup copy of the program. When Otto goes home, Ruggedo insists on showing him a mechanical mole he plans to use against Oz, but as soon as the Nome King crashes his invention, Otto is free to reach his computer.

Unfortunately, a computer virus is eating the game board and won't let Otto pull the kids out of virtual reality. Frank, however, realizes that the holographic replica of the Emerald City is so detailed, it includes a duplicate of his laptop, which he uses to create a gateway out of the crumbling world and go back to "Auntie Scraps" house. Otto insists he only played the prank because he resents not being really part of the Oz Kids; the kids respond by giving him a computer game of their own as a gift, but when he plays it, it deletes his entire hard drive.

Who Stole Santa?

Guest Cast: Santa Claus (Marc Allen Lewis), Jack, Sr. (Ross Mapletoft), Tommy Kwickstep (Andy Milder), Glinda (Erika Schikel), Wizard (Steve Stoliar).

As the kids wait eagerly for Christmas Day, Dorothy retells Santa's origins (a recap of Baum's *The Life and Adventures of Santa Claus*, of course). Miles away, in Laughing Valley, the elves discover that Santa has vanished, having been kidnapped by his old, monstrous enemies, the Awgwas. "Grownups don't tell that part of the story — they think it's too scary," says one of the elves. Having heard of the kids' previous exploits, the elf Wisk turns to them for help; the kids set off with the elves, telling their parents they're out to find a Christmas tree.

When they reach the Awgwas' Ice Castle, Tin Boy stays outside because the cold will freeze his joints. The others go forward, but an accident leaves Boris in Awgwa hands. They throw him in with Santa, whom they plan to keep imprisoned forever, destroying Christmas and making Earth's children as miserable as the hate-filled Awgwas themselves.

Santa tells Boris that after centuries of immortality, he's too weary to care about escape, but Boris convinces Santa that the world still needs him. After the usual adventures, Bella and Dot free Boris and escape; they join the others and return to Tin Boy, who has built sleds for the getaway. Despite repeatedly outwitting the pursuing Awgwas, the monsters keep coming, and losing, until they wind up going over a waterfall. After dropping Santa off, the kids return home, remembering at the last minute to

CHRISTMAS IN OZ

Guest Cast: Santa Claus (Marc Allen Lewis), Fred (Jarret Lennon), Prince Otto (Chauncey Leopardi), Jack, Sr. (Ross Mapletoft), Tommy Kwickstep (Andy Milder), Glinda (Erika Schikel), Wizard (Steve Stoliar).

Because of the Nome King's many attacks on Oz, Otto is the only person not invited to the Oz Kids' big Christmas party. Otto decides to spoil their fun by stealing Andrea's invitation, convincing her that she was never invited and working out a plan to use her magic to get even.

Meanwhile, the kids learn Rick won't be coming to the party. When they find him fishing, Rick explains that Christmas commercialism and years of Christmases spent alone have soured him on the holiday. The kids assure him that in Oz, where money doesn't exist, all gifts are homemade. Rick returns to the palace with them, but Andrea's magic turns their path into a treadmill that will keep them walking until after Christmas. When the kids learn why, they tell her she was indeed invited; she frees them, and puts Otto on the treadmill instead. The party takes place with not only Rick there but Santa Claus, Polychrome and her daughters and even the Brave Little Toaster (from an earlier Hyperion film).

A fairly traditional message about Christmas commercialism.

UNDERGROUND ADVENTURE

Guest Cast: Sam (Billy Mumy), Scraps (Lori Allen), Henna (LaCrystal Cooke), Teddy Bear (Miko Hughes), Hiro (Brian Ito), Dragonettes/Pinkie the Bear (Jarret Lennon), Zeb, Jack Sr. (Ross Mapletoft), Gwig (Andy Milder), Harriet (Remy Rayan), Wizard/George the Bear (Steve Stoliar).

With their parents traveling, the Oz Kids go to stay at Auntie Scraps's house, except Frank, who is visiting America with his dad. Over in San Francisco, Frank is caught in an earthquake that topples him and a school bus into the land of the Mangaboos (whom Frank recognizes from his father's stories). Blaming the intruders for the "rain of stones," the Mangaboos tie them up—but their vegetable ropes turn out to be edible. Frank, the kids and the bus driver return to the bus, where Frank intimidates the Mangaboos with humbug magic long enough to drive off.

As Frank and his new friends pass through the dragonet nest from *Dorothy and the Wizard in Oz*, the Wizard returns to Oz and word reaches the kids of Frank's plight. Dot remembers her mother's story of the underground adventure, so the kids set off to meet Frank when he emerges from Pyramid Mountain; Andrea sets out independently, figuring that if she saves Frank, the kids will be in her debt.

All the kids and Frank's California friends are caught by the wooden Gargoyles, but Rick has been trailing them and frees them. Returning to the Emerald City, the group wanders into Bear Center (from the *Lost Princess of Oz*) and pull a button off one baby teddy bear, whose indignant father demands a trial of the culprit, followed by execution. Dot is found guilty, but Sam the bus driver offers himself in her place; the bears are impressed enough to postpone the execution to 90 years from Thursday. Everyone returns to the city and the Wizard takes the Californians home (but not before one of the girls kisses Frank).

The opening sequence reveals the Tin Woodman, Scarecrow and Cowardly Lion have all bragged to their children about being the one who tossed water on the Wicked Witch of the West.

THE MONKEY PRINCE

Guest Cast: Wu Chen (Art Chudabala), Monkey Prince (Jonathan Charles Kaplan), Monkey King (Ross Mapletoft), Pig (Jarrett Lennon), Sea Dragon (Marc Allen Lewis), Gumpette (Jason Renfro), Sam (Billy Mumy).

Fascinated by the Chinese legends of the Monkey King and the mystical journeys he made, Neddy—unable to persuade his friends to visit China — goes alone in the balloon, with Toto. The other kids ask Andrea for help, and she suggests recreating the Gump from *The Land of Oz* to fly after him (though the Gump head is out being cleaned, so they use a young Gumpette head instead; despite the "ette" it sounds quite male).

In China, the Monkey King refuses his son's request to start a quest of his own (for the source of all waters), insisting that the boy isn't mature enough. When Ned lands, the Monkey Prince steals the computer, hoping it will guide him to the place he seeks.

Sam (the bus driver from *Underground Adventure*, now working as a tour guide) spots the balloon and shows up at the same time the Gump lands. Having no luck mastering the computer, the Prince kidnaps Sam to coerce the kids into helping his quest, even though they insist there is no source of all waters: "It's one of those hero-with-a-thousand-names questions." They're joined by Pig, son of the Pig who accompanied the Monkey King, and Wu Chen, a philosophical water buffalo.

The challenges of the journey begin to mature the prince, to the point that the kids want to help him complete the journey. They find the source of all waters (an immense waterfall) but entering the cavern behind it, Neddy and the Prince are caught by a cave demon. When the Prince finally admits he can't win alone, Andrea drives off the demon with her magic; the Prince emerges, knowing he finally has true friends. Wu Chen and Pig promise that when the Prince is ready for his real quest, they'll be there for him.

The kids go home by balloon (with Gumpette on board), but the computer crashes over the Nonestic Ocean and the balloon spirals down into a whirlpool ... and Neddy wakes up in the palace. The kids insist he was just dreaming (astonishingly he never throws in "and you were there, and you, and you—"), but at dinner, Dorothy tells them Sam just wrote to her, announcing his new job — as a tour-guide in China.

This gives a "next generation" slant to the characters of the Chinese classic, *Journey to the West* (by Wu Cheng-En, which presumably explains the name of the ox). The characters' quest for enlightenment has been described as a "Chinese *Wizard of Oz*" but a more probable reason for using it was the original Japanese audience: *Journey to the West* is the Chinese work most frequently adapted into anime.

THE RETURN OF MOMBI
 Guest Cast: Toby (Jarrett Lennon), Mombi (Darlene Conley), Woozy (Ross Mapletoft), Gumpette (Jason Renfrow), Mouse Queen/Glinda (Erika Schikel).

Years after Glinda took away Mombi's powers (and in this version, her memories) in *The Land of Oz*, Toby, a young Winged Monkey, wanders into the witch's old lair and finds her brewing a memory restoration potion — for which the last ingredient is a monkey's feather. Her memories restored, Mombi locks Toby away, then heads off to strike an alliance with the Nome King (Toby escapes soon after). To her displeasure, Ruggedo refuses to join a plan that involves destroying the Ozites rather than imprisoning them; moments later, Otto discovers that his father and Mombi have vanished.

Glinda is the next to vanish (like Ruggedo, bottled in Mombi's lair); visiting Andrea, the Oz Kids discover the disappearance, then Toby shows up and explains. Some of the kids go to the Emerald City; Andrea reassembles Gumpette to fly with Toby to Mombi's lair; and Boris and Bela stay at Glinda's to babysit Neddy on the grounds that this is too dangerous an adventure for the youngest Oz Kid.

Mombi arrives in Ozma's palace and captures the rest of the adults, but Otto shows up seeking help and narrowly beats her to his father's magic belt. When the other kids arrive, they join forces with Otto and escape into a Nome Tunnel, using the belt's magic to stay one step ahead of Mombi's sorcery.

Glinda's magic mirror shows Neddy and the cubs that Andrea's group crashlanded over the deadly poppy fields, but the Queen of the Field Mice has her subjects rope and pull Andrea and Toby to safety. Neddy asks the mirror to show Mombi, and they see her, right behind them. Toto shatters the mirror before Mombi can steal it, so the furious witch teleports the kids to her mountain home and imprisons them in a cell, then throws in Jack, Andrea and Gumpette when they arrive.

Otto and the kids emerge near the kalidahs, but the Woozy passes by and drives the beasts off with its fire-throwing eyes. Mombi appears and demands the belt in return for Toto's life, but the kids trick her into triggering the Woozy's flame blasts and escape back into the tunnel. Mombi captures everyone except Dot, who tricks the witch into drinking from the Forbidden Fountain, erasing her memory again. Convinced that she's a kindly old lady, Mombi willingly frees the other kids and helps Andrea disenchant their parents; rather than let the parents know the danger their children were in, Andrea also makes the adults forget everything that happened.

JOURNEY BENEATH THE SEA

Guest Cast: Merla (Lacey Chabert), Queen Aquamarine (Claudia Christian), Sacho (Jarrett Lennon), Anko (Marc Allen Lewis), Clia (Ashley Malinger), Zog (Ross Mapletoft), Octopus/Yell-Maker (Andy Milder), Joe (Steve Stoliar), Rick (James Keane).

When the kids and Rick visit Lake Quad, the boat holding Rick, Ned, Dot, Boris and Bella sinks inside a coastal cave. Mermaids intervene, turning them into merfolk and taking them underwater to the palace of Queen Aquamarine. There the kids and Rick meet King Enko the sea serpent and learn of his deadly enemy, the monstrous sorcerer Zog the Terrible.

The surface dwellers set out to explore the underwater world, whereupon Zog's sea devils capture them and bring them to Zog. Inside his castle, they meet Satcho, Zog's phlegmatic slave boy (saved from a sunken ship) and Joe, Rick's brother, lost at sea long ago. Zog tells the kids they're to serve as bait to lure Enko into a trap. Satcho and Joe help the others escape; Zog turns his magic and his monstrous servants loose on the kids, but Aquamarine matches his magic with her own. Zog emerges from his castle for a final battle, but Enko arrives and defeats the Wizard. Rick invites Joe back to Oz, but Joe decides to take the orphaned Satcho to his dream destination, Australia, instead.

An adaptation of Baum's *The Sea Fairies* (and a fairly faithful one, too).

Sliders: Into the Mystic. 3/1/96. Color, 48 mins., Fox.

Cast: Quinn Mallory (Jerry O'Connell), Arturo (John Rhys-Davies), Wade (Sabrina Lloyd), Rembrandt (Cleavant Derricks); Guests: Pavel Kurhenko (Alex Bruhanski), Nurse (Mikal Dughi), Bounty Hunter (Phil Fondacaro), Mrs. Mallory (Deanne Henry), Fortune Teller (Karin Konova), Ryan Simms (Nicholas Lea), Dr. Xang (Hrothgar Mathews), Mr. Gail (Christopher Neame), Ross J. Kelly (John Novak), Sorcerer (Red Wilson).

Credits: Director: Richard Compton; *Writer:* Tracy Torme.

Sliders centered on a quartet — science prodigy Quinn Mallory, pompous teacher Arturo, Quinn's semi-platonic buddy Wade and aging soul singer Rembrandt — sliding between parallel worlds using a malfunctioning invention of Quinn's. In the second-season opener, the quartet slides to a new world with Quinn critically injured from a gunshot received in the previous episode. Superstition and the occult rule the new world, but Quinn finds competent medical treatment from shaman Dr. Xang. When they can't pay, however, Xan demands Quinn's brain for his fee.

The Sliders go on the run with bounty hunters on their trail. Learning of a Sorcerer who can open gates to other worlds, they reach his forbidden castle (despite several obstacles in their path); the mage appears to them as a shimmering image, but they realize it's a hologram. The Sorcerer turns out to be one of Quinn's parallel world counterparts, who slid into this world and used technological trickery to set himself up as top wizard. His superior sliding equipment sends the travelers home, but when a fluke convinces them it's just a facsimile of their world, they resume sliding.

Creator Tracy Torme planned this to start a three-episode arc wrapping up plot threads from the previous season, but Fox executives didn't want that much continuity, so the most Torme could do was to resolve the gunshot.

High Incident. 4/1/96. Color.

A segment of this TV show tells, rather inaccurately, how Baum came to write The Wizard of Oz.

Shonen Santa No Daibouken [Also known as Young Santa Claus; The Adventures of Young Santa Claus; The Great Adventures of Young Santa]. 4/6/95–9/21/96. 24 episodes, color, animated, Japan, TBS television.

Voices: Mary (Megumi Hayashibara), Young Claus (Mifuyu Hóragi), May (Mika Kanai), Cathy (Urara Miura), Beezle (Tomohiro Nishimura), Ion (Rei Sakuma), Blinky (Hekiru Shiina), Nishil (Nobuko Shinokura), Marza (Mie Suzuki), Seegra Shiegral (Urara Takano), Ricky (Fumihiko Tatsuki), Flossy (Naoki Tatsuta), Goozle (Y?ji Ueda).

Credits: Animation Studio: K Factory; based on L. Frank Baum's *The Life and Adventures of Santa Claus*.

This was a Japanese anime adaptation of the book.

Power Rangers Zeo: It Came from Angel Grove. 9/11/96. Fox.

Cast: Adam Park/Green Ranger (Johnny Yong Bosch), Red Ranger Tommy Oliver/Tomacula (Jason David Frank), Rocky DeSantos/Blue Ranger/Lord Henry (Steve Cardenas), Yellow Ranger Tanya Sloan/Bride of Hackesack (Nakia Burrise), Pink Ranger Katherine Hilliard/Valencia (Catherine Sutherland), Billy Cranston/William von Hackensack (David Yost), Farkus "Bulk" Bulkmeier/Mummy (Paul Schrier), Eugene "Skull" Skullovitch/Professor (Jason Narvey), Ernie/Vampire Bartender (Richard Genelle), Lt. Jerome Stone/Burgermeister (Gregg Bullock), Zordon/Zordonicus (Robert L. Manahan, voice), Ay-gor (Donene Kistlter, voice), Alpha-5 (Richard Wood, voice), King Mondo (David Stenstrom, voice), Queen Machina (Alex Borstein, voice), Rita Repulsa (Carla Perez; Barbara Goodsun, voice), Lord Zedd (Ed Neil; Robert Axelrod, voice).

Credits: Using footage from *Chôriki Sentai Ohranger*; *Writer:* Joseph Kuhr; *Director:* Robert Radler; *Supervising producers:* Douglas Sloan, Scott Page-Pagter; *Co-producers:* Tony Oliver, Ann Knapp, Paul F. Rosenthal; *Producer:* Jonathan Tzachor; *Executive producers:* Haim Saban, Shuki Levy; *Photography:* Ilan Rosenberg; *Production design:* Yuda Ako; *From:* Saban Home Entertainment.

Adam — one of the six teens who transform into Power Rangers to battle King Mondo's Machine Empire — wears himself out studying and drifts off when he takes a break to watch his favorite horror film, *The Bride of Hackensack*. When he wakes, a black kitten leads him to the Rangers' old enemies, Zedd and Repulsa ("We'll get you — and your little cat too!"). They tell him Mondo has conquered the Earth and transformed the other rangers, but the cat will take Adam to a Wizard who can free them with the right talismans.

The cat leads Adam into a black-and-white Gothic world where Angel Grove's inhabitants are now characters in the Hackensack film (vampire, werewolf, mummy, etc.). The cat turns into an evil sorceress (Cat, the Pink Ranger) but Adam realizes her pendant is one of the talismans he needs and snatches it away; the witch vanishes.

The disembodied head of the Wizard Zordonicus (Zordon, the Rangers' alien mentor, who is always a disembodied head) tells Adam he must earn the cure by sending one of his friends to battle one of Mondo's monstrous warriors. Adam accidentally picks Red Ranger Tommy, and watches him battle and defeat a giant drilling machine. Zordonicus is suddenly replaced by Mondo, who gloats that Adam has enabled him to destroy the Wizard; as the Machine Warriors close in, Adam wakes to find his friends sitting around him, and tells them he had the most curious dream....

One of TV's weirdest success stories,

1994's *Mighty Morphing Power Rangers* mixed action clips from the Japanese adventure *Zyu Rangers* into scenes of wacky teen life in Angel Grove, thereby creating the impression that the actors playing Tommy, Cat, etc. were the ones in the suits battling monsters. The idea proved so successful (and cost-effective) it spawned several movies and numerous sequel series (*Power Rangers Wildstorm*, *Power Rangers Ninja Force*, etc.) of which *Power Rangers Zeo* was the first.

This particular episode is more a horror-movie parody than Oz, but the Oz element is there.

Earthworm Jim: The Wizard of Ooze. 11/23/96. 30 mins., color, animated, WB.

Voices: Earthworm Jim (Dan Castellaneta), Professor Monkey-for-a-Head (Charlie Adler), Peter Puppy/Narrator (Jeff Bennett), Psy-Crow/Bob the Killer Goldfish (Jim Cummings), Evil the Cat (Edward Hibbert), Snott/Henchrat (John Kassir), Queen Slug-for-a-Butt (Andrea Martin), Princess What's-Her-Name (Kath Soucie).

Credits: Producers: Kathi Castillo, Roy Smith II; *Executive producers:* David Perry IV, Douglas TenNapel.

Earthworm Jim is an earthworm who uses his special battlesuit to fight against evil, such as tyrannical Queen Slug-for-a-Butt of Insectica. In this episode, the queen's new weapon transports Jim and sidekick Peter Puppy to an alternate universe (where everything is in black-and-white) where everyone is a counterpart of a character in Jim's regular cast: The Queen is the Wicked Queen of the Southwest, Princess What's-Her-Name is Gilda the Good Witch of the Northwest and Jim himself is the powerful but slimy Wizard of Ooze.

Personal FX. 30 mins., color, F/X.

A series on collectibles focused this episode on one fan's Oz collection.

1997

The Rosie O'Donnell Show. 10/31/97. One hour, color, syndicated.

Cast: Dorothy (Rosie O'Donnell), Wicked Witch of the West/Glinda (Bette Midler), Band Leader/Scarecrow (John McDaniel), Percussionist (Ray Marchia), Guitarist/Tin Woodman (Rodney Jones), Saxophonist/Cowardly Lion (Morris Greenberg), Bass (Tracy Wormworth), The Village People (themselves).

Credits: Producer: Rosie O'Donnell; *Executive producer:* Daniel Kellison; *Music:* John McDaniel, Harold Arlen, Herbert Stothart, Keith Levenson; *From:* Kid-Ro.

A spoof of the MGM film.

1999

Priklyucheniya v izumrudnom goroda: Serebryanyye tufel'ki [Also known as, Adventures in the Emerald City: Silver Shoes]. Two 26-minute episodes, color, animated, NTV.

Cast: Mikhail Boyarsky, Yulia Bochanova, Vadim Guschchin, Era Zigarshina.

Credits: Director: Alexander Makarov; *Writer:* Yevgeni Markov (based on *The Wizard of Oz* and somewhat on *Wizard of the Emerald City*).

(Seen in Russian-language version)

A cyclone raised by the evil Witch of the East carries a farmhouse containing young Dorothy out of Russia and into Oz where the witch lives. Emerging from the farmhouse (which of course landed on top of the witch), Dorothy and her dog Toto meet the blue-clad Munchkins and the grandmotherly Good Witch of the North. The Wicked Witch's silver shoes appear on Dorothy's feet as the witch's body disintegrates, then the Good Witch and the girl take tea. The witch sends Dorothy to see the Wizard in the Emerald City.

Along the way, Dorothy is joined by the pudgy scarecrow Strasheela, the rusted Iron Woodman (who's been rusted in one spot so long, he's covered with cobwebs) and the Cowardly Lion, seeking respectively brains, heart and courage. In a mountain pass they're attacked by giant, savage lizards, but the Woodman chops down a tree to cross the nearest ravine (while the Lion holds off the beasts), then chops the bridge down once the travelers have crossed safely.

Next, a beautiful field of poppies puts Toto, Dorothy and the Lion to sleep. The Lion's too heavy to budge, but after the Iron Woodman saves the Queen of the Field Mice from a wildcat, an army of mice pulls the Lion out on a wooden wagon the Woodman makes. The Lion wakes, and is horrified at being surrounded by mice.

The travelers go rafting down a river, but the punting pole hooks in the river bottom, yanking Strasheela off the raft. A stork carries him to dry land and the group goes on to the Emerald City. Donning green spectacles, the group enters the city and has an audience with the Wizard, who takes a different form to greet each of them, but makes the same request each time: Slay the Wicked Witch of the West and win your wishes.

Dorothy and her friends set off, but the monocled witch sends wolves and crows against them, only to fall before Iron Woodman and Strasheela respectively (but unlike the results in Baum's story, they're routed, not killed). The Winged Monkeys, however, destroy Strasheela and the Woodman, then drag Dorothy, Toto and the Lion before the witch. The Witch cages the beasts, intimidates Dorothy into menial labor, then trips the girl with an invisible cord, knocking one silver shoe free. Her gloating unnerves Dorothy, who kicks over a water bucket, destroying the witch.

The Winkers rebuild Dorothy's friends and show her the cap that commands the Winged Monkeys. The monkeys fly everyone back to the Wizard's throne room, where the Wizard speaks to them invisibly — but they discover he's only hiding behind a secret panel, a fraud. The Winged Monkeys fly Dorothy to Glinda, who tells her how to use the shoes. Dorothy does, and magically reappears near her family farm.

For some reason, Russian TV turned to Baum rather than his Russian counterpart, Alexander Volkov, to create a new Oz story (though it uses elements from Volkov, such as the witch summoning Dorothy to Oz). It has some nice visual touches and is quite faithful to the book. A sequel followed in 2000.

Lexx: Woz. 3/19/99. One hour, color, Sci-Fi Channel.

Cast: Original Xev (Lisa Hynes), Skye (Kerry MacPherson), Calico (Stacy Smith), Guards (Robin Johnson, Laura Nason, Adrienne Horton), Holo-guard (Lori Heath), 7-90 (Jeffrey Hirschfield), Lexx (voice, Tom Gallant), Woz (Walter Borden), Dark Lady (Lenore Zann).

Credits: Gekko Film Corp/MGM; Salter Street Films, Time Film-und TV-Produktions GmbH, Screen Partners; *Executive producers:* Paul Donovan, Wolfram Tichy; *Producer:* Norman Denver; *Co-producer:* Bill Fleming; *Designed by* Mark Laing, Tim Boyd; *Visual effects:* Gary Mueller; *Mission Control—Post:* William Cairncross; *Costume designer:* Till Fuhrmann; *Photography:* Les Krizsan; *Music:* Marty Simon; *Editor:* Christopher Cooper; *Creative producers:* Cordell Wynne, Willie Stevenson; *Writer:* Paul Donovan, Lex Gigeroff; *Director:* David MacLeod.

In this comic SF show, the super-powerful space dreadnaught *Lexx* wound up controlled by janitor Stanley Tweedle and crewed by undead assassin Kai; Xev, an ugly housewife transformed into a sex slave; and the bodiless head of robot 7-90. As *Woz* opens, 7-90 reveals Xev's body will expire in 79 hours unless it is recharged in a Lustacon.

The only available Lustacon is on planet Woz. The crew takes a shuttle to the surface, but a tornado brings it down on a woman, leaving only her shoes visible. Nevertheless, Woz's unctuous theocrat, the Wozard, agrees to cure Xev if Kai assassinates the Dark Lady, who uses the Lustacon to create sex slaves who die in a week (in order to keep demand high). After Stanley and Kai leave, the Wozard admits he can't cure Xev, but restores her original body so she can die at peace with herself.

Kai breaks through the Dark Lady's defenses, but Stan gets caught by her gorgeous guards. The Wozard and his disciples widen the hole Kai punched in the defenses ("Ding, dong, the bitch will be dead!") and the surviving disciples confront Stanley's captors. The guards reveal the Wozard lied about the one-week expiration date, but the two groups kill each other anyway.

Kai confronts the deformed Dark Lady,

who tells him she uses the Lustacon to give other women beauty she cannot share. The Wozard enters and admits his real motive is that the Dark Lady made his wife beautiful; then she left him. The Wozard blows the fortress, himself and the Dark Lady to smithereens, but Kai and Stanley salvage the Lustacon component they need to save Xev. Back on the *Lexx*, a restored Xev tells her friends there's no place like home.

Walter Borden (the Woz) played several roles over the course of this series (including the voice of one of the arch-villains, His Shadow).

Rugrats: No Place Like Home. 10/2/99. 30 mins., animated, color, Nickelodeon.
Voices: Tommy Picles (Elizabeth Daily), Chuckie Finster (Nancy Cartwright), Phil DeVille/Lil DeVille/Betty Deville (Kath Soucie), Angelica Pickles (Cheryl Chase), Didi Pickles/Minka Pickles (Melanie Chartoff), Stu Pickles (Jack Riley), Drew Pickles/Chaz Finster (Michael Bell), Howard DeVille (Philip Proctor), Melinda Finster (Kim Cattrall), Grandpa Lou Pickles (Joe Alaskey), Charlotte Pickles (Tress MacNeille), Susie Carmichael (Cree Summer), Randy Carmichael (Ron Glass), Kira Finster (Julia Kato), Kimi Finster (Dianne Quan), Lulu Pickles (Debbie Reynolds).
Credits: Director: Becky Bristow; *Writers:* Barbara Herndon, Jill Gorey; *From:* Nickelodeon.

In this series, which focused on toddlers and infants trying to make sense of the world, this episode had little Susie going to hospital for a tonsilectomy. Under anesthesia, she dreams about going to Lots O' Tots Land where her sister, Alysa, is the Good Witch; bullying Angelica is the Wicked Witch; and Susie gets to wear magic pink fluffy slippers as she sets out to find the Magic Lizard who can take Susie to her mommy.

Traveling down Hopscotch Road, Susie meets a Scarecrow who has straw in his diapers (Tommy), the Tin Woodsmen (twins Phil and Lil in a trashcan) and the Cowardly Lion (ever-nervous Chuckie) before she finally gets to return to her family.

The *Rugrats* series also generated an Oz-based computer game, *Munchin Land*.

2000

Priklyucheniya v izumrudnom goroda: Printsessa Ozma [Also known as Adventures in the Emerald City: Princess Ozma]. Two 26-minute episodes, color, animated, NTV.
Cast: Mikhail Boyarsky, Yulia Bochanova, Vadim Guschchin, Era Zigarshina.
Credits: Directors: Denis Chernov, Ilya Maksimov; *Writers:* Mikhail Bartenev, Andrei Usachev (based on *The Land of Oz*).

Glinda catches her maids viewing romantic scenes in the moving illustrations of the Book of Records, and turns the book to current events: Strasheela ruling Oz, Iron Woodman ruling the Winkies, General Jinjur plotting revolution and the old witch Mombi. Mombi punishes her servant, Tip, by magically adding to the pile of peas he's shelling (he pops her with his pea-shooter as payback).

After Mombi steals the magic Powder of Life from sorcerer Dr. Pipt, she heads home only to recoil from a grotesque figure in her path, created by Tip from a pumpkin head and sticks. Mombi uses the powder to bring "Jack Pumpkinhead" to life, then decides that with him to serve her, she might as well turn Tip into a marble statue. Finding the prospect unappealing, Tip runs away, taking Jack and the powder. While showing Jack how Mombi brought him to life, Tip accidentally does the same to a sawhorse he's sitting on; they ride off, narrowly escaping Mombi's pursuit.

Tip falls off the speeding Sawhorse, which carries Jack to Strasheela in the Emerald City. Tip is caught by Jinjur and her all-woman army, and dragooned to pull a supply wagon. When the army arrives in the city, it starts looting emeralds, and Tip sneaks away into Strasheela's throne room; he, Strasheela and Jack ride off on the Sawhorse to meet the Iron Woodman while Mombi arrives in the city and allies herself with Jinjur.

Glinda, watching this in the book, turns a convenient insect into a human-size Woggle-Bug and sends it to Strasheela. The chattering Woggle-Bug gives Strasheela a gem that brings Dorothy back to Oz. They head back to the Emerald City, successfully overcoming the obstacles Mombi throws in their way. Strasheela calls on their old friend, the Queen of the Field Mice, and she agrees to let him carry some mice in his straw.

When the group reaches the throne room, Jinjur's army surrounds them, but flees in panic when the mice run out. Mombi summons a Nome drilling machine and descends to the Nome King's caverns. He reluctantly gives her a powder of transformation (she also swipes a diamond). The witch sneaks into the palace with a Nome platoon just as the good guys use the Powder of Life to turn some furniture and a hunting trophy into a flying Gump (the trophy head is quite horrified to see its new body).

The Gump flies into a mountain and crashes in a bird's nest, but after some quick repairs it flies the rest of the way to Glinda. Glinda tells the Scarecrow the long-lost Princess Ozma is Oz's true ruler (judging by the photos, Mombi kidnapped Ozma with no help from the Wizard). Glinda flies everyone back to the city and captures Mombi; the witch uses the Nome King's powder to turn into a spider, but doesn't get away.

Mombi confesses that she turned Ozma into a boy, at which Tip laughs until it sinks in whom she means. He resists being turned back, but when Mombi drops her vial of Nome powder, some of it gets on Tip and transforms him anyway. In the conclusion, Ozma becomes queen (and wings Mombi with her pea-shooter as the witch and Jinjur skulk, watching) and the Gump flies Dorothy home.

Some fine visual touches highlight this second installment, but Dorothy serves almost no purpose here.

Lost in Oz. Unaired, 44 mins.
Cast: Christine Laikin, Scott Schwartz.
Credits: Writer: Trey Callaway; *Story, executive producers:* Trey Callaway, Michael Katleman, Tim Burton, Joel T. Smith; *From:* Columbia-TriStar Syndication, A Band Apart.

A handful of Kansas residents—teacher Nancy Purinton; beautiful high-schooler Jade Welling; Theo Alred, who has a crush on Jade; Vance McCarver, a freewheeling 29 year old and his younger brother, Vince; and Kimber, a pierced, dyed drifter—wind up at Ponca's Emerald City service station. Everyone hides in Ponca's Winnebago when a twister hits, but the cyclone picks the vehicle up, eventually dropping it in what one review describes as a "psychedelic" version of Oz. The Kansans go looking for the Wizard, but he has disappeared (and no one knows what he looks like), and the kingdom is falling into chaos without him. It may be a while before the newcomers get home.

This pilot was developed for syndication (and reportedly was actually filmed), but it never aired. Instead, the production company, A Band Apart, went on to revise the concept for the WB network (see the next entry), though with no more success.

Stories about Oz falling into decline and doom have been a thriving sub-genre, including Caliber Comics' *Oz* series and Marv Wolfman's *The Oz Encounter*.

2002

Lost in Oz [Also known as Tales of Oz].
Never aired. 44 mins., WB.
Cast: Alex Wilder (Melissa George), Caleb Jansen (Colin Egglesfield), Lorielledere (Mia Sara), Brianna/Patchwork Girl (Sandra Allen), Bellaridere (Lynn Whitfield).
Credits: Director: Mick Garris; *Writer:* David Hayter; *Producer:* Darryl Sheen; *Executive producers:* Lawrence Bender, David Hayter, Kevin Brown, Joel Smith, Jeff Hayes; *From:* WB Network, A Band Apart.

Beautiful Alex Wilder is torn between marriage and a career, and not entirely sure either one will fulfil her, much to the bemusement of her cynical buddy, Brianna. While driving through Kansas, Alex is caught in a cyclone and carried to Oz. There she meets Caleb, a World War II fighter pilot (call sign Scarecrow) trapped in Oz since

1943 and unaware 50 years have passed since then.

In the decades since Dorothy visited, evil has grown strong enough for Lorielledere, the new Witch of the West, to imprison Princess Ozma in her magic labyrinth. Bellaridere the Good Witch confronts Alex and Caleb in her underwater city and gives them the choice of rescuing Ozma or becoming dinner for Bellaridere's tiger ally. Accompanied by the Patchwork Girl, Alex and Caleb travel across Oz, meeting the Wheelers from *Ozma of Oz*, and finding the ruins of the Munchkin village where Dorothy once landed.

When Alex and her friends confront the Wicked Witch in her labyrinth, they learn that if Alex destroys Lorielledere, she'll become the new Wicked Witch. Instead, they summon the twister to carry Lorielledere away, then return Ozma to Bellaridere. Unfortunately, with the twister gone, Alex is now trapped in Oz with Caleb, perhaps forever.

Like the previous *Lost in Oz* pilot, this one was finished but never saw the light of day until bootleg copies surfaced on eBay in 2004. The concept certainly seems to fit both the WB's revisionist slant on classic heroes (*Smallville*, *Tarzan*) and the wave of sexy butt-kicking women started in the 1990s by *Buffy the Vampire Slayer*. It was touted as a shoo-in for the schedule up to a few months before the 2002 fall season; although no definitive reason for its cancellation has been given, it wouldn't be the first series to be dropped at the last minute.

Another project that has yet to reach the screen is *Surrender Dorothy*, in which a grown-up Dorothy (Drew Barrymore) discovers the Witch of the West still lives, and wants both revenge on Dorothy and possession of the ruby slippers. *Surrender Dorothy* has been "in development" since 1999, with both Barrymore and producer Robert Kosberg putting other projects ahead of it.

Memories of Oz. 7/3/01. Turner Classic Movies.

Another documentary accompanying an airing of the MGM film, this time on the Turner Classic Movies channel.

Futurama: Anthology of Interest 2. 1/6/02. 30 mins., animated, color.

Voices: Phillip J. Fry/Zapp Brannigan/Professor Hubert Fansworth/Dr. Zoidberg (Billy West), Leela (Katey Sagal), Bender (John DiMaggio).

Credits: Director: Bret Haaland; *Writers:* Lewis Morton, David X. Cohen, Jason Gorbett, Scott Kirby; *Created by:* Matt Groening.

In this animated SF parody, Frye, a pizza boy thawed out from suspended animation in the distant future, wanders the universe with robot sleaze Bender, the eccentric Professor and one-eyed Leila. A recurring feature was anthology episodes, such as this one, in which the Professor showed alternate histories for the characters.

In the segment *Wizzin'*, Leela asks what life would be like if she'd found her unknown homeworld, but gets knocked out before the machine can answer. She dreams of herself as Dorothy, landing on Planet Ozz and stealing the witch's shoes, then joining the Tin Woodman (Bender) and the Lion (Professor Zoidberg, who doesn't run off from fear but to use the bathroom). They meet the Wizard (the Professor) whose giant head is real, though attached to a normal body.

The Wicked Witch (Mom, a ruthless CEO and recurring villain) sends the flying monkeys (her sons) to capture Leila, but only so Mom can adopt her. Leila is less than thrilled when her friends save her from a life of wealth, and with the Wizard's insistence that she return to her "poor, dirt-farming, teetotalling foster family." When she clicks her heels together, her real wish is to become a witch. She begins turning the others into frogs until the Lion splashes her with water, at which point she awakens to tell her friends about this curious dream she had.

That '70s Show: Tornado Prom. 2/5/02. 30 mins., color, Fox.

Cast: Eric Forman (Topher Grace), Jackie Beulah Burkhardt (Mila Kunis) Michael Kelso (Ashton Kutcher), Stephen Hyde (Danny Masterson),

Donna Pinciotti (Laura Prepon), Fes (Wilmer Valderrama), Kitty Foreman (Debra Jo Rupp), Red Forman (Kurtwood Smith); Guests: Joanne (Mo Gaffney), Rhonda (Cynthia Lamontagne), Cole (Timothy Bottoms), Coach Ferguson (Michael Milhoan), Wizard (Pamela Sue Martin).

Credits: Director: David Trainer; *Writer:* Dave Schiff; *Producers:* Rob DesHotel, Dean Batali, Mark Hudis, Gregg Mettler, Dave Schiff, Philip Stark, Patrick Kienlen; *Executive producers:* Bonnie Turner, Terry Turner, Mark Brazill, Caryn Mandabach, Marcy Carsey, Tom Werner, Jackie Filgo, Jeff Filgo; *From:* Carsey-Werner.

In this 1970s-set sitcom about small-town teens, vain, shallow Jackie is shell-shocked to learn she's only runner up as Prom Queen. Getting stoned to ease the pain, she dreams of walking down the yellow brick road with Scarecrow (her moronic boyfriend Michael), Tin Man (cynical Hyde) and the Cowardly Lion (socially inept Fez). None of the guys like the casting, nor does Donna (the Wicked Witch — made up to match the W.W. Denslow illustrations, rather than the MGM version) or Eric (a Winged Monkey).

Jackie escapes the witch and reaches Miss Wizard, who assures her that since good people are popular and only a popular girl could be Snow Queen, Jackie aspiring to be Snow Queen proves her inner goodness. Her view of the universe reconfirmed, Jackie wakes up and joins the rest of the cast in seeking shelter from a tornado.

Passions. 6/14–21/02. Six one-hour episodes, NBC.

Cast: David Hastings (Justin Carroll), Chad Harris (Charles Divins), Antonio Lopez-Fitzgerald (Christopher Douglas), Rebecca Hotchkiss (Andrea Evans), Luis Lopez-Fitzgerald (Galen Gering), Jessica Bennett (Jade Harlow), Nicholas Crane (Justin Hartley), Gwen Winthrop (Liza Huber), Sam Bennett (James Hyde), Ivy Winthrop Crane (Kim Johnston Ulrich), Whitney Russell (Brook Kerr), Theresa Lopez-Fitzgerald (Lindsay Korman), John Hastings (Jack Krizmanich), Liz Sanbourne (Amelia Marshall), Ethan Winthrop (Eric Martsolf), Julian Crane (Ben Masters), Beth Wallace (Kelli McCarty), Hank Bennett (Ryan McPartlin), Miguel Lopez-Fitzgerald (Jesse Metcalfe), Tabitha Lenox (Juliet Mills), Mrs. Wallace (Kathleen Noone), Simone Russell (Chrystee Pharris), Dr. Eve Russell (Tracey Ross), Grace Bennett (Dana Sparks), Charity Standish (Molly Stanton), Pilar Lopez-Fitzgerald (Eva Tamargo Lemus), T.C. Russell (Rodney Van Johnson), Sheridan Crane (McKenzie Westmore), Kay Bennett (Deanna Wright).

Credits: Directors: James Sayegh, Karen Wilkins; *Head writer:* James E. Reilly; *Writers:* Shawn Morrison, Mel Brez, Ethal Brez, Darrel Ray Thomas, Jr., Peggy Schibi, Nancy Williams Watt, Maralyn Thomas; *Producer:* Richard Schilling; *Executive producer:* Lisa Hesser; *Associate producer:* Denise Mark; *Production designer:* Barry Williams; *Costume designer:* Julie Rae Englesman; *Music directors:* John Henry & Wes Boatman; *From:* NBC Studios in association with Outpost Farms Productions.

Unlike typical soap-opera towns, Harmony, California, is not only burdened with amnesiacs and family feuds, but supernatural menace, courtesy of Tabitha, a lovable spinster who was really a 300-year-old witch seeking revenge on the town for burning her at the stake. At the time of this plotline, Tabitha had frozen Charity — a young girl gifted with magical powers by the forces of good — in ice and replaced her with "Zombie Charity," despite the fact that Tabby's familiar, Timmy (a literal living doll) had a crush on Charity.

Timmy leaves town seeking the Demon's Horn that can free Charity, and encounters Julian Crane, a wealthy scoundrel supposedly murdered (he survived and decided to hide until the killer was caught). Driving through a black-and-white landscape with Julian and Toto the dog, Timmy spots the Demon's Horn symbol on a billboard directing him to the Wizard at the Rainbow Hotel. Walking up a yellow brick road (everything becomes color) they find the hotel, which is filled with Munchkins. One of them eventually tells Timmy that to find the Wizard, he has to dress up as Dorothy, with Julian as the Cowardly Lion, then skip down the halls together.

Watching clairvoyantly, Zombie Charity sends an evil scarecrow to attack Timmy, but Julian sets it on fire with his cigar. The zom-

A computer-animated Ozma from the computer-animated *Patchwork Girl of Oz*. (Photograph credit: Thundertoad Animation.)

bie turns an empty can into a murderous Tin Man armed with a chain saw, but Julian destroys it with a can-opener. Flirtatious female Munchkins distract the libidinous Julian, while Timmy finds the Wizard behind the curtain; sick of the whole Oz thing, the Wizard refuses to help until he learns that Timmy is a friend of Tabitha's.

The Wizard's crystal shows Tabitha (dressed like Aunt Em) worrying over Timmy's absence, but the doll vows to press on. When they leave the hotel, Julian dismisses the experience as an acid trip, then discovers that the Munchkin girls swiped his wallet — and the hotel has vanished. Hitching a ride on a passing truck, they head out of this plotline.

A fairly typical story for this soap's nutty mix of soap shticks and supernatural menace.

In a 2001 episode, Tabitha had an Oz nightmare (with herself as the Wicked Witch, Charity as the Good Witch and Timmy as a flying monkey) in which she gets saddled with Charity and her family as unwanted houseguests.

2003

Road Trip: Movie Road Trip. 4/3/03.
Travel Channel.

This episode of the Travel Channel series paid tribute to classic movies by visiting sites where they were filmed or festivals saluting them. *Wizard of Oz* from MGM was covered, including interviews with four Munchkins.

The Patchwork Girl of Oz.

Credits: Animation director: Steve Young; *Producers:* D.J. Perry, Jeff Kennedy, Scott Reschke, Steve Young; *From:* Collective Development Inc., Thundertoad Animation.

Desperate for food, young Ojo and his uncle Unc Nunkie leave their home in the forest and visit Dr. Pipt and his wife Margolotte. Dr. Pipt has just completed six years' work creating a Powder of Life that will bring a patchwork doll to life as a servant for Margolotte. The powder works, but in coming to life, "Scraps" accidentally spills a petrifying potion on Nunkie and Margolotte.

She, Ojo and Pipt's glass cat set out to find the ingredients for an antidote, which leads them to encounters with that cubic creature, the Woozy; with cannibal plants; a giant porcupine that fires its quills; and the mountain realm of the Hoppers and the Horners before finally restoring Nunkie and Margolette to life again.

Thundertoad announced this computer-animated film for 2003, but as of early 2005, it hasn't aired.

8

Oz on Television: Commercials

1963

Contac. 9/29/63.

Sterling Holloway narrates how the miraculous cold-cure capsule successfully treats the combined symptoms of Scarecrow, Cowardly Lion and Tin Woodman (lifelike dolls). This first aired during an episode of *The Judy Garland Show*.

1965

Procter and Gamble.

The company, which sponsored this year's telecast of MGM's *The Wizard of Oz*, offers a line of Oz plastic hand puppets packaged with various products. A mail-in offer also lets consumers order a Wizard puppet, a theater and a script.

The company revived this campaign in 1969.

1979

Crispy Wheats-n-Raisins.

Geri Reischl of *The Brady Bunch Variety Hour* did an Oz-themed breakfast cereal commercial with herself in the Dorothy role.

1984

Lone Star Gas Company.

A film crew working on the water-throwing scene in the MGM *Wizard of Oz* uses a gas drier between takes to dry the costumes, leading Dorothy to observe that "There's no place like home for a gas dryer."

1987

3-in-1 Oil.

In this UK commercial, the Tin Woodman stays flexible even in drenching rain thanks to the miraculous properties of this "Wizard of Oilz."

1989

Krystal Commercial.

The hamburger chain promotes some Oz-related giveaways with scenes from the film.

Pfizer Chemicals.

The Tin Woodman testifies that Pfizer's arthritis treatment can help no matter how stiff your joints are.

Downey Fabric Softener.

A little girl tells the Wizard's doorman (Frank Morgan in a film clip from MGM's *Wizard*) about the amazing power of Downey Fabric Softener, which is coincidentally offering a rebate on the 50th anniversary video of the film.

Yamaha Electronic Keyboard.

A band plays a wild rock version of the MGM songs on the Yamaha keyboard.

Great Films Stamps.

A series of stamps commemorating the great films of 1939 is advertised, including MGM's *Wizard of Oz.*

Minolta Cameras.

In the hall of the Wizard of Oz, Dorothy wishes she had a photo, but the Lion is terrified to take one and Scarecrow doubts that he's smart enough. The announcer informs the audience that in reality, anybody can use a Minolta.

1990

Heinz Ketchup.

CGI-animated ants raid a picnic to the tune of the Winkie army's marching song in the MGM *Wizard.*

1991

Twin Peaks.

FBI agent Dale Cooper—the star of the eerie ABC TV series *Twin Peaks*—wakes from a nightmare crying out "Auntie Em!" and then sees his co-stars standing around his bed. He reveals a terrible nightmare "where we were airing on Saturdays, and you were there, and Lucy, and Nora…

The ad acknowledged the show had lost ratings when it moved to Saturday nights, and that it was relocating to Thursdays.

1993

Seattle Public Library.

In an animated commercial, the Scarecrow extols the virtues of reading, Tin Woodman reads a romance novel, the Cowardly Lion morbidly browses Poe, and Dorothy reads *Alice in Wonderland.*

1994

Energizer Batteries.

As part of the running battle between an evil battery manufacturer and the Energizer Bunny (which "keeps going and going and going" because of its choice of battery), the manufacturer hires the Wicked Witch (MGM version) as a hit woman. She tries to burn the rabbit ("How about a little fire, bunny?") which sets off an automatic sprinkler system, melting her.

1995

McDonald's.

Kids, animals and Oz characters sing the Big Mac theme.

1996

Jeff Foxworthy Show.

A tornado carries the cast of this sitcom from the drab, black-and-white world of ABC into the full-color NBC universe, where Glinda (Liz Torres of NBC's *The John Larroquette Show*) greets them.

The commercial satirizes ABC's decision to drop the show, which NBC picked up and ran through 1997.

2000

Federal Express.

As the Munchkins celebrate Dorothy's arrival in Oz, their voices begin to drop into a normal key. A Federal Express truck caught in the tornado crashes to the ground (crushing the Wicked Witch of the East) and the driver presents the Munchkins with some helium balloons, enabling them to talk squeaky again after they inhale. The Wicked Witch of the West skywrites "Be Absolutely Sure" overhead.

Federal Express has a tradition of wild Superbowl commercials; this one received some criticism on the grounds that the Munchkins were effectively promoting the use of inhalants.

2002

MasterCard.

Dorothy is so absorbed shopping on-line (sweater for Auntie Em, silver slippers for herself) she doesn't notice Toto barking a warning about an onrushing tornado. The cyclone ultimately skirts the farmhouse, showing metaphorically MasterCard's amazing power to protect against online credit-card fraud!

(Commercials this author has heard of but can't verify include a Subaru ad in which the driver encounters Dorothy and the Tin Woodman and a food commercial with Bobby Van as the Scarecrow doing a song-and-dance number).

9

Computer Games and Educational Software

1985

The Wizard of Oz. For: Apple, Commodore 64.
From: Windham Classics from Telarium.

This video game includes *Land of Oz* characters, but was primarily based on the MGM film, though the longer the plot progresses, the more it deviates from the movie. Like other Telarium games, it placed a heavy emphasis on puzzle-solving.

Return to Oz. For: Commodore 64.
From: U.S. Gold Commodore 64 games.

Presumably this game is based on the movie of the same name.

1992

Zim Greenleaf's Laboratory.

A downloadable game based on a character from the *Seven Blue Mountains of Oz* trilogy by Melody Grandy.

1993

The Wizard of Oz. For: Super NES.
From: Seta U.S.

Another game that follows the MGM movie (though with new adventures), with participants choosing whether to play Dorothy or one of her three friends. The MGM music was used in the background.

The Wizard of Oz. For: ZX Spectrum.
From: Jack Lockerby.

Another Oz-based game.

The Legends of Oz. Multicom Publishing.

This CD-Rom includes a matching game, pictures and film clips from the MGM movie, the complete text of *The Wizard of Oz* and animated storybooks of the three Roger S. Baum SillyOZbul books.

Reading Adventures in Oz. Davidson and Associates.

This software program includes lessons in reading, word recognition, phonics, problem solving and comprehension. The student (age three to nine) can select one of four characters to journey along the yellow brick road, and receives a wish from the Wizard at the end of the path.

1996

Yellow Brick Road. From: Synergy, Inc.

A CD-Rom game in which the player sends 3D versions of Tin Woodman and Cowardly Lion in search of the missing Scarecrow. There's reportedly a *Yellow Brick Road 2*.

Twisted.

In this satire, players become storm-chasers swept into a warped version of Oz, where they must solve a series of puzzles before they can return home and stop the tornado. Characters include Glinda Goodwrench, a Clintonesque Scarecrow, a Bob Dole Tin Man, the Wizard and Jack Pumpkinhead.

Creator Ray Dunakin said the idea began with the pun "Wicker Winch of the East," and built from there, incorporating a satire on the 1996 elections.

1999

Twisted Deluxe. For: Macintosh.

This is an updated, full-color version of *Twisted*, with some new scenes and added puzzles, and ambient and object-related sounds and music.

This game requires a 68030 processor (68040 or better strongly recommended); a color monitor; System 7.5 or higher; 6 MB of free RAM; and about 32 MB of hard drive space; it can also be ordered on CD.

2000

Oz: The Magical Adventure.
From: DK Publishing.

Players guide Scarecrow, Tin Woodman and Cowardly Lion around Oz seeking to rescue Dorothy in this CD game.

2003

Rugrats in Munchin Land.

A tornado carries off a carousel while the toddlers from *Rugrats* are riding it, and drops them off in the Land of Odd. The player must find the Whizzer of Odd, taking the role of Chuckie the Cowardly Lion, the Tin Twins, Tommy the Scarecrow or Kimmy from Kansas and trying to gather enough golden Paciflyers to enter Marigold City and meet the Wizard. The Wicked Witch Angelica tries to steal the Paciflyers, but the Good Witch Suzi can protect the toddlers with her kiss.

2004 (anticipated)

Wizard of Oz.
From: Carbon6.

This game takes place prior to *The Wizard of Oz*, when the land was scoured by brutal war and terrifying sorceress battles. With Oz's existence at stake, the rulers of the Realm of Night draw a man into Oz to save the people and turn them from destruction.

This announced game comes from American McGee, who did a similarly dark, bloody *Alice in Wonderland*.

10

Oz Web Sites

Any attempt to list all Oz sites would probably take up half this book, but many of them are just tributes to MGM's film. Included here are sites of interest to anyone interested in learning more about Oz.

mindspring.com/~daveh47/Oz.HTML.

An extensive site that links to a FAQ section about Oz, provides a wide variety of information and gives some of the author's thoughts about various Oz issues, such as whether Ozma should be shown in a romance (a very sensitive topic for some fans). At the linked *mindspring.com/~daveh47/Ozzy_FAQ.html,* visitors can register for Nonestica, an online Oz fan club/newsgroup.

put.com/oz/.

This site offers links to various Oz e-books and Baum's non–Oz e-books.

eskimo.com/~tiktok/.

Eric Gjovaag's excellent site is a great basic reference on almost every aspect of Oz: the MGM film, Oz adaptations, Oz books, Oz art, foreign productions and news of new Oz projects.

halcyon.com/piglet/.

This small press site includes an encyclopaedic listing of Oz places, people and significant objects.

timelineuniverse.net/Oz/Deadly-Desert.htm.

This site (devoted to fictional chronologies) includes several Oz timelines: official histories and books that fit with them, books that don't fit, and Dark Oz stories such as Caliber's *Oz.* It attempts to set dates and arrange in sequence as many Oz stories, canonical and not, as possible.

www.ozclub.org.

The International Wizard of Oz Club's site contains reference material on Oz books and movies, links to other sites, a message board for discussing Oz topics, a trading post for buying and selling, plus order forms for club merchandise, including many hard-to-find books. And of course, it's run by the premiere organization for Oz research and discussion, frivolous or serious.

hungrytigerpress.com.

An on-line store offering Oz related books and CDs.

booksofwonder.com.

Another bookstore, offering children's books, Oz books and assorted Oz merchandise.

www.geocities.com/Hollywood/Hills/6396/ozpage.htm

Jim Whitcomb, editor of the *Baum Bugle*'s "Odds and Ends" column, maintains this excellent site on the MGM film, covering the differences between MGM and Baum, why we don't see Miss Gulch at the end of the film (Whitcomb suggests that the twister killed her) and other matters.

http://www.geocities.com/Hollywood/Bungalow/2525/index.html.

Another good general reference site with links to lots of information and Oz sites (including an array of foreign ones—want to hear the movie reviewed in Thai?).

ozproject.egtech.net.

An impressive, on-going project listing every known Oz book, scholarly works about L. Frank Baum and Oz, non–Oz books by Baum, etc. An invaluable resource.

dorothyozma.topcities.com.

A site devoted to Oz games, including several downloadable computer games (some older ones you'll probably never find otherwise), a few text games and odds and ends of information.

11

Oz Allusions and References in Film, Television, and Video

1970

Brewster McCloud.

This was a peculiar black comedy from Robert Altman starring Bud Cort as a man seeking to master flight and Faye Dunaway as a mysterious woman killing anyone who threatens Cort's dream. When obnoxious old biddy Margaret Hamilton poses a threat, she's crushed under a house (a huge bird cage), with her red slippers sticking out.

1972–3

Electric Company. PBS.

In this educational skit, Dorothy (regular Denise Nickerson, dressed like Judy Garland in the MGM version of Oz) tries to demonstrate the meaning of the word "melt" by throwing water on a witch, without success.

This show was a *Sesame Street*-style educational series targeting slightly older viewers with more complicated words.

1973

Hunter. 1/9/73. CBS.

In this espionage-series pilot U.S. Agent Hunter assumes the identity of a fellow spy who's been brainwashed into launching a bioweapon attack on America. The brainwashing sequence reportedly includes some Oz scenes.

That's Entertainment!!!

This collection of clips from MGM's great musicals included several sequences of Judy Garland in *The Wizard of Oz*.

1976

Saturday Night Live. 11/27/76. NBC.

A businessman with a metal fetish has a humiliating experience trying to pass a metal detector, but the Tin Woodman is waved right through.

1977–78

Mr. Rogers' Neighborhood. PBS.

In one segment of the beloved, long-running children's show, Princess Margaret H. Witch—a lookalike for MGM's Wicked Witch of the West—visits the Royal Family of Makebelieve and astounds them with her magic, such as showing them their future in a crystal ball.

1977

The Young Sentinels: Wizard of Oz. 10/29/77. NBC.

The Sentinels, a trio of alien super-heroes, must enter another dimension in this episode to deactivate a reality warping device. As part of the warping, the path to the other dimension appears as a yellow brick road.

The Magnificent Major. 23 mins., color.

Daisy, a girl who hates to read — particularly *The Wizard of Oz*, since she's already seen the movie — is accidentally transported to the future by a friend's science fair project. The Elvis-like Grand Poloni rules the future and keeps children ignorant by repressing books and making kids play videogames. When Daisy refuses to burn the Baum book, Poloni puts her on trial, and the Magnificent Major defends her by reading the work aloud.

1978

Rainbow.

This Judy Garland biopic includes scenes of Garland working on MGM's *The Wizard of Oz*.

1979

Second City TV: Fantasy Island: . 1/13/79. Syndicated.

In a *Fantasy Island* parody, two rockers ask Mr. Roarke (Eugene Levy) and his assistant Patoo (John Candy) to turn the two musicians into comedians. The rockers become Hope and Crosby in one of the duo's "Road" pictures, then flee the cops in that film into *Casablanca*, where another film fantasy is taking place. When "Hope" rubs a magic lantern, "Glenda" appears and tells the duo to click their heels together to return to Kansas. "We're not from Kansas!" says one. "Buddy, shut up and click!" says the other. A tornado sweeps them away and they wake up to tell their band about this curious dream…

The Oz element was only one fraction of a sketch that sent up old movies, *Fantasy Island* and Montalban's then-current Oldsmobile commercials.

1980

The Muppet Show. 10/18/80. Syndicated.

When the Muppets put on *Alice in Wonderland*, starring Brooke Shields, dimwitted comic Fozzie Bear blithely comes on in the middle of the show as the Tin Woodman and asks, "Aren't we doing *Peter Pan*?" At the end of the episode, the still-confused bear comes back on stage and leads the cast in "We're Off to See the Wizard."

1981

Muppets Go to the Movies. 5/20/81. ABC.

In this collection of movie parodies, Miss Piggy briefly sings "Over the Rainbow" while dressed as Dorothy. Foo Foo played Toto, Gonzo played the Tin Woodman, Fozzie was the Cowardly Lion and Scooter was the Scarecrow.

1984

Top Secret.

At the end of this oddball comedy, the heroine says her goodbyes to her friends, then ends by flinging her arms around a Scarecrow. "I think I'll miss you most of all," she says.

1985

The Wizard of Ahh's.

This porn film opens in 2069, when all men have been locked up and women pleasure themselves with machines. On the planet Ahh's, three female astronauts meet the giant head of the Wizard of Ahh's (the body is very poorly blacked out) who decides to show them what sex is really like by sending them back to the present to work as sex surrogates (the rest of the film has no Oz elements).

That's Dancin'. 1/14/85.

This anthology of classic dance clips includes a five-minute dance by Ray Bolger's Scarecrow (in MGM's *Wizard*, of course) that was dropped for unknown reasons from the end of "If I Only Had a Brain." It's included on some video editions of the film, and a brief clip was used in *Invitation to Dance*, a music video by Kim Carnes using multiple clips from the movie.

M.A.S.K.: The Oz Effect. 10/10/85. Syndicated.

In this episode of the toyline-based action cartoon, agents of M.A.S.K. discover that the crime cartel V.E.N.O.M. has intimidated a native village into mining emeralds by having an agent pose as a wizard who can summon devastating whirlwinds.

The 13 Ghosts of Scooby-Doo: Horror-Scope Scooby. 11/30/85. ABC.

Semi-articulate Great Dane Scooby Doo and his friends spent this series working to recapture 13 horrific spirits who'd escaped from a chest of demons. After a sorcerer steals the chest, Scooby consults a fortune teller to find it. Much to the fortune teller's annoyance, a little girl appears in her crystal ball (not for the first time) crying out "Auntie Em! Auntie Em, where are you?"

1986

The Muppets — A Celebration of 30 Years. CBS.

This celebratory banquet honoring Jim Henson includes an Oz scene with the Muppets.

Transformers: Nightmare Planet. 10/30/86. Syndicated.

The Transformers — shapeshifting robots both good and evil — are trapped in this episode in a nightmare mindscape created by the alien Quintessons from the dreams of a young boy, Davey. The nightmare includes a malevolent witch, but Davey's subconscious fights to help his friends, providing a bucket of water to destroy the witch and creating a yellow brick road guiding the Transformers to the center of his mind for a showdown with the Quintessons.

1987

The New Adventures of Beans Baxter: There's No Place Like Omsk. 9/12/87. Fox.

In this sitcom (concerning teen spy Beans Baxter) episode, mysterious Agent Osborne — who communicates by projecting his enlarged face onto a screen — tells a Soviet defector who wants to return home that he'll allow her to emigrate only if she captures a rogue scientist armed with a shrinking ray. With the help of Beans, the defector not only captures the scientist but unmasks Oz-borne (despite orders to "Pay no attention to the Man behind the curtain") as a love-smitten spy trying to keep the defector from leaving the U.S.

1988

227: The Whiz Kid.

While staging a performance of *The Wiz*, the mother in this family sitcom also has to cope with a brainy 11-year-old college student staying with her.

1989

Murphy's Law: When You're Over the Hill, You Pick Up Speed. 2/11/89. ABC.

Sarcastic insurance investigator Murphy spends most of this episode trying to clear his friend Wes of murdering their malevolent boss, Morgana DuSade. Wes spends the episode suffering through hideous nightmares: Morgana crushed under a desk, shriveling up and leaving a pair of ruby slippers behind; Wes trying to contact his friend Kim on a crystal ball only to have Morgana's face replace Kim's: "HAHAHAHAHA! I'll give you Miss Finuchi!" Fortunately, Murphy exposes the real killer before the hour is up.

Dr. Caligari.

Sinister psychiatrist Dr. Caligari uses radical brain-altering techniques on the inmates of her asylum; an Oz hallucination takes place during one treatment.

ABC Saturday Morning Sneak Preview. Animated/live-action, 30 mins. ABC.

In this promotion for ABC's new fall Saturday morning slate, the characters from the *Family Matters* sitcom watch clips from the new fall cartoons with great enthusiasm for catching them all. The clips include the 1990 *Wizard of Oz* cartoon.

Late 1980s

Reunited. Greg Kihn Band music video.

A young couple driving through a black-and-white Kansas pass the Greg Kihn Band hitchiking. The requisite tornado separates the couple and drops the guy and the band in Munchkinland (switch to color), where the Wicked Witch turns the band into the Scarecrow, Tin Woodman, Lion and an donkey-headed man. Fortunately a farmhouse drops on top of the Witch and the girl emerges dressed as Dorothy outfit. She reunites with the young man, but a rather unattractive Glinda gets there first, magicking the man back to Kansas, then materializes beside him in the car.

1991

Growing Pains: Meet the Seevers. 3/6/91. ABC.

In this episode of the family sitcom, teenager Ben Seever is horrified to wake up and discover his home is a soundstage and the members of his family are just actors in the *Meet the Seevers* sitcom. The unseen director booms orders to the cast, but Ben finally confronts him (despite being told to "pay no attention" to the real man) and demands to go home. He then wakes and finds "you were there, and you, and you—"

Despite the Wizard-like director, this is closer to a remake of the *Twilight Zone* episode, *A World of Difference*, than to Oz.

1992

Picket Fences: Pilot. 9/18/92. CBS.

The opening episode of this philosophical mystery series has the police chief protagonist investigating the murder of the Tin Man during a local production of *The Wizard of Oz*.

1993

Hot Shots Part Deux.

In this parody (a sequel to *Hot Shots*), one-man army Topper Harley (Charlie Sheen) leads a special mission to rescue Desert Storm hostages from Iraq, as well as to bring back the previous rescue missions that Saddam Hussein captured. At the climax, as Topper and girlfriend Ramada (Valeria Golino) depart by helicopter, Saddam charges out, firing at them. A piano falls from the helicopter on top of the dictator, leaving only his legs sticking out, and they shrivel up just like the Wicked Witch of the East...

For Our Children: The Concert. 2/16/93. Disney.

This concert includes Bobby McFerrin performing "a unique version of *The Wizard of Oz*."

1995

Run Around. Blues Traveler music video (directed by Ken Fox).

Accompanied by Toto, the Scarecrow, Tin Woodman and the Lion, an under-age Dorothy tries and tries again to sneak inside a popular night club. When they finally make it inside, Toto accidentally tugs on a curtain and reveals that the hot young band playing is really lip-synching to the aging rockers behind the curtain.

Chicago Hope. 2/27/95. CBS.

A nurse dresses up as Dorothy to connect with a disturbed man obsessed with the movie.

General Hospital. ABC.

During a charity benefit at the title hospital, various cast members sing some of the MGM score.

1997

Pinky and the Brain: Brain Storm. 9/19/97. 30 mins. WB.

In his latest attempt at conquering the world, Brain, a genetically engineered super-genius lab mouse, attempts to take control of a tornado with the help of his dimwitted friend Pinky. Interference from a rival tornado-chaser results in the two mice, a scarecrow and Brain's man-sized armoured suit getting carried by the tornado to Oz.

Primarily a sendup of the same year's hit film *Twister*; the rodent duo had a more thoroughly Ozish adventure in the comic-book spinoff series, *Pinky and the Brain* (#23).

2001

Born to Fly. Sara Evans Music Video. 11/01. GAC TV.

While dressed as Dorothy — surrounded by the Kansas characters from MGM's version — Evans sings of wanting to take off and escape her limited world: "I'm gonna leave these fields behind, to find what's over the horizon." The cyclone comes and sweeps her away at the end.

2002

Answering Bell. 1/11/02. Ryan Adams music video (directed by Luke Scott).

After a blow to the head, Adams wakes up in Oz, where he finds a beautiful girl (Adams's girlfriend Leona Naess) in a poppy field with the Emerald City in the background, and winds up making out with her, while Elton John in a wizard's robe drifts down in Glinda's bubble from the MGM film and watches over the couple.

Adams says he came up with this idea while half delirious from flu medication. Counting Crows singer Adam Duritz provides background vocals.

Charmed: Happily Ever After. 9/29/02. WB.

The Halliwells, sister witches who use their magic to fight evil, found this episode pitting them against Snow White's evil stepmother after she escapes the secret vault where fairy-tale talismans (Cinderella's slipper, Sleeping Beauty's spindle, etc.) are preserved for eternity. Despite the queen's use of fairy-tale magic against the Halliwells, Piper Halliwell confronts her in the vault at the climax and destroys her with a magic potion: "I'm melting!" she cries. The keeper of the vault provides Piper with a pair of ruby slippers that teleport her home.

2003

Scarecrow. Montgomery Gentry music video.

The video, based on a song about cutting loose from the farm and heading off into the world, is supposed to include some Oz imagery.

12

Oz Title Allusions

1966

The New Three Stooges: The Three Wizards of Odds.

An ugly queen demands three wizards render her beautiful.

1976

Dynomutt: The Wizard of Ooze.

The superheroic Blue Falcon and his robot partner Dynomutt take on a master of muck and slime.

1984

Kangaroo: The Tail of the Cowardly Lion.

An episode of the sitcom cartoon about zoo animals.

1985

Moonlighting: Somewhere Over the Rainbow. 11/19/85.

The nutty detectives of the Addison-Hayes agency become involved with a woman who claims to be a leprechaun's daughter who has lost Dad's pot of gold.

Yogi's Treasure Hunt: Follow the Yellow Brick Gold.

Hanna Barbera cartoon characters race to find a golden treasure.

1988

The Snorks: The Wizard of Ice.

The underwater creatures called Snorks encounter a wizard living in the polar regions.

The Karate Kid: Over the Rainbow.

An episode of the cartoon that spun off from the popular *Karate Kid* film series.

1993

Over the Rainbow.

A British TV sitcom.

1994

Over the Rainbow, Under the Skirt.

A black sex comedy involving a cannibal landlord.

1998

Surrender Dorothy.

A psychosexual drama about a man who trains his male lover to become a submissive servant under the name Dorothy.

2003

The Boy from Oz.

A Broadway show about a man from Australia with strong ties to Judy Garland.

Index

Numbers in *italics* indicate photographs or illustrations.

A&E 221
A-KOM Productions, Ltd. 171
Aalda, Marianna 162
Aalerud, Nick 135
Abbott, Donald 50
ABC 159, 193, 195, 197, 199, 202, 203, 204, 211, 213, 218, 245, 246, 247
ABC Saturday Morning Sneak Preview 246
The ABC Saturday Superstar Movie 202
Abducted to Oz 54
Abe, Takashi 204
Able, Will B. 76
Abouda, Djura 109
Acinad Goes to the Emerald City 62
Acosto, Karen 109
Across Indiana — Round Barns in a Square 221
Adair, Tom 193
Adam 103
Adam Productions 172
Adams, Bill 127
Adams, Lis 136, 137
Adams, Mason 212
Adams, Ryan 247
Adema, Shirley 82
Adler, Charlie 218, 229
Adrian 148
Adventure Comics 122
An Adventure in the Land of Oz 70
Adventures in Odyssey 133–134
Adventures in Oz 77
Adventures in Oz with Cheryl 188–192, *191*
Adventures in the Emerald City 229–230, 231–232
Adventures in the Land of Oz 80–81
The Adventures of a Man in Search of a Heart 182
The Adventures of Jerry Lewis 121
The Adventures of Young Santa Claus 228

Afro Celt Sound System 109
After Harry Smith 152
Agahayan, Ray 197
Against All Oz 214
Ahlquist, Steven 124
Aik, Memet 155
Aires, Sônia 166
Aki, Tamio 175
Ako, Yuda 228
Alan, Lori 223, 224, 225
Alan Enterprises 165
Alaskey, Joe 231
Alazaraqui, Carlos 180
Albrecht, Margaret 183
Alcala, Alfredo 123
Alderton, John 159
Alesi, Gary 78
Alexander, Frank "Fatty" 144
Alexander, Irene 70
Alexander, John 167
Alexander, Larry J. 105
Alexander, Sara 95
Alexander, Van 202
Alexis, Alvin 162
Alf 217
Alfonso, Iona 116
Alftales 216, 217
Alien Massacre 153
Alien Productions 217
All, Harriet 76
All That 222
Allard, Scott 188
Allee, Pat 218
Allen, Billie 162
Allen, Debbie 206
Allen, Dede 162
Allen, Dorothy 76
Allen, Jack 133
Allen, Martin 161
Allen, Sandra 232
Alliance Films 141, 142, 143
Allison, Fran 193
Allison, Gladys W. 148
Alloway, Jackie 76
Aloni, Itzik 106
Altman, Robert 243

Amarillo Rojo Cafe 94
The Amber Flute of Oz 50
Amber-Thiessen, Tiffani 216
American Fairy Tales 142, 143
American Film Corporation 173
American General Pictures 153
American Heart Association 182, 183
Amico, Len Dell 89
Amusement parks 83
Anasti, Tedd 220
Anchor Bay Entertainment 185
Anders, Mark 107
Anderson, Andy 139, 143
Anderson, Harry 134
Anderson, Janet 185
Anderson, Jill 98
Anderson, John J. 184
Anderson, Kimberly C. 184
Anderson, Lynn 88
Anderson, Vet 146
Andrews, Kacy 185
Anfuso, Dennis 50
Angell, Jim 94
Angus, David 214
Animated Oz Productions 146, 147, 149, 152, 158, 165, 166, 170, 171, 173, 174, 176, 178, 179, 180, 181, 182, 183, 195, 196, 197, 198, 199, 200, 201, 202, 203, 204, 205, 206, 207, 208, 209, 210, 211, 212, 213, 214, 215, 216, 217, 218, 219, 220, 221, 222, 223, 224, 225, 226, 227, 228, 229, 230, 231, 232, 233, 235, 247
Aniskoff, Paulette 99
Answering Bell 247
Anthology of Interest 2, 233
Anthony, John 105
Antolini, Lea 96
Antonik, Vladimir 175
Anzelowitz, Amy 212
The Approach to Emerald City 152
Aragão, Caxa 166
Aragão, Paulo 166
Aragão, Renato 166, 167

249

Arden, Eve 164
Arefiev, Vladimir 106
Arena 221
Ariolli, Don 207
Aristov, L. 199
Arkin, Adam 164
Arlen, Harold 72, 76, 90, 96, 103, 106, 130, 148, 150, 184, 197, 229
Armstrong, Herb 203
Arnaz, Lucie 105
Aron, Kathi 91
Aroseva, Olga 199
Arrow Anthology 125
Arrow Comics 123, 125
Arsenov, Pavel 175
As the Clock Strikes Oz 54
Asher, William 194
Ashford, Nick 162
Ahshrov, Ariel 106
Ashrov, Azriel 106
Ashton, Rachel 168
Asnes, Andrew 99
Aspen Photography 98
Astar, Shay 222
Atalay, Harlun 155
Atari, Gal 103
Atkins, George 203
Atkinson, Vic 159, 196
Atlantic-Kushner-Locke, Inc. 171
Atlantic Records 86
Atwell, Judy 185
Atwood, Michael 221
Auberjonois, Rene 134
Audre 76
Aunt Em and Uncle Henry in Oz 56
Australian Film Commission 161
Avery, Victoria 96
Avila, Andrea 109
Axelrod, Craig 78
Axelrod, Robert 228
Ayers, Ashley 134, 136
Aysecik and the Bewitched Dwarfs in Dreamland 77, 155–158, *155, 156, 157*
Aysecik Ve Sihirli Cuceler Ruyular Ulkesinde 155–158, 155, 156, 157
Azlin, Justin 107

B&R Samizdat Express 60
Baakin, Haskell 203
Babay, Joey 188
Babbage Press 60
Babbs, Obie 101
Babes in Toyland 66, 68
Babs, Simon 101
Badalamenti, Angelo 171
Badham, John 163
Baer, Dale 158
Bahir, Vicky 103
Baird, Bil 82
Baiul, Oksana 106
Baker, Al 98
Baker, Buddy 193

Baker, Dee Bradley 134
Baker, Pam 183
Balchrovich, Misha 106
Balk, Fairuza 167, 185
Ball, Lucille 203
Ballas, John 148
Ballen, Tony 164
Balluck, Franz 148
Balluck, Josefine 148
Balsar, Robert 221
Balser, Robert 199
Baltimore, Vicki 162
Bambury, John T. 148
Banas, Carl 170, 195, 196
A Band Apart 232
Banjoko, Kashka 162
Banks, Keith 95, 96
Banno, Yoshimitsu 165
Barachois 109
Barantsev, Anatoli 199
Barbera, Joseph 203, 204, 205, 215
Barclay, William 186
Bardin, Garry 199
Bardin, V. 199
Barilla, Courtney 172
Barker, Bradley 127
Barker, Tod 91
Barlow, Joe 178
Barlow, Nate 50
Barnes, Will R. 64
Barnett, Robbie 168
Barnsley, Julie 98
A Barnstormer in Oz 54
Baron, Christy 105
Barr, Leonard 164
Barr, Roseanne 72
Barrett, Candace 134
Barrett, Clyde J. 162
Barrett, Sean 167
Barrington, Elizabeth 172
Barrison, Mabel 64
Barron, Robert 169
Barry, Gene 216
Barrymore, Drew 233
Barstock, Jeff 50, 51
Bartel, Paul 174
Bartenev, Mikhail 231
Bartlett, Scott 90
Barton, Fred 92, 93–94
Barty, Billy 164
Basaran, Tunc 155
Baslee, Sherron 76
Bass, Jules 195, 196, 197, 199, 202, 212
Bassman, George 106, 148
Batali, Dean 234
Batchelor, Joy 199
Bates, Cary 122
Battle, Hinton 84
The Battle for Christmas 213
Bauer, Fred 164
Baum, Frank J. 46, 47, 141, 143, 144, 145, 146
Baum, Kenneth Gage 51

Baum, L. Frank 3, 4, 7, 9, 10, 12, 13, 14, 18, 19, 21, 25, 27, 29, 30, 31, 35, 47, 48, 49, 61, 64, 65, 66, 67, 68, 69, 71, 76, 77, 78, 96, 106, 107, 109, 120, 122, 131, 138, 139, 140, 141, 142, 143, 150, 172, 183, 184, 196, 214, 221, 228, 229
Baum, L. Frank (as fictional character) 90, 91, 94, 100, 102, 107, 108, 113, 172, 198, 216–217
Baum, Maud Gage 10, 127, 130, 145, 147, 198
Baum, Roger S. 51, 178, 239
Baxley, Ron, Jr. 51
Bay, Frances 171
Bayley, Andree 70
Bazy, Robin 174
BBC 203
BBC Radio 4, 133
Beach Blanket Babyloz 52
Beard, Remy 96
Bebel, Andrea 88
Beck, Carl 88
Beck, Jenny 216
Becker, Charley 148
Beckford, Roxanne 221
Beckman, Henry 178
Beda, G. 199
Bednarski, Steven 206
Bedrock Productions 172
Beebee, John 133
Beecroft, Greg 212
Beenie in Oz 56
Beetlejuice 220
BEF Film Distributors 161
Before the Rainbow 108
Begley, Vincent 51
"The Believing Child" 30
Bell, Derrick 162
Bell, Michael 204, 231
Belveal, Carol 183
Ben-Yossef, Saar 103
Bender, Jack 172
Bender, Lawrence 232
Bening, Annette 134
Bennett, Eddie 135
Bennett, Jeff 229
Bennett, LeRoy 105
Bennett, Mairon 170
Bennett, Matthew 113
Benson, Robby 180
Benz, Rachel Berman 99
Berdan, Blain 108
Berends, Polly 51
Berg, Greg 212
Berg, Margaret 51
Berg, Mark Vander 136, 137
Bergen, Frances 194
Berger, Harvey 206
Berger, Richard H. 76
Bergh, Jerald E. 173
Bergman, Mary Kay 180
Beris, Gretchen 78
Berk, Ailsa 168
Berkley Books 54, 56

Index

Berlanti, Greg 99
Berle, Milton 158
Bernard, Susan 78
Bernardi, Herschel 158
Berner, Caroline 153
Bernett, Vic 98
Bernhardt, Eve 153
Berring, Douglas 162
Berry, Fred 213
Berry, Leigh 137
Berry, Tom 134, 135, 136, 137
Berti, Dehl 216
Besky, Freda 148
Besser, Joe 203
Besserer, Eugene 138
Betev, Vladimir 106
Betsy Bobbin in Oz 56
Bever, Blair Bruce 171
Beyond Phonics: The Wonderful Wizard of Oz 185
Bigode, Roberto 166
Bil and Cora Baird Marionettes 82
Bilik, Jerry 106
Billingsley, Barbara 212
Binn, William 206
Bird, P. George 91
Birguer, Maria 206
Birk, Raye 134
Birsef, Ozdemir 155
The Birthday Ban in Munchkin Land 59
Bishop, Gary 125
Bishop, Stuart 87
Bisson, Yannick 217
Biszewski-Eber, Susan 184
Black, G. Howe 144
Black, William 174
Blaine, Richard 52
Blake, Josh 212
Blanc, Mel 158, 194, 203
Blanch, Ana Gloria 94
Blanchard, Ken 184
Blanco, Toma's 153
Blandick, Clara 148
Blaney, Susan 182, 183
Blass, Bill 164
Blaushstein, Gili 106
Blewitt, David 164
Blewitt, David E. 184
Bliss, Thomas A. 171
Block, Stephanie J. 116
Blodgett, Ruth 183
Blonkvist, Heidi 178
Bloom, John 216
Blossom 52
Blossom, Henry S. 52
Blowin' in the Wind 215
Blue, Ben 194
Blue, Susan 180
The Blue Bird 195
The Blue Emperor of Oz 52
The Blue Witch of Oz 124
Blues Traveler 247
Bluestein, Steve 202

Bluth, Don 158
Blythe, Robin 202
Boa, Bruce 168
Boatman, Wes 234
Boaz, Charles 194
Bobbs-Merrill 47
Bochanova, Yulia 229, 231
Bock, Fred 94
Boddie, Aaron 162
Bode, Mark 126
Bode, Vaughn 126
Boe, Stephen 88
Boeke, Jom 164
Boers, Henry 148
Boers, Theodore 148
Boggs, Francis 68
Bogolobov, A. 199
Bogolobova, Y. 199
Bohanek, James 96
Bole, Cliff 211
Bolger, Ray 130, 148, 150, 197, 204
Boliver, Lucio 94
Boliver, Pilar 94
Bollheier, Barbara 81
Bond, Mischa 204
Bonestell, Jack 203
Boni, Gabrielle 223
Bonnet, Roland 161
Books of Wonder 49, 50
Boone, Maryeruth 146
Boone, Michael Kelly 90
Boorman, Christel Kruse 159
Boorman, John 159, 160, 161
Booth, Doug 203, 205
Booth, J.R. 146
Borden, Walter 230, 231
Born to Fly 247
Borough, Linda 109
Borstein, Alex 228
Bosch, Johnny Yong 228
Bosler, Mark 188
Bosworth, Chuck 114, 118
Bosworth, Hobart 138
Botsford, Diana Dru 171
Bottoms, Timothy 234
Bowe, John 95
Bowen, Andrea 113
Bowen-Merrill 47
Bowron, Gregory K. 218
Box, Bobby 90
Box of Bandits 143
Box Office Attraction Co. 140
The Boy from Oz 248
Boyarsky, Mikhail 229, 231
Boyd, Joshua 172
Boyd, Tim 230
Boyer, Sylvie 180
Boylan, Eleanor 83
Boyle, Sally 171
Boys' Choir of Harlem 105
Bracey, Sidney 66
Bradbury, Ray 134, 221
Bradley, Chris 134, 135
Bradley, Pat 164

The Brady Bunch Hour 202–203
The Braided Man of Oz 57
Brain Storm 247
Bransford, Bob 158
Branton, Allen 106
Brauer, Johnathan 106
Brave New Worlds 124
Brazill, Mark 234
Brealond, Tony 162
Brecher, Irving 148
Bressack, Gordon 219
Brewster Bunny and the Case of the Outrageous Enchantments in Oz 58
Brewster Bunny and the Purloined Pachyderms of Oz 62
Brewster McCloud 243
Brez, Ethal 234
Brez, Mel 234
Brice, Fanny 130
Brice, Matthew 96
Bridges, Lorraine 148
Bridgewater, Dee Dee 84
Bridgham, Pamela 87
Bridwell, E. Nelson 123
Briggle, Gary 88, 89
Briggs, Liatunah Johanna 52
Bright, Kelly 96
Bright, Patricia 202
Bright, Simon 214
Bristol, Frank 139
Bristow, Becky 231
Brittingham, Scott 215
Brody, Buster 148
Brohan, Paul 91
Bromilow, Peter 171
Brook, Tyler 148
Brooks, Claude 162
Brooks, David 172
Brophy, Colleen 78
Brown, Babo 222
Brown, Billie 95
Brown, Don 178
Brown, Duncan 185
Brown, Johnny 162
Brown, Kevin 232
Brown, Lisa 212
Brown, Ruth 164
Brown, William F. 84, 162
Brown, William H., Jr. 194
Browne, Jackson 105
Bruhanski, Alex 227
Bruskiewitz, Ann 87
Bryan, Bill 125
Bryant, Margaret 147
Bryer, Denise 166
Bryer, Jesse 107
Brzozowski, Annie 52
Buchanan, Mary 71
Buchanon, Mary 72
Buckethead Enterprises of Oz 50, 51, 52, 53, 54, 55, 56, 57, 58, 59, 60, 61, 62, 63
Buckley, Christopher Wayne 52
Buckley, Ora 140

Buckner, Susan 202
Buggy, Niall 159
Bukanov, A. 199
Bukanov, L. 199
Bullock, Gregg 228
Bumpass, Rodger 222
Bunce, Alan 220
Bungle and the Magic Lantern of Oz 55
The Bunglers and the Wizard of Oroz 166–167
The Bunny King of Oz 53
Burau, Janet 183
Buresh, Christie 148
Buresh, Eddie 148
Buresh, Lida 148
Burgess, Bobby 193
Burgess, Janell 109, 110
Burghardt, Arthur 133
Burke, Billie 148, 150
Burns, Andrea 113
Burns, Benn 98
Burns, Frank 68
Burridge, Walter 64, 66
Burrise, Nakia 228
Burroughs, Edgar Rice 7
Burstall, Dan 161
Burstyn, Thomas 172
Burt, Wayne 161
Burton, Corey 133
Burton, Tim 220, 232
Buscema, John 122
Bush, John 222
Bushman, Myrna 171
Busick, Armando 153
Butakovoi, N. 199
Butcher, Sandra J. 170
Butler, Daws 197, 203
Butler, Ted 162
Butteriss, Simon 97
Button Bright of Oz 58
Butz, Norbert Leo 116
The Buzzard of Oz 125
By the Book 212
Bynes, Amanda 222
Byrne, Connie 78
Byrne, Lisa 78
Byrne, Melanie 78
Byrne, Wendy 78
Byrns, Allen 165
Byron, Helen 64

Cabasa, Lisa Ann 171
Cabral, Ricardo 166
Cade, Michael 223
Caesar, Sid 204
Cage, Nicolas 171
Cahn, Sammy 158, 165
Cain, Betty Ann 148
Cairncross, William 230
Caldwell, Jeff 107
Caliber Press 125, 232
Callaway, Bill 204
Callaway, Trey 232
Camarata, Tutti 131, 132

Cameron, Ben 116
Cameron, Courtney 134
Cameron, Patsy 220
Campbell, Bill 52
Campbell, David 205
Campbell, Jenny 78
Campbell, Jeri 105
Campbell, John 133
Camston, Mimi 76
Candler, Cristy 116
Cannon, William H. 148
Cantor, Eddie 149
Capen, Diane 134, 135, 136, 137
Capitol Album 130
Caplan, Twink 164
Captain Salt in Oz 41, 53
Carbon6 240
Cardenas, Steve 228
The Careless Kangaroo of Oz 56
Carey, Richard A. 89
Carlson, Bob 158
Carlson, Jim 171
Carlson, Karyl 52
Carlson, Len 170, 220
Carlton, Bob 194
Carman, Michael 161
Carnes, Kim 245
Carpar, Salih 155
Carpenter, Angelica Shirley 184
Carpenter, Thelma 162
Carpenter, Willie 162
Carpentier-Alting, Neil 94
Carr, Alfred, Jr. 222
Carr, Mary 144
Carradine, John 153
Carrau, Bob 219
Carroll, Bruce 176
Carroll, Justin 176, 234
Carroll, Lewis 97, 123, 126
Carroll, Mickey 148
Carroll, Willard 52, 185, 222
Carroll-Bower, Mary 114
Carry, Lou 213
Carsey, Marcy 234
Carsey-Werner 234
Carter, Conlan 198
Carter, Dixie 180
Carter, Jim 95
Carter, Lin 52
Carter, Michael Patrick 216
Cartoon Corners 198
Cartwright, Nancy 231
Caruso, Frank A. 171
Casagrande, John 194
Cascone, Joe 107, 108
Case, Justin 167
The Case of the Framed Fairy of Oz 56
Casper, Colonel 148
Caspin, Yuval 103
Cassini, Joe 202
Cassling, Steve 96
Casson, Christopher 159
Castellaneta, Dan 229
Castillo, Kathi 229

Castles, Dolly 69
Cattrall, Kim 231
Cavalieri, Joey 123
Cavanagh, Terry 95
CBS 106, 151, 184, 204, 212, 216, 243, 247
CBS radio 130
Celep, Ferdi 155
Center for Drug Free Living 183
Century 48
Cerulli, Marc 185
Chabanenko, Anton 106
Chabert, Lacey 227
Chadwick, I.E. 144
Chadwick Pictures Corp. 144, 145, 146, 149
Chait, Melissa Bell 116
Chamberlain, Bryan 107
Chambers, Debbie 107
Chance, Nancy 170
Chapin, Frederic 66
Chapman, Elizabeth 71
Chapter Six 114, 118
Charendoff, Tara 170, 217
Charest, Micheline 207
Charles, John P. 94
Charles Santore Illustrates the Wizard of Oz 185
Charlottesville Performing Arts Center 98
Charlton, Kathryn 96
Charmed 247
The Charmed Gardens of Oz 56
Chartoff, Melanie 231
Chasan, Debbie 95, 96
Chasan, Nicole 95, 96
Chase, Cheryl 231
Chase, Chevy 164
The Cheerful Citizens of Oz 50
Chelton, Nick 96
Chenoweth, Kristin 115, *117*, 118, 119
Chernov, Denis 231
Cheshire, Denise 164
Chesnokov, Mikhail 106
Chicago Hope 247
Chihara, Paul 215
Children's Hour 127
Children's Theatre Company 88, 89, 90
China Beach 215
The China Dog of Oz 57
Choi, Marcus 116
Chôriki Sentai Ohranger 228
Christensen, Don 126, 158
Christian, Claudia 227
Christmas in Oz (book) 55
Christmas in Oz (cartoon) 204–205
Christmas in Oz (Oz Kids) 185, 225
Christmas in Ozland 82
Christmas in the Land of Oz 86
Christmas in the Land of Oz That Was 106

Index

Chudabala, Art 225
Church, Jeff 102
Church, Tony 95
Cihi, Jennifer 222
Cilento, Wayne 116
Cinar Productions 206, 207, 211
Cincinnati Playhouse in the Park 90
CineGroupe 178
Cinetron 153
Cippola, Tom 132
Cisi, Joe 171
Civic Light Opera Company 107
Clark, Lincoln 134, 136, 137
Civita, Diane 214
Clark, Bill 196
Clark, Jodie 96
Clark, Mary Cowles 47
Clark, Matt 167
Classics Illustrated, Jr. 83, 131
Clavel, Andre 180
Clay, Jamilah 105
Clayton, Sharlene 107
Cleghorne, Helen 221
Cleveland, Carlos 162
Cleveland, Doris 70
The Cloud King of Oz 52
Coats, William Alan 90
Cochrane, George 143
Coe, Frank A. 153
Cohen, David X. 233
Cohen, Dick 182, 183
Cohen, Edward H. 164
Cohen, Julie 204
Cohen, Marc 76
Cohen, Rob 86, 162, 163
Cohen, Yaacov 106
Cole, Evan 135, 136
Cole, Judy 76
Cole, Natalie 105
Collective Development Inc. 235
Colligan, Mike 184
Collins, Jason 107
Collison, Frank 171
Colonial Radio Theatre 134, 136, 137
The Colorful Kitten of Oz 53
Colt, Alvin 186
Columbia-TriStar Syndication 232
Combel, Paul 184
Combs, Sarah 90
Comic Lala 175
Committee of Russian Federation of Cinematograpy 175
Commodore 64, 239
Compton, Richard 227
Concordia Players Children's Theatre 78
Conklin, Chester 144
Conley, Darlene 226
Connell, Jim 203
Connell, Marcia 147
Connery, Sean 159, 160
Connor, John J. 215

Conried, Hans 130
Conroy, John 97
Contac commercial 236
Conway, James 214
Conway, Lyle 167
Conway, Susan 195, 196
Cooder, Ry 105
Coogan, Peter 214
Cook, Randy 98
Cooke, LaCrystal 225
Cooksey, Danny 215
Coolidge, Karl R. 143
Cooper, Christopher 230
Cooper, Joe 199
Cooper, Nona 148
Coppola, Nicolas 73, 74
Core, Traci 162
Corlett, Ian James 173
The Corn Mansion of Oz 59
Coronet Instructional Films 182
Corrigan, William 194
Le Corsaire, le Magician, le Voleur et les Enfants 186
Cort, Bud 243
Cortez, Miriam V. 111
Corwin, Norman 134
Corwin, Taylor 188
Cory in Oz 58
Cory, Fanny Y. 47
Cosby, Bill 159, 222
Cosgrove, Rachel 45
Costello, Gary 88
Cosumnes River College 183
Cottonaro, Tommy 148
Couch, Chuck 203
Couderc, Pierre 139, 140, 141
Coulter, Elizabeth 148
Count Features, Inc. 161
Countiss, Cathrine 143
The Country Circus 142
Court, Alyson 220
Coury, Susie 188
Cousins, Robin 105, 106
Cowan, Bernard 195
Cowan, Rob 217
The Cowardly Lion and the Hungry Tiger 48
The Cowardly Lion of Oz (book) 33,
The Cowardly Lion of Oz (Disneyland Records) 94, 131
Cowing, Heidi 91
Cox, Basil 202
Cox, Courtney 214
Cox, Karen 100
Cox, Olive 138
Coyne, Phoebe 66
Crabb, James 77
Craig, Dr. 98
Crane, John 221
Crawley Films 195
Crawley, F.R. 196
Creating the Wizard of Oz on Ice 105, 185
Creative Therapeutics 54

Creber, Inez 70
Crenshaw, Deloris 164
Crespo, Santiago 153
Cricket Records 131
Cricketone Chorus and Orchestra 131
Criscione, Frank 111, 115
Crispy Wheats-n-Raisins commercial 236
Crittenden, James 216
CRM Films 184
The Crocheted Cat in Oz 59
Croft, "Idaho Lewis" 148, 184
Cromosoma 221
Crosby, James A. 139, 140, 141, 143
Croteau, Libby 88
Crowder, Randy 216
The Crown of Oz 57
Cruise, Julee 88
Cruz, L.Q. "Missy" 183
Crystal, Kimberly 169
Crystal Clear 218
Cucksey, Frank 148
Cuiffo, Steven R. 153
Cukor, George 150
Cumberlidge, John 95
Cummings, Jim 180, 229
Cunningham, Davy 97
Cunningham, Ed 66
Cunningham, John 88
Cunningham, Leslie 78
Curreri, Lee 206
Curry, Tim 178
Curtin, Shaun 109
Curtis, Billy 148
Cusick, Kristoffer 116
Cutler, Andy 98
Cycle Toons 122

Dacre, Susan 168
Daemonstorm 125
Dafoe, Willem 171
Dagmar in Oz 53
Dai Won Animation Co. 173
Daily, Elizabeth 231
Dallimore, Maurice 194
Dalton, Cal 146
Daltrey, Roger 105
Daly, Candice 174
D'Amato, Brian 52
D'Amato Barbara 52
Dana, Al 212
Danacher, Lee 212
Dance productions 77, 78, 79, 98, 106, 109, 110,
Dandridge, Gregg 171
Daniel, Lois 76
Daniels, Bebe 138, 139
Daniels, Don 186, *188, 189, 190*
Danly, Linda 214
Danly, Mimi 214
Dante, Lisa 88
Danylkiw, John 165
Darbro, Kevin 178
Dark Horse Comics 124

Dark, Danny 204
Dark Oz 125
Daughters of Destiny 141
David, Eugene S., Jr. 148
David, Eulie H. 148
David, Jay 170
David, Mark 222
Davidson and Associates 239
Davies, Howard 140
Davis Equities Corporation Investment Partnerships 161
Davis, Ann B. 202
Davis, B.J. 174
Davis, Danny 131
Davis, Douglas 164
Davis, Gwen 131
Davis, Jim 158
Davis, Mildred 71
Davis, Rebecca 99
Davis, Zack 174
Dawson, Sid 148
A Day in Oz 71
The Day the Music Diede 219–220
Daywalt, Shawn 221
DC Comics 122, 123, 125
Deacon, Tim 178
Dead Head Water 126
The Deadly Desert Around Oz 53
Dean, Lloyd 107, 108
Dean, Nita 186
Deane, Sidney 66
Death Valley Days 198
deCamp, L. Sprague 52
DeCelles, Pierre 170
DeCrawley Films 194
Degen, Justin 95
Degirmencioglu, Hamdi 155
Degirmencioglu, Zeynep 155, *155, 156, 157*
Deitch, Kathy 116
Deitz, Phil 101
Dejon, Denise 162
de la Fuente, Eduardo Torre 153
de la Inglesia, Eloy German 153
DeLand, Bill 172
Delany, Dana 215
de Lavallade, Carmen 95
deLeon, Michael 88
DeLeon, Veronika 111
Dell Comics 121
Dell Junior Treasury Comics 121
Dell Publishing 121
DelRey 60
DeLuise, Dom 178
Dembeck, Karen 98
de Metto, Alberto 158
Dempsey, Barbara 135, 136
Demuza 167
Denberg, Lori Beth 222
Denis, Ethel W. 148
Denis, Mark 206
Denis, Prince 148
Dennen, Barry 174
Dennett, Matthew 107
Dennett, Tammie 107

Dennett, Yvonne 107
Dennis, Gil 168
Dennis, Jules 219
Dennis-Landman 58
Denniston, Robert F. 78
Denslow, W.W. 7, 49, 62, 64, 65, 69, 90, 120, 135, 234
Denslow's Scarecrow and the Tin Woodman 49, 120
Denslow's Scarecrow and Tin-Man 12, 49, 120
Denslow's Scarecrow and Tin-Man and Other Stories 49
Denver, Norman 230
Departmento de Cine of the Universidad de los Andes 98
Derbeneva, L. 199
Dern, Laura 171
De Rosier, G. Phillippe 76
Derricks, Cleavant 227
Derthick, Hazel I. 148
Descy, Rohanne 174
de Shields, Andre 84
DesHotel, Rob 234
Desio, Alfred 109
Det Lille Theater 83
Deverich, Nat G. 143
De Vita, Gina Marie 174
DeVries, Beth 106
DeWitt, Fay 132
Deyo, Blanche 66
De Young, Rusty 222
DeZuniga, Tony 122
D'Flon, Manuel 94
Diamond, Barry 221
Diamond, Dustin 216
Diamond, Laura 96
DIC 170, 217, 218, 222
Dickson, Jane 78
Diego, Juan 153
Diller, Phyliss 134
DiMaggio, John 233
Dinamonster of Oz 51
Dinapoli, Constance 99
Dingus, Don 98
Dinus, William 144
Dirik, Shana 136, 137
Dirk 45
Disclosure of the Great and Terrible 200
Discovery 196
The Disenchanted Princess of Oz 55
Disney, Melissa 180
Disney, Walt 147, 193, 194
Disney Channel 246
Disneyland 83
Disneyland (TV show) 193, 194
Disneyland Fourth Anniversary Show 193–194
Disneyland Records 131
DiStefano, Dan 220
Dittman, Dean 76
Divins, Charles 234
Dixon, Eddy 171

DK Publishing 240
Do It for Oz 53
Do Valle, Maurício 166
Dr. Angelina Bean in Oz 58
Dr. Caligari 246
Dodd, Jimmie 193
Dodson, Ed 98
Doe, John 174
Dog, Snoop Doggy 164
Doll, Daisy 148
Doll, Gracie 148
Doll, Harry 148
Doll, Tiny 148
Donahue, Ann 88, 215
Donatelli, Nick 222
Donato, Sam 137
Donavan, Mike 173
Donner, Robert 164
The Donny and Marie Show 203
Donovan, Paul 230
Doria, Vera 69
Dorn, Harding 76
Dorn, Margaret 212
Dorothy and Alice 99
Dorothy and Old King Crow 55
Dorothy and the Green Gobbler of Oz 58
Dorothy and the Lizard of Oz 54
Dorothy and the Magic Belt 59
Dorothy and the Scarecrow in Oz 138–139
Dorothy and the Seven Leaf Clover 55
Dorothy and the Wizard in Oz (book) 13, 68, 70, 78, 82, 194
Dorothy and the Wizard in Oz (Colonial radio) 134, 136
Dorothy and the Wizard in Oz, (record album) 130
Dorothy and the Wizard of Oz (Hotchner) 87
Dorothy and the Wooden Soldiers 59
Dorothy in the Land of Oz, (cartoon) 204–205
Dorothy in the Mysterious Land of Oz 78–79, *79, 80, 81*
Dorothy Meets Alice or The Wizard of Wonderland 96–97
Dorothy Meets Ozma of Oz 170
Dorothy of Oz 51
Dorothy: Return to Oz 60
Dorothy Returns to Oz (anthology) 62
Dorothy Returns to Oz (script treatment) 194
Dorothy: This Side of the Rainbow 51
Dorothy's Mystical Adventures in Oz 54
Dot and Tot in Merryland 10
Douglas, Ashanti 212
Douglas, Buddy 213
Douglas, Christopher 234

Index

Douglas, Jay 185
Dowling, Bairbre 159
Downey Fabric Softener 236
Downing, Al 72
Downs, David 100
Doyle, James P. 108
Doyle, Major 148
Drago, Barbara 222
Dragons in Oz 57
Drake, Alfred 212
Dramatic Feature Films 141, 143
Dranet, Leontine 139, 143
Draper, Douglas 89
Draper, John 183
Dream a Little Dream 219
The Dreamer of Oz 172–173
Drew, Norman 170
Driscoll, David 134, 137
Driver, John 88
Drobininoi, G. 199
Dryden, Mack 216
Duane, Diane 205
Dudynsky, Ivan 221
Dufau, Oscar 204, 205
Duff, Claudette 178
Duffy, Albert 193
Duggan, Lindsay 178
Dughi, Mikal 227
Dukas, James 132
Dulabone, Chris 53, 54, 55, 58, 62
Dumont, José 166
Dumont, Richard 206
Dunakin, Ray 240
Dunaway, Faye 243
Dunham, Duwayne 171
Dunlap, Romola (Remus) 212
Dunmore, Beatrice 162
Dunn, Roger 220
Dunn, Sophie 95, 96
Dunn, Tom 88
Dunsmure, John 69
Dunstan, Joy 161
Duran, Micki 222
Durham, Britain 173
Duritz, Adam 247
Dusenbury, Collin 99
Duval Freres 68
Dwan, Dorothy 144
Dworsky, Richard A. 89
Dworsky, Sally 88
Dynomutt 248
Dzhigarhanyan, Armen 175

E&G 221
E.C. Comics 122, 125
Eager, Edward 54
Eaglet Civic Theater 75
Eames, Curtis 176
Earthworm Jim 229
Eastern Michigan University 91, 94
Ebbs, Elizabeth 96
Eber, J. 184
Ebsen, Buddy 150
Edens, Michael 220

Education Reform in Kentucky: A Teacher's Search for the Wizard of Oz 184–185
Edward, Jennifer 198
Edward Stern 47
Edwards, Paul 99
Edwards, Sam 131, 132
Egglesfield, Colin 232
Egnor, Tara 91
Egor's Funhouse Goes to Oz 53
Ehrlich, Amy 222
Einhorn, Edward 54
Eiser, Shmuel 103
Ekran TV 199
El Camino College 77
El Mago de Oz (stage show) 94
El Mago de Oz Cuento de Frank Baum 94
Elam, Jack 216
Elder, Grace 68
The Electric Company 243
Elfman, Danny 220
Elimelech, Sharon 103
Elinosoi, A. 199
Elkhorn, John 130
Eller, Jamie 185
Elli in Magic Land 199
Elli Meets the Friends 202
Elliot, Peter 168
Elliot, Richard Bruce 218
Ellis, David 222
Ellison, Matthew 186, 187, 188, 189, 190
Ellzey, David 172
Elmes, Frederick 171
Elroi, Limor 103
Elton John 247
Elwes, Cassian 174
The Emerald Burrito of Oz 60
The Emerald City (alternate title, Wizard of Oz) 3
The Emerald City (Russian TV) 200
Emerald City of Oz (Colonial Radio) 136, 137
The Emerald City of Oz (Baum book) 4, 14–18, 48, 56, 121, 133, 211
The Emerald City of Oz (1969 play) 83
Emerald City Press 50, 52,54, 55, 60
The Emerald Ring of Oz 60
Emmons, Mrs. 140
The Enchanted Apples of Oz 123
The Enchanted Emeralds of Oz 61
The Enchanted Gnome of Oz 55
The Enchanted Island 50
The Enchanted Island of Oz 50
The Enchanted Island of Yew (book) 47
The Enchanted Island of Yew (de Lavallade) 95
The Enchanted Island of Yew (1937 play) 72

The Enchanted Princess of Oz 47
The Enchanted Tree of Oz 127
Endo, Masaharu 207
Energizer batteries commercial 237
Engerman, John 87
Englesman, Julie Rae 234
Ennals, Roger 168
Enoki 221
Eric Smith Puppet Theater 98
Erickson, Carl M. 148
Eroz, Mazhar 155
Escarrega, Geno 215
Eshbaugh, Ted 146
Eskenazi, Diane 173
Espindola, Carlos 94
Essex, Gregg R. 100
Estridge-Gray, Lisa 107
Estudio 5 y 3, 94
Eubank, Bill 71, 80, 82, 183
Evanier, Mark 205
Evans, Andrea 234
Evans, Bob 54
Evans, Jeramy 91
Evans, Robert J. 54
Evans, Sara 247
Evett, John 98
Evslin, Bernard 158
Experimental Performers Association 175
Eyster, Tim 172

Fables 126
Fahn, Melissa 116
Fainsinger, Liane 108
Fairfax, Marjorie 136
Fairy Circle in Oz 53
A Fairy Queen in Oz 57
Fairuza Returns to Oz 185
Fairylogue and Radio Plays 68–69, 138, 212
Faison, George 84
Falco, Ralph 94, 153
Fame 206
Family Vision Press 60
Famous Theatre Company 132
Fantagraphics Press 126
Fantasia III 153
The Fantastic Funhouse of Oz 53
Fantasy Island 211–212, 244
The Farewell to Oz 57
Farley, Chris 221
Farmer, Philip Jose 54
Farnon, Shannon 204
Farrell, Gene 196
Farrington, Mark Richard 106
The Fate of a Crown 141
Father Goose: His Book 3, 12
Father Goose in Oz 50
Faulkner, Gay 162
Faust 152
Favorite Children's Books 182
Fawcett Columbine 55
Fawcett Comics 121

Fearless 218
Federal Express commercial 237–238
Federer, Michelle 116
Fee, Kathleen 206
Fein, Mitzi 76
Feiss, David 217
Feld, Kenneth 105, 106
Feldman, Alexander O'Brien 214
Felix, Geoff 168
Felix, Philip J. 171
Feller, Sid 202
Fellner, Istvan 170
Fenn, Sherilyn 171
Fennell, George 134, 135, 136
Fennelly, Parker 127
Ferapontov, Vladimir 199
Fernandez, Juan 174
Fernandez, Martha 98
Fernstrom, Ray 193
Feuer, Otto 158
Fields, Gil 153
Fields, Herbert 148
Fields, W.C. 149, 150
The Fiery God of the Marrans 60
Filgo, Jackie 234
Filgo, Jeff 234
Filiminov, Vladimir 199
Fillian, Armand 134, 135, 136
Fillippov, Roman 199
Film Laboratories of Canada 146
Film Makers Cooperative Production 152
Filmation Associates 158
Fine, Sherry 76
Fink, Mark 203
Finn, Richard 180
Finnegan, Lynne "Patsy" 72
Finnson, Melissa 88
Finwall, Alyce 188
Fiorazo, Joe 98
Fiore, Roland 76
Firesign Theatre 134
Firestone, Diane 174
1st Books Library 59
First Comics 123, 124
First Comics Graphic Novels 123, 124
Fiscus, Deborah 188
Fisher, Adrienne 109, 110, 112
Fisher, Carrie 164
Fisher, Mark 106
Fitzgerald, Christopher 116
Flagg, Tom 90
Flagg, Tyler 111
Flaherty, Joe 215
Flake, Suanna 76
Flaviano, Péricles 166
Fleming, Bill 230
Fleming, Paul 87
Fleming, Victor 148, 150, 163
The Flight of the Gump 95
Florey, Thomas F. 89
The Flying Bus in Oz 58
Flynn, Matt 146

Flynn, Sissie 146
Focus on the Family 134
Follow the Yellow Brick Gold 248
Follow the Yellow Brick Road 80
Fondacaro, Phil 227
A Foolish Fable from Oz 62
For Our Children: The Concert 246
Foray, June 197
The Forbidden Fountain of Oz 49
Ford, Paul 158
Fordon, Leslie 108
Foren, Dale 91
The Forest Monster of Oz 54
The Forgotten Forest of Oz 124
Formica, Fern 148
Forum Theatre, Los Angeles 70, 146
Fournier, Gerry 220
Fox, Dorothy 162
Fox, Ken 247
Fox, Shayna 222
Fox, Ted 174
Fox-TV 222, 227, 228, 233, 245
Foxworthy, Jeff 237
Fragments of a Fate Forgotten 152
Fraley, Pat 218
Franchett, Andrea 88
Francis, Carol Ann 206
Franck, Tom 98
Francks, Cree Summer 170
Francoeur, Bill 112
Frank, Addie E. 148
Frank, Brent 106
Frank, Charles 216
Frank, Jason David 228
Frank, Sid 132
Franklin, Chester M. 143
Franklin, Sidney 143
Franks, Philip 133
Franz, Maybelle 76
Fraser, Brent 171
Freed, Arthur 148
Freedman, Jeff 54
Freedom Fighters 125
Freeman, J.E. 171
Frees, Paul 199
Frick, Hollee 91
Fricke, John 184
Friedkin, Gary 164
Friedman, Ed 158
Friedman, Marcia 134, 135
Frierson, Leon 222
Froebel, Kristen B. 88
The Frogman of Oz 57
Fuhrmann, Till 230
Fuji Eight Company Ltd. 173
Fuji Project 173
Fuji TV 214
Fujita, Toshiko 175
Fukube, Ichiro 221
Fukui, Masatoshi 205
Fukumoto, Tomo 205
Fuller, Robert 216
Fullilove, Donald 199

Fullmer, Richard 75
Funicello, Annette 193
The Funnies 121
Further Adventures of the Wizard of Oz 132
Fusco, Paul 217
Fuso Publishing, Inc. 173
Futurama 233
Fwiirp in Oz 62
F/X 229

G.W. Dillingham Co. 49
Gabrielson, Frank 72, 76, 90, 194
GAC-TV 247
Gaess, Hilary Lee 153
Gaffney, Mo 234
Gaffney, Simon 96
Gaffney, Tara 96
Gage, Jeffrey 135, 136, 137
Gage, Matilda 10
Galaxy Adventures of Space Oz 220–221
Galde Press 55
Gale, Ed 172
Gallant, Tom 230
Gallegos, Vernon 174
Galli, Allen 107
Gama, Ubirajara 166
Games People Play 211–212
Gannaway, Atticus 54
Gannaway, Ryan 54
Garafolo, Janeane 221
Garcia, Carolyn 101
Garcia, Hank 203
Garcia, Kyla 111, 114, 115
Garcia, Xavier 169
"garden of meats" 18, 19, 57
The Gardener's Boy of Oz 56
Gardner, Julian P. 212
Gardner, Martin 54
Gardner, Richard A. 54
Gardner, Thaisa L. 148
Gardner, Worth 90
Garfinkle, Gayle 206
Garigan, Tom 98
Garland, Judy 130, 148, 150, 151, 174, 197, 244, 248
Garman, Stephanie 211
Garrett, Pat 97
Garrick Theatre, Chicago 66
Garris, Mick 232
Gary, Linda 133
Gasco, Elaine 207
A Gathering of Guns 216
Gathering of Heroes 125
Gavras, Julie 186
Gay Men's Chorus 96
Gebbie, Melinda 124
Geffen, David 220
Geffen Film Company 220
Gekko Film Corp. 230
Gelbart, Allan 218
The Gene London Show 198
Genelle, Richard 228

Index

General Electric Show 'n Tell Picturesound 131
General Hospital 247
Gentry, Roger 153
Geo M. HIll Co. 7, 49
George, Lynda Day 211
George, Melissa 232
George, Rhett 116
George W. Ogilvie & Co. 49
Georges, Liz 218
Gerber, Joan 204
Gerdt, Zinovi 199
Gering, Galen 234
Gerlich, Jakob 148
Gersman, Shawn 98
Gets, Malcolm 113
GI Joe, Jr. 122
The Giant Garden of Oz 60
The Giant Horse of Oz 36–37
Gibbons, Cedric 148
Giblin, William A. 148
Gick, Greg 55
Gifford, Barry 171
The Gifts Are Divine Plan Is Awesome 185
Gigeroff, Lex 230
Gilbert, Willie 205
Gilberton Co. 121
Gilborn, Steve 172
Gillespie, Darlene 193
Gillis, Paulina 217, 220
Gimpel, Erica 206
Gingerbread Man 47
Gist, Rod 172
Gjovaag, Eric 52
Glamack, Mark 203
Glass, Ron 231
The Glass Cat in Oz 55
Glassboro New Jersey Center for the Arts 99
Glassboro Summer Children's Theatre 96
Glazer, Ethan 214
Gleason, Joanna 134
Gleitsman, Alan L. 165
Glennon, Herbert 139
Glicken, Jack 148
Glinda of Oz 30–31, 31, 59
Glover, Crispin 171
Glover, David 95
Glover, Susan 206
Glynn, Thomas 196
The Gnome King of Oz 35–36, 37
Godfrey, Hal 66, 68
Goding, Teresa 135
Goe, Bob 204, 205
Goff, John F. 164
Gogin, Michael Lee 164
Gold, Ari 212
Gold Key Comics 122
Goldberger, Amy Beth 186, 187, 188, 189, 190
Golden Orchestra 132
Golden Records 132
Goldstein, Eric 188

Goldstein, Stanley 188
Goldthwaite, Bobcat 178
Goldwyn, Samuel 149
Golin, Steve 171
Golino, Valeria 246
Golomb, I. 199
Gomavitz, Lewis 193
Gonçalves, Antônio 167
Gonzalez, Marissa 111, 116
Good, Frank 144
The Good Witch of Oz 57
Goodman, John 134
Goodspeed, Elizabeth Fuller 71
Goodsun, Barbara 228
Goodwin, James 214
Goodwin, Laura 214
Gorbett, Jason 233
Gorden, Daryl 78
Gorden, Debbie 78
Gordon, Anthony 164
Gordon, George 204, 205
Gorecki, Heather 88
Gorelov, Vladimir 199
Gorey, Jill 231
Gorky Films Studios 175
Gorski, Kristen Lee 116
Gosselaar, Mark-Paul 216
Gottschalk, Louis F. 20, 69, 108, 139, 141, 143
Gould, Bobbie 139
Gounod, Charles 152
Gow, Christine 202
Gowers, Bruce 222
Graas, John Christian 214
Grabe, Fred 158
Grace, Topher 233
Graeff, Tom 153
Graham, Ronny 202
Grammat, Georges 170, 171
Gramova, O. 199
Grampa in Oz 33, 127
Grand Opera House, Chicago 64
Grandy, Craig 199
Grandy, Melody 55, 239
Graney, John Link 223
Granger, Carolyn E. 148
Granite, Judy 76
Grapewin, Charley 148
Grasso, Joe 212
Graver, Ben 127
Gray, David A. 88
Gray, Richard 107
The Gray Nun of Belgium 141, 143
The Great Adventures of Young Santa 228
Great Film Stamps commercial 237
The Great Wishy Woz 133–134
The Great Wizard 82
Green, Seymour Willis 222
The Green Dolphin of Oz 57
The Green Goblins of Oz 62
The Green Star of Oz 51
Greenaway, David 168

Greenberg, Morris 229
Greene, Lorne 165
Greene, Stanley 162
Greenfield, Gary 203
Greenfield, John 98
Greenwood, Paul 95
Greenwood, Winifred 138
Greer, George 203
Greg Kihn Band 246
Grenke, David 99
Gresens, Gail 98
Grey, Joel 105, 116
Griffin, Kathy 178
Griffith, Ralph 125
Grilikhes, Michel M. 98
Grimes, Jack 131
Gringhuis, Dirk 45
Grizzard, Mark 114, 115
Groen, Pam 78
Groenendaal, Cris 87
Groening, Matt 233
Grogan, Clare 97
Gros, Irene Griffin 71
Gross, Michael 170
Grosser, Arthur 207
Growing Pains 246
GTRK 106
The Guiding Light 212
Guilherme, Roberto 166
Guillame, Robert 134
Guinness, Rowena 174
Gumus, Seyhan 155
Gunn, Archie 66
Gunn, Joe 98
Gurses, Yilzabram 155
The Guru of Ours 122
Guschchin, Vadim 229, 231
Gushman, Gerri 91
Gyerasimov, Yevgyeni 175

Haack, Bruce 73
Haaland, Bret 233
Haas, Dorothy 55
Haas, Mark E. 55
Hackady, Hal 199
Haddigan, Mark 95, 96
Hagopian, Dean 206, 207
Hague, Albert 206
Haid, Charles 172
Haines, David 107
Hairston, Charles 89
Hakosem! 103–104, 106
Hakosem Mae'Achorei Hakosem 184
Hakosem Me'Eretz Utz 106, 184
Hal Seeger Studios 182
Halas, John 199
Halas and Batchelor Cartoon Films 199
Haldeman, Harry F. 139, 140, 141, 143
Hale, Jennifer 134, 222
Haley, Jack 148, 204
Haley, Jack, Jr. 184
Halfpenny, John 220

Hall, Danny 146
Hall, Kevin Peter 214
Hallet, Morgan 206
Halliday, Karen 95
Halperin, Barbara 78
Halston 164
Hames, Ron 196
Hamill, Mark 134
Hamilton, Craig 126
Hamilton, Frank 172
Hamilton, Margaret 4, 72, 93, 94, 148, 152, 158, 196, 204, 243
Hamlett, Christina 95
Hamlin, Fred 64, 65
Hammond, Bill 135, 136, 137
Hammond, Earl 182, 212
Hample, Stu 202
Hancock, A. Wade 96
Hand, Robert 1265
Hand of Doom Publications 126
Hands, Terry 96
Handy Mandy in Oz 41–2
Haney, David 164
Hanky Pank Players 131
Hanna, Elizabeth 165, 170, 220
Hanna, William 203, 204, 205, 215
Hanna Barbera Productions 203, 204, 205, 215
Hansen, Juanita 143
Happily Ever After 247
Harburg, E.Y. 72, 76, 90, 96, 103, 106, 130, 148, 150, 184, 197
Harcourt, Brace and World 54
Hard Road 52
Harden, Bertran 109
Hardenbrook, Dave 55
Harding, Laverne 158
Hardy, Hagood 207
Hardy, Oliver 144, 145, 146
Hare, Todd 185
Harlow, Jade 234
Harmetz, Aljean 184, 204
Harnage, Phil 170
Harnell, Jess 180
Harney, Ben 84
Harper, Ken 84, 85, 162
Harper, William 102, 103, 104
Harriell, Marcy 113
Harris, Glenn Walker, Jr. 171
Harris, John H. 72
Harris, Mildred 141, 143
Harris, Renee 84
Harrison, Edith Ogden 13
Harrison, Gavin 223
Harrison, Jennilee 211
Harrison, Mary 90
Harrison, Tracy 88
Harsha, Amy 88
Hart, Peter 90
Hartley, Justin 234
Hartman, C.L. 158
Hartman, Becky 222
Hartzell, Linda 87, 107
Harvey Hits 122

Harvey Publications 122
Hasheian, Gwen 96
Hatchfield, Mark 183
Hathaway Group 184
Hauber, William 144
Haugen, Rana 88
The Haunted Castle of Oz 58
Hawkins, Cherie 168
Hawley, Wanda 144
Hawley Publications 121
Hayashabira, Megumi 175, 228
Hayden, J. Charles 140, 141
Hayes, Helen 149
Hayes, Jeff 232
Haynes, Tiger 84
Hayter, David 232
Hazelle, Little Play Theatre 77
Hazelton, Herb 158
HBO Nagai 207, 211
Healey, Denis 203
The Healing Power of Oz 56
Healy, Bart 97
The Heart That Changed Color 182
Heath, Lori 230
Hedningarna 109
Hehmeyer, Dick 202
Heinlein, Robert 55
Heinz Ketchup commercial 237
Helgenberger, Marg 215
Hellman, Caryn 99
Hello Kitty 170
Hello Kitty's Furry Tale Theater 170
Helms, Lyne 161
Helmsley, Sherman 216, 221
Hemphill, Shirley 213
Hemser, Ilhan 155
Henderson, A.J. 206, 207
Henderson, Donald 146
Henderson, Florence 202
Henderson, Marla 221
Henderson, Zenna 30
Hennessey, Dan 217
Hennessey, Ellen-Ray 217
Henry, Deanne 227
Henry, John 234
Henry, Mary Ann 186
Henry Ryan Films 186
Hensel, Howard 76
Henson, Brian 167, 214
Herbst, Joseph 148
Hern, Pat 164
Herndon, Barbara 231
Herrera, Manuel 116
Herrier, Mark 216
Herron, Joel 182, 183
Herron, Keith 88
Herron, Sandra 91
Hess, Robin 55
Hesser, Lisa 234
Heston, Charles 184
Hetherton, Drewe 107
Hewitt, Christopher 211
Hewitt, David L. 152

Heyward, Andy 170, 203, 217
Hi Spot Comics 121
Hibbert, Edward 229
Hickox, James 176
Hidaka, Noriko 223
The Hidden Prince of Oz 61
The Hidden Valley of Oz 45, 59
High Incident 228
Highley, Ronald 76
Higuchi, Masakazu 217
Hilfert, Susan 116
Hill, Arthur 64
Hill, Claudia 96
Hill, Glen 180
Hillier, Justin 95
Hinchey, Catie 88
Hine, Michele 168
Hirchhorn, Joel 171
Hirsch, Andrew 222
Hirschfield, Jeffrey 230
Hirsh, Michael 220
The His Majesty Scarecrow of Oz 21, 140, 141–142
Hisaishi, Joe 165
Hisar Films 155
Hita, Yubi 175
Hite, Mabel 66
Hoberg, Rick 204
Hodgeman, Lucille 71
Hodgson, Leslie 168
Hofbauer, Jakob 148
Hoffenstein, Samuel 148
Hoffer, Bernard 212
Hoffman, Jack 90
Hoffmeyer, Randy 87
Hogan, Bosco 159, 176
Hogg in Oz 122
Holbrook, Hal 180
Holcomb, Rod 215
Holder, Geoffrey 84, 85
Holdridge, Lee 172
Holiday in Oz 96
Holkeboer, John 91, 94
Holkeboer, Katherine 91
Holloway, Sterling 193, 194
The Hollywood Road to Oz 184
Hollywood Studio Orchestra 132
Holzman, Winnie 116
Home Again 216
Homme, Richard 207
Hook, Walter 76
Hopkins, Mark 168
Hopkinson, Marian 127
Horagi, Mifuyu 228
Horne, Lena 162
Horrocks, Jane 178
Horror-Scope Scoob 245
Horrors of the Red Planet 153
Horsley, Lee 216
Horton, Adrienne 230
Horton, John 119
Horvath, Jan 90
Horvitz, Louis J. 106
Horvitz, Wayne 99
Horwitz, Sandi 108

Hoshikawa, Yasuko 221
Hot Air 220
Hot Shots Part Deux 246
Hotchner, Kathy 87
Hotchner, Steve 87
Hoty, Tony 90
Houston, Margaret 97
How the Wizard Came to Oz 50
How the Wizard Saved Oz 50
Howard, Kisha 116
Howard, Ron 132
Howarton, Dana 133
Howat, Stacey 88
Howe, James 55
Howerton, Clarence C. 148
Hoxit, Linda 202
Hoy, Helen M. 148
Hoy, Marguerite A. 148
Hubbard, Al 126
Hubbert, Cork 164
Huber, Liza 234
Hudis, Mark 234
Huetter, Melani 183
Hughes, Miko 225
Huke, Steve 88
Hulan, David 55
Hulse, James R. 148
The Hungry Tiger of Oz 35
Hungry Tiger Press 54, 60
Hunsberger, Victor, Jr. 164
Hunt, Will 216
Hunter 243
Hunter, Greg 55, 56
Hunter, Tim 186
Hurley, Katie 111
Hurray for Oz 53
Hurst, Ben 218
Hurwitz, Harry 164
"Hutch" 146
Hutchins, Baden 161
Hutchinson, Sylvia 76
Hyde, James 234
Hyman, Earle 212
Hynes, Lisa 230
Hyperion Entertainment 222
Hyperion Pictures 185

I Married a Munchkin 184
I, Toto 52
I Want to Grow Up in Oz 62
IAC Film 106
The Ice King of Oz 124
Ickes, Alison 78, 80, 81
Imeni 175
Imperato, Carlo 206
In Dreamy Jungletown 143
In Other Lands Than Oz 62
In Search of Oz 221
Inbar, Noam 103
Inglis, Julia 56
Ingram, Donna Patrice 162
Iniesta, Fernando Martin 153
Innovsions/USA 165
Inter Planetary Pictures, Inc. 161

International Wizard of Oz Club 49, 50, 58, 61, 150, 176
Interset Press 50
Into the Mystic 227–228
Intropedi, Josie 69
Invisible Inzi of Oz 61
Irwin, Charles 148
Irvin Feld & Kenneth Feld Productions 106
Isacksen, Peter 164
Israeli Oz dramatizations 98, 103, 105, 106, 184
Issever, Murvet 155
Ista 76
It Came from Angel Grove 228
Ito, Brian 225
Itoman 207
It's a Heart 182
Itsuki, Natsumi 175
Ivanov, Andrei 175
Izzy the Religious Nut 101

Jabberwocky 132
Jack Haley Jr. Productions 184
Jack Pumpkinhead and the Sawhorse 48
Jack Pumpkinhead of Oz 37, 71
Jackson, Clinton 162
Jackson, Jackie 199
Jackson, Jermaine 199
Jackson, Marlon 199
Jackson, Michael 162, 199
Jackson, R. Eugene 106
Jackson, Tito 199
Jackson, Tom 203
The Jackson Five 199
Jacobs, Mark 96
Jafelice, Loretta 217
Jala, Jodi Kar 100
James, Blake 196
James, Bobb 91
James, Andrew Thomas 95
Jamison, Nick 180
Jansen, Juanita 139
Janson, Len 203
January, Lois 148
Japaneze Oz dramatizations, 86, 93, 98, 165, 166, 170, 171, 174, 205, 207, 208, 209, 210, 211, 214, 220, 221, 222, 223, 224, 225, 226, 227, 228
Jaquest, Christian 96
Jarman, Reginald 159
Jaumandreu, Francisco 153
Jean Gros French Marionettes 71
Jeff Foxworthy Show 237
Jellison, John 113
Jellison, L.J. 116
Jenkins, Carol Mayo 206
Jenkins, Patricia 130
Jenkins, Sarah 109
Jenks, Ethel 70
Jenne, Jeanne M. 94
Jewel 105–106
Jewison, Norman 197

Jim Henson Presents Mother Goose Stories 214
Jim Henson Productions 214
Jim Henson's Creature Shop 214
Jimenez, John 183
"Jimmy Bulber in Oz" 47
Jirafee, Momar 188
Joel, Gil S. 56
Johansen, Mila 99
John Dough and the Cherub 47, 69
John Dough and the Cherub (1910 film) 139
John R. Neill Visits Oz 61
Johnson, Anne-Marie 213
Johnson, Cage S. 171
Johnson, Carlton 162
Johnson, Jarrett 114, 118
Johnson, Jeremy 99
Johnson, Jimmy 131, 132
Johnson, Josef 70
Johnson, Katrina 222
Johnson, Louis 162
Johnson, Myron 89
Johnson, Patrick 183
Johnson, Robin 230
Joleron Production Company 182, 183
Jolly Bill and Jane 127
Jones, Chuck 197, 198
Jones, Dick 188
Jones, Freddie 171
Jones, Mark 203
Jones, Quincy 162
Jones, Rodney 229
Jones, Tamika 105
Jones, Vernon H. 198
Jordan, Glenn 76
Jose, Katherine 161
José, Fernando 166
Joseph, Al 153
Joseph, Karen 174
Joseph, Kristen 91
Journey Back to Oz (animated film) 158–159, 212
Journey Back to Oz (play) 94
Journey Beneath the Sea 227
Journey to the West 226
The Joust in Oz 52
Judge, Ian 96
The Judy Garland Show 197
Julsey, James 172
Junior League Plays 71, 72, 127
Jurman, Karl 97
Jurwich, Don 204, 205
Jutras, Benoit 109

K Factory 228
Kabo, Olga 175
Kabumpo in Oz 32
Kachivas, Lou 158
Kafkafi, Yaron 103
Kagan, Mike 202
Kahnert, Geoff 217
Kairo, Noriaki 171
Kalderon, Haldas 106

Kaliko in Oz 56
Kalisher, U. 199
Kaluza, Lesw 158
Kamijo, Osamu 221
Kaminsky, Stuart 56
Kamiyama, Takumi 207
Kanai, Mika 223, 228
Kane, John 96
Kaneko, Toshio 207
Kanevskii, Andrei 199
Kanezawa, Katsumata 221
Kangaroo 248
Kanter, Robert 148
Kapadia, Shaival 98
Kaplan, Jonathan Charles 223, 225
The Karate Kid 248
Karkar, Annaluna 174
Karr, Phyliss Ann 56
Karseler, Seda 155
Karseler, Semra 155
Karston, Joe 153
Karston-Hewitt Organization 153
Kasem, Casey 204, 205
Kasenow, Peggy L. 94
Kasha, Al 171
Kaskel, Stephanie 90
Kaspar in the Wonderful World of Oz 109
Kasradze, G. 199
Kassir, John 229
Kates, Kimberly 176
Katleman, Michael 232
Kato, Julia 231
Katsumasa, Ryuichi 221
Katten, Steven 184
Katz, Raymond 203
Katzenberg, Janet 78
Kaulbach, Helen 98
Kawahara, Sarah 106
Kawashi, Giosu 175
Kawaye, Janice 170
Kawtsu, Matsuhiko 175
Kay, Bob 174
Kay, Dee 202
Kayan, Orrin 76
Kaye, Stubby 87
Keane, James 227
Keaton, Diane 164
Keenan, William J. 199
Keene, William 194
Keighley, William 130
Keil, Bill 203, 204, 205
Kellerman, Sally 188
Kellison, Daniel 229
Kellogg, Jean 49, 197
Kelly, Brian 188
Kelly, Charles E. 148
Kelly, David Patrick 171
Kelly, Jessie E. 148
Kelly, Matt 112, 115
Kelly, Nancy 127
Kelly, Ned 161
Kelly, Tim 111
Kenmore, Joan 148

Kennedy, Jeff 235
Kennedy, Joanne 108
Kennedy, Shirley Ann 148
Kenney, Larry 212
Kent, Art 102
Kent School 77
Keown, Paul 97
Kerbel, Naomi 214
Kerr, Brook 234
Kerr, Kathy Fouche 94
Kerr, Stuart 125
Kerr, Wayne 169
Kerrigan, Michael J. 214
Kesden, Brad 217
Kesey, Ken 100, 101, 102
Kesey, Stephanie 100
Kesey, Zane 100
Kessel, LaVona 183
Kestelman, Sara 159
Ketamis, Peter 178
KG Productions 186
Kiblinger, Katherine 76
Kid-Ro 229
Kidder, Margot 206
Kids Radio 133
Kienlen, Patrick 234
Kikel, Frank 148
Kikuchi, Seiji 221
Kiman, Jay 105
Kimma, Aleksandr 199
King, Charlie 222
King, Craig 185
King, Dennis 214
King, Donald 162
King, Freeman 164
King, Mabel 84, 162
King, Peter 112
King, Reina 213
King, William 144
The King of Gee-Whiz 67
King Rinkitink 25
Kingdom of Bastinda 200
Kinney, Dave 222
Kino, Tatsuji 205
Kirby, Scott 233
Kirchner, Alexis 172
Kirsanoff 158
Kirschner, David 172
Kistler, Donene 228
Kitchen Sink Press 124
Kivitt, Ted 76
Klein, Kathy A. 94
Kleinbort, Barry 113, 114
Kleinschmitt, Carl 202
Klekolta, Paul 222
Kleputzkii, U. 199
Klima, Bernhard 148
Klinck, Elizabeth 207
Kline, K. 56
Kline, Paula 91
Knapp, Ann 228
Knight, Adrian 207
Knight, Chris 202
Knight, Keith 220
Knight, Sally 90

Knoll, Bill 171
Knopf 59
Ko Vert, Frederick 144
Kobata, Minoru 207
Kobayashi, Koji 165
Kodo 109
Koenenkamp, H.F. 144
Koestner, Emma 148
Koestner, Mitzi 148
Koestner, Willi 148
Kolvinovskii, L. 199
Konca, Cemal 155
Konchakova, A. 199
Kong, Emilie 204
Konova, Karin 227
Kopelow, Kevin 222
Korman, Lindsay 234
Kosberg, Robert 233
Kosiczky, Karl 148
Kosmachev, I. 199
Koste, Virginia (Glasgow) 91, 94, 95, 96
Kostich, Sonya 88
Kotula, Bobbi 107
Kouda, Mariko 220
Kozicki, Adam Edwin 148
Koziel, Joseph J. 148
Kramer, Dolly 148, 178
Kramer, Frank 44
Kramer, Marsha 87
Kranzler, Emil 148
Kraus, Ken 222
Kraus, Mary Ann 95
Krause, E. Jay 194
Krawford, Tom 94
Krebs, Nita 148
Kreisl, George 158
Krelatov, Yevgyenii 175
Krenz, Frank 105, 106
Krinit, David 134, 136, 137
Krizmanich, Jack 234
Krizsan, Les 230
Krofft, Marty 202, 203
Krofft, Sid 202, 203
Krofftette Dancers and Water Follies 202
Krukowski, Paul 158
Krumm, Paul 76
Kruschen, Jack 164
Kryczko, Ted 133
Krystal Commercial 236
Kubica, Cindy 186
Kugler, Carol 107, 108
Kuhn, Michael 171
Kuhr, Joseph 228
Kukla, Fran and Ollie 193
Kulleseid, Eleanor 183
Kulp, Nancy 87
Kunis, Mila 233
Kurtz, Gary 168
Kurtz, Roberta 214
Kushner, Donald 171
Kushnir, Todd 101
Kutcher, Ashton 233
Kutsu, Shiki 175

L. Frank Baum: The Royal Historian of Oz 184
L. Frank Baum's The Marvelous Land of Oz 88–90
LaBarbera, "Little Jeane" 148
Labrosse, Terrence 207
Lacey, Mike 222
Ladd, Diane 171
Ladd, Fred 158
Ladya 175
Lagler, Rene 202
Lahr, Bert 130, 148, 151
Lai, Carlene 109
Laikin, Christine 232
Laing, Mark 230
Lamarche, Maurice 180
Lamb, Gil 194
Lambrecht, Candace 101
Lamontagne, Cynthia 233
The Land Before Oz 62
The Land of Oz (Baum book) 4, 10–12, 14, 18, 21, 29, 47, 66, 68, 94, 95, 121, 153, 158, 159, 168, 169, 193, 195, 205, 208, 209, 231, 239
Land of Oz (Colonial Radio) 136
The Land of Oz (comic-book) 125
The Land of Oz (McClellan cartoon) 147
The Land of Oz (1928 play) 71
The Land of Oz (1933 cartoon) 146
The Land of Oz (Pasadenan Festival) 78, 82
The Land of Oz (Selig) 231
The Land of Oz (Shirley Temple Show) 194
The Land of Oz (theme park) 83, 155
Land of the Wizard Witch 77–78
Landau, Tina 113
Landisburg, Valerie 206
Lando, Brian 216
Landsburg, Dave 203
Lane, Daniel 105
Lane, Nathan 105
Lang, Paul Stewart 214
Lange, Hilda 148
Langen, Mandy 109, 111
Langley, Noel 148, 150
Lansbury, Angela 220
Lanza, Richard 183
Lapidot, Avi 106
LaPlante, William 145
La Prade, Jann 76
Larange, Stewart 167
Larkin, Alison 134
Laroque, Christine 207
Larson, Darrell 106
Larson, Ian 188
The Last Egyptian (book) 47
The Last Egyptian (movie) 140–141, 142
Latham, Larry 204

Latham, Lynn 202
Latifah, Queen 164
Latsham, George 193
Lattori, Gino 161
The Laughing Dragon of Oz 46–7
Laughlin, Anna 64
Laumer, Keith 56
Laumer, March 52, 56, 57
Laurents, Clyde 87
Laurie, Piper 167
Lauris, Anna 107
LaVancher, Donielle 96
The Lavender Bear of Oz 52
Lavi, Arik 103
Law, Leslie 107
Lawrence, Sheila R. 222
Lawrence, Steven 205
Laws, Maury 197, 202
Lawson, Lee 212
Lawson, Merrie 174
Lay, Carol 123
Laye, Dilys 95
Layton, Ron 173
Lea, Nicholas 227
Leach, Mecca 105
Leal, Johnny 148
Learned, Michael 134
Leavitt, Norman 194
Leder, Harvey 174
Lederer, Otto 144
Lee, Andy 98
Lee, Bill 132
Lee, Eugene 116
Lee, Harrison 90
Lee, Kyusang 98
Lee, Leon 144
Lee, Roberto 166
Lee, Sheryl 171
Leeds, Michael 186
The Legends of Oz 239
Legion of Super Heroes 125
Lehmann, Ted 164
Lehr, Wendy 88
Leialoha, Steve 126
Leigh, Katie 212
Leigh, Valli 171
Leitzell, Delilah 68
Lemire, Michel 178
Lemus, Eva Tamargo 234
Lenehen, Nancy 172
Lennick, Julie 107, 108
Lennon, Jarrett 223, 225, 226, 227
Lentz, Pat 133
Leonard, Brian 207
Leonard, Jack E. 158
Leonard, Robert 138
Leonard, Suzanne 164
Leopardi, Chauncey 222, 224, 225
Leopold, Glenn 203, 205
Leprechauns in Oz 55
LeRoy, Mervyn 148, 150
Leslie, Ann Rice 148
Lesser, Elana 178, 218
Lessons of Oz 95

Lester, Robie 131, 132
Levenson, Keith 106, 229
Levinskaya, V. 199
Levinthal, Marc 60
Levitow, Abe 197
Levitt, Zane W. 174
Levy, Shuki 169, 217, 228
Lewis, Bob 132
Lewis, Irene 161
Lewis, Irwin 182, 183
Lewis, Jerry 121
Lewis, Julia 95
Lewis, Marc Allen 222, 223, 224, 225, 227
Lewis, Mitchell 148
The Lexx 230–231
The Liberty Bell in Oz 61
The Life and Adventures of Santa Claus (animated film) 180
The Life and Adventures of Santa Claus (Baum book) 4, 10, 13, 47–8, 223, 228
The Life and Adventures of Santa Claus (graphic novel) 124
The Life and Adventures of Santa Claus (Rankin-Bass) 181, 212–213
Lightyear Entertainment 207
Like Babes in the Woods 143
Lim, Swee 168
Limata, J.F. 89
Lincoln Center Theater 113
Lind, Diane 134, 135, 136, 137
Lindsey, Mort 197
Linduska, James A. 76
Lineback, Richard 216
Linsenmann, George 154
Lintoff, Julia 95
Lion 125
The Lion of Oz 178–180
The Lion of Oz and the Badge of Courage (book) 51
The Lion of Oz and the Badge of Courage (film) 178–180
The Lion That Squeaked 219
Lionel, Rufus K. 57
Lipman, Maureen 133
Lippa, Christine 173
Lippert Company 194
Lipton, Lynne 212
Liquid Dreams 174–175
Little Dorothy and Toto 48
Little Oz Squad 125
"Little Wizard" Series 48, 53
Little Wizard Stories (Oz kids TV series) 224–227
Little Wizard Stories of Oz 48
Lively, Lee 185
The Lizard of Oz (book) 60
The Lizard of Oz (graphic novel) 126
Lloyd, Eric 222
Lloyd, Harold 139
Lloyd, Michael 171
Lloyd, Sabrina 227

Locke, Peter 171
Lockerby, Jack 239
Lockhart, Calvin 171
Lockman, Vic 122
Loder, Pegi 195, 196
Lodge, David 218
Loeb, Mark 91
Loew's, Inc. 148
Lofven, Chris 161
Loh, Terry 124
Lombard, Carol 131
London, Gene 198
Lone Star Gas Company commercial 236
Longden, Mike 217
Lookinland, Michael 202
Lopez, Mario 216
Loquasto, Santo 99
Lord, Stephen 198
Lorimar Telepictures 171, 212
The Lost Emeralds of Oz 59
Lost Girls 124
Lost in Oz (first pilot) 232
Lost in Oz (second pilot) 232–233
The Lost King of Oz 34–35
The Lost Princess of Oz (book) 25, 26, 225
The Lost Princess of Oz (play) 99
Loubert, Patrick 220
Loud, David 113
Loughram, Derek 172
Louise Reichlin & Dancers 109, 110, 111, 112
Love, Nick 171
Lowenberg, Johann 165
Loza, Veronica 89
Lucero, Amarante 107
Lucky Bucky in Oz 43–44
Ludviksen, Brian 178
Ludwig, Charley 148
Ludwig, Jerrold L. 172
Ludwig, Jon 90
Lugar, John 215
Lum, Benjamin 216
Lumet, Sidney 162, 163
Lunarr and Maureen in Oz 53
The Lunechien Forest of Oz 53
Lurie, John 171
Lurline and the White Ravens of Oz 58
Luske, Hamilton S. 193
Lustosa, Victor 166
Lux Radio Theatre 130
Luxford, Les 161
Lyberger, Amy 183
Lynch, David 171
Lynch, Kirstin 96
Lynde, Paul 158, 203
Lynn, Billy 130
Lynn, Joe 162
Lynn, Mari 194
Lyon Video, Inc. 186
Lytle, Bill 164
Lytton, Debbie 170

Macauley, Joseph 76
MacDonald, J. Farrell 139, 140, 141, 143
MacDonough, Glen 64
Mace, Fred 66, 68
Mackender, Greg 102
Mackie, Robert 134, 135, 136, 137
Mackintosh, Stewart 97
Maclean, Ewan 96
MacLeod, David 230
MacMillan, Eleanor T. 70
MacMillan, Norma 173
MacNeille, Tress 218, 231
MacNicol, Peter 223
MacPherson, Kerry 230
Macrae, Liz 207
MacVeigh, Rob Roy 50
Mad Magazine 122, 125
Madden, Onyx 58
Madhouse Studios 175
Madsen, Harry 162
Maekawa, Masahito 171
Maggiore, Susan 78
The Magic Behind the Wizard 184
The Magic Bon Bons 142–143
The Magic Book of Oz 176
The Magic Bowls of Oz 54
The Magic Chest of Oz 50
The Magic Cloak 143, 144
The Magic Cloak of Oz 140, 143–144, 145
The Magic Diamond of Oz 62
The Magic Dishpan of Oz 54
"The Magic Land" 46
The Magic Mirror of Oz 57
Magic Mushroom People of Oz 152
The Magic of Oz 4, 29–30, *30*
The Magic Ruby of Oz 56
The Magic Tapestry of Oz 58
The Magic Topaz of Oz 60
The Magical Land of Oz 71
Magical Mimics of Oz 44
The Magnificent Major 244
Magno, Alexandre 174
Magro, Dominick 148
Maguire, Gregory 58, 116, 118
Maher, Joseph 164
Mahin, John Lee 148
Mahon, Barry 153, 154
Mahon, Channy 153
Mahon, Clelle 153
Mahon, Peggy 153, 217
Mahoney, Kate 136
Mahway Ballet School 82
The Maid of Arran 3
Majestic Theatre, Los Angeles 69
Makarov, Alexander 229
The Making of the Oz Kids 185
The Making of the Wizard of Oz (book) 150, 152, 165, 184
The Making of the Wizard of Oz (documentary) 204
Mako 134, 164
Maksimov, Ilya 231
Maley, Stephen 64

Maliani, Lisa 218
Maliani, Michael 170, 218
Malinger, Ashley 223, 227
Malki, Sharon 103
Mallare, Mike 98
Maloney, Patty 164
The Maltese Falcon 164
Malugin, Alexander 175
Malyantovich, K. 199
Mamman, Ilan 103
Manahan, Robert L. 228
Mancini, Peter 135
Mandabach, Caryn 234
Mandel, Howie 182, 212
Mandel, Seymour 183
Mankiewicz, Herman J. 148, 150
Mann, Larry 195, 196
Mann, Nathaniel D. 64, 68
Mann, Rhoda 202
Manos, Mark 174
Mansfield, Betty Jane 147
Mantel, Bronwen 207
Mantello, Joe 116
Many Lands in Oz 61
Manzo, Carlos 148
Mapletoft, Ross 222, 223, 224, 225, 226, 227
Mar, Pons 168
Marchia, Ray 229
Marciano, David 215
Marco, Howard 148
Maren, Jerry 172
Margolin, Vladimir 103
Marguiles, Ellen 90
Marin Junior Theatre 80
Marion, Richard 172
Mark, Denise 234
Markie, Biz 221
Markov, Yevgeni 229
Marley, Yigal 103
Maroldo, Marie Denis 148
Maroney, Michael 218
Marquez, Lazaro 111
Marren, Jerry 148, 184
Marsh, Jean 167
Marshall, Amelia 234
Marshall, Rick 220
Marshall, Ron 182
Marshall, Sarah 78
Martell, Arlene 212
Martens, Anne Coulter 75
Martin, Andrea 215, 229
Martin, Dean Paul 214
Martin, Dick 46, 49, 50, 58
Martin, Jane 91
Martin, Pamela Sue 234
Martinez, Mike 199
Martini, Paul 106
Martsolf, Eric 234
Marue, Ramone 87
Marvel Comics 122, 123, 125
Marvel Treasury of Oz Featuring the Marvelous Land of Oz 123
The Marvelous Land of Oz (book) 10, 66, 120

The Marvelous Land of Oz (1964 Concordia play) 78
The Marvelous Land of Oz (Smithsonian Puppet Theatre) 84
The Marvelous Milkmaid of Mechanica 219
The Marvelous Misadventures of Ed Grimley 215
The Marvelous Monkeys in Oz 53
Marzulli, Debbie 98
Masamitsu, Cathy 78, *79*
M.A.S.K. 245
Maslansky, Paul 168
Mason, Bill 196
Mason, Brenda 102, *104*
Mason, Margaret 71
Mason, William 146
Masquerade in Oz 52
Massey, Walter 206, 207
Massin, Dona 148
Masten, Gordon 207
The Master Key 10
Mastercard commercial 238
Masters, Ben 234
Masterson, Danny 233
Masucci, Michael 109
Mathews, Hrothgar 227
Matina, Bele 148
Matina, Lajos "Leo" 148
Matina, Matthe 148
Matsubara, Chikako 205
Matsumoto, Yasunori 175
Matsuoka, Seiji 221
Matters, Graham 161
Matheson, Richard 172, 173
Matthews, Junius 127
Maus, Stef 178
Maxie's World 217
Maxwell, Paula 161
Maxwell House Good News 130
May, Aileen 64
May, Jim 188
May, Kit 188
Maybe the Miffin 56
Mayer, Louis B. 150
Mayer, Neal 105
Mayhem in Munchkinland 125
Maytalmah, Semra 155
McAfee, Anndi 214
McAfee, Scott 214
McAllister, Bill 172
McBain, Allison 58
McBride, Leslie 78
McCabe, Tom 91, 95
McCarty, Kelli 234
McClanahan, Rue 172
McClellan, Ken 147, 149
McClelland, Bill 98
McCloud, Scott 91
McClurg, Edie 134
McColl, Neil 161
McCormack, Maureen 202
McCormick, Pat 164
McCourt, Sean 116
McCubbin, Margaret 71

McCullough, Bill 185
McDaniel, John 229
McDonald, Kirk 113, 119
McDonald's commercial 237
McDonnell, Terrence 171
McDougall, Walt 120
McEachern, Shonna 135
McElwee, Theresa 91
McElya, Kate 91
McElya, Mitchel Roberts, Jr. 94
McFadden, Corrine 116
McFadden, Robert 212
McFerrin, Bobby 105, 106, 185, 246
McGee, American 240
McGee, Doug 183
McGee, Vic 153
McGehee, Read 98
McGill, Tom 76
McGovern, Francis M. 89
McGovern, Terry 132
McGraw, Eloise Jarvis 46, 49
McGraw, Lauren 46, 49
McIsaac, Sally 183
McKennon, Dal 131
McKennon, Dallas 158
McKenzie, Beatrice 66
McKillip, Kate 88
McKinney, Austin 153
McKinnion, Lloyd 71
McKinnon, Cameron 107
McKinnon, Christopher 108
McKinsey, Beverly 198
McLauchlan, Jenifer 87
McMillan, Violet 139, 141, 142, 143
McNamara, Sally 91
McNee, James 88
McNeil, Neil 64
McNeil, Scott 173, 178
McNellis, Sean 88
McNerney, Jennifer 78
McPartlin, Ryan 234
McQueen, Butterfly 84, 85
McWilliams, Daphne 162
Meadows, Tim 221
Mebes, Marcus 58
The Medicine Man of Oz 55
Medina, Lan 126
Meet the Seevers 246
Meglin, Ethel 146
Meglin Kiddies 146
Melo, Mano 166
Melville, Lisa 174
Memories of Oz 233
Menard, Luke 114, *118*
Menard, Ray 154
Mendonca, Carla 97
Mendoza, Linda 222
Menefee, Pete 202
Meneghel, Xuxa 166, 167
Menendez, Andres 94
Menville, Scott 222
Menz, Mike 98
Menzel, Idina 116, *117*, 119

Merge, Joycelyn 76
Merman, Ethel 158
Merrill, Lou 194
Merritt, A. 7
Merritt, John 160
Merritt, Theresa 162
Merry Go Round in Oz (book) 46, 59
Merry Go Round in Oz (play) 76, 77
Merwin, Rick 219
Messenger, Charlie 164
Messick, Don 197, 205
Messmer, Emily 101
Messmer, Lennon 101
Messmer, Lewis 101
Metcalf, Rosalind 96
Metcalfe, Jesse 234
Metchik, Aaron Michael 222
Metro-Goldwyn 149
Mettler, Gregg 234
Meugnio, Will 204
Meyers, Mike 221
MGM 4, 5, 122, 123, 148, 149, 150, 151, 170, 197, 230
MGM Children's Series 131
MGM's Marvelous Wizard of Oz 122–123
Michaels, Steve 207
Michanzyk, M. 57
Michelena, Beatriz 69
Michelle, Julianne 222
Middler, Bette 229
Mikhailovskaya, Katya 175
Milburn, Susan 199
Milder, Andy 222, 223, 224, 225, 227
Miles, Helene 182
Milhoan, Michael 234
Milkin, Mark 185
Miller, Kevin 105
Miller, Lara Jill 134
Miller, Lee 202
Miller, Lesley 212
Miller, Mark Thomas 214
Miller, Marvin 91
Miller, Maxine 178
Miller, Meredith 183
Miller, Paul 106
Miller, Sidney 193
Miller, Walter 148
Millichamp, Stephen 161
Millie 95
Mills, Jaqueline 214
Mills, Juliet 234
Mills, Stephanie 84
Milton, Emilya 199
Minguchi, Yuko 175
Ministeri, George 148
Minkovotzkii, Ilya 199
Minnelli, Liza 130, 151, 158
Minolta Cameras commercial 237
Mintz, Jack 148
Mintzer, William 90
Misfits of Science 214

Mishulin, Spartak 199
Miss Gulch Lives! 93–94
Miss Gulch Returns! 92, 93, 94
Mister Flint in Oz 59
Mr. Rogers Neighborhood 243
Mister Tinker in Oz 55
Mitchell, Adrian 97
Mitchell, Doris 64
Mitchell, John Cameron 172
Mitchell, Julian 64, 65, 66
Mitchell, Julie 78
Mitchell, Kel 222
Mitsuya, Yuji 175
Miura, Urara 228
Miyazaki, Akira 165, 207
Mizude, Hirokazu 221
Moffat, Pam 174
Moiseyev, B. 199
Molitor, Doug 218
Mongold, Harry E. 58
Monision, Tim 91
Monk, Stephen 107, 108
The Monkey Prince 225
Monkeys in Silk Productions 175
Monroney, Michael 88
Montalban, Ricardo 211
Monterey SoundWorks 137
Montgomery, Dave 64, 65, 66, 67
Montgomery, Monty 171
Montgomery, Pricilla 148
Montgomery County Ballet 77
Montgomery Gentry 247
Monty, Harry 148
Moonlighting 248
Moore, Alan 124
Moore, Frank 139, 140, 141
Moore, Frank Y. 69
Moore, Rachel 99
Moore, Sandee 183
Moorehead, Agnes 127, 194
Moppet Players 77
Moran, Peter 90
Moray, Yvonne 148
Morcillo, Fernando Garcia 153
More, Dotti Sue 78, *80, 81*
More, Greg 78, *81*
Morelli, Pascall 170
Moreno, Rita 222
Morgan, Aaron 99, 196
Morgan, Frank 130, 148, 150
Morgan, Ike 49
Morgan, J. Tommy 215
Morgan, Maitzi 204
Morgan, Nancy 172
Mori, Toshio 205
Moriber, Brooke Sunny 113
Morita, Hiromitsu 207
Moritz, Louisa 164
Morley, Justin, Jr. 76
Morosco, Oliver 69, 70
Morris, George 206
Morris, Redmon 160
Morris, Ruth 58
Morris, William 76
Morris, William C. 97

Morris A. Mechanic Theatre 84
Morrison, Bill 171
Morrison, Shawn 234
Morrison, Will 68
Morse, Robert 119
Morse, Susan 195, 196
Mortensen, Patty 132
Mortimer, Win 122
Morton, Greg 170
Morton, James C. 69
Morton, Lewis 233
Moses, Gilbert, III 84
Moskowitz, Laura 172
Most Happy Fellows 88
Mother Goose in Prose 3, 10, 214
Motherwell, Phil 161
Motown 86, 163, 199
Mouseketeers 193, 194
Moye, James 113
Mt. Holyoke College 88, 91, 94, 95, 106
Much to Do About Oz 82
Mudono, Asami 175
Mueller, Gary 230
Muhlpriedel, Michael 222
Muller, Romeo 59, 196, 199, 204
Muller-Rosen Productions 205
Multicom Publishing 239
Mulvaney, Michelle 134
Mumy, Billy 225
Munoz, Shawn 222
Munrow, David 160
Muppet Babies 212
Muppet Magazine 123
The Muppet Wizard of Oz 5, 212
The Muppet, Show 244
Muppets Go To the Movies 244
The Muppets — A Celebration of 30 Years 245
Murakami-Wolf-Swenson 205
Murakoshi, Shinji 109
Murch, Walter 168, 169
"A Murder in Oz" 12
Murder on the Yellow Brick Road 56
Murer, Michael 219
Murney, Julia K. 105
Murphy, Jamie Lisa 212
Murphy, Jim 137
Murphy's Law 245–246
Murray, Charles 144
Murray, Lee 148
Murray, Mike 222
Murvin, Robert 164
Musgrave, Lon 139
Mushi Productions 171
Music, John 114, *118*
Mussum 166
My Favorite Fairy Tales 169–170
Myars, Mark 116
Myers, Nancy 76
Myman, Robert M. 172
The Mysterious Cave 201
The Mysterious Caverns of Oz 58
The Mysterious Chronicles of Oz 58

The Mysterious Motr of Doov 122
A Mystical Magical SUper Adventure in Oz 62

Naden, Corrine J. 171
Nagai, Ichiro 207
Nagamine, Takafumi 207
Nakamura, Daiju 175
Nance, Jack 171
Napier, Carla 207
Napier, Charles 216
Napier, Sarah 88
Napoleon 164
Nardone, "Little Olga" C. 148
Narishkina, I. 199
Narvey, Jason 228
Naryshkina, Zinajda 199
Nash, Ogden 148
Nason, Laura 230
National Film Co. 144, 145
Nationwide 203
Nazaryk, V. 199
NBC 127, 151, 172, 193, 194, 203, 206, 214, 215, 216, 217, 234
NBC Productions 194
NBC Studios 234
Neame, Christopher 227
Negron, David 172
Neil, Ed 228
Neill, John R. 10, 13,14, 18, 19, 21, 25, 26, 27, 30, 31, 32, 33, 34, 35, 36, 37, 38, 39, 40 41, 42, 43, 47, 48, 49, 50, 61, 65, 69, 123, 169, 205
Nelson, Barrie 196
Nelson, Frank 204
Nelson, Haywood 213
Nelson, Jack 143
Nelson, Kelly 176
Nelson, Marty 212
Nelson, Nels 184
Nelson, Nels P. 148
Nelvana Productions 220
Nemark, Matthew 216
Nemelka, Gayle Cotterell 83
Ness, Michael 99
Neuberger, Jan 116
Neuland, Jennifer L. 105
Nevada County Performing Arts Guild 99
Neville, Kris 88
Nevinne, Vyacheslav 175
Nevison, Howard 76
The New Adventures of Beans Baxter 215, 245
New Shakespeare Company 83
The New Three Stooges 248
The New Wizard of Oz (book) 7
The New Wizard of Oz (Oz Films) 141
Newman, Peter 212
Newman, Richard 173
Newport, James William 215
Newton, Sally Anne 159
NHK-TV 206, 211

Nicholson, Toby 78
Nickelodeon 173, 222, 231
Nickerson, Denise 243
Nickloy, Margaret C.H. 148
Nicol, Lesley 97
Nicolo Marionettes 72–75, 86
Nielsen, Steven 109
Nielsen, Todd A. 94
Nightmare Planet 245
Nikolayev, I. 199
Nikulin, Valentin 199
Nine O'Clock Players 73
Nininger, Susan 87
Nishimura, Tomohiro 228
Nissan, Sigi 103
Niven, David, Jr. 184
Nizel, Jeanette 83
No Place Like Home 231
Noble, Eleanor 178
Noisom, George 148
The Nome King's Shadow in Oz 60
The Nome Prince and the Magic Belt 223
Noone, Kathleen 234
Norris, Patricia 171
Nosachev, V. 199
Nosik, Valyerii 175
Not in Kansas Anymore 206
Novak, David Alan 215
Novak, Frank 127
Novak, John 227
Novak, Russ 183
Novasio, Lenora 69
Noy, Tzahi 103
NTV 229, 231
Nucci, Natalie 222
Nufer, Beth 164
Number 13 152
The Number of the Beast 55
Nunes, Bill 158
The Nutcases and the Wizard of Oroz 166–167

O&O Associates, Ltd. 161
The O.Z. 164
O'Baugh, Franklin H. 148
O'Brien, Carl "Cubby" 193
O'Brien, Hugh 216
O'Brien, Laurie 212
Ocasek, Jeanne 76
O'Connell, Jerry 227
The Octopus 64
Oda, Yuichiro 165
Odd Tale of Osoenft in Oz 63
Oddyssey in Oz 90
O'Docharty, William H. 148
O'Donnell, Rosie 229
Odriozola, Dulcie 78, 82
O'Dwyer, Linda 207
Off to See the Wizard 197–198
The Official 50th Anniversary Pictorial History of the Wizard of Oz 184
O'Hara, Catherine 215
Ohta, Bennett 164

Ojo in Oz 39–40
Oksner, Bob 121
Okumura, Yoshiaki 221
Oldfield, Julian 84
Oliver, Barbara A. 173
Oliver, Tim 106
Oliver, Tony 173, 228
Olsen, Roger Scott 173
Olsen, Susan 202
Olson, Hildred C. 148
Olson, Thomas W. 89
O'Mahoney, Michael 219
On the Road to Oz 91, 96
On the Road to Wizdom ... Against All Oz 98
O'Neal, Gayle 185
O'Neil, Walter Winston 116
Online Computer Library Center 186
Operti, LeRoi 130
Oppenheimer, Alan 218
Oremus, Stephen 116
Oren, Torgut 155
Orion Pictures Company 164
Orme, Charles 159
Orsland, Gretchen 87
Orte, Peter C. 76
Ortiz, Ange'lica 94
Orton, Stan 76
Os Trapalhoes E O Magico De Oroz 167–168
Osborn, Justin 98
Osborne, Jefferson 140
Osbourn, Fred 146
Oseland, James 174
Osmond, Donny 203
Osmond, Marie 203
Ossman, David 134
Osterberg, Oliver 88
Ostrom, Harold 139, 140, 141, 143
Ostrove, Ilan 214
Otanu, Kosei 205
The Other Side of Time 56
O'Toole, Annette 172
Otto, Frederick E. 59
Ouimette, Stephen 220
Our Trip to Oz 61
Outpost Farms Productions 234
Over the Rainbow (dance film short) 98
Over the Rainbow (Karate Kid) 248
Over the Rainbow (1988 film strip)
Over the Rainbow (sitcom) 248
Over the Rainbow, Under the Skirt 248
Overmountain Press 51
Owen, R. 183
Owens, Laura 172
Oz (anime) 175
Oz (Australian film) 161–162, 212
Oz (Caliber) 125, 232
Oz (Paul Taylor) 99
Oz (Shanahan play) 102–103, *103, 104*

Oz; A Twisted Musical 111–113, *114, 115, 116*
Oz and the Three Witches 59
Oz Before the Rainbow 150
The Oz Effect 245
The Oz Encounter 61, 232
Oz Film Manufacturing Company 139–144, 221
The Oz Kids 222–227
Oz Kids Production Company 114
Oz No Maho Tsukai 206–211
Oz Squad 124
Oz-Story 46
Oz: The American Fairyland 185
Oz: The Magical Adventure 240
Oz University 147
The Oz Witch Project 176–178, *177, 178, 179*
The Oz-Wonderland War 123
Ozalooning in Oz 51
The Ozard of Wiz 99
Ozark, Jack 158
Ozian Seahorse Press 54, 62
Ozma and the Little Wizard 48
Ozma and the Wayward Wand 51
Ozma Gets Really Pissed Off and Cusses and Totally Offends (Almost) Everyone in Oz 52
Ozma of Oz (book) 12, 68, 70, 77, 78, 79, 82, 121, 168, 169, 171, 205, 211, 223
Ozma of Oz (Johansen) 99
Ozma of Oz (1935 play) 71
Ozma of Oz (1962 play) 73
Ozma of Oz (Zeder) 87–88, 107
Ozma, Ruler of Oz 77
The Ozmapolitan of Oz 58
Ozoplaning with the Wizard of Oz 42
Oz-Some Exercise Productions 188
Ozu No Mahotsukai 165–167

Pace, Lynne A. 94
Packard, Frank 148
Packer, Jack 76
Page, Nicholas 148
Page, Tara 109
Page-Pagter, Scott 228
Palacio, José 153
Palazzolo, Tom 184
Palermo, Andrew 116
Palhares, Carmen 166
Paliwoda, Amby 158
Palmer, Gerald 73
Palo Verde Emeralds 52, 58, 59
Palsson's Supper Club 93
Pamela West 119
Pan Latina 153
Panayiotou, Nicholas 95
Panmedia 207
Pape, Cynthia 134, 137
Papel, Geraldine 164
Paradise 216–217
Paradox in Oz 54

Paramount Pictures 139, 165, 202
Paris, Pat 203
Parker, Doug 173
Parker, Paula Jai 221
Parker, Ray 203, 207
Parker, Sarah Jessica 221
Parks, Leona M. 148
Parnes, Milli 106
Partok, Reuven 106
Passi, Christopher 88
Passi, Peter 88
Passions 234–235
Passmore, Angie 214
Paster, Uri 103, 105
The Patchwork Bride of Oz 60
The Patchwork Girl (Palace Theatre) 97–98
The Patchwork Girl of Oz (Baum book) 4, 18–19, 49, 72, 94, 121, 194
The Patchwork Girl of Oz (Louise Reichlin) 109–110, *110*, *111*, *112*, *113*
The Patchwork Girl of Oz (Mt. Holyoke) 94
Patchwork Girl of Oz (1964 play) 77
The Patchwork Girl of Oz (Oz film) 139–140, *141*, *142*, *143*, *144*, *146*
Patchwork Girl of Oz (Thundertoad) 5, 235
Patchwork Press 60, 124, 125
Patel, Chandi J. 176
Patrick, Tom 99
Patterson, Barbara 147
Patterson, Ray 203, 204, 205
Paul, Charles 130
Paul Taylor Dance Company 99
Paulsen, Rob 134
Pausch, Natalie. 109
Pavlov, Viktor 175
Pay No Attention to That Man Behind the Curtain 99
Payes, Rachel Cosgrove 49
PBS 212, 243
Pearce, Damon 162
The Pearl and the Pumpkin 66
Pearson, Kris Noel 169
Pearson, Virginia 144
Peçanha, Déa 167
Pegasus in Oz 52
Pellegrini, Margaret 184
Pelletier, Brian 109
Pelz, Roger 203
Pendleton, Karen 193
Pennell, Jon Maynard 216
Pentland, Alan 161
Penton Overseas 137
Pereira, Gilvan 166
Pereira, Sérgio Luis 166
Perez, Alex 112, 113
Perez, Carla 228
Perez, Gio 111, *115*
Perez, Manny 158

The Perhappsy Chaps 32
Perkins, Dwayne 105
Perkins, Robby 161
Perlus, Mik 178
Perrine, Paula 76
Perry, D.J. 235
Perry, David, IV 229
Perry, Jamie 162
Perry, Ruth F. 86
Perry, Ryan 113
Personal F/X 229
Peter Pan and the Warlords of Oz 126
Peters, Anthony 195
Peters, Pamela 183
Peterson, Melinda 134
Petrenko, Victor 106
Petri, Suzanne 88
Petrie, Diana 87
Pettiet, Christopher 172
Pettigrew, Jacques 178
Pfizer Chemicals 236
Pharris, Chrystee 234
Phillips, Charkie 202
Phillips, Eleanor 70
Phipps, Charles 59
Pian, Roberto 167
Picket Fences 246
Pickford, Mary 149
Pictures from the Wonderful Wizard of Oz 49
Pidgeon, Denise 170
Pierce, Betty 143
Pierce, Bradley 222
Pierce, Judson 134, 137
Pierce, Rik 137
Pierce, Sarah 147
Pies and Poetry 143
Piglet Press 133
Piltch, Robert 207
Pineschi, Olivia 166
Pinky and the Brain (cartoon) 247
Pinky and the Brain (comic book) 125
Pino, Haydee 98
Pinto, Patric 96
Pioneer Memorial Theatre 83
Piper, Devi 88
Piper, Elizabeth 88
The Pirate Wizard Thief and the Children 186
Pirates in Oz 38–9
Piro, Rita E. 59
Piskunov, Gennady 106
Pittu, David 113
Pizo 148
The Planet of Oz 204
Platt, Marc 116
Plazza, Diane Della 90
Plonk, Bill 98
Ploog, Michael 124
Plunkett, Gerard 178
Pogemiller, Barbara 207
Polacks, James 196
Polinsky, "Prince Leon" 148

Pollack, E. 68
Polygram/Propaganda Films 171
Ponce, Leyson 98
Poncho Theatre 87
Pony Canyon, Inc. 173
Poole, Duane 205
Pope, Tony 133
Popov, V. 199
Porn, Casey 178
Porter, Bobby 164
Porter, Lillian 148
Posnikov, Urii 175
Potterton, Gerald 207
Powell, Jane 197
Powell, Ray 59
Power Rangers Zeo 228
Powers, Francis 143
Powers, Jennifer 137
Powers, Jim 76
Prairie Rose Productions, Inc. 171
Prairie Strife 220
Pratt, Anthony 159
Pratt, Fletcher 52
Prell, Karen 214
Prendes 153
Prepon, Laura 234
Presbyterian Church, USA 185
Prescott, Norm 158
Price, Leigh Ann 134, 136
Price, Trevel 105
Priestley, Jason 178
Priklyucheniya v izumrudnom gorode: Printsessa Ozma 231
Priklyucheniya v izumrudnom gorode: Serebryanyye tufel'ki 229–230
Prince, Kenyatta 105
Prince Silverwings 13
The Princess of Cozytown 32
Proctor, David 143
Proctor, Phil 134
Proctor, Philip 231
Proctor and Gamble commercial 236
Producer's Club II Theatre 111
Production Associates, Ltd. 212
Prokop, Angela B. 88
Promenschenkel, George 186
Protea 55
Provance, Carol 100
Prudence, Gary 107, 108
Prud'homme, Anthony 99
Prymus, Ken 84
Pryor, Richard 162, 164
Ptitsen, Vladimir 175
Pufall, Nathan 114, *118*
Pulver, Pamela 87
Puppet productions 71, 72, 73, 77, 78, 79, 80, 81, 82, 83, 84, 90, 98, 193
Purple Prince of Oz 39
Puppetworks 72, 73, 75
Pyle, John 164
Pyramid Books 61

Quality Time Education, Inc. 185
Quan, Dianne 231
Queen Ann in Oz 52
Queen Zixi of Ix 3, 48, 143, 144
A Queer Quest for Oz 53
Queer Visitors From the Marvelous Land of Oz 49, 120
Quinby, Mike 214
Quinn, Aileen 165
Quinn, Daniel 171
Quinn, Richard G. 59

Raabe, Meinhardt 148, 184
Rabe, Anders 109
Rabe, Trulsa 109
Rabinovitch, Nadine 217
Race Through Oz 203
Raddatz, Virgil 158
Radio City Music Hall 98
Radio Play Company of America 68
Radio Works 136
Radler, Robert 228
Raeder, Henry 66
Ragaini, David 212
Ragaini, Robert 212
The Ragged Girl of Oz 140
Raggedys in Oz 59
Raia, Margie 148
Raia, Matthew 148
Rainbow 244
The Rainbow Road to Oz 131, 194, 212
The Rainbow's Daughter 70
Rainey, Doug 135, 136
Rampling, Charlotte 159, 160
Ramsay, Robin 161
Random House 51, 55, 59
Random House School Division 183
Rankin, Arthur, Jr. 195, 196, 199, 202, 212
Rankin/Bass 195, 196, 197, 199, 202, 212, 213
Rannow, Jerry 153
Ransom, Kenny 215
Rash, Steve 164
Ray, Gene Anthony 206
Rayan, Remy 225
Rayle, Hal 218
RCA-Columbia Pictures 207
Reading Adventures in Oz 239
The Real True Gen-U-Ine Wizard of Oz: L. Frank Baum 183
A Recall to Oz 94
The Red Reera Yookoohoo and the Enchanted Easter Eggs of Oz 59
Redgrave, Lynn 178
Reed, Bill 158
Reed, Edith 72
Reed, Ernie 153
Reed, Robert 202
Reed, Robin 72
Reed, Stuart 152
Reed, Vivian 140, 141, 143

Reed Marionettes 72
Regas, Jack 202
Reichlin, Louise 110
Reid, Tim 207
Reilly & Britton Co. 10, 13, 14, 18, 19, 21, 25, 47, 48, 49, 120
Reilly & Lee Co. 30, 32, 33, 34, 35, 36, 37, 38, 39, 40, 41, 42, 43, 44, 45, 46, 47, 49, 50, 76
Reilly, James E. 234
Reis, Dary 166
Reischl, Geri 202
Relph, Simon 159
The Remnants 222
Remus, Romola 68, 212
Renato Aragão Produções 166
Renee, Julene 222
Renfro, Jason 225, 226
Reno, Phil 186
Renzetti, Joe 164
Repple, Ron, Jr. 176
Republic Pictures 153
Reschke, Scott 235
Rescue of the Emerald City 218
The Return of Mombi 226
Return to Oz (animated film) 158
Return to Oz (computer game) 239
Return to Oz (Disney) 133, 167–169, 196, 212
Return to Oz (novelization) 60
Return to Oz (TV special) 196–197
Return to the Land of Oz 106
Reunited 245
The Rewolf of Oz 51
Reyes, Alisa 222
Reynolds, David 215
Reynolds, Debbie 231
Reynolds, Norman 168
Reynolds, Simon 217
Rhodes, "Little Billy" 148
Rhone-Alpes Cinema 186
Rhys-Davies, John 227
Riabov, Victor 106
Rice, Frederick 134, 136
Rice, Gertrude H. 148
Rice, Hazel 148
Rice, Rosemary 130
Richard, Winston 169, 173
Richardson, Arzinia 101
Richardson, Chelsea 111
Richardson, Frederick 48
Richardson, Nikki Ray 59
Richie Rich/Scooby-Doo Hour 205–206
Richman, Elizabeth 78
Rick Mill Productions 106
Rickabaugh, Kimber 106
Ricketts, Skiles 76
Riddles, Lawrence 105
Ridley, Emma 167
Ridgely, Bob 204
Ridiculous Rivals in Oz 62
Riley, Jack 231

Riley, Tom 133
Ring, Bert 222
Ringland, Louise 146
Ringling Brothers and Barnum & Bailey Circus 73, 105
Rinkitink in Oz 4, 21–25, 23, 24, 99
Ripley's Believe It or Not 130, 150, 206
Ritter, Friedrich 148
Ritter, Jason 172
Ritter, John 172
Rivers, Walter 130
Rizzo, Elvida 148
Rizzo, Steve 186, 187, 189, 190
Roach, Hal 139, 143
The Road to Oz (book) 14, 18, 53, 70, 94
The Road to Oz (Colonial Radio) 135–136
The Road to Oz (play) 86
Road Trip 235
Robbins, Brian 222
Robbins, Jerry 134, 136, 136, 137
Robbins, Kate 173
Roberge, Sean 170
Roberts, Andy 97
Roberts, Caryl 146
Roberts, Jerry 132
Roberts, Laine 132
Roberts, Marianne 107
Roberts, Steve 217
Robertson, Dale 198
Robertson, Elizabeth 178
Robinette, Joseph 97
Robins, A. 76
Robinson, Hal 78
Robinson, Mabel 162
Robison, Barry 89, 185
Robison, Lee 185
Roca, Baltasar 221
Rocket Trip to Oz 45, 46
Rodgers, Sarah 96
Rodrigeus, Arnaud 166
Rodrigo, David 94
Rodrigues, Arnaud 167
Rodriguez, Charles 162
Roeca, Sam 203
Roemer, Larry 195, 196
Roerick, William 212
Rogers, Andromeda 183
Rogers, Dana 106
Rogers, Katherine 10, 198
Rohlck, Lisabeth 94
Roka, Sandor 148
Rollins, Hazelle Hedges 78
Rollman, Eric S. 173
Roman, Susan 217
Romance in Rags 125
Romer, Ken 59
Rooney, Mickey 158
The Roots of Wonder in Oz 56
Rorke, Elizabeth 147
Rosa, Ellen 109, 110, 113
Rosario, Jose 96

Rose, Ralph 130
Rose, Tim 167
Rosen, Jimmie 148
Rosen, Robert L. 205
Rosenberg, Ilan 228
Rosenberg, Philip 162
Rosenthal, Paul F. 228
Rosette, Jorge 94
The Rosie O'Donnell Show 229
Rosine and the Laughing Dragon 47
Rosine in Oz 47
Ross, Carolyn 147
Ross, Dev 59
Ross, Diana 162, 163, 164
Ross, Ralph 184
Ross, Ted 84, 162
Ross, Tracey 234
Ross, Virgil 158
Rossellini, Isabella 171
Rosson, Dick 139, 143
Rosson, Harold 148
Roth, J.D. 212
Rotman, Michael 176, 177
Roundhouse 221–222
Routh, Matt 178
Rowe, Kathleen J. 94
Rowley, George 158
Roy, Deborah 134, 135
Roy, Deep 167
Roy, Rob 207
The Royal Book of Oz 32
Royal European Marionette Theatre 81
Royal Shakespeare Company 90, 95–96
Royal Wedding of Oz 94, 95
Royale, Charles F. 148
Royale, Helen J. 148
Royale, Stella A. 148
Royer, Mike 122
Rubell, Paul 206
Rubin, Ron 220
Rubinstein, Zelda 164
Ruble, George 196
Ruby, Cliff 178, 218
Rudder, Michael 207
Ruddinger, Albert 148
Rudick, Susan 186
Ruggles, Charlie 69
Rugrats 231, 240
Rugrats in Munchin Land 231, 240
Ruivivar, Catherine 105
Ruiz, Christina 112
Ruiz, Mia M. 171
Rumyanova, Klara 199
Run Around 247
The Runaway in Oz 49
Rundel, Clarence 139, 140, 141, 143
The Rundelstone of Oz 49
Running Away 221
Rupp, Debra Jo 234
Rushdie, Salman 221
Russell, Jordan 134

Russell, Nipsey 162
Russell, Raymond 139, 141, 143
Russell, Thomas 49
Russian Oz dramatizations 86, 106, 175, 176, 199, 200, 201, 202, 229, 230, 231, 232
Ruvinsky, Morrie 214
Ryan, Chris 88
Ryan, Jim 203
Ryan, Remy 223
Rydell, Steve 76
Ryerson, Florence 148, 150
Ryman, Geoff 59, 100, 114
Ryshpan, Howard 207

Saabay, Jay 203, 204
Saban, Haim 169, 217, 228
Saban Home Entertainment 228
Saban Productions 169, 173, 217
Sacret, Inc. 215
Safronov, Viktor 175
Sagal, Katey 233
Sager, Roy 70
Sail Away to Oz
St. Alban, Mary Ellen 184
St. Aubin, Parnell Elmer 148
St. James, Peter 95
St. Louis Muncipal Opera 72
St. Martin's 56
Saita, Shunji 171
Saito, Hiroshi 207
Saka, Osama 175
Sakai, Akio 207
Sakuma, Rei 228
Sale, Jo-Anne 95
Salenger, Meredith 176, 178, *178*, *179*
Salih, Kezi 96
Salisbury, Benjamin 185, 222
Salisbury, Frances 162
The Salt Sorcerer of Oz and Other Stories 60
Salter Street Films 230
Sammes, Mike 131
Sampson, Edward 87
Samuel, Peter 116
Samuel French 71, 127
Samuel Goldwyn Co. 171
Sanborn, David 106
Sanders, Alvin 173
Sanders, Annette 212
Sanders, Kelly 107
Sanders, Susan 108, 137
Sando, Ross 95
Sanina, A. 199
Sanrio Productions 170
Santana, Dedé 166
Santana, Dino 166
Santiago, Desiree 111
Sanusi, August 98
Sara, Mia 232
Sarbry, Jay 205
Saroyan, Hank 180
Sato, Ai 220
Saturday Night Live 215, 221, 243

Satz, Roxana 106
Saunders, Anna 180
Saunders, Susan 59
Saved by the Bell 216
Savelyev, Yuri 199
The Sawhorse of Oz 58
Sayegh, James 234
The Scalawagons of Oz 43
Scarecrow (comic book) 125
Scarecrow (music video) 247
The Scarecrow and the Tin Woodman 12
The Scarecrow and the Tin Woodman (Little Wizard Books) 48
The Scarecrow of Oz (book) 21, 22, 141
The Scarecrow of Oz (Meglin kiddies) 146
The Scarecrow, the Lion, the Tinman and Me 86
Scarfone, Jay 184
Schaeffer, William 90
Scharf, Walter 158
Scheerer, Robert 206
Scheimer, Lou 158
Schertzinger, Victor 69
Schibi, Peggy 234
Schieber, Phil 186
Schiff, Dave 233, 234
Schikel, Erica 222, 223, 224, 225, 226
Schiller, Justin 151
Schilling, Richard 234
Schlatter, George 197
Schneider, John 216
Schock, Harriett 180
Scholastic Book Services 59
Schooldays in the Land of Oz 70
Schrager, Rudy 130
Schramm, David 172
Schrier, Paul 228
Schrode, Joseph 68
Schroeder, Becky 98
Schubring, Donna 183
Schulenberg, Peter 60
Schumacher, Garth 88
Schumacher, Joel 162, 163
Schuster, Sunshine 101
Schwait, Shannon 109, *112*
Schwartz, Scott 232
Schwartz, Stephen 116, 117
Schwartz, Ted 202
Sci-Fi Channel 230
Scooby's Trip to Ahz 205–206
Scopp, Alfie 195, 196
Scott, Art 203
Scott, Jane 161
Scott, Jeffrey 204
Scott, Luke 247
Scraps 91
Scraps in Oz 71
Scraps! The Ragtime Girl of Oz! 94
Screen Partners 230
Scribner 52

Index

The Sea Fairies 3, 21, 48, 53, 223, 227
Seattle Children's Theatre 107
Seattle Public Library commercial 237
Second City Television 244
Second Story Players 83
The Secret Island of Oz 124
The Secret of Gingemma the Witch 201
The Secret of the Deserted Castle 61
Seelbach, Michael 116
Seeley, Stephanie 105
Segal, Misha 180
Seidl, Bia 166
Seki, Shuichi 207
Selen, Suna 155
Selig Polyscope Company 68, 69, 138, 139
Selig, William Nicholas 138, 139
Seltzer, Richard 60
Semon, Larry 144, 145, 146
Sen, Ali 155, *155*, *156*, *157*
Serezli, Metin 155, *155*, *156*, *157*
Sergachyov, Viktor 199
Serrano, Nestor 134
Server, Josh 222
Seta US 239
The Seven Blue Mountains of Oz (trilogy) 55, 239
Seven Day Magic 54
The Seven Underground Kings 60, 199
Sewell, Blanche 148
Sezgin, Sitki 155
Shaferan, I. 199
The Shaggy Man of Oz 44–45
Sha'ibi, Nir 103
Shale, Kerry 133
Shampain, Robert 107
Shanice 106
Shanower, Eric 49, 60, 123, 124
Shaw, Brad 102
Shaw, James 162
Shaw-Parker, David 97
Shchyerbakov, Boris 175
Shee, Neil 206
Sheehan, Tory 188
Sheen, Charley 232, 246
Sheffield, Buddy 222
Sheffield, Heather 222
Sheffield, Rita 222
Shelley, Carole 116
Shenton, Nadine 95
Shepard, Rod 112
Shepard, Valerie 148
Shepherd, Skip 217
Sheppard, Don 204
Sheppard, W. Morgan 171
Sherman, Joseph 220
Sherrerd, Norman 71
Shian, Chiou Wen 171
Shields, Brooke 244
The Shifting Sands of Oz 63

Shiina, Hekiru 228
Shilkret, Nathaniel 130
Shilling, Delton D. 76
Shimamoto, Sumi 207
Shimokawa, Gary 213
Shin, Nelson 171
Shinkyusei, Kyosei 175
Shinokura, Nobuku 228
Ship of the Old Sailor 201
Shire, David 168
Shirley, Jean 184
Shirley Temple Show 194, 195
Shishido, Phoydon 222
Shoen, Vic 194
Shonen Santa No Daibouken 228
Short, Martin 215
Shortt, Paul R. 90
Shultz, Elsie R. 148
Sibert, Roderick-Spencer 162
Sid & Marty Krofft 202
Siddall, Brianne 180
Sidebottom, Janice 185
Sider, Darby 98
Sidoni, David 222
Sighvatsson, Sigurjon 171
Silich, Cheryl Ann 188, 191, 192
Silich, Kathy L. 188
The Silly OZbul of Oz and the Magic Merry-Go-Round 51
The Silly OZbul of Oz and Toto 51
Silly OZbuls of Oz 51
Silva, Bill 183
Silva, P. Carol 60
Silver, Jonathan Randell 136
A Silver Elf in Oz 62
The Silver Princess of Oz 42
Silver Shoes
The Silver Shoes of Oz 62
The Silver Sorceress of Oz 54
Silverman, David 213
Silvern, Charles 148
Silvers, Edmund 199
Silvers, Sid 148
Silverstone, Lou 199
Simms, Willard 84
Simon, Jim 173
Simon, Marty 230
Simon, Murray E. 76
Simon, Sarah 90
Simon and Schuster 51
Simpson, Valerie 162
Sims, Larissa 91
Simukhinoai, S. 199
The Sing-a-Long Wizard of Oz 115–116
Singer, Lori 206
Sinister Gasses in Oz 54
Sir Harold and the Gnome King 52
Siriner, Rafet 155
Sirocco Productions 185
Skeaping, Colin 168
Skeezik and the Mys-Tree of Oz 63
Skiles, Sophia 99
Skinkle, Dorothy E. 83
Skinner, T.B.

Skipp, John 60
Skipper, Pat 172
Sky Island 21, 48–49
Skye, Robin 105
Slade, Jim 161
Slatten, Garland 148
Slavin, John 64
Sliders 227–228
Sloan, Douglas 228
Sloane, A. Baldwin 64
Slover, Karl 184
Slutsky, Jeff 186, 188
Smalls, Charlie 84, 85, 162
Smart, A.J. 183
Smart, Jack 127
Smekhov, Venyamin 199
Smirnov, L. 199
Smith, Alice 169
Smith, Clive A. 220
Smith, Cyril 203
Smith, Edgar 64
Smith, Gary 197
Smith, Harry 152
Smith, J.D. 220
Smith, Joel T. 232
Smith, Katy Broughton 214
Smith, Kurtwood 234
Smith, Leonard 144
Smith, Martin 164
Smith, Michael G. 178
Smith, Noah 106
Smith, Oliver 148
Smith, Philip 152
Smith, Robert B.
Smith, Ruth E. 148
Smith, Stacy 230
Smith, Walter 66
Smith, Roy, II 229
Smithson, Frank 66
Smolensky, Darlene 206
Smollet, Arthur 141
Smolyanov, V. 199
Smootie, Fredie 170
Smyk, Judith 107
Smyk, William 107
Smythe, Ernest 146
The Snorks 248
Snow, Jack 12, 44, 50
Snow, Lisa 107
Snow, Phoebe 106
The Snow White Meets the Wizard of Oz 77
Soares, Jofre 166
Sockwell, Sally 90
Socolov, R. 182
Sodaro, Craig 109
Soldiers to Gardeners 201
Solomon, Ed 158
Somerville, Phyliss 113
Somerville, Ralph 158
Somewhere Over the Radio (China Beach) 215
Somewhere Over the Rainbow (Moonlighting) 248
Sommers, Joan 97

Sondegaard, Gayle 150
Song of Oz 50
Songe, Cynthia 180
Sony Wonder 178
Sorrells, Robert 198
Soucie, Kath 180, 229, 231
Soule, Olan 204
South Hadley Oz Festival 91
Soviet Russia Publishers 60, 61
Space Oz No Boken 220–221
Spade, David 221
Spangler, Elmer 148
Sparks, Dana 234
The Speckled Rose of Oz 50
Spector, Ronnie 105
Speedy in Oz 40
Spelling, Aaron 211
Spelling Entertainment 172
Spence, Bruce 161
Spicer, Jerry 174
Spiderbaby Graphics 124
Spouse, Walt 121
Spradling, Charlie 171
Sprague, Gilbert M. 60
Stagno, Lisa 174
Stahl, Richard 164
Stair, Bill 160
Stalling, Carl W. 146
Stanley, Frank 164
Stanton, Harry Dean 171
Stanton, Molly 234
A Star Is Gone 219
Star Rover Press 59
Starglory of Oz 51
Stark, Don 174
Stark, Philip 234
Starlight Theater 76
Starnes, Amani 102, 103, 104
State Academic Children's Musical Theatre 106
Stathakis, Jonathan 89
Stauffer, Donald 127
Staunton, Imelda 95
Staz, Sharon 197
Steadman, Jeremy 60
Stearn, Don 196
Steffans, Roger 172
Stein, Lou 97
Stein, Milton 196
Stein, Ralph 132
Steinmann, Doree 183, 184
Steinmann Productions 183
Steinmetz, Richard 174
Stenstrom, David 228
Stepanova, Valentina 175
Stephan, Carl 148
Stephenson, John 203
Stevens, Alta M. 148
Stevens, Connie 76, 77, 132
Stevens, Ken 168
Stevens, Morgan 206
Stevens, Rise 158
Stevens, Robert 144
Stevens, Ronald "Smokey" 162
Stevenson, Guy 176

Stevenson, Willie 230
Stewart, Patrick 96
Stewart, Robin 78, 80, 81
Stewart, Susan, 203
Stewart, Tabori & Chang 52
Stillman, William 184
Stines, Darryl 99
Stockenstrom, Truda 88
Stocker, John 165, 217
Stockholm Marionette Theatre 82
Stockton, Kevin 162
Stoddart, Joe 107
Stodolski, Jean-Marie 111
Stoelk, Dave 221
Stofsky, Amy 171
Stole, Mink 174
Stoliar, Steve 22, 223, 224, 225, 227
Stoll, George E. 148
Stone, David 116
Stone, Edwin J. 64
Stone, Fred 64, 65, 66, 67, 130
Stone, Malcolm 214
Stoneburn, Melissa 76
Stonecipher, Aaron 114, 118
Storch, Larry 158
The Story and Songs from the Cowardly Lion of Oz 194
Stothart, Herbert 106, 148, 150, 184, 229
Stott, Jonathan 97
Stoughton, Richard 96
Stout, Bill 122
Strack, Amy 134, 135, 136, 137
Straightline 185
Stram, Henry 113
Strauch, Tim 183
Straussberg, Mandy 133
Straw and Sorcery 125
Street Fighter Marketing 186
Stringer, Robert W. 148
Strobl, Tony 122
Strong, Tara (Charendoff) 220
Stuart, Cindy 106
Studio Junio 174
Suchsie, George 148
Sudam 148
Sugarman, Maya 107
Sugiyama, Toyabi 175
Sugiyama, Toyomi 175
Sukhoverko, Rogvold 199
Sulakauri, K. 199
Sullivan, Charlotte V. 148
Sullivan, Mark 87
Summer, Cree 231
The Summer of Oz 59
Sun, Mine 155
Sundin, Michael 167
Sunset Post 185
Super NES 239
Surfside Over the Rainbow 217–218
Surratt, Harold 213
Surrender Dorothy 248
Surrender, Dorothy (Barrymore) 233

Susman, Judy 202
Sustarsic, Stephen 213
Sutherland, Catherine 228
Sutherland, Hal 158
Sutton, Laurie 219
Suzari Marionettes 72, 74
Suzuki, Mie 228
Suzuki, Shinichi 221
Sverbilova, Galina 106
Swale, Tom 202, 205
Swan, Billy 171
Swan, John 101
Swann, Leonard A., Jr. 185
Sweetin, Jodie 214
Swensen, August Clarence 148, 184
Swenson, Charles 204
Swickard, Josef 144
Swift, Jessica 159
Swingle, Vester 76
Switzer, Michael 214
Sylmar Chamber Ensemble 95
Syms, Richard 97
Synergy, Inc. 239
Szczesniak, Tom 207

Taboo 124
Tahara, Aruno 175
The Tail of the Cowardly Lion 248
Tails of the Cowardly Lion and Friends 51, 52, 53, 54, 55, 56, 60, 62
Taina Zabroshennovo Zamka 61
Takahashi, Shinya 207
Takami, Chika 93
Takano, Urara 228
Takayama, Fumihiko 165
Tale-Spinners for Children 132
Tales of Oz 232
The Tales of the Wizard of Oz 121, 195–196
Talit Productions 103
The Talking City of Oz 51
Tambarro, Chuck 215
Tambor, Jeffrey 212
Tan, Philip 168
Tanashian-Gentry, Lucy 222
Tanet, Ronald 89
Tanner, Betty 148, 184
Tarter, Dale 172
Tasha 188
Tatsuki, Fumihiko 228
Tavori, Eya 103
Taylor, Clarice 84
Taylor, Elizabeth 152
Taylor, Koko 171
Taylor, Paul 99
Taylor, Rip 87, 202
Taylor, Ross 73
Taylor, Russi 212
TB Books 59
TBS 222
Teaching Resources Film 161
Teague, David 222
Tedrow, Thomas L. 60

Index

Teeter, Al 193
Telarium 239
Telepictures Publications 123
Televisio de Catlunya 221
Tellez, Ramon 94
Telson, Bob 133
Temple, Shirley 150, 194, 195
The Ten Woodmen of Oz 57
Tenkauchi, Masaru 207
TenNapel, Douglas 229
The Terrific Takeover of Oz 125
Terry, Irwin 52
Tetty, Walter 127
Thalken, Joseph 113, 114
Thanksgiving in the Land of Oz 59, 204
That Girl in Wonderland 202
That Seventies Show 233–234
That Wonderful Wizard of Ourz 78
Thatcher, Wendy 165
That's Dancin' 245
That's Entertainment! 243
Theatre of the Young 94
Theodore Thomas Orchestra 68
There's No Place Like Omsk 245
Thexton, Christine 107
The Third Book of Oz 120
The Thirteen Ghosts of Scooby-Doo 245
Thirtle, Robert 168
Thomas, Asia 106
Thomas, Ben 97
Thomas, Charles 106
Thomas, Danny 158
Thomas, Ernest 213
Thomas, Jonathan Taylor 222
Thomas, Darrel Ray, Jr. 234
Thomas, Maralyn 234
Thomas, Marlo 202
Thomas, Mike 153
Thomas, Roy 122, 123
Thomas, Summer 216
Thomas, Tasha 84
Thompson, Kenan 222
Thompson, Kevin 213
Thompson, Mark 96
Thompson, Ruth Plumly 32, 33, 50, 61, 71, 76, 127, 131, 145, 147, 194, 195
Thompson, W.H. 66
Thompson, Wayne 188
Thomson, Russell 161
Thorn, Frankie 174
Thorns and Private Files in Oz 55
Thornton, Sigrid 216
Thorpe, Richard 148, 150
Three Girls in Oz 25
The Three Imps of Oz 53
3-in-1 Oil commercial 236
The Three Wizards of Odds 248
ThunderToad Animation 235
Tichy, Wolfram 230
Tierney, Lawrence 222
Tietjens, Paul 64, 65, 76, 108, 120

Tik-Tok and the Nome King 48
The Tik-Tok Man of Oz 13, 19, 66, 68, 69–70, 108, 109
Tik-Tok of Oz 13, 19, 20, 19–21, 70, 121
Tilstrom, Burr 193
Tim Burton, Inc. 220
Time Again in Oz 107
TiMe film-und-TV-Produktions GmbH 230
Time Town 219
Time Traveling in Oz 54
Timmins, Reuben 158
The Tin Castle of Oz 60
Tin Man 125
Tin Woodman 183
The Tin Woodman of Oz (book) 25–28
The Tin Woodman of Oz (Disneyland Records) 132
The Tin Woodman's Dream 152
Tina 174
Tingle, Mark 108
Tipper, Frank 146
Tippetarius of Oz 55
The Tired Tailor of Oz 52
Titus, David 186, 187, 189, 190
Tkachuk, Roman 199
TNT 105, 106, 151
Toby Nicholson School of Dance and Musical Theatre 78
Toby Tiger Tail 183
Toby's Rescue From the Planet 184
Tockar, Lee 173
Toda, Keiko 175
Todd, Ryan 172
Toei Doga Animation 205
Toho Co. 165
Tokmakovai, I. 199
Tokuda, Marilyn 174
Tolbert, Belinda 211
Tolkonnikova, Olga 106
Tollin, Michael 222
Tom, Nicholle 214
Tomei, Concetta 215
Tomino, Yuki 109
Tomney, Ed 174
Toms, Gordon 214
Top Secret 244
Top Shelf Productions 124
Topsy Turvy Time 127
Torme, Mel 197
Torme, Tracy 227
Tornado, Tony 166
Tornado Prom 233–234
Torres, John 98
Toto in Oz 53
Toto Lost in New York 223
Toto's Rescue 183
Tovar, Mario 94
Townsend, Robert 221
Townsend Television 221
Trachtenberg, Michelle 134
Tracy, Doreen 193
Trainer, David 234

Training Wheels Amateur Community Theatre Group 106
The Tramps and the Wizard of Oroz 166–167
Transformers 245
The Trapalhões 167
Travel Channel 235
Treacher, Arthur 194
Treadwell, Tom 105
Treasure Bay 59
The Triplets 221
Trofimov, U. 199
Trolmanden Fra Oz 83
Trouble in Oz 183
Truscello, Denise 174
Trusovoi, M. 199
Ts. K.V.I.O.S.M. Publishing House of Children's Literature 61
Tsaras, Philip 95
Tsu, Susan 107
Tsunoda, Tina 109
TSW Ltd. 214
Tucker, Tom 185
Tudor, Christopher 95
Tufeld, Dick 105
Tuller, Jane 98
Tullos, Jerry 87
Tundra Publishing 124
Turan, Suleyman 155, 155, 156, 157
Turevich, E. 199
Turevich, K. 199
Turevich, Y. 199
The Turkish Wizard of Oz 255
Turner, B.J. 96
Turner, Bonnie 234
Turner, J.T. 137
Turner, Otis 68, 138
Turner, Terry 234
Turner Classic Movies 151, 233
Turner Entertainment 184, 218
Turner Pictures Worldwide 106
Turvevich, Y.
Turyut, Hari 155
Tuttle, Lurene 204
Tuttle, Ruth 57
Tuttobene, Richard 222
TV Tokyo 207, 211, 221
20th Century Fox 85, 86, 160
20th Century Oz 161–162
Twin Peaks 237
Twisted 240
Twisted Deluxe 240
Twister! 100–102
Two Terrific Tales of Oz 56
227 245
Tyler, Ginny 131, 132
Tylo, Michael 212
Tzachor, Jonathan 228
Tzeits, Sergei 199
Tzioni, Lior 103

U.S. Gold Commodore 64, 239
UA Television 170
Udakov, N. 199

Ueda, Yuji 228
Ueno, Katsum 165
Uki, Tamio
Ulanet, Rachel 113
Ulrich, Kim Johnston 234
The Umbrellas of Oz 57
Unc Nunkie and the White King of Oz 56
Under the Rainbow 164–165
Underground Adventure 225, 226
Underhill, Barbara 106
Underhill, Beris 161
United Artists Records 132
Universal Film Manufacturing Co. 142
Universal Pictures 86, 116, 163, 180
University of Michigan Women's Athletic Association 147
University of Oklahoma 78
University of Utah 86
University of Virginia School of Medicine 98
The Unknown Witches of Oz 55
Unsworth, Geoffrey 159
Untermyer, Alice 78
Untermyer, Amy 78
Untermyer, Frank 78
The Unwinged Monkey of Oz 60
Upside Down Town 219
Uran, Irma 127
Urban, Jane 140
Urbano, Carl 203, 204, 205
Urfin Jus and His Wooden Soldiers 61, 199
Usachev, Andrei 231
Ushkov, Yevgeny 106
Uzzell, Bria 188

Vakili, Lilly Iran 88
Valderrama, Wilmer 234
Vale, Angelica 94
Valentine, Jan 87
Valentino, Charles 84
Valuable Gift from Oz 61
Valverde, Rawley 216
Vampires and Oz 59
Van, Billy 165
Van, Bobby 193
Van Baalen, Claire 107
Van Bruggen, John 220
Van Heusen, James 158
Van Johnson, Rodney 234
Van Scott, Glory 162
Van Volkenburg, Ellen 71
Vance, Pam 164
Vanitas Press 51, 52, 56, 57, 62
Varchak, Syergyeii 175
Varlye, Natalya 175
Varnado, Victor 188
Varttina 109
Vasilyeva, Vera 199
Vaughn, Glenna 146
The Vegetable Man of Oz 57
The Veggy Man of Oz 50

Velasquez, Alejandro 174
Viana, Wilson 166
Vicente, Jeffrey 111, 115
Victory, Fiona 168
Vidal, Gore 221
Video Anime E-Bon 171
Vidor, King 148, 150
Vierling, Arnold 148
Vigran, Herb 130
A Viking in Oz 53
Vilanch, Bruce 202
Vilaire, David 205
Villepique, Jean 99
Vince, Pruitt Taylor 171
Vingador, Alison 166
Vinge, Joan D. 60
Vinogradova, Mariya 199
Violet's Dreams 142
Virtual Oz 224
Visitors from Oz (Gardner book) 54
The Visitors from Oz (Kellogg book) 49
Vitha, Ashley 111
Vlasova, A. 199
Vlasova, G. 199
Volkov, Alexander 60, 61, 86, 106, 175, 199, 230
Volshebnik Izumrudnogo Goroda, (TV) 199–202
Volshebnik Izumrudnogo Goroda, (film) 175–176
Voorhees, Lark 216
Vorwald, Terrance 215
Voss, Gayla 102
Vrana, Vlasta 207
Vreeland, Theresa 76
Vysotsky, Vladimir 199

W.W. Denslow in Oz 62
Waddell, Gary 161
Wadsworth, George 153
Wagner, Harry L. 70
Wahlstrom, Gordon
Wainess, Richard 109
Wakefield, Marsha 216
Walcutt, Judith 134
Waldman, Myron 182, 183
Waldman, Robert 182, 183
Waldoch, Ryan 188
Walker, Benjamin 169
Walker, George 100
Walker, Jimmy 221
Walker, Mary 88
Walker, Phil 91
Walker Co. 171
Waller, James 105
Walsh, Barbara 113
Walsh, Bill 193
Walsh, Jessie May 139, 143
Walsh, Townsend 65
Walshe, Pat 148
Walston, Ray 216
Walt Disney Comics and Stories 122

Walt Disney Pictures Return to Oz 133
Walt Disney Presents the Scarecrow of Oz 131
Walt Disney Productions 147, 168, 193
Walter, Tracey 174
Walton, Bernard 133
Walton, Tony 162
Ward, B.J. 94, 218
Ward, Gregg 90
Ward, Peter 214
Ward, Sophie 168
Warde, Julie 88
Warner, Malcolm-Jamal 222
Warner Brothers 158, 164, 185, 220
Warner Home Video 184
Warren, Erin 107
Was (book) 59
Was (Lincoln Center) 113–114
Was (Northwestern University) 99–100
Washburn, Bryant 144
Wasko, George 76
Watanabe, Asami 175
Watanabe, Misa 223
Watassek, Deborah 90
Watkin, David 168
Watson, Bill 185
Watson, Bobby 148
Watson, Mary 71
Watt, Nancy Williams 234
Wauchope, Robert 61
Wauchope, Virginia 61
Wayne, Gary 164
Wayne, Gus 148
Wayne, Marie 139
WB 151, 229, 232, 233, 247
WCAU-TV 198
We All Dream of Oz 188
Weaver, Doodles 193
Weaver, Sarah 99
Web, Joy 153
Webb, Chloe 215
Webber, Tim 207
Weber, Chris 219
Wedwe, Rae Dawn 188
Weeki Wachi mermaids 82
Wegner, Kathleen 88
Weier, Amanda 99
Weigt, Jeff 183
Weinberg, Ronald A. 207
Weintrib, Lennie 205
Weis, Don 211
Weiser, Jaime 91
Weisker, John 183
Weiss, Dan 99
Welker, Frank 203, 212, 215, 218
Wells, Mai 140, 141, 143
Wentworth, Martha 131
We're Not in Kansas Any More 218–219
We're Off to Save the Wizard 109
We're Off to See … The Most Happy Fellows 88

We're Off to See the Munchkins 184
Werner, Tom 234
Weseluck, Cathy 173
Wesson, Michelle 214
West, Billy 233
West, Lorraine 161
Westbrook, Jay 96
Westgaard, Jon 88
Westmore, McKenzie 234
WFYI-TV 221
What If...? 125
What's Happenin' 213
What's Happenin' Now 213
Whelan, Aaron 107
Whelan, Kimberly 107
When You're Over the Hill, You Pick Up Speed 245–246
Where on Earth Is Carmen Sandiego? 222
Which Way to Oz 176
The Whimsical World of Oz 212
White, Elizabeth 88
White, Hollace 211
White, Viola 148
White Barn Theatre 95
Whitehouse, Steve 220
Whitfield, Lynn 232
Whiting, Barbara 173
Whitlock, Albert 162
Whitman 46
Whitmore, Dean 197
Whitney, Jamie 220
The Whiz Kid 245
Who Shrunk Saturday Morning? 216
Who Stole Santa? 185, 224
Who's Who in Oz 50
WICB-TV 197
Wicked 58, 116, 118
Wicked (stage musical) 115–119, 117
The Wicked Witch of Oz 49
The Wicked Witch Project 178
Wickwar, Gina 61
Wightman, Francis P. 47
Wild at Heart 171
Wild at Heart: The Story of Sailor and Lulu 172
Wildside Press 52
Wilhite, Thomas 222
Wilkerson, Laurnea 105
Wilkins, George 196
Wilkins, Karen 234
Will Vinton Productions 168
Williams, Barry 202, 234
Williams, Beth 70
Williams, Grace G. 148
Williams, Harvey B. 148
Williams, Liberty 204
Williams, Lori 88
Williams, Margaret 148
Williams, Martin 84
Williams, Mary Jeanne 76
Williams, Paul 203
Williams, Shelby 109
Williams, Ted 162
Williams, Wilson 109
Williamson, James 161
Williamson, Nicol 167
Willingham, Bill 126
Willis, Rod 196
Willis, Terry 172
Willow Grove Park Playhouse 77
Wilson, George E. 68
Wilson, Jennifer 178
Wilson, Joe, Jr. 188
Wilson, Karen 219
Wilson, Lisa 171
Wilson, Mak 167, 214
Wilson, Red 227
Wilson, Ross 161
Wilson, Thick 165, 217
Wimmer, Brian 215
Windham Classics 239
Winegardner, Bill 96
The Winged Monkeys of Oz 50
Winger, Debra 105
Winslow, Jean 70
Winters, Johnny 148
Winters, Jonathan 194, 215
Wishing Horse of Oz 40–41
The Witch Queen 143, 144
Witherspoon, John 221
Witney, Edwin 127
Wiz Kids 61, 62
Wiz Kids of Oz 61, 62
The Wiz (play) 84–86, 162, 163, 166, 245
The Wiz (film) 86, 162–164, 212
The Wizard of Aberdeen 198
The Wizard of Ahhs 244–245
The Wizard of Bahs 122
The Wizard of Clods 106–107
The Wizard of Cos 222
The Wizard of Emerald City (ballet) 106
The Wizard of Emerald City (film) 175–176
The Wizard of Foz 123
The Wizard of Ice 248
The Wizard of Malta 164
The Wizard of Mars 153
The Wizard of Oklahoma 78
The Wizard of Ooze (Beetlejuice) 220
Wizard of Ooze (Dynomutt) 248
The Wizard of Ooze (Earthworm Jim) 229
The Wizard of Ooze (Jerry Lewis) 121
The Wizard of Oz (ABC cartoon) 197, 218–220, 245
The Wizard of Oz (Alftales) 217
The Wizard of Oz (American Film Co.) 173–174
The Wizard of Oz (Baum book) 3–5, 8, 7–10, 21, 26, 29, 44, 46, 64, 68, 96, 102, 103, 106, 120, 121, 122, 130, 141, 147, 153, 161, 164, 171, 178, 183, 185, 202, 211, 212, 217 221, 228, 229, 239, 240, 244
The Wizard of Oz (BBC) 133
The Wizard of Oz (Bil Baird) 82–83
The Wizard of Oz (The Brooklyn College) 72
The Wizard of Oz (Carbon6) 240
The Wizard of Oz (CBS radio show) 130
The Wizard of Oz (Chapter Six) 114
The Wizard of Oz (Cinar) 206–211
The Wizard of Oz (Classics Illustrated) 121
The Wizard of Oz (Colonial Radio) 134–135
The Wizard of Oz (Crippled Children's Society) 80
The Wizard of Oz (Dell Publishing) 121
The Wizard of Oz (Disneyland Records) 131
The Wizard of Oz (El Paso high school) 81
The Wizard of Oz (Eric Smith Puppet Theater) 98
The Wizard of Oz (Eshbaugh cartoon) 146–147
The Wizard of Oz (Eubanks) 79–80
The Wizard of Oz (Fuji TV) 214
The Wizard of Oz (GE record) 131
The Wizard of Oz (Ice Capades) 72
The Wizard of Oz (Kappa Delta Sorority) 80
The Wizard of Oz (Koma Theatre) 98
The Wizard of Oz (Lorne Greene) 165–167
The Wizard of Oz (Mahwah Ballet School) 82
The Wizard of Oz (Martens play) 75
The Wizard of Oz (Melody Top) 87
The Wizard of Oz (MGM film), 4, 72, 73, 76, 77, 82, 87, 93, 96, 99, 105, 106, 114, 122, 130, 131, 146, 148–152, 163, 164, 165, 169, 177, 178, 184, 184, 186, 188, 195, 197, 198, 204, 205, 206, 215, 218, 220, 221, 222, 223, 229, 233, 235, 236, 237, 239, 243, 244
The Wizard of Oz (Monterey SoundWorks) 137
The Wizard of Oz (Mt. Holyoke College) 91
The Wizard of Oz: The Musical 107
The Wizard of Oz (Naden filmstrips) 171

The Wizard of Oz (Nationwide) 203
The Wizard of Oz (NBC radio show) 48, 127–130
The Wizard of Oz (New Masque Players) 77
The Wizard of Oz (New Shakespeare Company) 83
The Wizard of Oz (Nicolo Marionettes version) 72–74, 86
The Wizard of Oz (1902 Musical), 10, 12, 64–66, 67, 68, 69, 70, 108, 120, 130, 138, 140 150
The Wizard of Oz (1920s puppet show) 71
The Wizard of Oz (1925 film) 71, 144–146
The Wizard of Oz (1928 play) 71
The Wizard of Oz (1942 play) 72
The Wizard of Oz (1975 film strips) 161
The Wizard of Oz (1981 puppet show) 90
The Wizard of Oz (1983 Japanese version) 93
The Wizard of Oz (Oz Kids) 114
The Wizard of Oz (Page One Bookshop) 82
The Wizard of Oz (Piglet Press) 133
Wizard of Oz (possible sequel) 84
The Wizard of Oz (Puppetworks) 72, 73, 74, 72–75
The Wizard of Oz (Queen Latifah) 164
The Wizard of Oz (Reed Marionettes) 72
The Wizard of Oz (Ringling Brothers) 73
The Wizard of Oz (Royal European Marionettes) 81–82
The Wizard of Oz (Royal Shakespeare Company) 90, 95–96
The Wizard of Oz (Saban parody) 173, 174
The Wizard of Oz (Sayre Elementary School) 82
The Wizard of Oz (Second Story Players) 83
The Wizard of Oz (Skinkle) 83
The Wizard of Oz (Starlight Theater) 76–77
The Wizard of Oz (Stockholm Marionette) 82
The Wizard of Oz (Super NES) 239
The Wizard of Oz (Suzari Marionettes) 72
The Wizard of Oz (Swarthmore Swim Club) 81
The Wizard of Oz (Telarium) 239
The Wizard of Oz (Tupperware convention) 77
The Wizard of Oz (United Artists record) 132
The Wizard of Oz (Weeki Wachee Springs) 82
The Wizard of Oz (WICB) 197
The Wizard of Oz (WTAM) 127
Wizard of Oz (ZX Spectrum) 239
The Wizard of Oz (ZX Spectrum game) 239
The Wizard of Oz and the Magic Merry-Go-Round 51
Wizard of Oz/Babes in Toyland 131
The Wizard of Oz: Dorothy's Adventure 98
The Wizard of Oz: Fashion and Fanatsy 77
The Wizard of Oz in Concert 105–106
The Wizard of Oz in Hippieland 82
The Wizard of Oz in Story and Song 131
The Wizard of Oz in the Wild West 83–84
The Wizard of Oz Live! 98
The Wizard of Oz on Ice (UK) 73
The Wizard of Oz on Ice (US) 105, 106, 185
The Wizard of Oz Returns 132
The Wizard of Paws 170
The Wizard of Sales 186–188, 187, 188, 189, 190
The Wizard of Soul 199
Wizard of the City of Emeralds 199
The Wizard of the Emerald City (book) 61, 176, 229
The Wizard of the Emerald City (dance) 86
The Wizard of the Web 186
Wizzin' 233
WMAQ 127
Wogglebug 125
The Woggle-Bug 12, 66–68, 70
The Woggle-Bug Book 49
Wolf, Fred 204
Wolfangle, Karla 99
Wolfe, Ian 127
Wolff, Gladys V. 148
Wolfman, Marv 61, 232
The Wonder City of Oz 43
Wonder City of Oz (TV script) 76
A Wonderful Journey in Oz 54
The Wonderful Land of Oz (Eubanks) 82
Wonderful Wizard of Ourz 78
The Wonderful Wizard of Oz (Cincinnati) 90–91
The Wonderful Wizard of Oz (Civic Light Opera) 107–9
The Wonderful Wizard of Oz (film strip) 161
The Wonderful Wizard of Oz (Jabberwocky) 132
The Wonderful Wizard of Oz (Koste) 91–93
The Wonderful Wizard of Oz (1975)
The Wonderful Wizard of Oz (NPR) 134
The Wonderful Wizard of Oz (Selig) 138
The Wonderful Wizard of Oz (Walker Co.) 171
The Wonderful Wizard of Oz: 50 Years of Magic, 184
The Wonderful Wizard of Oz: The Making of a Movie Classic 220
The Wonderful World of Gene London 198
The Wonderful World of Oz 134–136, 135, 136, 137
The Wonderful Wizard of Oz (book) 7
The Wonderful Wizard of Oz ('65 playlet)
Wonderland (comic book) 123, 125
Wonderland (play) 66
The Wonderland of Oz 121
Wong, Carey 107
Wood, Gloria 193
Wood, Murray 148
Wood, Richard 228
Woodard, Alfre 105
Woods, Jane 207
Woods, Nan 215
Woodson, Bill 204
Woodson, William 132
Woodward, Fred 69, 70, 139, 140, 141, 142, 143
Wooglet in Oz 59
The Wooing of Ozma 59
Wooley, Peter W. 164
Woolf, Charles 204
Woolf, Edgar Allan 148, 150
Wooten, Regina 183
The Woozy of Oz 57
The Workteams and the Wizard of Oz 184
The World's Greatest Superfriends 204
Wormworth, Tracy 229
Worrall, Tom 218
Wow Comics 121
WoZ 230–231
Wright, Deanna 234
Wright, Ed 171
Wright, Max 214
Wright, Todd 139, 141
WTAM 127
Wycoff, Evelyn 72
Wyle, George 202
Wynn, Bessie 64
Wynn, Ed 150
Wynne, Cordell 230

Xiques, Marin Elizabeth 60, 62
Xlibris Copr. 51, 53, 54, 59

Yager, Hannah 91
Yajima, Akiko 223
Yakovlev, Andrei 106

Yamada, Katsuhisa 175
Yamadera, Kouchi 175
Yamaha Electronic Keyboard commercial 237
Yanase, Joji 207
Yaniv, Erez 103
Yankee in Oz 50
Yannai, Michal 103
Yanow, Carl 71
Yanowitz, Barri 112
Yaroshenko, Igor 106
Yasuhara, Tadashi 207
Yasulovitch, Igor 199
Yefremov, Igor 199
Yellow Brick Road 200, 239
Yellow Brick Road 2, 239
The Yellow Fog 61
The Yellow Knight of Oz (book) 38
The Yellow Knight of Oz (play) 75–6
Yemelyanov, Nikolai 175
Yildiz, Tayar 155
Yilmaz, Mustafa 155
Yogi's Space Race 203
Yogi's Treasure Hunt 248
Yokobi, Mari 175
York, Dick 211

Yoshida, Ayumi 223
Yoshikawa, Soji 221
Yoshikawa, Yoichiro 175
Yoshimizu, Kiku 175
Yoshimura, K.S. 207
Yost, David 228
Youmans, William 116
Young, Arthur 152
Young, Gary 161
Young, John Sacret 215
Young, Mike 180
Young, Ronnie 76
Young, Steve 235
Young Santa Claus 228
The Young Sentinels 243–244
Youngren, Milt 46
Younts, Caroline 176
Yue, Marion Kodama 215
Yukuba, Shin 171

Zabriskie, Grace 171
Zacarias 166
Zackery, Beulah 193
Zaconick, Dorothy 72
Zamparelli, Joseph, Jr. 135, 136, 137
Zann, Lenore 230
Zardoz 159

Zarnatha 167
Der Zauberer Von Oss 99
Zavada, Ervin 172
Zay, Tim 90
Zeder, Suzan 87, 88, 107
Zelenya, Rina 199
Zemke, Rick 91
Zeta Entertainment, LTD. 174
Zholtiy Tuman 61
Zigarshina, Era 229, 231
Zim Greenleaf's Laboratory 239
Zimbalist, Sam 144
Zimmer, Patricia Moore 94
Zimmerman, Gordon 164
Zimmet, Connie 132
Ziprin, Joanne 152
Ziprin, Lionel 152
Zisca 153
Zolotukhin, Valeri 199
Zuckerman, Alex 222
Zuckerman, Gabrielle 88
Zuckert, Bill 198
Zukor, Lou 158
Zvrakowska, Dianik 153
Zwerling, Darrel 171
ZX Spectrum 239
Zylberman, Noam 170